HISTORY OF THE GREAT WAR

BASED ON OFFICIAL DOCUMENTS

BY DIRECTION OF THE HISTORICAL SECTION OF THE COMMITTEE OF IMPERIAL DEFENCE

ORDER OF BATTLE OF DIVISIONS

• PART 2a •

The Territorial Force Mounted Divisions and The 1st-Line Territorial Force Divisions (42-56)

Compiled by
MAJOR A. F. BECKE
R.F.A. (Retired), Hon. M.A. (Oxon.)

The Naval & Military Press Ltd

Published by
The Naval & Military Press Ltd
Unit 10, Ridgewood Industrial Park,
Uckfield, East Sussex,
TN22 5QE England
Tel: +44 (0) 1825 749494
Fax: +44 (0) 1825 765701
www.naval-military-press.com
www.military-genealogy.com

ORDER OF BATTLE OF DIVISIONS

Part 1 The Regular British Divisions

Part 2a The Territorial Force Mounted Divisions and The 1st-Line Territorial Force Divisions (42-56)

Part 2b The 2nd-Line Territorial Force Divisions (57th-69th), with The Home-Service Divisions (71st-73rd) and 74th and 75th Divisions

Part 3 New Army Divisions (9-26 and 30-41) and 63rd (R.N.) Division

Part 4 The Army Council, G.H.Q.s, Armies, and Corps 1914–1918

Printed and bound by Antony Rowe Ltd, Eastbourne

PREFACE

Orders of Battle for the fifteen Regular British Divisions, which served in the Great War, were given in the first part of this Divisional Order of Battle Series. The present part gives the Orders of Battle for twenty of the Territorial Force Divisions (five mounted divisions, fourteen first-line infantry divisions, and one second-line infantry division).

No mounted divisions existed before August, 1914, but the three which were formed during the Great War, from first-line yeomanry units, are naturally included in this part; and, to complete the record of the mounted units of the Territorial Force and to facilitate reference in the future, the tables for the two second-line mounted divisions are also printed. For a somewhat analogous reason the tables for the 45th (2nd Wessex) Division have been given, as the number (45th) allotted to the 2nd Wessex Division is in the sequence of numbers (42nd-56th) which was used for the re-designation of the first-line Territorial Force divisions. The 2nd Wessex Division undoubtedly obtained this early number because its artillery and infantry went overseas in 1914, being the first units from a second-line division to leave the United Kingdom.

Succeeding parts of this Series, each containing about twenty divisions so as not to be too cumbersome, will be as follows: (2-B) Second-line Territorial Force Divisions; (3-A and B) New Army Divisions; and (4) Australian, Canadian, New Zealand, and Indian Divisions. The series will be concluded with a volume dealing with G.H.Q.s, Armies, and Corps.

It was intended originally to furnish tables only for divisions which served in a theatre of war. But, as the Great War went on, all the divisions at home were continually providing either units or drafts for the various fronts, and in this way most of their officers and men went abroad as they became trained and ready for service. Consequently it is necessary to put on record the ever changing composition of these home-service divisions. It is the more desirable to carry out the task for these divisions, as very few diaries are in existence for the divisions which remained at home; and the three divisions which went to India did not submit any diaries, as they reverted to peace service on landing in that country. The tables and narratives for the home-service mounted divisions and the three infantry divisions which went to India in 1914, have been compiled from returns, tables, telegrams, odd diaries, and some printed sources; officers who served with these divisions have given valuable assistance. The tables and narratives of the other fourteen divisions (two mounted and twelve infantry divisions) have been compiled from the war diaries of the formations and units concerned.

In the list of Commands and Staffs, temporary changes due to absences on short leave, at short courses, and at schools of instruction are not shown.

In the Divisional Tables the organization is given for each year in which the division served in a theatre of war, and the month selected is one which shows the division at some important period of its history: as it first went overseas, before one of the great battles, and its final organization in 1918. In the tables for the home-service mounted divisions, and for the three divisions which went to India, each considerable change in composition is given.

Appendix I. gives the peace establishment of a Territorial Force infantry division before August, 1914, and, in addition, the war establishment which was laid down for the division on the outbreak of the Great War, as well as the war establishments for a Territorial Force division in France in 1916, and in 1918. Appendices 2, 3, and 4 show respectively the authorized war establishments for the 2nd Mounted Division in Egypt (1915), for the 52nd (Lowland) Division in Gallipoli (1915), and for the 53rd (Welsh) Division in Palestine (1917).

By the end of 1914 there were already no fewer than five different field artillery establishments with the regular divisions then in France; and still another field artillery establishment was added in 1915, on the arrival of Territorial Force divisions. In addition, the low establishment of the latter divisional artilleries often entailed the provision of additional artillery from the regular divisions, so as to assist a territorial division in carrying out its appointed tasks. In 1916, partly by reducing the artillery of regular divisions in France to 64 guns and howitzers, similarity of field artillery establishment was at last secured for all divisions; and by this time the 15-pounder guns and 5-inch howitzers had been replaced by 18-pounders and 4·5-inch howitzers.

The 15-pounder Q.F. (Ehrhardt) guns (dating from the South African War), of the horse artillery batteries with the 2nd Mounted Division, were replaced in Egypt by 18-pounders. Some of these Ehrhardt guns were thereafter used to arm merchant ships. In these Ehrhardt equipments very few of the parts were interchangeable and the ammunition was a difficulty, as a special cartridge case was necessary.

As the 15-pounder B.L.C. guns[1] were replaced in the territorial infantry divisions, the equipments were returned to England and they became available for training units at home.

The 5-inch B.L. howitzer (first issued in 1896) only had a range of 4,900 yards with its 50-lb. lyddite shell. In April, 1915, a 40-lb. shell was fired with an increased charge, and by this means the range was lengthened to 6,100 yards. There were, however, other drawbacks to this howitzer. The piece had small buffers, giving a short recoil, and, although the carriage was fitted with drag-shoes, it had to be run up between rounds.

The replacement of the 15-pounders and 5-inch howitzers by 18-pounders and 4·5-inch howitzers, besides simplifying the ammunition supply, undoubtedly added to the effectiveness of the territorial batteries.[2] The delay in replacing the howitzers was due to the small output of 4·5-inch howitzers.

The numerous, intricate, and involved reorganizations and re-designations of the field artillery brigades and batteries are given in the notes to the various tables.

In the lists of Battles and Engagements, the periods when the divisional artillery, engineers, and pioneers were left in the line, after the relief of a division, are not shown.[3]

Neither the attachments to divisions of Army field artillery brigades (formed in France early in 1917 after the reorganization of divisional artilleries), nor the attachments of R.G.A. brigades, are shown in the General Notes to the tables. These attachments were so numerous, and often of such short duration, that their inclusion would have been misleading. All other attachments are given either in the order of battle table or in the general notes. In order that the table shall be as clear as possible, the numbered notes are printed on the page following the table.

---

[1]After the South African War the 15-pounder B.L. had been converted. The gun had its trunnions cut off and was fitted in a cradle, and the breech mechanism was converted to single motion.

[2]The following figures will show the part played by the 18-pounder and the 4·5-inch howitzer in the Great War. At the end of the War there were 3,970 18-pounder and 1,225 4·5-inch howitzer equipments with various units in the field. Of the 113,000,000 rounds of 18-pounder ammunition and 29,000,000 rounds of 4·5-inch howitzer ammunition shipped to the various theatres, 99,000,000 rounds of 18-pounder and 25,000,000 rounds of 4·5-inch howitzer were fired in France and Belgium.

[3]These extra tours of duty in the battle areas, after the relief of the infantry brigades of the division, were fairly numerous and sometimes of prolonged duration. To illustrate this, part of the experience of the 50th Division Artillery is given:—

1915. IV. Northumbrian (Howitzer) Brigade was in action from 10th May-23rd June, and then from 26th June-23rd October.

1916. 50th Division Artillery was engaged in February and March in support of the 17th Division, both on the 14th February in the Defence of the Bluff (when it was lost) and on the 2nd March in support of the attack, when the Bluff was regained.

Later in this year, in the Battles of the Somme, the 50th Division Artillery was in action from the 18th August-11th November.

1918. In the First Battles of the Somme, the 50th Division Artillery was in action from the 22nd March-7th and 8th April; and later in the year, in the Advance to Victory, the 50th Division Artillery was in action from the 21st October-8th November. (Also see General Notes, 50th Division, p. 95.)

During 1914 and early in 1915, the First-line Territorial Force Infantry Divisions were frequently called on to provide battalions and field companies to reinforce the Expeditionary Force on the Western Front. Although the sister Second-line Territorial Force battalion or field company was usually sent at once to the division to replace the unit which had gone overseas, yet second-line battalions had rarely received arms before joining the first-line division. The Territorial Force field artillery was often called on to provide many of its best field artillery horses for the Expeditionary Force. This constant provision of units, horses, and equipment, to meet the pressing needs of the situation in France, as well as the necessity of Home Defence, must be borne in mind whenever it is thought that any of the First-line Territorial Force Divisions were overlong in preparing for service overseas.[1]

In the lists of Battles and Engagements, occasional deviations have been made from the lists given in the *Report of the Battles Nomenclature Committee* (published in 1921), so as to include actions of which a division has reason to be particularly proud. In every case after the battle in which a division fought, there is given in square brackets the Corps and Army in which the division was serving at that time. If a division did not happen to be engaged during a whole year, in some specific battle or engagement, then only the year is shown, and this signifies that the division was on active service in the field during this period.

In the lists, the words " Action " and " Affair " have been omitted. Only the date and name are given of these engagements.[2]

Each divisional story was submitted for comment to the general officer who commanded the division in the field at the end of the Great War. In addition, the story of the division was sent to the general officer in command of the division of the Territorial Army which to-day is the descendant of the particular Territorial Force division which took part in the Great War. I am deeply grateful to all the divisional commanders, staff officers, and other officers of the divisions who have assisted in checking and correcting these tables and providing additional information. I have also received considerable assistance from the War Office Library and from " R " Records, War Office, in the elucidation of many obscure dates and details.

As in the preparation of the first part of this series, I am greatly indebted to the Staff of the Historical Section (Military Branch) for the specialized help which they have afforded so freely and so often ; and, in particular, my most grateful thanks are once more due to Mr. P. F. L. Wright, who has given me untiring assistance all through the compilation of this part.

Any corrections or amendments to these tables should be sent to the Secretary, Historical Section, Committee of Imperial Defence, 2, Whitehall Gardens, S.W.1.

A.F.B.

September, 1935.

[1]Forty battalions and seven field companies went overseas independently of their own Territorial Force divisions.

[2]The Second Action of Givenchy, 1915, is shown as " 15 and 16 June, Givenchy."

CONTENTS

Pages

List of Abbreviations .... vii—ix

1st MOUNTED DIVISION .... 1—7
- Commanders and Staff Officers .... 1—3
- Order of Battle Table 4, 5
- Notes on Table 6
- Formation and Narrative 7

(2nd/1st MOUNTED DIVISION was never formed)

2nd MOUNTED DIVISION (1st, 2nd, 3rd, and 4th Mtd. Bdes.) .... 9—17
- Commanders and Staff Officers .... 9—11
- Order of Battle Table 12, 13
- Notes on Table 14
- General Notes 15
- Formation, Battles, and Engagements 16, 17

2nd/2nd MOUNTED DIVISION .... 19—26
- Commanders and Staff Officers .... 19—21
- Order of Battle Table 22, 23
- Notes on Table and General Notes 24
- Formation and Narrative 25, 26

(3rd MOUNTED DIVISION, see 2nd/2nd Mtd. Div.)

4th MOUNTED DIVISION .... 27—30
- Commanders and Staff Officers 27
- Order of Battle Table 28
- Notes on Table and General Notes 29
- Formation and Narrative 30

YEOMANRY MOUNTED DIVISION (6th, 8th, and 22nd Mtd. Bdes.) .... 31—34
- Commanders and Staff Officers 31
- Order of Battle Table 32
- Notes on Table and General Notes 33
- Formation, Battles, and Engagements 34

42nd (EAST LANCASHIRE) DIVISION (125th, 126th, 127th Inf. Bdes.) .... 35—41
- Commanders and Staff Officers 35, 36
- General Notes 37
- Order of Battle Table 38
- Notes on Table 39
- Mobilization, Battles, and Engagements 40, 41

43rd (WESSEX) DIVISION .... 43—48
- Commanders and Staff Officers 43
- Order of Battle Table 44, 45
- Notes on Table 45
- General Notes 46
- Mobilization and Narrative 47, 48

44th (HOME COUNTIES) DIVISION .... 49—54
- Commanders and Staff Officers 49
- Order of Battle Table 50
- Notes on Table 51
- General Notes 52
- Mobilization and Narrative 53, 54

45th (2nd/WESSEX) DIVISION .... 55—60
- Commanders and Staff Officers 55
- Order of Battle Table 56
- Notes on Table 57
- General Notes 58
- Formation and Narrative 59, 60

46th (NORTH MIDLAND) DIVISION (137th, 138th, and 139th Inf. Bdes.) .... 61—67
- Commanders and Staff Officers 61, 62
- General Notes 63
- Order of Battle Table 64
- Notes on Table 65
- Mobilization, Battles, and Engagements 66, 67

47th (2nd LONDON) DIVISION (140th, 141st, and 142nd Inf. Bdes.) .... 69—75
- Commanders and Staff Officers 69, 70
- General Notes 71
- Order of Battle Table 72
- Notes on Table 73
- Mobilization, Battles, and Engagements 74, 75

Pages

48th (SOUTH MIDLAND) DIVISION (143rd, 144th, and 145th Inf. Bdes.) .... **77—83**
Commanders and Staff Officers 77, 78
General Notes 79
Order of Battle Table 80, 81
Notes on Table 81
Mobilization, Battles, and Engagements 82, 83

49th (WEST RIDING) DIVISION (146th, 147th, and 148th Inf. Bdes.)...................... **85—91**
Commanders and Staff Officers 85, 86
General Notes 87
Order of Battle Table 88
Notes on Table 89
Mobilization, Battles, and Engagements 90, 91

50th (NORTHUMBRIAN) DIVISION (149th, 150th, and 151st Inf. Bdes.) .... **93—100**
Commanders and Staff Officers 93, 94
General Notes 95
Order of Battle Table 96, 97
Notes on Table 98
Mobilization, Battles, and Engagements 99, 100

51st (HIGHLAND) DIVISION (152nd, 153rd, and 154th Inf. Bdes.) .... **101—107**
Commanders and Staff Officers 101, 102
General Notes 103
Order of Battle Table 104, 105
Notes on Table.. 105
Mobilization, Battles, and Engagements 106, 107

52nd (LOWLAND) DIVISION (155th, 156th, and 157th Inf. Bdes.) .... **109—115**
Commanders and Staff Officers 109, 110
General Notes 111
Order of Battle Table.. 112
Notes on Table.. 113
Mobilization, Battles, and Engagements 114, 115

53rd (WELSH) DIVISION (158th, 159th, and 160th Inf. Bdes.) .... **117—123**
Commanders and Staff Officers 117, 118
General Notes 119
Order of Battle Table.. 120
Notes on Table.. 121
Mobilization, Battles, and Engagements.................. 122, 123

54th (EAST ANGLIAN) DIVISION (161st, 162nd, and 163rd Inf. Bdes.) .... **125—131**
Commanders and Staff Officers.............................. 125, 126
General Notes 127
Order of Battle Table.. 128
Notes on Table.. 129
Mobilization, Battles, and Engagements 130, 131

55th (WEST LANCASHIRE) DIVISION (164th, 165th, and 166th Inf. Bdes.) .... **133—139**
Commanders and Staff Officers.............................. 133, 134
General Notes 135
Order of Battle Table.. 136
Notes on Table.. 137
Mobilization, Re-formation, Battles, and Engagements 138, 139

56th (1st LONDON) DIVISION (167th, 168th, and 169th Inf. Bdes.) .... **141—147**
Commanders and Staff Officers 141, 142
General Notes 143
Order of Battle Table.. 144
Notes on Table.. 145
Mobilization, Re-formation, Battles, and Engagements 146, 147

APPENDIX 1 — The changes in the establishment and composition of a T. F. Division on the Western Front during the Great War, 1914-1918 ...... **150, 151**

APPENDIX 2 ... War Establishment of the 2nd Mtd. Div. (Egypt), 1915..................... **152**

APPENDIX 3 — War Establishment of the 52nd (Lowland) Division (Gallipoli), 1915 ....**152, 153**

APPENDIX 4 — War Establishment of the 53rd (Welsh) Division (Palestine), 1917 .... **153**

INDEX OF FORMATIONS.. **155—157**

LIST OF ABBREVIATIONS

NOTE.—For the period of the Great War the titles of regiments have been taken from the 1914–1918 Army Lists.

A.

(A.-A.) ... ... (Anti-Aircraft).
A.-A. & Q.-M.-G. Assistant-Adjutant & Quarter-Master-General.
A. & S.H. ... ... Argyll & Sutherland Highlanders.
A.F.A. Bde. ... Army Field Artillery Brigade.
A.H.Q. ... ... Army Head-Quarters.
Amb. or Ambce. Ambulance.
Ammn. Coln. ... Ammunition Column.
Ammn. Park ... Ammunition Park.
A.R.O. ... ... Army Routine Order.
Arty. ... ... Artillery.
A.S.C.... ... ... Army Service Corps.
A.T. ... ... Army Troops.
Aux. ... ... Auxiliary.

B.

B.A.C. ... ... Brigade Ammunition Column.
Bde. ... ... Brigade.
Bedf. ... ... Bedfordshire Regiment.
Bedf. Yeo.... ... Bedfordshire Yeomanry.
B.E.F. ... ... British Expeditionary Force.
Berks. ... ... Berkshire.
B.F.T. ... ... British Forces in Turkey.
B.-G., R.A. ... Brigadier-General, Commanding Royal Artillery.
B.-G., R.H.A. ... Brigadier-General, Commanding Royal Horse Artillery.
B.L. ... ... Breech-loader.
B.L.C. ... ... B.L. Converted.
Bn. ... ... Battalion.
Bord. ... ... Border Regiment.
Br.-Gen. ... ... Brigadier-General.
Bty. ... ... Battery.
Bucks. ... ... Buckinghamshire.
Buffs ... ... Buffs (East Kent Regiment).
B.W. ... ... Black Watch (Royal Highlanders).

C.

Camb. ... ... Cambridgeshire Regiment.
Cam. H. ... ... Cameron Highlanders.
Cav. ... ... Cavalry.
C.B. ... ... Cavalry Brigade.
C.C.S. ... ... Casualty Clearing Station.
cd. ... ... command.
C.D.M.T. Coy. ... Cavalry Divisional Mechanical Transport Company.
Cdn. ... ... Canadian.
C.F.A. ... ... Combined Field Ambulance.
C.G. ... ... Coldstream Guards.
Ches. ... ... Cheshire Regiment.
C.I. ... ... Central India.
Col.-Cdt. ... ... Colonel-Commandant.
Comp. ... ... Composite.
Conn. Rang. ... Connaught Rangers.
Co. ... ... County.
Coy. ... ... Company.
Cos. ... ... Companies.
C.R.E. ... ... Commanding Royal Engineers.
C.R.H.A. ... ... Commanding Royal Horse Artillery.

D.

d. ... ... died.
D.A.C. ... ... Divisional Ammunition Column.
D.C.L.I. ... ... Duke of Cornwall's Light Infantry.
D.E. Coy. ... ... Divisional Employment Company.
Detnt. ... ... Detachment.
Devon ... ... Devonshire Regiment.
D.G. ... ... Dragoon Guards.
Dgns. ... ... Dragoons.
Disembkd. ... Disembarked.
Disembkn. ... Disembarkation.
Div. ... ... Division.
Divnl. ... ... Divisional.
D.L.I. ... ... Durham Light Infantry.
D.M.C. ... ... Desert Mounted Corps.
d. of w. ... ... died of wounds.
Dorset ... ... Dorsetshire Regiment.
Duke's ... ... Duke of Wellington's (West Riding Regiment).

E.

E. ... ... East ; or Eastern.
E.E.F. ... ... Egyptian Expeditionary Force.
E. Lanc. ... ... East Lancashire Regiment.
Embkd. ... ... Embarked.
Emplnt. or Emplynt. ... Employment.
Eng. ... ... Engineers.
Essex ... ... Essex Regiment.
E. Surr. ... ... East Surrey Regiment.
evacd. ... ... evacuated.
E. York. ... ... East Yorkshire Regiment.

F.

Fd. ... ... Field.

G.

G. B. or Garr. Bn. ... Garrison Battalion.
Gds. ... ... Guards.
G.G. ... ... Grenadier Guards.
G.H.Q. ... ... General Head-Quarters.
Glouc. ... ... Gloucestershire Regiment.
G.O.C. ... ... General Officer Commanding.
Gord. H. ... ... Gordon Highlanders.
Gr. How. ... ... Green Howards (Alexandra, Princess of Wales's Own Yorkshire Regiment).
G.S.O.1. ... ... General Staff Officer (1st Grade).

H.

(H.) ... ... (Howitzer).
H.A.C. ... ... Honourable Artillery Company.
Hants. ... ... Hampshire Regiment.
H.A.R. ... ... Heavy Artillery Reserve.
H.B. ... ... Heavy Battery.
H.D. Trps. ... Home Defence Troops.
Hereford ... ... Herefordshire.
Herts.... ... ... Hertfordshire Regiment.
H.L.I.... ... ... Highland Light Infantry.
Home Cties. ... Home Counties.
Househ'd.... ... Household.
How. Bde. ... Howitzer Brigade.
How. Bty. ... Howitzer Battery.
H.Q. ... ... Head-Quarters.
Hsrs. ... ... Hussars.
H.T. ... ... Horse Transport.
H.T.M.B. ... ... Heavy Trench Mortar Battery.
Hy. Bde. ... ... Heavy Brigade.
Hy. Bty. A.C. ... Heavy Battery Ammunition Column.

I.

I.G. ... ... Irish Guards.
Ind. ... ... Indian.
Inf. ... ... Infantry.
Ir. ... ... Irish.
It. ... ... Italian.

K.

K. or Kd. ... ... Killed.
K.E. Horse ... King Edward's Horse.
K.G.O. ... ... King George's Own.
King's ... ... King's (Liverpool Regiment).
K.O. ... ... King's Own (Royal Lancaster Regiment).
K.O.S.B. ... ... King's Own Scottish Borderers.
K.O.Y.L.I. ... King's Own (Yorkshire Light Infantry).
K.R.R.C. ... ... King's Royal Rifle Corps.
K.S.L.I. ... ... King's (Shropshire Light Infantry).

L.

Lcrs. ... ... Lancers.
Leic. ... ... Leicestershire Regiment.
Leic. Yeo. ... ... Leicestershire Yeomanry.
Leins. ... ... Leinster Regiment.
L.F. ... ... Lancashire Fusiliers.
L.G. ... ... Life Guards.
L.I. ... ... Light Infantry.
Linc. ... ... Lincolnshire Regiment.
L.N.L. ... ... Loyal North Lancashire Regiment.
L. of C. ... ... Line of Communications.
Lond. ... ... London Regiment.
Loyal ... ... The Loyal Regiment (North Lancashire).
L.R.B. ... ... London Rifle Brigade.
L.S. ... ... London Scottish.
L.Sec. ... ... Left Section.

M.

Manch. ... ... Manchester Regiment.
Med. ... ... Medium.
M.G.C. ... ... Machine Gun Corps.
M.G. Coy. ... Machine-Gun Company.
M.G. Sec. ... ... Machine-Gun Section.
M.G. Sqdn. ... Machine-Gun Squadron.
M.I. ... ... Mounted Infantry.
Midd'x. ... ... Middlesex Regiment.
Midld.... ... ... Midland.
Mk. ... ... Mark.
M.M.G. ... ... Motor Machine Gun.
Mobn. ... ... Mobilization.
Mob. Vety. Sec. Mobile Veterinary Section.
Mon. or Monm'th. Monmouthshire Regiment.
M.T. ... ... Mechanical Transport.
Mtd. ... ... Mounted.
Mtn. ... ... Mountain.

N.

N. ... ... North ; or Northern.
Newf'dld. ... ... Newfoundland.
N.F. ... ... Northumberland Fusiliers.
N. Irish H. ... North Irish Horse.
N.M. Fd. Coy. ... North Midland Field Company.
Norf. ... ... Norfolk Regiment.
Northants. Yeo. Northamptonshire Yeomanry.
North'bn. ... ... Northumbrian.
North'd. ... ... Northumberland.
North'n. ... ... Northamptonshire Regiment.
N. Som. ... ... North Somerset.
N. Staff. ... ... North Staffordshire Regiment.
N.S.W. ... ... New South Wales.
N.Z. & A. ... ... New Zealand and Australian.

O.

O. & B.L.I. ... Oxfordshire & Buckinghamshire Light Infantry.
Offrs. ... ... Officers.
O.R. ... ... Other ranks.

P.

(P.) ... ... (Pioneers).
P.E. ... ... Peace Establishment.
P.P.C.L.I. ... ... Princess Patricia's Canadian Light Infantry.
P.O. Rif. ... ... Post Office Rifles.
P.W.O. ... ... Prince of Wales's Own.

Q.

Q.O.O. Hsrs. ... Queen's Own Oxfordshire Hussars.
Q.O.R.R. Staff. Yeo. ... ... Queen's Own Royal Regiment, Staffordshire Yeomanry.
Queen's ... ... Queen's (Royal West Surrey Regiment.)
Q.V. Rif. ... ... Queen Victoria's Rifles.
Q.W. Rif. ... ... Queen's Westminster Rifles.

R.

R. ... ... Royal.
R.A.F. ... ... Royal Air Force.
R.A.S.C. ... ... Royal Army Service Corps.
R.B. ... ... Rifle Brigade.
R. Berks. ... ... Royal Berkshire Regiment.
R. Cdn. H.A. Bde. Royal Canadian Horse Artillery Brigade.
R.D.F. ... ... Royal Dublin Fusiliers.
R.E. ... ... Royal Engineers.
Regt. ... ... Regiment.
R.F. ... ... Royal Fusiliers.
R.F.A. ... ... Royal Field Artillery.
Rfts. ... ... Reinforcements.
R.G.A. ... ... Royal Garrison Artillery.
R.H.A. ... ... Royal Horse Artillery.
R.H.G. ... ... Royal Horse Guards.
Rid. ... ... Riding.
R. Innis. F. ... Royal Inniskilling Fusiliers.
R. Ir. F. ... ... Royal Irish Fusiliers.
R. Irish Regt. ... Royal Irish Regiment.
R. Ir. Rif. ... ... Royal Irish Rifles.
R.M.F. ... ... Royal Munster Fusiliers.
R.M.L.I. ... ... Royal Marine Light Infantry.
R.N.A.C.D. ... Royal Naval Armoured Car Division.
R.N.D. ... ... Royal Naval Division.
R. Scots. ... ... Royal Scots (Lothian Regiment).
R. Sec. ... ... Right Section.
R.S.F. ... ... Royal Scots Fusiliers.
R. Suss. ... ... Royal Sussex Regiment.
R.W. ... ... Royal Warrant.
R. War. ... ... Royal Warwickshire Regiment.
R.W.F. ... ... Royal Welsh Fusiliers.
R.W.K. ... ... Queen's Own (Royal West Kent Regiment).

S.

S. ... ... South ; or Southern.
S.A.A. Sec. ... Small-Arm-Ammunition Section.
S.B. ... ... Siege Battery.
S.B.A.C. ... ... Siege Battery Ammunition Column.
Sco. Rif. ... ... The Cameronians (Scottish Rifles).
Sea. H. ... ... Seaforth Highlanders.
Sec. ... ... Section.
S.G. ... ... Scots Guards.
Sher. For. ... Sherwood Foresters (Nottinghamshire & Derbyshire Regiment).

S.—*continued.*

Sig.	Signal.
S. Irish H. ...	South Irish Horse.
S. Lanc.	South Lancashire Regiment.
S. & M.	Sappers & Miners.
S.M. Fd. Coy. ...	South Midland Field Company.
Som. L.I.	Somerset Light Infantry.
Sqdn.	Squadron.
S. Staff.	South Staffordshire Regiment.
Suff.	Suffolk Regiment.
S.W.B.	South Wales Borderers.

T.

T.A.	Territorial Army.
T. & S. Coln. ...	Transport & Supply Column.
Tempy.	Temporary.
T.F.	Territorial Force.
T.M. Bty.	Trench Mortar Battery.
Trp.	Troop.

U.

U.K.	United Kingdom.

V.

Vety.	Veterinary.

W.

W.	West ; or Western.
w. or wd.	wounded.
War.	Warwickshire.
W.E.	War Establishment.
Welsh	Welsh Regiment.
W.G.	Welsh Guards.
Wilts.	Wiltshire Regiment.
Worc....	Worcestershire Regiment.
W. Rid.	West Riding.
W. York.	West Yorkshire Regiment.

Y.

Y. & L.	York & Lancaster Regiment.
Yeo.	Yeomanry.

NOTE.—To save space, some place-names have occasionally been shortened, e.g. :—

Burton-on-Trent appears as Burton,
Hebburn-on-Tyne ,, Hebburn,
Newcastle-on-Tyne ,, Newcastle,
etc.

1ST MOUNTED DIVISION

(In July, 1916, 1st Mounted Division became 1st Cyclist Division)

G.O.C.

5 August, 1914 ... ... Major-General E. A. H. ALDERSON.
29 September, 1914 ... ... Lieutenant-General R. G. BROADWOOD.

G.S.O. 1.

5 Aug., 1914...Col. W. E. PEYTON.
10 Sept., 1914...Col. R. C. B. LAWRENCE.
2 Feb., 1915...Lt.-Col. H. M. DURAND.
12 Nov., 1915...Lt.-Col. C. K. BURNETT.
28 July, 1916...Major C. J. THACKWELL (acting).
3 Aug., 1916...Lt.-Col. F. DE B. YOUNG.

A.-A. and Q.-M.-G.

5 Aug., 1914...Col. G. H. CARDEW.

C.R.H.A.

——

C.R.E.

19 Oct., 1914...Col. F. H. HORNIBLOW.
29 Oct., 1915 } Col. G. D. CLOSE.
3 May, 1916 }

AUGUST, 1914

EASTERN MOUNTED BDE.
[1 April, '12] *Br.-Gen. H. W. HODGSON.

1st S. MIDLAND MOUNTED BDE.
[28 June, '14] *Br.-Gen. E. A. WIGGIN.

2nd S. MIDLAND MOUNTED BDE.
[1 April, '12] *Br.-Gen. EARL OF LONGFORD.

NOTTS. and DERBY MOUNTED BDE.
[1 April, '12] *Br.-Gen. P. A. KENNA, V.C.

SEPTEMBER, 1914

EASTERN MOUNTED BDE.
[1 April, '12] *Br.-Gen. H. W. HODGSON.

S. WALES MOUNTED BDE.
[1 Jan., '13] *Br.-Gen. F. A. B. FRYER.

WELSH BORDER MOUNTED BDE.
[4 April, '12] *Br.-Gen. E. A. HERBERT.

N. MIDLAND MOUNTED BDE.
[1 Sep., '11] *Br.-Gen. C. WILLIAMS.

OCTOBER, 1915

S. WALES MOUNTED BDE.
[1 Jan., '13] *Br.-Gen. F. A. B. FRYER.

WELSH BORDER MOUNTED BDE.
[4 April, '12] *Br.-Gen. E. A. HERBERT.

2/1/S. WALES MOUNTED BDE.
[6 Jan., '15] Br.-Gen. F. C. MEYRICK.

2/1/N. MIDLAND MOUNTED BDE.
[12 Jan., '15] Br.-Gen. R. N. SMYTH.

MARCH, 1916

2/1/EASTERN MOUNTED BDE.
[10 Jan., '15] Br.-Gen. E. W. N. PEDDER.

2/1/WELSH BORDER MOUNTED BDE.
[20 Jan., '15] Br.-Gen. M. D. LITTLE.

2/1/S. WALES MOUNTED BDE.
[6 Jan., '15] Br.-Gen. F. C. MEYRICK.

2/1/N. MIDLAND MOUNTED BDE.
[12 Jan., '15] Br.-Gen. R. N. SMYTH.

*Br.-Gen. on 5 August, 1914.

APRIL, 1916

1st MOUNTED BDE.
(2/1/Highland)

[22 Jan., '15] Br.-Gen. J. E. DEWAR.

2nd MOUNTED BDE.
(2/2/South-Western)

[9 Jan., '15] Br.-Gen. H. H. J. W. DRUMMOND.
6 April, '16...Br.-Gen. F. A. B. FRYER.

3rd MOUNTED BDE.
(2/1/North Midland)

[12 Jan., '15] Br.-Gen. R. N. SMYTH.

4th MOUNTED BDE.
(2/1/South Wales)

[6 Jan., '15] Br.-Gen. F. C. MEYRICK.

JULY, 1916

1st CYCLIST BDE.

[22 Jan., '15] Br.-Gen. J. E. DEWAR.

2nd CYCLIST BDE.

[6 Jan., '15] Br.-Gen. F. C. MEYRICK.

3rd CYCLIST BDE.

[12 Jan., '15] Br.-Gen. R. N. SMYTH.

4th CYCLIST BDE.

[10 May, '16] Br.-Gen. A. D. MILLER.

Formed in August, 1914

1st MOUNTED DIVISION ORDER OF BATTLE, 1914-1916

Dates	YEOMANRY: Mounted (later Cyclist) Brigades	YEOMANRY: Regiments and attached Units	R.H.A. (T.F.): Brigade	R.H.A. (T.F.): Batteries	Engineers	Signal Service	Medical	Mobile Veterinary Sections	A.S.C.
1914 August (England)	Eastern................. 1st S. Midland[2] ... 2nd S. Midland[3] ... Notts. and Derby.[5] Attached	Suff. Yeo., K.O.R.R. Norf. Yeo., Essex Yeo.[1] War. Yeo., R. Glouc. Hsrs., Q.O. Worc. Hsrs. R. Bucks. Hsrs., Berks. Yeo., Q.O.O. Hsrs.[4] Sherwood Rgrs., S. Notts. Hsrs., Derby. Yeo. 6/Norf. (Cyclist Bn.), 6/Suff. (Cyclist Bn.), 6/R. Suss. (Cyclist Bn.), 25/Co. of London (Cyclist Bn.)	...	Essex and Ammn. Coln. Warwick[2] and Ammn. Coln. Berks.[3] and Ammn. Coln. Notts.[5] and Ammn. Coln.	...	London Wireless Sig. Coy. Southern Wireless Sig. Coy. 1 Sec., Scottish Cable Sig. Coy. 1 Sec., Scottish Cable Sig. Coy.	Eastern Fd. Amb. 1st S. Midland[2] Fd. Amb. 2nd S. Midland[3] Fd. Amb. Notts. and Derby.[5] Fd. Amb.	Eastern 1st S. Midland[2] 2nd S. Midland[3] Notts. and Derby.[5]	Eastern T. and S. Coln. 1st S. Midland[2] T. and S. Coln. 2nd S. Midland[3] T. and S. Coln. Notts. and Derby.[5] T. and S. Coln. 1st Mtd. Divnl. A.S.C.
1915 March (England)	Eastern[6] .... S. Wales[2]............ Welsh Border[3]...... N. Midland[5]; [8]...... Attached	Suff. Yeo., K.O.R.R. Norf. Yeo., 2/K.E. Horse[1]; [7] Pembroke. Yeo., Montgomery. Yeo., Glamorgan. Yeo. Shropshire Yeo., Ches. Yeo., Denbigh. Hsrs. Staff. Yeo., Lincoln. Yeo., Welsh Horse[7]; [9] 6/Norf. (Cyclist Bn.), 6/Suff. (Cyclist Bn.), 6/R. Suss. (Cyclist Bn.), 25/Co. of London (Cyclist Bn.)	...	Essex and Ammn. Coln. Glamorgan. and Ammn. Coln. Shropshire and Ammn. Coln. Leicester. and Ammn. Coln. 117th Hy. Bty., 41st Siege Bty.[10]	...	Eastern Sig. Trp. S. Wales Sig. Trp. Welsh Border Sig. Trp. N. Midland Sig. Trp. S. Cd. A.T. Sig. Coy. Scottish A.T. Sig. Coy. Lond. Wireless Sig. Sec.	Eastern Fd. Amb. S. Wales Fd. Amb. Welsh Border Fd. Amb. N. Midland Fd. Amb.	Eastern S. Wales Welsh Border N. Midland	Eastern A.S.C. S. Wales A.S.C. Welsh Border A.S.C. N. Midland A.S.C. 1st Mtd. Divnl. A.S.C.
1915 November (England)	S. Wales[11]........... Welsh Border[12] ... 2/1/S. Wales[6] .... 2/1/N. Midland[8] ... Attached	Pembroke. Yeo.,[13] Montgomery. Yeo.,[14] Glamorgan. Yeo.[13] Shropshire Yeo.,[15] Ches. Yeo.,[15] Denbigh. Hsrs.[16] 2/1/Pembroke. Yeo., 2/1/Montgomery. Yeo., 2/1/Glamorgan. Yeo., 2/1/Welsh Horse 2/1/Staff. Yeo., 2/1/Leicester. Yeo., 2/1/Lincoln. Yeo. 6/Norf. (Cyclist Bn.), 6/Suff. (Cyclist Bn.), 25/Co. of London (Cyclist Bn.),[17] 2/6/R. Suss. (Cyclist Bn.), 2/25/London (Cyclist Bn.)	...	Glamorgan.[18] and Ammn. Coln. Shropshire[19] and Ammn. Coln. Essex[20] and Ammn. Coln. 2/1/Glamorgan.[18] and Ammn. Coln. Leicester.[21] and Ammn. Coln. 2/1/Leicester.[22] and Ammn. Coln. 117 Hy. Bty.[23] 2/Devon. Hy. Bty.	...	S. Wales Sig. Trp. Welsh Border Sig. Trp. 2/1/S. Wales Sig. Trp. 2/1/N. Midland Sig. Trp. 1st Mtd. Divnl. Sig. Sqdn.	S. Wales Fd. Amb. Welsh Border Fd. Amb. 2/1/S. Wales Fd. Amb. 2/1/N. Midland Fd. Amb.	S. Wales Welsh Border 2/1/S. Wales 2/1/N. Midland	S. Wales A.S.C. Welsh Border A.S.C. 2/1/S. Wales A.S.C. 2/1/N. Midland A.S.C. 1st Mtd. Divnl. A.S.C.

1916 May (England)	**2/1/Eastern**[11]	2/1/Suff. Yeo., 2/1/K.O.R.R. Norf. Yeo., 2/1/**Essex** Yeo.	...	...	...	2/1/Eastern Sig. Trp.	2/1/Eastern Fd. Amb.	2/1/Eastern	2/1/Eastern A.S.C.
	2/1/N. Midland	2/1/Staff. Yeo., 2/1/Leic. Yeo., 2/1/Lincoln. Yeo.				2/1/N. Midland Sig. Trp.	2/1/N. Midland Fd. Amb.	2/1/N. Midland	2/1/N. Midland A.S.C.
	2/1/S. Wales	2/1/Pembroke. Yeo., 2/1/Montgomery. Yeo., 2/1/Glamorgan. Yeo.				2/1/S. Wales Sig. Trp.	2/1/S. Wales Fd. Amb.	2/1/S. Wales	2/1/S. Wales A.S.C.
	2/1/Welsh Border[12]	2/1/Shropshire Yeo., 2/1/Ches. Yeo., 2/1/Denbigh. Hsrs.		2/1/Shropshire[24] and Ammn. Coln.		2/1/Welsh Border Sig. Trp. 1st Mtd. Divnl. Sig. Sqdn.	2/1/Welsh Border Fd. Amb.	2/1/Welsh Border	2/1/Welsh Border A.S.C. 1st Mtd. Divnl. A.S.C.
1916 July (England)	1st (2/1/Highland)	2/1/Fife. & Forfar. Yeo., 2/1/Lovat's Scouts, 2/2/Lovat's Scouts	...	...	...	1st Mtd. Bde. Sig. Trp.	1st Mtd. Bde. Fd. Amb.	...	1st Mtd. Bde. A.S.C.
	2nd (2/2/S.-Western)	2/1/R. 1st Devon. Yeo., 2/1/R.N. Devon. Hsrs., 2/1/W. Som. Yeo.				2nd Mtd. Bde. Sig. Trp.	2nd Mtd. Bde. Fd. Amb.		2nd Mtd. Bde. A.S.C.
	3rd (2/1/N. Midland)	2/1/Staff. Yeo., 2/1/Leic. Yeo., 2/1/Lincoln. Yeo.				3rd Mtd. Bde. Sig. Trp.	3rd Mtd. Bde. Fd. Amb.		3rd Mtd. Bde. A.S.C.
	4th (2/1/S. Wales)	2/1/Pembroke. Yeo., 2/1/Montgomery. Yeo., 2/1/Glamorgan. Yeo.				4th Mtd. Bde. Sig. Trp. 1st Mtd. Divnl. Sig. Sqdn.	4th Mtd. Bde. Fd. Amb.		4th Mtd. Bde. A.S.C. 1st Mtd. Divnl. A.S.C.

In July, 1916, the 1st MOUNTED DIVISION became the 1st CYCLIST DIVISION

1916 September (England)	1st Cyclist	2/1/W. Som. Yeo.,[25] 2/1/Lovat's Scouts,[26] 2/2/Lovat's Scouts;[26] 2/25/London (Cyclist Bn.);[31] 6/Inf. Works Coy.	...	...	...	1st Cyclist Bde.[31] Sig. Trp.	1st Cyclist Bde.[31] Fd. Amb.	...	1st Cyclist Bde.[31] A.S.C.
	2nd Cyclist	2/1/Pembroke. Yeo.,[27] 2/1/R.N. Dev. Hsrs.,[28] 2/1/Glamorgan. Yeo.;[27] 6/Suff. (Cyclist Bn.)[31]				2nd Cyclist Bde.[31] Sig. Trp.	2nd Cyclist Bde.[31] Fd. Amb.		2nd Cyclist Bde.[31] A.S.C.
	3rd Cyclist[29]	2/1/Staff. Yeo., 2/1/Leicester. Yeo., 2/1/Lincoln. Yeo.; 2/7/Welsh (Cyclist Bn.)[32]				3rd Cyclist Bde.[32] Sig. Trp.	3rd Cyclist Bde.[32] Fd. Amb.		3rd Cyclist Bde.[32] A.S.C.
	4th Cyclist	2/1/Co. of Lond. Yeo.,[30] 2/1/City of Lond. Yeo.,[25] 2/3/Co. of Lond. Yeo.;[30] 6/Norf. (Cyclist Bn.)[32]				4th Cyclist Bde.[32] Sig. Trp.	4th Cyclist Bde.[32] Fd. Amb.		4th Cyclist Bde.[32] A.S.C.
	Attached	...	...	...	...	Cyclist Divnl. Sig. Coy. Northern Sig. Coy. (A.T.)			Cyclist Divnl. A.S.C.

By 16th November, 1916, the 1st CYCLIST DIVISION was broken up

NOTES

1 Regt. went to France and disembkd. at le Havre on 1/12/14. Regt. joined 8th Cav. Bde., 3rd Cav. Div., on 11/12/14. 2/K.E. Horse replaced Essex Yeo. in Eastern Mtd. Bde.

2 Bde. transferred to 2nd Mtd. Div. on its formation in Septr., 1914. Bde. was replaced by S. Wales Mtd. Bde.

3 Bde. transferred to 2nd Mtd. Div. on its formation in Septr., 1914. Bde. was replaced by Welsh Border Mtd. Bde.

4 Regt. went to France and disembkd. at Dunkirk on 22/9/14; joined 1st Cav. Div. on 31/10/14; and on 11/11/14 was posted to 4th Cav. Bde., 2nd Cav. Div. Q.O. Dorset Yeo. replaced Q.O.O. Hsrs. in 2nd S. Midland Mtd. Bde. (2nd Mtd. Div.).

5 Bde. transferred to 2nd Mtd. Div. on its formation in Septr., 1914. Bde. was replaced by N. Midland Mtd. Bde.

6 Bde. embkd. on 23/9/15 at Liverpool on *Olympic*, arrived Mudros 1/10/15, and landed at Anzac (Gallipoli) on 8 and 10/10/15. Welsh Horse had previously replaced 2/K.E.H. in Eastern Mtd. Bde. Bde. was replaced in 1st Mtd. Div. by 2/1/S. Wales Mtd. Bde.

7 Joined Cdn. Cav. Bde. at Maresfield. Cdn. Cav. Bde. handed over its horses to 2/1/S. Eastern Mtd. Bde. in May, 1915, entrained at Buxted Stn., on 4/5/15, arrived Boulogne, m/n. 4-5/5/15, reached Strazeele on 7/5/15. Bde. was attached to 1st Cdn. Div.

8 Bde. embkd. at Southampton on *Victorian*, *Mercian*, and *Nessian* on 27/10/15, for Salonika; destination was changed at sea, on 6/11/15, to Alexandria, and Bde. disembkd. at Alexandria between 10-20/11/15, and moved to Cairo. Bde. was replaced in 1st Mtd. Div. by 2/1/N. Mid. Mtd. Bde.

9 Regt. transferred to Eastern Mtd. Bde. to replace 2/K.E. Horse (see note 7). E. Riding Yeo. replaced Welsh Horse in N. Midland Mtd. Bde.

10 Bty. (4, 6-inch Hows.) disembkd. at le Havre on 10, 11, and 13/12/15, with XXXIV Hy. Arty. Bde., and reached Hazebrouck on 18/12/15. Bty. was made up to 6 hows. on 3/11/17.

11 Bde. disembkd. at Alexandria on 14 and 15/3/16. On 20/3/16 Bde. amalgamated with Welsh Border Mtd. Bde. and became 4th Dismtd. Bde. (see note 12). In Jany., 1917, 4th Dismtd. Bde. became 231st Bde., and the Bde. joined 74th (Yeo.) Div. on its formation in March, 1917. Bde. was replaced in 1st Mtd. Div. by 2/1/Eastern.

12 Bde. disembkd. at Alexandria on 15/3/16. On 20/3/16 Bde. amalgamated with S. Wales Mtd. Bde. and became 4th Dismtd. Bde. (see note 11). In Jany., 1917, 4th Dismtd. Bde. became 231st Bde., and the Bde. joined 74th (Yeo.) Div. on its formation in March, 1917. Bde. was replaced in 1st Mtd. Div. by 2/1/Welsh Border.

13 On 2/2/17 the two Regts. amalgamated and became 24/Welsh (Pembroke. and Glamorgan. Bn.) in 231st Bde., 74th Div.

14 On 4/3/17 the Regt. and the Welsh Horse amalgamated and became 25/R.W.F. (Montgomery. and Welsh Horse Bn.) in 231st Bde., 74th Div.

15 On 2/3/17 the two Regts. amalgamated and became 10/K.S.L.I. (Shropshire and Cheshire Bn.) in 231st Bde., 74th Div.

16 In Jany., 1917, the Regt. became 24/R.W.F. (Denbigh. Bn.) in 231st Bde. (later in 74th Div.).

17 Bn. went to India in Jany., 1916.

18 After the Bde. went to Egypt, the Bty. was posted in August, 1916, to CCXCIII Bde. with 58th (2/1/London) Div. (In Dec., 1915, the Bty. was rearmed with 4, 18-pdrs.) The Bde. disembkd. at le Havre on 22/1/17. Bde. became CCXCIII A.F.A. Bde. on 5/2/17. (2/1/Glamorgan. R.H.A. Bty. became 815 Fd. Bty. and remained in U.K.)

19 After the Bde. went to Egypt, the Bty. was posted in August, 1916, to CCXCIII Bde. with 58th (2/1/London) Div. The Bde. disembkd. at le Havre on 22/1/17. Bde. became CCXCIII A.F.A. Bde. on 5/2/17. (At Beccles on 30/12/15 the Bty. had been rearmed with 4, 18-pdr. guns.)

20 Bty. joined CCLXIV at Leicester on 13/1/16, embkd. at Devonport on 15 and 18/2/16, disembkd. at Port Said on 2/3/16, and joined 52nd (Lowland) Div. at el Qantara on 17/3/16. (See note 20, 52nd Div. Table.)

21 Bty. disembkd. at Alexandria on 25/2/16, and in March joined Anzac Mtd. Divnl. Arty. On 20/6/17 the Bty. was transferred to Yeo. Mtd. Div., and on 5/7/17 the Bty. joined XX R.H.A.

22 Bty. became A/CCXXIII (Home Counties) Bde. CCXXIII was transferred to 63rd (R.N.) Divnl. Arty. and became CCCXVIII. CCCXVIII disembkd. at le Havre on 3/7/16. On 10/7/16 CCCXVIII was renumbered CCXXV, and on 31/7/16 Bde. resumed its old number CCXXIII (Home Cos.) Bde. (G.H.Q., C.E. 1622 of 24/7/16).

23 Bty. (4, 60-pdr.) disembkd. at le Havre on 13/4/16, and arrived Bethune on 15/4/16 with XLIII Bde., R.G.A. (later XLIII H.A.G.).

24 Bty., after attachment to 1st Mtd. Div., joined CLVIII on the formation of the Bde. at Heytesbury on 13/4/17. The Bty. had been rearmed with 18-pdrs. CLVIII disembkd. at Boulogne on 24/5/17, and became an A.F.A. Bde. (Bty. armed with 18-pdrs.). On 6/7/17 the Bty. became A/CLVIII.

When the 1st Cyclist Division was broken up the following amalgamations and transfers took place:

25 2/1/W. Som. and 2/1/City of London (4th Cyclist Bde.) amalgamated and became 5th Bn., 2nd Cyclist Bde. Bn. joined 5th Cyclist Bde., 1st Mtd. Div., by May, 1917.

26 2/1 and 2/2/Lovat's Scouts amalgamated and became 1st Bn., 1st Cyclist Bde.

27 2/1/Pembroke. and 2/1/Glamorgan. amalgamated and became 2nd Bn. 1st Cyclist Bde.

28 2/1/R.N. Devon, Hsrs. and 2/1/R. 1st Dev. Yeo. (2nd Mtd. Bde., 1st Mtd. Div.) amalgamated and became 4th Bn., 2nd Cyclist Bde.

29 Bde. was transferred complete to 1st Mtd. Div. (originally 2/2nd Mtd. Div.) and became 2nd Mtd. Bde.

30 2/1 and 2/3/Co. of London amalgamated and became 6th Bn., 2nd Cyclist Bde.

31 Transferred to 1st Cyclist Bde.

32 Transferred to 2nd Cyclist Bde.

NOTE.—Orders for numbering the Mounted Brigades were issued on 31/3/16.

1st MOUNTED DIVISION

FORMATION AND NARRATIVE

The division had no existence before the outbreak of the Great War. Formed for Home Defence in August, 1914, immediately after the declaration of war, the division, composed of four existing mounted brigades (T.F.), was designated " Mounted Division." After assembling, the division established its headquarters at Bury St. Edmunds, the mounted brigades were at Ipswich, Diss, and Bury St. Edmunds (2), and the two cyclist battalions were at North Walsham and Saxmundham. Later in August, 1914, a concentration of mounted troops was ordered to take place at Churn, and the 1st S. Midland Mtd. Bde. moved to Newbury, the 2nd S. Midland Mtd. Bde. to Churn, and the Notts. and Derby. Mtd. Bde. to South Stoke. At the same time the Eastern Mtd. Bde. moved from Ipswich to Woodbridge.

At the end of August, 1914, it was decided to form another mounted division from the concentration of mounted brigades at and around Churn. The original Mounted Division was then designated 1st Mounted Division and the new division was known as the 2nd Mounted Division. The 1st Mounted Division, with its headquarters at Bury St. Edmunds, was now composed of the following 1st-line Mounted Brigades: Eastern (at Woodbridge), South Wales (at Aylsham), Welsh Border (at Bungay), and North Midland (at Diss). In February, 1915, the Welsh Border Mounted Brigade moved to Beccles, and the four cyclist battalions were stationed at North Walsham, Saxmundham, Holt, and Lowestoft.

As the 1st-line mounted brigades left for service overseas they were replaced by 2nd-line formations; but as late as July, 1915, there were 2nd-line R.H.A. Batteries without harness, guns, or wagons. (Some batteries only obtained two 12-pdr. guns, wagons, and harness in September, 1915.) In July, many 2nd-line signal troops were without the necessary equipment, even for training; machine-guns were still lacking; entrenching tools, swords, and rifles were required for instructional purposes; and very few men in 2nd-line units had fired a recruits' course of musketry. Not until October, 1915, were rifles available for every man.

By November, 1915, divisional headquarters had moved to Norwich, and the mounted brigades were around Cromer, Beccles, Yoxford, and Norwich, the cyclist battalions were at N. Walsham, Saxmundham, Lowestoft, Potter Heigham, and Holt, and the two heavy batteries were at Sheringham.

At the beginning of March, 1916, the last two 1st-line mounted brigades left for service overseas, and thenceforward the 1st Mounted Division was composed entirely of 2nd-line mounted brigades.

Early in July, 1916, the yeomanry regiments were dismounted and the horses were transferred to various remount depots. Bicycles were issued to the regiments, and they became yeomanry cyclist regiments. Later in July, 1916, the 1st Mounted Division was reorganized as a cyclist division and became the 1st Cyclist Division, in the Northern Army, Home Defence Troops. Divisional headquarters was at Bracondale (Norwich), and the four cyclist brigades had their headquarters at Beccles, Yoxford, Holt, and North Walsham, with the cyclist battalions at Beccles, Saxmundham, Holt, and North Walsham.

These stations were maintained until the middle of November, 1916, when the 1st Cyclist Division was broken up. The cyclist brigades were dispersed, and the regiments were amalgamated to form battalions in newly-formed cyclist brigades (see Notes, Order of Battle Table).

During its existence (from August, 1914, to November, 1916) the division served entirely in England and was employed on Home Defence.

2ND MOUNTED DIVISION

G.O.C.

31 August, 1914	Major-General W. E. PEYTON.
21 August, 1915	Br.-Gen. P. A. KENNA, V.C. (acting).
23 August, 1915	Major-General W. E. PEYTON.
13 November, 1915	Br.-Gen. MARQUIS OF TULLIBARDINE (acting).
14 November, 1915	Major-General W. E. PEYTON.

G.S.O. 1.

8 Sept.,1914...Col. Hon. H. A. LAWRENCE.
8 June, 1915...Col. W. J. C. BUTLER.
23 Aug., 1915...Captain P. R. CHAMBERS (acting).
4 Oct., 1915...Lt.-Col. C. N. MACMULLEN.

A.-A. and Q.-M.-G.

7 Sept., 1914...Col. W. J. C. BUTLER.
8 June, 1915...Major J. N. SINCLAIR (acting).
20 Aug., 1915...Lt.-Col. J. N. SINCLAIR (sick, 22/11/15).
22 Nov., 1915...Major A. C. ROBINSON (acting).

B.-G., R.H.A.

9 Sept., 1914...Br.-Gen. EARL OF DENBIGH AND DESMOND.

C.R.E.

——

2ND MOUNTED DIVISION

SEPTEMBER, 1914

1st MOUNTED BDE.
(1st South Midland)

[28 June, '14] *Br.-Gen. E. A. WIGGIN.

2nd MOUNTED BDE.
(2nd South Midland)

[1 April, '12] *Br.-Gen. EARL OF LONGFORD.

3rd MOUNTED BDE.
(Notts. and Derby.)

[1 April, '12] *Br.-Gen. P. A. KENNA, V.C.

4th MOUNTED BDE.
(London)

[25 May, '14] *Br.-Gen. A. H. M. TAYLOR.

In August, 1915, at Suvla :

1st MOUNTED BDE.
(1st S. Midland)

[28 June, '14] *Br.-Gen. E. A. WIGGIN.

2nd MOUNTED BDE.
(2nd S. Midland)

[1 April, '12] *Br.-Gen. EARL OF LONGFORD (killed, 21/8/15).

23 Aug., '15...Col. C. A. GRENFELL (acting) (sick, 26/8/15).

26 Aug., '15...Lt.-Col. E. T. TROYTE-BULLOCK (acting).

3rd MOUNTED BDE.
(Notts. and Derby.)

[1 April, '12] *Br.-Gen. P. A. KENNA, V.C.

20 Aug., '15...Col. E. H. COLE (acting) (wounded, 21/8/15).

21 Aug., '15...Major F. FITZ H. LANCE (acting).

24 Aug., '15...Br.-Gen. P. A. KENNA, V.C. (wounded, 29/8/15) (died of wounds, 30/8/15).

29 Aug., '15...Major F. FITZ H. LANCE (acting).

1 Sept., '15...Br.-Gen. F. FITZ H. LANCE.

4th MOUNTED BDE.
(London)

[25 May, '14] *Br.-Gen. A. H. M. TAYLOR.

5th MOUNTED BDE.
(Attached to 2nd Mounted Div. from 13/8/15.)

[19 Jan., '15] Br.-Gen J. D. T. TYNDALE-BISCOE.

On 4th September, 1915, the 2nd Mounted Division was reorganized :

1st COMPOSITE MOUNTED BDE.
(Formed 4/9/15.)

4 Sept., '15...Br.-Gen. E. A. WIGGIN (wounded, 18/9/15).

18 Sept., '15...Lt.-Col. T. A. WIGHT-BOYCOTT (acting).

1 Nov., '15...Br.-Gen. E. A. WIGGIN.

1st SCOTTISH HORSE MOUNTED BDE.
(Attached to 2nd Mounted Div. at Suvla on 2/9/15.)

[15 Aug., '14] Br.-Gen. MARQUIS OF TULLIBARDINE.

2nd COMPOSITE MOUNTED BDE.
(Formed 4/9/15.)

4 Sept., '15...Br.-Gen. A. H. M. TAYLOR.

1st HIGHLAND MOUNTED BDE.
(Attached to 2nd Mounted Div. at Suvla on 26/9/15.)

[9 Sept., '14] Br.-Gen. LORD LOVAT (sick, 11/10/15).

12 Oct., '15...Lt.-Col. A. STIRLING (acting).

24 Oct., '15...Br.-Gen. A. STIRLING.

*Br.-Gen. on 5 August, 1914.

On 1st December, 1915, the 2nd Mounted Division began reorganization at Cairo:

1st MOUNTED BDE.
(1st S. Midland)
1 Dec., '15...Br.-Gen. E. A. WIGGIN.

2nd MOUNTED BDE.
(2nd S. Midland)
1 Dec., '15...Br.-Gen. T. A. WIGHT-BOYCOTT.

3rd MOUNTED BDE.
(Notts. and Derby.)
1 Dec., '15...Br.-Gen. F. FITZ H. LANCE.

4th MOUNTED BDE.
(London)
1 Dec., '15...Br.-Gen. A. H. M. TAYLOR.

5th MOUNTED BDE.
1 Dec., '15...Lt.-Col. T. M. S. PITT (acting).

In January, 1916, after reorganization at Cairo :

1st MOUNTED BDE.
(1st S. Midland)
Br.-Gen. E. A. WIGGIN.

2nd MOUNTED BDE.
(2nd S. Midland)
Br.-Gen. T. A. WIGHT-BOYCOTT.

3rd MOUNTED BDE.
(Notts. and Derby.)
Br.-Gen. F. FITZ H. LANCE.

4th MOUNTED BDE.
(London)
Br.-Gen. A. H. M. TAYLOR.

Formed at Churn on 2nd September, 1914

2ND MOUNTED DIVISION ORDER OF BATTLE, 1914-1916

Dates	YEOMANRY		R.H.A. (T.F.)		Engineers	Signal Service	Medical	Mobile Veterinary Sections	A.S.C.
	Mounted Brigades	Regiments and attached Units	Brigades	Batteries					
1914 September (England)	1st S. Midland[1] .... 2nd S. Midland[2] ... Notts. and Derby.[4] London[5]	War. Yeo., R. Glouc. Hsrs., Q.O. Worc. Hsrs. R. Bucks. Hsrs., Q.O. Dorset. Yeo.,[3] Berks. Yeo. Sherwood Rgrs., S. Notts. Hsrs., Derby. Yeo. 1/Co. of Lond., 1/City of Lond., 3/Co. of Lond.	I.................... II....................	Warwick[6] and Ammn. Coln. Berks. & B., H.A.C.,[6] and Ammn. Colns. Notts. and Ammn. Coln. A, H.A.C., and Ammn. Coln.	...	1st S. Midland Sig. Trp. 2nd S. Midland Sig. Trp. Notts. and Derby. Sig. Trp. London Sig. Trp. 2nd Mtd. Divnl. Sig. Sqdn.	1st S. Midland Fd. Amb. 2nd S. Midland Fd. Amb. Notts. and Derby. Fd. Amb. London Fd. Amb.	1st S. Midland 2nd S. Midland Notts. and Derby. London	1st S. Midland A.S.C. 2nd S. Midland A.S.C. Notts. and Derby. A.S.C. London A.S.C. 2nd Mtd. Divnl. A.S.C.
1915 May (Egypt)	1st[7] (1st S. Midland) 2nd[7] (2nd S. Midland) 3rd[7] (Notts. and Derby.) 4th[7] (London)	War. Yeo., R. Glouc. Hsrs., Q.O. Worc. Hsrs. R. Bucks. Hsrs., Q.O. Dorset. Yeo., Berks. Yeo. Sherwood Rgrs., S. Notts. Hsrs., Derby. Yeo. 1/Co. of Lond., 1/City of Lond., 3/Co. of Lond.	I.................... II....................	B, H.A.C.,[6; 8] and Ammn. Coln. Berks.[9] and Ammn. Coln. Notts. and Ammn. Coln. A, H.A.C., and Ammn. Coln.	... .	1st S. Midland[13] Sig. Trp. 2nd S. Midland[13] Sig. Trp. Notts. and Derby.[13] Sig. Trp. London[13] Sig. Trp. 2nd Mtd. Divnl. Sig. Sqdn.	1st S. Midland[13] Fd. Amb. 2nd S. Midland Fd. Amb. Notts. and Derby.[13] Fd. Amb. London Fd. Amb.	A (1st S. Midland) B (2nd S. Midland) D (Notts. and Derby.) C (London)	1st S. Midland A.S.C. 2nd S. Midland A.S.C. Notts. and Derby. A.S.C. London A.S.C. 2nd Mtd. Divnl. A.S.C.
1915 August (Gallipoli)	1st (1st S. Midland) 2nd (2nd S. Midland) 3rd (Notts. and Derby.) 4th (London) Attached: 5th[10]...	War. Yeo., R. Glouc. Hsrs., Q.O. Worc. Hsrs. R. Bucks. Hsrs., Q.O. Dorset Yeo., Berks. Yeo. Sherwood Rgrs., S. Notts. Hsrs., Derby. Yeo. 1/Co. of Lond., 1/City of Lond., 3/Co. of Lond. Herts. Yeo.,[11] 2/Co. of Lond.[12]	...[13]	...[13]	... .	2nd Mtd. Divnl. Sig. Sqdn.	1st S. Midland[13] Fd. Amb. 2nd S. Midland Fd. Amb. Notts. and Derby.[13] Fd. Amb. London Fd. Amb.	...[13]	2nd Mtd. Divnl. A.S.C.

1915 September (Gallipoli)	1st Composite Mtd. Bde.[14] 2nd Composite Mtd. Bde.[15] **1st Scottish Horse Mtd. Bde.**[16] **1st Highland Mtd. Bde.**[17]	1st S. Midland Regt. (War., Glouc., and Worc. Yeo.); 2nd S. Midland Regt. (Bucks., Dorset., and Berks. Yeo.); 5th Yeomanry Regt. (Herts. and 2/Co. of Lond. Yeo.) 3rd Notts. and Derby. Regt. (Sherwood Rgrs., S. Notts. Hsrs., and Derby. Yeo.); 4th London Regt. (1st Co., 1st City, 3/Co. of Lond. Yeo.) 1/Scottish Horse, 2/1/Scottish Horse, 3/1/Scottish Horse Fife. and Forfar. Yeo., 1/Lovat's Scouts, 2/Lovat's Scouts	...[13]	...[13]	1/Kent Fd. Coy.[18] 2/Kent Fd. Coy.[18]	2nd Mtd. Divnl. Sig. Sqdn.	2nd S. Midland Fd. Amb. London Fd. Amb. Scottish Horse Fd. Amb. Highland Fd. Amb.	...[13]	2nd Mtd. Divnl. A.S.C.
1915 December (Reorganisation in Egypt)	1st (1st S. Midland) 2nd (2nd S. Midland) 3rd (Notts. and Derby.) 4th (London) 5th[19]...........	War. Yeo., R. Glouc. Hsrs., Q.O. Worc. Hsrs.; 1st S. Midland Sig. Trp. R. Bucks. Hsrs., Q.O. Dorset. Yeo., Berks. Yeo.; 2nd S. Midland Sig. Trp. Sherwood Rgrs., S. Notts. Hsrs., Derby. Yeo.; Notts. and Derby. Sig. Trp. 1/Co. of Lond., 1/City of Lond., 3/Co. of Lond.; London Sig. Troop Herts. Yeo., 2/Co. of Lond.							
1916 January (Egypt)	1st[20] (1st S. Midland) 2nd[21] (2nd S. Midland) 3rd[22] (Notts. and Derby.) 4th[23] (London)	War. Yeo., R. Glouc. Hsrs., Q.O. Worc. Yeo.; 1st S. Midland Sig. Trp. R. Bucks. Hsrs., Q.O. Dorset. Yeo., Berks. Yeo.; 2nd S. Midland Sig. Trp. Sherwood Rgrs., S. Notts. Hsrs., Derby. Yeo.; Notts. and Derby. Sig. Trp. 1/Co. of Lond., 1/City of Lond., 3/Co. of Lond.; London Sig. Trp.	I.................. II..................	A, H.A.C.,[24] B, H.A.C.,[25] and Bty. Ammn. Colns. Notts.,[26] Berks.,[21; 27] and Bty. Ammn. Colns.	...	2nd Mtd. Divnl.[28] Sig. Sqdn.	1st S. Midland[20] Fd. Amb. 2nd S. Midland[21] Fd. Amb. Notts. and Derby.[22] Fd. Amb. London[23] Fd. Amb.	1st S. Midland[20] 2nd S. Midland[21] Notts. and Derby.[22] London[23]	2nd Mtd. Divnl. A.S.C.

On 21/1/1916 the 2nd MOUNTED DIVISION was broken up

NOTES

1 Bde. transferred to 2nd Mtd. Div. (on formation) from 1st Mtd. Div.

2 Bde. transferred to 2nd Mtd. Div. (on formation) from 1st Mtd. Div.

3 Replaced Q.O.O. Hsrs. in Bde., after Q.O.O. Hsrs. left Churn for France. (Q.O.O. Hsrs. disembkd. at Dunkirk on 22/9/14.)

4 Bde. transferred to 2nd Mtd. Div. (on formation) from 1st Mtd. Div.

5 Bde. joined 2nd Mtd. Div., on formation of the Division.

6 Warwick Bty. went to France, disembkg. on 1/11/14 ; it was attached to 2nd Cav. Div. from 4/12/14—14/4/15, and was then transferred to 9th Cav. Bde. (1st Cav. Div.). On 27/11/16 the Bty. joined XV R.H.A. (29th Div.) and served with it for the remainder of the War. The Bty. was replaced in 1st S. Midland Mtd. Bde. by B, H.A.C.

7 The Mounted Brigades were numbered in May, 1915.

8 Bty. (armed with 4, 15-pdr. Erhardt Q.F. guns) embkd. at Suez on 14/7/15 and disembkd. at Aden on 19/7/15. Bty. re-embkd. at Aden on 17/9/15, disembkd. at Suez on 23/9/15, and proceeded to el Ferdan. Bty. rejoined the 2nd Mtd. Div. near Cairo on 13/12/15.

9 Bty. (armed with 4, 15-pdr. guns) embkd. at Suez on 14/7/15, disembkd. at Aden on 18/7/15, and was engaged at Sheikh Othman on 20/7/15. The Bty. re-embkd. at Aden on 17/9/15 and disembkd. at Suez on 23/9/15.

10 Bde. joined on 13/8/15 for service in Gallipoli with the 2nd Mounted Division. Bde. embkd. on 14/8/15 at Alexandria and disembkd. at Suvla on 18/8/15.

11 Regt. embkd. at Southampton on 10/9/14 on *Ionian*, and disembkd. at Alexandria on 25/9/14.

12 Regt. embkd. at Southampton, part on 4/9/14 on *Aragon* and part on *Avon* on 10/9/14. Regt. disembkd. at Alexandria on 25/9/14.

13 Left behind in Egypt.

14 Bde. (Br.-Gen. E. A. Wiggin) was formed on 4/9/15. Bde. left Suvla on 31/10/15, arrd. Mudros 1/11/15, embkd. Mudros 27/11/15, disembkd. Alexandria 1/12/15, and went to Mena Camp, Cairo.

15 Bde. (Br.-Gen. A. H. M. Taylor) was formed on 4/9/15. Bde. left Suvla on 2/11/15, arrd. Mudros 3/11/15, embkd. Mudros 24/11/15, disembkd. Alexandria 28/11/15, and went to Mena Camp, Cairo.

16 Bde. (Br.-Gen. Marquis of Tullibardine) landed at Suvla on 2/9/15 (from U.K.) and joined 2nd Mtd. Div. The Bde. remained in the 2nd Mtd. Div. at Suvla and took part in the Evacuation on the Night, 19-20/12/15. The Bde. reached Imbros on 20/12/15, and left the 2nd Mtd. Div. on 22/12/15. The Bde. embkd. at Imbros on 24/12/15, disembkd. at Alexandria on 28/12/15 and went to Sidi Bishr Camp. (On landing at Suvla the Bde. numbered 111 offrs. and 2,149 o.r.)

17 Bde. (Br.-Gen. Lord Lovat) landed at Suvla on 26/9/15 (from U.K.) and joined 2nd Mtd. Div. The Bde. remained in 2nd Mtd. Div. at Suvla and took part in the Evacuation on the Night, 19-20/12/15. The Bde. reached Imbros on 20/12/15, and left the 2nd Mtd. Div. on 22/12/15. The Bde. left Imbros on 23/12/15, arrd. Mudros on 24/12/15, left Mudros on 26/12/15, disembkd. at Alexandria on 28/12/15, and went to Sidi Bishr Camp. (On landing at Suvla the Bde. numbered 110 offrs. and 2,037 o.r.)

18 Both Fd. Cos. came from England to Suvla. 1/Kent arrd. Suvla on 7/10/15, and 2/Kent towards the end of Oct., 1915. Both Cos. were attached to the 2nd Mtd. Div. The Fd. Cos. were attached to the Div. until after the Evacuation of Suvla on 19-20/12/15. (On 1/2/17 the Fd. Cos. were renumbered 495 and 496.)

19 Bde. left Suvla on 31/10/15, arrd. Mudros on 1/11/15, embkd. Mudros on 26/11/15, disembkd. at Alexandria on 30/11/15, and went to Mena Camp, Cairo. Bde. left the 2nd Mtd. Div. on 7/12/15 for Western Frontier of Egypt. (Also see General Notes.)

20 Bde. left the Div. on 3 and 4/1/16 for Es Salhia. On 20/4/16 the Bde. was numbered 5th Mtd. Bde. It was renumbered 22nd Mtd. Bde., and served in Anzac Mtd. Div., Yeo. Mtd. Div., and 4th Cav. Div. (it was then renumbered 12th Cav. Bde.).

21 Bde. left the Div. on 17/1/16 for Western Frontier of Egypt. It was renumbered 6th Mtd. Bde. and served in Impl. Mtd. Div., Yeo. Mtd. Div., and 4th Cav. Div., and was renumbered 10th Cav. Bde.

22 Bde. left the Div. on 18 and 19/1/16. In Febry., 1916, the Bde. went to Salonika and was numbered 7th Mtd. Bde., returned to Egypt in June, 1917, joined 5th Cav. Div. in 1918, and was numbered 14th Cav. Bde.

23 Bde. left the Div. on 18/1/16 for Abbassia. It was numbered 8th Mtd. Bde., and served in Salonika from Nov., 1916—June, 1917. It then served in Yeo. Mtd. Div., and 4th Cav. Div., and was renumbered 11th Cav. Bde.

24 A, H.A.C. (4, 15-pdr. Erhardt guns) rejoined 2nd Mtd. Div. at Cairo on 13/12/15. On 20/12/15 the Bty. entrained for Alexandria, and on 7/1/16 it concentrated with its ammn. coln. at Mersa Matruh. Bty. returned to Alexandria on 6/3/16 and was rearmed with 4, 18-pdr. Q.F. Bty. returned to Canal Defences on 6/4/16, and rejoined 8th (formerly 4th) Mtd. Bde. In Febry., 1917, the Bty. joined the 4th A.L.H. Bde.

25 B, H.A.C., rejoined the Division at Cairo on 13/12/15 from Ismailia (Suez Canal Defences). B, H.A.C., left 2nd Mtd. Div. on 21/1/16, and in Febry., 1916, it was rearmed with 4, 13-pdr. Q.F. guns. The Bty. then moved to Balla (Suez Canal Defences), and remained there until 16/10/17, when it marched to join the (re-formed) 5th Mtd. Bde.

26 Notts. Bty. did not rejoin the Division at Cairo. On 28/11/15 the Bty. left Ismailia (Suez Canal Defences) for service with Western Frontier Force.

27 Berks. Bty. rejoined the Division at Cairo on 10/12/15, from Ismailia (Suez Canal Defences).

28 After taking part in the Evacuation of Suvla, 19-20/12/15, the Sig. Sqdn. disembarked at Alexandria on 27/12/15, and went to Mena Camp, Cairo.

GENERAL NOTES

5th Mounted Brigade (Br.-Gen. J. D. T. Tyndale-Biscoe). This Bde. was formed in Egypt on 19/1/15 with two Yeo. Cav. Regts. (Herts. and 2/County of London), which had reached Alexandria from England on 25/9/14. The Bde. was called Yeo. Mtd. Bde. until it joined 2nd Mtd. Div., when it was designated 5th Mtd. Bde. It served with the 2nd Mtd. Div. from 13/8/15-7/12/15 (see Table and notes 10, 11, 12, and 19). In July, 1918, the 5th Mtd. Bde. became 13th Cav. Bde., and in August, 1918, it joined the 5th Cav. Div.

2/South-Western Mounted Brigade.—(R. 1st Dev., R. N. Dev., W. Som., and Sig. Trp. and Fd. Amb., under Br.-Gen. R. Hoare) disembkd. at Suvla on 9/10/15, and until 15/11/15 was attached to the 13th Div. ; from 15/11/15 until 29/11/15 the Bde. was attached to the 2nd Mtd. Div., from 29/11/15-9/12/15 it served with the 53rd Div., and from 9/12/15-Evacuation of Suvla on 20/12/15, the Bde. was again attached to the 2nd Mtd. Div.

158th Inf. Bde. (53rd Division).—(5/R.W.F., 6/R.W.F., 7/R.W.F., and 1/Hereford, under Br.-Gen. S. F. Mott) was attached to the 2nd Mtd. Div. from 31/10/15-28/11/15.

159th Inf. Bde. (53rd Division).—(4/Ches., 7/Ches., 4/Welsh, and 5/Welsh, under Br.-Gen. R. O'B. Taylor) was attached to the 2nd Mtd. Div. from 29/11/15-9/12/15.

LV. Bde., R.F.A. (A, B, C, D Bties.—16, 18-pdrs.)—from 13th Divnl. Arty., was attached to the 2nd Mtd. Div. from 7/11/15–Evacuation of Suvla on Night of 19-20/12/15.

66th Field Coy. R.E.—from 10th Division—was attached to 2nd Mtd. Div. from 5/9/15 until the Fd. Coy. embkd. for Lemnos on 1/10/15.

1/4/Gurkha Rifles (29th Ind. Inf. Bde.)—was attached, during the Evacuation of Suvla on 18-20/12/15, to the 2nd Mtd. Div.

2ND MOUNTED DIVISION

FORMATION, NARRATIVE, AND BATTLES AND ENGAGEMENTS

Before the Great War the division did not exist, but late in August, 1914, it was decided to form a second mounted division. For this purpose four of the existing mounted brigades (T.F.) were concentrated around Churn, and, on the 2nd September, the 2nd Mounted Division came into existence and was attached to the Central Force. The mounted brigades were then at Newbury, Churn, South Stoke, and Streatley (the London Mounted Brigade had moved there from Hounslow). The brigades were dispersed, partly to give each a training area and partly because the water supply did not permit the division being concentrated at the camp at Churn. B. Battery, H.A.C., joined the division from Canterbury, and was attached to the 2nd S. Midland Mtd. Bde. At this time divisional and artillery headquarters were at Goring.

In the middle of November the 2nd Mounted Division moved to the Norfolk coast line, and the division was then disposed as follows:—Divisional headquarters was at Hanworth (in December divisional artillery headquarters moved from Cromer to Hanworth), the mounted brigades were around King's Lynn, Fakenham, Holt, and North Walsham, and the four horse artillery batteries were at Gayton, Little Walsingham, Leatheringsett, and Mundesley. The division still formed part of the Central Force.

Early in March, 1915, the 2nd Mounted Division was warned to prepare for service abroad. On the 3rd April, divisional headquarters left Avonmouth, and the mounted brigades followed between the 7th and 10th April. Divisional headquarters disembarked at Alexandria on the 19th April, and (with the exception of some details) the whole division had disembarked by the 29th April.

By the middle of May the division was disposed as follows: Divisional headquarters and the 2nd and 3rd Mounted Brigades were at Cairo, the 1st Mounted Brigade was at Alexandria, and the 4th Mounted Brigade and the four horse artillery batteries were attached to the Suez Canal Defences near Ismailia. On the 14th July, B Battery, H.A.C., and Berks. Battery left for Aden (disembarking on the 18th and 19th).

On the 10th August the 2nd Mounted Division (with the 5th Mounted Brigade attached) was directed to be ready to proceed overseas as a (reorganized) dismounted division. Each yeomanry regiment was ordered to leave in Egypt the headquarters of one squadron as well as the officers and men of two troops, to look after the horses. The horse artillery batteries, ammunition columns, mobile veterinary sections, motor cars, motor lorries, and riding horses were also to remain in Egypt.

On the 13th August the dismounted division began to entrain for Alexandria. The troops sailed in five transports on the 14th, and reached Mudros on the 17th. At Mudros the dismounted division transhipped, and on the night of 17th/18th August, the dismounted division (less the divisional transport left at Mudros) disembarked in Suvla Bay.

During its service in Egypt and Gallipoli the 2nd Mounted Division took part in the following operations :—

1915

THE BATTLES OF SUVLA

21 Aug. ... ...**Battle of Scimitar Hill** [IX. Corps].

21 Aug. ... ...**Attack on " W " Hills.**

Night, 19/20 Dec. ...**Evacuation of Suvla** [IX. Corps].

The 2nd Mounted Division had suffered such severe losses in the battle on the 21st August (the 2nd Mtd. Bde. lost 22 officers and 243 other ranks) and the wastage during August had been so heavy (by the 31st the strength of the 3rd Mtd. Bde. was reduced to 34 officers and 820 other ranks), that reinforcement and extensive reorganization became essential. On the 2nd September the 1st Scottish Horse Mtd. Bde. landed at Suvla and joined the division ; on the 4th September the original five mounted brigades (which had come from Egypt) were reorganized and became the 1st and 2nd Composite Mounted Brigades ; and on the 26th September the 1st Highland Mtd. Bde. arrived at Suvla and joined the division, completing a four-brigade organization (see Table). Even so, by the 7th October, wastage had reduced the effective strength of the 2nd Mounted Division to 255 officers and 4,868 other ranks. By the middle of October the 1st and 2nd Composite Mtd. Bdes. (formed from the original five mounted brigades which came from Egypt) were so weak and fatigued that they were temporarily unfit for further active operations, and between 31st October and 2nd November the 1st and 2nd Composite Brigades embarked for Mudros. The 1st and 2nd Composite Brigades then returned to Egypt to rest and recuperate. They reached Cairo between 28th November and 1st December and the reorganization of the division was undertaken (see Table). The B.-G., R.H.A., rejoined on the 13th December ; and, after the evacuation of Suvla on the 19th/20th December, the divisional headquarters rejoined the 2nd Mounted Division on the 27th December at Mena Camp, Cairo. The G.O.C. then resumed command of the original units, all of which had rejoined at Cairo by this time (except Notts. Battery, R.H.A., T.F.).

In December, however, the dismemberment of the re-formed mounted division began when A Battery, H.A.C., left the division for Mersa Matruh. This unit was speedily followed by others (see Notes 20-28, Order of Battle Table) ; and by the 19th January, 1916, all the units had been distributed to various commands. The B.-G., R.H.A., became C.R.A. Western Frontier Force, Egypt, the G.O.C. was transferred to the command of the same force, and on the 21st January, 1916, the 2nd Mounted Division passed out of existence.

2ND/2ND MOUNTED DIVISION

(On 20/3/16, 2nd/2nd Mounted Division became 3rd Mounted Division; in July, 1916, 3rd Mounted Division became 1st Mounted Division; and, on 4/9/17, 1st Mounted Division became The Cyclist Division.)

G.O.C.

6 March, 1915	... ...	Br.-Gen. J. F. BURN-MURDOCH.
26 May, 1916 ...	... ...	Major-General J. F. BURN-MURDOCH.
4 March, 1918	... ...	Major-General A. G. DALLAS.

G.S.O. 1.

25 May, 1915...Col. R. C. B. LAWRENCE.
23 Feb., 1916...Major F. R. DE BERTODANO (acting).
13 Mar., 1916...Lt.-Col. E. C. HAAG.
29 July, 1918...Lt.-Col. T. A. POLLOK-MORRIS

A.-A. and Q.-M.-G.

26 May, 1915...Lt.-Col. Hon. H. S. DAVEY.
2 Aug., 1918...Lt.-Col. C. H. G. COLLINS.

C.R.H.A.

———

C.R.E.

———

MARCH, 1915

2/1/NOTTS. and DERBY. MTD. BDE.

[1 Jan., '15] Br.-Gen. J. F. BURN-MURDOCH.

2/1/S. MIDLAND MOUNTED BDE.

[11 Jan., '15] Br.-Gen. G. L. PALMER.

2/2/S. MIDLAND MOUNTED BDE.

[13 Jan., '15] Br.-Gen. E. C. B. COTGRAVE.
20 Dec., '15...Br.-Gen. LORD G. BINNING.

2/1/LONDON MOUNTED BDE.

[8 Jan., '15] Br.-Gen. R. B. COLVIN.

APRIL, 1916

9th MOUNTED BDE.
(2/1/Notts. and Derby.)

[1 Jan., '15] Br.-Gen. J. F. BURN-MURDOCH.
14 April, '16...Br.-Gen. A. F. H. FERGUSON.

10th MOUNTED BDE.
(2/1/S. Midland)

[11 Jan., '15] Br.-Gen. G. L. PALMER.
15 May, '16...Br.-Gen. R. HOARE.

11th MOUNTED BDE.
(2/2/S. Midland)

[20 Dec., '15] Br.-Gen. LORD G. BINNING.

12th MOUNTED BDE.
(2/1/London)

[8 Jan., '15] Br.-Gen. R. B. COLVIN.
10 May, '16...Br.-Gen. A. D. MILLER.

JULY, 1916

1st MOUNTED BDE.

[20 Dec., '15] Br.-Gen. LORD G. BINNING.

2nd MOUNTED BDE.

[6 Jan., '15] Br.-Gen. F. C. MEYRICK.
[6 April, '16] Br.-Gen. F. A. B. FRYER.

3rd MOUNTED BDE.

29 July, '16...Br.-Gen C. K. BURNETT.

9th CYCLIST BDE.

[14 April, '16] Br.-Gen. A. F. H. FERGUSON.

NOVEMBER, 1916

1st MOUNTED BDE.
[20 Dec., '15] Br.-Gen. LORD G. BINNING.

2nd MOUNTED BDE.
[6 April, '16] Br.-Gen. F. A. B. FRYER.

[12 Jan., '15] Br.-Gen. R. N. SMYTH.

3rd MOUNTED BDE.
[29 July, '16] Br.-Gen. C. K. BURNETT.

5th CYCLIST BDE.
[14 April, '16] Br.-Gen. A. F. H. FERGUSON.

SEPTEMBER, 1917

11th CYCLIST BDE.
[5 Feb., '17] Br.-Gen. G. T. G. EDWARDS.

12th CYCLIST BDE.
[12 Jan., '15] Br.-Gen. R. N. SMYTH.

13th CYCLIST BDE.
[29 July, '16] Br.-Gen. C. K. BURNETT.

JANUARY, 1918

5th CYCLIST BDE.
[14 April, '16] Br.-Gen. A. F. H. FERGUSON.
21 June, '18...Br.-Gen. R. HAIG.

11th CYCLIST BDE.
[5 Feb., '17] Br.-Gen. G. T. G. EDWARDS.

12th CYCLIST BDE.
[12 Jan., '15] Br.-Gen. R. N. SMYTH.

Formed on the 6th March, 1915

2ND/2ND MOUNTED DIVISION — ORDER OF BATTLE, 1915-1918

Dates	YEOMANRY: Mounted (later Cyclist) Brigades	YEOMANRY: Regiments and attached Units	R.H.A. (T.F.): Brigades	R.H.A. (T.F.): Batteries	Engineers	Signal Service	Medical	Mobile Veterinary Sections	A.S.C.
1915 March (England)	2/1st Notts. and Derby. 2/1st S. Midland ... 2/2nd S. Midland... 2/1st London	2/1/Sherwood Rgrs., 2/1/S. Notts. Hsrs., 2/1/Derby. Yeo. 2/1/Warwick. Yeo., 2/1/R. Glouc. Hsrs., 2/1/Q.O. Worc. Hsrs. 2/1/R. Bucks. Hsrs., 2/1/Berks. Yeo., 2/1/Q.O.O. Hsrs. 2/1/Co. of Lond. Yeo., 2/1/City of Lond. Yeo., 2/3/Co. of Lond. Yeo.	...	2/1/Notts. and Ammn. Coln. 2/1/Warwick. and Ammn. Coln. 2/1/Berks. and Ammn. Coln. 2/A, H.A.C., and Ammn. Coln.	...	2/1/Notts. and Derby. Sig. Trp. 2/1/S. Midland Sig. Trp. 2/2/S. Midland Sig. Trp. 2/1/London Sig. Trp.	2/1/Notts. and Derby. Fd. Amb. 2/1/S. Midland Fd. Amb. 2/2/S. Midland Fd. Amb. 2/1/London Fd. Amb.	...	2/1/Notts. and Derby. A.S.C. 2/1/S. Midland A.S.C. 2/2/S. Midland A.S.C. 2/1/London A.S.C.

On 20/3/16, 2nd/2nd Mounted Division became 3rd MOUNTED DIVISION

Dates	Mounted (later Cyclist) Brigades	Regiments and attached Units	Brigades	Batteries	Engineers	Signal Service	Medical	Mobile Veterinary Sections	A.S.C.
1916 April (England)	2/1st Notts. and Derby. 2/1st S. Midland ... 2/2nd S. Midland... 2/1st London	2/1/Sherwood Rgrs., 2/1/S. Notts. Hsrs., 2/1/Derby. Yeo. 2/1 Warwick. Yeo., 2/1/R. Glouc. Hsrs., 2/1/Q.O. Worc. Hsrs. 2/1/R. Bucks. Hsrs., 2/1/Berks. Yeo., 2/1/Q.O.O. Hsrs. 2/1/Co. of Lond. Yeo., 2/1/City of Lond. Yeo., 2/3/Co. of Lond. Yeo.	...	2/1/Notts. and Ammn. Coln. 2/1/Warwick. and Ammn. Coln. 2/1/Berks. and Ammn. Coln. 2/A, H.A.C., and Ammn. Coln.	...	2/1/Notts. and Derby. Sig. Trp. 2/1/S. Midland Sig. Trp. 2/2/S. Midland Sig. Trp. 2/1/London Sig. Trp. 3rd Mtd. Divnl. Sig. Sqdn.	2/1/Notts. and Derby. Fd. Amb. 2/1/S. Midland Fd. Amb. 2/2/S. Midland Fd. Amb. 2/1/London Fd. Amb.	...	2/1/Notts. and Derby. A.S.C. 2/1/S. Midland A.S.C. 2/2/S. Midland A.S.C. 2/1/London A.S.C.
1916 July (England)	9th (2/1st Notts. and Derby.) 10th (2/1st S. Midland) 11th (2/2nd S. Midland) 12th[7] (2/1st London)	2/1/Sherwood Rgrs.,[1] 2/1/S. Notts. Hsrs.,[2] 2/1/Derby. Yeo.[2] 2/1/Warwick Yeo.,[3] 2/1/R. Glouc. Hsrs.,[4] 2/1/Q.O. Worc. Hsrs.[4] 2/1/R. Bucks. Hsrs.,[5] 2/1/Berks. Yeo.,[4] 2/1/Q.O.O. Hsrs.[6] 2/1/Co. of Lond. Yeo.,[7] 2/1/City of Lond. Yeo.,[7] 2/3/Co. of Lond. Yeo.[7]	...	2/1/Notts. and Ammn. Coln. 2/1/Warwick. and Ammn. Coln. 2/1/Berks. and Ammn. Coln. 2/A, H.A.C., and Ammn. Coln.	...	9th Mtd. Bde. Sig. Trp. 10th Mtd. Bde. Sig. Trp. 11th Mtd. Bde. Sig. Trp. 12th Mtd. Bde. Sig. Trp. 3rd Mtd. Divnl. Sig. Sqdn.	9th Mtd. Bde. Fd. Amb. 10th Mtd. Bde. Fd. Amb. 11th Mtd. Bde. Fd. Amb. 12th Mtd. Bde. Fd. Amb.	...	9th Mtd. Bde. A.S.C. 10th Mtd. Bde. A.S.C. 11th Mtd. Bde. A.S.C. 12th Mtd. Bde. A.S.C. 3rd Mtd. Divnl. A.S.C.

In July, 1916, 3rd Mounted Division became 1st MOUNTED DIVISION

Dates	Mounted (later Cyclist) Brigades	Regiments and attached Units	Brigades	Batteries	Engineers	Signal Service	Medical	Mobile Veterinary Sections	A.S.C.
1916 September (England)	1st Mounted .... 2nd Mounted .... 3rd Mounted .... 9th Cyclist	2/1/War. Yeo.,[3] 2/1/Sherwood Rgrs.,[1] 2/1/R. Bucks. Hsrs.[5] 2/1/R. 1st Devon. Yeo.,[8]; [16] 2/1/Montgomery. Yeo.,[9]; [17] 2/1/Fife. and Forfar. Yeo.[10]; [17] 2/1/Herts. Yeo.,[11] 2/1/Q.O. W. Kent. Yeo.,[12] 2/1/Essex Yeo.[13] 2/1/S. Notts. Hsrs.,[2] 2/1/Derby. Yeo.,[2] 2/1/Q.O.O. Hsrs.[6]	...	2/1/Notts.[14] and Ammn. Coln. 2/1/Warwick. and Ammn. Coln. 2/1/Berks.[15] and Ammn. Coln. 2/A, H.A.C., and Ammn. Coln.	...	1st Mtd. Bde. Sig. Trp. 2nd Mtd. Bde. Sig. Trp. 3rd Mtd. Bde. Sig. Trp. 9th Cyclist Bde. Sig. Trp. 3/2/Mtd. Divnl. Sig. Sqdn.	1st Mtd. Bde. Fd. Amb. 2nd Mtd. Bde. Fd. Amb. 3rd Mtd. Bde. Fd. Amb. 9th Cyclist Bde. Fd. Amb.	...	1st Mtd. Bde. A.S.C. 2nd Mtd. Bde. A.S.C. 3rd Mtd. Bde. A.S.C. 9th Cyclist Bde. A.S.C.

1916 November (England)	1st Mounted .... 2nd Mounted[18] .... 3rd Mounted .... Attached : 5th Cyclist[20]......	2/1/War. Yeo., 2/1/Sherwood Rgrs., 2/1/R. Bucks. Hsrs. 2/1/Staff. Yeo., 2/1/Leic. Yeo., 2/1/Linc. Yeo. 2/1/Q.O. Dorset. Yeo.,[19] 2/1/Herts. Yeo., 2/1/Essex Yeo. 2/1/S. Notts. Hsrs., 2/1/Derby. Yeo., 2/1/Q.O.O. Hsrs.;[25] 2/1/Kent (Cyclist Bn.),[21] 2/8/Essex (Cyclist Bn.)[22]	... .	... 2/A, H.A.C.,[23] and Ammn. Coln. 2/1/Warwick,[24] and Ammn. Coln.	...	1st Mtd. Bde. Sig. Trp. 2nd Mtd. Bde. Sig. Trp. 3rd Mtd. Bde. Sig. Trp. 1st Mtd. Divnl. Sig. Sqdn. 5th Cyclist Bde. Sig. Trp.	1st Mtd. Bde. Fd. Amb. 2nd Mtd. Bde. Fd. Amb. 3rd Mtd. Bde. Fd. Amb. 5th Cyclist Bde. Fd. Amb.	...	1st Mtd. Bde. A.S.C. 2nd Mtd. Bde. A.S.C. 3rd Mtd. Bde. A.S.C. 1st Mtd. Divnl. A.S.C. 5th Cyclist Bde. A.S.C.
1917 May (England)	1st Mounted[28]....... 2nd Mounted[29] .... 3rd Mounted[30]....... 5th Cyclist[31] .... Attached Troops...	2/1/War. Yeo., 2/1/Sherwood Rgrs., 2/1/R. Bucks. Hsrs. 2/1/Staff. Yeo., 2/1/Leic. Yeo., 2/1/Linc. Yeo. 2/1/Q.O. Dorset Yeo., 2/1/Herts. Yeo., 2/1/Essex Yeo. 2/1/S. Notts. Hsrs., 2/1/Derby. Yeo., 2/1/City of Lond. Yeo.[25] 7/Devon. (Cyclist Bn.),[26] 6/R. Suss. (Cyclist Bn.).[27]	... .	... 393 Bty. and Ammn Coln. 396 Bty. and Ammn. Coln.	...	1st Mtd. Bde. Sig. Trp. 2nd Mtd. Bde. Sig. Trp. 3rd Mtd. Bde. Sig. Trp. 5th Cyclist Bde. Sig. Trp. 1st Mtd. Divnl. Sig. Sqdn.	336 (E. Anglian) Fd. Amb. 337 (E. Anglian) Fd. Amb. 338 (Lowland) Fd. Amb. 339 (Lowland) Fd. Amb.	...	1st Mtd. Bde. A.S.C. 2nd Mtd. Bde. A.S.C. 3rd Mtd. Bde. A.S.C. 5th Mtd. Bde. A.S.C. 1st Mtd. Divnl. A.S.C.

On 4/9/1917, 1st MOUNTED DIVISION became THE CYCLIST DIVISION

1917 October (England)	11th Cyclist[28] ...... 12th Cyclist[29] ...... 13th Cyclist[30] ...... Attached Troops...	2/1/Sherwood Rgrs., 2/1/R. Bucks. Hsrs., 7/Devon. (Cyclist Bn.). 2/1/Staff. Yeo., 2/1/Leic. Yeo., 2/1/Linc. Yeo. 2/1/Q.O. Dorset Yeo., 2/1/Herts. Yeo., 2/1/Essex Yeo.	... .	... 393 Bty. and Ammn. Coln. 396 Bty. and Ammn. Coln.	...	11th Cyclist Bde. Sig. Sec. 12th Cyclist Bde. Sig. Sec. 13th Cyclist Bde. Sig. Sec. 1st Cyclist Divnl. Sig. Coy.	11th Cyclist Bde. Fd. Amb. 12th Cyclist Bde. Fd. Amb. 13th Cyclist Bde. Fd. Amb.	...	11th Cyclist Bde. A.S.C. 12th Cyclist Bde. A.S.C. 13th Cyclist Bde. A.S.C. 1st Cyclist Divnl. A.S.C.
1918 January—Armistice (England)	5th Cyclist[32]........ 11th Cyclist.......... 12th Cyclist......... Attached Troops...	2/1/S. Notts. Hsrs., 2/1/Derby. Yeo., 2/1/City of Lond. Yeo. 2/1/Sherwood Rgrs., 2/1/R. Bucks. Hsrs., 7/Devon. (Cyclist Bn.). 2/1/Staff. Yeo., 2/1/Leic. Yeo., 2/1/Linc. Yeo. 2/1/Kent (Cyclist Bn.).[35]	... .	... 393 Bty. and Ammn. Coln 396 Bty. and Ammn. Coln. 2/2/Lanc. Hy. Bty.[35] 2/1/War. Hy. Bty.[35]	... 563 Hunts.[35] Works Coy.	5th Cyclist Bde. Sig. Sec. 11th Cyclist Bde. Sig. Sec. 12th Cyclist Bde. Sig. Sec. Cyclist Divnl. Sig. Coy.	339 (Lowland) Fd. Amb. 336 (E. Anglian) Fd. Amb. 337 (E. Anglian) Fd. Amb. 126 Sany. Sec.[35]	... .	5th Cyclist Bde. A.S.C. 11th Cyclist Bde. A.S.C. 12th Cyclist Bde. A.S.C. Cyclist Divnl. A.S.C. 69th Railhead[35] Supply Detnt.

NOTES

On 3rd Mounted Division becoming 1st Mounted Division the following transfers took place:

1 To 1st Mtd. Bde.
2 To 9th Cyclist Bde. (later 5th Cyclist Bde.).
3 To 1st Mtd. Bde.
4 To 8th Cyclist Bde., in 2nd Cyclist Division.
5 To 1st Mtd. Bde.
6 To 9th Cyclist Bde. (later 5th Cyclist Bde.).
7 Became 4th Cyclist Bde., in 1st Cyclist Div.
8 Joined from 2nd (2/2/South-Western) Mtd. Bde. (in former 1st Mtd. Div.).
9 Joined from 4th (2/1/South Wales) Mtd. Bde. (in former 1st Mtd. Div.).
10 Joined from 1st (2/1/Highland) Mtd. Bde. (in former 1st Mtd. Div.).
11 Joined from 16th (2/1/Southern) Mtd. Bde., 4th Mtd. Div.
12 Joined from 14th (2/1/South-Eastern) Mtd. Bde., 4th Mtd. Div.
13 Joined from 13th (2/1/Eastern) Mtd. Bde., 4th Mtd. Div.

---

14 Bty. went overseas in June, 1917. Arrived at Basra on 13/8/17, joined CCXV (1 Wessex) Bde., R.F.A. (T.F.), and Bty. was numbered 812. (6, 18-pdrs.)

15 Bty. joined CLVIII Bde. (on formation of Bde.) at Heytesbury on 13/4/17; disembkd. (personnel only) at Boulogne on 24/5/17. CLVIII became an A.F.A. Bde. (Bty. armed with 18-pdrs.) On 6/7/17, 2/1/Berks. Bty. became C/CLVIII.

16 2/1/R. 1st Devon. Yeo. and 2/1/R.N. Devon. Hsrs. (2nd Cyclist Bde., 1st Cyclist Div.) amalgamated in Nov., 1916, and became 4th Bn., 2nd Cyclist Bde.

17 In Nov., 1916, 2/1/Montgomery. Yeo. amalgamated and became 3rd Bn., 1st Cyclist Bde.; and 2/1/Fife. and Forfar. Yeo. joined 6th Cyclist Bde.

18 Bde. (formerly 3rd, or 2/1/N. Midland, Mtd. Bde., later 3rd Cyclist Bde.) was transferred complete in Nov., 1916, from 1st Cyclist Div.

19 Transferred in Nov., 1916, from 7th Cyclist Bde., 2nd Cyclist Div.

20 Previously 9th Cyclist Bde.

21 Transferred in Nov., 1916, from 6th Cyclist Bde., 2nd Cyclist Div. By May, 1917, the Bn. was attached to 67th Div., Southern Army, H.D. Trps.

22 Transferred in Nov., 1916, from 8th Cyclist Bde., 2nd Cyclist Div. By May, 1917, the Bn. was attached to 226th Bde., Southern Army, H.D. Trps.

23 Bty. formed in Septr., 1914, as A (Reserve) Bty., H.A.C., and renamed 2/A, H.A.C. In Nov., 1915, the Bty. was armed with 4, 15-pdr.B.L.C. guns; and early in 1917 the Bty. was rearmed with 4, 18-pdr., Q.F. guns. In May, 1917, the Bty. joined the newly-formed CXXVI A.F.A. Bde., and the Bty. was made up to a 6-gun battery.

2/A Bty. went to France with CXXVI A.F.A. Bde., landing at Boulogne on 22/6/17. (2/B, H.A.C. also formed part of CXXVI A.F.A. Bde. 2/B had been formed at H.A.C. H.Q. on 26/9/14, and in July, 1915, became an overseas unit. In Dec., 1915, the Bty. received 4, 15-pdr. B.L.C. guns. In May, 1916, 2/B moved to Cupar (Fife.) and joined 14th Cyclist Bde. 2/B left Cupar on 10/5/17, and joined the newly-formed CXXVI A.F.A. Bde. at Heytesbury. 18-pdrs were issued to replace the 15-pdrs. The Bty. landed at Boulogne with the Bde. on 22/6/17.) After the Armistice both batteries (2/A, on 17/1/19 and 2/B, on 16/1/19) entered Germany.

24 In June, 1917, the Bty. went to France to join CXXVI A.F.A. Bde., and served with this Bde. for the rest of the War. After the Armistice the Bty. went into Germany, and the first and second-line Warwick. R.H.A. (T.F.) Bties. amalgamated.

25 In Nov., 1916, 2/1/City of London and 2/1/W. Som. Yeo. amalgamated and became 5th Bn., 2nd Cyclist Bde. This Bn. joined 5th Cyclist Bde. by May, 1917, to replace 2/1/Q.O.O.H., which had been transferred to 4th Cyclist Bde. at Wyvenhoe.

26 Until Nov., 1916, with 8th Cyclist Bde., 2nd Cyclist Div. Bn. left the Division by Aug., 1917, and by Oct., 1917, it had joined 11th Cyclist Bde.

27 Attached to (original) 1st Mtd. Div. in 1914 and 1915; and attached to 1st Mtd. Div. by May, 1917.

28 1st Mtd. Bde. became 11th Cyclist Bde., in Septr., 1917, and 7/Dev. (Cyclist Bn.) replaced 2/1/War. Yeo.

29 2nd Mtd. Bde. became 12th Cyclist Bde. in Septr., 1917.

30 3rd Mtd. Bde. became 13th Cyclist Bde. in Septr., 1917. 13th Cyclist Bde. was broken up in Dec., 1917, and 2/1/Q.O. Dorset. Yeo. and 2/1/Essex Yeo. joined 6th Cyclist Bde. in Ireland.

31 5th Cyclist Bde. became an Independent Bde. in Septr., 1917.

32 Replaced 13th Cyclist Bde.

33 Attached from March, 1918.

GENERAL NOTES

1/1/Inverness Bty. and 2/1/Inverness Bty., R.H.A. (T.F.) and Ammn. Colns. were attached to 2/1/S. Midland Mtd. Bde. from March, 1915. 2/1/Inverness Bty. left on 18/12/15 for Lark Hill; and, on 9/2/16, 1/1/Inverness Bty. left for service overseas. 1/1/Inverness Bty. disembkd. at Alexandria on 22 and 25/2/16, and the Bty. joined A. and N.Z. Mtd. Div. on its formation in mid-March, 1916. The Bty. joined IV. Bde. R.H.A. (T.F.); and in 1918 the Bty. joined XVIII. Bde. R.H.A. (T.F.), with A. and N.Z. Mtd. Div.

On 31/3/16 orders were issued for numbering the Mounted Bdes.

2ND/2ND MOUNTED DIVISION

FORMATION AND NARRATIVE

Early in 1915 the 2nd Mounted Division was selected for service abroad and it became necessary to complete the 2nd-line units which would replace it and form depots, and approval was given for the formation of the 2nd/2nd Mounted Division.

This 2nd-line division came into existence on the 6th March, 1915, but the units of which it was made up were by no means ready for war. Though the regiments were fairly strong in personnel (numbering between 410 and 498 men) yet they were short of horses (one had only 5, another had 99; and although a third had 354 horses for its 464 men, this regiment had only 83 rifles). Three of the regiments had no rifles, other regiments possessed 30, 83, and 90, and the maximum was 206. The four 2nd-line horse artillery batteries and ammunition columns were almost immobile. Three of the batteries were without any horses and the fourth had only 23. In personnel, three batteries averaged over 200 men each, but the fourth had only 91.

On the 6th March, when the division was formed, the units were still very scattered. The regiments were at Chatsworth, Ollerton, Retford, Warwick, Worcester, Gloucester, Sherborne, Buckingham, and Reading, and three were in London (Fulham and Putney). The horse artillery batteries were at Nottingham, Reading, Warwick, and Finsbury.

After the division had been assembled it was allotted to the First Army for the defence of the East Coast. Divisional headquarters was at King's Lynn, the four brigades were around Narborough, Hunstanton, King's Lynn, and Aylsham, with the batteries at Scarning and Wendling, South Creake, North Runcton, and Reepham.

The call for drafts, however, was so persistent that, by the end of October, 1915, three regiments of one brigade had been reduced in this way to the following strengths : 9 officers and 103 other ranks, 5 and 55, and 12 and 86, and the strength of the battery was 3 officers and 19 other ranks; though the strength of another brigade was 73 officers, 1,279 other ranks, and 1,504 horses. Musketry instruction could not be proceeded with because of lack of ammunition. So far no machine guns had been issued, the signal troops had no telephone equipment, and one battery had no gun ammunition. In November, 1915, the Japanese carbines were gradually being replaced by ·303" rifles. One battery, however, reported that its 15-pounder B.L.C. guns were "practically useless." Another battery only had sights issued for its 15-pounder, Mk.I., B.L. guns in December, 1915, and even then was without gun ammunition ; but on the 17th January, 1916, this battery (at North Runcton) received four 15-pounder B.L.C. guns, eight ammunition wagons, and 210 rounds of ammunition for each gun.

In March, 1916, after the 2nd/2nd Mounted Division had been in existence for twelve months, the designation of the division was changed to 3rd Mounted Division.

The organization of the division remained unaltered, though the mounted brigades were numbered 9th-12th. In July, 1916 (after the original 1st Mounted Division had become the 1st Cyclist Division), the 3rd Mounted Division was redesignated 1st Mounted Division, and the organization of the division was now changed, a cyclist brigade taking the place of the fourth mounted brigade (see Order of Battle Table). At this time the division formed part of the General Reserve, Home Defence Troops, and had its headquarters at Brentwood. Two of the mounted brigades were around Brentwood, the other mounted brigade was near Maidstone, and the cyclist brigade was at Bridge, Bishopsbourne, and Bekesbourne. In October the brigade at Maidstone was concentrated at West Malling and the cyclist brigade at Bridge. By November, 1916, the 2nd-line R.H.A. (T.F.) batteries had left ; and in this month the 9th Cyclist Brigade was renumbered and became 5th Cyclist Brigade.

2ND/2ND MOUNTED DIVISION

In May, 1917, the division still formed part of the General Reserve, Home Defence Troops, and had its headquarters at Sevenoaks. The mounted brigades were concentrated at Brentwood, West Malling, and Sevenoaks, the cyclist brigade was at Bridge Hill, the two attached batteries were at Canterbury and Westbere, and the cyclist battalions were at Margate and Wingham.

By the middle of August, 1917, the 1st Mounted Division had been issued with bicycles. It was then decided that this division should be utilised as a draft-finding unit for overseas cyclist units and the Army Cyclist Corps Training Centre at Chiseldon would be abolished. All category " A " men at Chiseldon were to be absorbed by the 1st Mounted Division, and all the trained cavalrymen with the division were to be transferred to Reserve Cavalry Regiments. On the 4th September, 1917, the title of the 1st Mounted Division was changed to The Cyclist Division, the 1st, 2nd, and 3rd Mounted Brigades became the 11th, 12th, and 13th Cyclist Brigades, and the yeomanry regiments became yeomanry cyclist regiments.

In March, 1918, The Cyclist Division (forming part of the Independent Force, Home Defence Troops) had its headquarters at Canterbury. One brigade was at Littlebourne, Ash, and Wingham, both the other brigades were at Canterbury, and the two attached batteries were at Westbere and Canterbury.

In November, 1918, at the end of the Great War, The Cyclist Division formed part of the Kent Force, Eastern Command, Forces in Great Britain. The Cyclist Divisional H.Q. and the three cyclist brigades were all at Canterbury, the two field batteries were at Westbere, and the two heavy batteries were at Minster and Wingham.

Disbandment of the units began in March, 1919, and by June, 1919, The Cyclist Division disappeared. During its existence (from March, 1915, to June, 1919) the division served entirely in England and was employed on Home Defence.

4TH MOUNTED DIVISION

(In July, 1916, 4th Mounted Division became 2nd Cyclist Division)

G.O.C.

Formation ... ... Br.-Gen. LORD LOVAT.
26 May, 1916 ... ... Major-General LORD LOVAT.

G.S.O. 1.

30 Mar., 1916...Lt.-Col. W. A. TILNEY.
18 June, 1916...Major H. H. POWELL (acting).
4 July, 1916...Lt.-Col. Hon. C. H. C. GUEST.

A.-A. and Q.-M.-G.

27 Mar., 1916...Lt.-Col. F. H. SYKES.
8 June, 1916...Lt.-Col. F. H. ALLHUSEN.

MARCH, 1916

13th MOUNTED BDE.
(2/1/Eastern)

[10 Jan., '15] Br.-Gen. E. W. N. PEDDER.

14th MOUNTED BDE.
(2/1/S.-Eastern)

[18 Jan., '15] Br.-Gen. T. O. W. CHAMPION DE CRESPIGNY.
6 April, '16...Br.-Gen. Hon. A. F. STANLEY.

15th MOUNTED BDE.
(2/1/S.-Western)

[25 Jan., '15] Br.-Gen. J. B. EDWARDS.
2 April, '16...Br.-Gen. F. LEE.

16th MOUNTED BDE.
(2/1/Southern)

Formation ...Br.-Gen. EARL OF SHAFTESBURY.

JULY, 1916

5th CYCLIST BDE.

[10 Jan., '15] Br.-Gen. E. W. N. PEDDER.

6th CYCLIST BDE.

[2 April, '16] Br.-Gen. F. LEE.

7th CYCLIST BDE.

[20 Mar., '16] Br.-Gen. EARL OF SHAFTESBURY.

8th CYCLIST BDE.

[July, '16] Br.-Gen. C. WILLIAMS.

Formed 20th March, 1916

4TH MOUNTED DIVISION ORDER OF BATTLE, 1916

Dates	YEOMANRY		R.H.A. (T.F.)		Engineers	Signal Service	Medical	Mobile Veterinary Sections	A.S.C.
	Mounted later Cyclist) Brigades	Regiments and attached Units	Brigades	Batteries					
1916 April (England)	13th Mounted (2/1st Eastern) 14th Mounted (2/1st S.-Eastern) 15th Mounted (2/1st S.-Western) 16th Mounted (2/1st Southern)	2/1/Suff. Yeo., 2/1/K.O.R.R. Norf. Yeo., 2/1/Essex Yeo.[1] 2/1/R. E. Kent. Mtd. Rif., 2/1/Q.O. W. Kent. Yeo.,[2] 2/1/Sussex Yeo.[3] 2/1/Wilts. Yeo., 2/1/N. Som. Yeo., 2/1/Hants. Yeo. 2/1/Q.O. Dorset Yeo., 2/1/Herts. Yeo.,[4] 2/1/Surrey Yeo.	...	...	...	13th Mtd. Bde. Sig. Trp. 14th Mtd. Bde. Sig. Trp. 15th Mtd. Bde. Sig. Trp. 16th Mtd. Bde. Sig. Trp. 4th Mtd. Divnl. Sig. Sqdn.	13th Mtd. Bde. Fd. Amb. 14th Mtd. Bde. Fd. Amb. 15th Mtd. Bde. Fd. Amb. 16th Mtd. Bde. Fd. Amb.	...	13th Mtd. Bde. A.S.C. 14th Mtd. Bde. A.S.C. 15th Mtd. Bde. A.S.C. 16th Mtd. Bde. A.S.C. 4th Mtd. Divnl. A.S.C.

In July, 1916, the 4th MOUNTED DIVISION became 2nd CYCLIST DIVISION

Dates	Mounted later Cyclist) Brigades	Regiments and attached Units	Brigades	Batteries	Engineers	Signal Service	Medical	Mobile Veterinary Sections	A.S.C.
1916 September (England)	5th Cyclist .... 6th Cyclist .... 7th Cyclist .... 8th Cyclist	2/1/Suff. Yeo.,[8] 2/1/K.O.R.R. Norf. Yeo.,[8] 2/1/Suss. Yeo.;[9] 8/Essex (Cyclist Bn.).[10] 2/1/Wilts. Yeo.,[11] 2/1/N. Som. Yeo.,[11] 2/1/Hants. Yeo.;[12] 2/1/Kent (Cyclist Bn.)[13] 2/1/R.E. Kent Mtd. Rif.,[14] 2/1/Q.O. Dorset. Yeo.,[15] 2/1/Surrey Yeo.;[9] 7/Devon. (Cyclist Bn.).[16] 2/1/R. Glouc. Hsrs.,[5]; [17] 2/1/Berks. Yeo.,[6]; [12] 2/1/Q.O. Worc. Hsrs.,[7]; [17] 2/8/Essex (Cyclist Bn.).[18]	...	...	...	5th Cyclist Bde.[19] Sig. Trp. 6th Cyclist Bde.[19] Sig. Trp. 7th Cyclist Bde.[20] Sig. Trp. 8th Cyclist Bde.[20] Sig. Trp. 2nd Cyclist Divnl. Sig. Sqdn.	5th Cyclist Bde.[19] Fd. Amb. 6th Cyclist Bde.[20] Fd. Amb. 7th Cyclist Bde.[19] Fd. Amb. 8th Cyclist Bde.[20] Fd. Amb.	...	5th Cyclist Bde.[19] A.S.C. 6th Cyclist Bde.[19] A.S.C. 7th Cyclist Bde.[20] A.S.C. 8th Cyclist Bde.[20] A.S.C. 2nd Cyclist Divnl. A.S.C.

By 16th November, 1916, the 2nd CYCLIST DIVISION was broken up

NOTES

On the 4th Mounted Division becoming the 2nd Cyclist Division (in July, 1916) the following transfers took place, and the following units joined :—

1 2/1/Essex Yeo., from 13th Mtd. Bde., to 3rd Mtd. Bde., 1st Mtd. Div.
2 2/1/Q.O. W. Kent. Yeo., from 14th Mtd. Bde. to 3rd Mtd. Bde., 1st Mtd. Div.
3 2/1/Sussex Yeo., from 14th Mtd. Bde., to 5th Cyclist Bde., 2nd Cyclist Div.
4 2/1/Herts. Yeo., from 16th Mtd. Bde., to 3rd Mtd. Bde., 1st Mtd. Div.
5 2/1/R. Glouc. Hsrs. joined 8th Cyclist Bde. from 10th Mtd. Bde., 3rd Mtd. Div.
6 2/1/Berks. Yeo., joined 8th Cyclist Bde. from 11th Mtd. Bde., 3rd Mtd. Div.
7 2/1/Q.O. Worc. Hsrs., joined 8th Cyclist Bde. from 10th Mtd. Bde., 3rd Mtd. Div.

When the 2nd Cyclist Division was broken up the following transfers and amalgamations took place :—

8 2/1/Suff. Yeo. and 2/1/K.O.R.R. Norf. Yeo. were amalgamated and became 7th Bn., 3rd Cyclist Bde.
9 2/1/Suss. Yeo. and 2/1/Surr. Yeo. were amalgamated and became 8th Bn., 3rd Cyclist Bde.
10 8/Essex (Cyclist Bn.) was attached to 3rd Cyclist Bde.
11 2/1/Wilts. Yeo. and 2/1/N. Som. Yeo. were amalgamated and became 10th Bn., 4th Cyclist Bde.
12 2/1/Hants. Yeo. and 2/1/Berks. Yeo. were amalgamated on 2/11/16 and became 11th Bn., 4th Cyclist Bde.
13 2/1/Kent (Cyclist Bn.) was attached to 3rd Cyclist Bde., and then in Nov., 1916, to 5th Cyclist Bde., with 1st Mtd. Div.
14 2/1/R.E. Kent Mtd. Rif. and 2/1/Q.O. W. Kent Yeo. (from 3rd Mtd. Bde., 1st Mtd. Div.) amalgamated and became 9th Bn., 3rd Cyclist Bde.
15 2/1/Q.O. Dorset Yeo. was transferred to 3rd Mtd. Bde., 1st Mtd. Div.
16 7/Devon. (Cyclist Bn.) was attached to 4th Cyclist Bde.
17 2/1/R. Glouc. Hsrs. and 2/1/Q.O. Worc. Hsrs. were amalgamated and became 12th Bn., 4th Cyclist Bde.
18 2/8/Essex (Cyclist Bn.) was attached to 4th Cyclist Bde.
19 Tranferred to 3rd Cyclist Bde.
20 Transferred to 4th Cyclist Bde., and then in Nov., 1916, to 5th Cyclist Bde., with 1st Mtd. Div.

GENERAL NOTES

2/1/**Berks. Bty., R.H.A. (T.F.)** was attached to the 7th Cyclist Bde. from Septr., 1916, until the division was broken up.

2/1/**Notts. Bty., R.H.A. (T.F.)** was attached to the 8th Cyclist Bde. from Septr., 1916, until the division was broken up.

Orders for numbering the Mounted Brigades were issued on 31/3/16.

4TH MOUNTED DIVISION

FORMATION AND NARRATIVE

The division was formed on the 20th March, 1916. It included three existing 2nd line mounted brigades and the newly formed 2/1/Southern Mounted Brigade. The headquarters of the 4th Mounted Division was at Colchester, and the four mounted brigades were at Wivenhoe, Canterbury, Kelvedon, and Manningtree.

Early in July, 1916, the yeomanry regiments were dismounted and the horses were transferred to various remount depots. Bicycles were then issued and the regiments became yeomanry cyclist regiments. Later in the month the 4th Mounted Division was reorganized as a cyclist division and became the 2nd Cyclist Division. The division formed part of the Southern Army, Home Defence Troops. Divisional headquarters was at Colchester, and the four cyclist brigades had their headquarters at Wivenhoe, Kelvedon, Manningtree, and West Malling.

In September, 1916, the division had its headquarters at Ipswich, and the four cyclist brigades had their headquarters at Wivenhoe, Wingham, Woodbridge, and Ipswich.

By the 16th November, the 2nd Cyclist Division was broken up, the cyclist brigades were dispersed, and the regiments were amalgamated to form battalions in newly formed cyclist brigades (see Notes, Order of Battle Table).

During its existence (from March to November, 1916) the division served in England and was employed on Home Defence.

YEOMANRY MOUNTED DIVISION

(On 24/4/18 the Yeomanry Mounted Division was reorganized and became 1st Mounted Division.)

G.O.C.

20 June, 1917	Major-General G. de S. Barrow.
1 October, 1917	Br.-Gen. C. S. Rome (acting).
7 October, 1917	Br.-Gen. F. A. B. Fryer (acting).
15 October, 1917	Major-General G. de S. Barrow.
7 November, 1917... ...	Br.-Gen. C. A. C. Godwin (acting).
9 November, 1917... ...	Major-General G. de S. Barrow.
30 December, 1917... ...	Br.-Gen. C. A. C. Godwin (acting).
6 January, 1918	Major-General G. de S. Barrow.
31 March, 1918	Br.-Gen. C. A. C. Godwin (acting).
22 April, 1918	Major-General G. de S. Barrow.

G.S.O. 1.

26 June, 1917...Major H. C. Robertson (acting).
15 July, 1917...Lt.-Col. W. J. Foster.

A.-A. and Q.-M.-G.

20 June, 1917...Lt.-Col. T. C. Robinson.

C.R.H.A.

(and Offr. Commdg. XX R.H.A.)

25 June, 1917...Lt. Col. O. L. Eugster (sick, 17/1/18).
17 Jan., 1918...Major H. E. Noel (acting).
26 Jan., 1918...Lt.-Col. O. L. Eugster.

C.R.E.

(The division had no C.R.E., but the O.C. Field Squadron, R.E., acted as such.)

6th MOUNTED BDE.
(2nd S. Midland)

(Joined on 27/6/17 from Impl. Mtd. Div.)

[17 July, '16]...Br.-Gen. T. M. S. Pitt.
28 Sept., '17...Lt.-Col. A. M. Pirie (acting).
1 Oct., '17...Lt.-Col. Sir R. L. Baker, Bt. (acting).
12 Oct., '17...Br.-Gen. C. A. C. Godwin.
7 Nov., '17...Lt.-Col. Hon. F. H. Cripps (acting).
9 Nov., '17...Br.-Gen. C. A. C. Godwin.
30 Dec., '17...Lt.-Col. Hon. F. H. Cripps (acting).
7 Jan., '18...Br.-Gen. C. A. C. Godwin.
31 Mar., '18...Lt.-Col. G. K. M. Mason (acting).
22 April, '18...Br.-Gen. C. A. C. Godwin.

8th MOUNTED BDE.
(1st London)

(Joined on 21/7/17 from Salonika.)

[25 May, '14] *Br.-Gen. A. H. M. Taylor.
6 Sept., '17...Br.-Gen. C. S. Rome.

22nd MOUNTED BDE.
(1st N. Midland)

(Joined on 6/7/17 from Anzac Mtd. Div.)

[29 Nov., '16] Br.-Gen. F. A. B. Fryer.
4 Dec., '17...Br.-Gen. P. D. FitzGerald.
7 April, '18...Br.-Gen. J. T. Wigan.

*Br.-Gen. on 5 August, 1914.

YEOMANRY MOUNTED DIVISION

ORDER OF BATTLE, 1917-1918

Formed at Khan Yunis between 20/6—22/7/17

Dates	CAVALRY		ARTILLERY		Engineers	Signal Service	Cavalry Field Ambulances	Mobile Veterinary Sections	Sanitary Section	Divisional Train
	Brigades	Regiments and attached Units	R.H.A. Brigade and Ammn. Coln.	R.H.A. Batteries	Field Squadron	Signal Squadron				
1917 July (Palestine)	6th Mounted[1] (2/S. Midland)	1/R. Bucks. Hsrs., 1/Q.O. Dorset. Yeo., 1/Berks. Yeo.; 17th M.G. Squadron; 6th Mtd. Bde. Signal Troop	XX4........	Hants.,[5] Berks.,[6] Leicester.[7]	6th[8]	Yeo. Mtd. Divnl.[9]	2/S. Midland,[10] 1/London,[11] 1/N. Midland[12]	3/1/N. Midland,[13] 4/1/N. Midland,[14] 3/1/Highland[15]	31st[16]	Yeomanry Mounted[17]
	8th Mounted[2] (1/London)	1/County of London (Middx. Yeo.), 1/City of London Yeo., 3/County of London Yeo.; 21st M.G. Squadron; 1/London Mtd. Bde. Signal Troop								
	22nd Mounted[3] (1/N. Midland)	1/Q.O.R.R. Staff. Yeo., 1/Linc. Yeo., 1/E. Riding Yeo.; 18th M.G. Squadron; 22nd Mtd. Bde. Signal Troop								
1918 March (Palestine)	6th Mounted[18]	1/R. Bucks. H.,[19] 1/Q.O. Dorset. Yeo.,[18] 1/Berks. Yeo.;[19] 17th M.G. Sqdn.;[18] 6th Mtd. Bde. Signal Troop[18]	XX[24]	Hants., Berks., Leicester.	6th[25]	Yeo. Mtd. Divnl.[26]	2/S. Midland,[27] 1/London,[28] 1/N. Midland[29]	3/1/N. Midland,[30] 4/1/N. Midland,[31] 3/1/Highland[32]	31st[33]	Yeomanry Mounted[34]
	8th Mounted[20].......	1/Co. of Lond. Yeo.,[20] 1/City of Lond. Yeo.,[21] 3/Co. of Lond. Yeo.;[21] 21st M.G. Sqdn.;[20] 1/Lond. Mtd. Bde. Signal Trp.[20]								
	22nd Mounted[22] ..	1/Q.O.R.R. Staff. Yeo.,[22] 1/Linc. Yeo.,[23] 1/E. Riding Yeo.;[23] 18th M.G. Sqdn.;[22] 22nd Mtd. Bde. Signal Troop[22]								

On 24/4/18 the YEOMANRY MTD. DIV. was reorganized, indianized, and designated 1st MOUNTED DIV.; and on 22/7/18 it was redesignated 4th CAVALRY DIV.

NOTES

1 The Bde. was transferred complete from the Impl. Mtd. Div., and joined at el Maraqeb on 27/6/17. M.G. Sqdn. was formed on 12/1/17.

2 The Bde. arrived complete at el Ferdan (Egypt) from Salonika on 8/6/17, moved forward on 7/7/17, and joined the Div. at el Fuqari on 21/7/17. The M.G. Sqdn. was formed in Egypt on 14/6/17.

3 The Bde. was transferred complete from the Anzac Mtd. Div., and joined at el Fuqari on 6/7/17. M.G. Sqdn. was formed on 8/1/17.

4 The Bde., CCLXIV (V Lowland), consisting of Hants. R.H.A., Essex R.H.A., and W. Riding R.H.A. Bties., concentrated at Leicester on 13/1/16, and the Bties. were rearmed with 4, 18-pdrs. each. Bde. embkd. at Devonport, 15-18/2/16, disembkd. at Port Said on 2/3/16, and joined 52nd Div. on 17/3/16 at el Qantara. On 28/5/16 the Bde. was numbered CCLXIII, and the Bties. were lettered A, B, and C; on 15/9/16 the Bde. was renumbered CCLXIV; and on 30/12/16 its number was changed back to CCLXIII, and C (W. Riding) was split up between A (Hants.) and B (Essex). At the end of June, 1917, arrangements were made to re-form CCLXIII as a horse artillery brigade. On 5/7/17, CCLXIII changed its 18-pdr. equipments for 13-pdr., became XX R.H.A., and joined the Yeo. Mtd. Div. at Khan Yunis leaving the Essex Bty. behind in the 52nd Div. On 17/9/17 the Essex Bty. joined the 7th Mtd. Bde., which had reached Egypt from Salonika on 29/6/17.

5 Joined with XX Bde. on 5/7/17 (see note 4). The Bty. was armed with 4, 13-pdr. guns.

6 The Bty. disembkd. at Alexandria on 26/4/15, and joined Canal Defence Force on 30/4/15. On 4/11/16 the Bty. joined 6th Mtd. Bde., and was transferred on 27/6/17, with 6th Mtd., to the Yeo. Mtd. Div. On 5/7/17, the Bty. joined XX Bde. The Bty. was armed with 4, 13-pdr. guns.

7 The Bty. disembkd. at Alexandria on 25/2/16. In March, 1916, the Bty. joined Anzac Mtd. Divnl. Arty., and on 20/6/17 it was transferred to Yeo. Mtd. Div., and joined XX Bde. on 5/7/17. The Bty. was armed with 4, 13-pdr. guns

8 Formed at el Maraqeb between 1-22/7/17.

9 Formed at Alexandria between 29/5—11/7/17, and joined Yeo. Mtd. Div. at Khan Yunis on 14/7/17.

10 Transferred on 27/6/17 from Impl. Mtd. Div.

11 Joined with 8th Mtd. Bde. (see note 2).

12 Transferred on 5/7/17 from Anzac Mtd. Div.

13 Joined with 22nd Mtd. Bde. (see note 3).

14 Joined with 6th Mtd. Bde. (see note 1).

15 Joined with 8th Mtd. Bde. (see note 2).

16 Transferred on 22/7/17 from Impl. Mtd. Div.

17 Joined at Khan Yunis, 22/7/17; it consisted of Nos. 999, 1,000, 1,001, 1,002 Coys., A.S.C.

18 Became part of 1st Mtd. Div. on 24/4/18. On 22/7/18, Bde. and Signal Troop were numbered 10th.

19 Left Bde. on 4/4/18 to form C Bn., M.G.C. Bn. disembkd. at Taranto on 21/6/18, reached Etaples on 28/6/18, and in mid-August was numbered 101.

20 Became part of 1st Mtd. Div. on 24/4/18. On 22/7/18, Bde. and Signal Troop were numbered 11th.

21 Left Bde. on 7/4/18 to form E Bn., M.G.C. Bn. disembkd. at Marseille on 1/6/18, reached Etaples on 8/6/18, and in mid-August was numbered 103.

22 Became part of 1st Mtd. Div. on 24/4/18. On 22/7/18, Bde. and Signal Troop were numbered 12th.

23 Left Bde. on 7/4/18 to form D Bn., M.G.C. Bn. disembkd. at Marseille on 1/6/18, reached Etaples on 8/6/18, and on 17/8/18 was numbered 102.

24 Became part of 1st Mtd. Div. on 24/4/18.

25 Became part of 1st Mtd. Div. on 24/4/18; and on 4/9/18 the Fd. Sqdn. was renumbered 4th.

26 Became part of 1st Mtd. Div. on 24/4/18, and renamed 1st Mtd. Divnl. Sig. Sqdn. On 22/7/18, the Sig. Sqdn. was numbered 4th.

27 On 11/5/18, 2/S Mid. and Mhow C.F.A.'s were amalgamated and became 6th Combd. Cav. Fd. Amb.; it was renumbered 10th on 22/7/18.

28 On 30/4/18, 1/Lond. and Lucknow C.F.A.'s were amalgamated and became 8th Combd. Cav. Fd. Amb.; it was renumbered 11th on 22/7/18.

29 On 24/4/18, 1/N. Mid. and Sialkot C.F.A.'s were amalgamated and became 22nd Combd. Cav. Fd. Amb.; it was renumbered 12th on 22/7/18.

30 3/1/N. Mid. reorganized with Sialkot M.V.S. on 26 and 27/4/18 and became 22nd M.V.S.; it was renumbered 12th on 22/7/18.

31 4/1/N. Mid. reorganized with Mhow M.V.S. on 11/5/18 and became 6th M.V.S.; it was renumbered 10th on 22/7/18.

32 3/1/Highland reorganized with Lucknow M.V.S. in April, 1918, and became 8th M.V.S.; it was renumbered 11th on 22/7/18.

33 Became part of 1st Mtd. Div. on 24/4/18, and of 4th Cav. Div. on 22/7/18.

34 Became part of 1st Mtd. Div. on 24/4/18 and was renamed 1st Mtd. Divnl. Train. On 22/7/18 it was designated 4th Cav. Divnl. Train.

GENERAL NOTES

The following also served with the Yeomanry Mounted Division:—

CAVALRY:—7th Mounted Brigade (Sherwood Rgrs. and S. Notts. Hussars) from 5/1/18–12/3/18 (transferred to D.M.C.).

7th Mounted Brigade from 2/4/18–6/5/18 (transferred to XXI. Corps). **34/Poona Horse and 20/Deccan Horse** (formerly of Secunderabad Cav. Bde.) joined 7th Mtd. Bde. on 26 and 27/4/18 (respectively), and left with the 7th Mtd. Bde. on 6/5/18.

Warwickshire Yeo. (from 5th Mtd. Bde.) and **S. Notts. Hussars** (from 7th Mtd. Bde.) were attached from 2–7/4/18. On 3/4/18 the two Regiments amalgamated and became B. Bn., M.G.C. The Bn. reached France in May, 1918; and on 19/8/18 B. Bn. was numbered 100.

2/County of London Yeo. (from Corps Troops, XXI. Corps) was attached from 6–8/4/18; whilst reorganizing as F. Bn., M.G.C. The Bn. reached France on 1/6/18; and in mid-August, 1918, F. Bn. was numbered 104.

YEOMANRY MOUNTED DIVISION

FORMATION, BATTLES, AND ENGAGEMENTS

In accordance with Eastern Force Order, No. 53, the mounted troops of the Desert Column, E.E.F., were formed into three mounted divisions.

As a result of this order, the Yeomanry Mounted Division came into existence, between 20/6-22/7/17, at Khan Yunis (Palestine).

Of its three mounted brigades: the 6th was transferred from the Imperial Mounted Division (redesignated on 20/6/17 Australian Mtd. Div.); the 8th came from Salonika; and the 22nd was transferred from the Anzac Mtd. Div. The XX. Bde., R.H.A., was the CCLXIII. Bde. (52nd Div. Arty.) re-formed, rearmed, and redesignated (see note 4). The field squadron and the signal squadron were new formations.

During its brief existence the Yeomanry Mounted Division served with the Egyptian Expeditionary Force in Palestine and was engaged in the following operations:—

1917

THIRD BATTLE OF GAZA

31 Oct. ... ...**Capture of Beersheba** [In G.H.Q. Reserve].

6 Nov. ... ...**Capture of the Sheria Position** [Desert Mounted Corps].

---

13 and 14 Nov. ... ...**El Maghar** [Desert Mounted Corps].

17-24 Nov. ... ...**Battle of Nabi Samweil** [D.M.C.; attached on 23/11 to XXI. Corps].

27-29 Nov. ... ...**Turkish counter-attacks in Turkish Defence of Jerusalem** [XXI. Corps; attached on 28/11 to XX. Corps].

1918

By G.H.Q., E.E.F., Order of 12/4/18, the mounted troops of the E.E.F. were reorganized when the Indian units arrived. In consequence of this order the Yeomanry Mounted Division underwent reorganization at Deir el Bela. On the 24th April, 1918, its designation was changed to 1st Mounted Division; the division was indianized, and its yeomanry story ended.*

*In its turn the 1st Mounted Division was redesignated 4th Cavalry Division on 22/7/18. The further war service, of what had originally started as the Yeo. Mtd. Div., will be given in Part IV., under the 1st Mtd. and 4th Cav. Division.

42ND (EAST LANCASHIRE) DIVISION

G.O.C.

5 May, 1913 ... ... Major-General W. DOUGLAS.
24 July, 1915 ... ... Major-General W. R. MARSHALL (tempy.).
8 August, 1915 ... ... Major-General W. DOUGLAS (invalided, 29/12/15).
29 December, 1915 ... ... Br.-Gen. H. C. FRITH (acting).
21 January, 1916 ... ... Major-General W. DOUGLAS.
2 March, 1917 ... ... Br.-Gen. H. C. FRITH (acting).
10 March, 1917 ... ... Major-General B. R. MITFORD.
1 October, 1917 ... ... Br.-Gen. W. W. SEYMOUR (acting).
15 October, 1917 ... ... Major-General A. SOLLY-FLOOD.

G.S.O. 1.

1 April, 1912...Captain A. W. TUFNELL (G.S.O. 2).
5 Aug., 1914...Lt.-Col. A. W. TUFNELL.
10 Jan., 1916...Lt.-Col. A. CROOKENDEN (invalided, 27/4/17).
28 April, 1917...Lt.-Col. R. G. PARKER (tempy.).
30 April, 1917...Major B. C. BATTYE (acting).
8 June, 1917...Lt.-Col. B. J. CURLING.
29 Jan., 1918...Lt.-Col. R. F. GUY.

A.-A. and Q.-M.-G.

1 Jan., 1911...Captain R. S. ALLEN (D.-A.-A. and Q.-M.-G.).
5 Aug., 1914...Col. W. H. CUMMINGS (invalided, 3/5/15).
3 May, 1915...Colonel E. S. HERBERT.
6 Sept., 1915...Lt.-Col. H. F. L. GRANT.
30 Nov., 1915...Lt.-Col. R. J. SLAUGHTER.

B.-G., R.A.

5 Aug., 1914...*Br.-Gen. A. D'A. KING.
1 June, 1916...Lt.-Col. J. H. DUDGEON (acting).
2 July, 1916...Br.-Gen. A. D'A. KING.
12 Oct., 1916...Br.-Gen. F. W. H. WALSHE (wounded, 29/9/17).
29 Sept., 1917...Lt.-Col. A. BIRTWHISTLE (acting).
12 Oct., 1917...Br.-Gen. F. W. H. WALSHE.
16 Feb., 1918...Lt.-Col. D. J. MASON (acting).
9 Mar., 1918...Br.-Gen. F. W. H. WALSHE.

C.R.E.

12 Mar., 1913...Lt.-Col. C. E. NEWTON.
31 Aug., 1914...Lt.-Col. S. L. TENNANT.
16 April, 1916...Lt.-Col. E. N. MOZLEY (Tempy. C.R.E., 54th Div., 23/5/15).
24 May, 1916...Major L. F. WELLS (acting).
21 June, 1916...Lt.-Col. E. N. MOZLEY.
26 Sept. 1916...Major A. N. LAWFORD (acting).
21 Nov., 1916...Lt.-Col. E. N. MOZLEY (invalided, 8/1/17).
8 Jan., 1917...Major A. N. LAWFORD (acting).
13 Feb., 1917...Lt.-Col. E. N. MOZLEY (invalided, 20/5/17).
20 May, 1917...Major J. G. RIDDICK (acting).
3 June, 1917...Lt.-Col. D. S. MACINNES.
22 Dec., 1917...Lt.-Col. R. E. B. PRATT.
21 June, 1918...Major J. H. MOUSLEY (acting).
28 June, 1918...Major J. G. RIDDICK (acting).
8 July, 1918...Lt.-Col. A. T. SHAKESPEAR (Transferred to C.R.E., 12th Div., 12/7/18).
12 July, 1918...Lt.-Col. J. G. RIDDICK.

*Br.-Gen. on 5 August, 1914.

125th BDE.
(Lanc. Fus. Bde.)

30 May, '14...*Br.-Gen. H. C. FRITH.
10 Jan., '16...Lt.-Col. G. W. ROBINSON (acting).
21 Jan., '16...Br.-Gen. H. C. FRITH.
25 Jan., '16...Lt.-Col. G. W. ROBINSON (acting).
26 Feb., '16...Br.-Gen. H. C. FRITH.
2 Mar., '17...Lt.-Col. R. L. LEES (acting).
12 Mar., '17...Br.-Gen. H. C. FRITH.
23 June, '17...Br.-Gen. H. FARGUS.

126th BDE.
(E. Lanc. Bde.)

20 July, '14...*Br.-Gen. D. G. PRENDERGAST.
13 July, '15...Br.-Gen. VISCOUNT HAMPDEN.
27 Dec., '15...Lt.-Col. G. W. ROBINSON (acting).
10 Jan., '16...Br.-Gen. A. W. TUFNELL.
13 Sept., '17...Lt.-Col. E. C. LLOYD (acting).
14 Sept., '17...Br.-Gen. A. C. JOHNSTON (wounded, 16/9/17).
16 Sept., '17...Lt.-Col. E. C. LLOYD (acting).
19 Sept., '17...Br.-Gen. W. W. SEYMOUR.
25 May, '18...Br.-Gen. G. H. WEDGWOOD.
1 Sept., '18...Lt.-Col. E. V. MANGER (acting).
5 Sept., '18...Br.-Gen. T. H. S. MARCHANT.

127th BDE.
(Manch. Bde.)

1 Sept., '11...*Br.-Gen. N. LEE (wounded, 4/6/15).
4 June, '15...Lt.-Col. W. G. HEYS (acting).
4 June, '15...Lt.-Col. LORD ROCHDALE (acting).
21 June, '15...Br.-Gen. HON. H. A. LAWRENCE.
6 July, '15...Lt.-Col. H. C. DARLINGTON (acting).
27 July, '15...Br.-Gen. HON. H. A. LAWRENCE.
19 Aug., '15...Lt.-Col. A. CANNING (acting).
26 Aug., '15...Br.-Gen. HON. H. A. LAWRENCE.
17 Sept., '15...Lt.-Col. A. CANNING (acting).
22 Sept., '15...Br.-Gen. G. S. McD. ELLIOT.
17 Feb., '16...Lt.-Col. A. CANNING (acting).
1 Mar., '16...Br.-Gen. V. A. ORMSBY (killed, 2/5/17).
2 May, '17...Lt.-Col. H. C. DARLINGTON (acting).
5 May, '17...Br.-Gen. HON. A. M. HENLEY.

*Br.-Gen. on 5 August, 1914.

GENERAL NOTES

2nd Lancashire Heavy Battery, R.G.A. (Liverpool), (4, 4·7-inch guns),. went to France independently of the Division. The Heavy Battery disembarked at le Havre on 9/2/16, and on 15/2/16 it joined XVI. Hy. Bde., R.G.A.

The following Units also served with the 42nd Div. :—

South-Eastern Mtd. Bde., Br.-Gen. H. Clifton-Brown—1/R.E. Kent, 1/W. Kent (Q.O.), 1/Sussex, with Signal Troop, and S.-E. Mtd. Bde. Fd. Amb., joined 42nd Div. on 8/10/15 at Helles (to act as infantry). The Bde. served at Helles with the division until 30/12/15 when it embarked with the division for Mudros. On 2/1/16 the Bde. left the 42nd Division at Mudros.

3rd Dismounted Bde., Br.-Gen. H. W. Hodgson—1/Norfolk Yeo., 1/Suffolk Yeo., 1/Welsh Horse ; and 1/R.E. Kent, 1/W. Kent (Q.O.), 1/Sussex, with M.G. Coy., 3rd Dismtd. Bde. Signal Troop, 1/Eastern Mtd. Bde. Fd. Amb., and 1/S.-E. Mtd. Bde. Fd. Amb., was formed on 22/2/16 by the amalgamation of the Eastern Mtd. Bde. (Br.-Gen. H. W. Hodgson) with the South-Eastern Mtd. Bde. (Br.-Gen. H. Clifton-Brown). The 3rd Dismtd. Bde. was attached to the 42nd Div. from 14/3/16–26/7/16.

42nd Division Artillery. At Helles from 9/8/15 until the Evacuation, the 42nd Div. Arty. had no separate existence, as the Artillery of the VIII. Corps at Helles was formed into Groups for that period.

42nd Divnl. Mobile Ammn. Coln. The Mobile Ammn. Coln. was formed on 1/9/16 and served with the division until 12/2/17, when the Column was disbanded and the personnel and animals rejoined their respective Ammn. Colns.

Bde. Light T.M. Battery. The T.M.B. joined the division by 31/5/16, and it was attached to 126th Infantry Bde. until the end of February, 1917, when the 42nd Div. left Egypt for France.

13th Divisional Cyclist Coy. This Coy. was attached to the division from 2/3–7/6/16, when the Coy. left to embark for Mesopotamia.

22nd Sanitary Section. The Sec. joined the division in Egypt on 9/2/16, and served with it until 8/4/17, when the Section was transferred to the XIX. Corps.

N.B.—**125th (Lancashire Fusilier) Bde.** was attached to the 29th Division from 5–8/5/15.

On 19/2/18 the reorganization of the division on a 9-battalion basis was completed ; and on 1/3/18 the pioneer battalion (7/N.F.) was reorganized on a 3-company basis.

42ND[1] (EAST LANCASHIRE) DIVISION

ORDER OF BATTLE, 1914-1918

Dates	INFANTRY		Mounted Troops	ARTILLERY							Engineers	Signal Service	Pioneers	M.G. Units	Field Ambu-lances	Mobile Vety. Secn.	Divnl. Emplmt. Coy.	Divnl. Train
				Field Artillery			Heavy Arty.	Trench Mortar B'ties.		Divnl. Ammn. Coln.								
	Brigades	Battalions and attached Units		Brigades	Batteries	Bde. Ammn. Colns.		Medium	Heavy		Field Cos.	Divnl. Signal Coy.						
1914 Sept. (Egypt)	Lanc. Fus.[2] E. Lanc.[3] ... Manch.[4] ...	5/L.F., 6/L.F., 7/L.F., 8/L.F. 4/E. Lanc., 5/E. Lanc., 9/Manch., 10/Manch. 5/Manch., 6/Manch., 7/Manch., 8/Manch.	A. Sqdn.,[5] D. of Lanc. Yeo.	I E. Lanc.[6] III E. Lanc.[7]	4/Lanc., 5/Lanc., 6/Lanc. 18/Lanc., 19/Lanc., 20/Lanc.	I E. Lanc. B.A.C. III. E. Lanc. B.A.C.	...	...	...	...	1st E. Lanc.[8] 2nd E. Lanc.[8]	E. Lanc.[9]	...	...	1st E. Lanc.[10] 2nd E. Lanc.[10] 3rd E. Lanc.[10]	...	...	E. Lanc.[11] Divnl. T. & S. Coln.
1915 Sept. (Galli-poli)	125th[12] (Lanc. Fus.) 126th[12] (E. Lanc.) 127th[12] (Manch.)	5/L.F., 6/L.F., 7/L.F., 8/L.F. 4/E. Lanc., 5/E. Lanc., 9/Manch., 10/Manch. 5/Manch., 6/Manch., 7/Manch., 8/Manch.	A. Sqdn., D. of Lanc. Yeo.	I. E. Lanc.[13] II E. Lanc.[14] III E. Lanc.[15] IV E. Lanc. (H.)[16]	4/Lanc., 5/Lanc., 6/Lanc. 15/Lanc., 16/Lanc., 17/Lanc. 18/Lanc., 19/Lanc., 20/Lanc. 1/Cumbd. (H.), 2/Cumbd. (H.)	I E. Lanc. B.A.C. II E. Lanc. B.A.C. III E. Lanc. B.A.C. IV E. Lanc. (H.) B.A.C.	...	...	...	42nd (W. Lanc.) D.A.C.[17]	1st E. Lanc. 2nd E. Lanc. 2nd W. Lanc.[18]	42nd (E. Lanc.)	...	...	1st E. Lanc. 2nd E. Lanc. 3rd E. Lanc.	...	...	42nd[19] (E. Lanc.)
1916 June (Egypt)	125th...... 126th...... 127th......	5/L.F., 6/L.F., 7/L.F., 8/L.F.; 125th Bde., M.G. Coy.[20] 4/E. Lanc., 5/E. Lanc., 9/Manch., 10/Manch.; 126th Bde. M.G. Coy.[20] 5/Manch., 6/Manch., 7/Manch., 8/Manch.; 127th Bde. M.G. Coy.[20]	A. Sqdn.,[21] D. of Lanc. Yeo.	CCX[22] (I E. Lanc.) CCXI[23] (II E. Lanc.) CCXII[24] (III E. Lanc.) CCXIII (H.)[25] (IV E. Lanc.)	A, B, C A, B, C A, B, C A (H.), B (H.)	CCX B.A.C. CCXI B.A.C. CCXII B.A.C. CCXIII (H.) B.A.C.	...	...	...	42nd D.A.C.[26]	1st E. Lanc. 2nd E. Lanc. 3rd E. Lanc.[27]	42nd	...	...	1st E. Lanc. 2nd E. Lanc. 3rd E. Lanc.	19th[28]	...	42nd[29]
1917 June (France)	125th...... 126th...... 127th......	5/L.F., 6/L.F.,[30] 7/L.F., 8/L.F.; 125th M.G. Coy.;[44] 125th T.M. Bty.[31] 4/E. Lanc.,[32] 5/E. Lanc., 9/Manch.,[33] 10/Manch.; 126th M.G. Coy.;[44] 126th T.M. Bty.[31] 5/Manch., 6/Manch., 7/Manch., 8/Manch.;[34] 127th M.G. Coy.;[44] 127th T.M. Bty.[31]	...	CCX.......... CCXI[35]	A, B, C; D (H.). A, B, C; D (H.).	...[58]	...	X.42[36] Y.42[36] Z.42[36]	V.42[37]	42nd D.A.C.[38]	427th[39] (1st E. Lanc.). 428th[39] (2nd E. Lanc.). 429th[39] (3rd E. Lanc.).	42nd	...	...	1st E. Lanc. 2nd E. Lanc. 3rd E. Lanc.	19th	239th[40]	42nd[41]
1918 March (France)	125th...... 126th...... 127th......	5/L.F., 7/L.F., 8/L.F.; 125th T.M. Bty. 5/E. Lanc., 8/Manch.,[34] 10/Manch.; 126th T.M. Bty. 5/Manch., 6/Manch., 7/Manch.; 127th T.M. Bty.	...	CCX.......... CCXI	A, B, C; D (H.). A, B, C; D (H.).	...	...	X.42[42] Y.42[42]	...[42]	42nd D.A.C.	427th 428th 429th	42nd	7/N.F. (P.)[43]	No. 42 Bn.[44] M.G.C.	1st E. Lanc. 2nd E. Lanc. 3rd E. Lanc.	19th	239th	42nd

NOTES

1 E. Lancashire Div. was designated 42nd (E. Lanc.) on 26/5/15. (Authy., W.O. letter—40/W.O./2481 (A.G.1) of 7/5/15.)

2 Bde. H.Q. were at Preston. The Bns. came from Bury (1), Rochdale (1), and Salford (2). The L.F. Bde. was numbered 125th on 26/5/15.

3 Bde. H.Q. were at Manchester. The Bns. came from Blackburn, Burnley, Ashton-under-Lyne, and Oldham. The E. Lanc. Inf. Bde. was numbered 126th on 26/5/15.

4 Bde. H.Q. were at Manchester. The Bns. came from Wigan (1), Manchester (2), and Ardwick (1). The Manch. Inf. Bde. was numbered 127th on 26/5/15.

5 Stationed at Manchester. Embarked on 9/9/14 with the 42nd Div. for Egypt. The Sqdn. remained in Egypt in 1915.

6 Bde. H.Q., 1 Bty., and the B.A.C. were at Blackburn; the other 2 Btics. were at Church and Burnley. Bties. were armed with 4, 15-pdrs. each.

7 The whole Bde. came from Bolton. Bties. were armed with 4, 15-pdrs. each.

8 Both Fd. Cos. came from Old Trafford, Manchester.

9 The Sig. Coy. came from Old Trafford.

10 The 3 Field Ambces. came from Manchester.

11 Hd. Qrs. and the 4 Cos.: H.Q. Coy., L.F. Bde. Coy., E. Lanc. Bde. Coy., and Manch. Bde. Coy. all came from Manchester.

12 Inf. Bdes. were designated 125th, 126th, and 127th on 26/5/15.

13 5th Bty. and 6th Bty. (less 1 Sec.) arrived Helles on 9/5/15. 4th Bty. and 1 Sec. 6th Bty. arrived at Helles on 23/9/15. The B.A.C. remained in Egpyt.

14 Quartered in 1914 at Manchester. The Bties. were armed with 4, 15-pdrs. each. The Bde. reached Alexandria (from England) by 14/6/15, and joined 42nd Div. The Bde. remained in Egypt.

15 18th Bty. disembkd. at Helles on 25/7/15. The rest of the Bde. reached Helles on 24/9/15.

16 With the exception of an outlying Bty. at Carlisle, the Bde., in 1914, was quartered at Workington. Bties. were armed with 4, 5-inch Hows. each. The Bde. reached Alexandria by 14/6/15 and joined 42nd Div. The Bde. landed at Helles between 9 and 11/7/15.

17 Formed after the outbreak of war as 1/W. Lanc. D.A.C. Sent out to Egypt as 42nd D.A.C., and arrived Alexandria on 6/6/15. Between 30/10—2/11/15 42nd D.A.C. sent all its animals, vehicles, and equipt. to Salonika to refit 29th D.A.C. (torpedoed in *Marquette* on 23/10/15). 42nd D.A.C. joined 42nd Divnl. Arty. on 21/1/16 at Mena Camp, Cairo.

18 Quartered at St. Helens in 1914. Arrived at Alexandria on 10/7/15, and joined 42nd Div. at Helles on 28/8/15. The Coy. was transferred on 10/5/16 to the Comp. Bde. at Mudros.

19 The Cos. of the Divnl. Train were renumbered 447, 448, 449, and 450 on 17/1/16.

20 Cos. were formed in Egypt: 125th on 4/3/16; and 126th and 127th on 14/3/16.

21 Transferred to 53rd Div. on 29/1/17.

22 Bde. was rearmed on 29/2/16 with 18-pdrs. On 6/5/16 the Bde. was numbered CCX, and the bties. were lettered A, B, C. On 26/12/16 the Bde. was reorganized; A was split up between B and C, and then B became A and C became B; B/CCXIII (H.) joined and became C (H.). On 11/2/17 the Bde. was again reorganized: C (H.) became D (H.), and A/CCXII joined and became C (see note 23). On 23/6/17 D (H.) was made up to 6 hows. by 1 sec. of personnel from C/CCCXXXII (First Army Arty. Bde., and formerly 66th Divnl. Arty.).

23 Bde. was rearmed on 29/2/16 with 18-pdrs. On 29/5/16 the Bde. was numbered CCXI, and bties. were lettered A, B, C. On 26/12/16 the Bde. was renumbered CCXII, and it was reorganized: B was split up between A and C, and then C became B. On 21/2/17 CCXII was broken up: A joined CCX. as C/CCX; and B went to CCXI as C/CCXI. (CCXII B.A.C. went to France—see note 38.)

24 Bde. was rearmed on 27/2/16 with 18-pdrs. On 31/5/16 the Bde. was numbered CCXII, and bties. were lettered A, B, C. On 25/12/16 the Bde. was renumbered CCXI, and it was reorganized: C was split up between A and B; and A/CCXIII (H.) joined and became C (H.). On 10/2/17 the Bde. was again reorganized: C (H.) became D (H.); and B/CCXII joined and became C (see note 23). On 19/6/17 D (H.) was made up to 6 hows., by 1 sec. from C/CCXCVIII (formerly in 59th Divnl. Arty.).

25 Bde. was rearmed in 1916 in Egypt with 4.5-inch Hows. On 31/5/16 the Bde. was numbered CCXIII (H.), and the bties. were lettered A (H.), B (H.). On 26/12/16 the Bde. was broken up: A (H.) became C (H.)/CCXI (see note 24), and B (H.) became C (H.)/CXX.

26 42nd (W. Lanc.) D.A.C. was left behind at el Arish on 31/1/17 (on the transfer of the div. to France) to perform the duties of Sub-Park.

27 Arrived from England and joined the div. on 24/7/16.

28 The Sec. left England on 5/3/15 for service with R.N. Div. On 18/2/16 the Sec. was transferred to 42nd Div.

29 The Train (447—450 Cos.) was left behind in Egypt, and on 20/3/17 it was attached to the 53rd Div. for the Gaza Operations. On 1/4/17 the Train joined 74th Div. (then forming), and on 13/4/17 its nomenclature was changed from 42nd to 74th Divnl. Train.

30 Transferred on 19/2/18 to 197th Bde., 66th Div. On 20/2/18 it was amalgamated with 2/6/L.F., and became 6/L.F.

31 125th and 126th T.M. Bties. joined on 26/3/17; and 127th (formed on 1/4/17) joined on 23/4/17.

32 Transferred on 14/2/18 to 198th Bde., 66th Div. On 19/2/18 it amalgamated with 2/4/E. Lanc. and became 4/E. Lanc.

33 Transferred on 19/2/18 to 198th Bde., 66th Div. On 20/2/18 it amalgamated with 2/9 Manch. and became 9/Manch.

34 Transferred from 127th Bde. on 19/2/18, to 126th Bde.

35 Formerly III E. Lanc. R.F.A. Bde. (see note 24).

36 The 3 Medium T.M. Bties. joined on 23/3/17.

37 Joined 23/3/17.

38 On arrival of the Div. in France a new D.A.C. was formed on 19/3/17. CCX B.A.C. was used to form No. 1 Sec., CCXI B.A.C. formed No. 2 Sec., and CCXII B.A.C. (see note 23) formed No. 3 Sec.

39 The Fd. Cos. were numbered on 3/2/17.

40 The Employment Coy. arrived on 1/6/17. It was numbered 239th by 30/6/17.

41 Nos. 428, 429, 430, and 431 Cos., A.S.C., landed in France by 2/3/17. The Cos. joined 42nd Div. at Pont Remy on 4/3/17 to form the Divnl. Train.

42 The Divnl. T.M. Bties. were reorganized on 3/2/18. Z. was absorbed by X. and Y.; and V (Heavy) left to become I Corps H.T.M.B.

43 Joined on 12/2/18 from 149th Bde., 50th Div.

44 Bn. was formed on 23/2/18. It consisted of 125th, 126th, 127th, and 268th M.G. Cos. 268th Coy. (formed in England in Oct., 1917) joined the 42nd Div. on 20/1/18.

42ND (EAST LANCASHIRE) DIVISION

MOBILIZATION, BATTLES, AND ENGAGEMENTS

The division—an existing T.F. division—was drawn from Manchester and Salford and the Cotton and Colliery Towns of East Lancashire, with the divisional headquarters in Manchester. The twelve infantry battalions came from Bury, Rochdale, Salford (2), Blackburn, Burnley, Ashton-under-Lyne, Oldham, Wigan, and Manchester (3). The artillery was very scattered: headquarters was at Nantwich (Cheshire); the I. E. Lanc. Bde. had its headquarters, one battery, and its ammunition column at Blackburn, with two outlying batteries at Church and Burnley; and the III. E. Lanc. Bde. was concentrated at Bolton. (The other two artillery brigades of the division did not go overseas until June, 1915—see Order of Battle Table. In 1914 the II. E. Lanc. Bde. was concentrated in Manchester, and the IV. E. Lanc. (How.) Bde. was at Carlisle, with an outlying battery at Workington.) There was no divisional ammunition column at the outbreak of the Great War. Except the heavy battery (which came from Liverpool) the remainder of the division—field companies, signal company, field ambulances, and the Divnl. T. and S. Column—came from Manchester.

The order to mobilize was received at 5-30 p.m. on the 4th August, and units were billeted within reach of their respective headquarters. On the 10th August the Territorial Force was invited to volunteer for foreign service; and, on the 20th, the division, having accepted the liability, moved out into camps for training. On the 5th September, the division was warned that it would be sent to Egypt. On the 9th it began to entrain for Southampton, and the first transport sailed on the 10th. The East Lancashire Division possesses the proud distinction of being the first division of the Territorial Force to leave England for foreign service.

The division began its disembarkation at Alexandria on the 25th September. The Manchester Inf. Bde. (less 1½ battalions) remained at Alexandria. This brigade sent a half-battalion to garrison Cyprus and one battalion to Khartoum. The rest of the division concentrated around Cairo for training. Towards the end of October some detachments were sent to strengthen the Canal Zone, and on the 5th November Great Britain declared war against Turkey. During the Great War the 42nd Division was engaged in the following operations in Egypt, Gallipoli, France, and Belgium :—

1914

1915

3 and 4 Feb. ... ...**Defence of the Suez Canal** (A Sqdn., D. of L. Yeo., III. E. Lanc. R.F.A. Bde., 1st E. Lanc. Fd. Coy., and E. Lanc. Sig. Coy.).

On the 1st May the division began to embark at Alexandria for Gallipoli. The first transports left on the 2nd and the last followed on the 6th. By the evening of the 9th, Divnl. H.Q. and all the infantry had landed at Helles. The strength embarking for Gallipoli was 14,224 all ranks, with 24 15-pdr. B.L.C. guns, and 24 machine guns.

THE BATTLES OF HELLES

6–8 May ... ...**Second Battle of Krithia** (125th Bde.) [with 29th Div.].

4 June ... ...**Third Battle of Krithia** [VIII. Corps].

6–13 Aug. ... ...**Krithia Vineyard** [VIII. Corps].

On 26th December the division was ordered to prepare to leave Helles. Between 27-31 December the division (with the S.E. Mtd. Bde.) reached Mudros (less the Divisional Artillery, detnt. of R.E., and 1st and 3rd Fd. Ambces., which were all attached to the 13th Division, and with it took part in the Evacuation of Helles, 7th/8th January, 1916).

1916

The division embarked for Egypt between 12–16 January and concentrated at Mena on 22nd January, its effective strength on this day was 6,669 all ranks. On 29th January the division began to take over part of the IX. Corps front, Canal Defences.

4 and 5 Aug. ... ...**Battle of Romani** [No. 3 Section, Canal Defences].

1917

On the 28th January, after reaching El Arish, orders were received that the division would leave Egypt. By the 12th February the division had been withdrawn to Moascar (near Ismailia), and on the 22nd it began embarking at Alexandria for Marseille. On the 15th March the last train reached Pont Remy, thus completing the move of the division from Egypt. For the remainder of the Great War the 42nd Division served on the Western Front in France and Belgium, and was engaged in the following operations :—

24 Sept.-18 Nov.... ...**Operations on the Flanders Coast** [XV. Corps, Fourth Army].

1918

FIRST BATTLES OF THE SOMME

24 and 25 March... ...**Battle of Bapaume** [VI. Corps, Third Army].

28 March ... ...**First Battle of Arras** [IV. Corps, Third Army].

5 April ... ...**Battle of Ancre** [IV. Corps, Third Army].

THE ADVANCE TO VICTORY

SECOND BATTLES OF THE SOMME

21–23 Aug. ... ...**Battle of Albert** [IV. Corps, Third Army].

31 Aug.–3 Sept. ... ...**Second Battle of Bapaume** [IV. Corps, Third Army].

BATTLES OF THE HINDENBURG LINE

27–29 Sept. ... ...**Battle of the Canal du Nord** [IV. Corps, Third Army].

9–12 Oct. ... ...**The Pursuit to the Selle** [IV. Corps, Third Army].

THE FINAL ADVANCE IN PICARDY

17–23 Oct. ... ...**Battle of the Selle** [IV. Corps, Third Army].

The division was withdrawn into IV. Corps Reserve and halted around Beauvois from 24th October–3rd November, when the advance was resumed. On the 10th November the division captured Hautmont and Fort Hautmont. This was the end of its fighting in the Great War. On the 11th November the 42nd Division was halted astride the Sambre at Hautmont, with its most advanced troops on the Maubeuge–Avesnes road. The division did not proceed to the Rhine as part of the Army of Occupation, and during November it remained at Hautmont. On the 1st December the division was visited by H.M. the King. Between 14th–19th December the division moved into the Charleroi area; and by m/n. 15th/16th March, 1919, it had been reduced to cadre strength. In April, 1920, the division began to re-form at home.

43RD (WESSEX) DIVISION

G.O.C.

10 February, 1911 ... ... —Disembarkation in India } Major-General C. G. DONALD (Became Inspector of Territorials (India) from November, 1914, until April, 1915).

G.S.O. 1.

8 May, 1914...Major F. A. BUZZARD (G.S.O. 2).

5 Aug., 1914 —Embarkation } Lt.-Col. F. A. BUZZARD.

A.-A. and Q.-M.-G.

6 Aug., 1914 —Embarkation } Lt.-Col. A. F. MOCKLER-FERRYMAN.

D.-A.-A. and Q.-M.-G.

19 April, 1912 —April, 1915 } Major A. MUDGE.

B.-G., R.A.

1 Oct., 1913...*Br.-Gen. E. A. FANSHAWE.
16 Sept., 1914...Lt.-Col. G. R. FITZ R. TALBOT (acting).

21 Sept., 1914 —Embarkation } Br.-Gen. J. J. MACMAHON.

C.R.E.

1 April, 1908 —Embarkation } Lt.-Col. S. KEEN.

HAMPSHIRE BDE.

14 Feb., 1914 —Embarkation } *Br.-Gen. G. H. NICHOLSON.

SOUTH-WESTERN BDE.

16 Jan., 1914 —Embarkation } *Br.-Gen. G. S. McD. ELLIOT.

DEVON and CORNWALL BDE.

16 July, 1913 —5 Oct., 1914 } *Br.-Gen. R. J. PINNEY.

*Br.-Gen. on 5 August, 1914.

43RD (WESSEX) DIVISION

ORDER OF BATTLE, 1914-1918

Dates	INFANTRY		Mounted Troops	ARTILLERY							Engineers	Signal Service	Pioneers	M.G. Units	Field Ambulances	Mobile Vety. Sec.	Divnl. Emplnt. Coy.	Divnl. Train
	Brigades	Battalions		Field Artillery			Heavy Artillery	Trench Mortar B'ties.		Divnl. Ammn. Coln.	Field Cos.	Divnl. Signal Coy.						
				Brigades	Batteries	Bde. Ammn. Colns.		Medium	Heavy									
1914 August (England)	Hants. ..... South-Western Devon and Cornwall	4/Hants., 5/Hants., 6/Hants., 7/Hants. 4/Som. L.I., 5/Som. L.I., 4/Dorset., 4/Wilts. 4/Devon., 5/Devon., 6/Devon., 4/D.C.L.I.	...	I Wessex...... II Wessex (H.). III Wessex.... IV Wessex ...	1/Hants., 2/Hants., 3/Hants. 4/Hants. (H.), 5/Hants. (H.). 6/Hants., 1/Dorset., 1/Wilts. 1/Devon., 2/Devon., 3/Devon.	I Wessex* II Wessex* (H.). III Wessex* IV Wessex*	Wessex*1 (Hampshire) Hy. Bty., and Ammn. Coln.	...	...	...	1/Wessex*2 2/Wessex*2	Wessex*2	...	...	1st Wessex*3 2nd Wessex*3 3rd Wessex*3	...	...	Wessex*4 Divnl. T. and S. Coln.
1915 June (India)	[128th (1/1st Hants.)] [129th (1/1st S.-W.)] [130th (1/1st D. and C.)]	1/4/Hants.,[5] 1/5/Hants., 1/6/Hants., 1/7/Hants. 1/4/Som. L.I.,[6] 1/5/Som. L.I., 1/4/Dorset.,[7] 1/4/Wilts. 1/4/Devon.,[8] 1/5/Devon., 1/6 Devon.,[9] 1/4/D.C.L.I.[10]	...	I Wessex[11] ... II Wessex (H.)[11] III Wessex[11] IV Wessex[11]	1/1/Hants., 1/2/Hants., 1/3/Hants. 1/4/Hants. (H.)[12] 1/5/Hants. (H.)[13] 1/6/Hants., 1/1/Dorset., 1/1/Wilts. 1/1/Devon., 1/2/Devon., 1/3/Devon.	...	...	...	...	...	...	...	...	...	...	...	...	...
1916 July (India)	[128th] ..... [129th] ..... [130th]	1/5/Hants., 1/6/Hants., 1/7/Hants. 1/5/Som. L.I.,[14] 1/4/Wilts. 1/5/Devon.,[15] 1/4/D.C.L.I.[16]	...	CCXV[17] (I Wessex) CCXVI (H.). (II Wessex) CCXVII (III Wessex) CCXVIII (IV Wessex)	1/1/Hants., 1/2/Hants., 1/3/Hants. 1/4/Hants. (H.)[18] 1/6/Hants.,[19] 1/1/Dorset.,[19] 1/1/Wilts.[19] 1/1/Devon.,[20] 1/2/Devon.,[20] 1/3/Devon.[20]	...	...	...	...	...	...	...	...	...	...	...	...	...
1917 July (India)	[128th] ..... [129th]	1/5/Hants., 1/6/Hants.,[21] 1/7/Hants.[22] 1/4/Wilts.[23]	...	CCXVI .... CCXVII ...... CCXVIII	1089 (1/4/Hants.) 1097 (2/1/Hants.)[24] 1104 (2/1/Wilts.)[25] 79 (H.),[26] 1091 (1/6/Hants.), 1093 (1/1/Wilts.). 1094 (1/1/Devon.), 1096 (1/3/Devon.)	...	...	...	...	...	...	...		...	...	...	...	...

1918 Nov. (India)	[128th]	1/5/Hants.,[27] 1/7/Hants.[22] •	...	CCXVI .... CCXVII[29]..... CCXVIII	1089,[28] 1097 79 (H.), 1091, 1093 1094, 1096,[30] 1104.[25]; [31]	...	...	...	...	...	...	...	...	...	...	...	...	...

NOTES

• These units did not go to India. Inf. Bde. H.Q. remained in England.

1 On 17/1/15 the Bty. sent 8 offrs. and 170 o.r. to the 28th D.A.C. (many of them returned later on), and practically a new Bty. had to be formed. On 22/4/16 the Bty. sailed for France, and joined XLI H.A. Group on 25/4/16.

2 Joined 27th Div. at Winchester on 20/11/14.

3 Joined 8th Div. near Winchester in Oct., 1914, and numbered 24th, 25th, and 26th Fd. Ambces.

4 T. and S. Coln. formed 29th Divnl. Train, and 27th Divnl. Res. Park. Train joined 29th Div. in Feb., 1915, and served with 29th Div. until 17/3/16, when it was transferred in Egypt to 53rd (Welsh) Div.

5 Arrived at Basra on 17/3/15 with 33rd Bde., 12th Ind. Div. On 12/2/16, 1/4/Hants. (less 1 Coy.) joined 35th Bde., 14th Ind. Div. H.Q. and 1 Coy., 1/4 Hants. (attached to 30th Bde., 6th Ind. Div. in Kut) were beseiged in Kut, 7/12/15—29/4/16, and surrendered there.

6 Landed at Basra on 23/2/16 and joined 37th Ind. Bde.; on 5/5/16 Bn. was transferred to 41st Ind. Bde. (on L. of C.).

7 Landed at Basra on 23/2/16, and joined 42nd Ind. Bde. (This Bde. joined 15th Ind. Div. on 10/5/16.)

8 Arrived at Basra on 2/3/16 and joined 41st Ind. Bde. (on L. of C.). Bn. was transferred on 5/5/16 to 37th Ind. Bde.

9 Arrived at Basra on 6/1/16 with 36th Ind. Bde. (This Bde., on 12/5/16, joined 14th Ind. Div.)

10 Bn. served at Aden from 28/1/16—8/2/17.

11 In 1916 Bdes. were numbered and bties. were lettered A, B, and C in each Bde. Subsequently 1 Bty. in each Bde. was broken up and distributed amongst the other 2, thus making the surviving bties. up to 6 guns each. Bties. were given numbers, and the 15-pdr. batteries were rearmed with 18-pdr. Q.F. guns.

12 Bty. served at Aden from 13/9/15—14/8/16, with Aden Expeditionary Force.

13 Bty. landed at Basra on 23/3/15 and joined 6th Ind. Div. Engaged with Div. at Battle of Ctesiphon, 22-24/11/15, and in the Defence of Kut, 7/12/15—29/4/16, where it surrendered. (The guns were blown up on 28/4/16; and, owing to lack of forage, the bty. horses had all been killed by the end of March.)

14 Landed at Suez on 11/5/17, and on 25/5/17 joined 233rd Bde. (on formation). On 25/6/17, the Bde. joined 75th Div. (on formation).

15 Landed at Suez on 4/4/17 and joined 232nd Bde. on 14/4/17. On 25/6/17, Bde. joined 75th Div. (on formation).

16 Embkd. at Aden 8/2/17 and disembkd. Suez on 13/2/17 and employed on L. of C. On 14/4/17 the Bn. joined 232nd Bde. The Bn. was attached 233rd Bde. on 4/6/17, and joined 234th Bde. (75th Div.) on 25/6/17.

17 In July, 1916, the Bde. was rearmed with 18-pdrs. The Bde. (and a B.A.C.) reached Basra on 12 and 13/10/16, and joined 3rd Ind. Div. on 8/12/16. Bties. were numbered 1086, 1087, and 1088 on 7/8/17; and 1087 was broken up between 1086 and 1088. On 4/10/17 the Bde. was transferred to the 15th Ind. Div.

18 On return to India the Bty. was rearmed with 18-pdrs., and in 1917 it became 1089 Bty. It was completed to 6 guns by 1 Sec. from CCXXVIII (45th Div.).

19 Bties. numbered 1091, 1092, 1093 in 1917; and 1092 broken up between 1091 and 1093.

20 Bties. numbered 1094, 1095, and 1096 in 1917; and 1095 broken up between 1094 and 1096.

21 Landed at Basra 18/9/17, and joined 52nd Bde., 15th Ind. Div. on 24/9/17. (52nd Bde. was transferred on 1/10/17 to 17th Ind. Div.)

22 Bn. served at Aden from 8/1/18—May, 1919.

23 Landed at Suez on 25/9/17, and joined 233rd Bde., 75th Div., on 15/10/17.

24 Joined CCXVI Bde. by April, 1917, from CCXXV Bde. (45th Div.).

25 Joined CCXVI Bde. by April, 1917, from CCXXVII Bde. (45th Div.). 1104 Bty. was transferred to CCXVIII Bde. by July, 1918.

26 79 (H.) Bty., R.F.A. (formerly in VI (H.) Bde. R.F.A.), joined CCXVII Bde. by July, 1917.

27 Served throughout the War in India. On the outbreak of the Third Afghan War (6/5—8/8/19) the Bn. joined the 46th Mobile Ind. Bde. at Kohat in May, 1919. The Bn. was withdrawn in June, 1919, and embarked for England 15/10/19. It reached Southampton on 8/11/19, having been away 5 years.

28 In 1919 the Bty. took part in the Third Afghan War with the 47th Mobile Ind. Bde.

29 In 1919 the Bde. took part in the Third Afghan War with the 16th Ind. Div.

30 In 1919 the Bty. took part in the Third Afghan War with the 46th Mobile Ind. Bde., and later with the Kohat-Kurrum Field Force.

31 In 1919 the Bty. took part in the Third Afghan War in XXI Bde., R.F.A., with the 4th Ind. Div.

43RD (WESSEX) DIVISION

GENERAL NOTES

In May, 1915, the territorial designations of the Division and of the Infantry Brigades were discontinued, and numbers were substituted for them. The 1st Wessex Div. was then designated 43rd (Wessex) Div., and the Inf. Bdes. were merely numbered. (Authy., W.O. letter, 40/W.O./2481 (A.G.1.) of 7/5/15.)

In 1918 **1/4/Hants.** entered Persia on 2nd January (with Lt.-Col. C. L. Matthews's Column). On 26th August, C. Coy. occupied Krasnovodsk, and then pushed on to Merv ; and D. Coy. occupied Resht and Enzeli. A detachment of 40 rifles, under Lieut. L. E. R. Fisher, was at Baku from 4/8—15/9/18. At the Armistice 1/4/Hants. (less C. Coy. at Merv) was at Zinjan (on the Tabriz road). In June, 1919, two Cos. were attached to Lt.-Col. Matthews's Motor Mobile Column, and fought with it at Resht in August, 1919.

During the Great War the following Wessex battalion had extensive service in the East :—

1/9 (Cyclist Bn.)/Hants. sailed for India on 4/2/16 with 2/6/R. Sussex, 25/London, and 1/1/Kent, and the Bns. went to Bangalore. In October, 1918, 1/9/Hants. sailed from Bombay and landed at Vladivostock on 28/11/18. Bn. proceeded to Omsk (3,000 miles) and arrived on 7/1/19. In May, 1919, 1/9/Hants. moved to Ekaterinburg and remained there until August, 1919, when it withdrew via Omsk to Vladivostock. On 1/11/19 the Bn. sailed from Vladivostock for Vancouver, and it returned across Canada to England. On 5/12/19, after a world tour of 50,000 miles, the Bn. disembarked at Southampton, and 1/9/Hants. was then disbanded. (In November, 1915, the 1/9/Hants. relinquished its cycles and became an infantry battalion.)

43RD (WESSEX) DIVISION

MOBILIZATION AND NARRATIVE

The division—an existing T.F. division—was drawn chiefly from the south-western counties of England, with the divisional headquarters in Exeter. The twelve infantry battalions came from Winchester, Portsmouth, Southampton, Dorchester, Bournemouth, Trowbridge, Bath, Taunton, Exeter, Barnstaple, Plymouth, and Truro. The field batteries were at Portsmouth (2), Gosport, Ventnor, Freshwater, Bournemouth, Bridport, Swindon, Exeter, Paignton, and Tavistock ; and the heavy battery was at Cosham. The field companies were at Bath and Weston-super-Mare ; the field ambulances at Portsmouth, Exeter, and Plymouth ; and the T. and S. Column was at Exeter.

On the 26th July, 1914, the Wessex Division was on Salisbury Plain, carrying out its annual training in camp. On the 29th July the G.O.C. was informed that precautionary measures were to be taken. On the 30th July, divisional headquarters moved to Exeter, and precautionary posts were occupied in Somerset, Devon, and Cornwall. On the 3rd August the infantry brigades were ordered to the defended ports, and the brigades reached them on the 4th August ; and at 6.8 p.m. on the same day the order to mobilize was received. On the 10th August, the division began to concentrate on Salisbury Plain ; and, on the 13th, divisional headquarters moved from Exeter to Tidworth. All ranks were impressed by the transition from peace training, with its usual accompaniment of luxuries, to the more spartan simplicity of service conditions.

On the 22nd September, India consented to send to Europe 32 British regular battalions and 20 Indian battalions in exchange for 43 partially-trained T.F. battalions. By the 24th September, at the special request of Field-Marshal Earl Kitchener, Secretary of State for War, the Wessex Division accepted liability for service in India in order to relieve regular units of the permanent garrison of India. It was then decided to send at once from the Wessex Division, the 4 artillery brigades (brigade staffs and 11 batteries, but no brigade ammunition columns) and the 12 infantry battalions (the infantry brigade staffs were to be left behind).

All the selected units embarked at Southampton on the 9th October—a total of 447 officers, 11,250 other ranks, 3 horses, 36 guns, 8 howitzers, and 88 four-wheeled vehicles. The transports sailed on the 9th October, and the convoy was safeguarded by two British cruisers as far as Gibraltar, from Malta to Port Said it was accompanied by two French battleships and a gunboat, and from Suez to Bombay the transports were escorted by the French cruiser *Dupleix*. Three battalions (4/, 5/, and 6/Devon), destined for the Punjab, disembarked at Karachi on the 11th November. The remainder of the convoy went direct to Bombay, and the troops disembarked there on the 9th November. Batteries arrived in India each armed with 4, 15-pdr. B.L.C. guns, or with 4, 5-inch B.L. howitzers, and each battery went ashore with 5 officers and 140 other ranks. The battalions landed with 30 officers and 800 other ranks.

The British regular garrison in India, owing to response to urgent calls, had by this time been reduced to three cavalry regiments, three R.F.A. brigades, and eight infantry battalions. Undoubtedly the prompt arrival of the territorial units in India had a steadying effect on the native population, because it proved conclusively that Great Britain, far from being at the end of her tether, had still plenty of troops available.

Major-General C. G. Donald (with a staff officer—Major A. Mudge) went out in command of troops during the voyage to India. On arrival, General Donald reported to the Commander-in-Chief, and was then appointed Inspector of Territorials (India). General Donald proceeded to visit all the territorial batteries and battalions at their stations, scattered over the length and breadth of India and in Burma. By the end of April, 1915, when General Donald and Major Mudge returned to England, they had travelled over 20,000 miles on this tour of inspection.

Meanwhile, on arrival in India, all the territorial units reverted at once to peace-service conditions, and batteries and battalions were allotted to various stations. At first the 15-pdr. batteries were quartered at Lahore (2), Peshawar, Ambala, Bareilly, Delhi, Allahabad, Dinapore, and Barrackpore, with the two howitzer batteries at Lucknow; and the battalions were stationed at Bombay, Ferozepore, Multan, Lahore, Bareilly, Jullundur, Ambala, Delhi, Rawal Pindi, Allahabad, Agra, Mhow, and Meerut.

On arrival at their respective stations the infantry not only had to provide guards for everything which could be guarded, including German prisoners, but they had to furnish men as telegraphists, for the government dairies, for the Y.M.C.A., etc.; and both the artillery and the infantry had to push on as rapidly as possible with their training, so as to become ready for field service. In this training for war they were successful; and, as the call for men became more insistent and more urgent, drafts were provided for British units already serving in Mesopotamia. In addition, as early as March, 1915, two Wessex units (5/Hants. How. Battery and 4/Hants. Regiment) moved to the Mesopotamian theatre of war, and in September, 1915, the 4/Hants. How. Battery joined the Aden Expeditionary Force. It was during 1915 that the Wessex battalions were rearmed with the short rifle. In 1915 no drafts were sent out from England to the Wessex Division, but numbers of time-expired men were sent home and the units slowly dwindled. (By July, 1915, one battalion had been reduced to about 500 all ranks from this cause.)

Even early in 1916, the seriousness of the general situation on land in every theatre and the growing submarine menace made it clear that it had become impossible to recall the Wessex Division to France, as had been originally intended; consequently, in 1916, the training was pushed on in India. At the same time reinforcing drafts were provided for the various theatres of war, whilst many of the best N.C.O.'s were taken away to train as officers; and, as they arrived from home, drafts were assimilated. The artillery was rearmed with the 18-pdr. Q.F.; and during the year the I Wessex (18-pdr.) Bde. and four battalions left for service in Mesopotamia, one battalion went to Aden, and the howitzer battery at Aden returned to India. As units left India for service in a theatre of war they were replaced from England by second-line territorial units and by garrison battalions.*

During 1917 the drain on all units still remained continuous. As well as providing drafts to replace casualties in the field, officers and men were constantly being transferred all over India to fill numerous posts and perform various duties. In addition, one battalion was sent to Mesopotamia, three battalions went to Palestine, and the battalion at Aden went on to Palestine. It was during this year that the artillery brigades of the Wessex Division were reorganized and surviving batteries became 6-gun organizations (see Table for details).

By the beginning of 1918, of the original Wessex units which landed in India in November, 1914, only five batteries and two battalions still remained in the country. Of these units, one battalion was sent to Aden in January, 1918; and, of the remainder, four of the original batteries and one battalion were employed in the Third Afghan War (May–August, 1919).

In many cases the men sent home in 1919 from Mesopotamia, for demobilization, were detained in India and formed into provisional battalions on account of local civil disorders, and they were then retained for the Third Afghan War. Otherwise units were gradually reduced to cadre and sent back to England in 1919. During 1920 the division was re-formed in England.

*The first garrison battalions to reach India, early in 1916, were: 1st G.B. Norfolk Regt., 1st G.B. Lincoln Regt., 1st G.B. Yorkshire Regt., and 18th G.B. Rifle Bde.; but in no sense did these battalions ever belong to the Wessex Division. During the Great War between 50,000–60,000 Territorial troops were sent to India.

44th (HOME COUNTIES) DIVISION

G.O.C.

25 October, 1912 —Disembarkation in India } Major-General J. C. Young.

G.S.O. 1.

16 Jan., 1913...Major B. Atkinson (G.S.O. 2).

5 Aug., 1914 —Embarkation } Lt.-Col. B. Atkinson.

A.-A. and Q.-M.-G.

1 April, 1912...Capt. H. W. Grubb (D.-A.-A. and Q.-M.-G.).

5 Aug., 1914 —Embarkation } Lt.-Col. R. H. L. Warner.

B.-G., R.A.

1 Oct., 1913 —Embarkation } *Br.-Gen. C. T. Caulfeild.

C.R.E.

12 July, 1913 —Embarkation } Lt.-Col. W. F. Cheesewright.

SURREY BDE.

1 April, 1913 —Embarkation } *Br.-Gen. J. Marriott.

MIDDLESEX BDE.

26 Dec., 1912 —Embarkation } *Br.-Gen. W. R. Clifford.

KENT BDE.

1 July, 1911 Colonel V. T. Bunbury.

5 Aug., 1914 —Embarkation } *Br.-Gen. L. Combe.

*Br.-Gen. on 5 August, 1914.

44TH (HOME COUNTIES) DIVISION ORDER OF BATTLE, 1914-1918

Dates	INFANTRY: Brigades	INFANTRY: Battalions	Mtd. Trps.	ARTILLERY: Field Artillery: Brigades	ARTILLERY: Field Artillery: Batteries	ARTILLERY: Field Artillery: Bde. Ammn. Colns.	ARTILLERY: Heavy Artillery	ARTILLERY: Trench Mortar B'ties.: Medium	ARTILLERY: Trench Mortar B'ties.: Heavy	ARTILLERY: Divnl. Ammn. Coln.	Engineers: Field Cos.	Signal Service: Divnl. Signal Coy.	Pioneers	M.G. Units	Field Ambulances	Mobile Vety. Sec.	Divnl. Emplnt. Coy.	Divnl. Train
1914 August (England)	Surrey ……. Midd'x …… Kent……….	4/Queen's, 5/Queen's, 5/E. Surr., 6/E. Surr. 7/Midd'x.,*1 8/Midd'x.,*2 9/Midd'x., 10/Midd'x.; 4/Border,3 4/K.S.L.I.;3 1/Brecknockshire (S.W.B.).4 4/Buffs, 5/Buffs, 4/Q.O.R.W. Kent, 5/Q.O.R.W. Kent.	…	I Home Counties. II Home Counties III Home Counties (Cinque Ports) IV Home Counties (H.)*5	1/Sussex, 2/Sussex, 3/Sussex 4/Sussex, 5/Sussex, 6/Sussex 1/Kent, 2/Kent, 3/Kent 4/Kent (H.),*5 5/Kent (H.)*5	I Home Counties* II Home Counties* III Home Counties* (Cinque (Ports) IV. Home Counties5* (How.)	Home Counties*6 (Kent) Hy. Bty., and Ammn. Coln.*	…	…	…	1st Home Counties*7 2nd Home Counties*8	Home Counties*9	…	…	1st Home Counties*10 2nd Home Counties*10 3rd Home Counties*10	…	…	Home Counties*11 Divnl. T. and S. Coln.
1915 June (India)	[131st (1/1st Surrey)] [132nd (1/1st Midd'x.)] [133rd (1/1st Kent)]	1/4/Queen's, 1/5/Queen's,12 1/5/E. Surr., 1/6/E. Surr. 1/9/Midd'x., 1/10/Midd'x., 1/4/Border, 1/4/K.S.L.I.,13 1/Brecknockshire(S.W.B.),4 2/4/Border.14 1/4/Buffs,15 1/5/Buffs,16 1/4/Q.O.R.W. Kent, 1/5/Q.O.R.W. Kent.	…	I Home Counties17 II Home Counties III Home Counties18 (Cinque Ports)	1/1/Sussex, 1/2/Sussex, 1/3 Sussex 1/4/Sussex, 1/5/Sussex, 1/6/Sussex 1/1/Kent, 1/2/Kent, 1/3/Kent	…	…	…	…	…	…	…	…	…	…	…	…	…
1916 July (India)	[131st]……. [132nd]…… [133rd] ……	1/4/Queen's, 1/5/E. Surr., 1/6/E. Surr.19 1/9/Midd'x., 1/10/Midd'x., 1/4/Border, 1/4/K.S.L.I.20 1/4/Buffs, 1/4/Q.O.R.W. Kent, 1/5/Q.O.R.W. Kent. ——— 1/1/Brecknockshire (S.W.B.), 2/4/Border.	…	CCXX21 (I Home Counties) CCXXI22 (II Home Counties)	1/1/Sussex, 1/2/Sussex, 1/3/Sussex 1/4/Sussex, 1/5/Sussex, 1/6/Sussex	…	…	…	…	…	…	…	…	…	…	…	…	…
1917 July (India)	[131st]……. [132nd]…… [133rd] ……	1/4/Queen's, 1/5/E. Surr.,23 1/6/E. Surr.19 1/9/Midd'x.,24 1/10/Midd'x., 1/4/Border. 1/4/Buffs, 1/4/Q.O.R.W. Kent, 1/5/Q.O.R.W. Kent25 ——— 1/1/Brecknockshire (S.W.B.), 2/4/Border.	…	CCXX26 ….. CCXXI27 …	1064 (1/1/Sussex) 1066 (1/3/Sussex) 1067 (1/4/Sussex) 1068 (1/5/Sussex)	…	…	…	…	…	…	…	…	…	…	…	…	…
1918 November (India)	[131st]……. [132nd]…… [133rd] ……	1/4/Queen's,28 1/6/E. Surr. 1/10/Midd'x., 1/4/Border29 1/4/Buffs, 1/4/Q.O.R.W. Kent30 ——— 1/1/Brecknockshire (S.W.B.), 2/4/Border31	…	…	…	…	…	…	…	…	…	…	…	…	…	…	…	…

NOTES

* These units did not go to India. Inf. Bde. H.Q. remained in England.

1 Served at Gibraltar, 9/9/14—8/2/15. Joined 23rd Bde., 8th Div., in France on 15/3/15.

2 Served at Gibraltar, 17/9/14—8/2/15. Joined 85th Bde., 28th Div., in France on 11/3/15.

3 Joined Div. on embkn. to replace 7/ and 8/Middx.

4 Arrived at Bombay, with Div., on 3/12/14; transhipped there, and arrived at Aden, 16/12/14; the Bn. returned to India, 5/8/15.

5 Went to France on 21/12/14 as 27th D.A.C. Returned to England late in 1915, and again went to France on 10/3/16 as CCCXVIII (H.)—4.5-inch H. Joined R.N.D. on 18/7/16, and the B.A.C. was absorbed into the D.A.C. on 22/7/16. The Bde. was renumbered CCXXV on 19/7/16, and CCXXIII on 31/7/16.

6 Joined XVI H.A. Bde. in France on 31/12/15.

7 Joined 8th Div. in France on 2/2/15.

8 Joined 5th Div. in France on 2/2/15.

9 Joined 28th Div. at Winchester on 5/1/15.

10 Joined 27th Div. at Winchester in Nov. '14, and were numbered 81st, 82nd, and 83rd Fd. Ambces.

11 H.C.T. and S. Coln. in Nov., 1914, joined 27th Div. at Winchester as its Train. It went to France in Dec., 1914. The Cos. were numbered 95, 96, 97, and 98. On 1/1/16 the Train was transferred in France to 55th Div., and joined on 2-4/1/16.

12 Landed at Basra on 10/12/15, and joined 34th Bde., 15th Ind. Div. The Bn. was transferred on 11/1/16 to 12th Bde., 15th Div.

13 Bn. arrived Rangoon on 10/12/14, and detached 1½ Cos. to Andaman Is. from 10/12/14—4/4/15. On 10/2/15 the Bn. (less 1½ Cos.) reached Singapore, and on 10/4/15 the Andaman Detnt. rejoined. 1 Coy. was sent on to Hong Kong, and arrived there on 5/4/15, and 2 more Cos. followed on 18/4/15. Two detachments (each 1 offr. and 40 o.r.) sailed to Australia (Melbourne, Sydney, and Brisbane) as escort to German prisoners, and were away from 10/4-23/5/15. The Bn. also sent a column of 160 to operate in Kelantan between 2-17/5/15. In 1916 the Bn. was reorganized in 4 Cos.

14 Bn. was sent to replace 4/K.S.L.I.; left England on 4/3/15, arrived Bombay 31/3/15, and proceeded to Rangoon.

15 Bn. served at Aden from 4/8/15—28/1/16.

16 Landed at Basra on 6/12/15, and joined 35th Bde., 14th Ind. Div.

17 Bde. (armed with 15-pdr. B.L.C.) landed at Basra, 7-12/12/15, and joined III Corps in Jany., 1916. Bde. returned to India, July, 1916.

18 Bde. (subsequently numbered CCXXII) landed at Basra on 21/5/16, and joined 15th Ind. Div. between 21/5/16 and 2/1/17. (Bties. had 4, 18-pdr. Q.F. each.) Bties. were lettered A, B, and C, and later were numbered 1070, 1071, and 1072. On 11/9/17, 1071 was broken up: R. Sec. went to 1070 and L. Sec. to 1072.

19 Bn. served at Aden from 7/2/17—8/1/18.

20 Bn. remained at Singapore and Hong Kong in 1916. On relief by 25/Mdd'x., the Cos. rejoined from Hong Kong on 13/4/17, and the Bn. left Singapore on 14/4/17. The Bn. was in Ceylon from 19/4—3/5/17, reached Durban 23/5, and Cape Town on 30/5/17. The Bn. left Cape Town 29/6/17, and arrived Plymouth on 27/7/17; re-embarked at Southampton, and reached Havre 29/7/17. The Bn. joined the 190th Bde., 63rd (R.N.) Div. On 4/2/18 the Bn. was transferred to 56th Bde., 19th Div. The Bn. gained the *Croix de Guerre avec Palmes* (French) on 6/6/18 (Award d/d. 21/8/1918), and the presentation was made by General Berthelot at Shrewsbury on 3/6/1922.

21 In 1916 the Bde. was numbered and the Bties. lettered, A, B, and C. In 1917 Bties. were rearmed with 18-pdr. Q.F., and numbered 1064, 1065, and 1066; 1065 was then broken up between 1064 and 1066.

22 In 1916 the Bde. was numbered and the Bties. lettered A, B, and C. In 1917 Bties. were armed with 18-pdr. Q.F., and numbered 1067, 1068, and 1069. 1069 was then broken up between 1067 and 1068.

23 Landed at Basra on 27/12/17, and joined 55th Bde., 18th Ind. Div., on 10/2/18.

24 Landed near Basra on 24/11/17, with 53rd Bde.; and on 24/12/17, with Bde., joined 18th Ind. Div. (on formation).

25 Landed at Basra 11/12/17, and joined 54th Bde. on 26/12/17; and, with Bde., joined 18th Ind. Div. on 3/1/18.

26 Bde. (with a B.A.C.) returned to Mesopotamia and landed at Basra 18-23/10/17. Bde. joined 17th Ind. Div. on 11/11/17.

27 Bde. (with a B.A.C.) landed at Basra 18-25/10/17, and joined 17th Ind. Div. on 16/11/17.

28 In 1919 took part in Third Afghan War, in Peshawar Area.

29 In 1919 took part in Third Afghan War with 47th Mobile Ind. Bde.

30 In 1919 took part in Third Afghan War with 57th Bde., 4th Ind. Div.

31 In 1919 took part in Third Afghan War, in Peshawar Area.

44TH (HOME COUNTIES) DIVISION

GENERAL NOTES

In May, 1915, the territorial designations of the Division and of the Infantry Brigades were discontinued and numbers were substituted for them. The 1st Home Counties Div. was then designated 44th (Home Counties) Div., and the Inf. Bdes. were merely numbered. (Authy., W.O. letter, 40/W.O./2481 (A.G.I.) of 7/5/15.)

During the Great War the following Home Counties unit had extensive service in the East:—

25th, Garrison Bn., Middlesex Regt.—Raised in October, 1915, as the 25th (Reserve) Bn. (Pioneers) Midd'x. Regt. In July, 1916, the Bn. changed its designation and became a Foreign Service Garrison Bn. On 22/12/16 the Bn. embarked at Devonport on the *Tyndareus* for Singapore and Hong Kong, so as to relieve 1/4/K.S.L.I. for service on the Western Front in France (see Note 20). On 6/2/17, immediately after leaving Cape Town, the *Tyndareus* was damaged by an explosion. The Bn. was then brought back to Cape Town in the *Oxfordshire* and the *Umaeus*. The Bn. was quartered at Wynberg until 25/2/17, when it re-embarked on the *Ingoma*, and sailed at once for Singapore and Hong Kong. Two Coys. were left at Singapore, and H.Q. and two Coys. arrived on 1/4/17 at Hong Kong. On 11/7/18 one officer and six o.r., 25/Midd'x., left for Australia, escorting prisoners of war. On 27/7/18, 25/Midd'x. (both Hong Kong and Singapore Wings) sailed under sealed orders. (1st Garr. Bn. Manchester Regt. relieved 25th Midd'x. at Singapore and Hong Kong.) 25/Midd'x. disembarked at Vladivostock on 3/8/18. 25/Midd'x. (less a detnt.) left Vladivostock on 6/8/18 and detrained at Slagena. On 20/8/18 a withdrawal was made to Svagena, and the Bn. came temporarily under the Japanese. On 23 and 24/8/18, 25/Midd'x. took part in the Battle of Dukhovskaya. After this victory, 25/Midd'x. (less a detnt. of 250) on 29 and 30/9/18 entrained at Spascoe for Western Siberia. The Bn. proceeded via Harbin, Chita, Lake Baikal, and Irkutsk, and reached Omsk on 26/10/18. On 9/11/18, Bn. H.Q. and a detnt. (the band and 100 men) proceeded to Ekaterinburg, and next day crossed the Ural to General Galitzin's H.Q. This detnt. also visited the Lisvin Front and Cheliyabinsk, and returned on 17/11/18 to Omsk. (On 7/1/19, 1/9/Hants. reached Omsk—see 43rd Div. Notes.) On 21/5/19, 25/Midd'x. left Omsk for Vladivostock, and arrived in June. On 7/9/19, 25/Midd'x. sailed for England (via Vancouver), disembarked at Glasgow in November, and then returned, via Catterick Camp, to London, where the unit was disbanded.

44TH (HOME COUNTIES) DIVISION

MOBILIZATION AND NARRATIVE

The division—an existing T.F. division—was drawn chiefly from the south-eastern counties of England, with the divisional headquarters at Hounslow. The twelve infantry battalions came from Willesden Green, Ravenscourt Park (London, W.), Hornsey, Hounslow, Croydon, Wimbledon, Kingston, Guildford, Bromley, Tonbridge, Ashford, and Canterbury. The field batteries were at Erith (two howitzer), Brighton (2), Eastbourne, Bexhill, St. Leonard's, Folkestone, Dover, and Ramsgate ; and the heavy battery was at Faversham. The field companies were at Eastbourne and St. Leonard's; the field ambulances were at Surbiton, Maidstone, and Ashford ; and the T. and S. Column was at Hounslow.

Early in September, 1914, the division was ordered to send two battalions to Gibraltar, to relieve regular battalions of that garrison. 7/ and 8/Midd'x. were selected, and the two battalions sailed for Gibraltar on the 4th and 10th September.

In accordance with the plan for relieving most of the regular garrison of India by partially-trained territorial units (see Narrative, 43rd Division) the Home Counties Division accepted the liability for service in India. On the 17th October India was informed that 3 artillery brigades (9, 15-pdr. B.L.C. batteries, but no ammunition columns) and 13 battalions of the Home Counties Division were being sent out immediately. Infantry brigade staffs and all the regular adjutants were to be left behind.

To replace 7/ and 8/Midd'x. in the Middlesex Inf. Bde., two battalions—4/Border (from Carlisle) and 4/K.S.L.I. (from Shrewsbury)—joined the division on embarkation. The Brecknockshire Bn., S.W.B. (from Brecon), also joined the division on embarkation, in order to provide an extra battalion for garrison duty at Aden.

All the units embarked at Southampton ; and the division sailed on the 30th October. Disembarkation took place at Bombay between 1st–3rd December. The Brecknockshire Bn. transhipped at Bombay and left for Aden on the 9th December, landing there on the 16th.

Major-General J. C. Young (accompanied by a staff officer) went out in command of the troops during the voyage, and returned at once to England after handing over the units in India.

On arrival in India all the territorial units at once reverted to peace-service conditions, and batteries and battalions were allotted to various stations in India and Burma. At first the 15-pdr. batteries were quartered at Kamptee, Mhow (2), Jullundur, Multan, Ferozepore, and Jubbulpore (3) ; and the 10 battalions in India were stationed at Lucknow (2), Cawnpore, Fyzabad, Mhow, Kamptee, Jubbulpore, Jhansi, Dinapore, and Fort William, and the two battalions in Burma were at Rangoon and Maymyo. On arrival at their respective stations, the units at once proceeded to push on with their training so as to become ready for field service.

1/4/K.S.L.I., immediately after reaching Rangoon on 10th December, 1914, sent a detachment to the Andaman Islands. Then, on 21st January, 1915, the battalion was called on to disarm a native infantry battalion of the Rangoon garrison which was on the verge of mutiny. This duty was carried out within a few hours and without a shot being fired. Shortly afterwards, on the 6th February, a mutiny at Singapore caused the sudden despatch there of the bulk of the 1/4/K.S.L.I. from Rangoon ; and in April the battalion was divided between Singapore and Hong Kong. Its place at Rangoon had been taken by 2/4/Border, which arrived there in April from England. (See Table.) In August the Brecknockshire Bn. returned to India from Aden, and it was replaced at Aden by the 1/4/Buffs.

During 1915 units were called on to find numerous drafts to replace the casualties incurred by British units serving in Mesopotamia. Many of the best N.C.O.'s were taken away to train as officers; officers and men were constantly being transferred all over India to fill numerous posts and to perform various duties, and reinforcing drafts from England had to be assimilated as they arrived. During the year the battalions were rearmed with the short rifle. In December the following Home Counties units : I. Home Counties Fd. Arty. Bde. (armed with 15-pdr. B.L.C. guns) and 1/5/Queen's and 1/5/Buffs proceeded to the Mesopotamian theatre of war.

By early in 1916 it was apparent that it had become impossible to recall the Home Counties Division to France, as had been intended originally, and the units of the division continued their training for war in India.

In January, 1916, 1/4/Buffs returned to India from Aden. In May, III. Home Counties Fd. Arty. Bde. went to Mesopotamia ; and, in July, I. Home Counties Fd. Arty. Bde. returned to India from Mesopotamia. During this year (1916) the Home Counties artillery was rearmed with the 18-pdr. Q.F.

The drain of draft and duty finding remained steady and continuous throughout the year, and also persisted during the remainder of the division's service in India.

In 1917 the artillery brigades were reorganized, and the surviving batteries became 6-gun organizations. (See Table for details.) In February the 1/6/E. Surrey went to Aden. In April 1/4/K.S.L.I. left Hong Kong and Singapore for the Western Front in France (see Table) ; and the Bn. was replaced at Hong Kong and Singapore by the 25th, Garrison Bn., Midd'x. Regt., which had come out from England (see General Notes). The demands of the Mesopotamian theatre also had to be met ; and in October the CCXX. (I. Home Counties) Fd. Arty. Bde. returned to that theatre, and the remaining artillery brigade, CCXXI. (II. Home Counties), moved there. In November, 1/9 Midd'x. went to Mesopotamia, to be followed in December by 1/5/Q.O.R.W. Kent and 1/5/E. Surrey.

At the beginning of 1918, of the original Home Counties units which landed in India in December, 1914, only seven battalions still remained in the country ; but, in January, 1/6/E. Surrey returned to India from Aden. Of these units, three of the original battalions as well as 2/4/Border Regt. were employed in the Third Afghan War (May–August, 1919).

During 1919 units were gradually reduced and sent back to England ; and in 1920 the division was re-formed in England.

45TH (2ND/WESSEX) DIVISION

G.O.C.

9 October, 1914 ... ... Br.-Gen. R. J. PINNEY.
11 October, 1914 –Embarkation ... ... Br.-Gen. G. S. McD. ELLIOT.

G.S.O. 1.

Formation–Embarkation } Captain H. I. NICHOL.

A.-A. and Q.-M.-G.

Formation–Embarkation } Lt.-Col. A. F. MOCKLER-FERRYMAN.

B.-G., R.A.

Formation–Embarkation } Br.-Gen. J. J. MACMAHON.

C.R.E.

———

2nd/1st/HAMPSHIRE BDE.

Formation–Disembarkation in India } Br.-Gen. G. H. NICHOLSON.

2nd/1st/SOUTH-WESTERN BDE.

Formation–Embarkation } Br.-Gen. G. S. McD. ELLIOT.

2nd/1st/DEVON and CORNWALL BDE.

Formation–Embarkation } Br.-Gen. LORD ST. LEVAN.

45th (2nd/Wessex) Division

Order of Battle, 1914-1918

Dates	Infantry		Mtd. Trps.	Artillery							Engineers	Signal Service	Pioneers	M.G. Units	Field Ambu-lances	Mobile Vety. Secn.	Divnl. Emplnt Coy.	Divnl. Train
	Brigades	Battalions		Field Artillery			Heavy Artillery	Trench Mortar Batteries		Divnl. Ammn. Coln.	Field Cos.	Divnl. Signal Coy.						
				Brigades	Batteries	Bde. Ammn. Colns.		Medium	Heavy									
1914 December (England)	2nd/1st/Hants.... 2nd/1st/South-Western 2nd/1st/Devon and Cornwall	2/4/Hants., 2/5/Hants., 2/6/Hants.,*[1] 2/7/Hants. 2/4/Som. L.I., 2/5/Som. L.I., 2/4/Dorset., 2/4/Wilts. 2/4/Devon., 2/5/Devon.,*[2] 2/6/Devon., 2/4/D.C.L.I.	...	2nd/I Wessex..... 2nd/II Wessex (H.)*[3] 2nd/III Wessex 2nd/IV Wessex	2/1/Hants., 2/2/Hants., 2/3/Hants. 2/4/Hants. (H.),* 2/5/Hants.(H.).* 2/6/Hants., 2/1/Dorset., 2/1/Wilts. 2/1/Devon., 2/2/Devon., 2/3/Devon.	...	...	...	...	...	...	...	...	...	...	...	...	...
1915 June (India)	[134th (2nd/1st/Hants.)] [135th (2nd/1st/S.-W.)] [136th (2nd/1st/D. & C.)]	2/4/Hants., 2/5/Hants., 2/7/Hants. 2/4/Som. L.I., 2/5/Som. L.I., 2/4/Dorset., 2/4/Wilts. 2/4/Devon., 2/6/Devon., 2/4/D.C.L.I.	...	2nd/I Wessex..... 2nd/III Wessex 2nd/IV Wessex	2/1/Hants., 2/2/Hants., 2/3/Hants. 2/6/Hants., 2/1/Dorset., 2/1/Wilts. 2/1/Devon., 2/2/Devon., 2/3/Devon.	...	...	...	...	...	...	...	...	...	...	...	...	...
1916 July (India)	[134th] .... [135th] .... [136th]	2/4/Hants.,[4] 2/5/Hants.,[5] 2/7/Hants. 2/4/Som. L.I., 2/5/Som. L.I., 2/4/Dorset., 2/4/Wilts. 2/4/Devon., 2/6/Devon., 2/4/D.C.L.I.	...	CCXXV[6] (2nd/I Wessex) CCXXVII[6] (2nd/III Wessex) CCXXVIII[6] (2nd/IV Wessex)	2/1/Hants.,[7] 2/2/Hants.,[8] 2/3/Hants.[9] 2/6/Hants.,[10] 2/1/Dorset.,[11] 2/1/Wilts.[12] 2/1/Devon.,[13] 2/2/Devon.,[14] 2/3/Devon.[15]	...	...	...	...	...	...	...	...	...	...	...	...	...
1917 July (India)	[134th] .... [135th] .... [136th]	2/7/Hants.[16] 2/4/Som. L.I.,[17] 2/5/Som. L.I., 2/4/Dorset,[18] 2/4/Wilts. 2/4/Devon.,[19] 2/6/Devon.,[20] 2/4/D.C.L.I.	...	CCXXVII ...	1098 (2/2/Hants.), 1103 (2/1/Dorset.), 1105 (H.)[21] (2/1/Devon.).	...	...	...	...	...	...	...	...	...	...	...	...	...
1918 November (India)	[135th] .... [136th]	2/5/Som. L.I., 2/4/Wilts. 2/4/D.C.L.I.	...	CCXXVII ...	1098, 1103, 1105 (H.)[21]	...	...	...	...	...	...	...	...	...	...	...	...	...

NOTES

• These units did not go to India. Inf. Bde. H.Q. remained in England (in Dec., 1914).

---

1 The Bn. did not go to India. It moved to Petersfield and joined a Provisional Bn. on 13/2/15. This Bn. became Hants. Bde. Bn., 84th Prov. Bn., and finally 17/Hants.—a draft-finding Bn. It did not go overseas, and it was broken up in May, 1919.

2 Bn. went to Egypt in Septr., 1915. It was disbanded in June, 1916, and the personnel was distributed between 1/4, 1/5, and 1/6 Devon.

3 Bde. formed directly after departure of 1/II Wessex (How.) Bde. for India. The Bde. did not go to India, and in 1915 it was moved to the Isle of Wight. In Jany., 1916, the Bde. moved to Winchester, and later became part of "E" Reserve Bty. It was at Bordon from Oct., 1916—Oct., 1918, and then at Larkhill until Jany., 1919.

4 Landed at Suez on 15/5/17, and joined 233rd Bde. (on formation) on 25/5/17. The Bde. joined 75th Div. (on formation) on 25/6/17. The Bn. went to France, June, 1918, and joined 186th Bde., 62nd Div., on 5/6/1918.

5 Landed at Suez on 5 April, 1917, and joined 232nd Bde. (on formation) on 14/4/17. The Bde. joined 75th Div. (on formation) on 25/6/17. In July, 1918, the Bn. was disbanded.

6 In 1916 Bdes. were numbered and batteries were lettered A, B, and C in each Bde. Subsequently 1 Battery in each Bde. was broken up and distributed amongst the other 2, thus making the surviving batteries up to 6 guns each. Bties. were given numbers and they were rearmed with 18-pdr. Q.F. guns.

7 Transferred to CCXVI (43rd Div.) by April, 1917. (No. 1097.)

8 Transferred to IV Combined Wessex Bde. (later CCXXVII) by April, 1917. (No. 1098.)

9 Broken up in 1917. (No. 1099.)

10 Broken up in 1917. (No. 1102.)

11 Received number 1103 in 1917.

12 Transferred to CCXVI (43rd Div.) by April, 1917 (No. 1104), and transferred to CCXVIII (43rd Div.) by July, 1918.

13 Went to Aden 12/8/1916. Rearmed in Aden with 5-inch B.L. Hows. Received number 1105 in 1917. The Bty. remained at Aden until March, 1919.

14 Broken up in 1917. (No. 1106.)

15 Transferred to XXI Bde., R.F.A., by April, 1917— (No. 1107); and with XXI, in 1919, took part in Third Afghan War with 4th Ind. Div.

16 Reached Basra 11/9/17 and Kut on 15/9/17. Bn. was employed on L. of C. until Septr., 1918, when it was attached to 40th Bde., 13th Div., until 27/12/18.

17 Landed at Suez on 25/9/17, and joined 232nd Bde., 75th Div., on 16/10/17.

18 Arrived at Suez on 29/8/17, and joined 234th Bde., 75th Div., by 25/9/17. Bn. was attached to 233rd Bde. on 25/4/18, lent to 232nd Bde. on 1/5/18, and transferred to 233rd Bde. on 2/5/18. The Bn. was disbanded on 3/8/18.

19 Disembarked at Qantara on 26/10/17, and employed on L. of C. On 13/12/17 the Bn. joined 234th Bde., 75th Div. The Bn. was disbanded on 17/8/18.

20 Landed at Basra on 14/9/17, and employed on L. of C.

21 At Aden until March, 1919.

45TH (2ND/WESSEX) DIVISION

GENERAL NOTES

In May, 1915, the territorial designations of the Division and of the Infantry Brigades were discontinued and numbers were substituted for them. The 2/1st Wessex Div. was then designated 45th (Wessex) Div., and the Inf. Bdes. were merely numbered. (Authy., W.O. letter, 40/W.O./2481 (A.G.I.) of 7/5/15.)

2/1/Wessex (Hampshire) Heavy Battery, R.G.A., was formed in 1914. This battery never went overseas, and it was used to provide drafts for the 1/1/Wessex (Hampshire) Heavy Battery, R.G.A. (see 43rd Division Table).

45TH (2ND/WESSEX) DIVISION

FORMATION AND NARRATIVE

This Territorial Force division had no existence before the outbreak of the Great War.

In September, 1914, it was decided to raise 14 additional T.F. divisions which would be composed of 2nd-line T.F. units, and all liable for service overseas. In this way the 2nd Wessex Division came into existence early in October. Although a few of the units (e.g. 2/1/Wessex Bde., R.F.A., and 2/5/Hants. Regt.) were formed late in September, most of the units of this division were only raised immediately after the departure of the 1st Wessex Division for India. Any officers and men left behind by a 1st-line unit were used to serve as a nucleus for the 2nd-line unit which was being formed.

On the 13th November, so as to continue the relief of more of the regular units still in India, by partially-trained territorial units, it was decided to send the Welsh Division (T.F.) to India. On the 25th November, however, it was arranged to substitute 3 Field Artillery Brigades (9 batteries armed with the 15-pdr. B.L.) and 10 battalions of the 2nd Wessex Division, for the Welsh Division, and, on the 30th, notification of this change was sent to India. The embarking strength of the batteries was to be 5 officers, 140 other ranks, and 4 guns, and that of the battalions 30 officers and 800 other ranks. Machine guns, horses, 1st-line transport, and train transport, were not to be taken. So far the units now proceeding to India had been scattered in various towns. The artillery was at Fort Fareham, Bournemouth, Bridport, Swindon, Exeter, and Exmouth ; and the infantry was in Winchester, Southampton, Dorchester, Bournemouth, Trowbridge, Bath, Taunton, Exmouth, Barnstaple, and Newquay.

On the 12th December, 1914, the 3 artillery brigades (9 batteries) and 10 battalions—a total of 283 officers, 9,344 other ranks, and 36 guns—embarked at Southampton. The 2/4/D.C.L.I. and 2/4/Hants. went direct from Aden to Karachi and arrived on the 9th January ; and the remainder all disembarked at Bombay between the 4th and 8th January, 1915. Br.-Gen. G. H. Nicholson with one staff officer (Major G. E. Kenrick) went out in command of the troops during the voyage. Gen. Nicholson and Major Kenrick returned to England after handing over the troops on disembarkation in India. These two officers reached England on the 3rd February, 1915.

On arrival in India the units were transferred at once to peace-service conditions. The artillery brigades were quartered at Kirkee, Secunderabad, and Bangalore ; and the infantry battalions were stationed at Bombay, Poona, Secunderabad (2), Bangalore, Ahmednagar, Karachi, Quetta, Wellington, and Meiktilia.

Unfortunately in March, 1915, it was discovered that 18 obturator pads for the 15-pdr. B.L. guns were made of wood, thus 18 of the 36 guns could not be used for practice until these pads had been replaced from England. In the infantry, in some battalions, the rifles brought out from England were unfit for use. In consequence, no musketry could be carried out in these units until the obsolete rifles had been replaced by the long rifles, after the latter had been discarded by the sister first-line territorial battalions. This only occurred late in 1915 after the first-line battalions had been rearmed with the short rifle.

After the units had been trained, they were repeatedly called on to send drafts of varying strengths to those first-line territorial units which had already proceeded to Mesopotamia (e.g., between March, 1915, and April, 1917, 2/4/Hants. Regt. sent 17 officers and over 700 other ranks to the 1/4/Hants. Regt. in Mesopotamia). In addition to finding drafts, many of the best N.C.O.'s were taken away to be trained as officers ; officers and men were constantly being transferred all over India to fill numerous posts and to perform various duties, and reinforcing drafts from England had to be assimilated as they arrived.

45TH (2ND/WESSEX) DIVISION

Early in 1916 it was apparent that it had become impossible to recall the 2nd Wessex Division to France, as had been originally intended ; and the units of the division continued their training for war in India. During this year the artillery was gradually re-armed with the 18-pdr. Q.F., the artillery brigades were numbered, and the batteries in each brigade were for a time designated by letters (see Table). In August, 2/1/Devon Bty. (then A/CCXXVIII., and later 1105 H.) went to Aden. The Bty. was armed at Aden with howitzers, and it remained attached to the Aden Expeditionary Force until after the Armistice with Turkey (on the 31st October, 1918).

In 1917 the artillery brigades were entirely reorganized, the batteries were numbered, the surviving batteries became 6-gun organizations, and two batteries (2/1/Hants. and 2/1/Wilts.) were transferred to a brigade in the 43rd Division (see Tables). During the year five battalions went to Palestine between April and October, and two battalions left for the Mesopotamian theatre in September (see Table).

By the beginning of 1918, of the original Wessex second-line territorial units which had landed in India in January, 1915, only four batteries (two with the 43rd Division) and three battalions still remained in the country. Of these units, one battery (1104, 2/1/Wilts., attached to XXI. Bde., R.F.A., with 4th Indian Division), took part in the Third Afghan War (May–August, 1919).

During 1919 units were gradually reduced and sent back to England, and the division passed out of existence.

46TH (NORTH MIDLAND) DIVISION

G.O.C.

1 June, 1914 ... ... Major-General HON. E. J. MONTAGU-STUART-WORTLEY.
6 July, 1916 ... ... Br.-Gen. H. M. CAMPBELL (acting).
8 July, 1916 ... ... Major-General W. THWAITES.
2 September, 1918 ... ... Br.-Gen. F. G. M. ROWLEY (acting).
5 September, 1918 ... ... Major-General G. F. BOYD.

G.S.O. 1.

17 Mar., 1914...Major W. H. F. WEBER (G.S.O. 2).
5 Aug., 1914...Lt.-Col. W. H. F. WEBER.
8 Mar., 1915...Lt.-Col. F. LYON.
14 July, 1915...Capt. L. A. E. PRICE-DAVIES, V.C. (acting).
18 July, 1915...Lt.-Col. P. W. GAME.
19 Mar., 1916...Lt.-Col. T. H. C. NUNN (invalided, 3/4/16).
3 April, 1916...Major G. THORPE (acting).
9 April, 1916...Lt.-Col. A. F. HOME.
14 June, 1916...Lt.-Col. G. THORPE.
28 May, 1917...Major V. N. JOHNSON (acting).
13 June, 1917...Lt.-Col. G. THORPE.
13 Oct., 1917...Lt.-Col. F. H. DORLING.
23 July, 1918...Lt.-Col. C. F. JERRAM.

A.-A. and Q.-M.-G.

1 Oct., 1913...Captain F. H. DANSEY (D.-A.-A. and Q.-M.-G.).
5 Aug., 1914...Colonel J. W. FEARON.
27 Oct., 1914...Lt.-Col. E. ALLEN.
17 July, 1916...Lt.-Col. W. H. M. FREESTUN.
11 Sept., 1918...Major H. N. FORBES (acting).
12 Sept., 1918...Lt.-Col. R. DUCKWORTH.

B.-G., R.A.

1 Aug., 1914...*Br.-Gen. H. M. CAMPBELL (wounded, 13/3/18).
13 Mar., 1918...Lt.-Col. SIR S. H. CHILD, BT. (acting).
22 Mar., 1918...Br.-Gen. SIR S. H. CHILD, BT.

C.R.E.

25 May, 1912...Lt.-Col. W. E. HARRISON (invalided, 19/10/14).
19 Oct., 1914...Br.-Gen. C. V. WINGFIELD-STRATFORD.
2 May, 1918...Lt.-Col. E. J. WALTHEW (killed, 22/5/18).
22 May, 1918...Major W. D. ZELLER (acting).
1 June, 1918...Lt.-Col. H. T. MORSHEAD (wounded, 25/9/18).
25 Sept., 1918...Captain H. J. C. MARSHALL (acting).
25 Sept., 1918...Major W. H. HARDMAN (acting).
27 Sept., 1918...Lt.-Col. H. T. MORSHEAD (tempy.).
28 Sept., 1918...Lt.-Col. W. GARFORTH.
10 Nov., 1918...Lt.-Col. H. T. MORSHEAD.

*Br.-Gen. on 5 August, 1914.

137th BDE.

(Staffordshire Bde.)

10 Oct., '12...*Br.-Gen. W. BROMILOW (sick, 25/3/15).
2 April, '15...Br.-Gen. E. FEETHAM (sick, 18/5/16).
18 May, '16...Lt.-Col. R. R. RAYMER (acting).
5 June, '16...Br.-Gen. H. B. WILLIAMS.
9 Nov., '16...Lt.-Col. W. A. ODLING (acting).
17 Nov., '16...Br.-Gen. J. V. CAMPBELL, V.C.
10 Nov., '18...Br.-Gen. M. L. HORNBY.

138th BDE.

(Linc. and Leic. Bde.)

9 Aug., '13...*Br.-Gen. A. W. TAYLOR.
22 Feb., '15...Br.-Gen. W. R. CLIFFORD.
15 Aug., '15...Br.-Gen. G. C. KEMP (sick, 29/4/17).
29 April, '17...Lt.-Col. C. A. EVILL (acting).
28 May, '17...Lt.-Col. G. THORPE (acting).
13 June, '17...Lt.-Col. C. A. EVILL (acting).
16 June, '17...Br.-Gen. F. G. M. ROWLEY.

139th BDE.

(Sherwood Forester Bde.)

9 Sept., '11...*Br.-Gen. C. T. SHIPLEY.
27 May, '17...Br.-Gen. G. G. S. CAREY.
26 Mar., '18...Br.-Gen. P. R. WOOD.
24 July, '18...Br.-Gen. J. HARINGTON.

*Br.-Gen. on 5 August, 1914.

GENERAL NOTES

On 23/12/15, the 46th Div. was ordered to proceed overseas, leaving in France the D.A.C. (for the 55th Div.), the Train (for the 56th Div.), and the Mob. Vety. Sec. The rest of the Div. entrained for Marseille ; and D.H.Q. (part), 137th Bde. (complete), 138th Bde. (less two Bns.), the Cyclist Coy., the R.E. (less one Field Coy.), and the Pioneer Bn. all reached Egypt by 13/1/16. On 21/1/16 the move of the division to Egypt was countermanded, and on 5/2/16 the last unit left Alexandria to return to France. The 46th Division was reassembled at Pont Remy (near Amiens) by 14/2/16, and the D.A.C., Mob. Vety. Sec., and Divnl. Train rejoined.

The following Units also served with the 46th Division :—

INFANTRY :—4/King's, transferred from Sirhind Bde., Lahore Div., on 10/11/15, and attached to 137th Bde., until 3/12/15, when the Bn. was transferred to 56th Bde., 19th Div., and on 19/12/15 to 58th Bde., 19th Div.

4/Suff., transferred from Jullundur Bde., Lahore Div., on 10/11/15, and attached to 137th Bde. until 15/11/15, when the Bn. was transferred to 46th Bde., 15th Div.

4/B.W., transferred from Bareilly Bde., Meerut Div., on 6/11/15, and attached to 139th Bde. until 14/11/15, when the Bn. was transferred to 44th Bde., 15th Div.

4/Sea. H., transferred from Dehra Dun Bde., Meerut Div., on 6/11/15, and attached to 137th Bde. until 16/11/15, when the Bn. was transferred to 46th Bde., 15th Div.

3/London, transferred from Dehra Dun Bde., Meerut Div., on 6/11/15, and attached to 139th Bde. until 16/11/15, when the Bn. was transferred to 142nd Bde., 47th Div.

4/London, transferred from Ferozepore Bde., Lahore Div., on 11/11/15, and attached to 137th Bde. until 15/11/15, when the Bn. was transferred to the 140th Bde., 47th Div.

ARTILLERY :—N. Midland (Staffordshire) Heavy Battery, R.G.A. (Stoke-on-Trent), (4, 4.7-inch guns), after mobilization was quartered at Bishop's Stortford. The Hy. Bty. went to France with the Div., landed at le Havre on 1/3/15, went into action on 23/3/15, and on 18/4/15 joined XIII. Hy. Bde., R.G.A.

512 (H.) Bty., R.F.A.—See note 29.

ENGINEERS :—57th Fd. Coy., R.E., attached on 7/4/15 (from 3rd Div.), and transferred on 10/7/15 to 49th Div.

OTHER UNITS :—17th Sanitary Section, joined on 4/3/15 (from England) ; transferred on 21/3/17 to V. Corps.

46th (N. Midl'd.) Divnl. Ambce. Workshop, joined 1/3/15 (from England) ; on 6/4/16 it was transferred to Divnl. Supply Coln.

On 31/1/18 the reorganization of the division on a 9-battalion basis was completed ; and on 5/6/18 the pioneer battalion (1/Mon.) was reorganized on a 3-company basis.

46TH[1] (NORTH MIDLAND) DIVISION

ORDER OF BATTLE, 1915-1918

Dates	INFANTRY		Mounted Troops	ARTILLERY						Engineers	Signal Service	Pioneers	M.G. Units	Field Ambulances	Mobile Vety. Secn.	Divnl. Emplnt. Coy.	Divnl. Train
				Field Artillery			Trench Mortar Btties.										
	Brigades	Battalions and attached Units		Brigades	Batteries	Bde. Ammn. Colns.	Medium	Heavy	Divnl. Ammn. Coln.	Field Cos.	Divnl. Signal Coy.						
1915 March (France)	Staffordshire[2] Lincoln and Leicester[3] Sherwood Forester[4]	5/S. Staff., 6/S. Staff., 5/N. Staff., 6/N. Staff. 4/Linc., 5/Linc., 4/Leic., 5/Leic. 5/Sher. For., 6/Sher. For., 7/Sher. For., 8/Sher. For.	B Sqdn.,[5] 1/Yorkshire Hsrs. N.Midl'd.[6] Cyclist Coy.	I N. Midland[7] II N. Midland[8] III N. Midland[9] IV N. Midland[10] (H.)	1/Linc., 2/Linc., 3/Linc. 1/Staff., 2/Staff., 3/Staff. 4/Staff., 5/Staff., 6/Staff. 1/Derby (H.), 2/Derby (H.).	I N. Midland II N. Midland III N. Midland IV N. Midland (H.).	...	...	N. Midl'd. D.A.C.[11]	2nd N. Midland[12] 2/1st N. Midland[13]	N. Midl'd.[14]	...	...	1st N. Midl'd.[15] 2nd N. Midl'd.[15] 3rd N. Midl'd.[15]	1st N. Midl'd.[16]	...	N. Midl'd.[17]
1915 September (France)	137th[18] ..... (Staffordshire) 138th[18] ..... (Linc. & Leic.) 139th[18] ..... (Sherwood Forester)	5/S. Staff., 6/S. Staff., 5/N. Staff., 6/N. Staff. 4/Linc., 5/Linc., 4/Leic., 5/Leic. 5/Sher. For., 6/Sher. For., 7/Sher. For., 8/Sher. For.	B Sqdn., 1/Yorkshire Hsrs.[19] N. Midl'd.[20] Cyclist Coy.	I N. Midland[21] II N. Midland[22] III N. Midland[23] IV N. Midland (H.)[24]	1/Linc., 2/Linc., 3/Linc. 1/Staff., 2/Staff., 3/Staff. 4/Staff., 5/Staff., 6/Staff. 1/Derby (H.), 2/Derby (H.).	I N. Midland II N. Midland III. N. Midland IV N. Midland (H.).	...	...	46th D.A.C. (N. Midl'd.)	1st N. Midl'd.[25] 2nd N. Midl'd. 2/1st N. Midl'd.	46th (N. Midl'd.)	1/Mon.[26] (P.)	...	1st N. Midl'd. 2nd N. Midl'd. 3rd N. Midl'd.	1st N. Midl'd.	...	46th (N. Midl'd.)
1916 June (France)	137th .... 138th 139th	5/S. Staff., 6/S. Staff., 5/N. Staff., 6/N. Staff.; 137th Bde. M.G. Coy.;[27] 137th T.M. Bty.[28] 4/Linc., 5/Linc., 4/Leic., 5/Leic.; 138th Bde. M.G. Coy.;[27] 138th T.M. Bty.[28] 5/Sher. For., 6/Sher. For., 7/Sher. For., 8/Sher. For.; 139th Bde. M.G. Coy.;[27] 139th T.M. Bty.[28]	...	CCXXX .... (I N. Midl'd.) CCXXXI (II N. Midl'd.) CCXXXII[29] (III N. Midl'd.) CCXXXIII[30] (IV N. Midl'd.)	A,[31] B,[31] C;[32] D (H.)[34] A,[32] B,[33] C;[33] D (H.)[34] A, B, C;[35] D (H.)[36] A,[31] B,[33] C[32]	...[37]	X.46[38] Y.46[38] Z.46[38]	V.46[39]	46th D.A.C.[37]	1st N. Midl'd. 2nd N. Midl'd. 2/1st N. Midl'd.	46th	1/Mon. (P.)	...	1st N. Midl'd. 2nd N. Midl'd. 3rd N. Midl'd.	1st N. Midl'd.	...	46th
1917 June (France)	137th .... 138th 139th	5/S. Staff., 6/S. Staff., 5/N. Staff.,[40] 6/N. Staff.; 137th M.G. Coy.;[47] 137th T.M. Bty. 4/Linc.,[41] 5/Linc., 4/Leic., 5/Leic.; 138th M.G. Coy.;[47] 138th T.M. Bty. 5/Sher. For., 6/Sher. For., 7/Sher. For.,[42] 8/Sher. For.; 139th M.G. Coy.;[47] 139th T.M. Bty.	...	CCXXX .... CCXXXI ...	A, B, C; D (H.) A, B, C; D (H.)	...	X.46 Y.46 Z. 46	V.46	46th D.A.C.	465th[43] (1st N. Midl'd.) 466th[43] (2nd N. Midl'd.) 468th[43] (2/1st N. Midl'd.)	46th	1/Mon. (P.)	178th M.G. Coy.[44]	1st N. Midl'd. 2nd N. Midl'd. 3rd N. Midl'd.	1st N. Midl'd.	240th[45]	46th
1918 March (France)	137th .... 138th 139th	5/S. Staff., 6/S. Staff., 6/N. Staff.; 137th T.M. Bty. 5/Linc., 4/Leic., 5/Leic.; 138th T.M. Bty. 5/Sher. For., 6/Sher. For., 8/Sher. For.; 139th T.M. Bty.	...	CCXXX .... CCXXXI ...	A, B, C; D (H.) A, B, C; D (H.)	...	X.46[46] Y.46[46]	...[46]	46th D.A.C.	465th 466th 468th	46th	1/Mon. (P.)	No. 46 Bn.,[47] M.G.C.	1st N. Midl'd. 2nd N. Midl'd. 3rd N. Midl'd.	1st N. Midl'd.	240th	46th

NOTES

1 N. Midland Div. was designated 46th (N. Midland) Div. on 12/5/15. (Authy. W. O. letter—40/W.O./2481 (A.G.1) of 7/5/15.)

2 Bde. H.Q. was at Stafford. The Bns. came from Walsall, Wolverhampton, Hanley, and Burton-on-Trent.

3 Bde. H.Q. was at Grantham. The Bns. came from Lincoln, Grimsby, Leicester, and Loughborough.

4 Bde. H.Q. was at Nottingham. The Bns. came from Derby, Chesterfield, Nottingham, and Newark. On 19/2/15 the Bde. designation was changed from Notts. and Derby. Bde. (Div. Order, 1248.)

5 Stationed at York. The Sqdn. joined the Division at Luton, and disembkd. at le Havre on 28/2/15.

6 Formed on 11/11/14 at Luton. Disembkd. at le Havre on 28/2/15.

7 The 3 Bties. (4, 15-pdrs. each) came from Boston, Grimsby, and Louth.

8 The 3 Bties. (4, 15-pdrs. each) came from Stoke-on-Trent (2) and Leek.

9 The 3 Bties. (4, 15-pdrs. each) came from Wolverhampton, West Bromwich, and Stafford.

10 The How. Bde. came from Derby. (Bties. armed with 4, 5-inch Hows. each.)

11 Formed at Luton. It disembkd. at le Havre on 4/3/15.

12 The Fd. Coy. came from Cannock.

13 Formed after mobilization. It disembkd. at le Havre on 1/3/15. It was detached on disembkn. to G.H.Q. and rejoined the Div. on 10/7/15.

14 H.Q. and No. 1 Sec. were at Hanley. The Bde. Secs. were at Stafford, Grantham, and Nottingham.

15 The Fd. Ambces. came from Derby, Leicester, and Wolverhampton.

16 Joined in the mobn. area. It disembkd. at le Havre on 1/3/15.

17 Formed from North Midland Divnl. T. and S. Coln., which had companies at Birmingham, Handsworth, Leicester, and Nottingham. The Train disembkd. at le Havre between 28/2-5/3/15. The Cos. were numbered 451, 452, 453, and 454 Cos., A.S.C.

18 The Inf. Bdes. were designated 137th, 138th, and 139th on 12/5/15.

19 Entrained for Marseille 11/1/16, detrained at Marseille 13/1/16, entrained at Marseille 27/1, and detrained at Pont Remy, 29/1/16. The Sqdn. joined XVII Corps Cav. Regt. on 5/5/16.

20 Embkd. at Marseille 5/1/16, disembkd. at Alexandria 12/1/16; re-embkd. at Alexandria 4/2/16, disembkd. at Marseille 9/2/16, and rejoined 46th Div. on 12/2/16. The Cyclist Coy. joined XVII Corps Cyclist Bn. on 9/5/16.

21 Bties. were rearmed with 4, 18-pdrs. each on 19-22/11/15. On 19/4/16 D Bty. (4, 18-pdrs.) was formed. On 12 and 13/5/16 the Bde. was numbered CCXXX and the Bties. were lettered A, B, C, and D. On 23/5/16 D (18-pdrs.) was transferred to CCXXXIII and became A/CCXXXIII, in exchange for A/CCXXXIII (formerly 1st Derby Bty., 4, 4.5-inch. Hows.), which then became D (H.)/CCXXX.

22 Bties. were rearmed with 4, 18-pdrs. each on 19-22/11/15. On 25/4/16 D Bty. (4, 18-pdrs.) was formed. On 13/5/16 the Bde. was numbered CCXXXI and the Bties. were lettered A, B, C, and D. On 23/5/16 D (18-pdrs.) was transferred to CCXXXIII and became B/CCXXXIII, in exchange for R. Bty./CCXXXIII (formerly A/CLIV, 4, 4.5-inch Hows.), which then became D (H.)/CCXXXI.

23 Bties. were rearmed with 4, 18-pdrs. each on 19-22/11/15. On 4/5/16 D Bty. (4, 18-pdrs.) was formed. On 13/5/16 the Bde. was numbered CCXXXII and the Bties. were lettered A, B, C, and D. On 23/5/16 D (18-pdrs.) was transferred to CCXXXIII and became C/CCXXXIII, in exchange for B/CCXXXIII (formerly 2nd Derby Bty., 4, 4.5 Hows.), which then became D (H.)/CCXXXII.

24 1st and 2nd Derby (H.) Bties. were rearmed with 4, 4.5-inch Hows. each on 16/12/15. A (H.)/CLIV(H.) joined the Bde. on 28/2/16 from 36th Div., and became R(H.)/IV N. Mid. Bde. on 8/3/16. On 13/5/16 the Bde. was numbered CCXXXIII and the Bties. were lettered A, B, and R. On 23/5/16 the Bde. was reorganized: D/CCXXX was exchanged with A/CCXXXIII (note 21); D/CCXXXI with R/CCXXXIII (note 22); and D/CCXXXII with C/CCXXXIII (note 23). D/CCXXX became A/CCXXXIII, D/CCXXXI became B/CCXXXIII, and D/CCXXXII became C/CCXXXIII. The Bde. was now 3, 18-pdr. bties.

25 The Fd. Coy. came from Smethwick. It mobilized (1-17/1/15) with the 28th Div., went to France with 28th Div., disembkg. at le Havre on 19/1/15. The Fd. Coy. rejoined the N. Mid. Div., in France, on 6/4/15.

26 Joined (from 28th Div.) as divnl. pioneers on 3/9/15.

27 The M.G. Cos. were formed: 137th on 7/3/16; 138th on 22/2/16; and 139th on 16/2/16.

28 The T.M. Bties. joined as follows: 137/1 (formerly 423 T.M.B.) on 2/3/16 and 137/2 on 22/4/16, the T.M. Bties. were amalgamated by 6/6/16; 138/1 (formerly 422 T.M.B.) joined on 2/3/16, and 138/2 on 23/3/16—amalgamated on 14/6/16; 139/1 joined on 9/3/16 and 139/2 on 29/4/16—amalgamated by 7/6/16.

29 Bde. became an A.F.A. Bde. on 3/1/17. 512 (H.) joined the Bde. on 27/10/16 and became C (H.) on 3/11/16; C (H.) was broken up on 2/1/17 and 1 Sec. joined D (H.)/CCXXX and 1 Sec. joined D (H.)/CCXXXI. C/CCXLVII joined Bde. on 3/1/17 and became C/CCXXXII (18-pdrs.).

30 Bde. was broken up on 29/8/16.

31 A/CCXXXIII was broken up, 28/8/16; R. Sec. joined A/CCXXX and L. Sec. joined B/CCXXX, completing A and B to 6, 18-pdrs. each.

32 C/CCXXXIII was broken up, 28/8/16; R. Sec. joined A/CCXXXI and L. Sec. joined C/CCXXX, completing them to 6, 18-pdrs. each.

33 B/CCXXXIII was broken up, 28/8/16; R. Sec. joined B/CCXXXI and L. Sec. joined C/CCXXXI, completing them to 6, 18-pdrs. each.

34 C (H.)/CCXXXII (see n. 29) was broken up on 2/1/17; and 1 Sec. joined D (H.)/CCXXX and 1 Sec. went to D (H.)/CCXXXI—making them 6, 4.5-inch H.'s each.

35 C was broken up, 28/8/16; R Sec. went to A and L Sec. to B/CCXXXII, completing A and B to 6, 18-pdrs. each. (Also see n. 29.)

36 1 Sec. D (H.)/CCXLVII joined D (H.)/CCXXXII on 3/1/17, and made the Bty. up to 6, 4.5-inch Hows.

37 B.A.C.'s abolished and D.A.C. reorganized on 22/5/16.

38 X. joined on 9/3/16; and Y. and Z. were formed by 17/3/16.

39 V. joined on 20/6/16.

40 On 29 and 30/1/18 the Bn. was broken up between 2/5, 1/6, 2/6, and 9/N. Staff.

41 On 30/1/18 the Bn. was broken up between 2/4, 1/5, and 2/5/Linc.

42 On 31/1/18 the Bn. was broken up between 1/5, 1/6, 2/7, and 1/8/Sher. For.

43 The Fd. Cos. were numbered on 12/2/17.

44 The 178th M.G. Coy. joined (from England) on 28/3/17.

45 The D.E. Coy. was formed on 25/6/17.

46 The T.M. Bties. were reorganized on 3/2/18: Z. was absorbed by X. and Y.; and V (Heavy) partly by X. and Y., and partly by I Corps H.T.M. Bty.

47 The Bn. was formed on 28/2/18; it comprised 137th, 138th, 139th, and 178th M.G. Cos.

46TH (NORTH MIDLAND) DIVISION

MOBILIZATION, BATTLES, AND ENGAGEMENTS

The division—an existing T.F. division—was drawn chiefly (as indicated by the titles of the artillery and infantry brigades) from the North Midland Counties of England.

Divisional headquarters was at Lichfield. The twelve infantry battalions came from Walsall, Wolverhampton, Burton, Hanley, Leicester, Loughborough, Lincoln, Grimsby, Newark, Nottingham, Derby, and Chesterfield. In the artillery brigades: the I. N. Midland was at Grimsby, with outlying batteries at Louth and Boston; the II. N. Midland was at Stoke-on-Trent, with one battery at Leek; the III. N. Midland was at Wolverhampton, with outlying batteries at West Bromwich and Stafford; and the howitzer bde. was concentrated at Derby. The field companies came from Smethwick and Cannock; the field ambulances from Derby, Leicester, and Wolverhampton; and the companies of the T. and S. Column were at Birmingham, Leicester, Handsworth, and Nottingham.

The 1st N. Midland (Stafford) Heavy Battery (4, 4·7-inch) was detached from the N. Midland Division on arrival in France. The heavy battery disembarked at le Havre on 1/3/15, and on 18/4/15 the battery joined XIII. Bde., R.G.A.

The order for the division to mobilize was received on the 4th August. Divnl. H.Q. then moved to Derby, and soon afterwards the division was invited to volunteer for foreign service. This liability having been accepted, the division, in the middle of August, concentrated for training at Luton, and the division became part of the Third Army, Central Force. In November the division moved to Bishop's Stortford, Much Hadham, Sawbridgeworth, Saffron Walden, Braintree, and Dunmow; and in this area its war training was completed.

On the 19th February, 1915, H.M. the King inspected the division prior to its embarking for active service. On the 23rd the divisional advance party arrived at Boulogne, and on the 28th the units began to arrive. By the 8th March the division had completed its concentration in France, and thus it gained the distinction of being the first complete territorial division to arrive in any theatre of war.

With the exception of some units, which were sent to Egypt early in 1916 and returned immediately to France (see General Notes), the 46th Division served throughout the War on the Western Front in France and Belgium, and was engaged in the following operations:

1915

30 and 31 July ... ...**The Liquid-fire Attack, Hooge** (139th Bde. and Artillery) [V. Corps, Second Army].

BATTLE OF LOOS

13–15 October ... ...**Hohenzollern Redoubt** [XI. Corps, First Army].

1916

BATTLES OF THE SOMME

1 July ... ...**Gommecourt** [VII. Corps, Third Army].

1917

ADVANCE TO THE HINDENBURG LINE

1–13 March ... ...**Operations on the Ancre** [XVIII. Corps, Third Army, until 7/3/17; then V. Corps, Fifth Army].

4 March ... ...**Occupation of Gommecourt Defences** [XVIII. Corps].

12 March ... ...**Attack of Rettemoy Graben** [V. Corps].

14–22 March ... ...**German Retreat to the Hindenburg Line** [V. Corps, Fifth Army].

1 July ... ...**Attack on Liévin** [I. Corps, First Army].

15–25 August ... ...**Battle of Hill 70** [I. Corps, First Army].

1918

THE ADVANCE TO VICTORY

BATTLES OF THE HINDENBURG LINE

29 Sept.–2 Oct. ... ...**Battle of the St. Quentin Canal** [IX. Corps, Fourth Army].

29 Sept. ... ...**Passage at Bellenglise** [IX. Corps].

3–5 Oct. ... ...**Battle of the Beaurevoir Line** [IX. Corps, Fourth Army].

8 and 9 Oct. ... ...**Battle of Cambrai** [IX. Corps, Fourth Army].

THE FINAL ADVANCE IN PICARDY

17 and 18 Oct. ... ...**Battle of the Selle** [IX. Corps, Fourth Army].

4 Nov. ... ...**Battle of the Sambre** [IX. Corps, Fourth Army].

On the 11th November, the 46th Division had two brigades (137th and 138th) at Sains du Nord (four miles S.E. of Avesnes), the 139th Bde. at Boulogne (three miles S.S.W. of Avesnes), and Divnl. H.Q. at Prisches (eight miles S.W. of Avesnes).

On the 14th and 15th November the division moved back into billets in and west of Landrecies, and here it was employed in salvage work and in removing all traces of war, so as to hand back to the inhabitants the area for which it was responsible. On the 1st December, H.M. the King visited the division at Landrecies, and on the next day His Majesty, accompanied by Major-General Boyd, visited the St. Quentin Canal at Bellenglise, the scene of the division's triumph on the 29th September, 1918.

Early in January, 1919, the division moved to the le Cateau area, and here demobilization was steadily proceeded with. In June, the cadres of units began returning to England, and the war service of the 46th Division came to an end. In 1920 the division was re-formed in England.

47TH (2ND LONDON) DIVISION

G.O.C.

31 March, 1912 ... ... Major-General C. C. MONRO.
5 August, 1914 ... ... Major-General T. L. N. MORLAND.
3 September, 1914 ... ... Major-General C. ST. L. BARTER.
28 September, 1916 ... ... Br.-Gen. W. H. GREENLY (tempy.).
2 October, 1916... ... ... Major-General SIR G. F. GORRINGE.
14 October, 1917... ... ... Br.-Gen. R. McDOUALL (acting).
26 October, 1917... ... ... Br.-Gen. J. F. ERSKINE (acting).
5 November, 1917 ... ... Major-General SIR G. F. GORRINGE.

G.S.O. 1.

17 Feb., 1912...Lt.-Col. W. THWAITES.
1 June, 1915...Lt.-Col. HON. W. P. HORE-RUTHVEN.
20 Aug., 1915...Lt.-Col. B. BURNETT HITCHCOCK.
15 June, 1916...Lt.-Col. J. T. WEATHERBY (sick, 23/10/16).
23 Oct., 1916...Lt.-Col. A. J. TURNER (tempy.).
6 Nov., 1916...Lt.-Col. A. J. TURNER.
20 Feb., 1918...Lt.-Col. C. M. DAVIES.
12 July, 1918...Major M. LEWIS (acting).
14 July, 1918...Lt.-Col. B. L. MONTGOMERY.

A.-A. and Q.-M.-G.

2 Oct., 1911...Major H. V. M. DE LA FONTAINE (D.-A.-A. and Q.-M.-G.)
5 Aug., 1914...Colonel A. N. LYSAGHT.
24 Aug., 1914...Lt.-Col. R. M. FOOT.
5 Feb., 1916...Lt.-Col. S. H. J. THUNDER.
29 Oct., 1918...Major A. J. STEPHENSON-FETHERSTONHAUGH (acting).
30 Nov., 1918...Lt.-Col. S. H. J. THUNDER.

B.-G., R.A.

1 April, 1912...*Br.-Gen. J. C. WRAY.
5 Feb., 1916...Br.-Gen. E .W. SPEDDING.
31 Mar., 1917...Br.-Gen. E. N. WHITLEY.

C.R.E.

15 April, 1910...Lt.-Col. H. H. TAYLOR.
1 Sept., 1914...Col. A. H. KENNEY.
30 July, 1915...Lt.-Col. S. D'A. CROOKSHANK.
27 Nov., 1916...Lt.-Col. W. S. TRAILL.
24 May, 1917...Lt.-Col. H. S. CHRISTIE.
26 Nov., 1917...Lt.-Col. A. B. CAREY.
1 Nov., 1918...Lt.-Col. H. J. COUCHMAN.

*Br.-Gen. on 5 August, 1914.

140th BDE.
(4th London Bde.)

9 Oct., '13...*Br.-Gen. F. J. HEYWORTH.
26 Nov., '14...Br.-Gen. G. J. CUTHBERT.
12 July, '16...Lt.-Col. W. F. MILDREN (acting).
15 July, '16...Br.-Gen. VISCOUNT HAMPDEN (sick, 6/5/17).
6 May, '17...Lt.-Col. W. F. MILDREN (acting).
18 May, '17...Br.-Gen. H. B. P. L. KENNEDY.

141st BDE.
(5th London Bde.)

14 July, '13...*Br.-Gen. C. FITZ CLARENCE, V.C.
29 Aug., '14...Br.-Gen. G. C. NUGENT (killed, 31/5/15).
31 May, '15...Lt.-Col. J. GODDING (acting).
2 June, '15...Br.-Gen. W. THWAITES.
5 July, '16...Br.-Gen. R. J. BRIDGFORD.
19 Aug., '16...Br.-Gen. R. McDOUALL.
28 Dec., '16...Lt.-Col. W. C. W. HAWKES (acting).
28 Jan., '17...Br.-Gen. R. McDOUALL.
14 Oct., '17...Lt.-Col. W. F. MILDREN (acting).
26 Oct., '17...Br.-Gen. J. F. ERSKINE.
26 Oct., '17...Lt.-Col. W. F. MILDREN (acting).
5 Nov., '17...Br.-Gen. J. F. ERSKINE (sick, 16/12/17).
16 Dec., '17...Lt.-Col. W. W. HUGHES (acting).
18 Dec., '17...Lt.-Col. W. F. MILDREN (acting).
2 Jan., '18...Br.-Gen. W. F. MILDREN.

142nd BDE.
(6th London Bde.)

11 April, '12 *Br.-Gen. HON. C. S. HEATHCOTE-DRUMMOND-WILLOUGHBY (sick, 10/6/15).
10 June, '15...Lt.-Col. W. G. SIMPSON (acting).
14 Aug., '15...Br.-Gen. F. G. LEWIS.
26 Dec., '16...Lt.-Col. H. B. P. L. KENNEDY (acting).
5 Feb., '17...Br.-Gen. V. T. BAILEY.
6 Nov., '17...Lt.-Col. W. F. MILDREN (acting).
27 Nov., '17...Br.-Gen. V. T. BAILEY (wounded and captured, 24/3/18).
25 Mar., '18...Lt.-Col. A. MAXWELL (acting).
3 April, '18...Br.-Gen. R. McDOUALL.

*Br.-Gen. on 5 August, 1914.

GENERAL NOTES

4th London Inf. Bde., on 4th August, 1914, consisted of 13/, 14/, 15/, and 16/London Regt. Three of these battalions: 13/, 14/, and 16/London Regt., were transferred from the 4th Lond. Inf. Bde. and went to France independently (see below).

13/Lond. (Kensington), disembkd. at le Havre on 4/11/14, and the Bn. joined 25th Bde., 8th Div., on 13/11/14. The Bn., on 20/5/15, was transferred to G.H.Q. Troops, and on 11/2/16 it joined 168th Bde., 56th Div.

14/Lond. (London Scottish), disembkd. at le Havre on 16/9/14, and employed on L. of C. The Bn. concentrated on 27/10/14, at G.H.Q., St. Omer, reached Ypres on 30/10/14, and was engaged in the Battles of Ypres, 31/10–11/11/1914. On 7/11/14 the Bn. joined 1st (Guards) Bde., 1st Div.; it served with the 1st Bde. until 8/2/16, when it was transferred to 168th Bde., 56th Div., and it joined 168th Bde. on 8/2/16.

16/Lond. (Queen's Westminster Rifles), disembkd. at le Havre on 2/11/14. The Bn. joined 18th Bde., 6th Div., on 12/11/14; and on 10/2/16 the Bn. joined 169th Bde., 56th Div.

2nd London Hy. Bty., R.G.A. (4, 4.7-inch guns), went to France with the division on 15/3/15; and on 31/3/15 the Hy. Bty. joined I. Group, H.A.R.

The following Units also served with the 47th Division:—

INFANTRY:—3/Lond., joined 142nd Bde. on 16/11/15 (from 139th Bde., 46th Div.) and transferred to 167th Bde., 56th Div., on 9/2/16.

4/Lond., joined 140th Bde. on 15/11/15 (from 137th Bde., 46th Div.) and transferred to 168th Bde., 56th Div., on 9/2/16.

ARTILLERY:—I. Lond. Bde. (CCLXXX.) (from 16th Div.), served with the 47th Div. from 3/1–26/1/16. (It eventually joined 56th Divnl. Arty. on 25/2/16.)

III. Lond. Bde. (CCLXXXII.) (from 38th Div.), served with the 47th Div. from 27/1/16–19/2/16, when it was transferred to the 56th Divnl. Arty., and joined on 25 and 26/2/16.

523 (How.) Bty., R.F.A.—See note 32.

50th Div. Artillery (CCL. and CCLI.), from 13–25/8/18 (taken over from 58th Div., and transferred to 3rd Aus. Div.).

MACHINE-GUN COY.:—239th M.G. Coy.—See note 46.

OTHER UNITS:—2nd London (later 47th) Sanitary Section, was formed in England. It disembkd. at le Havre on 18/3/15. It served with the 47th Div. until 18/4/17 when it was transferred to Second Army. (From Sept., 1916–31/1/17 the Sec. was designated No. 19 Sanitary Sec.)

2nd London (later 47th) Divnl. Ambce. Workshop, was formed in England and joined the Div. in France by 1/4/15. The unit served until 3/4/16, when it was transferred to the 47th Divnl. Supply Coln.

The following **Portuguese** units: IV. Fd. Arty. Bde., 1st Eng. Fd. Coy., and two infantry battalions—23rd and 35th—were attached to the 47th Division; artillery, 14/10–16/11/18; engineers, 8–15/11/18; and infantry, 9–19/11/18.

On 2/2/18 the reorganization of the division on a 9-battalion basis was completed; and on 27/2/18 the pioneer battalion was reorganized on a 3-company basis.

47TH[1] (2ND LONDON) DIVISION

ORDER OF BATTLE, 1915-1918

Dates	INFANTRY: Brigades	INFANTRY: Battalions and attached Units	Mounted Troops	ARTILLERY: Field Artillery: Brigades	ARTILLERY: Field Artillery: Batteries	ARTILLERY: Field Artillery: Bde. Ammn. Colns.	ARTILLERY: Trench Mortar B'ties.: Medium	ARTILLERY: Trench Mortar B'ties.: Heavy	ARTILLERY: Divnl. Ammn. Coln.	Engineers: Field Cos.	Signal Service: Divnl. Signal Coy.	Pioneers	M.G. Units	Field Ambu-lances	Mobile Vety. Secn.	Divnl. Emplnt. Coy.	Divnl. Train
1915 March (France)	4th London[2] 5th London[3] 6th London[4]	6/Lond.,[5] 7/Lond.,[5] 8/Lond. (P.O. Rif.),[6] 15/Lond. (P.W.O. Civ. Ser. Rif.). 17/Lond., 18/Lond. (Lond. Ir. Rif.), 19/Lond., 20/Lond. 21/Lond., 22/Lond. (Queen's), 23/Lond., 24/Lond. (Queen's)	C Sqdn., 1st K.E. Horse[7] 2nd London Divnl. Cyclist Coy.[8]	V London[9]...... VI London[10]... VII London[11] VIII London[12] (H.)	12/Lond., 13/Lond., 14/Lond. 15/Lond., 16/Lond., 17/Lond. 18/Lond., 19/Lond., 20/Lond. 21/Lond. (H.), 22/Lond. (H.)	V London VI London VII London VIII London (H.)	...	...	2nd London[13] D.A.C.	3rd London[14] 4th London[15]	2nd London[16]	...	...	4th London[17] 5th London[17] 6th London[17]	2nd London[18]	...	2nd London[19]
1915 September (France)	140th[20] (4th London) 141st[20] (5th London) 142nd[20] (6th London)	6/Lond., 7/Lond., 8/Lond., 15/Lond. 17/Lond., 18/Lond., 19/Lond., 20/Lond. 21/Lond., 22/Lond., 23/Lond., 24/Lond.	C Sqdn., 1st K.E. Horse[21] 47th Divnl. Cyclist Coy.[22]	V London[23] .... VI London[24]... VII London[25] VIII London[26] (H.)	12/Lond., 13/Lond., 14/Lond. 15/Lond., 16/Lond., 17/Lond. 18/Lond., 19/Lond., 20/Lond. 21/Lond. (H.), 22/Lond. (H.)	V London VI London VII London VIII London (H.)	...	...	47th D.A.C. (2nd Lond.)	3rd London 4th London 2/3rd London[27]	47th (2nd Lond.)	4/R.W.F. (P.)[28]	...	4th London 5th London 6th London	2nd London	...	47th (2nd Lond.)
1916 June (France)	140th ..... 141st 142nd	6/Lond., 7/Lond., 8/Lond., 15/Lond.; 140th Bde. M.G. Coy.;[29] 140th T.M. Bty.[30] 17/Lond., 18/Lond., 19/Lond., 20/Lond.; 141st Bde. M.G. Coy.;[29] 141st T.M. Bty.[30] 21/Lond., 22/Lond., 23/Lond., 24/Lond.; 142nd Bde. M.G. Coy.;[29] 142nd T.M. Bty.[30]	...	CCXXXV[31] (V London) CCXXXVI[32] (VI London) CCXXXVII[33] (VII London) CCXXXVIII[34] (VIII London)	A, B, C; D (H.) A, B, C; D (H.) A, B, C. 34,[23] B, C; D (H.)	...[35]	X.47[36] Y.47[36] Z.47[36]	V.47[37]	47th D.A.C.[35]	3rd London 4th London 2/3rd London	47th	4/R.W.F. (P.)	...	4th London 5th London 6th London	2nd London	...	47th
1917 June (France)	140th ..... 141st 142nd	6/Lond.,[38] 7/Lond.,[39] 8/Lond.,[40] 15/Lond.; 140th M.G. Coy.;[48] 140th T.M. Bty. 17/Lond.,[41] 18/Lond., 19/Lond., 20/Lond.; 141st M.G. Coy.[48]; 141st T.M. Bty. 21/Lon.,[42] 22/Lond., 23/Lond., 24/Lond.; 142nd M.G. Coy.;[48] 142nd T.M. Bty.	...	CCXXXV[31] ... CCXXXVI[32]...	A, B, C; D (H.) A, B, C; D (H.)	...	X.47[43] Y.47[43] Z.47[43]	V.47[44]	47th D.A.C.	517th[45] (3rd London) 518th[45] (4th London) 520th[45] (2/3rd London)	47th	4/R.W.F. (P.)	255th M.G. Coy.[46]	4th London 5th London 6th London	2nd London	241st[47]	47th
1918 March (France)	140th ..... 141st 142nd	15/Lond., 17/Lond.,[41] 21/Lond.;[42] 140th T.M. Bty. 18/Lond., 19/Lond., 20/Lond.; 141st T.M. Bty. 22/Lond., 23/Lond., 24/Lond.; 142nd T.M. Bty.	...	CCXXXV..... CCXXXVI....	A, B, C; D (H.) A, B, C; D (H.)	...	X.47[43] Y.47	...	47th D.A.C.	517th 518th 520th	47th	4/R.W.F. (P.)	No. 47 Bn.,[48] M.G.C.	4th London 5th London 6th London	2nd London	241st	47th

NOTES

1 The 2nd London Div. was designated 47th (London) Div. on 11/5/15. (Authy. W.O. letter—40/W.O./2481 (A.G.1) of 7/5/15.)

2 The 4 original Bns. (see General Notes) came from Kensington, Westminster (2), and the Strand. The headquarters of 6/, 7/, and 8/London were all situated in the East Central Postal District.

3 The Bns. came from Chelsea, Bow, Camden Town, and Blackheath.

4 The Bns. came from Camberwell, Bermondsey, Kennington, and Clapham.

5 Joined the Bde. on 5/11/14 (from 2nd London Bde., 1st London Div.).

6 Joined the Bde. on 6/11/14 (from 2nd London Bde., 1st London Div.).

7 Disembkd. at le Havre on 22/4/15, and joined the div. on 25/4/15.

8 Formed in the concentration area. It disembkd. at le Havre, 16/3/15.

9 The 3 Bties. (4, 15-pdrs. each) came from Kennington (2), and Paddington.

10 The Bde. was concentrated at Brixton. (Bties. had 4, 15-pdrs. each.)

11 The 3 Bties. (4, 15-pdrs. each) came from Fulham (2), and Shepherd's Bush.

12 The Bde. was concentrated at Woolwich. (Bties. had 4, 5-inch. Hows. each.)

13 The D.A.C. was formed after mobilization. It disembkd. at le Havre on 21/3/15.

14 The Fd. Coy. came from Chelsea. It went to Winchester on 26/12/14 and joined 28th Division, and went to France in Jany., 1915, with the 28th Div. On 6/4/15 the Fd. Coy. was transferred back to the 2nd London Div. (in France) and rejoined on 8/4/15.

15 The Fd. Coy. came from Chelsea.

16 The Signal Coy. came from Chelsea.

17 The Fd. Ambces. came from Woolwich, Greenwich, and Chelsea.

18 Joined in Aug., 1914, and arrived in the divnl. area in France on 20/3/15.

19 Formed from 2nd London Divnl. T. and S. Coln. (from Chelsea). It disembkd. at le Havre between 10-18/3/15. The 4 companies were renumbered 455, 456, 457, 458 Cos., A.S.C., in 1915.

20 The Bdes. were designated: 140th on 12/5/15; 141st on 11/5/15; and 142nd on 14/5/15.

21 The Sqdn. joined IV Corps Cav. Regt. on 1/6/16.

22 The Cyclist Coy. joined IV Corps Cyclist Bn. on 1/6/16.

23 Bties. were rearmed with 4, 18-pdrs. each on 6/11/15. 34th Bty. joined on 20/4/16 (from XXXVIII of 6th Div.); 34th Bty. on 14/5/16 was transferred to CCXXXVIII. On 14/5/16 the Bde. was numbered CCXXXV, and the bties. were lettered A, B, and C. D (H.)—formerly R/VIII Lond.—joined CCXXXV on 14/5/16.

24 Bties. were rearmed with 4, 18-pdrs. each on 16/11/15. On 17/5/16 the Bde. was numbered CCXXXVI, and the bties. were lettered A, B, and C. D (H.)—formerly 22/Lond. (H.) of VIII Lond.—joined 17/5/16.

25 Bties. were rearmed with 4, 18-pdrs. each on 16/11/15. On 14/5/16 the Bde. was numbered CCXXXVII, and the bties. were lettered A, B, and C. R/VII Lond., which had joined the Bde. on 20/4/16, was transferred on 14/5/16 to CCXXXVIII and became C/CCXXXVIII.

26 The How. Bties. were rearmed with 4, 4.5-inch Hows. each on 19/1/16. On 4/2/16 B/CLXXVI and on 4/4/16 R (H.) joined VIII Lond. On 14/5/16 the Bde. was numbered CCXXXVIII, and R (H.) was transferred to CCXXXV and became D (H.); 34th Bty. was transferred from CCXXXV on 14/5/16; B/CLXXVI became B; R/VII Lond. joined and became C; and 21/Lond. (H.) remained and became D (H.)/CCXXXVIII.

27 Formed in Oct., 1914, and joined 2/2nd Lond. Div. Went to France June, '15, and joined 47th Div. on 25/6/15.

28 Became Pioneers 1/9/15, and was transferred from 3rd Bde., 1st Div., to 47th Div. on 1/9/15.

29 The M.G. Cos. were formed: 140th by 13/12/15; 141st on 12/12/15; and 142nd on 10/12/15.

30 On 12/6/16 the two light trench mortar bties. with each Bde. were amalgamated, and became the Bde. T.M. Bty.

31 Bde. reorganized on 27/11/16: A was divided between B and C; B then became A, and C became B; A/CCXXXVII, made up to 6 guns by 1/2 C/CCXXXVII, joined CCXXXV on 27/11/16 and became C; and D (H.) remained. On 19/1/17 D (H.) sent 1 Sec. to D/CCXXXVI, and D/CCXXXVIII then joined D/CCXXXV, and made D/CCXXXV up to 6 hows.

32 Bde. reorganized between 21-27/11/16: C was divided between A and B; 523 (H.) which had joined the Divnl. Arty. on 19/10/16 (from England) joined CCXXXVI on 27/11/16 and became C (H.); and D (H.) remained. On 19/1/17, C (H.) was broken up: R. Sec. joined D/CIV. A.F.A. Bde., and L. Sec. joined D/CLXXXIX A.F.A. Bde.; C/CCXXXVIII joined CCXXXVI and became C; and 1 sec. D/CCXXXV joined D/CCXXXVI and made it up to 6 hows.

33 Bde. broken up on 29/11/16, and the bties. joined CCXXXV and CCXXXVIII (see notes 31 and 34).

34 Bde. reorganized on 27/11/16: 34 and 1/2 B became 34; C and 1/2 B became B; B and 1/2 C joined from CCXXXVII on 27/11/16 and became C; and D (H.) remained. On 20 and 21/1/17 CCXXXVIII was broken up; 34 joined CLXXXIX A.F.A. Bde.; B became C/CIV A.F.A. Bde.; C became C/CCXXXVI; and D (H.) was transferred to CCXXXV and made up D/CCXXXV to 6 hows.

35 Between 15-20/5/16 the B.A.C.'s were abolished and the D.A.C. was reorganized.

36 Nos. 7 and 8 T.M. Bties. joined the Div. on 17/11/15, and became X and Y on 28/5/16; Z was formed in April, 1916.

37 V. was formed by 6/11/16.

38 On 30/1/18 drafts were sent to 15/Lond. and 18/Lond.; and between 31/1—2/2/18 the remdr. amalgamated with 2/6/Lond. and became 6/Lond. in 174th Bde., 58th Div.

39 On 29/1/18 a draft was sent to 19/Lond.; and on 2/2/18 the remdr. amalgamated with 2/7/Lond. and became 7/Lond. in 174th Bde., 58th Div.

40 On 1/2/18 a draft was sent to 17/Lond.; and on 2/2/18 the remdr. amalgamated with 2/8/Lond. and became 8/Lond. in 174th Bde., 58th Div.

41 Transferred on 1/2/18 to 140th Bde.

42 Transferred on 1/2/18 to 140th Bde.

43 Reorganized on 1/2/18: X was absorbed by Y and Z; and on 13/2/18 Z became X.

44 Became V Corps H.T.M.Bty. by 16/2/18.

45 Fd. Cos. were designated by numbers on 1/2/17.

46 239th M.G. Coy. joined from England on 17/7/17. The Coy. left the Div. on 1/10/17 for Mesopotamia and arrived there on 7/11/17; it was replaced in the 47th Div. on 19/11/17 by the 255th M.G. Coy. (from England).

47 The Coy. was formed in May, 1917, and was numbered 241st in June.

48 The Bn. was formed on 1/3/18; it comprised 140th, 141st, 142nd, and 255th M.G. Cos.

47TH (2ND LONDON) DIVISION

MOBILIZATION, BATTLES, AND ENGAGEMENTS

The division—an existing T.F. division—was drawn chiefly from the south-western and south-eastern districts of London.

Divisional headquarters was at the Duke of York's Headquarters, Chelsea, and here also were King Edward's Horse, the two field companies, the signal company, one field ambulance (the other two were at Greenwich and Woolwich), and the Divnl. T. and S. Column. The twelve infantry battalions came from the following districts: Kensington, Westminster (2), Strand, Chelsea, Bow, Camden Town, Blackheath, Camberwell, Bermondsey, Clapham, and Kennington. (Before the division went abroad the three battalions from Kensington and Westminster (2) were replaced by three from Farringdon Rd., Finsbury Sq., and Bunhill Row—see Table and General Notes.)

In the artillery: the V. London Bde. had two batteries in Kennington Lane and one battery in Paddington; the VI. London Bde. was concentrated at Brixton; the VII. London Bde. had two batteries in Fulham and one battery in Shepherd's Bush; and the VIII. London (How.) Bde. was concentrated at Woolwich. The 2nd London Heavy Battery (4, 4·7-inch guns) came from Islington (see General Notes).

Two of the artillery brigades had completed their annual training just before the outbreak of the Great War, but the remainder of the division had only just settled down in its August camps on Salisbury Plain when war was declared. Thereupon the division at once returned to its London headquarters to carry out its mobilization. By the middle of August the 2nd London Division was completed for war, and the units then marched away to their war stations in the country around St. Albans, to form part of the Third Army, Central Force, and to carry on the division's progressive training for war. By the end of October, 1914, the 2nd London Division was selected as one of the T.F. Divisions which would proceed direct to France.

On 2nd March, 1915, the division was ordered to prepare to move to France. On the 6th, the 2/2nd London Division took over details who were to remain in England, and on the 8th and 9th March the 2nd London Division began its move to the Western Theatre of War. The leading brigade (5th London) landed at le Havre on the 9th and 10th March, and moved to Cassel; but, on arrival in France, the remainder of the division moved into the Bethune area and was concentrated there by the 22nd March, and the 5th London Inf. Bde. rejoined. The division was the second complete territorial division to arrive in France.

The 47th Division served throughout the War on the Western Front in France and Belgium, and was engaged in the following operations:—

1915

9 May ... ...**Battle of Aubers Ridge** [I. Corps, First Army].

15–25 May ... ...**Battle of Festubert** [Barter's Force, I. Corps, First Army].

25 Sept.–1 Oct. ... ...**Battle of Loos** [IV. Corps, First Army].

13–19 Oct. ... ...**Actions of Hohenzollern Redoubt** [IV. Corps, First Army].

1916

21 May ... ...**Vimy Ridge** [IV. Corps, First Army].

BATTLES OF THE SOMME

15–19 Sept. ... ...**Battle of Flers-Courcelette** [III. Corps, Fourth Army].
15 Sept. ... ...**Capture of High Wood** [III. Corps].
1–9 Oct. ... ...**Battle of the Transloy Ridges** [III. Corps, Fourth Army].
1–3 Oct. ... ...**Capture of Eaucourt l'Abbaye** [III. Corps].
7 and 8 Oct. ... ...**Attacks on Butte de Warlencourt** [III. Corps].

1917

7–13 June ... ...**Battle of Messines** [X. Corps, Second Army].
18 Aug.–2 Sept., and 8–17 Sept. ...**BATTLES OF YPRES** [II. Corps, Fifth Army; and I. Anzac, Second Army].
31 July–2 Aug. ... ...**Battle of Pilckem Ridge** [In reserve, X. Corps, Second Army].

BATTLE OF CAMBRAI

28 Nov. ... ...**Capture of Bourlon Wood** [IV. Corps, Third Army].
30 Nov.–3 Dec. ... ...**The German Counter-attacks** [IV. Corps; then, from 1st December, V. Corps, Third Army].

1918

FIRST BATTLES OF THE SOMME

21–23 March ... ...**Battle of St. Quentin** [V. Corps, Third Army].
24 and 25 March ...**First Battle of Bapaume** [V. Corps, Third Army].
5 April ... ...**Battle of the Ancre** [V. Corps, Third Army].

THE ADVANCE TO VICTORY

SECOND BATTLES OF THE SOMME

22 and 23 Aug. ... ...**Battle of Albert** [III. Corps, Fourth Army].
31 Aug.–3 Sept. ... ...**Second Battle of Bapaume** [III. Corps, Fourth Army].

THE FINAL ADVANCE IN ARTOIS

2 Oct.–11 Nov. ... ...**Operations in Artois** [XI. Corps, Fifth Army].
28 Oct. ... ...**Official Entry into Lille** [Fifth Army].

On the 10th November the divisional advanced guard (142nd Bde.) reached the line Frasnes lez Buissenal-Moustier (N. of Leuze).

On the 11th November the III. Corps took over that part of the Fifth Army Front which had been occupied by the XI. Corps, and on this day the 47th Division marched back and concentrated around Tournai. On the 13th November the 140th and 141st Inf. Bdes. began working on the repair of the Tournai-Ath railway; on the 15th the rest of the division moved back to the Cysoing area, and on the 19th the 140th and 141st Bdes. rejoined. On the 26th November the 47th Division began to move into the Bethune area. By the 29th the move was completed, and the division proceeded to settle down in the small mining and agricultural villages around Bethune to await demobilization. Between the 1st and 10th January, 1919, the first parties left for England. Thenceforward the division rapidly dwindled, and by the 28th March the units were all at cadre strength. The 47th (London) Division was then replaced by the 47th Divisional Group of Cadres. In 1920 the division began to re-form in England.

48th (SOUTH MIDLAND) DIVISION

G.O.C.

1 July, 1912 ... ... Major-General J. L. Keir.
27 July, 1914 ... ... Major-General E. R. C. Graham.
5 August, 1914 ... ... Major-General H. N. C. Heath (sick, 7/5/15).
7 May, 1915 ... ... Br.-Gen. W. K. McClintock (acting).
31 May, 1915 ... ... Major-General R. Fanshawe.
20 June, 1918 ... ... Br.-Gen. J. Steele (acting).
4 July, 1918 ... ... Major-General Sir H. B. Walker.

G.S.O. 1.

4 Mar., 1914...Captain A. L. C. Clarke (G.S.O. 2).
5 Aug., 1914...Lt.-Col. A. L. C. Clarke.
1 April, 1915...Lt.-Col. H. A. D. Simpson-Baikie.
20 April, 1915...Lt.-Col. J. S. J. Baumgartner.
2 April, 1916...Lt.-Col. H. R. Cumming.
27 Aug., 1916...Lt.-Col. A. I. R. Glasfurd.
9 July, 1917...Major T. J. Leahy (acting).
16 July, 1917...Lt.-Col. H. C. L. Howard.

A.-A. & Q.-M.-G.

26 Feb., 1913...Captain W. H. P. Law (D.-A.-A. and Q.-M.-G.).
5 Aug., 1914...Col. J. A. H. Reilly.
23 Aug., 1915...Lt.-Col. H. A. Boyce.
24 Nov., 1915...Major M. R. Walsh (acting).
30 Nov., 1915...Lt.-Col. G. N. T. Smyth-Osbourne.
24 Dec., 1916...Lt.-Col. G. H. Barnett.

B.-G., R.A.

20 Mar., 1911...Colonel D. G. Prinsep.
18 July, 1914...*Br.-Gen. H. H. Butler.
11 May, 1915...Br.-Gen. C. M. Ross-Johnson.
30 Jan., 1916...Lt.-Col. A. R. B. Cossart (acting).
6 Feb., 1916...Br.-Gen. H. D. O. Ward.
8 May, 1917...Br.-Gen. W. Strong.

C.R.E.

11 May, 1912...Lt.-Col. E. S. Sinnott.
19 April, 1915...Lt.-Col. H. J. M. Marshall.
27 Feb., 1917...Major A. D. Walker (acting).
3 Mar., 1917...Lt.-Col. V. Giles.
25 Jan., 1918...Major G. S. J. F. Eberle (acting).
18 Feb., 1918...Major E. Briggs (acting).
13 Mar., 1918...Lt.-Col. E. Briggs.

*Br.-Gen. on 5 August, 1914.

143rd BDE.
(Warwickshire)

1 June, '11...*Br.Gen. C. H. L. JAMES.
4 May, '16...Lt.-Col. G. C. SLADEN (acting).
8 May, '16...Br.-Gen. B. C. DENT.
2 Sept., '16...Br.-Gen. G. C. SLADEN.

144th BDE.
(Gloucester and Worcester)

7 Dec., '10...*Br.-Gen. E. K. DAUBENEY.
27 Mar., '15...Br.-Gen. G. H. NICHOLSON.
4 Mar., '17...Lt.-Col. H. T. DOBBIN (acting).
9 Mar., '17...Br.-Gen. H. R. DONE.

145th BDE.
(South Midland)

1 July, '11...*Br.-Gen. W. K. McCLINTOCK.
7 May '15...Col. O. PEARCE-SEROCOLD (acting).
31 May '15...Br.-Gen. W. K. McCLINTOCK.
12 Dec., '15...Lt.-Col. J. H. COLLETT (acting).
15 Dec., '15...Br.-Gen. H. R. DONE.
20 Nov., '16...Lt.-Col. R. J. CLARKE (acting).
22 Nov., '16...Br.-Gen. D. M. WATT.
27 Aug., '18...Br.-Gen. W. W. PITT-TAYLOR.
14 Oct., '18...Lt.-Col. L. L. C. REYNOLDS (acting).
29 Oct., '18...Br.-Gen. G. W. HOWARD.

*Br.-Gen. on 5 August, 1914.

GENERAL NOTES

South Midland (Warwickshire) Hy. Bty., R.G.A. (4, 4.7-inch guns), went to France with the Division on 31/3/15; joined Second Army Artillery on 16/4/15; XVI. Bde., R.G.A., on 10/6/15; and VIII. Bde., R.G.A., on 3/7/15.

The following Units also served with the Division :—

ARTILLERY :—531 (H.) Bty., R.F.A.—See note 32.

ENGINEERS :—7th Fd. Coy., R.E., joined on 29/4/15 (from the 4th Div.), and was transferred to the 50th Div. on 17/6/15.

1/W. Lanc. Fd. Coy., R.E., attached from 18/4/15–28/4/15, when the Fd. Coy. returned to the 55th Div.

OTHER UNITS :—S. Midl'd. (later 48th) Sanitary Section, was formed in the concentration area on 21/2/15; it disembkd. with the Div. at le Havre on 1/4/15, and it was transferred to III. Corps on 4/4/17.

S. Midl'd. (later 48th) Divnl. Ambce. Workshop, joined in the concentration area; it disembkd. with the Div. at Boulogne on 2/4/15, and it was absorbed by the Divnl. Supply Coln. on 4/4/16.

On 12/9/18 the reorganization of the 48th Division on a 9-battalion basis was completed. The pioneer battalion had been reorganized on a 3-company basis by May, 1918.

48TH[1] (SOUTH MIDLAND) DIVISION — ORDER OF BATTLE, 1915-1918

Dates	INFANTRY: Brigades	INFANTRY: Battalions and attached Units	Mounted Troops	ARTILLERY: Field Artillery: Brigades	ARTILLERY: Field Artillery: Batteries	ARTILLERY: Field Artillery: Bde. Ammn. Cols.	ARTILLERY: Trench Mortar B'ties.: Medium	ARTILLERY: Trench Mortar B'ties.: Heavy	ARTILLERY: Divnl. Ammn. Coln.	Engineers: Field Cos.	Signal Service: Divnl. Signal Coy.	Pioneers	M.G. Units	Field Ambu-lances	Mobile Vety. Secn.	Divnl. Emplnt. Coy.	Divnl. Train
1915 March (France)	Warwickshire[2] Gloucester[3] and Worcester South Midland[4]....	5/R. War., 6/R. War., 7/R. War., 8/R. War. 4/Glouc., 6/Glouc., 7/Worc., 8/Worc. 5/Glouc., 4/O. and B.L.I., 1/Bucks. Bn./O. and B.L.I., 4/R. Berks.	B Sqdn.,[5] 1st K.E. Horse; South Midland[6] Divnl. Cyclist Coy.	I South Midland[7] II South Midland[8] III South Midland[9] IV South Midland (H.)[10]	1/Glouc., 2/Glouc., 3/Glouc. 1/Worc., 2/Worc., 3/Worc. 1/War., 2/War., 3/War. 4/War. (H.), 5/War. (H.)	I S. Midland II S. Midland III S. Midland IV S. Midland (H.)	...	...	South Midl'd.[11] D.A.C.	1st S. Midland[12] 2nd S. Midland[12]	S. Midl'd.[13]	...	...	1st S. Midl'd.[14] 2nd S. Midl'd.[14] 3rd S. Midl'd.[14]	1st South Midl'd.[15]	...	1st South Midl'd.[16]
1915 September (France)	143rd[17] (Warwick.) 144th[17] (Glouc. and Worc.) 145th[17] (S. Midland)	5/R. War., 6/R. War., 7/R. War., 8/R. War. 4/Glouc., 6/Glouc., 7/Worc., 8/Worc. 5/Glouc., 4/O. and B.L.I., 1/Bucks. Bn./O. and B.L.I., 4/R. Berks.	B Sqdn.,[18] 1st K.E. Horse; S. Mid.[19] Divnl. Cyclist Coy.	I S. Midland[20] II S. Midland[21] III S. Midland[22] IV S. Midland (H.)[23]	1/Glouc., 2/Glouc., 3/Glouc. 1/Worc., 2/Worc., 3/Worc. 1/War., 2/War., 3/War. 4/War. (H.), 5/War. (H.)	I S. Midland II S. Midland III S. Midland IV S. Midland (H.)	...	...	48th D.A.C. (S. Midl'd.)	1st S. Midland 2nd S. Midland 2/1st S. Midland[24]	48th (S. Midl'd.)	5/R. Suss.[25] (P.)	...	1st S. Midl'd. 2nd S. Midl'd. 3rd S. Midl'd.	1st South Midl'd.	...	48th (S. Midl'd.)
1916 June (France)	143rd........ 144th........ 145th........	5/R. War., 6/R. War., 7/R. War., 8/R. War.; 143rd Bde. M.G. Coy.;[26] 143rd T.M. Bty.[27] 4/Glouc., 6/Glouc., 7/Worc., 8/Worc.; 144th Bde. M.G. Coy.;[26] 144th T.M. Bty.[28] 5/Glouc., 4/O. and B.L.I., 1/Bucks. Bn./O. and B.L.I., 4/R. Berks.; 145th Bde. M.G. Coy.;[26] 145th T.M. Bty.[29]	...	CCXL[30] (I S. Midl'd.) CCXLI[31] (II S. Midl'd.) CCXLII[32] (III S. Midl'd.) CCXLIII[33] (IV S. Midl'd.)	A, B, C; D (H.) A, B, C; D (H.) A, B, C; D (H.) A, B, C	..[34]	X.48[35] Y.48[35] Z.48[35]	V.48[36]	48th D.A.C.[34]	1st S. Midland 2nd S. Midland 2/1st S. Midland	48th	5/R. Suss. (P.)		1st S. Midl'd. 2nd S. Midl'd. 3rd S. Midl'd.	1st South Midl'd.	...	48th
1917 June (France)	143rd........ 144th........ 145th........	5/R. War., 6/R. War., 7/R. War., 8/R. War.; 143rd M.G. Coy.;[45] 143rd T.M. Bty. 4/Glouc., 6/Glouc., 7/Worc., 8/Worc.; 144th M.G. Coy.;[45] 144th T.M. Bty. 5/Glouc., 4/O. and B.L.I., 1/Bucks. Bn./O. and B.L.I., 4/R. Berks.; 145th M.G. Coy.;[45] 145th T.M. Bty.	...	CCXL[30] ...... CCXLI[31]	A, B, C; D (H.) A, B, C; D (H.)	...	X.48[37] Y.48[37] Z.48[37]	V.48[38]	48th D.A.C.	474th (1st S. Midl'd.)[39] 475th (2nd S. Midl'd.)[39] 477th (2/1st S. Midl'd.)[39]	48th	5/R. Suss. (P.)	251st M.G. Coy.[40]	1st S. Midl'd. 2nd S. Midl'd. 3rd S. Midl'd.	1st South Midl'd.	242nd[41]	48th
1918 April (Italy)	143rd........ 144th........ 145th........	5/R. War., 6/R. War., 7/R. War., 8/R. War.;[42] 143rd T.M. Bty. 4/Glouc., 6/Glouc., 7/Worc., 8/Worc.;[43] 144th T.M. Bty. 5/Glouc.,[44] 4/O. and B.L.I., 1/Bucks. Bn./O. and B.L.I., 4/R. Berks.; 145th T.M. Bty.	...	CCXL ...... CCXLI	A, B, C; D (H.) A, B, C; D (H.)	...	X. 48 Y. 48	...	48th D.A.C.	474th 475th 477th	48th	5/R. Suss. (P.)	No. 48 Bn.[45] M.G.C.	1st S. Midl'd. 2nd S. Midl'd. 3rd S. Midl'd.	1st South Midl'd.	242nd	48th

1918 October (Italy)	143rd	5/R. War., 6/R. War., 7/R. War.; 143rd T.M. Bty.	...	CCXL	A, B, C; D (H.)		X. 48 Y. 48	...	48th D.A.C.	474th 475th 477th	48th	5/R. Suss. (P.)	No. 48 Bn. M.G.C.	1st S. Midl'd. 2nd S. Midl'd. 3rd S. Midl'd.	1st South Midl'd.	242nd	48th
	144th	4/Glouc., 6/Glouc., 7/Worc.; 144th T.M. Bty.		CCXLI	A, B, C; D (H.)												
	145th	4/O. and B.L.I., 1/Bucks. Bn. /O. and B.L.I., 4/R. Berks.; 145th T.M. Bty.															

NOTES

1 The 1st South Midland Div. was designated 48th (South Midland) Div. on 12/5/15. (Authy. W.O. letter 40/W.O./2481 (A.G.1.) of 7/5/15.)

2 The Bns. came from Birmingham (2), Aston, and Coventry.

3 The Bns. came from Bristol (2), Worcester, and Kidderminster.

4 The Bns. came from Reading, Oxford, Aylesbury, and Gloucester.

5 Regtl. H.Q. was in Chelsea. B Sqdn. disembkd. at le Havre on 22/4/15, and joined S Midl'd. Div. on 24/4/15

6 Formed by the Division at Chelmsford on 3/12/14; it disembkd. at le Havre on 31/3/15.

7 The Bties. (4, 15-pdrs. each) were at Clifton (2) and Gloucester.

8 The Bties. (4, 15-pdrs. each) were at Worcester, Kidderminster, and Redditch. The Bde. Ammn. Coln. was at Malvern.

9 The Bde. (15 pdrs.) was concentrated at Stoney Lane, Birmingham.

10 The Bties. (4, 5-inch Hows. each) were at Coventry and Rugby.

11 Formed after mobilization: it disembkd. with the Div. at le Havre on 1/4/15.

12 Both Fd. Cos. came from Bristol. 1st S. Midl'd. Fd. Coy. joined 27th Div. at Winchester, 4/12/14, and disembkd. with the 27th at le Havre on 22/12/14. The Coy. was attached to the 3rd Div. on 17/3/15; to the 5th Div., 24/3/15; to the 6th Div. on 10/4/15; and it rejoined the S. Midl'd. Div. on 1/5/15.

13 The H.Q. and No. 1 Sec. came from Bristol.

14 The 3 Fd. Ambces. came from Birmingham (2) and Bristol.

15 The Mob. Vety. Sec. joined the Div. in the concentration area, and it disembkd. with the Div. at le Havre on 1/4/15.

16 Formed, during concentration, from Divnl. T. and S. Coln. The companies came from Taplow, Stroud, Harborne, and Aston. The Train disembkd. with the Div. at le Havre between 23-31/3/15. The companies were numbered 459, 460, 461, and 462 Cos., A.S.C.

17 On 12/5/15 the Inf Bdes. were designated 143rd, 144th, and 145th.

18 The Sqdn. joined IV Corps Cav. Regt. on 13/5/16.

19 The Cyclist Coy. joined VIII Corps Cyclist Bn. on 14/5/16.

20 Bties. were rearmed with 4, 18-pdrs. each on 21/7/15. D Bty. (18-pdrs.) was formed by 6/4/16. On 18/5/16 the Bde. was numbered CCXL, and the old bties. were lettered A, B, and C; D was transferred to CCXLIII and became A/CCXLIII; and 4/War. (H.) joined the Bde. from CCXLIII and became D (H.)/CCXL.

21 Bties. were rearmed with 4, 18-pdrs. each on 21/7/15. D Bty. (18-pdrs.) was formed on 3/4/16. On 18/5/16 the Bde. was numbered CCXLI, and the old bties. were lettered A, B, and C; D was transferred to CCXLIII and became B/CCXLIII; and 5/War. (H.) joined the Bde. from CCXLIII and became D (H.)/CCXLI.

22 Bties. were rearmed with 4, 18-pdrs. each on 21/7/15. D Bty. (18-pdrs.) was formed on 5/5/16. On 18/5/16 the Bde. was numbered CCXLII, and the old batteries were lettered A, B, and C; D was transferred to CCXLIII and became C/CCXLIII; and D (H.) joined the Bde. from CCXLIII and became D (H.)/CCXLII.

23 Bties. were rearmed with 4, 4.5 inch Hows. each on 6/1/16. D (H.) from CXXVI (37th Div.) joined CCXLIII on 7/2/16. On 18/5/16 the Bde. was numbered CCXLIII; and 4/War. (H.) was transferred to CCXL as D (H.); 5/War. (H.) went to CCXLI as D (H.); and D (H.)/CCXLIII became D (H.)/CCXLII. In exchange D/CCXL joined and became A, D/CCXLI joined and became B, and D/CCXLII joined and became C. (3, 18-pdr. bties.)

24 This Fd. Coy., raised after the outbreak of war, reached le Havre on 7/6/15, and joined the Div. on 10/6/15.

25 Joined on 21/8/15 as Pioneers (from 2nd Bde., 1st Div.).

26 The M.G. Cos. were formed: 143rd on 8/1/16; 144th on 23/1/16; and 145th on 11/1/16.

27 86 and 109 T.M. Bties. were attached to the Bde. by 10/1/16; they were replaced by 143/1 (on 21/3) and 143/2 (on 24/4/16). 143rd T.M. Bty. formed on 14/6/16.

28 82 (from 10/2/16) and 100 (in Nov., '15) T.M. Bties. were attached to the Bde.; they were replaced by 144/1 and 144/2 on 21/4/16. 144th T.M.B. was formed on 14/6/16.

29 80 (in Dec., '15) and 95 (on 3/1/16) T.M. Bties. were attached to the Bde.: they were replaced by 145/1 (on 18/3/16) and 145/2 (on 25/4/16). 145/1 and 145/2 were amalgamated on 14/6/16 and formed 145th T.M. Bty.

30 Bde. was reorganized on 18/10/16: A and 1/2 C joined from CCXLIII and completed A, B, and C/CCXL to 6-gun bties. On 16/1/17 1/2 C (H.) joined from CCXLII and completed D (H.)/CCXL to 6 hows.

31 Bde. was reorganized on 18/10/16: B and 1/2 C joined from CCXLIII and completed A, B, and C/CCXLI to 6-gun bties. On 18/1/17 1/2 C (H.) joined from CCXLII and completed D (H.)/CCXLI to 6 hows.

32 Bde. was reorganized on 10/10/16: C was absorbed by A and B, thus completing A and B to 6-gun bties.; 531 (H.) joined Bde. from England on 28/10/16, and was lettered C (H.). On 16/1/17 CCXLII was again reorganized: C (H.) went 1/2 to D/CCXL and 1/2 to D/CCXLI; 1 Sec. C (H.) of CLXXXVIII (from 40th Div.) joined on 16/1/17 and made D (H.)/CCXLII up to 6 hows.; and on 20/1/17 A/CCLII (from 50th Div.) joined and became C/CCXLII. On 20/1/17 CCXLII became an A.F.A. Bde.

33 On 18/10/16 CCXLIII was broken up: A and 1/2 C went to CCXL, and B and 1/2 C to CCXLI, to complete their 18-pdr. bties. to 6 guns each.

34 On 15/5/16 the B.A.C.'s were abolished and the D.A.C. was reorganized.

35 The Medium T.M. Bties. were formed by 15/3/16.

36 V H.T.M. Bty. was formed on 21/4/16.

37 On 21/3/18 Z was absorbed by X and Y.

38 V was abolished on 10/11/17, and its personnel was distributed between CCXL, CCXLI, and the D.A.C.

39 The Fd. Cos. were numbered by 11/2/17.

40 The Coy. (formed at Grantham) disembkd. at le Havre on 13/11/17, and joined the Div. on 16/11/17.

41 Formed in the Div. by 16/6/17.

42 8/R. War. left the Div. on 11/9/18 to proceed to B.E.F., France; and the bn. joined 75th Bde., 25th Div.

43 8/Worc. left the Div. on 12/9/18 to proceed to B.E.F., France; and the bn. joined 75th Bde., 25th Div.

44 5/Glouc. left the Div. on 11/9/18 to proceed to B.E.F., France; and the bn. joined 75th Bde., 25th Div.

45 Bn. was formed on 22/3/18; it comprised 143rd, 144th, 145th, and 251st M.G. Cos.

48TH (SOUTH MIDLAND) DIVISION

MOBILIZATION, BATTLES, AND ENGAGEMENTS

The division—an existing T.F. division—was drawn chiefly from Warwickshire, Worcestershire, and Gloucestershire, with divisional headquarters at Warwick. The three brigade headquarters were at Warwick, Cheltenham, and Oxford; and the 12 infantry battalions came from Thorp St., Birmingham (2), Aston, Coventry, Kidderminster, Worcester, Bristol (2), Gloucester, Oxford, Aylesbury, and Reading.

In the artillery: the I. S.M. Bde. was at Clifton, with an outlying battery at Gloucester; the II. S.M. Bde. was at Worcester, with outlying batteries at Kidderminster and Redditch, and its ammunition column at Malvern; the III. S.M. Bde. was concentrated at Stoney Lane, Birmingham; the IV. S.M. (How.) Bde. had its two batteries at Coventry and Rugby; and the S.M. (Warwickshire) Heavy Battery (4, 4.7-inch guns) came from Saltley (see General Notes).

The two field companies and the H.Q. and No. 1 Section of the Signal Company all came from Bristol; the three field ambulances were at Gt. Brook St., Birmingham (2), and Bristol; and the companies of the Divnl. T. and S. Coln. were at Aston, Harborne, Stroud, and Taplow.

On the outbreak of the Great War the division was mobilized, and during August it concentrated around Chelmsford. In this area the division was part of the Central Force. Progressive training for war was carried on, and in due course the division was selected to proceed to France.

On the 13th March, 1915, the division received orders to prepare to embark for France, and the entrainment of the units began on the 22nd March. Divnl. H.Q., the Gloucester and Worcester Bde., and the S. Midland Bde. crossed from Folkestone to Boulogne; but the R.A., the R.E., the Warwickshire Bde., the Cyclist Coy., and all the transport crossed from Southampton to le Havre. By the 1st April disembarkation had been effected, and by the 3rd April the division completed its concentration to the south and east of Cassel.

The division served on the Western Front in France and Belgium until the 21st November, 1917, when it began entraining for the Italian Front on which it served for the remainder of the War.

From 1915 to 1918 the 48th Division was engaged in the following operations:

1915

1916

BATTLES OF THE SOMME

1 July	...**Battle of Albert** [VIII. Corps, Fourth Army].
15–17 July ...	...**Battle of Bazentin Ridge** [X. Corps, Reserve Army].
17 July	...**Capture of Ovillers** [X. Corps].
23–27 July, and 13–28 Aug. ...	**Battle of Pozières Ridge** [X. Corps, until 24th July; and then II. Corps, Reserve Army].
3–11 Nov. ...	...**Battle of the Ancre Heights** [III. Corps, Fourth Army].
13–18 Nov. ...	...**Battle of the Ancre** [III. Corps, Fourth Army].

1917

14 March–5 April ...**German Retreat to the Hindenburg Line** [III. Corps, Fourth Army].

18 March ... ...**Occupation of Péronne** [III. Corps].

BATTLES OF YPRES

16–18 Aug. ... ...**Battle of Langemarck** [XVIII. Corps, Fifth Army].

28 Sept.–3 Oct. ... ...**Battle of Polygon Wood** [XVIII. Corps, Fifth Army].

4 Oct. ... ...**Battle of Broodseinde** [XVIII. Corps, Fifth Army].

9 Oct. ... ...**Battle of Poelcappelle** [XVIII. Corps, Fifth Army].

On the 10th November orders were received from G.H.Q. that the 48th Division would be moved to Italy. Entrainment began on the 21st November, and by the 1st December detrainment was completed around Legnago (on the Adige). On the 2nd December the division began moving northwards into the XI. Corps area.

1918

On the 1st March the 48th Division completed the relief of the 7th Division [XIV. Corps] in the front line of the Montello Sector on the Piave Front, and held the line until relieved on the 16th March. On the 1st April the 48th Division moved westward, into reserve for the middle sector of the Asiago Plateau Front.

BATTLE OF THE PIAVE

15 and 16 June ...**The Fighting on the Asiago Plateau** [XIV. Corps, Sixth (It.) Army].

BATTLE OF VITTORIO VENETO

1–4 Nov. ... ...**The Fighting in the Val d'Assa** [XII. (It.) Corps, Sixth (It.) Army].

On the 3rd November, at Osteria del Termine (eight miles north-west of Asiago) the 48th Division surrounded and captured the commander of the Austrian III. Corps (General von Ritter Romer), three divisional commanders, and a force of about 14 battalions. By 3 p.m. on the 4th November (Armistice with Austria-Hungary) the leading troops of the 48th Division had pushed forward into the Trentino, eight miles north-westward of Levico.

After the conclusion of hostilities the 48th Division was withdrawn from the front line, and by the 10th November it had moved back to the Granezza area. Here, on the 11th, news was received (as the last troops of the division left Austria) that the Armistice had been signed with Germany. By the 15th the division completed its withdrawal to the plains around Trissino (West of Vicenza), and on the 27th November the 48th Division was represented at the review of the British Forces in Italy, held by H.M. the King of Italy at the aerodrome at Castelgomberto (N.E. of Trissino).

In 1919 demobilization began and was carried on with increasing speed. Finally, on the 31st March, the service of the 48th Division in the Great War came to an end with the departure for England of the cadre of divisional headquarters. The division was re-formed in England in 1920.

49TH (WEST RIDING) DIVISION

G.O.C.

19 September, 1911 ... ... Major-General T. S. BALDOCK (wounded, 16/7/15).
17 July, 1915 ... ... Major-General E. M. PERCEVAL.
20 October, 1917... ... ... Major-General N. J. G. CAMERON.

G.S.O. 1.

4 Sept., 1913...Major H. ST. C. WILKINS (G.S.O. 2).
5 Aug., 1914...Lt.-Col. H. ST. C. WILKINS.
5 Nov., 1914...Col. G. W. W. SAVILE (A.-A. and Q.-M.-G., acted as G.S.O. 1).
14 Jan., 1915...Lt.-Col. J. B. G. TULLOCH.
20 April, 1915...Lt.-Col. C. H. HARINGTON.
13 Sept., 1915...Lt.-Col. HON. A. M. HENLEY.
5 May, 1917...Lt.-Col. S. J. P. SCOBELL.

A.-A. and Q.-M.-G.

1 Oct., 1913...Major A. G. PRATT (D.-A.-A. and Q.-M.-G.).
5 Aug., 1914...Col. G. W. W. SAVILE.
3 June, 1915...Lt.-Col. W. K. LEGGE.
19 Dec., 1915...Major C. H. BINGHAM (acting).
18 Jan., 1916...Lt.-Col. W. K. LEGGE.
27 Oct., 1916...Major W. E. SCAFE (acting).
5 Dec., 1916...Lt.-Col. W. E. SCAFE.

B.G., R.A.

1 Jan., 1913...*Br.-Gen. S. D. BROWNE.
5 Jan., 1915...Br.-Gen. C. T. CAULFIELD (sick, 12/3/16).
12 Mar., 1916...Lt.-Col. C. CLIFFORD (acting).
13 April, 1916...Br.-Gen. W. H. KAY (injured, 26/6/17).
27 June, 1917...Lt.-Col. HON. O. H. STANLEY (acting).
18 July, 1917...Br.-Gen. A. B. FORMAN.

C.R.E.

8 Dec., 1912...Lt.-Col. A. E. BINGHAM.
3 Nov., 1914...Lt.-Col. R. B. HEYWOOD.
26 July, 1915...Major F. G. HOWARD (acting).
3 Aug., 1915...Lt.-Col. F. G. HOWARD (killed, 19/10/15).
19 Oct., 1915...Major C. M. CARPENTER (acting).
27 Oct., 1915...Lt.-Col. T. E. KELSALL.
8 July, 1917...Major O. G. D. JONES (acting).
19 July, 1917...Lt.-Col. D. OGILVY.

*Br.-Gen. on 5 August, 1914.

146th BDE.
(I. W. Riding)

25 Nov., '13...*Br.-Gen. F. A. MacFarlan.
20 Dec., '15...Lt.-Col. W. K. Legge (acting).
17 Jan., '16...Br.-Gen. M. D. Goring-Jones.
18 Oct., '17...Br.-Gen. G. A. P. Rennie.

147th BDE.
(II. W. Riding)

11 May, '12...*Br.-Gen. E. F. Brereton.
13 Sept., '16...Br.-Gen. C. G. Lewes.
2 Sept., '18...Br.-Gen. H. H. S. Morant.

148th BDE.
(III. W. Riding)

1 April, '12...*Br.-Gen. R. Dawson.
7 June, '16...Br.-Gen. R. L. Adlercron.
24 Oct., '17...Br.-Gen. L. F. Green-Wilkinson.

*Br.-Gen. on 5 August, 1914.

GENERAL NOTES

West Riding Hy. Bty., R.G.A. (4, 4.7-inch guns), was ordered to mobilize at York on 4/8/14. The Hy. Bty. moved to Hedon on 16/8/14, received its orders to serve in France on 6/4/15, disembkd. at le Havre on 17/4/15, and joined VIII. Bde., II. Group, H.A.R., on 24/4/15. The Hy. Bty. returned to 49th Div. on 13/5/15 and served with the Div. until 28/6/15, when the Hy. Bty. joined VIII. Bde., R.G.A.

1/West Riding Fd. Coy., R.E. (from Sheffield), joined the 29th Division at Kineton on 6/2/15, and the Fd. Coy. served with the 29th Div. throughout the Great War. (On 1/2/17 the 1/W. Rid. Fd. Coy. was numbered 455th Coy.)

The following Units also served with the 49th Division :—

ARTILLERY :—**518 (H.) Bty., R.F.A.**—See note 31.

M.G. UNIT :—**254th M.G. Coy.**—See notes 43 and 45.

OTHER UNITS :—**W. Riding (later 49th) Sanitary Section,** mobilized at York on 1/4/15, and disembkd. with the Div. at le Havre on 14/4/15. It left the Div. on 2/4/17, on allotment to an XI. Corps Sanitary Area..
W. Riding (later 49th) Divnl. Ambce. Workshop, left Grove Park for Bulford on 10/4/15, embkd. at Southampton on 16/4/15, disembkd. at Rouen on 17/4/15, and joined the Div. on 21/4/15. On 4/4/16 the Unit was absorbed by the Supply Column.

On 30/1/18 the reorganization of the 49th Division on a 9-battalion basis was completed ; and by 22/2/18 the pioneer battalion (19/L.F.) had been reorganized on a 3-company basis.

49TH[1] (WEST RIDING) DIVISION

ORDER OF BATTLE, 1915-1918

Dates	INFANTRY		Mounted Troops	ARTILLERY						Engineers	Signal Service	Pioneers	M.G. Units	Field Ambu-lances	Mobile Vety. Secn.	Divnl. Emplnt. Coy.	Divnl. Train
				Field Artillery			Trench Mortar B'ties.		Divnl. Ammn. Coln.								
	Brigades	Battalions and attached Units		Brigades	Batteries	Bde. Ammn. Colns.	Medium	Heavy		Field Cos.	Divnl. Signal Coy.						
1915 April (France)	I W. Riding[2] II W. Riding[3] III W. Riding[4]	5/W. York., 6/W. York., 7/W. York., 8/W. York. 4/Duke's, 5/Duke's, 6/Duke's, 7/Duke's. 4/K.O.Y.L.I., 5/K.O.Y.L.I., 4/Y. and L., 5/Y. and L.	C Sqdn., 1/York. Hsrs.;[5] 1/W. Riding Divnl. Cyclist Coy.[6]	I W. Riding[7]... II W. Riding[8] III W. Riding[9] IV W. Riding (H.)[10]	1/W. Rid., 2/W. Rid., 3/W. Rid. 4/W. Rid., 5/W. Rid., 6/W. Rid. 7/W. Rid., 8/W. Rid., 9/W. Rid. 10/W. Rid. (H.), 11/W. Rid. (H.)	I W. Riding II W. Riding III W. Riding IV W. Riding (H.)	...	...	W. Riding[11] D.A.C.	2/W. Riding[12]	W. Riding[13]	...	...	1/W. Riding[14] 2/W. Riding[14] 3/W. Riding[14]	1/W. Riding[15]	...	1/W. Rid.[16]
1915 September (France)	146th[17] (I W. Riding) 147th[17] (II W. Riding) 148th[17] (III W. Riding)	5/W. York., 6/W. York., 7/W. York., 8/W. York. 4/Duke's, 5/Duke's, 6/Duke's, 7/Duke's. 4/K.O.Y.L.I., 5/K.O.Y.L.I., 4/Y. and L., 5/Y. and L.	C Sqdn., 1/York. Hsrs.;[18] 1/W. Riding Divnl. Cyclist Coy.[19]	I W. Riding[20] II W. Riding[21] III W. Riding[22] IV W. Riding[23] (H.)	1/W. Rid., 2/W. Rid., 3/W. Rid. 4/W. Rid., 5/W. Rid., 6/W. Rid. 7/W. Rid., 8/W. Rid., 9/W. Rid. 10/W. Rid. (H.), 11/W. Rid. (H.)	I W. Riding II W. Riding III W. Riding IV W. Riding (H.)	...	...	49th D.A.C. (W. Riding)	57th[24] 2/W. Riding 2/1/W. Riding[25]	49th (W. Rid.)	3/Mon. (P.)[26]	...	1/W. Riding 2/W. Riding 3/W. Riding	1/W. Riding	...	49th (W. Rid.)
1916 June (France)	146th........ 147th........ 148th........	5/W. York., 6/W. York., 7/W. York., 8/W. York.; 146th Bde. M.G. Coy.;[27] 146th T.M. Bty.[28] 4/Duke's, 5/Duke's, 6/Duke's, 7/Duke's; 147th Bde. M.G. Coy.;[27] 147th T.M. Bty.[28] 4/K.O.Y.L.I., 5/K.O.Y.L.I., 4/Y. and L., 5/Y. and L.; 148th Bde. M.G. Coy.;[27] 148th T.M. Bty.[28]	...	CCXLV[29] (I. W. Riding) CCXLVI[30] (II W. Riding) CCXLVII[31] (III W. Riding) CCXLVIII[32] (IV W. Riding)	A, B, C; D (H.) A, B, C; D (H.) A, B, C; D (H.) A, B, C	...[33]	X.49[34] Y.49[34] Z.49[34]	V.49[35] W.49[35]	49th D.A.C.[33]	57th 2/W. Riding 2/1/W. Riding	49th	19/L.F. (P.)[36]	...	1/W. Riding 2/W. Riding 3/W. Riding	1/W. Riding	...	49th
1917 June (France)	146th........ 147th........ 148th........	5/W. York., 6/W. York., 7/W. York., 8/W. York.;[37] 146th M.G. Coy.;[45] 146th T.M. Bty. 4/Duke's, 5/Duke's,[38] 6/Duke's, 7/Duke's; 147th M.G. Coy.;[45] 147th T.M. Bty. 4/K.O.Y.L.I., 5/K.O.Y.L.I.,[39] 4/Y. and L., 5/Y. and L.; 148th M.G. Coy.;[45] 148th T.M. Bty.	...	CCXLV[29] .... CCXLVI[30] ...	A, B, C; D (H.) A, B, C; D (H.)	...	X.49 Y.49 Z.49[40]	V.49[41]	49th D.A.C.	57th 456th[42] (2/W. Rid.) 458th[42] (2/1/W. Riding)	49th	19/L.F. (P.)	199th M.G.[43] Coy.	1/W. Riding 2/W. Riding 3/W. Riding	1/W. Riding	243rd[44]	49th
1918 March (France)	146th........ 147th........ 148th........	5/W. York., 6/W. York., 7/W. York.; 146th T.M. Bty. 4/Duke's, 6/Duke's, 7/Duke's; 147th T.M. Bty. 4/K.O.Y.L.I., 4/Y. and L., 5/Y. and L.; 148th T.M. Bty.	...	CCXLV........ CCXLVI......	A, B, C; D (H.) A, B, C; D (H.)	...	X.49 Y.49	...	49th D.A.C.	57th 456th 458th	49th	19/L.F. (P.)	No. 49[45] Bn., M.G.C.	1/W. Riding 2/W. Riding 3/W. Riding	1/W. Riding	243rd	49th

NOTES

1 The 1st West Riding Div. was designated 49th (West Riding) Div. on 12/5/15. (Authy. W.O. letter 40/W.O./2481 (A.G.1.) of 7/5/15.)

2 The Bns. came from York, Bradford, and Leeds (2).

3 The Bns. came from Halifax, Huddersfield, Skipton in Craven, and Milnsbridge.

4 The Bns. came from Wakefield, Doncaster, Sheffield, and Rotherham.

5 The Sqdn. joined the Div. during concentration. It disembkd. at le Havre on 16/4/15.

6 The Coy. was formed by the Div. during concentration. It disembkd. at le Havre on 14/4/15.

7 The Bties. were at Leeds (2) and Bramley. The 15-pdr. Mk. I guns were exchanged on 7/4/15 for 15-pdr. Mk. IV., B.L.C., from 1st London Div.

8 The Bties. were at Bradford, Halifax, and Heckmondwike. The 15-pdrs., Mk. I, were exchanged before embkn. for 15-pdrs., Mk. IV, B.L.C.

9 The Bde. was concentrated at Norfolk Bks., Sheffield. The 15-pdrs., Mk. I, were exchanged before embkn. for 15-pdrs., Mk. IV., B.L.C.

10 The Bties. (4, 5-inch. Hows. each) were at Otley and Ilkley, and the B.A.C. was at Burley.

11 The D.A.C. was formed after mobilization. On 9/4/15 it moved from Sheffield to Blackheath to complete its own mobilization. The D.A.C. disembkd. at le Havre on 16/4/15.

12 The Fd. Coy. came from Sheffield.

13 H.Q. and No. 1 Sec. were at Sheffield.

14 The Fd. Ambces. came from Leeds (2) and Sheffield.

15 Formed after the outbreak of War; it joined the Div. in the concentration area, and it disembkd. at le Havre on 17/4 15.

16 Formed from W. Rid. Divnl. T. and S. Coln., which had Companies at York and Leeds (3). The Train disembkd. at le Havre on 14/4/15. The Cos. were numbered 463, 464, 465, and 466 Cos., A.S.C.

17 The Inf. Bdes. were designated 146th, 147th, and 149th on 12/5/15.

18 The Sqdn. joined XVII Corps Cav. Regt. on 8/5/16.

19 The Cyclist Coy. joined X Corps Cyclist Bn. on 26/5/16.

20 On 25 and 26/10/15 the Bties. were rearmed with 4, 18-pdrs. each. On 3/4/16 the Bde. was numbered CCXLV and the Bties. were lettered A, B, and C; and on 17 and 18/4/16 D Bty. (18-pdrs.) arrived. By 21/5/16 the Bde. was reorganized: C was transferred to CCXLVIII; D became C/CCXLV; and 11/W. Rid. (How.) Bty. joined from CCXLVIII and became D (H.)/CCXLV.

21 On 20/10/15 the Bties. were rearmed with 4, 18-pdrs. each. D Bty. (18-pdrs.) was formed on 16/4/16; and on 1/5/16 the Bde. was numbered CCXLVI; 5/W. Rid. Bty. was transferred to CCXLVIII, and 4/W. Rid. Bty. became A, 6/W. Rid. Bty. became B, and D became C; and 10/W. Rid. (How.) Bty. joined from CCXLVIII and became D (H.)/CCXLVI.

22 On 21/10/15 the Bties. were rearmed with 4, 18-pdrs. each. D Bty. (18-pdrs.) was formed on 19/4/16. The Bde. was numbered CCXLVII on 13/5/16; the old bties. were lettered A, B, and C; D was transferred to CCXLVIII; and D (H.)/CCXLVIII joined the Bde. and became D (H.)/CCXLVII.

23 Bties. were rearmed with 4, 4.5-inch Hows. each between 4–31/1/16. D (H.)/CLXIV (4.5 H.)—from 32nd Div.—joined on 16/2/16 and became D (H.)/IV. W.R. Bde. On 1/5/16 the Bde. was numbered CCXLVIII, and by 21/5/16 it was reorganized: 10/W. Rid. (H.) Bty. went to CCXLVI as D (H.)/CCXLVI; 11/W. Rid. (H.) Bty. went to CCXLV as D (H.)/CCXLV; and D (H.) went to CCXLVII as D (H.)/CCXLVII. At the same time C/CCXLV joined and became A/CCXLVIII; 5/W. Rid. Bty./CCXLVI joined and became B/CCXLVIII; and D/CCXLVII joined and became C/CCXLVIII.

24 The Coy. went to France with the 3rd Div. in Aug., '14. It was attached to the 46th (N. Mid.) Div. from 7/4–10/7/15, on which date it was transferred to the 49th Div.

25 Formed after the outbreak of war. The Coy. disembkd. at le Havre on 21/6/15, and it joined the Division on 23/6/15.

26 Joined on 2/9/15 from the 28th Div., and became Divnl. Pioneers on 18/9/15. The Bn. was transferred to G.H.Q. Troops on 9/8/16. The Bn. was broken up for drafts by 31/8/16.

27 The M.G. Cos. were formed: 146th on 27/1/16; 147th on 26/1/16; and 148th on 6/2/16.

28 The T.M. Bties. were formed on 12/6/16, by the amalgamation of Nos. 1 and 2 T.M. Bties. in each Bde.

29 Bde. was reorganized on 18/10/16: C was broken up to make A and B up to 6 guns each; A/CCXLVIII (originally C/CCXLV) rejoined and became C/CCXLV, and it was made up to 6 guns by R. Sec. of C/CCXLVIII. On 8/1/17 D (H.) was completed to 6 hows. by R. Sec. of B (H.)/CCXLVII.

30 Bde. was reorganized on 18/10/16: C was broken up to make A and B up to 6 guns each; B/CCXLVIII rejoined and became C/CCXLVI, and it was made up to 6 guns by L. Sec. of C/CCXLVIII. On 8/1/17 D (H.) was completed to 6 hows. by L. Sec. of B (H.)/CCXLVII.

31 Bde. was reorganized between 18–29/10/16; on 18/10/16 B was broken up to complete A and C to 6 guns each; on 29/10/16, 518(H.) joined from England, and on 4/12/16 it became B (H.); and on 8/1/17 B (H.) was broken up, the R. Sec. went to D (H.)/CCXLV, and the L. Sec. to D (H.)/CCXLVI. On 1/1/17 A and 1 Sec. D (H.) went to CL A.F.A. Bde. (from 30th Div.), and C and 1 Sec. D (H.) went to CCXXXII A.F.A. Bde. (from 46th Div.); and on 28/2/17 the Bde. ceased to exist.

32 Bde. was broken up on 18/10/16: A and R. Sec. of C went to CCXLV, and B and L. Sec. of C went to CCXLVI.

33 On 19/5/16 the B.A.C.'s were abolished and the D.A.C. was reorganized.

34 34, 37, and 48 T.M. Bties. were with the Div. from Dec., 1915, until the formation of X, Y, and Z T.M. Bties. by 4/4/16.

35 V was formed on 18/4/16 and W on 17/5/16. V absorbed W by 7/6/17.

36 Joined on 7/8/16 from 32nd Div.

37 On 30/1/18 the Bn. was transferred to 185th Bde., 62nd Div., and amalgamated with 2/8/W. York, becoming 8/W. York.

38 Part of Bn. was drafted in 147th Bde. on 29/1/18; and on 30/1/18 the remdr. joined 62nd Div. and amalgamated with 2/5/Duke's, becoming 5/Duke's in 186th Bde.

39 Part of Bn. was drafted to 4/K.O.Y.L.I. on 30/1/18, and remdr. amalgamated with 2/5/K.O.Y.L.I. in 62nd Div. and became 5/K.O.Y.L.I. in 187th Bde.

40 Between 4-9/2/18, Z was absorbed by X and Y.

41 Became X Corps H.T.M.B. on 7/2/18.

42 The Fd. Cos. were numbered on 1/2/17.

43 199th Coy., formed at Grantham, disembkd. at le Havre on 15/12/16, and joined the Div. on 19/12/16. 199th Coy. left the 49th Div. on 29/10/17 on transfer to 41st Div. It was replaced by 254th M.G. Coy., which disembkd. at le Havre on 15/11/17, and 254th Coy. joined 49th Div. on 26/11/17.

44 The Coy. was formed in the Div. by 16/6/17, and it was numbered by 7/7/17.

45 The Bn. was formed on 1/3/18. It comprised 146th, 147th, 148th, and 254th M.G. Cos. (see note 43).

49TH (WEST RIDING) DIVISION

MOBILIZATION, BATTLES, AND ENGAGEMENTS

The division—an existing T.F. division—was drawn from the West Riding of Yorkshire, with divisional headquarters in York. The three brigade headquarters were in York, Skipton, and Sheffield; and the twelve infantry battalions came from York, Bradford, Leeds (2), Halifax, Huddersfield, Skipton, Milnsbridge, Wakefield, Doncaster, Sheffield, and Rotherham.

In the artillery: the I. W. Riding Bde. was at Leeds, with an outlying battery at Bramley; the II. W. Riding Bde. had its batteries at Bradford, Halifax, and Heckmondwike; the III. W. Riding Bde. was concentrated in Norfolk Barracks, Sheffield; the IV. W. Riding (How.) Bde. had the batteries at Otley and Ilkley, and its ammunition column at Burley; and the W. Riding Heavy Battery (4, 4.7-inch guns) came from York.

The field companies and the H.Q. and No. 1 Sec. of the Signal Company all came from Sheffield; the three field ambulances were at Leeds (2) and Sheffield; and the four companies of the Divnl. T. and S. Coln. were at York and Leeds (3).

Towards the end of July, 1914, units left their headquarters for their annual training camps, but on the 3rd and 4th August units received orders to return to their headquarters, with the exception of the II. West Riding Infantry Brigade, which proceeded direct from Camp for immediate duty. On the 4th August mobilization was ordered, and the Great War had begun. Units then proceeded to their allotted war stations as part of the Central Force, Home Defence, and progressive training for war was carried out.

On the 31st March, 1915, the West Riding Division was informed that it had been selected to proceed to France as a complete division, and embarkation would take place in April.

On the 7th April a small advance party left Doncaster for le Havre, on the 12th April the division began to entrain so as to proceed to France, and, on the 13th, Divnl. H.Q. and the H.Q. of the Divnl. Artillery left Doncaster and crossed from Folkestone to Boulogne. The infantry of the division also crossed from Folkestone to Boulogne; but the mounted troops, R.A., R.E., signal company, field ambulances, sanitary section, veterinary section, and the train, all went from Southampton to le Havre. By the 19th April the division completed its concentration behind the Lys, in the area Estaires—Merville—Neuf Berquin.

The 49th Division served on the Western Front in France and Belgium throughout the Great War, and was engaged in the following operations:—

1915

9 May ... ... **Battle of Aubers Ridge** [Defensive Front, IV. Corps, First Army].

19 Dec. ... ... **First Phosgene Gas Attack** [VI. Corps, Second Army].

1916

BATTLES OF THE SOMME

1–3 July ... ...**Battle of Albert** [X. Corps, Fourth Army].

14–17 July ... ...**Battle of Bazentin Ridge** [X. Corps, Reserve Army].

23 July–18 Aug ; and 27 Aug.–3 Sept. ... ...**Battle of Pozières Ridge** [X. Corps, until 24/7 ; then II. Corps, Reserve Army].

15–22 Sept. ... ...**Battle of Flers-Courcelette** [II. Corps, Reserve Army].

1917

12 July–23 Sept. ... ...**Operations on the Flanders Coast** [XV. Corps, Fourth Army].

BATTLES OF YPRES

9 Oct. ... ...**Battle of Poelcappelle** [II. Anzac Corps, Second Army].

1918

BATTLES OF THE LYS

10 and 11 April ... ...**Battle of Estaires** (147th Bde.) [XV. Corps, First Army].

10 and 11 April ... ...**Battle of Messines** (148th Bde.) [IX. Corps, Second Army].

13–15 April ... ...**Battle of Bailleul** [IX. Corps, Second Army].

13 and 14 April ... ...**Defence of Neuve Eglise** (148th Bde.).

17–19 April ... ...**First Battle of Kemmel Ridge** [IX. Corps, Second Army ; 146th Bde. under XXII.].

25 and 26 April ... ...**Second Battle of Kemmel Ridge** [XXII. Corps, Second Army].

29 April ... ...**Battle of the Scherpenberg** [XXII. Corps, Second Army].

THE ADVANCE TO VICTORY

10–12 Oct. ... ...**Pursuit to the Selle** [Cdn. Corps, First Army].

THE FINAL ADVANCE IN PICARDY

17 and 18 Oct. ... ...**Battle of the Selle** [XXII. Corps, First Army].

1 and 2 Nov. ... ...**Battle of Valenciennes** [XXII. Corps, First Army].

At the end of the Battle of Valenciennes the 49th Division was relieved in the front line. On the 5th November the division moved back to the north of Douai and was transferred to the VIII. Corps, and it was still resting on the 11th November. The division did not proceed to the Rhine but remained in the Douai area. Here, on the 16th December, the 49th Division was inspected, on a ceremonial parade, by Lieut.-General Sir A. J. Godley, Commanding XXII. Corps.

Demobilization began in January, 1919, and went steadily on until the 30th March, by which date the division had been reduced to cadre. The division was re-formed in England in 1920.

50TH (NORTHUMBRIAN) DIVISION

G.O.C.

1 March, 1912 ... ... Major-General B. BURTON.
9 April, 1915 ... ... Major-General SIR W. F. L. LINDSAY.
29 June, 1915 ... ... Major-General THE EARL OF CAVAN.
5 August, 1915 ... ... Major-General P. S. WILKINSON.
25 February, 1918 ... ... Br.-Gen. C. COFFIN, V.C. (tempy.).
17 March, 1918 ... ... Br.-Gen. A. U. STOCKLEY (acting).
23 March, 1918 ... ... Major-General H. C. JACKSON.

G.S.O. 1.

16 Mar., 1912...Major L. HUME-SPRY (G.S.O. 2).
5 Aug., 1914...Lt.-Col. L. HUME-SPRY.
10 May, 1915...Lt.-Col. G. V. HORDERN.
29 Jan., 1916...Lt.-Col. A. G. STUART (killed, 4/6/16).
4 June, 1916...Major H. W. B. THORP (acting).
12 June, 1916...Lt.-Col. D. FORSTER (wounded, 17/6/16).
18 June, 1916...Major H. W. B. THORP (acting).
27 June, 1916...Lt.-Col. H. KARSLAKE.
17 Sept., 1917...Lt.-Col. E. C. ANSTEY (invalided, 13/10/18).
14 Oct., 1918...Major A. F. MILLER (acting).
20 Oct., 1918...Lt.-Col. A. K. GRANT.

A.-A. and Q.-M.-G.

1 April, 1912...Capt. A. W. B. WALLACE (D.-A.-A. and Q.-M.-G.).
5 Jan., 1915...Col. C. M. CARTWRIGHT.
25 Feb., 1918...Lt.-Col. A. C. H. DUKE.

B.-G., R.A.

1 Oct., 1913...*Br.-Gen. A. H. HUSSEY.
12 Sept., 1914...Br.-Gen. C. G. HENSHAW.
25 Dec., 1915...Br.-Gen. W. A. ROBINSON (invalided, 21/5/16).
21 May, 1916...Lt.-Col. A. U. STOCKLEY (acting).
20 June, 1916...Br.-Gen. A. U. STOCKLEY.
17 Mar., 1918...Lt.-Col. F. B. MOSS-BLUNDELL (acting).
24 Mar., 1918...Br.-Gen. A. U. STOCKLEY (invalided, 29/3/18).
1 April, 1918...Br.-Gen. W. STIRLING.

C.R.E.

23 May, 1907...Col. F. S. CRAWF[illegible].
16 April, 1915...Lt.-Col. J. E. MCPHERSON.
16 July, 1915...Lt.-Col. C. W. SINGER.
23 Dec., 1916...Major E. C. HENDERSON (tempy.).
25 Mar., 1917...Lt.-Col. C. W. SINGER.
4 April, 1917...Major J. A. MCQUEEN (acting).
9 April, 1917...Lt.-Col. H. E. F. RATHBONE.
5 Feb., 1918...Lt.-Col. J. A. MCQUEEN.
24 June, 1918...Major J. MCCLELLAN (acting).
30 July, 1918...Lt.-Col. P. DE H. HALL.

*Br.-Gen. on 5 August, 1914.

149th BDE.
(Northumberland)

3 July, '11...*Br.-Gen. J. F. RIDDELL (killed, 26/4/15).
26 April, '15...Lt.-Col. A. J. FOSTER (acting).
26 April, '15...Lt.-Col. A. H. COLES (acting).
27 April, '15...Br.-Gen. G. P. T. FEILDING.
29 June, '15...Br.-Gen. H. F. H. CLIFFORD (killed, 11/9/16).
11 Sept., '16...Lt.-Col. C. TURNER (acting).
14 Sept., '16...Br.-Gen. R. M. OVENS.
6 Mar., '17...Lt.-Col. G. SCOTT-JACKSON (acting).
10 Mar., '17...Br.-Gen. H. C. REES (invalided, 17/8/17).
17 Aug., '17...Lt.-Col. G. SCOTT-JACKSON (acting).
2 Oct., '17...Br.-Gen. E. P. A. RIDDELL (wounded, 27/5/18).
27 May, '18...Major I. M. TWEEDY (acting).
3 June, '18...Lt.-Col. L. D. SCOTT (acting).
7 June, '18...Br.-Gen. P. M. ROBINSON.

150th BDE.
(York. and Durham)

18 June, '11...*Br.-Gen. J. E. BUSH (invalided, 25/1/16).
24 Jan., '16...Lt.-Col. G. O. SPENCE (acting).
4 Feb., '16...Br.-Gen. B. G. PRICE.
25 Feb., '18...Lt.-Col. J. A. R. THOMSON (acting).
27 Feb., '18...Br.-Gen. H. C. REES (captured, 27/5/18).

[The Bde. H.Q. ceased to exist (temporarily) on 27/5/18 ; and it was re-formed on 31/5/18.]

1 June, '18...Br.-Gen. F. J. MARSHALL.
13 July, '18...Br.-Gen. C. P. HEYWOOD.
29 Sept., '18...Br.-Gen. G. ROLLO.

151st BDE.
(Durham Light Infantry)

30 Mar., '13...*Br.-Gen. J. W. SEARS.
16 Dec., '14...Br.-Gen. H. MARTIN.
4 July, '15...Br.-Gen. J. S. M. SHEA.
16 May, '16...Br.-Gen. P. T. WESTMORLAND.
6 Sept., '16...Br.-Gen. N. J. G. CAMERON.
20 Oct., '17...Br.-Gen. C. T. MARTIN (killed, 27/5/18).
27 May, '18...Lt.-Col. F. WALTON (acting).
7 June, '18...Br.-Gen. R. E. SUGDEN.

*Br.-Gen. on 5 August, 1914.

GENERAL NOTES

After the German onslaught on the 27th May, 1918 (Battle of the Aisne), certain regroupings took place at once in the Division :—

(1). On the **29th May**, Lt.-Col. N. W. Stead's Comp. Bn. (950) was formed ; and on **30th May** it joined 74th Bde., 8th Div., and served until the **8th June**, when the Bn. was broken up and the personnel then rejoined the Bde. Bns. in Br.-Gen. F. J. Marshall's Force.

(2). On the **2nd June**, a Comp. Bn. (1,000) was formed from the 50th Div., it was then divided into two Bns. and placed under Br.-Gen. F. J. Marshall (150th Inf. Bde.). On the **3rd June**, Marshall's Force was increased by another Bn. and the three Bns. were then designated 149th Inf. Bn. (Lt.-Col. L. D. Scott), 150th Inf. Bn. (Major A. C. Barnes), and 151st Inf. Bn. (Lt.-Col. F. Walton). On the **5th June**, Marshall's Force joined the 19th Div., and between **6–19th June** Marshall's Force held part of the 19th Div. Front. On relief it rejoined the 50th Division.

(3). On the **23rd June**, the 50th Comp. Bde. (Br.-Gen. P. M. Robinson) was formed. It consisted of 149th, 150th, and 151st Inf. Bde. Bns. and one T.M. Bty.

(4). On the **25th June**, the 50th Comp. Div. (50th Comp. Bde. and 25th Div. Comp. Bde.) was formed, and was designated " Jackson's Force." On the **3rd July**, " Jackson's Force " moved behind the British Front (into XXII. Corps area) ; and, on the **7th July**, the 25th Comp. Bde. was broken up.

MACHINE GUNS :—On the **2nd June**, No. 50 Bn., M.G.C., formed an Inf. Coy. (5 officers, 180 m. grs., and three Vickers guns, and 2 offrs. and 60 o.r. from the 149th Inf. Bde.), and the Coy. was attached to the 19th Div. On the **4th June**, 13 more Vickers guns were sent up to the Coy.

On the **19th June**, the Coy. rejoined No. 50 Bn., M.G.C.

On the **15th July**, the 50th Division (then in the Dieppe area of the L. of C.) was reduced to training cadre, the Division was reconstituted on the **16th July**, and on the **18th July**, the nine cadre Bns. (see notes 49–51) left the 50th Division. On the **1st October**, the 50th Division went back into the line (XIII. Corps).

50th Division Artillery (June–October, 1918).

All June, 1918, was spent in reorganizing and re-equipping ; and during July the divnl. artillery was training, calibrating, and preparing to go into the line. On the 1st August, the 50th Div. Artillery went into the line under 18th Div. (III. Corps) ; on 6/8/18, it was transferred to 58th Div. (Battle of Amiens) ; and on 13/8/18, it was transferred to 47th Div. (III. Corps). From 25/8/18–1/9/18, the 50th Div. Arty. served with 3rd Aus. Div., Aus. Corps (Battle of Albert). From 5–10/9/18, the 50th Div. Arty. was with the 11th Div. (XXII. Corps). Between 22/9–2/10/18, CCLI. was under 4th Cdn. Div., Cdn. Corps (Battle of the Canal du Nord) ; and from 23/9–3/10/18, CCL. was under 56th Div., XIII. Corps (Battle of the Canal du Nord). On 6 and 7/10/18 the 50th Div. Arty. took over the line and covered 12th Div. (VIII. Corps). On 12/10/18, the 50th Div. Arty. was relieved ; on 20/10/18, it rejoined 50th Div. at Maretz, and was then engaged in the Battle of the Selle.

Northumbrian (N. Riding) Heavy Battery, R.G.A. (4, 4.7-inch), came from Middlesbrough. On 5/8/14, the Hy. Bty. moved to Monkseaton, and on **1/9/14**, to Newcastle. On 12/4/15 embkn. orders were received ; the Hy. Bty. entrained on 19/4/15, and disembkd. at le Havre on 21/4/15. The Hy. Bty. was transferred on 6/5/15 from 50th Division to XIII. Bde., R.G.A.

2/Northumbrian Field Ambulance came from Darlington. On 21/12/14 this Fd. Ambce. joined the 28th Division at Winchester, and in January, 1915, it went to France with the 28th Division. The Fd. Ambce. served with the 28th Division throughout the Great War and until 1923. It was designated 86th Field Ambulance.

The following Formation and Units served with the 50th Division :—

25th (Div.) Comp. Bde. (11/L.F., 6/Ches., 8/Bord., 4/S. Staffs., 9/L.N.L., with 7th, 74th, 75th, Lt. T.M. Bties., and 106th Fd. Coy., R.E., 75th Bde. Signal Sec., 6/S.W.B. (P.), and 75th Fd. Ambce.), which had been formed on the 22nd June, served with the 50th Div. from 25th June until 7th July, 1918, on which day the 25th Comp. Bde. was broken up at Huppy.

OTHER UNITS :—**Northumbrian (later 50th) Sanitary Section**, was formed after mobn. It went to France with the Division, and disembkd. at le Havre on 19/4/15. On 3/4/17 the Sany. Sec. took over duties in the Fourth Army area.

Northumbrian (later 50th Divnl.) Ambce. Workshop, was mobd. at Grove Park on 3-8/4/15. The unit went from Avonmouth to le Havre (via Southampton) on 17-19/4/15, and it joined the 50th Div. at Hazebrouck on 23/4/15. On 3/4/16 the unit was absorbed by the Divnl. T. and S. Coln.

On 12/2/18 the reorganization of the 50th Division on a 9-battalion basis was completed ; and on 23/2/18 the pioneer battalion (7/D.L.I.) was reorganized on a 3-company basis.

50TH[1] (NORTHUMBRIAN) DIVISION

ORDER OF BATTLE, 1915-1918

Dates	INFANTRY		Mounted Troops	ARTILLERY						Engineers	Signal Service	Pioneers	M.G. Units	Field Ambu-lances	Mobile Vety. Secn.	Divnl. Emplnt. Coy.	Divnl. Train
	Brigades	Battalions and attached Units		Field Artillery: Brigades	Field Artillery: Batteries	Field Artillery: Bde. Ammn. Colns.	Trench Mortar B'ties.: Medium	Trench Mortar B'ties.: Heavy	Divnl. Ammn. Coln.	Field Cos.	Divnl. Signal Coy.						
1915 April (France)	Northumber-land[2] York and Durham[3] Durham L.I.[4]	4/N.F., 5/N.F., 6/N.F., 7/N.F. 4/E. York., 4/York., 5/York., 5/D.L.I. 6/D.L.I., 7/D.L.I.,[5] 8/D.L.I., 9/D.L.I.	A Sqdn.,[6] 1/York. Hsrs. 1/ North'bn.[7] Cyclist Coy.	I North'bn.[8] II North'bn.[9] III North'bn[10] IV North'bn.[11] (H.)	1/North'd., 2/North'd., 3/North'd. 1/E. Rid., 2/E. Rid., 3/N. Rid. 1/Durham, 2/Durham, 3/Durham. 4/Durham (H.), 5/Durham (H.)	I North'bn. II North'bn. III North'bn. IV North'bn. (H.)	...	...	North'bn.[12] D.A.C.	2/ North'bn.[13]	North'bn.[14]	...	...	1/ North'bn.[15] 3/ North'bn.[16] 2/2/ North'bn.[17]	1/ North'bn.[18]	...	1/ North'bn.[19]
1915 September (France)	149th[20] (North'd.) 150th[20] (Y. and D.) 151st[20] (D.L.I.)	4/N.F., 5/N.F., 6/N.F., 7/N.F., 5/Bord.[21] 4/E. York., 4/York., 5/York., 5/D.L.I. 6/D.L.I., 8/D.L.I., 9/D.L.I., 5/L.N.L.[22]	A Sqdn.,[23] 1/York. Hsrs. 1/ North'bn.[24] Cyclist Coy.	I North'bn.[25] II North'bn.[26] III North'bn.[27] IV North'bn.[28] (H.)	1/North'd., 2/North'd., 3/North'd. 1/E. Rid., 2/E. Rid., 3/N. Rid. 1/Durham, 2/Durham, 3/Durham. 4/Durham (H.), 5/Durham (H.)	I North'bn. II North'bn. III North'bn. IV North'bn.	...	...	50th D.A.C. (North'bn.)	7th[29] 1/ North'bn.[30] 2/ North'bn.	50th (North'bn.)	7/D.L.I. (P.)[5]	...	1/ North'bn. 3/ North'bn. 2/2/ North'bn.	1/ North'bn.	...	50th (North'bn.)
1916 June (France)	149th ..... 150th 151st	4/N.F., 5/N.F., 6/N.F., 7/N.F.; 149th Bde. M.G. Coy.;[31] 149th T.M. Bty.[32] 4/E. York., 4/York., 5/York., 5/D.L.I.; 150th Bde. M.G. Coy.;[31] 150th T.M. Bty.[32] 5/Bord.,[21] 6/D.L.I., 8/D.L.I., 9/D.L.I.; 151st Bde. M.G. Coy.;[31] 151st T.M. Bty.[32]	...	CCL[33] (I North'bn.) CCLI[34] (II North'bn.) CCLII[35] (III North'bn.) CCLIII[36] (IV North'bn.)	A, B, C; D (H.) A, B, C; D (H.) A, B, C; D (H.) A, B, C.	...[37]	X.50[38] Y.50[38] Z.50[38]	V.50[39]	50th D.A.C.[37]	7th 1/North'bn. 2/North'bn.	50th	7/D.L.I. (P.)	...	1/ North'bn. 3/ North'bn. 2/2/ North'bn.	1/ North'bn.	...	50th

1917 June (France)	149th	4/N.F., 5/N.F., 6/N.F., 7/N.F.;[40] 149th M.G. Coy.;[53] 149th T.M. Bty.	...	CCL[33]	A, B, C; D (H.)	...	X.50 Y.50 Z.50[44]	V.50[45]	50th D.A.C.	7th 446th[46] (1/ North'bn.) 447th[46] (2/ North'bn.)	50th	7/D.L.I. (P.)	245th M.G. Coy.[47]	1/ North'bn. 3/ North'bn. 2/2/ North'bn.	1/ North'bn.	244th[48]	50th
	150th	4/E. York., 4/York., 5/York., 5/D.L.I.;[41] 150th M.G. Coy.;[53] 150th T.M. Bty.		CCLI[34]	A, B, C; D (H.)												
	151st	5/Bord.,[42] 6/D.L.I., 8/D.L.I., 9/D.L.I.;[43] 151st M.G. Coy.;[53] 151st T.M. Bty.															
1918 March (France)	149th	4/N.F.,[49] 5/N.F.,[49] 6/N.F.;[49] 149th T.M. Bty.	...	CCL	A, B, C; D (H.)	...	X.50 Y.50	...	50th D.A.C.	7th 446th 447th	50th	7/D.L.I. (P.)[52]	No. 50 Bn.,[53] M.G.C.	1/ North'bn. 3/ North'bn. 2/2/ North'bn.	1/ North'bn.	244th	50th
	150th	4/E. York.,[50] 4/York.,[50] 5/York.;[50] 150th T.M. Bty.		CCLI	A, B, C; D (H.)												
	151st	5/D.L.I.,[41];[51] 6/D.L.I.,[51] 8/D.L.I.;[51] 151st T.M. Bty.															
After reconstitution 1918 August (France)	149th	3/R.F.,[54] 13/B.W.,[55] 2/R.D.F.;[56] 149th T.M. Bty.	...	CCL	A, B, C; D (H.)	...	X.50 Y.50	...	50th D.A.C.	7th 446th 447th	50th	5/R. Ir. Regt.[63] (P.)	No. 50 Bn., M.G.C.	1/ North'bn. 3/ North'bn. 2/2/ North'bn.	1/ North'bn.	244th	50th
	150th	2/N.F.,[57] 7/Wilts.,[58] 2/R.M.F.;[59] 150th T.M. Bty.		CCLI	A, B, C; D (H.)												
	151st	6/R. Innis. F.,[60] 1/K.O.Y.L.I.,[61] 4/K.R.R.C.;[62] 151st T.M. Bty.															

NOTES

1 The 1st Northumbrian Div. was designated 50th (North'bn.) Div. on 14/5/15. (Authy. W.O. letter 40/W.O./2481 (A.G.1) of 7/5/15.)

2 The Bns. came from Hexham, Newcastle (2), and Alnwick.

3 The Bns. came from Hull, Northallerton, Scarborough, and Stockton.

4 The Bns. came from Bishop Auckland, Sunderland, Durham, and Gateshead.

5 The Bn. became Divnl. Pioneers on 16/11/15.

6 The Sqdn., then at Harlow, was ordered on 4/4/15 to join the North'bn. Div. It disembkd. at le Havre on 18/4/15.

7 The Coy. was formed in the Div. during concentration. It disembkd. at le Havre on 18/4/15.

8 The Bde. (15-pdrs.) was concentrated at Newcastle.

9 The Bties. (15-pdrs.) were at Hull (2) and Scarborough.

10 The Bties. (15-pdrs.) were at Seaham Harbour, Durham, and West Hartlepool.

11 The Bties. (5-inch Hows.) were at South Shields and Hebburn.

12 The D.A.C. was formed at Seaham Harbour on 20/11/14 from III and IV North'bn. Res. Bdes. It moved to Newcastle on 9/1/15, went to Willesden on 10/4/15 to complete for war, and disembkd. at le Havre on 23/4/15.

13 The Coy. came from Newcastle.

14 H.Q. and No. 1 Sec. came from Newcastle.

15 The Fd. Ambce. came from Newcastle.

16 The Fd. Ambce. came from Hull.

17 This reserve unit was raised after the outbreak of war; it joined the Div. in the concentration area, and it disembkd. at le Havre on 20/4/15.

18 Formed after the outbreak of War. It disembkd. at le Havre on 19/4/15.

19 Formed from North'bn. Divnl. T. and S. Coln., which had Cos. at Gateshead, Newcastle, Hull, and Sunderland. The Train disembkd. at le Havre on 17/4/15. The Cos. were numbered 467, 468, 469, and 470 Cos., A.S.C.

20 The Inf. Bdes. were designated 149th, 150th, and 151st on 14/5/15.

21 The Bn. reached France on 26/10/14 and was employed on L. of C. It joined the North'd. [149th] Bde. on 5/5/15; and the Bn. was transferred to the 151st Bde. on 20/12/15.

22 The Bn. was transferred on 11/6/15 to 151st Bde. from 16th Bde., 6th Div. On 21/12/15 the Bn. joined 26th Bde., 9th Div. (tempy.), and on 8/1/16 it was transferred to 166th Bde., 55th Div.

23 The Sqdn. joined XVII Corps Cavy. on 10/5/16.

24 The Cyclist Coy. joined V Corps Cyclist Bn. on 20/5/16.

25 Between 23-25/11/15 the Bties. were rearmed with 4, 18-pdrs. each. On 9/5/16 D Bty. (18-pdrs.) was completed. On 16/5/16 the Bde. was numbered CCL and the (old) Bties. were lettered A, B, and C; and D was transferred to CCLIII and became A/CCLIII. On 16/5/16, 4/Durh. (H.) Bty. joined from CCLIII and became D (H.)/CCL.

26 On 23/11/15 the Bties. were rearmed with 4, 18-pdrs. each. On 11/5/16 D Bty. (18-pdrs.) was completed. On 16/5/16 the Bde. was numbered CCLI and the (old) Bties. were lettered A, B, and C; and D was transferred to CCLIII and became B/CCLIII. On 16/5/16, 5/Durh. (H.) Bty. joined from CCLIII. and became D(H)/CCLI.

27 On 25/11/15 the Bties. were rearmed with 4, 18-pdrs. each. D Bty. (18-pdrs.) arrived by 30/4/16. On 16/5/16 the Bde. was numbered CCLII and the (old) Bties. were lettered A, B, and C.; and D was transferred to CCLIII and became C/CCLIII. On 16/5/16, D (H.)/LXI joined from CCLIII and became D (H.)/CCLII.

28 On 17/1/16 the Bties. were rearmed with 4, 4.5-inch Hows. each. On 21/2/16 D (H.) LXI joined from the Guards Div. On 16/5/16 the Bde. was numbered CCLIII and re-organized: 4/Durh. (H.) Bty. was transferred to CCL and became D (H.)/CCL; 5/Durh. (H.) Bty. became D (H.)/CCLI; and D (H.)/LXI became D (H.)/CCLII. D/CCL, D/CCLI, and D/CCLII (18-pdr. Bties.) joined CCLIII on 16/5/16 and became A, B, and C/CCLIII.

29 The Fd. Coy. joined on 17/6/15 from the 48th Div.

30 1/North'bn. Fd. Coy. joined the 28th Div. on 26/12/14 at Winchester, it disembkd. at le Havre on 19/1/15, and on 2/6/15 the Coy. was transferred back to the 50th Div.

31 The M.G. Cos. were formed: 150th on 1/2/16; and 149th and 151st on 6/2/16.

32 The Bde. T.M. Bties. were formed between 12-18/6/16 by the amalgamation of Nos. 1 and 2 T.M. Bties. in each Bde.

33 On 16/11/16 A and 1 Sec. C joined from CCLIII and made A, B, and C/CCL up to 6 guns each. On 16/1/17 R Sec. of D (H.)/CCLII joined and made D (H.)/CCL up to 6 hows.

34 On 16/11/16 B and 1 Sec. C joined from CCLIII and made A, B, and C/CCLI up to 6 guns each. On 16/1/17 L. Sec. of D (H.)/CCLII joined and made D (H.)/CCLI up to 6 hows.

35 The Bde. was reorganized on 16/11/16: R. Sec. of B completed A to 6 guns, and C completed B to 6 guns. On 16/1/17 D (H.) was split up and transferred: R. Sec. went to D (H.)/CCL; and L Sec. to D (H.)/CCLI. On 20/1/17 CCLII was broken up: A became C/CCXLII A.F.A. Bde.; and B became C/LXXII A.F.A. Bde.

36 On 16/11/16 CCLIII was broken up: A and 1 Sec. C went to CCL, and B and 1 Sec. C went to CCLI.

37 On 10/5/16 the B.A.C.'s were abolished and the D.A.C. was reorganized.

38 31, 29, and 23 T.M. Bties. became X, Y, and Z by 5/3/16.

39 V joined in July, 1916.

40 On 10/2/18 the Bn. was transferred to 42nd Div. as Pioneers; it joined on 12/2/18.

41 On 12/2/18 the Bn. was transferred to the 151st Bde.

42 On 12/2/18 the Bn. was transferred to 66th Div. as Pioneers; it joined on 13/2/18.

43 On 12/2/18 the Bn. was transferred to 62nd Div. as Pioneers.

44 Z was absorbed by X and Y by 1/3/18.

45 On 11/2/18 V.50 (with W/8) became V/VIII Corps H.T.M.B.

46 The Fd. Cos. were numbered on 3/2/17.

47 The Coy. joined on 30/7/17, from Grantham.

48 The D.E. Coy. was formed in the Div. by 9/6/17, and it was numbered by 30/6/17.

49 The 3 Bns. were reduced to cadre on 15/7/18, they moved to the Dieppe area (L. of C.) on 19/7/18, and on 16/8/18 the Bns. joined 118th Bde., 39th Div., at le Havre.

50 The 3 Bns. were reduced to cadre on 15/7/18, they moved to the Dieppe area (L. of C.) on 19/7/18, and on 16/8/18 the Bns. joined 116th Bde., 39th Div., at Cucq.

51 The 3 Bns. were reduced to cadre on 15/7/18, they moved to the Dieppe area (L. of C.) on 19/7/18, and on 16/8/18 the Bns. joined 117th Bde., 39th Div., at Rouen.

52 On 20/6/18 the Bn. was transferred (as Pioneers) to 8th Div.

53 The Bn. was formed on 1/3/18; it consisted of 149th, 150th, 151st, and 245th M.G. Cos.

RECONSTITUTED DIVISION

54 On 26/6/18 the Bn. was transferred from 85th Bde., 28th Div. (Macedonia) to B.E.F. (France); and on 15/7/18 the Bn. joined 149th Bde. at Martin Eglise.

55 The 13/B.W. (Scottish Horse Bn.) was transferred on 11/6/18 from 81st Bde., 27th Div. (Macedonia) to B.E.F. (France); and on 15/7/18 the Bn. joined 149th Bde. at Martin Eglise.

56 The Bn. went to France on 22/8/14 with 10th Bde., 4th Div.; it joined 48th Bde., 16th Div., on 16/11/16; it was reduced to cadre on 21/4/18; on 1/6/18 it joined 94th Bde., 31st Div.; on 6/6/18 it was re-formed and absorbed 7/R.D.F.; on 16/6/18 the Bn. was transferred to L. of C.; and on 15/7/18 it joined 149th Bde. at Martin Eglise.

57 On 21/6/18 the Bn. was transferred from 84th Bde., 28th Div. (Macedonia) to B.E.F. (France); and on 16/7/18 the Bn. joined 150th Bde. at Martin Eglise.

58 The Bn. served with the 79th Bde., 26th Div., in France (23/9/15—13/11/15) and in Macedonia (21/11/15—16/6/18); and on 15/7/18 the Bn. joined 150th Bde. at Martin Eglise.

59 The Bn. went to France on 14/8/14 with the 1st Gds. Bde., 1st Div.; the Bn. became Army Troops on 4/9/14; it was transferred to the 3rd Bde., 1st Div., on 9/11/14; it joined 48th Bde., 16th Div., on 3/2/18; it joined 94th Bde., 31st Div., on 31/5/18; the Bn. was re-formed and absorbed 6/R.M.F. on 6/6/18; it was transferred to L. of C. on 16/6/18; and on 15/7/18 the Bn. joined 150th Bde. at Martin Eglise.

60 The Bn. served with the 31st Bde., 10th Div. at Suvla (7/8/15—1/10/15); in Macedonia (16/10/15—18/9/17); in Egypt (disembkd. 21/9/17); and in Palestine (8/10/17—6/5/18). The Bn. was transferred to France (disembkd. at Marseille on 1/6/18); it joined 43rd Bde., 14th Div., on 7/6/18; it served with 103rd Bde., 34th Div. (18–28/6/18); it was transferred to L. of C. on 29/6/18; and on 16/7/18 the Bn. joined 151st Bde. at Martin Eglise.

61 On 20/6/18 the Bn. was transferred from 83rd Bde., 28th Div. (Macedonia) to B.E.F. (France); and on 15/7/18 the Bn. joined 151st Bde. at Martin Eglise.

62 On 12/6/18 the Bn. was transferred from 80th Bde., 27th Div. (Macedonia) to B.E.F. (France); and on 16/7/18 the Bn. joined 151st Bde. at Martin Eglise.

63 The Bn. served as the Pioneer Bn. of the 10th Div. at Suvla (landed, 7/8/15); in Macedonia (disembkd., 6/10/15); in Egypt (disembkd., 16/9/17); and in Palestine (2/10/17—1/4/18). On 3/4/18 the Pioneer Bn. joined 52nd Div., and it embkd. at Alexandria on 10/4/18, disembkd. at Marseille on 17/4/18, and left the 52nd Div. on 31/5/18 on transfer to L. of C. On 14/7/18 the Bn. joined 50th Div., as Pioneer Bn., at Martin Eglise.

50TH (NORTHUMBRIAN) DIVISION

MOBILIZATION, BATTLES, AND ENGAGEMENTS

The division—an existing Territorial Force division—was drawn from Northumberland, Durham, and the North and East Ridings of Yorkshire, with the divisional headquarters in the Castle at Richmond. The three brigade headquarters were at Newcastle, Malton, and Durham; and the twelve infantry battalions came from Alnwick, Newcastle (2), Hexham, Stockton, Northallerton, Scarborough, Hull, Gateshead, Sunderland, Durham, and Bishop Auckland. In the artillery: the I. Northumbrian Bde. was concentrated at Newcastle; the II. Northumbrian Bde. was at Hull, with an outlying battery at Scarborough; the III. Northumbrian Bde. was at Seaham Harbour, with batteries at Durham and West Hartlepool; the IV. Northumbrian (How.) Bde. was at South Shields, with a battery at Hebburn; and the Northumbrian (North Riding) Heavy Battery (4, 4.7-inch guns) came from Middlesbrough.

The field companies and the H.Q. and No. 1 Sec. of the Signal Company were all at Newcastle; the three field ambulances were at Newcastle, Darlington, and Hull; and the four companies of the Divisional T. and S. Column were at Newcastle, Gateshead, Sunderland, and Hull.

Towards the end of July, 1914, units went into their annual training camps. On the 3rd August they returned to their peace stations, and, on the 4th, orders to mobilize were received. The mobilized division then became part of the Central Force, Home Defence; it garrisoned the Tyne Defences and training for war was proceeded with.

Early in April, 1915, the 50th Division was informed that it would shortly be sent to France; embarkation orders were issued on the 5th, and on the 16th April the division began to entrain for the ports of embarkation (Southampton and Folkestone).

After crossing over to France, the 50th Division completed its concentration in the vicinity of Steenvoorde on the 23rd April. On the next day it went into action.

Throughout the Great War the 50th Division served on the Western Front in France and Belgium, and was engaged in the following operations:—

1915

BATTLES OF YPRES

24 April–3 May ... ...**Battle of St. Julien** [V. Corps, Second Army, until 28/4; then Plumer's Force].

11–13 May ... ...**Battle of Frezenberg Ridge** [V. Corps, Second Army].

24 and 25 May ... ...**Battle of Bellewaarde Ridge** [V. Corps, Second Army].

---

16 June ... ...**Bellewaarde** (149th Bde.) [V. Corps, Second Army].

1916

BATTLES OF THE SOMME

15–22 Sept. ... ...**Battle of Flers-Courcelette** [III. Corps, Fourth Army].

25–28 Sept. ... ...**Battle of Morval** [III. Corps, Fourth Army].

1–3 Oct. ... ...**Battle of the Transloy Ridges** [III. Corps, Fourth Army].

1917

BATTLES OF ARRAS

11–14 April ... ...**First Battle of the Scarpe** [XVIII. Corps until 11/4; then VII. Corps, Third Army].

13–15 April ... ...**Capture of Wancourt Ridge** [VII. Corps].

23 and 24 April... ...**Second Battle of the Scarpe** [VII. Corps, Third Army].

BATTLES OF YPRES

26 Oct.–9 Nov. ... ...**Second Battle of Passchendaele** [XIV. Corps, until 29/10; then XIX. Corps, Fifth Army].

1918

BATTLES OF THE SOMME

21–23 March ... ...**Battle of St. Quentin** [Fifth Army Reserve on 21/3; then XIX. Corps, Fifth Army].

23 March ... ...**Actions at the Somme Crossings** [XIX. Corps].

26 and 27 March ...**Battle of Rosières** [XIX. Corps, Fifth Army].

BATTLES OF THE LYS

9–11 April ... ...**Battle of Estaires** [XV. Corps, First Army].

12 April ... ...**Battle of Hazebrouck** [XV. Corps, First Army].

On Friday, 26th April, the division entrained for the Aisne Front. On Sunday, 28th April, it completed detrainment and joined the IX. Corps, which was under the Sixth (French) Army. On Monday, 6th May, the 50th Division moved into the line and took over the Beaurieux Sector from the 51st (French) Division.

27 May–6 June ... ...**Battle of the Aisne** [IX. Corps, Sixth (French) Army].

Between the 3rd and 5th July the 50th Division returned to the British Zone, and by Sunday, 14th July, the division was concentrated in the Dieppe area, where it was reorganized (see Order of Battle Table).

THE ADVANCE TO VICTORY

BATTLES OF THE HINDENBURG LINE

1 Oct. ... ...**Battle of the St. Quentin Canal** [XIII. Corps, Fourth Army].

3–5 Oct. ... ...**Battle of the Beaurevoir Line** [XIII. Corps, Fourth Army].

8 Oct. ... ...**Battle of Cambrai** [XIII. Corps, Fourth Army].

---

11 and 12 Oct. ... ...**Pursuit to the Selle** [XIII. Corps, Fourth Army].

THE FINAL ADVANCE IN PICARDY

17 and 18 Oct. ... ...**Battle of the Selle** [XIII. Corps, Fourth Army].

4 Nov. ... ...**Battle of the Sambre** [XIII Corps, Fourth Army].

After crossing the Sambre, the 50th Division remained in the line until it was relieved on the 10th November. By this date it had fought its way forward to Solre le Château. On the 11th November the division was in billets between Flourcies and Monceau (astride the Maubeuge–Avesnes road). On the 2nd December H.M. the King, accompanied by Major-General Jackson, visited le Catelet, where the division had crossed the St. Quentin Canal in October; and on the 3rd His Majesty visited the division in its billeting area. In the middle of the month the division moved back to billets in the le Quesnoy area.

Demobilization started in December, and continued steadily until units were reduced to cadre strength. On Wednesday, 19th March, 1919, the 50th Division was reduced to cadre and ceased to exist in France. In April, 1920, the division was formed again in England under its old title of Northumbrian Division.

51st (HIGHLAND) DIVISION

G.O.C.

3 March, 1914 ... ... Major-General C. J. MACKENZIE.
23 August, 1914... ... ... Br.-Gen. D. A. MACFARLANE (acting).
27 August, 1914... ... ... Major-General R. BANNATINE-ALLASON.
24 September, 1915 ... ... Major-General G. M. HARPER.
11 March, 1918 ... ... Br.-Gen. L. C. L. OLDFIELD (acting).
16 March, 1918 ... ... Major-General G. T. C. CARTER-CAMPBELL.

G.S.O. 1.

1 April, 1912...Major A. J. G. MOIR (G.S.O. 2).
5 Aug., 1914...Lt.-Col. A. J. G. MOIR.
5 May, 1915...Lt.-Col. G. N. CORY.
19 June, 1915...Lt.-Col. I. STEWART.
11 Nov., 1916...Lt.-Col. J. K. DICK-CUNYNGHAM.
7 April, 1918...Col. A SYMONS.
30 May, 1918...Lt.-Col. R. S. McCLINTOCK.

A.-A. and Q.-M.-G.

22 June, 1912...Capt. W. N. NICHOLSON (D.-A.-A. and Q.-M.-G.).
6 Aug., 1914...Col. G. M. V. HUNT.
9 Dec., 1914...Major SIR W. K. JENNER, BT. (acting).
19 Dec., 1914...Capt. W. N. NICHOLSON (acting).
30 Dec., 1914...Lt.-Col. C. W. GARTSIDE-SPAIGHT.
14 Mar., 1915...Major J. L. WESTON (acting).
20 Mar., 1915...Col. M. W. J. EDYE.
22 May, 1915...Lt.-Col. A. J. G. MOIR.
23 Mar., 1917...Lt.-Col. J. L. WESTON.
12 July, 1918...Lt.-Col. P. F. FITZ GERALD.
17 Oct., 1918...Lt.-Col. A. R. G. GORDON.

B.-G., R.A.

15 May, 1913...*Br.-Gen. H. A. BRENDON.
8 July, 1915...Br.-Gen. M. J. MACCARTHY.
4 July, 1916...Br.-Gen. L. C. L. OLDFIELD.
11 Mar., 1918...Lt.-Col. L. M. DYSON (acting).
16 Mar., 1918...Br.-Gen. L. C. L. OLDFIELD (wounded, 28/4/18).
28 April, 1918...Lt.-Col. L. M. DYSON (acting).
3 July, 1918...Br.-Gen. L. C. L. OLDFIELD.

C.R.E.

9 July, 1910...Lt.-Col. G. A. CORNWALL.
22 Jan., 1915...Lt.-Col. C. L. SPENCER.
25 May, 1915...Lt.-Col. H. W. WEEKES.
23 Mar., 1916...Lt.-Col. C. F. RUNDALL.
9 Jan., 1917...Lt.-Col. H. W. WEEKES (sick, 25/3/17).
25 Mar., 1917...Major J. G. ALLAN (acting)
28 Mar., 1917...Lt.-Col. J. G. FLEMING.
14 June, 1918...Lt.-Col. N. W. NAPIER-CLAVERING.

*Br.-Gen. on 5 August, 1914.

152nd BDE.
(1st Highland)
[Seaforth and Cameron Bde.]

9 May, '11...*Br.-Gen. D. A. MACFARLANE
13 Nov., '14...Br.-Gen. W. C. ROSS.
9 July, '16...Lt.-Col. A. H. SPOONER.
16 July, '16...Br.-Gen. H. P. BURN.
7 April, '18...Br.-Gen. J. K. DICK-CUNYNGHAM (captured, 12/4/18).
13 April, '18...**Major A. A. DUFF (acting).
15 April, '18...Lt.-Col. J. M. SCOTT (acting).
17 April, '18...Br.-Gen. E. I. DE S. THORPE.
28 April, '18...Br.-Gen. R. LAING.
8 Aug., '18...Br.-Gen. W. H. E. SEGRAVE.

153rd BDE.
(2nd Highland)
[Gordon Bde.]

22 Jan., '12...*Br.-Gen. G. C. I. STOCKWELL.
1 Feb., '15...Br.-Gen. D. CAMPBELL.
6 May, '17...Br.-Gen. A. F. GORDON (wounded, 29/7/17; died of wounds, 31/7/17).
29 July, '17...Lt.-Col. H. G. HYSLOP (acting).
2 Aug., '17...Br.-Gen. A. T. BECKWITH (wounded, 11/4/18).
11 April, '18...Lt.-Col. L. M. DYSON (acting).
13 April, '18...**Major W. H. NEWSON (acting).
13 April, '18...Lt.-Col. J. M. SCOTT (acting).
15 April, '18...Br.-Gen. W. GREEN.

154th BDE.
(3rd Highland)
[Argyll and Sutherland Bde.]

1 June, '11...*Br.-Gen. ST. G. E. W. BURTON.
19 April, '15...Br.-Gen. G. L. HIBBERT (wounded, 1/10/15).
1 Oct., '15...Lt.-Col. R. HINDLE (acting).
7 Oct., '15...Br.-Gen. G. T. G. EDWARDS.

(On 6/1/16 the original 154th Bde. left the 51st Div., it was transferred to the 55th Div., and it then became 164th Bde.)

154th Bde.
(The Bde. was re-formed on 6/1/16.)

6 Jan., '16...Br.-Gen. C. E. STEWART (killed, 14/9/16).
14 Sept., '16...Lt.-Col. H. G. HYSLOP (acting).
17 Sept., '16...Br.-Gen. J. G. H. HAMILTON.
26 Sept., '17...Br.-Gen. K. G. BUCHANAN.

*Br.-Gen. on 5 August, 1914.

**From 3 p.m. on 13/4/18 to 1 p.m. on 15/4/18, Lt.-Col. J. M. Scott was in command of 152nd Bde. Comp. Bn. (Major A. A. Duff), 153rd Bde. Comp. Bn. (Major W. H. Newson), and 8/R. Scots (Pioneers).

GENERAL NOTES

The following Units belonged to the Highland Division in August, 1914, but they went overseas independently :—

IV. Highland Mtn. Arty. Bde. (Argyll, Ross and Cromarty, and Bute Mtn. Bties.—2.75-inch, 10-pdrs.), mobd. on 4/8/14, and concentrated at Bedford on 10/8/14. The Bde. (less Bute Bty.) was transferred on 10/3/15 to the 29th Div., and left Avonmouth on 16/3/15. Bute Mtn. Bty. left England on 6/9/16, and disembkd. at Salonika on 20/9/16.

2/Highland Fd. Coy. (Aberdeen), joined the 7th Div. in France on 17/1/15 ; and on 31/1/16 it rejoined the 51st (Highland) Division, in exchange with 3/Durham Fd. Coy.

4/Seaforth Highlanders (Dingwall), landed in France on 7/11/14, and on 18/12/14 joined Dehra Dun Bde., Meerut Div. ; on 15/11/15 the Bn. was transferred to 46th Bde., 15th Div., and on 7/1/16 to 154th Bde., 51st Div.

4/Gordon Highlanders (Aberdeen), joined 8th Bde., 3rd Div., in France, on 27/2/15 ; it was transferred on 19/10/15 to 76th Bde., 3rd Div. ; and on 23/2/16 it joined 154th Bde., 51st Div.

6/Gordon Highlanders (Keith), joined 20th Bde., 7th Div., in France, on 5/12/14. On 5/1/16 the Bn. was transferred to L. of C. Troops, and joined 152nd Bde., 51st Div., on 1/6/16.

4/Cameron Highlanders (Inverness), joined 24th Bde., 8th Div., in France, on 23/2/15 ; on 8/4/15 it was transferred to 21st Bde., 7th Div., and on 20/12/15 to 91st Bde., 7th Div. On 7/1/16 the Bn. joined 154th Bde., 51st Div., and served with the 51st Div. until 26/2/16 (see below).

7/Argyll and Sutherland Highlanders (Stirling), joined 10th Bde., 4th Div., in France, on 6/1/15 ; and on 1/3/16 the Bn. was transferred to 154th Bde., 51st Div. (Also see 9/A. and S.H. below.)

9/Argyll and Sutherland Highlanders (Dumbarton), joined 81st Bde., 27th Div., in France, on 23/2/15 ; transferred to 10th Bde., 4th Div., on 21/5/15, and amalgamated with 7/A. and S.H. on 29/5/15. The Bn. resumed its independent formation on 20/7/15, and joined VI. Corps Troops on 22/7/15. On 27/2/16 the Bn. was sent to the Base, and on 22/3/16 it became a draft-producing bn.

1/Highland Field Ambulance (Aberdeen), was transferred to the 29th Division, and joined on 23/1/15 at Nuneaton. The Fd. Ambce. (numbered 89th) served with the 29th Div., in Gallipoli, Egypt, and France.

FLEMING'S FORCE (Battles of the Lys, 1918). From 12–15/4/18, Lt.-Col. J. G. Fleming (C.R.E.) commanded a Comp. Bde. formed from the 51st Div., and the Force held part of the First Army Line in front of Robecq. Fleming's Force was composed of : Echelon B and Reinforcements of 154th Bde. (400), Party of 152nd Bde. (100), Party of 153rd Bde. (200), No. 1 and B Special Cos., R.E. (300), 2 Cos., 11th (Cdn.) Rly. Bn. (250), one Coy., 51st M.G. Bn., and one Coy., 39th M.G. Bn.

The following Units also served with the 51st Division :—

INFANTRY :—4/B.W., landed in France on 26/2/15, and, on 4/3/15, joined Bareilly Bde., Meerut Div. On 6/11/15 the Bn. was transferred to 139th Bde., 46th Div., and on 14/11/15 to 44th Bde., 15th Div. On 6/1/16 the Bn. was transferred to 154th Bde., and on 25/2/16 the Bn. left on transfer to 118th Bde., 39th Div. (joined 29/2/16).

5/B.W., joined 24th Bde., 8th Div. (from U.K.) on 13/11/14, and became Pioneers on 18/10/15. On 6/1/16 the Bn. was transferred to the 154th Bde., and left on 25/2/16 on transfer to 118th Bde., 39th Div. (joined 29/2/16). N.B.—4/ and 5/B.W. were amalgamated into 4/5/B.W. (118th Bde.) on 16/3/16.

4/Cam. H., joined 154th Bde. on 7/1/16 (from 91st Bde., 7th Div.) ; and on 26/2/16 the Bn. was sent to the Base and drafted. (Also see General Notes, under 4/Cam. H., above.)

ARTILLERY :—Highland (Fifeshire) Heavy Battery (4, 4.7-inch guns), from Dunfermline, went to France with 51st Division, and landed on 4/5/15. The Hy. Bty. reached la Gorgue on 5/5/15, and joined II. Group, H.A.R., and on 3/7/15 the Hy. Bty. joined IV. Hy. Bde., R.G.A.

ENGINEERS :—3/Durham Fd. Coy., landed at le Havre on 18/9/15, and joined 51st Division on 19/9/15. The Fd. Coy. was transferred to the 7th Division on 30/1/16, in exchange with 2/Highland Fd. Coy.

OTHER UNITS :—51st Sanitary Section, went to France with 51st (Highl'd.) Division, and was transferred to XVII. Corps Sanitary Area by 11/4/17.

51st Divnl. Motor Amb. Workshop, joined 51st (Highl'd.) Division in France by 9/5/15 ; and on 6/4/16 it was absorbed in the Divnl. Supply Coln.

On 7/2/18 the division was reorganized on a 9-battalion basis ; and on 25/2/18 the pioneer battalion was reorganized on a 3-company basis.

51st[1] (HIGHLAND) DIVISION

ORDER OF BATTLE, 1915-1918

Dates	INFANTRY		Mounted Troops	ARTILLERY						Engineers	Signal Service	Pioneers	M.G. Units	Field Ambu-lances	Mobile Vety. Secn.	Divnl. Emplnt. Coy.	Divnl. Train
	Brigades	Battalions and attached Units		Field Artillery			Trench Mortar B'ties.		Divnl. Ammn. Coln.	Field Cos.	Divnl. Signal Coy.						
				Brigades	Batteries	Bde. Ammn. Colns.	Medium	Heavy									
1915 May (France)	152nd[2] (1st Highl'd.) 153rd[3] (2nd Highl'd.) 154th[4] (3rd Highl'd.)	5/Sea. H., 6/Sea. H., 6/A. & S.H.,[5] 8/A. & S.H.[5] 6/B.W.,[6] 7/B.W.,[6] 5/Gord. H., 7/Gord. H. 4/K.O.,[7] 8/King's,[7] 2/5/L.F.,[8] 4/L.N.L.[7]	D Sqdn., N. Irish H.[9] 51st (Highl'd.) Divnl. Cyclist Coy.[10]	I Highl'd.[11]... II Highl'd.[12] III Highl'd.[13] (H.)	1/Aberdeen, 2/Aberdeen, 3/Aberdeen. Forfarshire. Fifeshire. Dundee. 1/Renfrew (H.), 2/Renfrew (H.)	I Highl'd. B.A.C. II Highl'd. B.A.C. III Highl'd. B.A.C. (H.)	...	...	51st (Highl'd.) D.A C.[14]	1/Highl'd.[15] 2/2/ Highl'd.[16]	51st[17] (Highl'd.)	...	...	2/ Highl'd.[18] 3/ Highl'd.[19] 2/1/ Highl'd.[20]	1/ Highl'd.[21]	...	51st[22] (Highl'd.)
1915 September (France)	152nd........ 153rd .... 154th[24]	5/Sea. H., 6/Sea. H., 6/A. & S.H.,[23] 8/A. & S.H. 6/B.W., 7/B.W., 5/Gord. H., 7/Gord. H. 4/K.O.,[24] 8/King's,[24] 2/5/L.F.,[24] 6/Sco. Rif.,[25] 4/L.N.L.[24]	D Sqdn., N. Irish H.[26] 51st Divnl. Cyclist Coy.[27]	I Highl'd.[28] II Highl'd.[29] III Highl'd.[30] (H.)	1/Aberdeen, 2/Aberdeen, 3/Aberdeen. Forfarshire, Fifeshire, Dundee. 1/Renfrew (H.), 2/Renfrew (H.)	I Highl'd. B.A.C. II Highl'd. B.A.C. III Highl'd. B.A.C. (H.)	...	...	51st D.A.C.	1/Highl'd. 2/2/ Highl'd.	51st	8/R. Scots[31] (P.)	...	2/ Highl'd. 3/ Highl'd. 2/1/ Highl'd.	1/ Highl'd.	...	51st
1916 June (France)	152nd........ 153rd .... 154th[32]	5/Sea. H., 6/Sea. H., 6/Gord. H.,[33] 8/A. & S.H.; 152nd Bde. M.G. Coy.;[34] 152nd T.M. Bty.[35] 6/B.W., 7/B.W., 5/Gord. H., 7/Gord. H.; 153rd Bde. M.G. Coy.;[34] 153rd T.M. Bty.[35] 9/R. Scots.,[36] 4/Sea. H.,[37] 4/Gord. H.,[38] 7/A. & S.H.;[39] 154th Bde. M.G. Coy.;[34] 154th T.M. Bty.[35]	...	CCLV[40] (I Highl'd.) CCLVI[41] (II Highl'd.) CCLVIII[42] (III Highl'd.) CCLX[43] (I Lowland)	A, B, C; D (H.) A, B, C; D (H.) A, B, C. A, B, C; D (H.)	...[44]	X.51[45] Y.51[45] Z.51[45]	V.51[46]	51st D.A.C.[44]	1/Highl'd. 2/ Highl'd.[47] 2/2/ Highl'd.	51st	8/R. Scots (P.)	...	2/ Highl'd. 3/ Highl'd. 2/1/ Highl'd.	1/ Highl'd.	...	51st
1917 June (France)	152nd........ 153rd 154th	5/Sea. H., 6/Sea. H., 6/Gord. H., 8/A. & S.H.;[48] 152nd M.G. Coy.;[56] 152nd T.M. Bty. 6/B.W., 7/B.W., 5/Gord. H.,[49] 7/Gord. H.; 153rd M.G. Coy.,[56] 153rd T.M. Bty. 9/R. Scots.,[50] 4/Sea. H., 4/Gord. H., 7/A. & S.H.; 154th M.G. Coy.;[56] 154th T.M. Bty.	...	CCLV .... CCLVI	A, B, C; D (H.) A, B, C; D (H.)	...	X.51[51] Y.51[51] Z.51[51]	V.51[52]	51st D.A.C.	400th (1/High'ld.) 401st (2/Highl'd.) 404th (2/2/ Highl'd.)	51st	8/R. Scots (P.)	232nd M.G. Coy.[53]	2/ Highl'd. 3/ Highl'd. 2/1/ Highl'd.	1/ Highl'd.	245th[54]	51st
1918 March (France)	152nd ...... 153rd........ 154th	5/Sea. H., 6/Sea. H., 6/Gord. H.;[55] 152nd T.M. Bty. 6/B.W., 7/B.W., 7/Gord. H.;[55] 153rd T.M. Bty. 4/Sea. H., 4/Gord. H., 7/A. & S.H.; 154th T.M. Bty.	...	CCLV .... CCLVI	A, B, C; D (H.) A, B, C; D (H.)	...	X.51 Y.51	...	51st D.A.C.	400th 401st 404th	51st	8/R. Scots (P.)	No. 51 Bn.,[55] M.G.C.	2/ Highl'd. 3/ Highl'd. 2/1/ Highl'd.	1/ Highl'd.	245th	51st

1918 October (France)	152nd	5/Sea. H., 6/Sea. H., 6/7/Gord. H.;[55] 152nd T.M. Bty.	...	CCLV	A, B, C; D (H.)	...	X.51	...	51st D.A.C.	400th 401st 404th	51st	8/R. Scots (P.)	No. 51 Bn., M.G.C.	2/Highl'd. 3/Highl'd. 2/1/Highl'd.	1/Highl'd.	245th	51st
	153rd	6/B.W., 7/B.W., 6/A. & S.H.;[57] 153rd T.M. Bty.		CCLVI	A, B, C; D (H.)		Y.51										
	154th	4/Sea. H., 4/Gord. H., 7/A. & S.H.; 154th T.M. Bty.															

NOTES

1 Highland Div. was numbered 51st Div. on 12/5/15. (Authy. W.O. letter—40/W.O./2481 (A.G.1.) of 7/5/15.)

2 The Sea. and Cam. Bde. was renamed 1st Highl'd., after reorganization, and numbered 152nd on 12/5/15. The Bns. came from Golspie, Elgin, Paisley, and Dunoon (see note 5).

3 The Gord. Bde. was renamed 2nd Highl'd., after reorganization, and numbered 153rd on 12/5/15. The Bns. came from Perth, St. Andrews, Peterhead, and Banchory (see note 6).

4 N. Lanc. Bde. (with 8/King's replacing 5/L.N.L. and 2/5/L.F. replacing 5/K.O.) was transferred by 18/4/15 from W. Lanc. Div. to Highl'd. Div. at Bedford. Bde. was renamed 3rd Highl'd. Bde., and on 12/5/15 it was numbered 154th. The Bns. came from Ulverston, Liverpool, Bury, and Preston. (Also see Notes 7, 8, and 24.)

5 Transferred from 2nd Highl'd. Bde. on 15/4/15.

6 Transferred from B.W. Inf. Bde., Scottish Coast Defences, on 16/4/15.

7 Transferred from N. Lanc. Inf. Bde., W. Lanc. Div., by 18/4/15.

8 Raised at Bury after the outbreak of war. Joined at Bedford by 18/4/15. After arrival in France the Bn. was sent for further training from 19/5—9/7/15.

9 The Sqdn. joined at Bedford. It disembkd. at le Havre on 2/5/15.

10 Formed at Bedford. The Coy. disembkd. at le Havre on 2/5/15.

11 The Bde. (15-pdrs.) came from Aberdeen.

12 The Bties. (15-pdrs.) came from Dundee, Arbroath, and Leven.

13 The Bties. (5-inch Hows.) came from Greenock, and the Ammn. Coln. from Cathcart.

14 Formed at Bedford on 17/4/15; mobd. at Blackheath, 19/4—3/5/15; and disembkd. at le Havre on 6/5/15.

15 The Coy. came from Glasgow.

16 The Coy. was raised after the outbreak of war. It disembkd. at le Havre on 3/5/15.

17 H.Q. and No. 1 Sec. came from Aberdeen.

18 Came from Aberdeen.

19 Came from Dundee.

20 Raised after the outbreak of war. It disembkd. at le Havre on 3/5/15.

21 Formed after the outbreak of war. It disembkd. at le Havre on 4/5/15.

22 The Train was formed by the Highl'd. Divnl. T. and S. Coln. (Cos. at Perth, Stirling, Aberdeen, and Dundee). The Train disembkd. at le Havre on 1/5/15. The Cos. were numbered 471, 472, 473, and 474 Cos., A.S.C.

23 Bn. joined divnl. troops on 1/6/16, and on 12/6/16 it was transferred as Pioneers to the 5th Div.

24 Transferred to 55th Div. on 6/1/16 to form 164th Bde., and joined 55th on 7/1/16.

25 Joined on 2/6/15 from 23rd Bde., 8th Div.; the Bn. remained in the 154th Bde. after the re-formation of the Bde, on 6/1/16. The Bn. was transferred to divnl. troops on 12/1/16 and trained as Pioneers. On 21/2/16 the Bn. joined 33rd Div., and on 25/2/16 the Bn. was posted to 100th Bde., 33rd Div.

26 Transferred to VII Corps Cav. Regt. on 10/5/16.

27 Transferred to XVII Corps Cyclist Bn. on 9/5/16.

28 Bde. rearmed with 18-pdrs. on 24/8/15. D Bty. (18-pdrs.) was formed on 14/4/16. Bde. was numbered CCLV on 15/5/16, and reorganized: the old batteries were lettered A, B, and C; D became A/CCLVIII; and 1/Renfrew (H.) was transferred from CCLVIII and became D (H.)/CCLV.

29 Bde. rearmed with 18-pdrs. on 28/8/15. D Bty. (18-pdrs.) was formed on 7/4/16. Bde. was numbered CCLVI on 19/5/16, and reorganized: the old batteries were lettered A, B, and C; D became B/CCLVIII; and R (H.) was transferred from CCLVIII and became D (H.)/CCLVI.

30 Bde. rearmed with 4.5-inch H. on 11/1/16. On 8/2/16 D (H.)/CLI joined Bde. and became R (H.). Bde. was numbered CCLVIII on 17/5/16, and it was reorganized: 1/Renfrew became D (H.)/CCLV; 2/Renfrew became D (H.)/CCLX; and R (H.) became D (H.)/CCLVI. Three 18-pdr. bties. joined: D/CCLV, D/CCLVI, and D/CCLX, and became A, B, and C.

31 The Bn. (then in 22nd Bde., 7th Div.) became Pioneers on 27/7/15; and on 19/8/15 the Bn. was transferred as Pioneer Bn. to the 51st Div.

32 The original 154th Bde. was transferred to 55th Div., as 164th Bde., on 7/1/16 (see note 24). 154th Bde. was re-formed on 6/1/16.

33 Transferred from L. of C., and joined Bde. on 1/6/16 (see General Notes).

34 The M.G. Cos. were formed: 152nd on 16/1/16; 153rd on 12/1/16; and 154th on 14/1/16.

35 The Bde. T.M. Bties. were formed as follows: 4/4 T.M. Bty. joined 152nd Bde. on 17/3/16 and became 152/1, and 152/2 joined by May, 1916. 152/1 and 2 amalgamated by July, 1916. 417 T.M. Bty. joined on 2/3/16 and on 15/3/16 became 153/1; 153/2 joined by May, 1916. 153/1 and 2 became 153 T.M. Bty. by July, 1916. 154/1 joined on 17/3/16, and 154/2 by 10/5/16, and the 2 bties. amalgamated by 22/6/16.

36 Joined on 1/3/16 from Third Army Troops. (In Aug., 1914, the Bn. belonged to the Lothian Inf. Bde.)

37 Joined on 7/1/16 from 46th Bde., 15th Div. (see General Notes).

38 Joined on 23/2/16 from 76th Bde., 3rd Div. (see General Notes).

39 Joined on 1/3/16 from 10th Bde., 4th Div. (see General Notes).

40 Bde. reorganized between 21—23/8/16: A and R. Sec. C/CCLVIII joined and made A, B, and C up to 6, 18-pdrs. each. On 25/1/17 R. Sec. C (H.)/CCLX joined and made D (H.) up to 6 hows.

41 Bde. reorganized on 23/8/16: B and L. Sec. C/CCLVIII joined and made A, B, and C up to 6, 18-pdrs. each. On 25/1/17 L. Sec. C (H.)/CCLX joined and made D (H.) up to 6 hows.

42 Bde. broken up on 21/8/16: A and R. Sec. C was transferred to CCLV, and B and L. Sec. C was transferred to CCLVI.

43 1/Lowland R.F.A. Bde. (detached from Lowland Div.) arrived at le Havre on 24/10/15 and was rearmed with 18-pdrs. The Bde. joined 51st Div. on 10/11/15; it was numbered CCLVII on 15/5/16, and renumbered CCLX on 3/6/16. On 15/5/16 the 4 batteries were lettered A, B, C, and D; D was transferred and became C/CCLVIII, and 2/Renfrew (H.) joined from CCLVIII and became D (H.). On 23/8/16 the Bde. was again reorganized, C was split up between A and B; and, on 18/11/16, 535 (H.) joined and became C (H.). On 28/1/17 CCLX was broken up: A became C/CCCXV A.F.A. Bde., B became C/LXXXI A.F.A. Bde.; R. Sec. C (H.) made D (H.)/CCLV up to 6 hows., and L. Sec. C (H.) made up D (H.)/CCLVI; and D (H.) became D (H.)/LXXXIV A.F.A. Bde.

44 The D.A.C. was reorganized between 15-17/5/16, and the B.A.C.'s were abolished.

45 The T.M. Bties. joined: X by 28/4/16; Y by 16/3/16; and Z on 17/3/16.

46 V H.T.M.B. joined 18/10/16.

47 2/Highl'd. Fd. Coy. joined on 31/1/16 (on transfer from 7th Div.).

48 Transferred on 7/2/18 to 183rd Bde., 61st Div.

49 Transferred on 2/2/18 to 183rd Bde., 61st Div.

50 Transferred on 6/2/18 to 183rd Bde., 61st Div.

51 In Feb., 1918, the 3, 4-mortar bties. were reorganized as 2, 6-mortar bties., X and Y.

52 Left the division in Feb., 1918, and became H.T.M.B., IV Corps.

53 The M.G. Coy. arrived from England on 13/7/17, and joined the Div. on 20/7/17.

54 Joined 16/6/17, and numbered 245th by 4/8/17.

55 7/Gord. H. was transferred on 5/10/18 from 153rd to 152nd Bde.; and, on 6/10/18, 6/Gord. H. and 7/Gord. H. were amalgamated.

56 Bn. was formed on 19/2/18. (It consisted of 152nd, 153rd, 154th, and 232nd M.G. Cos.)

57 Joined on 6/10/18 from 5th Div. (See note 23.)

51st (HIGHLAND) DIVISION

MOBILIZATION, BATTLES, AND ENGAGEMENTS

The division—an existing T.F. division—was drawn from the Highlands of Scotland, with the divisional headquarters in Perth. The three brigade headquarters were at Inverness, Aberdeen, and Stirling, and the original 12 battalions came from Dingwall, Golspie, Elgin, Inverness, Aberdeen, Peterhead, Keith, Banchory, Paisley, Stirling, Dunoon, and Dumbarton.

In the artillery : the I. Highland Bde., R.F.A., was at Aberdeen ; the II. Highland Bde., R.F.A., was at Dundee, with outlying batteries at Arbroath and Leven ; the III. Highland (How.) Bde., R.F.A., was at Greenock, with its ammunition column at Cathcart ; the IV. Highland Mountain Artillery Bde., R.G.A., had its headquarters and one battery at Rothesay, and the other two batteries were at Campbeltown and Lochcarron, with the ammunition column at Tarbert ; and the Highland (Fifeshire) Heavy Battery, R.G.A. (4, 4.7-inch guns) came from Dunfermline (see General Notes).

The field companies came from Glasgow and Aberdeen, and the H.Q. and No. 1 Section of the Signal Company from Aberdeen. Two field ambulances came from Aberdeen and the third from Dundee ; and the companies of the Divnl. T. and S. Column were at Perth, Stirling, Aberdeen, and Dundee.

On the 29th July, 1914, the Warning Order arrived at Divisional Hd. Qrs. at Perth, and at 5-35 p.m. on the 4th August, the order to mobilize was received. Mobilization began on the 5th August. On the 12th, the Highland Division was ordered to move to Bedford, on the 15th entrainment began, and the concentration of the division at Bedford was completed by the 17th August. The division now formed part of the First Army, Central Force, and training for war was carried on. On the 22nd October H.M. the King inspected the Highland Division.

Between early in November, 1914, and the middle of March, 1915, the following units left the division to join other formations in the field, viz. : IV. Highland Mtn. Arty. Bde., 2/Highland Fd. Coy., 4/Seaforth Highlanders, 4/ and 6/Gordon Highlanders, 4/ Cameron Highlanders, 7/ and 9/Argyll and Sutherland Highlanders, and 1/Highland Fd. Ambce. (See General Notes.) To replace some of the units which it had lost, the division had transferred to it by the middle of April, 1915, two Black Watch battalions, and three Lancashire battalions (the latter from the West Lancashire Division), as well as the following 2nd-line units : one battalion, one field company, and one field ambulance. The infantry brigades were then reorganized and redesignated (see Order of Battle Table).

On the 13th April, the Highland Division was ordered to prepare for service overseas. Between the 30th April and the 3rd May, 1915, the division crossed to France : the mounted troops, artillery, engineers, field ambulances, transport of units, veterinary and sanitary sections, and the divisional train proceeded from Southampton to le Havre, and the rest of the division crossed from Folkestone to Boulogne. By the 6th May, the division completed its concentration at Lillers, Busnes, and Robecq.

The 51st Division served throughout the War in France and Belgium, and was engaged in the following operations :—

1915

19–25 May ... ...**Battle of Festubert** [Alderson's Force from 19–22/5 ; then Indian Corps, First Army].

15 and 16 June ... ...**Givenchy** [IV. Corps, First Army].

1916

21 July–7 Aug.; and 4 Oct.–24 Nov.	**BATTLES OF THE SOMME**
21–30 July ...	...**Attacks on High Wood** [XV. Corps, Fourth Army].
13–18 Nov. ...	...**Battle of the Ancre** [V. Corps, Fifth Army].
13 Nov.	...**Capture of Beaumont Hamel.**

1917

	BATTLES OF ARRAS
9–11 April ...	...**First Battle of the Scarpe** [XVII. Corps, Third Army].
23 and 24 April	...**Second Battle of the Scarpe** [XVII. Corps, Third Army].
13–16 May ...	...**Capture and Defence of Roeux** [XVII. Corps, Third Army].
	BATTLES OF YPRES
31 July–2 Aug. ...	...**Battle of Pilckem Ridge** [XVIII. Corps, Fifth Army].
20–24 Sept. ...	...**Battle of the Menin Road Ridge** [XVIII. Corps, Fifth Army].
	BATTLE OF CAMBRAI
20 and 21 Nov. ...	...**The Tank Attack** [IV. Corps, Third Army].
23 Nov.	...**Capture of Bourlon Wood** [IV. Corps, Third Army].
1–3 Dec. ...	...**German Counter-Attacks** [VI. Corps, Third Army].

1918

	FIRST BATTLES OF THE SOMME
21–23 Mar. ...	...**Battle of St. Quentin** [IV. Corps, Third Army].
24 and 25 March	...**Battle of Bapaume** [IV. Corps, Third Army].
	BATTLES OF THE LYS
9–11 April ...	...**Battle of Estaires** [XI. Corps, First Army].
12–15 April ...	...**Battle of Hazebrouck** [XI. Corps, First Army].
	THE ADVANCE TO VICTORY
	BATTLES OF THE MARNE
20–31 July ...	...**Battle of Tardenois** [XXII. Corps, Fifth (French) Army].
	SECOND BATTLES OF ARRAS
26–30 Aug. ...	...**Battle of the Scarpe** [Cdn. Corps, First Army].
11 and 12 Oct. ...	...**Pursuit to the Selle** [Cdn. Corps, First Army].
	THE FINAL ADVANCE IN PICARDY
17–25 Oct. ...	...**Battle of the Selle** [XXII. Corps, First Army].

On the 29th October the 51st Division (less the artillery) was withdrawn from the Front Line, and on the 31st the division was placed in First Army Reserve. On the 11th November the 51st Division was billeted in the Schelde Valley in the Cambrai—Iwuy area. During December units were mainly employed in educational training and salvage work, and 1,200 coal-miners left for demobilization in the United Kingdom. In January, 1919, the division moved forward to a new area north of Binche, and between the 27th and 29th January H.R.H. the Prince of Wales visited the units of the division.

In February, three battalions (6/Black Watch, 4/Seaforth, and 4/Gordon Highlanders) left the division for Germany; and in April these three battalions were posted to a Highland Division in the Army of the Rhine. Gradually the 51st (Highland) Division faded away, and by the middle of March, 1919, it and all its units were reduced to cadre strength. The last of its units to leave France was 8/Argyll and Sutherland Highlanders. In 1920 the division was re-formed in Scotland.

52ND (LOWLAND) DIVISION

G.O.C.

21 March, 1914 ... ... Major-General G. G. A. EGERTON.
17 September, 1915 ... ... *Major-General Hon. H. A. LAWRENCE.
27 June, 1916 ... ... Br.-Gen. H. G. CASSON (acting).
11 July, 1916 ... ... Major-General W. E. B. SMITH.
11 September, 1917 ... ... Major-General J. HILL.
23 September, 1918 ... ... Major-General F. J. MARSHALL.

G.S.O. 1.

19 Feb., 1914...Major F. W. H. WALSHE (G.S.O. 2).
5 Aug., 1914...Lt.-Col. F. W. H. WALSHE.
21 April, 1916...Lt.-Col. C. M. DAVIES.
2 Nov., 1916...Major W. F. STIRLING (acting).
6 Nov., 1916...Lt.-Col. R. E. M. RUSSELL.
1 Mar., 1917...Lt.-Col. G. W. V. HOLDICH.
[17 Nov., 1918...Lt.-Col. A. G. THOMPSON].

B.-G., R.A.

1 April, 1913...**Br.-Gen. F. B. JOHNSTONE. (On 2/11/15, as the Div. Arty. was so scattered, the B.-G., R.A., was transferred to the 10th Division. Between 4–17/3/16 52nd Div. Arty. was re-formed at el Qantara.)
4 Mar., 1916...Br.-Gen. J. L. PARKER (sick, 23/12/16).
25 Dec., 1916...Lt.-Col. A. BIRTWISTLE (acting).
24 Jan., 1917...Br.-Gen. H. G. SANDILANDS (Tempy., returned to 54th Div. 17/2/17).
17 Feb., 1917...Lt.-Col. J. HENRY (acting).
2 April, 1917...Br.-Gen. E. C. MASSY (sick, 14/8/17).
14 Aug., 1917...Lt.-Col. J. FARQUHAR (acting).
24 Aug., 1917...Br.-Gen. E. C. MASSY. (On 31/3/18 52nd Div. Arty. was exchanged with 7th Ind. Div. Arty.)
1 April, 1918...Br.-Gen. A. D. MUSGRAVE. (Between 10/5/18 and 21/6/18 the R.A. Staff, 52nd Div., was under instruction; it was replaced temporarily by R.A. Staff, 14th Div.)
10 May, 1918...Br.-Gen. E. HARDING-NEWMAN (tempy.).
21 June, 1918...Br.-Gen. A. D. MUSGRAVE (wounded, 2/8/18).
2 Aug., 1918...Lt.-Col. H. J. COTTER (acting).
4 Aug., 1918...Br.-Gen. A. D. MUSGRAVE.
15 Oct., 1918...Br.-Gen. G. T. MAIR.

A.-A. and Q.-M.-G.

10 Sept., 1910...Major C. A. H. MACLEAN (D.-A.-A. and Q.-M.G.).
5 Aug., 1914...Major C. A. H. MACLEAN (acting).
15 June, 1915...Lt.-Col. A. MUDGE.
28 Aug., 1915...Lt.-Col. C. A. H. MACLEAN.
19 Nov., 1917...Capt. J. T. TULLOCH (acting).
24 Nov., 1917...Lt.-Col. W. H. J. THORNTON.
2 April, 1918...Lt.-Col. C. G. MAUDE.

C.R.E.

28 Feb., 1911...Lt.-Col. T. SYMINGTON (sick, May, 1915).
16 June, 1915...Lt.-Col. G. B. MOTHERWELL (sick, 22/8/15).
22 Aug., 1915...Capt. L. C. PITMAN (acting).
10 Sept., 1915...Lt.-Col. R. L. WALLER.
3 Feb., 1916...Major M. S. SPENCE (acting).
4 Mar., 1916...Lt.-Col. R. L. WALLER.
24 Nov., 1916...Lt.-Col. L. F. WELLS.

*From 12/4/16–27/6/16 the G.O.C. 52nd Div. also commanded No. 3 (Northern Section), Suez Canal Defences. On 27/6/16 the commands were separated and Major-Gen. Hon. H. A. Lawrence took over command of No. 3 Section.

**Br.-Gen. on 5 August, 1914.

155th BDE.
(South Scottish Bde.)

19 May, '11...*Br.-Gen. J. F. ERSKINE (sick, 2/8/15).
2 Aug., '15...Lt.-Col. J. B. POLLOK-McCALL (acting).
5 Aug., '15...Br.-Gen. J. F. ERSKINE.
14 Aug., '15...Br.-Gen. J. B. POLLOK-McCALL.
11 Jan., '18...Lt.-Col. J. ANDERSON (acting).
8 April, '18...Br.-Gen. P. S. ALLAN.
19 June, '18...Br.-Gen. J. FORBES-ROBERTSON, V.C.
23 Sept., '18...Br.-Gen. G. H. HARRISON.

156th BDE.
(Scottish Rifle Bde.)

20 Aug., '12...*Br.-Gen. S. W. HARE.
18 Feb., '15...Br.-Gen. W. SCOTT-MONCRIEFFE (killed, 28/6/15).
29 June, '15...Lt.-Col. P. C. PALIN (acting).
20 July, '15...Br.-Gen. H. G. CASSON.
30 July, '15...Lt.-Col. W. C. PEEBLES (acting).
11 Aug., '15...Lt.-Col. and Hony. Col. A. YOUNG (acting).
13 Aug., '15...Br.-Gen. L. C. KOE.
19 June, '16...Lt.-Col. G. T. B. WILSON (acting).
3 July, '16...Br.-Gen. E. S. GIRDWOOD.
3 Mar., '17...Br.-Gen. A. H. LEGGETT.

157th BDE.
(Highland Light Inf. Bde.)

8 June, '11...*Br.-Gen. P. W. HENDRY (sick, 10/7/15).
10 July, '15...Lt.-Col. W. H. MILLAR (acting).
31 July, '15...Br.-Gen. H. G. CASSON.
2 Oct., '16...Col. F. L. MORRISON (acting).
5 Oct., '16...Br.-Gen. C. D. HAMILTON-MOORE.
4 Nov., '18...Lt.-Col. J. G. P. ROMANES (acting).
10 Nov., '18...Br.-Gen. B. G. PRICE.
[5 Dec., '18...Br.-Gen. C. D. HAMILTON-MOORE.]

*Br.-Gen. on 5 August, 1914.

GENERAL NOTES

The following Units belonged to the Lowland Division in August, 1914, but they went overseas independently :—

I. Lowland Bde., R.F.A., T.F. (1/Edinburgh, 2/Edinburgh, and Midlothian Bties. (4, 15-pdrs. each) and B.A.C.) remained behind in the Forth Defences, and went to France in October, 1915. The Bde. landed at le Havre on 24/10/15, and was then rearmed with 18-pdrs. On 10/11/15 the Bde. joined 51st (Highland) Division (see note 43, p. 105).

III. Lowland Bde., R.F.A., T.F. (1/, 2/, and 3/Glasgow Bties. (4, 15-pdrs. each) and B.A.C.) was left behind when the Lowland Div. embkd. for Egypt and Gallipoli. The Bde. was rearmed with 18-pdrs. before proceeding abroad. The Bde. embkd. on 27/2/16 and landed at Alexandria on 10/3/16. The Bde. rejoined 52nd Div. at El Qantara on 17/3/16 (see note 19).

Lowland (Edinburgh) Heavy Battery, R.G.A., T.F. (4, 4.7-inch guns), mobilized at Edinburgh, 4–14/8/14; moved to its war station, Stirling, 15/8/14; and moved to Cupar, 25/10/15. On 26/1/16 the Hy. Bty. reached Woolwich to prepare for France. The Hy. Bty. disembkd. at le Havre on 16/2/16, and on 18/2/16 the Bty. joined XVII. Bde., R.G.A., at Authie.

1/Lowland Fd. Coy., R.E., T.F., embkd. at Southampton on 15/12/14, landed at le Havre on 16/12/14. and joined 1st Division on 28/12/14. The Fd. Coy. served with the 1st Division for the remainder of the War. (In 1917 the Fd. Coy. was numbered 409th.)

2/Lowland Fd. Coy., R.E., T.F., joined 29th Division at Southam on March, 1915, and served with the 29th Division until 24/2/16, when the Fd. Coy. was transferred back to the 52nd Division.

5/Scottish Rifles, joined 19th Bde., 6th Division, on 19/11/14, and served with the 19th Bde. for the remainder of the War. (The 19th Bde. served in the 6th Div. until 31/5/15; in the 27th Div. until 19/8/15; in the 2nd Div. until 25/11/15; it then joined the 33rd Div., and served in the 33rd Div. for the remainder of the War.)

6/Scottish Rifles, joined 23rd Bde., 8th Division, on 24/3/15; was transferred to 154th Bde., 51st Division, on 2/6/15; was transferred to 51st Divisional Troops on 12/1/16; joined 100th Bde., 33rd Division, on 25/2/16. On 29/5/16 the Bn. was transferred to L. of C. and then broken up for drafts.

9/Highland Light Infantry, joined 5th Bde., 2nd Division, on 23/11/14; was transferred to G.H.Q. Troops on 30/1/16. On 29/5/16 the Bn. joined 100th Bde., 33rd Div., and served there for the remainder of the War.

The following Units also served with the 52nd Division :—

Lowland Mounted Bde. (Br.-Gen. F. Lee, with Ayrshire Yeo. and Lanarkshire Yeo.—46 offrs. and 921 o.r.) landed at Helles on 11/10/15, and reinforced the 52nd Div. The Bde. remained with the 52nd Div. until 31/12/15, when the Bde. left Helles and went to Mudros. The Bde. arrived back in Egypt on 7/2/16 and then joined 1st Dismtd. Bde.

1st Dismounted Bde. (Br.-Gen. Marquis of Tullibardine (5/2/16–16/10/16), with the Ayrshire Yeo., Lanarkshire Yeo., 1/Sco. Horse, 2/Sco. Horse, 3/Sco. Horse, 1st Dismtd. Bde., Sig. Coy., 1st Dismtd. Bde., M.G. Coy., 1/Lowland Mtd. Bde. Fd. Amb., and 1/Sco. Horse Fd. Amb.) was attached from 8/2/16–28/6/16 to the 52nd Div. in No. 3 (Northern) Section, Suez Canal Defences. (The 1st Dismtd. Bde. was disbanded on 16/10/16).

MOUNTED TROOPS :—One Troop, 4/Hussars and Detnt., VIII. Corps Cyclist Bn., were attached to the 52nd Div. from 30th October–11th November, 1918 (Armistice).

ARTILLERY :—**52nd (1-pdr.) Pom-Pom Bty.**, served throughout June, 1917, with the 52nd Div.

ENGINEERS :—**3/Kent Fd. Coy., R.E., T.F.**, left Mudros on 28/10/15 in H.M.S. *Hythe* to join 52nd Div. at Helles. *Hythe* sank after a collision, and 1 offr. and 128 o.r. were drowned. The remainder (4 offrs. and 85 o.r.) returned to Mudros in H.M.S. *Sarnia*. On 20/11/15 the Fd. Coy. (4 offrs. and 78 o.r.) embkd. again and landed the same day at Helles, and was attached to the 52nd Div. until 26/2/16, when the Fd. Coy. was transferred (in Egypt) to the 29th Div.

OTHER UNITS :—**52nd Sanitary Section** left Glasgow on 3/6/15, embkd. at Devonport on 4/6/15, disembkd. at Port Said on 18/6/15, and landed at Mudros on 27/7/15. Early in October, 1915, the Sany. Sec. sailed for Salonika, attached to the 10th Div. The Sec. returned to Alexandria on 19/9/17 (with the 10th Div.), and on 22/10/17, 52nd Sany. Sec. rejoined 52nd Div. On 17/4/18 the Sany. Sec. disembkd. at Marseille (with the 52nd Div.), and on 4/5/18 the Sany. Sec. was transferred to XI. Corps Sanitary Area.

18th Sanitary Section, from the L. of C., joined the 52nd Div. in October, 1915, at Mudros, and remained with the 52nd Div. until 24/10/17, when 18th Sany. Sec. was transferred to the 10th Div. at Shellal.

52nd Divnl. Motor Amb. Workshop (formerly 31st Divnl. Motor Amb. W'kshp.) joined the 52nd Div. by 21/4/16, and served with the 52nd Div. until June, 1917, when it was absorbed in the Divnl. Supply Coln.

NOTE A.—Between 25–30/12/16 arrangements were made to complete 18-pdr. batteries of the Divisional Artillery to six guns each (see notes 18, 19, and 20). But the extra section per battery was retained for the defence of El Qantara and later of El Arish. It was not until 25/6/17 (at Inseirat) that these extra sections rejoined the 52nd Div., and completed their respective 18-pdr. batteries to six guns each.

In France, on 28/6/18, the 52nd Division was reorganized on a 9-battalion basis.

52ND[1] (LOWLAND) DIVISION

ORDER OF BATTLE, 1915-1918

Dates	INFANTRY		Mounted Troops	ARTILLERY						Engineers	Signal Service	Pioneers	M.G. Units	Field Ambu-lances	Mobile Vety. Secn.	Divnl. Emplmt. Coy.	Divnl. Train.
				Field Artillery			Trench Mortar Bties.										
	Brigades	Battalions and attached Units		Brigades	Batteries	Bde. Ammn. Colns.	Medium	Heavy	Divnl. Ammn. Coln.	Field Cos.	Divnl. Signal Coy.						
1915 June (Gallipoli)	155th[1]; [2] [Sth. Scottish] 156th[1]; [3] [Scottish Rifle] 157th[1]; [4] [H.L.I.]	4/R.S.F., 5/R.S.F., 4/K.O.S.B., 5/K.O.S.B. 4/R. Scots.,[5] 7/R. Scots.,[5] 7/Sco. Rif., 8/Sco. Rif. 5/H.L.I., 6/H.L.I., 7/H.L.I., 5/A. & S.H.[6]	52nd (Lowland) Divnl. Cyclist Coy.[7]	II Lowland[8] IV Lowland[9] (H.)	1/Ayr, 2/Ayr, Kirkcudbright. 4/Glasgow (H.), 5/Glasgow (H.)	II Lowland IV Lowland (H.)	...	...	52nd D.A.C.[10] (Low-land)	2/1/Low-land[11] 2/2/Low-land[11]	52nd[12] (Low-land)	...	...	1/Low-land[13] 2/Low-land[13] 3/Low-land[13]	1/Low-land[14]	...	52nd[15] (Low-land)
1916 June (Egypt)	155th........ 156th........ 157th........	4/R.S.F., 5/R.S.F., 4/K.O.S.B., 5/K.O.S.B.; 155th Bde. M.G. Coy.[16] 4/R. Scots., 7/R. Scots., 7/Sco. Rif., 8/Sco. Rif.; 156th Bde. M.G. Coy.[16] 5/H.L.I., 6/H.L.I., 7/H.L.I., 5/A. and S.H.; 157th Bde. M.G. Coy.[16]	Hd. Qrs. and C Sqdn., R. Glasgow Yeo.[17] 52nd Divnl. Cyclist Coy.[7]	CCLXI[18] (II Lowland) CCLXII[19] (III Lowland) CCLXIV[20] (V Lowland) CCLXIII[21] (H) (IV Lowland)	A (1/Ayr), B (2/Ayr), C (Kirkcudbright). A (1/Glasgow), B (2/Glasgow), C (3/Glasgow). A (Hants. R.H.A.), B (Essex R.H.A.), C (W. Riding R.H.A.). A (H.) (4/Glasgow), B (H.) (5/Glasgow)	CCLXI (II Lowland) CCLXII (III Lowland) CCLXIV (V Lowland) CCLXIII (H.) (IV Lowland)	...	...	...[10]	2/Low-land[22] 2/1/Low-land 2/2/Low-land	52nd	...	...	1/Low-land 2/Low-land 3/Low-land	1/Low-land	...	52nd[15]
1917 June (Palestine)	155th........ 156th........ 157th........	4/R.S.F., 5/R.S.F., 4/K.O.S.B., 5/K.O.S.B.; 155th M.G. Coy.;[37] 155th T.M. Bty.[23] 4/R. Scots., 7/R. Scots., 7/Sco. Rif., 8/Sco. Rif.; 156th M.G. Coy.;[37] 156th T.M. Bty.[23] 5/H.L.I., 6/H.L.I., 7/H.L.I., 5/A. & S.H.; 157th M.G. Coy.;[37] 157th T.M. Bty.[23]	Hd. Qrs. and C Sqdn., R. Glasgow Yeo.[24] 52nd Divnl. Cyclist Coy.[25]	CCLXI[26] ..... CCLXII[27] .... CCLXIV[28] ..	A, B; C (H.) A, B A; C (H.)	...[29]	X.52[30] Y.52[30] Z.52[30]	...	52nd D.A.C.[29]	410th (2/Low-land) 412th (2/1/Low-land) 413th (2/2/Low-land)	52nd	...	...	1/Low-land 2/Low-land 3/Low-land	1/Low-land	...	52nd
1918 May (France)	155th........ 156th........ 157th........	4/R.S.F., 5/R.S.F., 4/K.O.S.B., 5/K.O.S.B.;[31] 155th T.M. Bty. 4/R. Scots., 7/R. Scots., 7/Sco. Rif., 8/Sco. Rif.;[31] 156th T.M. Bty. 5/H.L.I., 6/H.L.I., 7/H.L.I., 5/A. & S.H.;[31] 157th T.M. Bty.	...	IX[32] .... LVI[33]	19, 20, 28; D/LXIX (H.) A, B, C; 527 (H.)	...	X.52[34] Y.52[34]	...	52nd D.A.C.[35]	410th 412th 413th	52nd	5/R. Ir. Rgt.[36] (P.)	No. 52[37] Bn., M.G.C.	1/Low-land 2/Low-land 3/Low-land	1/Low-land	984th[38]	52nd
1918 August (France)	155th........ 156th........ 157th........	4/R.S.F., 5/R.S.F., 4/K.O.S.B.; 155th T.M. Bty. 4/R. Scots., 7/R. Scots., 7/Sco. Rif.; 156th T.M. Bty. 5/H.L.I., 6/H.L.I., 7/H.L.I.; 157th T.M. Bty.	...	IX .... LVI	19, 20, 28; D/LXIX (H.) A, B, C; 527 (H.)	...	X.52 Y.52	...	52nd D.A.C.	410th 412th 413th	52nd	17/N.F. (P.)[39]	No. 52 Bn., M.G.C.	1/Low-land 2/Low-land 3/Low-land	1/Low-land	984th	52nd

NOTES

1 The Lowland Division was numbered 52nd Division on 11/5/15, and the Inf. Bdes. were numbered 155th, 156th, 157th on the same day. (Authy. W.O. letter—40/W.O./2481 (A.G.1) of 7/5/15.)

2 The Bns. came from Kilmarnock, Ayr, Galashiels, and Dumfries. The Bde. landed at Helles on 6 and 7/6/15; the 4/K.O.S.B. on 14/6/15.

3 The 4 original Bns. came from Glasgow (3) and Hamilton; and 4/ and 7/R. Scots. came from Edinburgh. The Bde. landed at Helles on 12-14/6/15.

4 The 4 original Bns. came from Glasgow; and 5/A. & S.H. from Greenock. The Bde. landed at Helles on 3/7/15.

5 4/ and 7/R. Scots. joined on 24/4/15, from Lothian Bde. (Scottish Coast Defences). The Bns. sailed from Liverpool on 24/5/15.

6 Joined on 24/4/15 at Dunfermline, from Black Watch Bde. (Scottish Coast Defences). Bn. embarked on 1/6/15 at Devonport.

7 Formed during war training period, and embkd. on 5/6/15 at Devonport. The Coy landed at Helles, and on 1/8/15 it was broken up as reinforcements. On 27/3/16 the Cyclist Coy. was reformed at El Qantara.

8 The Bties. (4, 15-pdrs. each) came from Irvine, Kilmarnock, and Kirkcudbright, with the B.A.C. at Ardrossan. The Bde. remained in Egypt, and rejoined Div. at El Qantara on 5 and 6/3/16.

9 The Bde. was concentrated at Glasgow; and bties. were armed with 5-inch hows. Bde. H.Q. and 4/Glasgow Bty. landed at Helles on 21/6/15, and 5/Glasgow Bty. at Anzac on 24/6/15. Bde. H.Q. and 4th Bty. went to Anzac on 27/7/15, and then to Suvla on 20/8/15. Both Bties. took part in the Evacuations on 19-20/12/15. One 5-inch How. was destroyed at Anzac. Bde. rejoined Div. at Cairo on 11/1/16.

10 Raised at Glasgow on 25/4/15; went to Blackheath on 7/5/15, and drew its equipment; embkd. at Devonport on 4/6/15, and disembkd. at Port Said on 17/6/15. The D.A.C. remained in Egypt. The D.A.C. was broken up on 17/3/16.

11 Raised after mobn. The Cos. embkd. at Devonport on 9 and 10/6/15, disembkd. at Port Said on 23 and 22/6/15, and both landed at Helles on 29/6/15.

12 Hd. Qrs. and No. 1 Sec. came from Rutherglen. The Coy. embkd. at Liverpool on 24/5/15, disembkd. at Alexandria, 4/6/15; and the Coy. landed at Helles on 21/6/15.

13 The Fd. Ambces. came from Glasgow (2) and Edinburgh. They embkd. at Devonport on 5/6/15, and 1 and 2 landed at Helles on 28/6/15, and 3 landed at Helles on 3/7/15.

14 The Sec. left Stirling on 9/6/15, embkd. at Devonport on 10/6/15, disembkd. at Port Said on 22/6/15, and on 1/11/15 it joined 52nd Divnl. Details at Ismailia.

15 Formed during mobn. from Lowland Divnl. T. and S. Coln. Tpt. Sec. sailed from Devonport on 9/6/15 and disembkd. Port Said on 23/6/15. It was transferred to 10th Div. in Oct. 1915, and landed at Salonika on 19 and 20/10/15. Supply Sec. sailed for Gallipoli with Hd. Qrs. of Div. on 24/5/15 and served throughout the War with the 52nd Div. Between 1-10/3/16 Tpt. Sec. of 31st Div. was transferred to 52nd Div., and thenceforward Tpt. Sec., 31st Div., and Supply Sec., 52nd Div., formed 52nd Divnl. Train. The Cos. were numbered 217, 218, 219, and 220 Cos., A.S.C.

16 The M.G. Cos. were formed: 155th on 23/3/16; 156th on 16/3/16; and 157th on 14/3/16.

17 Hd. Qrs. and C Sqdn. disembkd. at Port Said on 22/6/15, and on 10/10/15 joined 52nd Div. at Helles (9 offrs. and 149 o.r.).

18 Bties. were rearmed with 18-pdrs. on 27 and 28/4/16. The Bde. was numbered CCLX and Bties. lettered A, B, C, on 28/5/16; and on 15/9/16 the Bde. was renumbered CCLXI. On 25/12/16 C Bty. was broken up, and R. Sec. joined A, and L. Sec. joined B. On 30/12/16 A (H.)/CCLXIII (H.) joined and became C (H.)/CCLXI.

19 Bde. rejoined Div. at El Qantara on 17/3/16. Bties. were rearmed with 18-pdrs. before embkn. The Bde. was numbered CCLXI and Bties. lettered A, B, C, on 28/5/16; and on 15/9/16 the Bde. was renumbered CCLXII. On 25/12/16 C Bty. was broken up and 1 sec. went to A and 1 sec. to B. On 30/12/16 B (H.)/CCLXIII (H.) joined and became C (H.)/CCLXII.

20 The Bde. concentrated at Leicester on 13/1/16, embkd. at Devonport on 15 and 18/2/16, disembkd. at Port Said on 2/3/16, and joined 52nd Div. at El Qantara on 17/3/16. Before sailing the 3 R.H.A. (T.F.) Bties. had been rearmed with 18-pdrs. Bde. was numbered CCLXIII and Bties. lettered A, B, C, on 28/5/16; on 15/9/16 the Bde. was renumbered CCLXIV, and on 30/12/16 its number was changed again to CCLXIII. On 30/12/16 C Bty. was split up: 1 sec. went to A, and 1 sec. to B. On 5/7/17 CCLXIII changed its 18-pdr. equipt. for 13-pdr., and became XX R.H.A. (Hants., Berks., and Leciester R.H.A. (T.F.) Bties.). XX R.H.A. joined Yeo. Mtd. Div. on 5/7/17 at Khan Yunis. Essex R.H.A. (T.F.) Bty. joined 7th Mtd. Bde. (later in 2nd Mtd. Div.) on 17/9/17.

21 The Bde. was numbered CCLXII (H.) and Bties. lettered A, B, C, on 28/5/16. On 28/6/16 Bties. were rearmed with 4.5-inch Hows. On 15/9/16 the Bde. was renumbered CCLXIII; and on 30/12/16 the Bde. was broken up: A (H.) became C (H.)/CCLXI; and B (H.) became C (H.)/CCLXII.

22 On 24/2/16 the Coy. was transferred back from 29th Div.

23 155th was formed on 24/5/17; 156th by 27/6/17; and 157th by 11/6/17.

24 Joined XXI Corps Cav. Regt. on 21/8/17.

25 Joined XXI Corps Troops by 8/12/17. The Coy. returned to 52nd Div. at Sarafand on 1/4/18, went to France with 52nd Div., and on 4/5/18 was transferred to Cyclist Base Depot at Rouen, and broken up for drafts.

26 Bde. was transferred on 3/4/18 to 7th Ind. Div. at Nahr el Auja.

27 Bde. transferred on 3/4/18 to 7th Ind. Div. at Nahr el Auja. On 5/4/18, 438 (H.) joined the Bde. and became C (H.)/CCLXII.

28 Bde. formed on 1/7/17 from A/CCLXXII and C (H.)/CCLXII which became A and C (H.)/CCLXIV. On 27/2/18, 422 and 423 Bties. (each 6, 18-pdrs.) joined the Bde. On 3/4/18, CCLXIV was transferred to 7th Ind. Div. at Nahrel Auja. (A rejoined CCLXXII, 54th Div., on 2/3/18.)

29 On 1/1/17 52nd D.A.C. was reformed from B.A.C.'s of CCLXI, CCLXII, and CCLXXII, and the B.A.C.'s were abolished. On 3/4/18 the D.A.C. was transferred to the 7th Ind. Div. at Arsuf.

30 X, Y, and Z joined 52nd Div. on 3/10/17 at Deir el Bela. On 3/4/18 X, Y, and Z were transferred to 7th Ind. Div.

31 The 3 Bns. left the 52nd Div. on 28/6/18 and joined 103rd Bde., 34th Div.

32 Bde. transferred on 1/4/18 from 7th Ind. Div. at Moascar. Bde. (with 133 and 134 T.M. Bties., No. 1 Sec. D.A.C., and 413 Coy., R.E.) embkd. on 4/4/18 at Alexandria in *Kingstonian*. This ship was torpedoed on 11/4/18 and all the equipt. was lost. Personnel reached Marseille on 12/4/18 in *Lychnis* and *Berberis*. New guns, wagons, harness, etc., were drawn on 23-26/4/18.

33 Bde. transferred on 1/4/18 from 7th Ind. Div. at Moascar, and went to France in April with 52nd Div. Previous service of the Bde. had been with 10th and 13th Divs.

34 133, 134, 135 Med. T.M. Bties. (without any equipt.) joined 7th Ind. Div. on 31/1/18. 135 was split up between 133 and 134; and on 3/4/18 the 2 T.M.B.'s were transferred to 52nd Div. at El Qantara, and went to France in April. On 1/5/18, 133 and 134 formed X.52, and Y.40 became Y.52. On 8/5/18 X and Y joined 52nd Div. from the T.M. School. (Also see note 32.)

35 7th Ind. D.A.C. was reorganized at Moascar on 1/4/18 into Nos. 1 and 2 Secs. and B Echelon and became 52nd D.A.C. It embkd. at Alexandria on 3/4/18 (also see note 32) and arrived at Marseille on 12/4/18.

36 Joined at Sarafand on 3/4/18 (from 10th Div.) and was transferred to L. of C. on 31/5/18. The Pioneer Bn. joined 50th Div. on 14/7/18 (see 50th Div., note 63).

37 Bn. formed on 28/4/18; it consisted of 155th, 156th, 157th, and 211th M.G. Cos. 211th Coy. was formed by 15/9/17 in XXI Corps in Palestine, and joined 52nd Div. on 1/4/18 at Sarafand.

38 Coy. formed in France by 27/4/18.

39 In Nov., '15, the Bn. went to France with the 32nd Div. as Pioneers, and in Nov., '17 the Bn. was transferred to G.H.Q. Troops and worked as a Rly. Pioneer Bn. On 31/5/18 the Bn. joined 52nd Div. (tempy.) as Pioneers, and on 30/6/18 it was posted permanently.

52ND (LOWLAND) DIVISION

MOBILIZATION, BATTLES, AND ENGAGEMENTS

The division—an existing T.F. division—was drawn from that part of Scotland lying south of a line from the Firth of Forth to Loch Lomond, with the divisional headquarters in Glasgow. The three brigade headquarters were at Ayr and Glasgow (2); and the original 12 battalions came from Kilmarnock, Ayr, Galashiels, Dumfries, Glasgow (7), and Hamilton.

In the artillery: the I. Lowland Bde. was at Edinburgh; the II. Lowland Bde. was at Irvine, with outlying batteries at Kilmarnock and Kirkcudbright, and the ammunition column at Ardrossan; the III. Lowland Bde. was at Glasgow; the IV. Lowland (How.) Bde. was also in Glasgow; and the Lowland (City of Edinburgh) Heavy Battery came from Edinburgh (see General Notes).

The field companies came from Coatbridge and Rutherglen; and the H.Q. and No. 1 Section of the Signal Company from Rutherglen. Two field ambulances came from Glasgow and the third from Edinburgh; and the companies of the Divnl. T. and S. Column were at Glasgow (2), Edinburgh, and Motherwell.

On Tuesday, the 4th August, 1914, the order to mobilize was received by telegram and, by the 10th August, mobilization was completed. The Lowland Division was assigned to the coast defence of Scotland. The division moved to Bridge of Allan, Stirling, Falkirk, and Dunfermline, and training for war was proceeded with.

Between mid-November, 1914, and the end of March, 1915, the following units left the division to join other formations, viz.: 1/Lowland Fd. Coy., 2/Lowland Fd. Coy., 5/Scottish Rifles, 6/Scottish Rifles, 9/Highland Light Infantry (see General Notes). In April, 1915, to replace these units, the division had transferred to it two second-line field companies (2/1/Lowland and 2/2/Lowland), and three first-line battalions (4/R. Scots and 7/R. Scots, from the Lothian Infantry Brigade; and 5/Argyll and Sutherland Highlanders, from the Black Watch Infantry Brigade).

On the 5th April the division received information that it would shortly proceed overseas. On the 7th May it was warned that it would be employed in Gallipoli, and between the 18th May and the 8th June the division embarked at Devonport and Liverpool. The movement to Liverpool was marked by a tragedy. On the 22nd May the troop-train carrying headquarters and two companies, 7/R. Scots (156th Brigade) was involved in a collision near Gretna in which 3 officers and 207 other ranks were killed and 5 officers and 219 other ranks were injured; only 7 officers and 57 other ranks were uninjured.

The division left behind two of its field artillery brigades, in the Forth Defences, as well as its heavy battery (see General Notes).

Only the 155th Brigade (less 4/K.O.S.B.) went direct to Mudros, arriving on the 29th May; the other transports went to Alexandria and Port Said, arriving between 4th–23rd June, 1915. On the 6th June the first units of the division landed at Cape Helles; and by the first week in July, the rest of the division had reached the Gallipoli Peninsula. The division left behind in Egypt the II. Lowland Brigade, the divisional ammunition column, and the transport section of the train.

During the Great War the 52nd Division served in Gallipoli, then in Egypt and Palestine, and lastly in France and Belgium, and was engaged in the following operations:

1915

28 and 29 June ... ...**Gully Ravine** (156th Bde.) [with 29th Div., VIII. Corps].
12 and 13 July ... ...**Achi Baba Nullah** [VIII. Corps].
29 Dec. ... ...**Krithia Nullahs** [VIII Corps].

1916

Night of 7/8 Jan. ...**Evacuation of Helles** [VIII. Corps].

After the Evacuation of Helles the 52nd Division moved to Egypt, and by the end of January the division had concentrated at Abbassia (near Cairo). The division then moved to El Qantara, and on the 2nd March it took over part of No. 3 Section of the Suez Canal Defences (under XV. Corps; until 12/4/16).

22 April ... ...**Dueidar** (4/ and 5/R.S.F. of 155th Bde.).
4 and 5 Aug. ... ...**Battle of Romani** [No. 3 Section, Canal Defences].

1917

INVASION OF PALESTINE

26 and 27 March ...**First Battle of Gaza** (In Reserve) [Eastern Force].
17–19 April ... ...**Second Battle of Gaza** [Eastern Force].
1–7 Nov. ... ...**Third Battle of Gaza** [XXI. Corps].
8 Nov. ... ...**Wadi el Hesi** [XXI. Corps].
12 Nov. ... ...**Burqa** (156th Brigade).
13 Nov. ... ...**El Maghar** (155th Brigade) [with Yeo. Mtd. Div., XXI. Corps].
14 Nov. ... ...**Capture of Junction Station** [XXI. Corps].
20–24 Nov. ... ...**Battle of Nabi Samweil** [XXI. Corps].
21 and 22 Dec. ... ...**Battle of Jaffa** [XXI. Corps].
21 Dec. ... ...**Passage of the Nahr el Auja.**

1918

Until March the division remained in the line near Arsuf. On the 24th March XXI. Corps warned the 52nd Division that it would be relieved by the 7th (Indian) Division, and the 52nd Division would be transferred to the Western Front. The relief was completed, and the whole of the 52nd Div. Artillery was exchanged with the 7th (Indian) Div. Artillery. The 52nd Division left Alexandria between the 4th and 11th April, and reached Marseille between the 12th and 17th. The division concentrated near Abbeville by 23rd April, and on the 29th it moved to Aire and continued war training. On the 6th May the division moved to the Vimy area and its units took over front line trenches in the various sectors. On the 23rd July the division went into G.H.Q. Reserve, and on the 31st July it moved up into the front line to the north-east of Arras, and was engaged in the following battles:

THE ADVANCE TO VICTORY

SECOND BATTLES OF THE SOMME

23 Aug. ... ...**Battle of Albert** [VI. Corps, Third Army].

SECOND BATTLES OF ARRAS

26 and 27 Aug. ... ...**Battle of the Scarpe** [XVII. Corps, Third Army].
2 and 3 Sept. ... ...**Battle of the Drocourt-Quéant Line** [XVII. Corps, Third Army].

BATTLES OF THE HINDENBURG LINE

27 Sept.–1 Oct. ... ...**Battle of the Canal du Nord** [XVII. Corps, Third Army].

On 7th October, 52nd Division (less Divnl. Arty. and M.G. Bn. left in line, with XVII. Corps) was transferred to VIII. Corps, First Army. The M.G. Bn. rejoined on the 11th and the Divnl. Artillery on the 20th. On the 28th October, 52nd Division again went into the line to the north-east of St. Amand, on the left of the VIII. Corps front, and took part in :—

28 Oct.–11 Nov. ...**FINAL ADVANCE IN ARTOIS** [VIII. Corps, First Army].

On the 11th November, the 52nd Division was in the front line beyond Condé, to the north of the Mons Canal, and, clearing Herchies, had reached by 11 a.m. the Nimy-Jurbise road to the north-west of Mons.

After the Armistice the division was employed in training and in clearing up the area. On the 5th December H.M. the King drove through the divisional area. Drafting and demobilization proceeded and units and formations gradually dwindled to cadre. At the end of January, 1919, the strength of the division was 584 officers, and 10,665 other ranks, but finally, on the 31st May, 1919, when the last cadres entrained for the United Kingdom, the division had shrunk to 57 officers and 969 other ranks. In 1920 the division was re-formed in Scotland.

53RD (WELSH) DIVISION

G.O.C.

14 October, 1913 ... ... Major-General HON. J. E. LINDLEY.
19 August, 1915... ... ... Major-General HON. H. A. LAWRENCE (tempy.).
25 August, 1915... ... ... Major-General W. R. MARSHALL.
9 September, 1915 ... ... Br.-Gen. W. J. C. BUTLER (acting).
13 September, 1915 ... ... Major-General W. R. MARSHALL.
23 December, 1915 ... ... Br.-Gen. R. O'B. TAYLOR (acting).
27 December, 1915 ... ... Br.-Gen. W. J. C. BUTLER (acting).
11 January, 1916 ... ... Major-General A. G. DALLAS (sick, 6/3/16).
8 March, 1916 ... ... Br.-Gen. A. H. SHORT (acting).
11 March, 1916 ... ... *Major-General A. G. DALLAS.
20 May, 1916 ... ... Br.-Gen. A. H. SHORT (acting).
28 June, 1916 ... ... Major-General A. G. DALLAS.
10 April, 1917 ... ... Major-General S. F. MOTT.

G.S.O. 1.

29 Sept., 1913...Major W. DE L. WILLIAMS (G.S.O. 2).
5 Aug., 1914...Lt.-Col.W. DE L. WILLIAMS.
10 April, 1915...Lt.-Col. J. D. MCLACHLAN.
20 June, 1915...Major W. F. WALTER (acting).
7 July, 1915...Lt.-Col. G. A. S. CAPE.
27 May, 1916...Lt.-Col. A. B. ROBERTSON.
23 Sept., 1916...Lt.-Col. A. E. M. SINCLAIR-THOMSON.
15 June, 1918...Major H. B. D. WILLCOX (acting) (sick, 24/6/18).
24 June, 1918...Capt. A. M. T. EVE (acting).
25 June, 1918...Lt.-Col. W. C. GARSIA.

A.-A. and Q.-M.-G.

1 April, 1912...Capt. A. DERRY (D.-A.-A. and Q.-M.-G.).
5 Aug., 1914...Col. F. S. L. PENNO (invalided, 23/11/15).
23 Nov., 1915...Lt.-Col. A. DERRY (invalided, 24/3/16).
24 Mar., 1916...Major G. P. C. BLOUNT (acting).
9 April, 1916...Lt.-Col. G. P. C. BLOUNT.
9 Aug., 1917...Lt.-Col. C. H. G. COLLINS.
15 May, 1918...Major H. E. P. PATESHALL (acting).
16 June, 1918...Lt.-Col. R. W. OPPENHEIM.

B.-G., R.A.

12 Aug., 1912...**Br.-Gen. W. K. MCLEOD.
5 April, 1915...Br.-Gen. W. A. MACBEAN.
(In July, 1915, when the Division embarked for Gallipoli, the Divisional Artillery remained at Bedford.)
19 Nov., 1915...Lt.-Col. F. J. BONNALIE (acting).
(The Divisional Artillery and D.A.C. went to France in November, 1915, and concentrated at Pont Remy by 25/11/15.)
24 Nov., 1915...Br.-Gen. A. H. SHORT.
(On 3/2/16 the Divisional Artillery and a party from the D.A.C. embarked for Egypt, and on 22/2/16 rejoined the Division near Wardan (see General Notes and Notes 14–18).)
8 Mar., 1916...Lt.-Col. F. J. BONNALIE (acting).
11 Mar., 1916...Br.-Gen. A. H. SHORT.
18 May, 1916...Lt.-Col. F. J. BONNALIE (acting).
27 June, 1916...Br.-Gen. A. H. SHORT.
24 Oct., 1916...Lt.-Col. T. W. PEARSON (acting).
7 Nov., 1916...Lt.-Col. F. J. BONNALIE (acting).
30 Nov., 1916...Br.-Gen. R. E. A. LE MOTTÉE (sick, 22/10/17).
20 Oct., 1917...Br.-Gen. J. W. HOPE (sick, 5/11/17).
5 Nov., 1917...Lt.-Col. J. W. WALKER (acting).
24 Nov., 1917...Br.-Gen. J. W. WALKER.

C.R.E.

16 Nov., 1910...Lt.-Col. R. L. HUTCHISON (invalided, 29/9/15).
29 Sept., 1915...Major T. A. ISAAC (acting).
11 Nov., 1915...Lt.-Col. R. P. T. HAWKSLEY.
8 Nov., 1916...Major R. A. NEVILL (acting).
25 Jan., 1917...Lt.-Col. R. P. T. HAWKSLEY.
24 Mar., 1917...Lt.-Col. F. R. H. EUSTACE.

*From 1/4/16–20/5/16 the G.O.C. 53rd Div. also commanded N.W. Force; from 20/5/16–21/6/16 he took over the Western Frontier Force; and then he commanded 53rd Div. as well as No. 2 Sec., Suez Canal Defences.

**Br.-Gen. on 5 August, 1914.

158th BDE.
(N. Wales Bde.)

26 July, '12...*Br.-Gen. F. C. LLOYD (wounded, 17/8/15).
17 Aug., '15...Major J. GOING (acting).
20 Aug., '15...Br.-Gen. S. F. MOTT.
10 April, '17...Lt.-Col. G. DRAGE (acting).
12 April, '17...Br.-Gen. C. S. ROME.
29 Aug., '17...Lt.-Col. T. H. HARKER (acting).
3 Sept., '17...Br.-Gen. C. S. ROME.
4 Sept., '17...Br.-Gen. H. A. VERNON.
27 Sept., '18...Lt.-Col. F. H. BORTHWICK (acting).
30 Sept., '18...Br.-Gen. E. H. WILDBLOOD.

159th BDE.
(Cheshire Bde.)

25 June, '14...*Br.-Gen. E. A. COWANS (wounded, 14/8/15).
14 Aug., '15...Lt.-Col. H. BACKHOUSE (acting).
24 Aug., '15...Br.-Gen. W. J. C. BUTLER.
21 Sept., '15...Br.-Gen. E. A. COWANS (invalided, 12/11/15).
12 Nov., '15...Lt.-Col. G. H. SWINDELLS (acting).
19 Nov., '15...Br.-Gen. R. O'B. TAYLOR.
27 Mar., '16...Lt.-Col. H. J. KINSMAN (acting).
29 Mar., '16...Br.-Gen. J. H. DU B. TRAVERS (sick, 27/10/17).
27 Oct., '17...Lt.-Col. H. M. LAWRENCE (acting).
28 Oct., '17...Br.-Gen. N. E. MONEY.

160th BDE.
(Welsh Border Bde.)

1 July, '10...*Br.-Gen. J. J. F. HUME (invalided, 31/8/15).
1 Sept., '15...Col. F. D. WATNEY (acting).
22 Sept., '15...Br.-Gen. W. J. C. BUTLER (sick, 29/11/15).
30 Nov., '15...Lt.-Col. E. J. F. VAUGHAN (acting).
5 Dec., '15...Br.-Gen. S. W. HARE.
15 Dec., '15...Lt.-Col. E. J. F. VAUGHAN (acting).
27 Dec., '15...Br.-Gen. W. J. C. BUTLER.
27 Dec., '15...Lt.-Col. E. J. F. VAUGHAN (acting).
11 Jan., '16...Br.-Gen. W. J. C. BUTLER (invalided, 29/4/17).
29 April, '17...Lt.-Col. H. ST. C. WILKINS (acting).
10 May, '17...Br.-Gen. V. L. N. PEARSON.
30 Sept., '18...Lt.-Col. T. H. HARKER (acting).
1 Oct., '18...Br.-Gen. F. H. BORTHWICK.

*Br.-Gen. on 5 August, 1914.

GENERAL NOTES

The following Units belonged to the Welsh Division in August, 1914, but they went overseas independently :—

DIVISIONAL ARTILLERY :—

I. Welsh (How.) Bde., R.F.A., T.F. (Bties. 4, 5-inch H. each)
II. Welsh Bde., R.F.A., T.F. (Bties. 4, 15-pdrs. each)
Cheshire Bde., R.F.A., T.F. (Bties. 4, 15-pdrs. each)
IV. Welsh Bde., R.F.A., T.F. (Bties. 4, 15-pdrs. each)
53rd (Welsh) D.A.C.

In 1915, when the 53rd Div. went to Gallipoli, the Arty. Bdes., B.A.C.s, and D.A.C. (less S.A.A. Sec.—see note 10) remained behind in Bedford.

In October, 1915, Bties. were rearmed with 18-pdrs. and 4.5-inch Hows., and on 8/11/15 the old 15-pdr. and 5-inch How. equipments were handed over to the 68th (2/Welsh) Div. Arty.

On 20/11/15 the 53rd Div. Arty. began embkg. for France, and by 25/11/15 it had concentrated at Pont Remy. Bties. and parties from the Bdes. and Ammn. Colns. were attached for instruction to various divnl. artilleries. On 30/1/16 Bdes. were ordered to prepare to rejoin the 53rd Div. in Egypt. On 1/2/16 entrainment began at Pont Remy, on 3/2/16 embkn. began at Marseille, and disembkn. at Alexandria on 11/2/16. By 22/2/16 the 53rd Div. Arty. had completed its concentration at Beni Salama (see notes 14–18).

Welsh (Caernarvonshire) Hy. Bty., R.G.A., T.F. (4, 4.7-inch guns), was left behind by the Div. at Bedford. On 16/2/16 the Hy. Bty. went to Woolwich to mobilize, embkd. at Southampton on 2/3/16, disembkd. at le Havre on 3/3/16, and joined XXIII. H.A. Group in March, 1916. The Hy. Bty. was in action on 17/3/16, and was engaged in the Battles of the Somme from 24/6/16.

Cheshire Fd. Coy., R.E., T.F., left Welsh Div. for France on 8/12/14, embkd. on 9/12/14, disembkd. at le Havre on 10/12/14, and joined 3rd Div. on 22/12/14.

4/R. Welsh Fusiliers (Wrexham) left Welsh Div. for France on 5/11/14, and on 7/12/14 joined 3rd Bde., 1st Div. On 1/9/15 the Bn. was transferred to 47th Div. as Pioneers.

5/Cheshire (Chester) left Div. for France on 14/2/15, and on 19/2/15 joined 14th Bde., 5th Div., became Divnl. Pioneers on 29/11/15, and on 13/2/16 was transferred to 56th Div. as Divnl. Pioneers.

6/Cheshire (Stockport) left Div. for France on 9/11/14, joined 15th Bde., 5th Div., on 17/12/14, and was transferred on 1/3/15 to G.H.Q. Troops.

1/Monmouth (Newport) left Div. for France on 13/2/15, joined 84th Bde., 28th Div., on 27/2/15, and was transferred on 3/9/15 to 46th Div. as Divnl. Pioneers.

2/Monmouth (Pontypool) left Div. for France on 5/11/14, joined 12th Bde., 4th Div., 20/11/14, amalgamated (in 84th Bde., 28th Div.) with 1/Mon. and 3/Mon. on 27/5/15. Bn. resumed independent formation on 24/7/15, rejoined 12th Bde., 4th Div., on 25/7/15, transferred to L. of C. on 30/1/16, and on 1/5/16 became Divnl. Pioneers, 29th Div.

3/Monmouth (Abergavenny) left Div. for France on 13/2/15, joined 83rd Bde., 28th Div., on 3/3/15, and on 2/9/15 was transferred to 49th Div. and became Divnl. Pioneers on 18/9/15. Bn. was transferred to G.H.Q. Troops on 9/8/16, and by 31/8/16 it was broken up for drafts.

53rd (Welsh) Divisional Train was left behind by the Div. in July, 1915. On 13/6/16 the Train was allotted to the 11th Div., and it embarked for France on 1/7/16. The Cos. were numbered 479, 480, 481, and 482.

Hd. Qrs. and No. 1 Sec., 53rd (Welsh) Divnl. Sig. Coy.
(a) attached at Suvla to 54th Div. from 10–23/8/15, then handed over to 54th Divnl. Sig. Coy. and rejoined 53rd Div.;
(b) after leaving Suvla, ordered on 15/12/15 to proceed to Salonika. Disembkd. at Salonika on 19/12/15, and joined XII. Corps as signal unit on 27/12/15. Re-embkd. at Salonika on 16/1/16, arrived Alexandria on 21/1/16, and rejoined 53rd Div. at Wardan on 22/1/16.

3rd Welsh Field Ambulance was attached to the 54th Div. at Suvla, from 11–18/8/15.

The following Units also served with the 53rd Division :—

(i) **Before embarkation :—**

Westmorland and Cumberland Yeo.	18/8/14–21/6/15 ;
Sqdn., South Irish Horse...	22/6/15–19/7/15 ;
2/6/Ches., 2/4/R.W.F., and 2/2/Mon.	22/11/14–22/4/15 ;
2/5/Ches., 2/1/Mon., and 2/3/Mon.	18/2/15–22/4/15.

(ii) **After embarkation : 2/S. Western Mtd. Bde.** (Br.-Gen. R. Hoare), at Suvla, from 29/11/15–9/12/15.

4th Dismounted Bde. (Br.-Gen. E. A. Herbert) consisting of Welsh Border and South Wales Mtd. Bdes., was attached to the 53rd Div. from 15/3/16—21/6/16 (transferred to Western Frontier Force).

A. Sqdn., 1/Linc. Yeo.—from 19/12/16–14/1/17.

A. Sqdn., 2/County of London Yeo. (Westminster Dragoons)—from 12/1/17–28/1/17.

2/1/London R., **2/3/London R.** } joined at Wardan on 15/1/16, from 29th Div.
2/2/London R., **2/4/London R.** } joined at Wardan on 22/2/16

All four Bns. left the 53rd Div. in April, 1916, to move to France. The four Bns. disembkd. at Marseille on 24/4/16 ; and in May, 1916, all four Bns. were broken up in France and drafted.

53rd Sanitary Section—formed at Cardiff on 22/4/15, the Section arrived at Bedford on 29/5/15 ; it sailed for Egypt on 19/7/15, and disembkd. at Suvla on 9/8/15. During the remainder of the Great War the Section served with the 53rd (Welsh) Division.

The following Bdes. were attached to the **2nd Mounted Division** at Suvla :—

158th Bde., from 31/10/15–28/11/15 ; and
159th Bde., from 29/11/15–9/12/15.

53RD[1] (WELSH) DIVISION ORDER OF BATTLE, 1915-1918

Dates	INFANTRY		Mounted Troops	ARTILLERY						Engineers	Signal Service	Pioneers	M.G. Units	Field Ambulances	Mobile Vety. Secn.	Divnl. Emplnt. Coy.	Divnl. Train
				Field Artillery			Trench Mortar Bties.										
	Brigades	Battalions and attached Units		Brigades	Batteries	Bde. Ammn. Colns.	Medium	Heavy	Divnl. Ammn. Coln.	Field Cos.	Divnl. Signal Coy.						
1915 August (Gallipoli)	158th[1]; [2] (North Wales) 159th[1]; [4] (Cheshire) 160th[1]; [6] (WelshBorder)	5/R.W.F., 6/R.W.F., 7/R.W.F., 1/Hereford.[3] 4/Ches., 7/Ches., 4/Welsh,[5] 5/Welsh[5] 2/4/Queen's,[7] 4/R. Suss.,[8] 2/4/R.W.K.,[7] 2/10/Midd'x.[7]	53rd[9] (Welsh) Divnl. Cyclist Coy.	...	...	...	...	...	53rd[10] (Welsh) D.A.C.	1/Welsh 2/1/ Cheshire[11]	53rd (Welsh)	...	...	1/Welsh 2/Welsh 3/Welsh	53rd[12] (Welsh)	...	...
1916 June (Egypt)	158th........ 159th........ 160th........	5/R.W.F., 6/R.W.F., 7/R.W.F., 1/Hereford.; 158th Bde. M.G. Coy.[13] 4/Ches., 7/Ches., 4/Welsh, 5/Welsh; 159th Bde. M.G. Coy.[13] 2/4/Queen's, 4/R. Suss., 2/4/R.W.K., 2/10/Midd'x.; 160th Bde. M.G. Coy.[13]	53rd Divnl. Cyclist Coy.	CCLXV (H.)[14] (I Welsh (H.)) CCLXVI[15] (II Welsh) CCLXVII[16] (Cheshire) CCLXVIII[17] (IV Welsh)	1/Glamorgan (H.), 2/Glamorgan (H.) 3/Glamorgan, 4/Glamorgan, Cardigan 1/Cheshire, 2/Cheshire, 3/Cheshire 1/Monmouth, 2/Monmouth, 3/Monmouth	CCLXV (H.)[14] (I Welsh (H.)) CCLXVI (II Welsh) CCLXVII (Cheshire) CCLXVIII (IV Welsh)	...	...	53rd[18] D.A.C.	1/Welsh 2/1/Welsh[19] 2/1/Cheshire	53rd	...	...	1/Welsh 2/Welsh 3/Welsh	53rd	...	53rd[20]
1917 June (Palestine)	158th........ 159th........ 160th........	5/R.W.F., 6/R.W.F., 7/R.W.F., 1/Hereford.;[21] 158th M.G. Coy.; 158th T.M. Bty.[22] 4/Ches.,[23] 7/Ches.,[24] 4/Welsh, 5/Welsh; 159th M.G. Coy.; 159th T.M. Bty.[22] 2/4/Queen's,[25] 4/R. Suss.,[26] 2/4/R.W.K., 2/10/Midd'x.; 160th M.G. Coy.; 160th T.M. Bty.[22]	A Sqdn., Duke of Lanc.'s Own Yeo.[27] 53rd Divnl. Cyclist Coy.	CCLXV[14]; [16] CCLXVI[15]; [17] CCLXVII[15]; [16]	A, B; C (H.) A, B; C (H.) A, B	...[18]	...	...	53rd D.A.C.	436th[28] (1/Welsh) 437th[28] (2/1/Welsh) 439th[28]; [29] (2/1/Cheshire)	53rd	...	...	1/Welsh 2/Welsh 3/Welsh	53rd	...	53rd
1918 July (Palestine)	158th........ 159th........ 160th........	5/R.W.F.,[30] 6/R.W.F.,[30] 7/R.W.F.,[31] 4/11/Gurkha Rif.,[32] 3/153/Inf.;[33] 158th T.M. Bty. 4/Welsh,[34] 5/Welsh,[34] 3/152/Inf.,[35] 2/153/Inf.;[36] 159th T.M. Bty. 2/4/R.W.K.,[37] 2/10/Midd'x.,[38] 21/Punjabis,[39] 110/Mahratta L.I.;[40] 160th T.M. Bty.	53rd Divnl. Cyclist Coy.	CCLXV .... CCLXVI .... CCLXVII	A, B; C (H.) A, B; C (H.) A, B; 439 (H.)[41]	...	...	...	53rd D.A.C.	436th 437th 72nd Coy.,[42] 3/S. & M.	53rd	...	No. 53 Bn.,[43] M.G.C.	1/Welsh[44] 2/Welsh[45] 3/Welsh[46] 113 C.F.A.[47]	53rd	...	53rd
1918 September (Palestine)	158th........ 159th........ 160th........	5/6/R.W.F., 4/11/Gurkha Rif., 3/153/Inf., 3/154/Inf.;[48] 158th T.M. Bty. 4/5/Welsh, 3/152/Inf., 1/153/Inf.,[49] 2/153/Inf.; 159th T.M. Bty. 7/R.W.F.,[31] 17/Inf.,[50] 21/Punjabis, 1/Cape Corps;[51] 160th T.M. Bty.	53rd Divnl. Cyclist Coy.	CCLXV .... CCLXVI .... CCLXVII	A, B; C (H.) A, B; C (H.) A, B; 439 (H.)	...	...	...	53rd D.A.C.	436th 437th 72nd Coy., 3/S. & M.	53rd	155th (P.)[52]	No. 53 Bn., M.G.C.	113 C.F.A. 170 C.F.A.[53] 171 C.F.A.[54]	53rd	...	53rd

NOTES

1 The Welsh Division was numbered 53rd Division on 13/5/15, and the Inf. Bdes. were numbered 158th, 159th, and 160th on the same day. (Authy. W.O. letter—40/W.O./2481 (A.G.1) of 7/5/15.)

2 After reorganization, the Bns. came from Flint, Caernarvon, Newtown, and Hereford (see note 3).

3 Transferred from Welsh Border Bde. on 24/4/15.

4 After reorganization, the Bns. came from Birkenhead, Macclesfield, Carmarthen, and Pontypridd (see note 5).

5 Transferred from S. Wales Bde., Army Troops, Western Command, on 17/4/15. At Suvla on 8/10/15 the 2 Bns. were amalgamated as 4/Welsh Comp. Bn. The 2 Bns. resumed independent formation in Egypt on 20/2/16.

6 Bde. was re-formed on 24/4/15 (see notes 7 and 8).

7 These 3 2nd-Line Bns., raised after the outbreak of war, joined the Bde. on 24/4/15.

8 4/R. Suss. (Horsham) joined the Bde. on 24/4/15.

9 Coy. formed at Stockport in May and June, 1915, went to Bedford on 3/7/15, sailed for Egypt on 16/7/15, and landed at Suvla on 10/8/15.

10 D.A.C. was formed during mobilization. Between 6—14/7/15 the S.A.A. Sec. (184 all ranks, 202 horses, 41 vehicles) was specially organized to proceed with the Div. The S.A.A. Sec. embkd. on 16/7/15 and disembkd. at Suvla between 12—15/8/15.

11 Coy. joined Div. to replace 1/Ches. Fd. Coy. (see General Notes), and landed at Suvla on 9/8/15.

12 Formed at Bedford on 27/6/15. It was left behind by the Div., and sailed for Egypt on 21/3/16. The Sec. disembkd. at Alexandria on 10/4/16, and it rejoined 53rd Div. on 11/4/16.

13 M.G. Cos. were formed: 158th on 26/4/16; 159th on 20/4/16; and 160th on 11/5/16.

14 Bde. (also see General Notes) rejoined Div. in Egypt between 15-22/2/16. On 26/5/16 Bde. was numbered CCLXV (H.), and batteries lettered A (H.) and B (H.). CCLXV (H.) was broken up on 25/12/16; and CCLXVII became CCLXV. A (H.) became C (H.) in new CCXLV, and B (H.) became C (H.) in new CCLXVI; and B.A.C. was divided between new CCLXV and new CCLXVI.

15 Bde. (also see General Notes) rejoined Div. in Egypt between 11-15/2/16. On 26/5/16 Bde. was numbered CCLXVI, and batteries lettered A, B, and C. On 25/12/16 A was broken up between B and C, and B became A and C became B; and the Bde. was renumbered CCLXVII.

16 Bde. (also see General Notes) rejoined Div. in Egypt between 18-21/2/16. On 26/5/16 Bde. was numbered CCLXVII, and batteries lettered A, B, and C. On 25/12/16 A was broken up between B and C, and B became A and C became B; and the Bde. was renumbered CCLXV. A (H.) from old CCLXV (note 14) joined and became C (H.) new CCLXV. B.A.C. new CCLXV was formed from B.A.C. of old CCLXVII and 1/2 B.A.C. of old CCLXV.

17 Bde. (also see General Notes) rejoined Div. in Egypt between 18-22/2/16. On 26/5/16 Bde. was numbered CCLXVIII, and batteries lettered A, B, and C. On 25/12/16 C was broken up between A and B; and the Bde. was renumbered CCLXVI. B (H.) from old CCLXV (note 14) joined and became C (H.) new CCLXVI. B.A.C. new CCLXVI was formed from B.A.C. of old CCLXVIII and 1/2 B.A.C. of old CCLXV.

18 D.A.C. remained in England on departure of Div. (see note 10). The D.A.C. went to France and disembkd. at le Havre on 25/11/15. Between 27-31/1/16, 53rd and 54th D.A.C.s (in France) exchanged personnel and riding horses: 53rd D.A.C. (vehicles and draught horses, with personnel and riding horses of 54th D.A.C.) then became 54th D.A.C. Only a party of 1 offr. and 34 o.r., from D.A.C., embkd. at Marseille on 14/2/16, and joined 53rd Div. at Wardan on 22/2/16.

Between 23-27/11/16 B.A.C.'s were abolished and the D.A.C. was reformed at Moascar.

19 Coy. left U.K. on 4/10/15, disembkd. at Suvla on 24/10/15, and it was attached to the IX Corps until 2/12/15, when the Fd. Coy. joined 53rd Div. at Lala Baba. The Coy. embkd. for Mudros on 13/12/15, and reached Wardan on 19 and 20/12/15.

20 Train of 29th Div. (formerly Train of Wessex Div.) was transferred at Suez to 53rd Div., and joined on 17/3/16. It consisted of 246, 247, 248, and 249 Cos., A.S.C.

21 Left Bde. on 1/6/18, embkd. Alexandria on 17/6/18, disembkd. at Taranto on 22/6/18, arrived Proven on 30/6/18, and joined 102nd Bde., 34th Div., on 1/7/18.

22 158th formed on 22/7/17; 159th joined from T.M. School on 28/6/17; and 160th joined from T.M. School on 26/6/17.

23 Left Bde. on 31/5/18, embkd. Alexandria on 17/6/18, disembkd. at Taranto on 22/6/18, arrived Proven on 30/6/18, and joined 102nd Bde., 34th Div., on 1/7/18.

24 Left Bde. on 1/6/18, embkd. Alexandria on 17/6/18, disembkd. at Taranto on 22/6/18, arrived Proven on 30/6/18, and joined 102nd Bde., 34th Div., on 1/7/18.

25 Left Bde. on 31/5/18, embkd. Alexandria on 15/6/18, disembkd. at Taranto on 21/6/18, arrived Proven on 29/6/18, and joined 101st Bde., 34th Div., on 30/6/18.

26 Left Bde. on 30/5/18, embkd. Alexandria on 17/6/18, disembkd. at Taranto on 22/6/18, arrived Proven on 30/6/18, and joined 101st Bde., 34th Div., that day.

27 Joined Div. at El Arish on 1/2/17. Sqdn. left Div. on 23/8/17 to join XXI Corps Cav. Regt. (A/Duke of Lanc.'s Own, A/1/Herts., and C/R. Glasgow Yeo.).

28 Fd. Cos. were numbered on 4/2/17.

29 Transferred to 74th Div. at Ramle on 9/4/18.

30 Amalgamated on 2/8/18, and became 5/6/R.W.F.

31 On 24/6/18 the Bn. was transferred to 160th Bde.

32 Bn. formed at Sarafand on 24/5/18, from platoons and companies of 2/3, 3/3, 2/7, and 1/8 Gurkhas. On 4/6/18 Bn. joined 158th Bde. near Ram Allah.

33 Bn. formed at Sarafand on 24/5/18, from companies of 123 and 125/Rif., and 105/Mahratta L.I. (on 1/6/18). On 10/6/18 Bn. joined 158th Bde. at Et Taiyibe.

34 Amalgamated on 30/7/18, and became 4/5/Welsh.

35 Bn. formed at Sarafand on 24/5/18, from Cos. of 20/, 27/, and 28/Punjabis. On 4/6/18 Bn. joined 159th Bde. near Ram Allah.

36 Bn. formed at Sarafand on 27/5/18, from Cos. of 91/ and 92/Punjabis, and 93/Burma Inf. (on 1/6/18). On 5/6/18 Bn. joined 159th Bde. near Ram Allah.

37 Bn. left Bde. on 25/8/18; and was afterwards employed on repair of roads, etc.

38 Bn. left Bde. on 19/8/18 for El Qantara, and it was broken up for drafts.

39 Bn. embkd. at Karachi on 5/3/18, disembkd. Suez 18/3/18, arrived Lydda 21/5/18, and joined Bde. on 26/5/18.

40 Bn. embkd. at Karachi on 11/5/18, disembkd. Suez 21/5/18, arrived Lydda 12/6/18 (from Tell el Kebir), joined Bde. on 28/6/18 near Ram Allah. On 19/7/18 Bn. left Bde. on transfer to Desert Corps, and on 20/7/18 joined 20th Ind. Inf. Bde. at El Ghoraniye.

41 Bty. (4, 4.5-inch H.) was formed on 8/4/18, with equipments from C (H.)/CXVII and personnel from 53rd and 60th D.A.s, and 9th (Br.) Mtn. Bty., R.G.A.; and joined CCLXVII.

42 Coy. embkd. at Karachi on 18/5/18, disembkd. Suez 29/5/18, arrived Ramle (from Tell el Kebir) on 10/6/18, and on 5/8/18 joined 53rd Div. near Ram Allah.

43 Bn. formed at Ain Sinia on 15-25/4/18. It was composed of 158th, 159th, and 160th M.G. Cos., and was completed on 17/9/18 by Cape Corps M.G. Coy.

44 Transferred on 21/8/18 to Desert Mtd. Corps.

45 Absorbed into 170 C.F.A. on 11/9/18, and supernumerary details left for Base on 18/9/18.

46 Absorbed into 171 C.F.A. on 8-11/9/18, and supernumerary details left for Base on 18/9/18.

47 Disembkd. on 4/5/18 at Suez (from Mesopotamia), and joined 53rd Div. on 3/7/18 near Latrun.

48 Bn. disembkd. on 5/7/18 at Suez (from Mesopotamia), reached Lydda on 17/7/18, and joined 158th Bde. on 3/8/18, near Jerusalem.

49 Formed at Diyala on 18/5/18 from Cos. of 82/, 87/, and 90/Punjabis. Bn. arrived Amara on 23/5/18, left for Egypt 20/6/18, disembkd. Suez 5/7/18, reached Lydda 17/7/18, and joined 159th Bde. on 2/8/18, near Jerusalem.

50 Bn. entrained at Dinapur on 4/6/18, embkd. at Bombay 7/6/18, disembkd. at Suez 19/6/18; arrived Lydda on 31/7/18 (from Tell el Kebir), and joined 160th Bde. on 6/8/18, near Enab.

51 Moved on 15 and 16/7/18 from El Arish to Lydda; joined 160th Bde. on 22/7/18 near Latrun.

52 Bn. disembkd. at Suez on 11/7/18; reached Lydda on 6/8/18 (from El Qantara), and joined 53rd Div. on 12/8/18 near Ram Allah.

53 Joined 53rd Div. near Ram Allah on 29/8/18. On 11/9/18 it absorbed part of 2/Welsh Fd. Amb. (Note 45.)

54 Landed at Suez on 12/8/18, joined 53rd Div. on 23/8/18 near Ram Allah. On 8-11/9/18 it absorbed part of 3/Welsh Fd. Amb. (Note 46.)

53RD (WELSH) DIVISION

MOBILIZATION, BATTLES, AND ENGAGEMENTS

The division—an existing T.F. division—was chiefly drawn from North, Mid, and South Wales, the Marches, and Cheshire, with the divisional headquarters in Shrewsbury. The three brigade headquarters were at Wrexham, Chester, and Shrewsbury; and the original 12 battalions came from Wrexham, Flint, Caernarvon, Newtown, Newport, Pontypool, Abergavenny, Hereford, Birkenhead, Chester, Stockport, and Macclesfield.

In the artillery: the I. Welsh (How.) Bde. came from Swansea, with one battery at Neath and the ammunition column at Morriston; the II. Welsh Bde. was at Cardiff, with an outlying battery at Aberystwyth; the Cheshire Bde. was at Chester; and the IV. Welsh Bde. was at Newport, with outlying batteries at Risca and at Griffithstown; and the Welsh (Caernarvonshire) Heavy Battery was at Bangor with its ammunition column at Llandudno.

The field companies came from Birkenhead and Carmarthenshire; H.Q. and No. 1 Section of the Signal Company were at Cardiff; the three field ambulances came from Ebbw Vale, Cardiff, and Swansea; and the companies of the Welsh Divnl. T. and S. Column were at Weobley, Birkenhead, Ruthin, and in the Rhondda.

At 5 p.m. on Tuesday, the 4th August, 1914, the order to " Mobilize " was received at Shrewsbury. On the 11th, units completed concentration at Shrewsbury, Wellington, Oswestry, and Fort Scoveston (Pembrokeshire); and units were asked to ascertain the number of men who volunteered for service overseas. On the 12th August mobilization was complete, except for some horses and ordnance stores; and at the end of August the division moved to Northampton.

Between early November, 1914, and mid-February, 1915, the following units left the division to join other formations in the field: Cheshire Fd. Coy., 4/R.W. Fusiliers, 5/, and 6/Cheshire, 1/, 2/, and 3/Monmouth (see General Notes). The battalions were gradually replaced by second-line territorial battalions which arrived clothed and partly equipped, but not armed. (In several cases these second-line battalions sent drafts out to their first-line battalions overseas.)

On the 18th November the division was warned that it would proceed to India on the 30th, but on the 25th this move was cancelled. In December the division moved to Cambridge, and on the 11th February, 1915, it was inspected by H.M. the King. Between the 17th–24th April the infantry brigades were reorganized and six battalions joined to replace the unarmed battalions (see Table and Notes). In May the division moved to Bedford, and on the 2nd July was ordered to refit for service in the Mediterranean. The divisional artillery (except S.A.A. ammunition column) and Train (except a few details) remained at Bedford. The rest of the 53rd Division left between the 14th–19th July for embarkation at Devonport. The transports went via Alexandria (25th–30th July), and reached Lemnos between 29th July–7th August. On the 9th August the 53rd Division landed at Suvla.

During the Great War the 53rd Division served in Gallipoli, Egypt, and Palestine, and was engaged in the following operations:—

1915

BATTLES OF SUVLA

9–15 Aug. ... ...**The Landing at Suvla** [IX. Corps].

By the 30th November, after the blizzard, the effective fighting strength of the 53rd Division had shrunk to 162 officers and 2,428 other ranks. On the 11th and 12th December the 53rd Division left Suvla for Mudros, and, on arrival, it transhipped to proceed to Alexandria. The division began to arrive at Alexandria on the 20th December, and entrained for Wardan. The last unit reached Wardan on the 23rd. (The divisional artillery rejoined the division at Wardan between 11–22/2/16.)

1916

4 and 5 Aug. ... ...**Battle of Romani** (158th Bde.) [with 52nd Division, No. 3 Section, Canal Defences].

1917

INVASION OF PALESTINE

26 and 27 March ...**First Battle of Gaza** [Eastern Force].

17–19 April ... ...**Second Battle of Gaza** [Eastern Force].

27 Oct.–7 Nov. ... ...**Third Battle of Gaza** [XX. Corps].

31 Oct. ... ...**Capture of Beersheba** [XX. Corps].

3–7 Nov. ... ...**Capture of Tell Khuweilfe** [XX. Corps, until 6-30 a.m., 6/11 ; then Desert Mtd. Corps].

7–9 Dec. ... ...**Capture of Jerusalem** [XX. Corps].

27–30 Dec. ... ...**Defence of Jerusalem** [XX. Corps].

1918

8–12 March ... ...**Tell 'Asur** [XX. Corps].

Between 4/6–29/8/18 the division (with the exception of the artillery) was changed to the Indian establishment ; the infantry brigades were re-formed with one British and three Indian Army battalions each ; and an Indian S. and M. Company, an Indian pioneer battalion, and three combined field ambulances joined the division (see Table).

THE FINAL OFFENSIVE

THE BATTLES OF MEGIDDO

18–21 Sept. ... ...**Battle of Nablus** [XX. Corps].

By the end of the battle the advanced troops of the division reached the line Beit Dejan-Beit Furik (south-east of Nablus), and for a few days the division was employed in clearing the battlefield and working on the Nablus road. On the 26th September, the division moved back to the Tell 'Asur area, and by the 12th October it had moved down into the Ramle area. On the 27th the division began entraining for Alexandria ; and at noon on the 31st October, the Armistice with Turkey came into force. By the 15th November the division had completed its move to Alexandria. On the 20th December demobilization instructions were received, and on the 22nd the first party left for embarkation. The 155th Pioneers left for Mersina on the 25th January, 1919 ; on the 24th February, the 72nd S. and M. Company left to join the 75th Division, and, as transports became available, the Indian infantry battalions returned to India. By the 7th March the 159th Brigade was reduced to cadre, and all units gradually shrank as demobilization proceeded. On the 15th May the first half of the 1/Cape Corps moved to Suez to return to South Africa. By the 7th June the division was reduced to an effective strength of 75 officers and 1,429 other ranks. On the 15th June divisional details and cadres moved to Port Said en route for the United Kingdom ; and in 1920 the division was re-formed at home.

54TH (EAST ANGLIAN) DIVISION

G.O.C.

7 June, 1913 ... ... Major-General F. S. INGLEFIELD (sick, 6/10/15).
6 October, 1915 ... ... Br.-Gen. F. F. W. DANIELL (acting).
11 October, 1915 ... ... Major-General F. S. INGLEFIELD (sick, 14/10/15).
14 October, 1915 ... ... Br.-Gen. H. W. HODGSON (of Eastern Mtd. Bde.) (acting).
13 November, 1915 ... ... Major-General F. S. INGLEFIELD.
27 April, 1916 ... ... Major-General S. W. HARE (sick, 31/3/17).
31 March, 1917 ... ... Br.-Gen. H. G. SANDILANDS (acting).
12 April, 1917 ... ... Major-General S. W. HARE (leave, 4/1/18).
4 January, 1918 ... ... Br.-Gen. D. B. STEWART (acting).
16 March, 1918 ... ... Major-General S. W. HARE.

G.S.O. 1.

8 Mar., 1913...Major C. STIRLING (G.S.O. 2).
5 Aug., 1914...Lt.-Col. E. C. DA COSTA.
13 May, 1916...Lt.-Col. A. H. C. KEARSEY.
3 May, 1917...Lt.-Col. W. C. GARSIA.
25 June, 1918...Major J. I. BENSON. (acting).
15 Aug., 1918...Lt.-Col. C. L. C. GUEST (sick, 28/8/18).
28 Aug., 1918...Lt.-Col. S. H. KERSHAW.

A.-A. and Q.-M.-G.

4 Jan., 1912...Major E. EVANS (D.-A.-A. and Q.-M.-G.).
5 Aug., 1914...Lt.-Col. A. B. KING (invalided, 11/9/15).
11 Sept., 1915...Lt.-Col. E. EVANS.
29 April, 1917...Lt.-Col. ST.G. B. ARMSTRONG.
10 Aug., 1917...Lt.-Col. K. H. BRUCE.
11 June, 1918...Lt.-Col. B. H. W. TAYLOR.
[15 Nov., 1918...Lt.-Col. G. P. C. BLOUNT].

B.-G., R.A.

1 Jan., 1913...*Br.-Gen. G. W. BIDDULPH.
4 Nov., 1916...Lt.-Col. R. M. LAURIE (acting).
9 Nov., 1916...Col. EARL OF STRADBROKE (acting).
14 Nov., 1916...Lt.-Col. R. M. LAURIE (acting).
22 Nov., 1916...Lt.-Col. MARQUESS OF EXETER (acting).
30 Nov., 1916...Br.-Gen. H. G. SANDILANDS (tempy. B.G., R.A., 52nd Div., 24/1/17).
24 Jan., 1917...Col. EARL OF STRADBROKE (acting).
17 Feb., 1917...Br.-Gen. H. G. SANDILANDS.
4 April, 1917...Lt.-Col. J. HENRY (acting).
12 April, 1917...Br.-Gen. H. G. SANDILANDS.
18 Nov., 1917...Lt.-Col. R. M. LAURIE (acting).
11 Dec., 1917...Br.-Gen. D. B. STEWART.
5 Jan., 1918...Lt.-Col. R. M. LAURIE (acting).
4 Feb., 1918...Br.-Gen. D. B. STEWART.
16 Feb., 1918...Lt.-Col. R. M. LAURIE (acting).
15 Mar., 1918...Br.-Gen. D. B. STEWART.

C.R.E.

22 July, 1911...Lt.-Col. G. H. WELLS.
23 May, 1916...Lt.-Col. E. N. MOZLEY (tempy. from C.R.E., 42nd Div.).
15 June, 1916...Lt.-Col. D. M. GRIFFITH (sick, 23/6/16).
23 June, 1916...Capt. A. W. STOKES (acting).
11 July, 1916...Major A. W. STOKES (acting).
8 Aug., 1916...Lt.-Col. A. W. STOKES.

*Br.-Gen. on 5 August, 1914.

161st BDE.
(Essex Bde.)

30 June, '13...*Br.-Gen. S. T. B. LAWFORD.
9 Sept., '14...Br.-Gen. F. F. W. DANIELL.
19 June, '16...Br.-Gen. W. MARRIOTT-DODINGTON.
24 July, '17...Lt.-Col. JOHN BROWN (acting).
31 July, '17...Br.-Gen. W. MARRIOTT-DODINGTON.
8 Feb., '18...Lt.-Col. B. C. WELLS (acting).
12 Feb., '18...Br.-Gen. H. B. H. ORPEN-PALMER.

162nd BDE.
(East Midland Bde.)

21 Aug., '11...*Br.-Gen. C. DE WINTON.
15 Aug., '15...Lt.-Col. P. C. BYRNE (acting).
28 Aug., '15...Br.-Gen. A. MUDGE (sick, 25/5/17).
25 May, '17...Lt.-Col. E. W. BRIGHTEN (acting).
23 June, '17...Br.-Gen. A. MUDGE (leave, 12/6/18).
12 June, '18...Lt.-Col. J. F. S. WINNINGTON (acting).
20 June, '18...Lt.-Col. E. W. BRIGHTEN (acting).
25 Aug., '18...Br.-Gen. A. MUDGE.

163rd BDE.
(Norfolk and Suffolk Bde.)

9 Oct., '11...*Br.-Gen. R. BAYARD.
24 May, '15...Br.-Gen. C. M. BRUNKER.
19 Aug., '15...Br.-Gen. F. F. W. DANIELL (tempy.).
19 Aug., '15...Lt.-Col. E. EVANS (acting).
10 Sept., '15...Br.-Gen. T. WARD.
24 April, '18...Lt.-Col. O. M. TORKINGTON (acting).
27 April, '18...Br.-Gen. A. J. MCNEILL.

*Br.-Gen. on 5 August, 1914.

GENERAL NOTES

The following Units belonged to the East Anglian Division, August, 1914, but they went overseas independently :—

DIVISIONAL ARTILLERY :—

I. E. Anglian Bde., R.F.A., T.F. (Bties. 4, 15-pdrs. each)
II. E. Anglian Bde., R.F.A., T.F. (Bties. 4, 15-pdrs. each)
III. E. Anglian (How.) Bde., R.F.A., T.F. (Bties. 4, 5-inch Hows. each)
IV. E. Anglian Bde., R.F.A., T.F. (Bties. 4, 15-pdrs. each)
54th (E. Anglian) D.A.C.

In 1915, when the 54th Div. went to Gallipoli, the Arty. Bdes., B.A.C.s, and D.A.C. (less a Divnl. S.A.A. Coln. and Divnl. Ammn. Park—see note 8) remained behind at Brandon and Thetford.

After the division had left, the Bties. were re-armed with 18-pdrs. and 4.5-inch Hows.; and on 12/11/15 the 54th Div. Arty. began to move to France. It embarked at Southampton on 17/11/15 for le Havre, and on 21/11/15 the Divnl. Arty. was concentrated round Blaringhem, attached to the 33rd Div., and officers and men were attached to the 2nd, 7th, and 12th Div. Artilleries in the Front Line.

On 30/12/15 the 54th Div. Arty. was warned that it would be sent to Egypt, and on 11/1/16 it began to move to Marseille. Embkn. started on 30/1/16, and the artillery completed disembkn. at Alexandria by 14/2/16. Between 8–15/2/16 the Divnl. Arty. rejoined the 54th Div. at Mena Camp (Cairo). The S.A.A. Coln. and Park rejoined the Divnl. Arty. on 14/2/16; and the D.A.C. was then 1 offr. and 34 o.r. i/c. ammunition. (See notes 14–18.)

East Anglian (Essex) Heavy Bty., R.G.A., T.F. (4, 4.7-inch guns), was left behind in England by the 54th Div. in July, 1915. The Hy. Bty. went to France and disembkd. at le Havre on 14/3/16; and on 16/3/16 the Hy. Bty. joined XXIII. H.A. Group.

1/E. Anglian Fd. Coy., R.E., T.F., disembkd. at le Havre on 25/12/14, and joined 2nd Div. on 5/1/15. The Fd. Coy. served with the 2nd Div. for the remainder of the Great War.

4/Suffolk disembkd. at le Havre on 9/11/14, and joined Jullundur Bde., Lahore Div.; on 4/12/14, it was attached to Bareilly Bde., Meerut Div., on 31/1/15, and rejoined Jullundur Bde. on 8/3/15. The Bn. joined 46th Bde., 15th Div., on 15/11/15; it joined 98th Bde., 33rd Div., on 28/2/16; and on 15/2/18 the Bn. became Pioneer Bn., 58th Div.

1/Cambridgeshire disembkd. at le Havre on 15/2/15, and joined 82nd Bde., 27th Div., on 18/2/15. The Bn. was transferred to VII. Corps Troops on 15/11/15, joined 118th Bde., 39th Div., on 29/2/16; and on 10/5/18 it joined 35th Bde., 12th Div., and absorbed 7/Suffolk on 19/5/18.

1/Hertfordshire disembkd. at le Havre on 6/11/14, and joined 4th (Guards) Bde., 2nd Div., on 20/11/14. The Bn. was transferred to 6th Bde., 2nd Div., on 19/8/15, and to G.H.Q. Troops on 28/2/16. The Bn. joined 118th Bde., 39th Div., on 8/3/16, it was transferred to 116th Bde., 39th Div., on 8/2/18; and it joined 112th Bde., 37th Div., on 10/5/18, and absorbed 6/Bedford on 22/5/18.

1/E. Anglian Fd. Ambce. (Ipswich) joined 29th Division in January, 1915, at Leamington. It was numbered 88th, and it served with the 29th Division throughout the Great War.

54th (East Anglian) Divisional Train was left behind by the Div. in July, 1915. On 28/11/15 the Train was re-allotted to the 27th Div., and it embarked for Salonika, 16–23/1/16. The Cos. were numbered 483, 484, 485, and 486. The Train reached Salonkia on 21/2/16.

The following Units also served with the 54th Division :—

Hd. Qrs. and No. 1 Section, 53rd (Welsh) Divisional Signal Coy., was attached at Suvla to 54th Divnl. H.Q. from 10/8/15–23/8/15, when it handed over to 54th Divnl. Sig. Coy. 53rd Signal Coy. rejoined 53rd Div.

3rd Welsh Field Ambulance was attached at Suvla to 54th Div., from 11/8/15–18/8/15, when 3/Welsh Fd. Amb. rejoined 53rd Div.

54th Divnl. Sanitary Section was formed in England after mobilization, and went abroad with the 54th Div., embarking at Devonport on 23/7/15. The Sec. landed at Suvla on 10/8/15, and served there until 9/12/15; it reached Alexandria on 18/12/15, and served for the remainder of the Great War with the 54th Div. in Egypt and Palestine.

Détachement Français de Palestine et Syrie (less cavalry)—Colonel P. de Piépape—was attached to the 54th Division from 12/9–28/9/18, for co-operation in the Battle of Sharon (Battles of Megiddo). **D.F.P.S.** comprised 7e/1er Tirailleurs Algériens, 9e/2e Tirailleurs Algériens, 1er and 2e Bns. Arméniens, 1 Territorial Bn., 1 Coy. Syrians, 1 Sqdn. (dismtd.) Spahis, and 1, 80-mm., 1, 75-mm., and 1, 65-mm. (mountain) Batteries. (D.F.P.S. was approximately a Brigade.)

The 54th Division was not indianized or reorganized in 1918, so that, if necessity arose, it could be sent at once to France.

54TH[1] (EAST ANGLIAN) DIVISION

ORDER OF BATTLE, 1915-1918

Dates	INFANTRY: Brigades	INFANTRY: Battalions and attached Units	Mounted Troops	ARTILLERY: Field Artillery: Brigades	ARTILLERY: Field Artillery: Batteries	ARTILLERY: Field Artillery: Bde. Ammn. Colns.	ARTILLERY: Trench Mortar Bties.: Medium	ARTILLERY: Trench Mortar Bties.: Heavy	ARTILLERY: Divnl. Ammn. Coln.	Engineers: Field Cos.	Signal Service: Divnl. Signal Coy.	Pioneers	M.G. Units	Field Ambu-lances	Mobile Vety. Secn.	Divnl. Emplnt. Coy.	Divnl. Train
1915 August (Gallipoli)	161st[1]; [2] (Essex) 162nd[1]; [3] (E. Midland) 163rd[1]; [5] (Norfolk & Suffolk)	4/Essex, 5/Essex, 6/Essex, 7/Essex 5/Bedf., 4/North'n., 10/Lond.,[4] 11/Lond.[4] 4/Norf., 5/Norf., 5/Suff., 8/Hants.[6]	54th (E. Anglian)[7] Cyclist Coy.	...	...	...	...	...	54th (E. Anglian) D.A.C.[8]	2/E. Anglian 2/1/E. Anglian[9]	54th (E. Anglian)	...	...	2/E. Anglian 3/E. Anglian 2/1/E.[10] Anglian	...	...	54th[11] (E. Anglian)
1916 June (Egypt)	161st ...... 162nd 163rd	4/Essex, 5/Essex, 6/Essex, 7/Essex; 161st Bde. M.G. Coy.[12] 5/Bedf., 4/North'n., 10/Lond., 11/Lond.; 162nd Bde. M.G. Coy.[12] 4/Norf., 5/Norf., 5/Suff., 8/Hants.; 163rd Bde. M.G. Coy.[12]	Hd. Qrs.[13] and A Sqdn., 1/Herts. Yeo. 54th Divnl. Cyclist Coy.	CCLXX[14] (I E. Anglian) CCLXXI[15] (II E. Anglian) CCLXXII[16] (H.) (III E. Anglian (H.)) CCLXXIII[17] (IV E. Anglian)	1/Norfolk, 2/Norfolk, 3/Norfolk. 1/Essex, 2/Essex, 3/Essex. 1/Suffolk (H.), 2/Suffolk (H.). 1/Herts., 2/Herts., North'n.	CCLXX (I E. Anglian) CCLXXI (II E. Anglian) CCLXXII[16] (H.) (III E. Anglian (H.)) CCLXXIII (IV E. Anglian)	...	...	54th D.A.C.[18]	2/E. Anglian 2/1/E. Anglian 1/Kent[19]	54th	...	...	2/E. Anglian 3/E. Anglian 2/1/E. Anglian	54th[20] (E. Anglian)	...	54th[21]
1917 June (Palestine)	161st ...... 162nd 163rd	4/Essex, 5/Essex, 6/Essex, 7/Essex; 161st M.G. Coy.;[33] 161st T.M. Bty.[22] 5/Bedf., 4/North'n., 10/Lond., 11/Lond.; 162nd M.G. Coy.;[33] 162nd T.M. Bty.[22] 4/Norf., 5/Norf., 5/Suff., 8/Hants.; 163rd M.G. Coy.;[33] 163rd T.M. Bty.[22]	Hd. Qrs.[23] and A. Sqdn., 1/Herts. Yeo. 54th[24] Divnl. Cyclist Coy.	CCLXX[17] CCLXXI[15]; [25] CCLXXII[14]; [26]	A, B; C (H.)[16] A, B B; C (H.)[16]; [25]	...[25]	X.54[27] Y.54[27] Z.54[27]	...	54th D.A.C.[28]	484th[29] (2/E. Anglian) 486th[29] (2/1/E. Anglian) 495th[29] (1/Kent)	54th	...	...	2/E. Anglian 3/E. Anglian 2/1/E. Anglian	54th	...	54th
1918 September (Palestine)	161st ...... 162nd 163rd	4/Essex, 5/Essex, 6/Essex, 7/Essex; 161st T.M. Bty. 5/Bedf., 4/North'n., 10/Lond., 11/Lond.; 162nd T.M. Bty. 4/Norf., 5/Norf., 5/Suff., 8/Hants.; 163rd T.M. Bty.	...	CCLXX .... CCLXXI ...... CCLXXII	A, B; C (H.) A, B; 440[30] (H.) A,[31] B; C (H.)	...	...[32]	...	54th D.A.C.	484th 486th 495th	54th	...	No. 54 Bn.,[33] M.G.C.	2/E. Anglian 3/E. Anglian 2/1/E. Anglian	54th	...	54th

NOTES

1 By mid-May, 1915, the East Anglian Division was numbered 54th Division; and the Inf. Bdes. were numbered 161st, 162nd, and 163rd. (Authy. W.O. letter—40/W.O./2481 (A.G.1) of 7/5/15.)

2 The Bns. came from Brentwood, Chelmsford, West Ham, and Walthamstow.

3 After reorganization, the Bns. came from Bedford, Northampton, Hackney, and Pentonville.

4 Transferred from 3rd Lond. Inf. Bde., 1st Lond. Div., and joined at Norwich: 10/Lond. in April, 1915; and 11/Lond. on 24/4/15.

5 After reorganization, the Bns. came from Norwich, East Dereham, Bury St. Edmunds, and Newport (I. of W.).

6 Transferred from Southern Command (unattached), and joined on 19/4/15. (Bn. had adopted the 4-Coy. organization on 19/1/15.).

7 Coy. formed after mobilization, embkd. at Devonport on 29/7/15, and landed at Suvla on 16/8/15.

8 Formed after mobilization. For the Dardanelles, the B.A.C.s formed a Divnl. S.A.A. Coln., and the D.A.C. formed a Divnl. Ammn. Park. Coln. and Park embkd. at Devonport on 28/7/15, and landed at Suvla on 16/8/15. Remdr. of D.A.C. was left behind with Divnl. Arty.

9 Coy. formed after mobilization; embkd. at Devonport on 28/7/15.

10 Formed after mobilization; embkd. at Devonport on 22/7/15.

11 Train formed after mobn. from E. Anglian T. & S. Coln. Only some S. and T. details accompanied 54th Div. to Gallipoli. The original Cos. were numbered 483, 484, 485, 486, and they embkd. at Devonport on 16/1/16, disembkd. at Salonika on 21/2/16, and became 27th Divnl. Train.

12 Bde. M.G. Cos. were formed in Egypt: 161st on 23/4/16; 162nd on 26/4/16; and 163rd on 1/5/16.

13 Hd. Qrs., M.G. Sec., and A. Sqdn. joined 54th Div. at Mena on 20/3/16.

14 Bde. (also see General Notes) rejoined Div. in Egypt between 11-15/2/16. On 26/5/16 Bde. was numbered CCLXX, and batteries lettered A, B, and C. On 21/12/16 C was broken up between A and B; and Bde. was renumbered CCLXXII.

15 Bde. (also see General Notes) rejoined Div. in Egypt between 8-15/2/16. On 26/5/16 the Bde. was numbered CCLXXI, and batteries lettered A, B, and C. On 20/12/16 C was broken up between A and B, and Bde. kept its old number, CCLXXI; and A (H.)/CCLXXII (H.) joined and became C (H.)/CCLXXI.

16 Bde. (also see General Notes) rejoined Div. in Egypt between 11-15/2/16. On 28/5/16 Bde. was numbered CCLXXII (H.) and batteries were lettered A (H.) and B (H.). On 21/12/16 CCLXXII (H.) was broken up, and A (H.) became C (H.)/CCLXXI, and B (H.) became C (H.)/CCLXX. The B.A.C. was divided between CCLXX and CCLXXI B.A.C.'s.

17 Bde. (also see General Notes) rejoined Div. in Egypt between 11-15/2/16. On 29/5/16 Bde. was numbered CCLXXIII and batteries lettered A, B, and C. On 21/12/16 B was broken up between A and C, and C then became B, and Bde. was renumbered CCLXX; and B (H.)/CCLXXII (H.) joined and became C (H.)/CCLXX.

18 The original D.A.C. (also see note 8) remained in England on departure of Div. for Gallipoli; and the D.A.C. disembkd. at le Havre on 18/11/15 and concentrated with Divnl. Arty. in France (see General Notes) on 21/11/15. On 29/1/16 54th D.A.C. took over equipt. and horses from 53rd D.A.C. and became 55th D.A.C.; and 1 offr. and 34 o.r. from 54th D.A.C. accompanied Divnl. Arty. to Egypt.

19 Coy. left England on 25/9/15, landed at Suvla on 7/10/15, and joined 2nd Mtd. Div. The Coy. left Suvla on 13/12/15 and reached Alexandria on 18/12/15, and joined 54th Div. on 1/7/16 on Suez Canal.

20 Joined Div. at Shallufa on 11/4/16.

21 Train was formed at Alexandria between 5-24/2/17, and the Cos. were numbered 428, 429, 430, and 431. On 18/4/17 the Cos. were renumbered and became 921, 922, 923, and 924 Cos., A.S.C.

22 Bde. T.M. Bties. were formed: 161st by 17/5/17; 162nd by 5/5/17; and 163rd by 4/5/17.

23 Hd. Qrs., M.G. Sec., and A Sqdn. were transferred on 26/8/17 to XXI Corps Cav. Regt. (Duke of Lanc.'s Own, Herts., and R. Glasgow).

24 In Febry., 1917, when the 54th Div. left the Suez Canal, the 54th Divnl. Cyclist Coy. came under Southern Canal Section. On 19/12/17 54th Divnl. Cyclist Coy. left Southern Canal Section, and on 28/12/17 the Coy. joined XXI Corps Mtd. Troops at Ramle.

25 C (H.) (see note 15) was transferred on 26/6/17 to CCLXXII.

26 Bde. was reorganized on 26/6/17: B remained, and C (H.)/CCLXXI joined and became C (H.)/CCLXXII. A/CCLXXII was transferred on 1/7/17 to CCLXIV, 52nd Divnl. Arty. (Also see note 30.)

27 X, Y, and Z T.M. Bties. arrived at Sheikh Sabasi on 3/10/17, and joined the Divnl. Arty.

28 The D.A.C. was formed on 20/7/17 at Deir el Balah, by the absorption of the three B.A.C.'s and 54th Mobile D.A.C.

29 The Fd. Cos. were numbered on 1/2/17.

30 Bty. arrived from the Base and joined CCLXXI on 5/6/18.

31 Bty. (formerly A/CCLXIV) joined CCLXXII on 2/3/18. (A/CCLXIV had previously been A/CCLXXII—see note 26).

32 Divnl. T.M. Bties. were replaced by Corps T.M. Bties., 10-12/2/18; and the personnel of 54th Divnl. T.M. Bties. proceeded to the Base on 2/3/18.

33 Bn. was formed on 19/4/18. It consisted of 161, 162, and 163 Bde. M.G. Cos.

54TH (EAST ANGLIAN) DIVISION

MOBILIZATION, BATTLES, AND ENGAGEMENTS

The division—an existing T.F. division—was chiefly drawn from the Eastern Counties and the Eastern Midlands, with the divisional headquarters at Warley. The three brigade headquarters were at Brentwood, Bedford, and Norwich ; and the original twelve battalions came from Brentwood, Chelmsford, West Ham, Walthamstow, Bedford, Northampton, Cambridge, Hertford, Norwich, East Dereham, Ipswich, and Bury St. Edmunds.

In the artillery : the I. E. Anglian Bde. was at Norwich, with an outlying battery at Yarmouth ; the II. E. Anglian Bde., at Stratford, had outlying batteries at Romford and Grays ; the III. E. Anglian (How.) Bde. was at Ipswich, with one battery and the ammunition column at Lowestoft ; the IV. E. Anglian Bde., with headquarters and ammunition column at Hertford, had its batteries at St. Albans, Watford, and Peterborough ; and the E. Anglian (Essex) Heavy Battery was at Stratford.

Both field companies came from Bedford ; H.Q. and No. 1 Section of the Signal Company were also at Bedford ; the three field ambulances came from Norwich, Ipswich, and Walthamstow ; and the companies of the East Anglian T. and S. Column were at Ilford, Stratford, Northampton, and King's Lynn.

In many units the fortnight's annual training began on the 27th July, 1914, and the first week's work was according to programme ; but on the 4th August the order to mobilize was received. Units mobilized immediately at their headquarters and then moved at once to their war stations. By the 10th August the 54th Division was concentrated around Brentwood, and on the 20th August the division moved to Chelmsford, Bury St. Edmunds, and Norwich. In January, 1915, the battalions were reorganized on the 4-company basis.

Between early November, 1914, and mid-February, 1915, the following units left the division to serve with other formations in the field, viz. : 1/E. Anglian Fd. Coy., 4/Suffolk, 1/Cambridgeshire, 1/Hertfordshire, and 1/E. Anglian Fd. Ambce. (see General Notes). In April, 1915, the three battalions were replaced by 8/Hants. (Newport, I. of W.), 10/London (Hackney), and 11/London (Pentonville), and the field company and field ambulance were replaced by second-line units.

The division was employed on coast-defence until May, 1915, when it concentrated around St. Albans to prepare for overseas, and on the 8th July it was ordered to prepare for service in Gallipoli. The Divisional Artillery (except S.A.A. column and park) and Train (except a few details) were left behind when the remainder of the division left St. Albans between 20th–30th July for embarkation at Devonport and Liverpool. Some of the transports went direct to Mudros, whilst others went via Alexandria, and the division began to reach Lemnos on the 6th August. On the 10th August the 54th Division began landing at Suvla ; and by nightfall on the 11th, 10 battalions and divisional headquarters were ashore.

54TH (EAST ANGLIAN) DIVISION

During the Great War the 54th Division served at first in Gallipoli, then in Egypt, and lastly in Palestine and Syria, and was engaged in the following operations :—

1915

10–15 Aug. ... ...**The Landing at Suvla** [IX. Corps].

On the 26th November orders were received for the division to re-embark for Mudros, and between 3rd–8th December the move was carried out. With reinforcements, the strength of the division on the 9th December was 240 officers and 4,480 other ranks. On 13th December the division began to embark for Egypt. Alexandria was reached on the 18th, and on the 19th December the division concentrated at Sidi Bishr, and from there moved to Mena Camp, Cairo. In connection with the Senussi rising, the 161st Inf. Bde. moved into the Western Desert on 28/12/15.

1916

Between 11–15/2/16 the divisional artillery (from France) rejoined the 54th Division at Mena Camp, Cairo ; and on 5/3/16 the 161st Inf. Bde. (less 4/Essex) also rejoined the division at Cairo (4/Essex rejoined 161st Inf. Bde. on 23/3/16). On 2/4/16 the 54th Division took over No. 1 (Southern) Section, Suez Canal Defences.

1917

INVASION OF PALESTINE

26 and 27 March ...**First Battle of Gaza** [Eastern Force].
17–19 April ... ...**Second Battle of Gaza** [Eastern Force].
27 Oct.–7 Nov. ... ...**Third Battle of Gaza** [XXI. Corps].
1–7 Nov.... ... ...**Capture of Gaza** [XXI. Corps].
21 and 22 Dec. ... ...**Battle of Jaffa** [XXI. Corps].

1918

12 March ... ...**Fight at Ras el'Ain** (162nd Bde.) [XXI. Corps].
9 and 10 April... ...**Berukin** [XXI. Corps].

THE FINAL OFFENSIVE
THE BATTLES OF MEGIDDO

19–23 Sept. ... ...**Battle of Sharon** [XXI. Corps].

On the 24th September the 54th Division concentrated at Hable (N.E. of Jaljulye) ; and on the 27th the division was ordered to move to Haifa, and the advance began on the 28th, via 'Athlith. The concentration of the division at Haifa was completed on the 4th October, and the division was then employed on the improvement of communications. On the 20th the division was ordered to begin to move to Beirut, by brigade groups at one day's interval. On the 23rd the advance began, the brigades moving via Acre, Ras en Naqura, Es Sur (Tyre), and Saida (Sidon). The division concentrated at Beirut between 31st October and the 5th November ; but, at noon on the 31st October, hostilities had ceased with Turkey.

On the 24th November the division was warned that it would be moved back by sea to El Qantara, and the embarkation of 163rd brigade began on the 28th. On arrival at El Qantara the troops marched to Helmie, and the division (less artillery and train) concentrated at Helmie on the 7th December. By the 14th the divisional artillery and train arrived, having come by sea to El Qantara, except CCLXXII. Brigade, which marched from Beirut to Tul Qarm and then entrained on the 9th for Helmie.

On the 6th January, 1919, the three brigade trench mortar batteries were disbanded, the first serious step in the demobilization of the 54th Division. During the month the divisional education scheme made good progress and gradual demobilization began. On the 22nd May the 54th Division was reorganized, and only six of its twelve battalions remained. On the 29th, the 77th Brigade joined and was renumbered 161st; and on the 1st June CII. Brigade joined and became 54th Division Artillery. Gradually the Territorial units were reduced to cadre, the war-time formations were disbanded, and on the 30th September, 1919, the 54th Division disappeared in Egypt. In 1920 the division began to re-form in the Eastern Command at home.

55TH (WEST LANCASHIRE) DIVISION

G.O.C.

3 June, 1912 ... ... Major-General W. F. L. LINDSAY.
5 August, 1914... ... ... Major-General F. HAMMERSLEY.
3 September, 1914 ... ... Major-General J. B. FORSTER.

. . . .

3 January, 1916 ... ... Major-General H. S. JEUDWINE.

G.S.O. 1.

19 Feb., 1914...Major E. J. BUCKLEY (G.S.O. 2).
5 Aug., 1914...Lt.-Col. E. J. BUCKLEY.
24 Jan., 1915...Lt.-Col. C. W. GWYNN.

. . . .

3 Jan., 1916...Lt.-Col. J. K. COCHRANE.
4 Dec., 1916...Major R. S. POPHAM (acting).
4 Jan., 1917...Lt.-Col. J. K. COCHRANE.
5 April, 1917...Major V. A. JACKSON (acting).
28 April, 1917...Lt.-Col. J. K. COCHRANE.
29 May, 1917...Lt.-Col. T. R. C. PRICE.
5 Aug., 1918...Major H. E. PICKERING (acting).
15 Aug., 1918...Lt.-Col. R. T. LEE.

A.-A. and Q.-M.-G.

21 April, 1914...Capt. A. G. MCCLINTOCK (D.-A.-A. and Q.-M.-G.).
5 Aug., 1914...Col. J. G. PANTON.

. . . .

3 Jan., 1916...Lt.-Col. C. G. LIDDELL.
4 Dec., 1916...Lt.-Col. S. H. EDEN.

B.-G., R.A.

1 April, 1914...*Br.-Gen. A. W. GAY.
4 Jan., 1915...Br.-Gen. J. J. MACMAHON.

. . . .

(Divnl. Arty. rejoined from 2nd Cdn. Div., 2-4/1/16.)
[4 Jan., 1915] Br.-Gen. J. J. MACMAHON (sick, 10/6/16).
10 June, 1916...Lt.-Col. J. P. REYNOLDS (acting).
11 June, 1916...Lt.-Col. E. HARDING NEWMAN (tempy., from XXVIII. Bde., 5th Div.).
26 June, 1916...Br.-Gen. A. M. PERREAU.

C.R.E.

1 April, 1913...Lt.-Col. G. E. SAYCE.

. . . .

3 Jan., 1916...Lt.-Col. J. E. E. CRASTER.
17 June, 1916...Lt.-Col. C. B. BONHAM (leave, 6/10/16).
6 Oct., 1916...Major C. T. BROWN (acting).
22 Oct., 1916...Lt.-Col. O. G. BRANDON.

*Br.-Gen. on 5 August, 1914.

N. LANCASHIRE BDE.

17 Feb., '13...*Br.-Gen. G. L. HIBBERT.
(Bde. transferred on 18/4/15 to Highland Div.)

LIVERPOOL BDE.

11 May, '12...*Br.-Gen. A. R. GILBERT.

S. LANCASHIRE BDE.

3 Oct., '11...*Br.-Gen. A. L. MACFIE.

. . . .

164th Bde.
(N. Lancashire)

(Bde. rejoined on 7/1/16 from 51st (Highland) Div.)

[7 Oct., '15]...Br.-Gen G. T. G. EDWARDS (leave, 16/9/16).
18 Sept., '16...Br.-Gen. C. I. STOCKWELL.

165th Bde.
(Liverpool)

(Bde. re-formed on 3—26/1/16 at Hallencourt and Yanville.)

3 Jan., '16...Br.-Gen. F. J. DUNCAN.
11 April, '17...Br.-Gen. L. B. BOYD-MOSS.

166th Bde.
(S. Lancashire)

(Bde. re-formed on 3—8/1/16 around Merelessart.)

3 Jan., '16...Br.-Gen. L. F. GREEN-WILKINSON.
25 April, '17...Br.-Gen. F. G. LEWIS (wounded, 1/12/17).
1 Dec., '17...Lt.-Col. J. L. A. MACDONALD (acting).
4 Dec., '17...Br.-Gen. R. J. KENTISH.

*Br.-Gen. on 5 August, 1914.

GENERAL NOTES

1st Lancashire Heavy Battery, R.G.A., T.F. (4, 4.7-inch guns), joined the 57th (2/W. Lanc.) Div., after the 55th Div. had been broken up to reinforce the B.E.F. in France. On 28/12/15 the Hy. Bty. left the 57th Div., at Canterbury, and moved to Woolwich to prepare for service overseas. The Hy. Bty. disembkd. at le Havre on 26/1/16, and joined XXIX. Heavy Brigade, R.G.A. by 1/2/16.

2/5/Lancashire Fusiliers was raised at Bury after the outbreak of war. The Bn. joined the N. Lanc. Bde. to replace 5/K.O. (see notes 2 and 3), and was transferred with the Bde. to 51st Div., at Bedford by 18/4/15. With its Bde., the Bn. rejoined the (re-formed) 55th Div. in France on 7/1/16 (see note 22).

The following Units also served with the 55th Division :—

C Sqdn., King Edward's Horse, from 25/10/18–21/11/18.

A Coy., VIII. Corps Cyclist Bn., from 18/10/18–18/11/18.

2/10/King's, transferred from 172nd Bde., 57th Div., on 20/4/18, and remained until the Bn. was distributed on 30/4/18 to 1/10/King's and 55th Divnl. Rft. Camp.

No. 55 Sanitary Section, joined from England on 16/1/16. It was transferred on 12/4/17 to an VIII. Corps Sanitary Area.

55th Divnl. Amb. Workshop, joined from England on 6/1/16. On 3/4/16 it was absorbed by 55th Divnl. Supply Coln.

On 4/2/18 the reorganization of the division on a 9-battalion basis was completed ; and on 1/3/18 the pioneer battalion was reorganized on a 3-company basis.

55th[1] (WEST LANCASHIRE) DIVISION

ORDER OF BATTLE, 1914-1918

Dates	INFANTRY		Mounted Troops	ARTILLERY						Engineers	Signal Service	Pioneers	M.G. Units	Field Ambu-lances	Mobile Vety. Secn.	Divnl. Emplnt. Coy.	Divnl. Train
				Field Artillery.			Trench Mortar Bties.										
	Brigades	Battalions and attached Units		Brigades	Batteries	Bde. Ammn. Colns.	Medium	Heavy	Divnl. Ammn. Coln.	Field Cos.	Divnl. Signal Coy.						
1914 August (England)	N. Lancashire[2] Liverpool[5] S. Lancashire[10]	4/K.O.,[2] 5/K.O.,[3] 4/L.N.L.,[2] 5/L.N.L.[4] 5/King's,[6] 6/King's,[7] 7/King's,[8] 8/King's[9] 9/King's,[11] 10/King's,[12] 4/S. Lanc.,[13] 5/S. Lanc.[14]	Lancashire Hussars[15]	I W. Lanc.[16] II W. Lanc.[16] III W. Lanc.[16] IV W. Lanc.[16] (H.)	1/Lanc., 2/Lanc., 3/Lanc. 9/Lanc., 10/Lanc., 11/Lanc. 12/Lanc., 13/Lanc., 14/Lanc. 7/Lanc. (H.), 8/Lanc. (H.)	I W. Lanc. II W. Lanc. III W. Lanc. IV W. Lanc. (H.)	...	...	...	1/W. Lanc.[17] 2/W. Lanc.[18]	W. Lanc.	...	...	1/W. Lanc.[19] 2/W. Lanc.[20] 3/W. Lanc.	...	...	W. Lanc.[21] Divnl. T. & S. Coln.
1916 January (Re-formed in France)	164th[22] ...... 165th[23] ...... 166th[28]	4/K.O., 8/King's, 2/5/L.F., 4/L.N.L. 5/King's,[24] 6/King's,[25] 7/King's,[26] 9/King's[27] 5/K.O.,[3]; [29] 10/King's,[30] 5/S. Lanc.,[31] 5/L.N.L.[4]; [32]	A Sqdn., N. Irish H.[33] 55th Divnl. Cyclist Coy.[34]	I W. Lanc.[35] II W. Lanc.[36] III W. Lanc.[37] IV W. Lanc.[38] (H.)	1/Lanc., 2/Lanc., 3/Lanc. 9/Lanc., 10/Lanc., 11/Lanc. 12/Lanc., 13/Lanc., 14/Lanc. 7/Lanc. (H.), 8/Lanc. (H.)	I W. Lanc. II W. Lanc. III W. Lanc. IV W. Lanc. (H.)	...	...	55th D.A.C.[39]	1/W. Lanc.[40] 2/1/W. Lanc.[41] 2/2/W. Lanc.[41]	55th[42] (W. Lanc.)	4/S. Lanc.[43] (P.)	...	3/W. Lanc.[44] 2/1/W. Lanc.[44] 2/1/Wessex[44]	1/W. Lanc.[45]	...	55th[46]
1916 June (France)	164th .... 165th 166th	4/K.O., 8/King's, 2/5/L.F., 4/L.N.L.; 164th Bde. M.G. Coy.;[47] 164th T.M. Bty.[48] 5/King's, 6/King's, 7/King's, 9/King's; 165th Bde. M.G. Coy.;[47] 165th T.M. Bty.[48] 5/K.O., 10/King's, 5/S. Lanc., 5/L.N.L.; 166th Bde. M.G. Coy.;[47] 166th T.M. Bty.[48]	...	CCLXXV[49] CCLXXVI[50] CCLXXVII[51] CCLXXVIII[52]	A, B, C; D (H.) A, B, C; D (H.) A, B, C; D (H.) A, B, C	...[39]	X.55[53] Y.55[53] Z.55[53]	V.55[54]	55th D.A.C.	1/W. Lanc. 2/1/W. Lanc. 2/2/W. Lanc.	55th	4/S. Lanc. (P.)	...	3/W. Lanc. 2/1/W. Lanc. 2/1/Wessex	1/W. Lanc.	...	55th
1917 June (France)	164th .... 165th 166th	4/K.O., 8/King's,[55] 2/5/L.F., 4/L.N.L.; 164th M.G. Coy.;[61] 164th T.M. Bty. 5/King's, 6/King's, 7/King's, 9/King's;[56] 165th M.G. Coy.;[61] 165th T.M. Bty. 5/K.O., 10/King's, 5/S. Lanc., 5/L.N.L.;[57] 166th M.G. Coy.;[61] 166th T.M. Bty.	...	CCLXXV ... CCLXXVI....	A, B, C; D (H.) A, B, C; D (H.)	...	X.55 Y.55 Z.55[53]	V.55	55th D.A.C.	419th[58] (1/W. Lanc.) 422nd[58] (2/1/W. Lanc.) 423rd[58] (2/2/W. Lanc.)	55th	4/S. Lanc. (P.)	196th M.G. Coy.[59]	3/W. Lanc. 2/1/W. Lanc. 2/1/Wessex	1/W. Lanc.	246th[60]	55th
1918 March (France)	164th .... 165th 166th	4/K.O., 2/5/L.F., 4/L.N.L.; 164th T.M. Bty. 5/King's, 6/King's, 7/King's; 165th T.M. Bty. 5/K.O., 10/King's, 5/S. Lanc.; 166th T.M. Bty.	...	CCLXXV .... CCLXXVI....	A, B, C; D (H.) A, B, C; D (H.)	...	X.55 Y.55	...[54]	55th D.A.C.	419th 422nd 423rd	55th	4/S. Lanc. (P.)	No. 55 Bn.,[61] M.G.C.	3/W. Lanc. 2/1/W. Lanc. 2/1/Wessex	1/W. Lanc.	246th	55th

NOTES

1 Between Nov., 1914, and March, 1915, the W. Lancashire Div. sent 9 of its battalions to France to reinforce the B.E.F., and the remaining 3 joined the Highland Div. in April, 1915 (note 2). In Jany., 1916, the 55th Div. was reformed in France.

2 Bde. (with 8/King's replacing 5/L.N.L. and 2/5/L.F. replacing 5/K.O.) was transferred by 18/4/15 to 51st (Highland) Div. at Bedford, and became 154th Bde.

3 Disembkd. at le Havre on 15/2/15, joined 83rd Bde., 28th Div., on 3/3/15, and was transferred on 21/10/15 to 2nd Bde., 1st Div.

4 Disembkd. at le Havre on 13/2/15, joined 16th Bde., 6th Div., on 15/2/15, transferred to 151st Bde., 50th Div., on 11/6/15, and on 21/12/15 joined 26th Bde., 9th Div. (tempy.).

5 Bde. was broken up after its battalions had gone to France in Feb. and March, 1915.

6 Disembkd. at le Havre on 22/2/15, joined 6th Bde., 2nd Div., on 24/2/15, and transferred to 99th Bde., 2nd Div., on 15/12/15.

7 Disembkd. at le Havre on 25/2/15, joined 15th Bde., 5th Div., on 27/2/15, and was transferred to Third Army Troops on 18/11/15.

8 Disembkd. at le Havre on 8/3/15, joined 6th Bde., 2nd Div., on 12/3/15, transferred to 5th Bde., 2nd Div., on 4/9/15, and joined 22nd Bde., 7th Div., on 11/11/15.

9 Transferred to N. Lanc. Bde. to replace 5/L.N.L. (note 4), and was transferred with N. Lanc. Bde. to 51st Div. (note 2).

10 Bde. was broken up after its battalions had gone to France between Nov., 1914, and March, 1915.

11 Disembkd. at le Havre on 13/3/15, joined 2nd Bde., 1st Div., on 24/3/15, and was transferred to 3rd Bde., 1st Div., on 12/11/15.

12 Disembkd. at le Havre on 3/11/14, and joined 9th Bde., 3rd Div., on 25/11/14.

13 Disembkd. at le Havre on 13/2/15, joined 7th Bde., 3rd Div., on 24/2/15, and became Pioneers on 12/10/15.

14 Disembkd. at le Havre on 13/2/15, joined 12th Bde., 4th Div., on 16/2/15, and was transferred (tempy. with Bde.) to 36th Div. on 7/11/15.

15 When the W. Lancashire Div. broke up in 1915, the Regt. left between 29/10-14/11/15 to form the divnl. cavy. sqdns. of 30th, 31st, and 35th Divs. On 4/5/16 the Regt. became Corps Cavy., VIII Corps; on 15/7/17 it was transferred to XIV Corps, and on 24/9/17 it amalgamated with 18/King's (21st Bde., 30th Div.), and in Feb., 1918, the Bn. was transferred to 89th Bde., 30th Div.

16 The 4 Bdes. of Divnl. Arty. were attached to the 2nd Cdn. Div. and completed disembkn. at le Havre on 1/10/15. The 4 Bdes. concentrated at Locre and Berthen by 3/10/15. The 4 Bdes. rejoined the 55th Div. at Hallencourt between 2-4/1/16. Before leaving England the 15-pdrs. were replaced by 18-pdrs, and the 5-inch Hows. by 4.5-inch Hows.

17 Disembkd. at le Havre on 3/1/15, joined 4th Div. on 14/2/15, and between 18/4-28/4/15 the Fd. Coy. was attached (tempy.) to the 48th Div.

18 Arrived at Alexandria on 10/7/15, and joined 42nd Div. at Helles on 28/8/15. The Fd. Coy. was transferred on 10/5/16 to Comp. Bde., Mudros; embkd. for Salonika on 30/6/17, and served there with Army Troops for the rest of the War. The Fd. Coy. was numbered 420.

19 Joined 29th Div. in Jany., 1915, near Leamington, and was numbered 87th, embkd. at Avonmouth on 18/3/15, and served for the rest of the War with the 29th Div.

20 Left on 22/10/15 to join 30th Div. Joined at Lark Hill on 2/11/15, and was numbered 98th

21 The Train remained at home, and carried out Supply duties until 1917. The Cos. were numbered 505, 506, 507, and 508 Cos., A.S.C. The Train was allotted to 57th (2/W .Lanc.) Div., and embkd. for France on 10/2/17.

22 154th Bde. (formerly N. Lanc. Bde., see note 2) was transferred complete from the 51st Div. to the 55th Div., and joined on 7/1/16 at Hallencourt; the Bde. was then renumbered 164th.

23 The Bde. H.Q. was re-formed at Hallencourt on 3/1/16.

24 Rejoined on 7/1/16, from 99th Bde., 2nd Div.

25 Rejoined on 26/1/16, from Third Army Troops.

26 Rejoined on 7/1/16, from 22nd Bde., 7th Div.

27 Rejoined on 7/1/16, from 3rd Bde., 1st Div.

28 The Bde. H.Q. was re-formed at Hallencourt on 3/1/16.

29 Rejoined on 8/1/16, from 2nd Bde., 1st Div.

30 Rejoined on 8/1/16, from 9th Bde., 3rd Div.

31 Rejoined on 6/1/16, from 12th Bde. (attached tempy.), 36th Div.

32 Rejoined on 8/1/16, from 26th Bde., 9th Div.

33 The Sqdn. landed at le Havre on 19/8/14. On 4/1/16 it joined 55th Div. from G.H.Q. Troops. Sqdn. was transferred on 10/5/16 to VII Corps Cav. Regt.

34 Coy. formed on 12/1/15, became 57th Cyclist Coy. on 14/8/15; rejoined 55th Divn. at Hallencourt on 16/1/16, and was numbered 55th Cyclist Coy. On 11/5/16 the Coy. was transferred to VII Corps Cyclist Bn.

35 Bde. rejoined on 3/1/16 from 2nd Cdn. Div. On 7/5/16 D Bty. (18-pdrs.) was formed. On 15/5/16 the Bde. was numbered CCLXXV, and the Bties. lettered A, B, C, D. On 23/5/16 D was transferred and became A/CCLXXVIII; and B (H.)/CCLXXVIII joined and became D (H.)/CCLXXV.

36 Bde. rejoined on 2/1/16 from 2nd Cdn. Div. In May, 1916, D Bty. (18-pdrs.) was formed. On 15/5/16 the Bde. was numbered CCLXXVI, and the Bties. lettered A, B, C, D. On 23/5/16 D was transferred and became B/CCLXXVIII; and A (H.)/CCLXXVIII joined and became D (H.)/CCLXXVI.

37 Bde. rejoined on 4/1/16 from 2nd Cdn. Div. On 5/5/16 D Bty. (18-pdrs.) was formed. On 15/5/16 the Bde. was numbered CCLXXVII, and the Bties. lettered A, B, C, D. On 23/5/16 D was transferred and became C/CCLXXVIII; and C (H.)/CCLXXVIII joined and became D (H.)/CCLXXVII.

38 Bde. rejoined on 3/1/16 from 2nd Cdn. Div. On 9/2/16 B (H.)/LXXXV (H.) (from 18th Divnl. Arty.) joined and became C (H.). On 15/5/16 the Bde. was numbered CCLXXVIII and Bties. lettered A, B, C. On 23/5/16 the Bde. was reorganized: B (H.) became D (H.)/CCLXXV, A (H.) became D (H.)/CCLXXVI, and C (H.) became D (H.)/CCLXXVII; and D/CCLXXV, D/CCLXXVI, and D/CCLXXVII joined and became A, B, and C/CCLXXVIII.

39 54th D.A.C. became 55th D.A.C. on 29/1/16, and joined on 17/2/16. On 18/5/16 B.A.C.s were abolished and the D.A.C. was reorganized.

40 Rejoined on 28/2/16, from 4th Div. (See note 17.)

41 The Cos. joined from England, 2/1 on 17/1/16, and 2/2 on 16/1/16.

42 Rejoined from England on 14/1/16.

43 Transferred as Pioneer Bn. from 3rd Div., and joined on 9/1/16 (see note 13).

44 The Fd. Ambces. joined from England, 3/W. Lanc. and 2/1/Wessex on 16/1/16, and 2/1/W. Lanc. on 17/1/16.

45 Joined from England on 15/1/16.

46 Formerly 27th Divnl. Train. It joined 55th Div. at Hallencourt, 2—4/1/16; it consisted of 95, 96, 97, 98 Cos., A.S.C. (Originally Home Cties. Divnl. T. and S. Coln.)

47 M.G. Cos. formed: 164th on 19/2/16; 165th on 26/2/16; and 166th by 1/3/16.

48 164th and 165th T.M. Bties. joined in March, 1916, and 166th T.M. Bty. on 2/3/16.

49 On 5/10/16 B was broken up between A and C, and on 6/10/16 A/CCLXXVIII joined and became B/CCLXXV. On 18/1/17 D (H.) was made up to 6 Hows. by the addition of left sec. of C (H.)/CCLXXVI.

50 On 4/10/16 C was broken up between A and B; and on 8/10/16 530 (How.) joined and became C (H.)/CCLXXVI. On 18/1/17 D (H.) was made up to 6 Hows. by the addition of right sec. of C (H.)/CCLXXVI; and A/CCLXXVII became C/CCLXXVI.

51 On 4/10/16 A was broken up between B and C, and on 7/10/16 B/CCLXXVIII joined and became A/CCLXXVII. On 18/1/17 the Bde. became an A.F.A. Bde., and A was transferred and became C/CCLXXVI. A/CLXXIX (from 39th Div.) joined and became A/CCLXXVII, and D (H.) was made up to 6 Hows. by 1 sec. of D (H.)/CLXXIX (from 39th Div.).

52 On 4/10/16 C was broken up between A and B; and on 19/10/16 the Bde. was broken up; A became B/CCLXXV (on 6/10/16) and B became A/CCLXXVII (on 7/10/16).

53 X, Y, and Z were formed by 3/6/16; and on 29/1/18 Z was broken up between X and Y.

54 V was formed on 25/5/16; and on 29/1/18 V was transferred to Corps Artillery.

55 On 31/1/18, 8/King's and 2/8/King's were amalgamated, and became 8/King's in 171st Bde., 57th Div.

56 On 1-6/2/18, 9/King's and 2/9/King's were amalgamated, and became 9/King's in 172nd Bde., 57th Div.

57 On 4/2/18, 5/L.N.L. and 2/5/L.N.L. were amalgamated, and became 5/L.N.L. in 170th Bde., 57th Div.

58 The Fd. Cos. were numbered by 1/2/17.

59 Coy. disembkd. at le Havre on 16/12/16, and joined 55th Div. on 22/12/16.

60 Joined Div. by 16/6/17.

61 Formed on 7/3/18. It consisted of 164th, 165th 166th, and 196th M.G. Cos.

55TH (WEST LANCASHIRE) DIVISION

MOBILIZATION, RE-FORMATION, BATTLES, AND ENGAGEMENTS

The division—an existing T.F. division—was chiefly drawn from the western part of Lancashire, between the Lune and the Mersey, with the divisional headquarters at Liverpool. The three brigade headquarters were at Lancaster and Liverpool (2) ; and the original 12 battalions came from Ulverston, Lancaster, Preston, Bolton, Liverpool (5), Bootle, Warrington, and St. Helens. The attached yeomanry regiment had its headquarters in Liverpool. In the artillery : the I. W. Lancashire Bde. was concentrated in Windsor Barracks, Liverpool ; the II. W. Lancashire Bde. was at Preston, with outlying batteries at Lancaster and Blackpool ; the III. W. Lancashire Bde. was in Liverpool, with outlying batteries at Garston and Widnes ; the IV. W. Lancashire (How.) Bde. was at Edge Lane, Liverpool ; and the heavy battery was at Sefton Barracks, Liverpool.

Both field companies as well as H.Q. and No. 1 Section of the Signal Company were at St. Helens ; the three field ambulances were in Liverpool (2) and at St. Helens (with one section at Kendal) ; and the companies of the W. Lanc. Divnl. T. and S. Column were at Southport, Liverpool (2), and Warrington.

Annual training had just begun when war was declared, and all units at once returned to their peace stations for mobilization.

To provide reinforcements for the B.E.F., eight battalions left for France between November, 1914, and March, 1915 ; and with the transfer, in April, 1915, of the N. Lanc. Inf. Bde. to the Highland Division, the last of the infantry disappeared from England, and the rest of the W. Lanc. Div. joined the 2/1/W. Lanc. Div. (later 57th Div.).

In November, 1915, the Army Council authorized the re-formation of the 55th (W. Lancashire) Division in France; and, on the 3rd January, 1916, the division began to assemble around Hallencourt, in the Third Army area. The original battalions all returned, the artillery rejoined from the 2nd Canadian Division (with which it had embarked for France in October, 1915), and the 55th Division was complete by the 27th January, 1916.

For the remainder of the Great War the 55th Division served on the Western Front in France and Belgium, and was engaged in the following operations :—

1916

BATTLES OF THE SOMME

4–6 Sept. ... ...**Battle of Guillemont** [XV. Corps, Fourth Army].

9 Sept. ... ...**Battle of Ginchy** [XV. Corps, Fourth Army].

17–22 Sept. ... ...**Battle of Flers-Courcelette** [XV. Corps, Fourth Army].

25–28 Sept. ... ...**Battle of Morval** [XV. Corps, Fourth Army].

1917

BATTLES OF YPRES

31 July–2 Aug. ... ...**Battle of Pilckem Ridge** [XIX. Corps, Fifth Army].

20–23 Sept. ... ...**Battle of Menin Road Ridge** [V. Corps, Fifth Army].

BATTLE OF CAMBRAI

20 and 21 Nov. ... ...**The Tank Attack** [VII. Corps, Third Army].

30 Nov.–3 Dec. ... ...**German Counter-Attacks** [VII. Corps, Third Army].

1918

THE BATTLES OF THE LYS

9–11 April ... ...**Battle of Estaires** [XI. Corps, First Army].

9–17 April ... ...**Defence of Givenchy** [XI. Corps, until 8 a.m., 12/4 ; then I. Corps].

12–15 April ... ...**Battle of Hazebrouck** [I. Corps, First Army].

THE ADVANCE TO VICTORY

24 Aug. ... ...**Capture of Givenchy Craters** [I. Corps, Fifth Army].

17 Sept. ... ...**Capture of Canteleux Trench** (165th Bde.) [I. Corps, Fifth Army].

THE FINAL ADVANCE IN ARTOIS

2 Oct.–11 Nov. ... ...**The Pursuit to Mons** [I. Corps, until 8 October ; then III. Corps, Fifth Army].

On the 2nd October the Germans started to withdraw on the divisional front, and the 55th Division pressed forward and occupied la Bassée the same day. The line of the Haute Deule Canal was forced, 14th–16th October, and Ath was captured early on the 11th November.

By 11 a.m., 11th November, when the Armistice put an end to hostilities, the leading troops of the division had reached the line Thoricourt–Bassilly (seven miles east of Ath).

On the 15th November orders were issued for the division to advance into Germany as part of the Second Army. On the 21st, however, the 55th Division was transferred to the Fifth Army and its advance into Germany was cancelled. During the latter part of the month the division was chiefly employed on railway reconstruction and road repair in the Leuze area. On the 7th December the division was visited by H.M. the King. On the 15th the division began to move to Brussels, and on the 18th this move was completed ; and during this month educational work was carried on extensively. On the 3rd January, 1919, the division was reviewed by H.M. the King of the Belgians, and on the 26th the 55th Division was represented at a ceremonial parade in Brussels. During the month demobilization proceeded, and the division gradually dwindled. The G.O.C. left on the 15th March to take over command of a division in the Army of Occupation ; on the 5th April the G.S. Office ceased to exist, and by the end of the month the strength of the division had shrunk to 158 officers and 2,192 other ranks. Its war service was over ; and in April, 1920, it began to re-form in the Western Command at home.

56TH (1ST LONDON) DIVISION

G.O.C.

22 February, 1912 ... ... Major-General W. FRY.

. . . .

6 February, 1916 ... ... Major-General C. P. A. HULL (sick, 20/7/17).
20 July, 1917 ... ... Br.-Gen. G. H. B. FREETH (acting).
24 July, 1917 ... ... Major-General W. DOUGLAS SMITH.
9 August, 1917... ... ... Br.-Gen. G. H. B. FREETH (acting).
10 August, 1917... ... ... Major-General F. A. DUDGEON (sick, 25/4/18).
25 April, 1918 ... ... Br.-Gen. G. H. B. FREETH (acting).
4 May, 1918 ... ... Major-General SIR C. P. A. HULL.

G.S.O. 1.

12 Dec., 1913...Major H. A. BOYCE (G.S.O. 2).
5 Aug., 1914...Lt.-Col. H. A. BOYCE.

. . . .

5 Feb., 1916...Lt.-Col. J. E. S. BRIND.
30 Oct., 1916...Lt.-Col. A. BRYANT.
23 Dec., 1916...Lt.-Col. G. DE LA P. B. PAKENHAM.

A.-A. and Q.-M.-G.

1 April, 1912...Major J. McC. STEELE (D.-A.-A. and Q.-M.-G.).
5 Aug., 1914...Col. G. COCKBURN.

. . . .

5 Feb., 1916...Lt.-Col. H. W. GRUBB.
3 Dec., 1917...Lt.-Col. W. M. SUTTON.

B.-G., R.A.

29 July, 1912...*Br.-Gen. G. S. DUFFUS.

. . . .

(Divnl. Artillery rejoined on 25 and 26/2/16.)
[9 Oct., 1915]...Br.-Gen. R. J. G. ELKINGTON.

C.R.E.

28 Jan., 1913...Lt.-Col. G. W. WALTERS.

. . . .

5 Feb., 1916...Lt.-Col. H. W. GORDON.
15 Oct., 1917...Lt.-Col. E. N. MOZLEY.

*Br.-Gen. on 5 August, 1914.

1st LONDON BDE.

9 Dec., '12...*Br.-Gen. EARL OF LUCAN.
(Bde. embkd. for Malta on 4/9/14.)

2nd LONDON BDE.

30 July, '10...Col. R. SCOTT KERR.
30 July, '14...Lt.-Col. G. D. M. MOORE (acting).
11 Aug., '14...Br.-Gen. EARL OF CAVAN.
9 Sept., '14...Lt.-Col. G. D. M. MOORE (acting).

3rd LONDON BDE.

1 Jan., '13...*Br.-Gen. C. S. O. MONCK.

. . . .

167th BDE.
(1st London)

(Bde. formed at Hallencourt, 5–9/2/16.)
5 Feb., '16...Br.-Gen. F. H. NUGENT (sick, 22/7/16).
22 July, '16...Lt.-Col. E. J. KING (acting).
27 July, '16...Br.-Gen. G. H. B. FREETH.
20 July, '17...Lt.-Col. P. L. INGPEN (acting).
23 July, '17...Br.-Gen. G. H. B. FREETH.
26 April, '18...Lt.-Col. R. H. HUSEY (acting).
6 May, '18...Br.-Gen. G. H. B. FREETH.

168th BDE.
(2nd London)

(Bde. formed at Yanville, 5–11/2/16.)
7 Feb., '16...Br.-Gen. G. G. LOCH (sick, 31/10/18).
31 Oct., '18...Lt.-Col. A. F. MARCHMENT (acting).
12 Nov., '18...Br.-Gen. G. G. LOCH.

169th BDE.
(3rd London)

(Bde. formed at Hallencourt, 5–13/2/16.)
5 Feb., '16...Br.-Gen. E. S. DE E. COKE.

*Br.-Gen. on 5 August, 1914.

GENERAL NOTES

1st London Heavy Battery, R.G.A., T.F. (4, 4.7-inch guns), joined the 58th (2/1/London) Div., after the 1st London Div. had been broken up to reinforce the B.E.F. in France. On 11/2/16 the Hy. Bty. left the 58th Div. and moved to Woolwich to prepare for service overseas. The Hy. Bty. disembkd. at le Havre on 3/3/16, and on 5/3/16 it joined XXVII. H.A. Group, R.G.A.

The following Units also served with the 56th Division :—

ARTILLERY :—**CCL. Bde.** (of 50th Div. Arty.), joined from 11th Div. on 23/9/18, and was transferred to 12th Div. on 3/10/18.
B (H.) and C (H.)/LVII. (H.) Bde. (of 10th Div. Arty.). See note 18.
500 (H.) Bty. See note 57.

OTHER UNITS :—**No. 56 Sanitary Section,** joined from England on 11/2/16, and it was transferred on 1/4/17 to a VII. Corps Sanitary Area.
56th Divnl. Amb. Workshop, joined from England on 28/2/16, and was absorbed by the Supply Column on 31/3/16.

On 30/1/18 the reorganization of the Division on a 9-battalion basis was completed; and on 6/3/18 the pioneer battalion was reorganized on a 3-company basis.

56TH[1] (1ST LONDON) DIVISION ORDER OF BATTLE, 1914-1918

Dates	INFANTRY Brigades	INFANTRY Battalions and attached Units	Mounted Troops	ARTILLERY Field Artillery Brigades	ARTILLERY Field Artillery Batteries	ARTILLERY Field Artillery Bde. Ammn. Colns.	ARTILLERY Trench Mortar Bties. Medium	ARTILLERY Trench Mortar Bties. Heavy	ARTILLERY Divnl. Ammn. Coln.	Engineers Field Cos.	Signal Service Divnl. Signal Coy.	Pioneers	M.G. Units	Field Ambulances	Mobile Vety. Secn.	Divnl. Emplnt. Coy.	Divnl. Train
1914 August (England)	1st London[2] 2nd London[7] 3rd London[10]	1/Lond.,[3] 2/Lond.,[4] 3/Lond.,[5] 4/Lond.[6] 5/Lond. (L.R.B.),[8] 6/Lond.,[9] 7/Lond.,[9] 8/Lond. (P.O. Rif.)[9] 9/Lond. (Q.V. Rif.),[11] 10/Lond.,[12] 11/Lond.,[12] 12/Lond. (Rangers)[13]	2/Co.[14] of Lond. Yeo. (Westminster Dgns.)	I City of London[15] II London[16] III London[17] IV London[18] (H.)	1/City of Lond., 2/City of Lond., 3/City of Lond. 4/Co. of Lond., 5/Co. of Lond., 6/Co. of Lond. 7/Co. of Lond., 8/Co. of Lond., 9/Co. of Lond. 10/Co. of Lond. (H.), 11/Co. of Lond. (H.)	I London II London III London IV London (H.)	...	...	...	1/London[19] 2/London[20]	1/London[21]	...	...	1/London[22] 2/London[23] 3/London[23]	...	...	1/London[24] Divnl. T. & S. Coln.
1916 February (Re-formed in France)	167th[25] 168th[30] 169th[35]	7/Middx.,[26] 8/Middx.,[27] 1/Lond.,[28] 3/Lond.[29] 4/Lond.,[31] 12/Lond. (Rgrs.),[32] 13/Lond. (Kensington),[33] 14/Lond. (L.S.)[34] 2/Lond.,[36] 5/Lond. (L.R.B.),[37] 9/Lond. (Q.V. Rif.),[38] 16/Lond. (Q.W. Rif.)[39]	B Sqdn., 2/K.E. Horse;[40] 1/Lond. Divnl.[41] Cyclist Coy.	I City of London[42] II London[43] III London[44] IV London[45] (H.)	1/City of Lond., 2/City of Lond., 3/City of Lond. 4/Co. of Lond., 5/Co. of Lond., 6/Co. of Lond. 7/Co. of Lond., 8/Co. of Lond., 9/Co. of Lond. 10/Co. of Lond. (H.), 11/Co. of Lond. (H.), R. (H.)	I London II London III London IV London (H.)	...	...	56th D.A.C.[46]	2/1/London[47] 2/2/London[47]	56th[48] (London)	5/Ches. (P.)[49]	...	2/1/London[50] 2/2/London[50] 2/3/London[50]	1/London[51]	...	56th[52]
1916 June (France)	167th 168th 169th	1/Middx., 8/Middx., 1/Lond., 3/Lond.; 167th Bde. M.G. Coy.;[53] 167th T.M. Bty.[54] 4/Lond., 12/Lond., 13/Lond., 14/Lond.; 168th Bde. M.G. Coy.;[55] 168th T.M. Bty.[54] 2/Lond., 5/Lond., 9/Lond., 16/Lond.; 169th Bde. M.G. Coy.;[53] 169th T.M. Bty.[54]	...	CCLXXX[55] CCLXXXI[56] CCLXXXII[57] CCLXXXIII[58]	A, B, C; D (H.) A, B, C; D (H.) A, B, C; D (H.) A[93], B[109], C	...[45]	X.56[59] Y.56[59] Z.56[59]	V.56[60]	56th D.A.C.	1/Edinburgh[61] 2/1/London 2/2/London	56th	5/Ches. (P.)	...	2/1/London 2/2/London 2/3/London	1/London	...	56th
1917 June (France)	167th 168th 169th	7/Middx., 8/Middx., 1/Lond., 3/Lond.;[62] 167th M.G. Coy.;[68] 167th T.M. Bty. 4/Lond., 12/Lond.,[63] 13/Lond., 14/Lond.; 168th M.G. Coy.;[68] 168th T.M. Bty. 2/Lond., 5/Lond., 9/Lond.,[64] 16/Lond.; 169th M.G. Coy.;[68] 169th T.M. Bty.	...	CCLXXX CCLXXXI	93, A, C; D (H.) 109, A, B; D (H.)	...	X.56 Y.56 Z.56[59]	V.56[60]	56th D.A.C.	416th[65] (1/Edinburgh) 512th[65] (2/1/London) 513th[65] (2/2/London)	56th	5/Ches. (P.)	193rd M.G. Coy.[66]	2/1/London 2/2/London 2/3 London	1/London	247th[67]	56th
1918 March (France)	167th 168th 169th	7/Middx., 8/Middx., 1/Lond.; 167th T.M. Bty. 4/Lond., 13/Lond., 14/Lond.; 168th T.M. Bty. 2/Lond., 5/Lond., 16/Lond.; 169th T.M. Bty.	...	CCLXXX CCLXXXI	93, A, C; D (H.) 109, A, B; D (H.)	...	X.56 Y.56	...	56th D.A.C.	416th 512th 513th	56th	5/Ches. (P.)	No. 56 Bn.,[68] M.G.C.	2/1/London 2/2 London 2/3 London	1/London	247th	56th

Div. sent 1 Lond. Inf. Bde. to Malta and 6 Bns. to reinforce the B.E.F. in France; 2 Fd. Cos. and 3 Fd. Ambces. also left; and in April, 1915, the last 2 Bns. were transferred to the 54th Div. In Febry., 1916, the 56th Div. was re-formed in France.

2 The Bde. embkd. on 4/9/14 and disembkd. at Malta on 14/9/14. As the Bns. left Malta for France, they were replaced by their 2nd-Line Bns. (see Notes 3—6).

3 Disembkd. at Malta on 14/9/14; left Malta on 11/2/15 and went to France (via England), disembkd. at le Havre on 11/3/15, joined 25th Bde., 8th Div., on 14/3/15.

4 Disembkd. at Malta on 14/9/14; left Malta on 2/1/15, disembkd. at Marseille on 6/1/15, joined 17th Bde., 6th Div., on 21/2/15, and on 14/10/15 was transferred (with 17th Bde.) to 24th Div.

5 Disembkd. at Malta on 14/9/14; left Malta on 2/1/15, disembkd. at Marseille on 6/1/15, joined Ferozepore Bde., Lahore Div., on 10/2/15, transferred to Garhwal Bde., Meerut Div., on 17/2/15, transferred to Dehra Dun Bde., Meerut Div., on 4/11/15, to 139th Bde., 46th Div., on 6/11/15, and to 142nd Bde., 47th Div., on 16/11/15.

6 Disembkd. at Malta on 14/9/14; left Malta on 2/1/15, disembkd. at Marseille on 6/1/15, joined Ferozepore Bde., Lahore Div., on 20/2/15, transferred to 137th Bde., 46th Div., on 11/11/15, and to 140th Bde., 47th Div., on 15/11/15.

7 The Bde. was broken up in Nov., 1914, after 3 Bns. had been transferred to 4th Lond. Bde., 2nd Lond. Div., and the L.R.B. had gone to France.

8 Joined 11th Bde, 4th Div., in France, on 17/11/14, was transferred to G.H.Q. on 19/5/15; joined 8th Bde., 3rd Div., on 25/10/15.

9 The 3 Bns. joined 4th Lond. Bde., 2nd Lond. Div., on 5 and 6/11/14. On 31/1.-2/2/18 the 3 Bns. were transferred to 174th Bde., 58th Div., and on joining were amalgamated with their 2nd-Line Bns.

10 The Bde. was broken up in April, 1915; 2 Bns. had gone to France, and 2 Bns. joined E. Midland Bde., E. Anglian Div.

11 Joined 13th Bde., 5th Div., in France on 27/11/14. From 3/3-7/4/15 the Bn. was attached (tempy.) to 83rd Bde.

12 The 2 Bns. were transferred to E. Midland Bde., E. Anglian Div., at Norwich in April, 1915, and they served with the 54th (E. Anglian) Div. throughout the War.

13 Joined G.H.Q. Troops, France, on 4/1/15, joined 28th Div. on 30/1/15, and posted to 84th Bde. on 8/2/15. On 20/5/15 Bn. was transferred to G.H.Q. Troops.

14 Joined 2nd Mtd. Div. in Egypt on 13/8/15 (with 5th Mtd. Bde.), served with it at Suvla from 18/8-31/10/15, and returned to Alexandria on 30/11/15.

15 Rearmed with 18-pdrs. on joining 36th Div. in Septr., 1915, disembkd. at le Havre on 4/10/15, transferred to 38th Div. on 11/12/15, to 16th Div. on 1/1/16, to 47th Div. on 3/1/16, and to 16th Div. on 26/1/16.

16 Rearmed with 18-pdrs. on joining 36th Div. in Septr., 1915, disembkd. at le Havre on 4/10/15, transferred to 38th Div. on 11/12/15, and to IV Corps Artillery on 1/1/16.

17 Rearmed with 18-pdrs. on joining 36th Div. in Septr., 1915, disembkd. at le Havre on 5/10/15, transferred to 38th Div. on 11/12/15, to IV Corps Artillery on 1/1/16, and to 47th Div. on 27/1/16.

18 Rearmed with 4.5-inch Hows. on joining 36th Div. in Septr., 1915, and B (H.) and C (H.)/LVII (Hows.) were attached to IV London Bde. Bde. and attached Bties. disembkd. at le Havre on 4/10/15. On 18/11/15 B and C/LVII (H.) left for Marseille to join 10th Divnl. Arty. at Salonika. IV Lond. Bde. was transferred to 38th Div. on 12/12/15, and to Dismtd. Cav. Div. on 3/1/16.

Joined 8th Div. in France on 23/12/14, and served with it throughout the War.

20 Joined 29th Div. in Jany., 1915, and served with it throughout the War.

21 1 Sec. went to Malta in Septr., 1914, with 1st Lond. Inf. Bde.

22 Disembkd. at Malta on 14/9/14 with 1st Lond. Inf. Bde. Left Malta 30/3/16 and arrived in England 5/4/16; left for Egypt and Salonika in June, 1916, disembkd. at Salonika on 4/7/16, and became 30th Staty. Hospital.

23 The 2 Fd. Ambces. joined 28th Div. at Winchester on 21/12/14, and served with the Div. throughout the War. The 2 Ambces. were numbered 84 and 85 on 29/1/15.

24 The Cos. formed Nos. 170, 171, 172, and 173 Cos.; they were allotted as 28th Divnl. Train and joined on 21/12/14; the Train embkd. for France on 15/1/15. On 13/11/15 the Cos. left 28th Div. and were re-allotted as 33rd Divnl. Train. On 25/11/15 No. 172 Coy. joined 2nd Divnl. Train and was replaced by No. 8 Coy. from 2nd Div.

25 Bde. formed at Hallencourt on 5-9/2/16.

26 Formerly in Middx. Inf. Bde., Home Cties. Div.; served at Gibraltar 9/9/14-8/2/15, joined 23rd Bde., 8th Div., in France on 15/3/15, and joined 167th Bde., on 9/2/16.

27 Formerly in Middx. Inf. Bde., Home Cties. Div.; served at Gibraltar 17/9/14-8/2/15; joined 85th Bde., 28th Div., in France on 11/3/15, joined 8th Div. on 21/6/15, and amalgamated with 7/Middx. until 2/8/15; posted to 25th Bde., 8th Div., on 27/8/15, and to 70th Bde., 8th Div., on 23/10/15; and joined 167th Bde. on 9/2/16.

28 Rejoined on 8/2/16, from 25th Bde., 8th Div.

29 Rejoined on 9/2/16, from 142nd Bde., 47th Div.

30 Bde. formed at Yanville on 5-11/2/16.

31 Rejoined on 9/2/16, from 140th Bde., 47th Div.

32 Rejoined on 11/2/16, from G.H.Q. Troops.

33 See General Notes, 47th Div. Joined 168th Bde. on 11/2/16, from G.H.Q. Troops.

34 See General Notes, 47th Div. Joined 168th Bde. on 8/2/16, from 1st Bde., 1st Div.

35 Bde. formed at Hallencourt on 5-13/2/16.

36 Rejoined on 10/2/16, from 17th Bde., 24th Div.

37 Rejoined on 10/2/16, from 8th Bde., 3rd Div.

38 Rejoined on 13/2/16, from 13th Bde., 5th Div.

39 See General Notes, 47th Div. Joined 169th Bde. on 10/2/16, from 18th Bde., 6th Div.

40 Sqdn. joined from XIV Corps Troops on 23/3/15; and on 30/5/15 the Sqdn. rejoined Comp. Cav. Regt. in XIV Corps.

41 Joined from England on 26/4/16, and on 11/5/16 the Coy. was transferred to VI Corps Cyclist Bn.

42 Bde. rejoined on 25/2/16, from 16th Div. On 15/4/16 93 (from XVIII, originally with Lahore Div., and then with 2nd Cdn. Div.) joined Bde. On 11/5/16 Bde. was numbered CCLXXX and Bties. lettered A, B, C, and D [93rd]. On 28/5/16. D [93rd] was transferred and became A/CCLXXXIII; and B (H.) joined from CCLXXXIII and became D (H.)/CCLXXX.

43 Bde. rejoined on 25/2/16, from IV Corps Arty. On 15/4/16, 109 (from XXIII, with 3rd Div.) joined Bde. On 12/5/16 the Bde. was numbered CCLXXXI and Bties. lettered A, B, C, and D [109th]. On 26/5/16, D [109th] was transferred and became B/CCLXXXIII, and A (H.) joined from CCLXXXIII and became D (H.)/CCLXXXI.

44 Bde. rejoined on 25 and 26/2/16 from 47th Div. On 16/4/16, R Bty. (formed from 93rd and 109th Bties) joined Bde. On 11/5/16 Bde. was numbered CCLXXXII and Bties. lettered A, B, C, and D [R]. On 28/5/16, D was transferred and became C/CCLXXXIII, and C (H.) joined from CCLXXXIII and became D (H.)/CCLXXXII.

45 B (H.)/CLXVII (H.) (from 33rd Div.) joined Bde. on 14/2/16, and became R (H.). Bde. rejoined on 26/2/16 from Dismtd. Cav. Div. On 12/5/16 Bde. was numbered CCLXXXIII and Bties. lettered A, B, and C [R]. On 26/5/16 Bde. was reorganized: A (H.) became D (H.)/CCLXXXI, B (H.) became D (H.)/CCLXXX, and C (H.) became D (H.)/CCLXXXII; and D [93]/CCLXXX joined and became A; D [109]/CCLXXXI became B; and D [R]/CCLXXXII became C.

46 Formed as 10th D.A.C.; sent with 1st Lond. Divnl. Arty. to 36th Div. in Septr., 1915; disembkd. at le Havre on 5 and 6/10/15 with Divnl. Arty.; joined 56th Div. on 27/2/16, and became 56th D.A.C. On 17/5/16 B.A.C.s were abolished and the D.A.C. was reorganized.

47 Left 58th Div. for France on 21/2/16, and joined on 24/2/16.

48 Left 58th Div. for France on 12/2/16, disembkd. at le Havre on 13/2/16, and joined on 16/2/16.

49 Joined on 13/2/16, from Pioneers, 5th Div. (Served with 14th Bde., 5th Div., from 19/2-29/11/15, and then became Pioneers.)

50 Left 58th Div. for France on 21/2/16, and joined on 24/2/16.

51 Arrived from England on 14/3/16.

52 Joined from England on 13/2/16. It consisted of 213, 214, 215, and 216 Cos., A.S.C. (Formed originally as 11th Divnl. Train.)

53 The M.G. Cos. were formed: 167th on 22/3/16; 168th on 16/3/16; and 169th on 17/4/16.

54 167th T.M. Bty. was formed on 14/6/16, from 167/1 and 167/2; 168th T.M.B. by 13/6/16; and 169th T.M.B. by 17/6/16, from 169/1 and 169/2.

55 On 5/11/16 B was broken up between A and C, and 93 (formerly A/CCLXXXIII) joined. On 23/1/17 R. Sec. of A (H.)/CCLXXXII joined D (H.)/CCLXXX.

56 On 5/11/16 C was broken up between A and B, and 109 (formerly B/CCLXXXIII) joined. On 23/1/17 L. Sec. of A (H.)/CCLXXXII joined D (H.)/CCLXXXI.

57 On 5/11/16 A was broken up between B and C; and by 6/12/16 500 (H.) joined and became A (H.). On 23/1/17 A (H) was broken up between D (H.)/CCLXXX and D (H)/CCLXXXI; and B/CXXVI (of 37th Divnl. Arty.) joined and became A/CCLXXXII, and 1 sec. of D (H.)/CXXVI (of 37th Divnl. Arty.) made D (H.)/CCLXXXII up to 6 Hows.; CCLXXXII then became an A.F.A. Bde.

58 On 5/11/16 C was broken up between A [93] and B [109]; and Bde. was broken up: 93 joined CCLXXX, and 109, CCLXXXI.

59 X, Y, and Z were formed by the middle of May, 1916. In Febry., 1918, Z was broken up between X and Y.

60 V was formed by May, 1916; and in Febry., 1918, V was transferred to Corps Arty.

61 A Fortress Coy., T.F., in Aug., 1914, it became a Fd. Coy. It embkd. at Devonport on 19/12/15, disembkd. at Port Said on 3-5/1/16, and was allotted to Army Troops. Employed on Suez Canal Defences, 10/1-12/4/16. The Fd. Coy. embkd. Alexandria on 17/4/16, disembkd. Marseille on 24/4/16, and joined 56th Div. 27/4-4/5/16.

62 Transferred to 173rd Bde., 58th Div., and amalgamated with 2/3/Lond. on 31/1/18. Bn. became 3/Lond.

63 Transferred to 175th Bde., 58th Div., and amalgamated with 2/12/Lond. on 31/1/18. Bn. became 12/Lond.

64 Transferred to 175th Bde., 58th Div., and amalgamated with 2/9/Lond. on 1/2/18. Bn. became 9/Lond.

65 Fd. Cos. were numbered on 30/1/17.

66 Joined by 24/12/16.

67 Formed by 23/6/17.

68 Formed on 1/3/18. Bn. consisted of 167, 168, 169, and 193 M.G. Cos.

56TH (1ST LONDON) DIVISION

MOBILIZATION, RE-FORMATION, BATTLES, AND ENGAGEMENTS

The division—an existing T.F. division—was chiefly drawn from the northern, eastern, and south-eastern districts of London, with the divisional headquarters in New Broad St. The three brigade headquarters were in New Broad St. and in Buckingham Gate (2); and the original 12 battalions came from Bloomsbury, Westminster, Hampstead, City Road, Bunhill Row (2), Farringdon Road, Finsbury Sq., Berkeley Sq., Hackney, Pentonville, and Bedford Square. The attached yeomanry regiment had its headquarters in Westminster. In the artillery: the I. City of London Bde. was concentrated in Bloomsbury; the II. London Bde. was at Woolwich, with an outlying battery at Eltham; the III. London Bde. was in the Artillery Barracks, City Road; the IV. London (How.) Bde. was at Lewisham; and the heavy battery was at Islington.

Both field companies as well as H.Q. and No. 1 Section of the Signal Company were at Bethnal Green; the three field ambulances were at Chelsea; and the companies of the 1st London Divnl. T. and S. Coln. were all at Plumstead.

Annual training had just begun when war was declared, and all units promptly mustered at their headquarters for mobilization.

To relieve the regular garrison of Malta, the 1st London Inf. Bde. embarked on 4th September, 1914, for garrison duty in that fortress (see Notes on Table). . Early in November, three battalions were transferred to the 4th London Bde., 2nd London Div., three more battalions left for France between the middle of November, 1914, and early in January, 1915, and what remained of the 1st London Div. then joined the 2/1st London Div. (later 58th Div.). In April, 1915, the two remaining battalions were transferred to the E. Midland Bde., E. Anglian Div.; and in September, 1915, the Artillery was selected for service in France and joined the 36th (Ulster) Div. (see Notes on Table).

On the 7th January, 1916, the Army Council authorized the re-formation in France, as soon as circumstances would allow, of the 56th (1st London) Division; and on the 5th February, 1916, the division began to assemble around Hallencourt, in the Third Army area. Seven of the original battalions returned and the artillery rejoined (see Table).

By the 21st February the bulk of the division had assembled.

For the remainder of the Great War the 56th Division served on the Western Front in France and Belgium, and was engaged in the following operations:—

1916

BATTLES OF THE SOMME

1 July ... ...**Gommecourt** [VII. Corps, Third Army].

9 Sept. ... ...**Battle of Ginchy** [XIV. Corps, Fourth Army].

15–22 Sept. ... ...**Battle of Flers-Courcelette** [XIV. Corps, Fourth Army].

25–27 Sept. ... ...**Battle of Morval** [XIV. Corps, Fourth Army].

26 Sept. ... ...**Capture of Combles.**

1–9 Oct.... ... ...**Battle of the Transloy Ridges** [XIV. Corps, Fourth Army].

1917

14 March–5 April ...**German Retreat to the Hindenburg Line** [VII. Corps, Third Army].

BATTLES OF ARRAS

9–14 April ... ...**First Battle of the Scarpe** [VII. Corps, Third Army].
3 and 4 May ... ...**Third Battle of the Scarpe** [VI. Corps, Third Army].

BATTLES OF YPRES

16 and 17 Aug.... ...**Battle of Langemarck** [II. Corps, Fifth Army].

BATTLE OF CAMBRAI

21 Nov. ... ...**Capture of Tadpole Copse** [IV. Corps, Third Army].
23–28 Nov. ... ...**Capture of Bourlon Wood** [IV. Corps, until m/n. 24/11; then VI. Corps, Third Army].
30 Nov.-2 Dec. ... ...**German Counter-attacks** [VI. Corps, Third Army].

1918

FIRST BATTLES OF THE SOMME

28 March ... ...**First Battle of Arras** [XIII. Corps, First Army].

THE ADVANCE TO VICTORY

SECOND BATTLES OF THE SOMME

23 Aug. ... ...**Battle of Albert** [VI. Corps, Third Army].

SECOND BATTLES OF ARRAS

26–30 Aug. ... ...**Battle of the Scarpe** [XVII. Corps, Third Army].

BATTLES OF THE HINDENBURG LINE

27 Sept.–1 Oct. ... ...**Battle of the Canal du Nord** [XXII. Corps, First Army].
8 and 9 Oct. ... ...**Battle of Cambrai** [XXII. Corps, First Army].
9–12 Oct. ... ...**Pursuit to the Selle** [XXII. Corps until 5 p.m., 11/10; then Cdn. Corps, First Army].

THE FINAL ADVANCE IN PICARDY

4 Nov. ... ...**Battle of the Sambre** [XXII. Corps, First Army].
5–7 Nov. ... ...**Passage of the Grande Honnelle** [XXII. Corps, First Army].

By m/n. on the 10th November the division was relieved in the front line and drawn back into support to the XXII. Corps, but the 56th Division Artillery remained in action until the 'Cease Fire' sounded at 11 a.m. on the 11th November. At that time, the leading infantry brigade of the 56th Division (advancing between Maubeuge and Mons) had reached Harveng.

During the 1,010 days of its existence (since its re-formation) the division spent 330 days in rest,* 195 days in a quiet sector of the Western Front, 385 days in an active sector, and 100 days in active operations.

After the Armistice the division remained around Harveng and was employed on road-mending, etc. The 56th Division was selected to accompany the advance to the Rhine, but the order was cancelled on the 21st November; and, during December, the troops were engaged chiefly in educational training, road-mending, and clearing obstructions. On the 5th, H.M. the King passed through the divisional area. On the 12th, the first party of coal-miners left for demobilization, and thereafter demobilization proceeded steadily, and the division gradually dwindled. On the 18th May, 1919, the Divisional H.Q. cadre entrained at Jemappes for Antwerp, en route for England; and in April, 1920, the division began to re-form in the London District.

*The divisional artillery was frequently left in the line after the withdrawal of the infantry of the division.

APPENDICES

1, 2, 3, & 4

ENGLAND, 1914. Peace Establishment.
Authority—P.E., Part II., T.F. Estblnts., 1913-14.

Divnl. H.Q.

Infantry :
3 Brigades
(12 Inf. Battalions, with 2 Machine Guns each).

Mounted Troops :
1 Yeomanry Regiment
(with 2 Machine Guns).

Artillery :
H.Q., Divnl. Artillery ;
3 Field Artillery Bdes. (15-pdrs.) and 3 B.A.C.s ;
1 Field Artillery (How.) Bde. (5" Hows.) and 1 (How.) B.A.C. ;
1 Heavy Battery (4.7" Guns) and Hy. Bty. A.C.

Engineers :
H.Q., Divnl. Engineers ;
2 Field Companies.

Signal Service :
1 Signal Company.

3 Field Ambulances.

1 Divnl. Transport and Supply Column.

OCTOBER, 1914. War Establishment.
W.E., Territorial Divisions, 23/Oct./

Divnl. H.Q.

Infantry :
3 Brigades
(12 Inf. Battalions, with 2 Machine each).

Mounted Troops :
1 Yeomanry Sqdn. ;
1 Cyclist Coy.

Artillery :
H.Q., Divnl. Artillery ;
3 Field Artillery Bdes. (15-pdrs.) a
B.A.C.s ;
1 Field Artillery (How.) Bde. (5" Hows
1 (How.) B.A.C. ;
1 Heavy Battery (4.7" Guns) and Hy.
A.C. ;
1 A.-A. Gun Detachment (1-pdr.) ;
1 Divnl. Ammn. Coln.

Engineers :
H.Q., Divnl. Engineers ;
2 Field Companies.

Signal Service :
1 Signal Company.

3 Field Ambulances.
1 Motor Ambulance Workshop.
1 Mobile Veterinary Section.

1 Divnl. Train.

	Peace Establishment, 1914.		**War Establishment, OCTOBER, 1914.**	
All Ranks		17,484		17,37
Horses		2,267		4,17
Guns		48		4
15-pdr. B.L.C.	36		36	
5" Hows.	8		8	
4.7" Guns, Q.F.	4		4	
1-pdr., Q.F.			1	
Trench Mortars				
Stokes				
Medium (2")				
Heavy (9.45")				
Machine Guns		26		2
Vickers	26		24	
Lewis				
Carts and Vehicles		266		80
Cycles		61		4
Motor Cycles		8		2
Motor Cars				1
Motor Lorries				
Motor Ambulance Cars				2

'TEMBER, 1916. War Establishment (Western ront).
W.E., Part VII., 18/Sept./1916.

Divnl. H.Q.

ntry :
Brigades
(12 Inf. Battalions, with 12 Lewis Guns each) ;
Brigade Machine-Gun Companies (16 Vickers M.G. each) ;
Brigade Light Trench Mortar Batteries (8, 3" Stokes Mortars each).

llery :
.Q., Divnl. Artillery ;
4 Field Artillery Brigades
(18-pdrs. and 4·5" Hows.) ;
3 Medium Trench Mortar Batteries
(4, 2" Mortars each) ;
1 Heavy Trench Mortar Battery
(4, 9.45" Mortars) ;

1 Divnl. Ammn. Coln.

neers :
Q., Divnl. Engineers ;
3 Field Companies.

l Service :
Signal Company.

eers :
Pioneer Battalion
(12 Lewis Guns).

Field Ambulances.
Sanitary Section.
Mobile Veterinary Section.
Divnl. Train.

OCTOBER, 1918. War Establishment (Western Front).
W.E., Part VII. A., Series I. (France), 31/Oct./1918.

Divnl. H.Q.

Infantry :
3 Brigades
(9 Inf. Battalions, with 36 Lewis Guns each) ;

3 Light Trench Mortar Batteries
(8, 3" Stokes Mortars each).

Artillery :
H.Q., Divnl. Artillery ;
2 Field Artillery Brigades
(18-pdrs. and 4.5" Hows.) ;
2 Medium Trench Mortar Batteries
(6, 2" Mortars each) ;

1 Divnl. Ammn. Coln.

Engineers:
H.Q., Divnl. Engineers ;
3 Field Companies.

Signal Service :
1 Signal Company.

Pioneers :
1 Pioneer Battalion
(12 Lewis Guns).

Machine-Gun Unit :
1 Machine-Gun Battalion
(4 Companies, with 16 Vickers M.G. each).

3 Field Ambulances.
1 Mobile Veterinary Section.
1 Divnl. Employment Company.
1 Divnl. Train.

Establishment, SEPTEMBER, 1916.		War Establishment, OCTOBER, 1918.		
	19,372		16,035	All Ranks.
	5,145		3,838	Horses.
	64		48	Guns.
18-pdrs. 48		36		18 pdrs.
4.5" Hows. 16		12		4.5" Hows.
				4.7" Q.F.
				1-pdr. Q.F.
	40		36	Trench Mortars.
24		24		Stokes.
12		12		Medium (2").
4				Heavy (9.45").
	204		400	Machine Guns.
48		64		Vickers.
156		336		Lewis.
	942		870	Carts and Vehicles.
	372		341	Cycles.
	24		44	Motor Cycles.
	13		11	Motor Cars.
	3		3	Motor Lorries.
	21		21	Motor Amb. Cars.

WAR ESTABLISHMENT OF 2nd MOUNTED DIVISION, T.F. (Egypt), 5

Appendix 2.

2nd MOUNTED DIVISION (Egypt).
Authority—W.E., d/d. 12/Oct./1914.

Mtd. Divnl. H.Q.

4 Mounted Brigades
(3 Yeomanry Regts., 6 Machine Guns, and 1 Signal Troop each).

Artillery :
H.Q., Mtd. Divnl. Artillery;
2 Horse Artillery Brigades
(2 Bties. and Ammn. Colns. each).

Signal Service :
1 Mtd. Divnl. Signal Squadron.

4 Mounted Brigade Field Ambulances.

H.Q., Mtd. Divnl. A.S.C.

WAR ESTABLISHMENT, 1914.

All Ranks	7,903
Horses	7,792
15-pdr. Q.F. Guns	16
Machine Guns	24
Carts and Vehicles	337
Cycles	368
Motor Cycles	26
Motor Cars	23

NOTE.—For the Organization of 2nd Mounted Division at Suvla (Gallipoli), August—December, 1915, see Tables, pp. 12 and 13.

52nd (LOWLAND) DIV

Divnl. H.Q.

Infantry :
3 Brigades
(4 Inf. Battalion

Mounted Troops :
H.Q. and M.-G. S
1 Yeomanry Sqdn
1 Cyclist Coy.

Artillery :
H.Q., Divnl. Artil
3 Field Artillery
1 Field Artillery (
1 Divnl. Ammn.

Engineers :
H.Q., Divnl. Engi
2 Field Companies

Signal Service :
1 Signal Company

3 Field Ambulanc

1 Motor Ambulan

1 Mobile Veterina

1 Divnl. Train.

WAR ESTABLISHME

All Ranks ....
Horses ....
Guns ....
15-pdr. B.L.C
5" Hows. .....
Machine Guns.....
Carts and Vehicle
Cycles ....
Motor Cycles ......
Motor Cars ....
Motor Lorries......
Motor Ambulance

NOTE.—For th
at Helles (Gallipoli) in

...ION (Gallipoli), and 53rd DIVISION (Palestine).

Appendix 3.

...ll).
...ority—W.E., d/d. 9/May/1915.

...hine Guns each).

...ry Regt.;

...) and 3 B.A.C.s;
..." Hows.) and 1 (How.) B.A.C.;

...shop

...on.

...	17,853
...	5,101
...	44
......36	
...... 8	
...	50
...	980
...	427
...	25
...	12
...	3
...	21

... of the 52nd Division on arrival ... Tables, p. 112.

Appendix 4.

53rd (WELSH) DIVISION (Palestine).
Authority—W.E., Part XI. (Egypt) d/d. 30/Aug./1917.

Divnl. H.Q.

Infantry:
- 3 Brigades
  (4 Inf. Battalions, with 16 Lewis Guns each);
- 3 Machine-Gun Companies
  (16 Vickers M.G. each);
- 3 Light Trench Mortar Batteries
  (8, 3" Stokes Mortars each).

Mounted Troops:
- 1 Yeomanry Squadron;
- 1 Cyclist Company.

Artillery:
- H.Q., Divnl. Artillery;
- 3 Field Artillery Bdes.
  (2 Bties. of 18-pdrs. and 1 Bty. of 4·5" Hows. each);
- 1 Divnl. Ammn. Coln.

Engineers:
- H.Q., Divnl. Engineers;
- 3 Field Companies.

Signal Service:
- 1 Signal Company.

3 Field Ambulances.

1 Sanitary Section.

1 Mobile Veterinary Section.

1 Divnl. Train.

WAR ESTABLISHMENT, 1917.

All Ranks		17,990
Horses		5,175
Guns		48
18-pdrs.	36	
4.5" Hows.	12	
Trench Mortars (3" Stokes)		24
Machine Guns		240
Vickers	48	
Lewis	192	
Carts and Vehicles		743
Cycles		533
Motor Cycles		24
Motor Cars		9
Motor Lorries		3
Motor Ambulance Cars		21

NOTE.—For the Organization of the 53rd Division in Palestine in June, 1917, and July, 1918, see Tables, p. 120.

INDEX OF FORMATIONS

BRIGADES AND DIVISIONS

BRIGADES

Artillery—

R.H.A., T.F.—
I, 12; 13.
II, 12; 13.
XX, 31; 32; 33; 34; 113 (note 20).

R.F.A.—
IX, 112; 113; 115.
LV, 15.
LVI, 112; 113; 115.
LVII (H.), 143; 145 (note 18).
CII, 131.

R.F.A., T.F.—
CCX (I East Lancashire), 38; 39; 40.
CCXI (II East Lancashire), 38; 39; 40.
CCXII (III East Lancashire), 38; 39; 40.
CCXIII (IV East Lancashire), 38; 39; 40.
CCXV (I Wessex), 44; 45; 47; 48.
CCXVI (II Wessex), 44; 45; 47; 48.
CCXVII (III Wessex), 44; 45; 47; 48.
CCXVIII (IV Wessex), 44; 45; 47; 48.
CCXX (I Home Counties), 50; 51; 53; 54.
CCXXI (II Home Counties), 50; 51; 53; 54.
CCXXII (III Home Counties), 50; 51; 53; 54.
CCXXIII (IV Home Counties), 50; 51 (note 5).
CCXXV (2nd/I Wessex), 56; 57; 59; 60.
CCXXVI (2nd/II Wessex), 56; 57 (note 3).
CCXXVII (2nd/III Wessex), 56; 57; 59; 60.
CCXXVIII (2nd/IV Wessex), 56; 57; 59; 60.
CCXXX (I North Midland), 64; 65; 66.
CCXXXI (II North Midland), 64; 65; 66.
CCXXXII (III North Midland), 64; 65; 66.
CCXXXIII (IV North Midland), 64; 65; 66.
CCXXXV (V London), 72; 73; 74.
CCXXXVI (VI London), 72; 73; 74.
CCXXXVII (VII London), 72; 73; 74.
CCXXXVIII (VIII London), 72; 73; 74.
CCXL (I South Midland), 80; 81; 82.
CCXLI (II South Midland), 80; 81; 82.
CCXLII (III South Midland), 80; 81 (notes 9, 22, and 32); 82.
CCXLIII (IV South Midland), 80; 81 (notes 10, 23, and 33); 82.
CCXLV (I West Riding), 88; 89; 90.
CCXLVI (II West Riding), 88; 89; 90.
CCXLVII (III West Riding), 88; 89; 90.
CCXLVIII (IV West Riding), 88; 89; 90.
CCL (I Northumbrian), 95; 96; 97; 98; 99; 143.
CCLI (II Northumbrian), 95; 96; 97; 98; 99.
CCLII (III Northumbrian), 96; 98; 99.
CCLIII (IV Northumbrian), ii (f.n. 3); 96; 98; 99.
CCLV (I Highland), 104; 105; 106.
CCLVI (II Highland), 104; 105; 106.
CCLVIII (III Highland), 104; 105; 106.
CCLX (I Lowland), 104; 105; 111; 114.
CCLXI (II Lowland), 112; 113; 114; 115.
CCLXII (III Lowland), 111; 112; 113; 114; 115.
CCLXIII (IV Lowland), 33 (note 4); 112; 113; 114.
CCLXIV (V Lowland), 33 (note 4); 112; 113 (note 20).

R.F.A.—(*Continued*)
CCLXV (I Welsh), 119; 120; 121; 122.
CCLXVI (II Welsh), 119; 120; 121; 122.
CCLXVII (Cheshire), 119; 120; 121; 122.
CCLXVIII (IV Welsh), 119; 120; 121; 122.
CCLXX (I East Anglian), 127; 128; 129; 130.
CCLXXI (II East Anglian), 127; 128; 129; 130.
CCLXXII (III East Anglian), 127; 128; 129; 130; 131.
CCLXXIII (IV East Anglian), 127; 128; 129; 130.
CCLXXV (I West Lancashire), 136; 137; 138.
CCLXXVI (II West Lancashire), 136; 137; 138.
CCLXXVII (III West Lancashire), 136; 137; 138.
CCLXXVIII (IV West Lancashire), 136; 137; 138.
CCLXXX (I City of London), 71; 144; 145; 146; 147.
CCLXXXI (II London), 144; 145; 146; 147.
CCLXXXII (III London), 71; 144; 145; 146; 147.
CCLXXXIII (IV London), 144; 145; 146; 147.

R.G.A.—

Mountain, T.F.—
IV (Highland), 103; 106.

Cavalry Brigades—
10th, 14 (note 21).
11th, 14 (note 23).
12th, 14 (note 20).
14th, 14 (note 22).

Cyclist Brigades—
1st, 3; 5; 6; 7.
2nd, 3; 5; 6; 7.
3rd, 3; 5; 6; 7.
4th, 3; 5; 6; 7.
5th, 21; 23; 24; 25; 26; 27; 28; 30.
6th, 27; 28; 30.
7th, 27; 28; 29; 30.
8th, 27; 28; 29; 30.
9th, 20; 22; 25.
11th, 21; 23; 24; 26.
12th, 21; 23; 24; 26.
13th, 21; 23; 24; 26.

Detachments and Forces—
Détachement Français de Palestine et Syrie, 127.
Alderson's Force, 106.
Fleming's Force, 103.
Independent Force, 26.
Jackson's Force, 95 (note 4).
Marshall's Force, 95 (notes 1 and 2).
Plumer's Force, 99.

Dismounted Brigades—
1st, 111.
3rd, 37.
4th, 119.

Infantry Brigades—

19th, 111 (under note on 5/Sco. Rif.).
25th Div. Composite, 95 (note 4).
74th, 95 (note 1).
77th, 131.

Infantry Brigades, T.F.—

125th (Lancashire Fusilier), 36 ; 37 ; 38 ; 39 ; 40.
126th (East Lancashire), 36 ; 38 ; 39.
127th (Manchester), 36 ; 38 ; 39 ; 40.
128th (Hampshire), 43 ; 44 ; 46 ; 47.
129th (South-Western), 43 ; 44 ; 46 ; 47.
130th (Devon and Cornwall), 43 ; 44 ; 46 ; 47.
131st (Surrey), 49 ; 50 ; 51 ; 52 ; 53.
132nd (Middlesex), 49 ; 50 ; 51 ; 52 ; 53.
133rd (Kent), 49 ; 50 ; 51 ; 52 ; 53.
134th (2nd/1st Hampshire), 55 ; 56 ; 58.
135th (2nd/1st South-Western), 55 ; 56 ; 58.
136th (2nd/1st Devon and Cornwall), 55 ; 56 ; 58.
137th (Staffordshire), 62 ; 63 ; 64 ; 65 ; 67.
138th (Lincoln and Leicester), 62 ; 63 ; 64 ; 65 ; 67.
139th (Sherwood Forester), 62 ; 63 ; 64 ; 65 ; 66 ; 67.
140th (4th London), 70 ; 71 ; 72 ; 73 ; 75.
141st (5th London), 70 ; 72 ; 73 ; 75.
142nd (6th London), 70 ; 72 ; 73 ; 75.
143rd (Warwickshire), 78 ; 80 ; 81 ; 82.
144th (Gloucester and Worcester), 78 ; 80 ; 81 ; 82.
145th (South Midland), 78 ; 80 ; 81 ; 82.
146th (I West Riding), 86 ; 88 ; 89 ; 90 ; 91.
147th (II West Riding), 86 ; 88 ; 89 ; 90 ; 91.
148th (III West Riding), 86 ; 88 ; 89 ; 90 ; 91.
149th (Northumberland), 94 ; 95 ; 96 ; 97 ; 98 ; 99.
150th (York and Durham), 94 ; 95 ; 96 ; 97 ; 98 ; 99.
151st (Durham Light Infantry), 94 ; 95 ; 96 ; 97 ; 98 ; 99.
152nd (1st Highland, formerly Seaforth and Cameron), 102 ; 104 ; 105 ; 106.
153rd (2nd Highland, formerly Gordon), 102 ; 104 ; 105 ; 106.
154th (3rd Highland, formerly Argyll and Sutherland), 102 ; 104 ; 105 ; 106.
155th (South Scottish), 110 ; 112 ; 113 ; 114 ; 115.
156th (Scottish Rifle), 110 ; 112 ; 113 ; 114 ; 115.
157th (Highland Light Infantry), 110 ; 112 ; 113 ; 114.
158th (North Wales), 15 ; 118 ; 119 ; 120 ; 121 ; 122 ; 123.
159th (Cheshire), 15 ; 118 ; 119 ; 120 ; 121 ; 122 ; 123.
160th (Welsh Border), 118 ; 120 ; 121 ; 122.
161st (Essex), 126 ; 128 ; 129 ; 130 ; 131.
162nd (East Midland), 126 ; 128 ; 129 ; 130 ; 131.
163rd (Norfolk and Suffolk), 126 ; 128 ; 129 ; 130 ; 131.
164th (North Lancashire), 134 ; 136 ; 137 ; 138.
165th (Liverpool), 134 ; 136 ; 137 ; 138 ; 139.
166th (South Lancashire), 134 ; 136 ; 137 ; 138.
167th (1st London), 142 ; 144 ; 145 ; 146.
168th (2nd London), 142 ; 144 ; 145 ; 146.
169th (3rd London), 142 ; 144 ; 145 ; 146.
Black Watch, 114.
Lothian, 114.
50th Composite, 95 (notes 3 and 4).

Mounted Brigades—

Eastern, 2 ; 4 ; 6 ; 7 ; 37.
2/1/Eastern, 2 ; 5 ; 6 ; 27 ; 28 ; 30.
1st Highland, 10 ; 13 ; 14 ; 17.
2/1/Highland, 3 ; 5.
1st London, 10 ; 11 ; 12 ; 13 ; 14 ; 16 ; 31 ; 32 ; 33 ; 34.
2/1/London, 20 ; 22 ; 25.
Lowland, 111.
1st North Midland, 2 ; 4 ; 6 ; 7 ; 31 ; 32 ; 33 ; 34.
2/1/North Midland, 2 ; 3 ; 4 ; 5 ; 6.
1st Notts. and Derby, 2 ; 4 ; 6 ; 7 ; 10 ; 11 ; 12 ; 13 ; 14 ; 16 ; 17.
2/1/Notts. and Derby, 20 ; 22 ; 25.
1st Scottish Horse, 10 ; 13 ; 14 ; 17.
2/1/Southern, 27 ; 28 ; 30.
South-Eastern, 37.
2/1/South-Eastern, 27 ; 28 ; 30.
1st South Midland, 2 ; 4 ; 6 ; 7 ; 10 ; 11 ; 12 ; 13 ; 14 ; 16.
2/1/South Midland, 20 ; 22 ; 25.
2nd South Midland, 2 ; 4 ; 6 ; 7 ; 10 ; 11 ; 12 ; 13 ; 14 ; 16 ; 31 ; 32 ; 33 ; 34.
2/2/South Midland, 20 ; 22 ; 25.
South Wales, 2 ; 4 ; 6 ; 7 ; 119.
2/1/South Wales, 2 ; 3 ; 4 ; 5 ; 6.
2/1/South-Western, 27 ; 28 ; 30.
2nd South-Western, 15 ; 119.
2/2/South-Western, 3 ; 5.
Welsh Border, 2 ; 4 ; 6 ; 7 ; 119.
2/1/Welsh Border, 2 ; 5 ; 6.
1st, 3 ; 5 ; 10 ; 11 ; 12 ; 13 ; 14 ; 16 ; 20 ; 21 ; 22 ; 23 ; 24 ; 25 ; 26.
2nd, 3 ; 5 ; 10 ; 11 ; 12 ; 13 ; 14 ; 16 ; 17 ; 20 ; 21 ; 22 ; 23 ; 24 ; 25 ; 26.
3rd, 3 ; 5 ; 10 ; 11 ; 12 ; 13 ; 14 ; 16 ; 17 ; 20 ; 21 ; 22 ; 23 ; 24 ; 25 ; 26.
4th, 3 ; 5 ; 10 ; 11 ; 12 ; 13 ; 14 ; 16.
5th, 10 ; 11 ; 12; 13 ; 14 (note 19) ; 15 ; 16.
6th, 14 (note 21) ; 31 ; 32 ; 33 ; 34.
7th, 14 (note 22) ; 33 (General Notes).
8th, 14 (note 23) ; 31 ; 32 ; 33 ; 34.
9th, 20 ; 22 ; 25.
10th, 20 ; 22 ; 25.
11th, 20 ; 22 ; 25.
12th, 20 ; 22 ; 25.
13th, 27 ; 28 ; 29 ; 30.
14th, 27 ; 28 ; 29 ; 30.
15th, 27 ; 28 ; 30.
16th, 27 ; 28 ; 29 ; 30.
22nd, 14 (note 20) ; 31 ; 32 ; 33 ; 34.
1st Composite, 10 ; 13 ; 14 ; 17.
2nd Composite, 10 ; 13 ; 14 ; 17.

DIVISIONS

Cavalry—

4th, 32 ; 34 (f.n.).

Cyclist—

1st (see 1st Mounted Division), 1 ; 5 ; 7.
2nd (see 4th Mounted Division), 27 ; 28 ; 29 ; 30.
The Cyclist Division (see 2nd/2nd Mounted Division), 19 ; 23 ; 26.

Infantry—

8th, 95 (note 1).
19th, 95 (note 2) ; 95.

Infantry, T.F.—

42nd (East Lancashire), 35—41.
43rd (Wessex), 43—48 ; 59.
44th (Home Counties), 49—54.
45th (2nd Wessex), 55—60.

Infantry, T.F.—(*Continued*)

46th (North Midland), 61—67.
47th (2nd London), 69—75.
48th (South Midland), 77—83.
49th (West Riding), 85—91.
50th (Northumbrian), 93—100.
50th Composite, 95 (note 4).
51st (Highland), 101—107.
52nd (Lowland), 109—115; 123; 152; 153.
53rd (Welsh), 59; 117—123; 153.
54th (East Anglian), 125—131.
55th (West Lancashire), 105 (note 7); 106; 133—139.
56th (1st London), 141—147.
75th, 123.

Mounted—

Australian, 34.
Anzac, 31; 33; 34.
Imperial, 31; 33; 34.
The Mounted Division (see 1st Mounted Division), 7.
1st, 1—7; 19; 22; 23; 24; 25; 26; 31; 32; 34.
2nd/1st [never formed].
2nd, 7; 9—17; 119; 152.
2nd/2nd, 19—26.
3rd (see 2nd/2nd Mounted Division), 19; 22; 24; 25.
4th, 27—30.
Yeomanry, 31—34.

ADDITIONAL UNITS

R.G.A., T.F.—

Heavy Batteries—

2nd/1st Devon, 4; 7.
East Anglian (Essex), 127; 130.
Highland (Fifeshire), 103; 106.
Home Counties (Kent), 50; 51; 53.
1st Lancashire, 135; 138.
2nd Lancashire, 37; 40.
2nd/2nd Lancashire, 23; 26.
1st London, 143; 146.
2nd London, 71; 74.
Lowland (Edinburgh), 111; 114.
North Midland (Staffordshire), 63; 66.
Northumbrian (North Riding), 95; 99.
South Midland (Warwickshire), 79; 82.
2nd/1st Warwickshire, 23; 26.
Welsh (Caernarvonshire), 119; 122.
Wessex (Hampshire), 44; 45; 47.
2nd/1st Wessex (Hampshire), 58.
West Riding, 87; 90.

Infantry Battalions—

1/4th Hants. Regt., 46.
1/9th (Cyclist Bn.) Hants. Regt., 46.
1st G.B. Lincoln Regt., 48 (f.n.).
25th G.B. Middlesex Regt., 52; 54.
1st G.B. Norfolk Regt., 48 (f.n.).
18th G.B. Rifle Bde., 48 (f.n.).
1st G.B. Yorkshire Regt., 48 (f.n.).

Printed under the authority of His Majesty's Stationery Office,
By Charles Birchall & Sons, Ltd., James Street, Liverpool, 2.
32482/556, 550, 2/36. C.B.&S.Ltd.

S.O. Code No. 70-307-2-1.

HISTORY OF THE GREAT WAR

BASED ON OFFICIAL DOCUMENTS

BY DIRECTION OF THE HISTORICAL SECTION OF THE COMMITTEE OF IMPERIAL DEFENCE

ORDER OF BATTLE OF DIVISIONS

• PART 2b •

The 2nd-Line Territorial Force Divisions (57th-69th), with The Home-Service Divisions (71st-73rd) and 74th and 75th Divisions

Compiled by

MAJOR A. F. BECKE

R.F.A. (Retired), Hon. M.A. (Oxon.)

The Naval & Military Press Ltd

Published by
The Naval & Military Press Ltd
Unit 10, Ridgewood Industrial Park,
Uckfield, East Sussex,
TN22 5QE England
Tel: +44 (0) 1825 749494
Fax: +44 (0) 1825 765701
www.naval-military-press.com
www.military-genealogy.com

ORDER OF BATTLE OF DIVISIONS

Part 1 The Regular British Divisions

Part 2a The Territorial Force Mounted Divisions and
The 1st-Line Territorial Force Divisions (42-56)

Part 2b The 2nd-Line Territorial Force Divisions (57th-69th),
with The Home-Service Divisions (71st-73rd)
and 74th and 75th Divisions

Part 3 New Army Divisions (9-26 and 30-41)
and 63rd (R.N.) Division

Part 4 The Army Council, G.H.Q.s, Armies, and Corps 1914–1918

Printed and bound by Antony Rowe Ltd, Eastbourne

PREFACE

Orders of Battle for the fifteen regular British divisions which served in the Great War were given in Part 1 of this series. Part 2-A gave the Orders of Battle of twenty Territorial Force divisions (five mounted, fourteen 1st-line, and one 2nd-line). This Part (2-B) contains the Orders of Battle of eighteen divisions: thirteen 2nd-line Territorial Force divisions (57th–69th), three home-service divisions (71st–73rd), and the 74th and 75th Divisions.*

Succeeding parts of this series, each giving about fifteen divisions, will be as follows: (3-A and B), New Army Divisions; and (4-A and B), Australian, Canadian, New Zealand, and Indian Divisions. The series will be concluded with a volume dealing with G.H.Q.s, Armies, and Corps.

The eighteen divisions contained in this Part were war-time formations; not a single one was in existence at the outbreak of the Great War. Of the eighteen divisions, nine served abroad in various theatres of war; the other nine remained at home, and at different times were responsible for a share in Home Defence.

In raising men for the Territorial Force during 1914–1918, London bore its full share. The capital produced one-seventh of the whole Territorial Force of England and Wales; over 450,000 men passed through the ranks of the London units. During the Great War, London Territorial Force units served on the Western Front (in France and Belgium), in Egypt, in Gallipoli, in Macedonia, in Palestine, and in North Russia, as well as in Turkey (1919–1922).

So far as the record of service in the field is concerned, the tables and narratives of the nine divisions which served in the field have been compiled from the existing war diaries, kept in the field by the formations and units. For the service at Home, however, the war diaries of these divisions are laconic, or do not exist at all, although this period covers the formation, raising, equipping, and training of these new formations. Probably the numerous difficulties which had to be surmounted in the early days were regarded merely as matters of routine, or it was not thought worth the trouble of recording many of the improvisations and temporary expedients which had to be adopted to meet the urgent needs of the first fifteen months.

The compilation of the tables and narratives of the nine home-service divisions was even more difficult and more arduous than recording the changes in composition and the services of the nine divisions which served in the field. In preparing the record of the home-service divisions, the chief difficulty to be overcome was the few orders or diaries which exist for these divisions. A comparison will make this clear: for the 4th Division (which served throughout the war in the field) 162 boxes are available in the Military Branch, 30 boxes exist for the 66th Division (which went to France in March, 1917), and there are 29 boxes for the 75th Division (which was not formed until June, 1917, at el 'Arish). The whole of the available records, however, for the nine home-service divisions only require 14 boxes. Even such diaries as do exist are often not very informative. The only entry for October, 1915, in the diary of one home-service battalion ran: "*I beg to submit a Nil Return please*"—merely providing a distressing example of italics

---

* The two last-named divisions were formed in the Egyptian Expeditionary Force in 1917. The infantry of the 74th Division at first consisted of dismounted yeomanry regiments, and it was intended that the infantry of the 75th Division should be composed of Territorial Force battalions from India. To complete the war record of the Territorial Force, and to facilitate reference, the tables of the 74th and 75th Divisions are included in this Part.

The 70th Division was never formed.

and the please-habit. With the opening of 1916 the majority of the existing home-service diaries became nil returns; and on the 1st April, 1916, arrived the fatal order: "Units are no longer required to render war diaries." No order was ever obeyed with such alacrity and thoroughness.

In the absence of war diaries, the record of these nine home-service divisions has been completed from returns, tables, and a few printed sources. Several officers, who served with the home-service divisions, have given valuable assistance, and for this help I am indeed grateful.

In the narratives, contained in this Part, a considerable amount of the available space has been allotted to the description of the raising and training of the 2nd-line Territorial Force divisions. The time which elapsed before any 2nd-line division was able to embark for a theatre of war is amply explained by the difficulties which confronted these divisions in the first fifteen months of their existence, the slowness with which arms and equipment arrived, and the constant provision of drafts for the 1st-line formations which were already in the field.

As in the previous Parts of this series, the lists of Commanders and Staff Officers do not show temporary changes due to absences on short leave, at short courses, and at schools of instruction.

In the Divisional Tables each considerable change in composition is shown. In any case, the organization of the division is given for each year, and at one or more important periods in its history.

The numerous reorganizations and re-designations of the field artillery brigades and batteries are given in the notes to the various tables.

In the lists of Battles and Engagements occasional deviations have been made from the lists given in the *Report of the Battles Nomenclature Committee* (published in 1921), in order to include actions of which a division has reason to be proud. In every case, after the battle in which a division fought, the corps and Army in which the division served at the time is given in square brackets. If a division did not happen to be engaged during a whole year in some specific action, then only the year is shown, but this signifies that the division was on active service in the field during this period.

In the lists, the words "Action" and "Affair" have been omitted and only the date and name of these engagements are given.* The periods when the divisional artillery, engineers, and pioneers were left in the line, after the relief of a division, are not shown.

Neither the attachments to a division of Army field artillery brigades (formed in France early in 1917, after the final reorganization of the divisional artilleries), nor the attachment of R.G.A. brigades, are shown in the General Notes to the Tables. All other attachments are given either in the Tables or in the General Notes. In order that the Tables shall be as clear as possible, the numerous notes are printed on the page following each Table.

The first four Appendices at the end of this Part give short descriptions of the following: (1) The Central Force, and (1-A) its Commanders; (2) Graduated Battalions; (3) The 90-mm. gun; and (4) Work of the Army Ordnance Department at Home, 1914–1918.

Appendices (5), (6), and (7) give the War Establishments of 57th (2nd/West Lancashire) Division (England), 1915; 58th (2nd/1st London) Division (France), 1918; and 60th (2nd/2nd London) Division (Palestine), 1918. Appendices (8), (9), and (10) give the War Establishments for Home Defence of 73rd Division, 1917; 69th (2nd/East Anglian) Division, 1918; and The Cyclist Division, 1918.

---

* The Actions of Villers Bretonneux, 24th and 25th April, 1918, are shown as "24 and 25 April, Villers Bretonneux."

Each divisional story was submitted for comment to the general officer who commanded the division at the end of the Great War. In addition, the story of the division was sent to the general officer in command of the division of the Territorial Army which is the present-day descendant of the particular 1st-line Territorial Force division which took part in the Great War. Copies were sent to any officer who had served for a long period with a division, and many Territorial Army Associations had copies submitted to them. I am very grateful to all the divisional commanders and other officers who have assisted in checking and correcting these tables and for providing additional information. I have also received a considerable amount of assistance both from the War Office Library and from " R " Records, War Office. Without the help of the latter many dates could not have been recovered.

I am also greatly indebted to the Staff of the Historical Section (Military Branch) for the skilled help which they have given me so freely on numerous occasions. In particular, my most grateful thanks are due to Mr. P. F. L. Wright and to Mr. S. Woolgar for the continued and valuable assistance they have both given to me during the compilation of this Part.

Any corrections or amendments to these Tables should be sent to the Secretary, Historical Section, Committee of Imperial Defence, 2 Whitehall Gardens, S.W.1.

A. F. B.

February, 1937.

CONTENTS

	Pages
List of Abbreviations	vii—ix
57th (2nd/WEST LANCASHIRE) DIVISION (170th, 171st, and 172nd Inf. Bdes.)	**1—7**
Commanders and Staff Officers ... 1, 2	
General Notes ... 3	
Order of Battle Table ... 4	
Notes on Table ... 5	
Formation, Battles, and Engagements ... 6, 7	
58th (2nd/1st LONDON) DIVISION (173rd, 174th, and 175th Inf. Bdes.)	**9—15**
Commanders and Staff Officers ... 9, 10	
General Notes ... 11	
Order of Battle Table ... 12, 13	
Notes on Table ... 13	
Formation, Battles, and Engagements ... 14, 15	
59th (2nd/NORTH MIDLAND) DIVISION (176th, 177th, and 178th Inf. Bdes.)	**17—23**
Commanders and Staff Officers ... 17, 18	
General Notes ... 19	
Order of Battle Table ... 20	
Notes on Table ... 21	
Formation, Battles, and Engagements ... 22, 23	
60th (2nd/2nd LONDON) DIVISION (179th, 180th, and 181st Inf. Bdes.)	**25—32**
Commanders and Staff Officers ... 25, 26	
General Notes ... 27	
Order of Battle Table ... 28, 29	
Notes on Table ... 29, 30	
Formation, Battles, and Engagements ... 31, 32	
61st (2nd/SOUTH MIDLAND) DIVISION (182nd, 183rd, and 184th Inf. Bdes.)	**33—39**
Commanders and Staff Officers ... 33, 34	
General Notes ... 35	
Order of Battle Table ... 36, 37	
Notes on Table ... 37	
Formation, Battles, and Engagements ... 38, 39	
62nd (2nd/WEST RIDING) DIVISION (185th, 186th, and 187th Inf. Bdes.)	**41—48**
Commanders and Staff Officers ... 41, 42	
General Notes ... 43	
Order of Battle Table ... 44	
Notes on Table ... 45	
Formation, Battles, and Engagements ... 46–48	
63rd (2nd/NORTHUMBRIAN) DIVISION (188th, 189th, and 190th Inf. Bdes.)	**49—54**
Commanders and Staff Officers ... 49, 50	
General Notes ... 51	
Order of Battle Table ... 52	
Notes on Table ... 53	
Formation and Narrative ... 54	
64th (2nd/HIGHLAND) DIVISION (191st, 192nd, and 193rd Inf. Bdes.)	**55—59**
Commanders and Staff Officers ... 55	
Order of Battle Table ... 56, 57	
Notes on Table and General Notes ... 58	
Formation and Narrative ... 59	
65th (2nd/LOWLAND) DIVISION (194th, 195th, and 196th Inf. Bdes.)	**61—65**
Commanders and Staff Officers ... 61	
Order of Battle Table ... 62, 63	
Notes on Table and General Notes ... 64	
Formation and Narrative ... 65	
66th (2nd/EAST LANCASHIRE) DIVISION (197th, 198th, 199th, and South African Inf. Bdes.).	**67—74**
Commanders and Staff Officers ... 67, 68	
General Notes ... 69; 72	
Order of Battle Table ... 70	
Notes on Table ... 71	
Formation, Battles, and Engagements ... 73, 74	
67th (2nd/HOME COUNTIES) DIVISION (200th, 201st, 202nd, and 214th Inf. Bdes.)	**75—82**
Commanders and Staff Officers ... 75, 76	
General Notes ... 77	
Order of Battle Table ... 78, 79	
Notes on Table ... 80	
Formation and Narrative ... 81, 82	

Pages

68th (2nd/WELSH) DIVISION (203rd, 204th, and 205th Inf. Bdes.) .... **83—90**
Commanders and Staff Officers 83, 84
General Notes 85
Order of Battle Table 86, 87
Notes on Table 88
Formation and Narrative 89, 90

69th (2nd/EAST ANGLIAN) DIVISION (206th, 207th, and 208th Inf. Bdes.) .... **91—98**
Commanders and Staff Officers 91, 92
General Notes 93
Order of Battle Table 94, 95
Notes on Table 96
Formation and Narrative 97, 98

70th DIVISION (209th, 210th, and 211th Inf. Bdes.) **99**

71st DIVISION (212th, 213th, and 214th Inf. Bdes.) .... **101—105**
Commanders and Staff Officers 101
Order of Battle Table 102
Notes on Table 103
General Notes 104
Formation and Narrative 105

72nd DIVISION (215th, 216th, and 217th Inf. Bdes.) .... **107—110**
Commanders and Staff Officers 107
Order of Battle Table 108
Notes on Table and General Notes 109
Formation and Narrative 110

73rd DIVISION (218th, 219th, and 220th Inf. Bdes.) .... **111—116**
Commanders and Staff Officers 111, 112
General Notes 113
Order of Battle Table 114, 115
Notes on Table 115
Formation and Narrative 116

74th (YEOMANRY) DIVISION (229th, 230th, and 231st Inf. Bdes.) .... **117—122**
Commanders and Staff Officers 117
Order of Battle Table 118
Notes on Table 119
General Notes 120
Formation, Battles, and Engagements 121, 122

75th DIVISION (232nd, 233rd, and 234th Inf. Bdes.) .... **123—130**
Commanders and Staff Officers 123, 124
General Notes 125
Order of Battle Table 126
Notes on Table 127, 128
Formation, Battles, and Engagements 129, 130

APPENDICES .... **131—143**

APPENDIX 1 ... Central Force **133**

APPENDIX 1A Commanders of Central Force and of First, Second, and Third Armies, Home Defence Forces. **134**

APPENDIX 2 ... Graduated Battalions **135**

APPENDIX 3 ... 90-mm. Field Gun **136**

APPENDIX 4 ... Work of the Army Ordnance Department at Home, 1914–1918 **137—138**

APPENDIX 5 War Establishment of 57th (2nd/W. Lanc.) Division, England, 1915. .... **140**

APPENDIX 6 War Establishment of 58th (2nd/1st London) Division, France, 1918. .... **140, 141**

APPENDIX 7 War Establishment of 60th (2nd/2nd London) Division, Palestine, 1918. .... **141**

APPENDIX 8 ... War Establishment of 73rd Division, England, 1917.......... **142**

APPENDIX 9 War Establishment of 69th (2nd/E. Anglian) Division, England, 1918. .... **142, 143**

APPENDIX 10 ... War Establishment of The Cyclist Division, England, 1918.......... **143**

INDEX OF FORMATIONS .... **145—147**

LIST OF ABBREVIATIONS

NOTE.—For the period of the Great War the titles of regiments have been taken from the 1914-1918 Army Lists.

A.

(A.-A.) ... ... (Anti-Aircraft).
A.-A. & Q.-M.-G. Assistant-Adjutant & Quarter-Master-General.
A.C.C. ... ... Army Cyclist Corps (Home Service).
A. & S.H. ... ... Argyll & Sutherland Highlanders.
A.F.A. Bde. ... Army Field Artillery Brigade.
A.H.Q. ... ... Army Head-Quarters.
Amb. or Ambce. Ambulance.
Ammn. Coln. ... Ammunition Column.
Ammn. Park ... Ammunition Park.
A.R.O. ... ... Army Routine Order.
Arty. ... ... Artillery.
A.S.C.... ... ... Army Service Corps.
A.T. ... ... Army Troops.
Aux. ... ... Auxiliary.

B.

B.A.C. ... ... Brigade Ammunition Column.
Bde. ... ... Brigade.
Bedf. ... ... Bedfordshire Regiment.
Bedf. Yeo.... ... Bedfordshire Yeomanry.
B.E.F. ... ... British Expeditionary Force.
Berks. ... ...Berkshire.
B.F.T. ... ... British Forces in Turkey.
B.-G., R.A. ... Brigadier-General, Commanding Royal Artillery.
B.-G., R.H.A. ... Brigadier-General, Commanding Royal Horse Artillery.
B.L. ... ... Breech-loader.
B.L.C. ... ... B.L. Converted.
Bn. ... ... Battalion.
Bord. ... ... Border Regiment.
Br.-Gen. ... ... Brigadier-General.
Bty. ... ... Battery.
Bucks. ... ... Buckinghamshire.
Buffs ... ... Buffs (East Kent Regiment).
B.W. ... ... Black Watch (Royal Highlanders).
B.W.I. ... ... British West Indies Regiment.

C.

Camb. ... ... Cambridgeshire Regiment.
Cam. H. ... ... Cameron Highlanders.
Cav. ... ... Cavalry.
C.B. ... ... Cavalry Brigade.
C.C.S. ... ... Casualty Clearing Station.
cd. ... ... command
C.D.M.T. Coy. ... Cavalry Divisional Mechanical Transport Company.
Cdn. ... ... Canadian.
C.F.A. ... ... Combined Field Ambulance.
C.G. ... ... Coldstream Guards.
Ches. ... ... Cheshire Regiment.
C.I. ... ... Central India.
Col.-Cdt. ... ... Colonel-Commandant.
Comp. ... ... Composite.
Conn. Rang. ... Connaught Rangers.
Co. ... ... County.
Coy. ... ... Company.
Cos. ... ... Companies.
C.R.E. ... ... Commanding Royal Engineers.
C.R.H.A. ... ... Commanding Royal Horse Artillery.

D.

d. ... ... died.
D.A.C. ... ... Divisional Ammunition Column.
D.C.L.I. ... ... Duke of Cornwall's Light Infantry.
D.E. Coy. ... ... Divisional Employment Company.
Detnt. ... ... Detachment.
Devon. ... ... Devonshire Regiment.
D.G. ... ... Dragoon Guards.
Dgns. ... ... Dragoons.
Disembkd. ... Disembarked.
Disembkn. ... Disembarkation.
Div. ... ... Division.
Divnl.... ... ... Divisional.
D.L.I. ... ... Durham Light Infantry.
D.M.C. ... ... Desert Mounted Corps.
D. of L. Own Yeo. Duke of Lancaster's Own Yeomanry.
d. of w. ... ... died of wounds.
Dorset. ... ... Dorsetshire Regiment.
Duke's ... ... Duke of Wellington's (West Riding Regiment)

E.

E. ... ... East ; or Eastern.
E.E.F. ... ... Egyptian Expeditionary Force.
E. Lanc. ... ... East Lancashire Regiment.
Embkd. ... ... Embarked.
Emplnt. or Emplynt. ... Employment.
Eng. ... ... Engineers.
Entg. Bn. ... Entrenching Battalion.
Essex ... ... Essex Regiment.
E. Surr. ... ... East Surrey Regiment.
evacd. ... ... evacuated.
E. York. ... ... East Yorkshire Regiment.

F.

Fd. ... ... Field.

G.

(G.) ... ... (Graduated Battalion).
Garr. Gd. ... ... Garrison Guard Battalion.
G. B. or Garr. Bn. ... Garrison Battalion.
Gds. ... ... Guards.
G.G. ... ... Grenadier Guards.
G.H.Q. ... ... General Headquarters.
Glam. ... ... Glamorganshire.
Glouc. ... ... Gloucestershire Regiment.
G.O.C. ... ... General Officer Commanding.
Gord. H. ... ... Gordon Highlanders.
Gr. How. ... ... Green Howards (Alexandra, Princess of Wales's Own Yorkshire Regiment).
G.S.O.1. ... ... General Staff Officer (1st Grade).

H.

(H.) ... ... (Howitzer).
H.A.C. ... ... Honourable Artillery Company.
Hants. ... ... Hampshire Regiment.
H.A.R. ... ... Heavy Artillery Reserve.
H.B. ... ... Heavy Battery.

H—*continued.*

H.D. Trps. ... Home Defence Troops.
Hereford. ... ... Herefordshire.
Herts. ... ... Hertfordshire Regiment.
H.L.I.... ... ... Highland Light Infantry.
Home Cties. ... Home Counties.
Househ'd. ... ... Household.
How. Bde. ... Howitzer Brigade.
How. Bty. ... Howitzer Battery.
H.Q. ... ... Headquarters.
Hsrs. ... ... Hussars.
H.T. ... ... Horse Transport.
H.T.M.B. ... ... Heavy Trench Mortar Battery.
Hy. Bde. ... ... Heavy Brigade.
Hy. Bty. A.C. ... Heavy Battery Ammunition Column.

I.

I.G. ... ... Irish Guards.
Ind. ... ... Indian.
Inf. ... ... Infantry.
Ir. ... ... Irish.
It. ... ... Italian.

K.

k. or kd. ... ... killed.
K.E. Horse ... King Edward's Horse.
K.G.O. ... ... King George's Own.
King's ... ... King's (Liverpool Regiment).
K.O. ... ... King's Own (Royal Lancaster Regiment).
K.O.S.B. ... ... King's Own Scottish Borderers.
K.O.Y.L.I. ... King's Own (Yorkshire Light Infantry.)
K.R.R.C. ... ... King's Royal Rifle Corps.
K.S.L.I. ... ... King's (Shropshire Light Infantry).

L.

Lcrs. ... ... Lancers.
Leic. ... ... Leicestershire Regiment.
Leic. Yeo. ... ... Leicestershire Yeomanry.
Leins. ... ... Leinster Regiment.
L.F. ... ... Lancashire Fusiliers.
L.G. ... ... Life Guards.
L.I. ... ... Light Infantry.
Linc. ... ... Lincolnshire Regiment.
L.N.L. ... ... Loyal North Lancashire Regiment.
L. of C. ... ... Line of Communications.
Lond. ... ... London Regiment.
L.R.B. ... ... London Rifle Brigade.
L.S. ... ... London Scottish.
L.Sec. ... ... Left Section.

M.

Manch. ... ... Manchester Regiment.
Med. ... ... Medium.
M.E.F. ... ... Mediterranean Expeditionary Force [Gallipoli].
M.G.C. ... ... Machine Gun Corps.
M.G. Coy. ... Machine-Gun Company.
M.G. Sec. ... Machine-Gun Section.
M.G. Sqdn. ... Machine-Gun Squadron.
M.I. ... ... Mounted Infantry.
Midd'x. ... ... Middlesex Regiment.
Midld. ... ... Midland.
Mk. ... ... Mark.
M.M.G. ... ... Motor Machine Gun.
Mobn. ... ... Mobilization.
Mob. Vety. Sec. Mobile Veterinary Section.
Mon. or Monm'th. Monmouthshire Regiment.
Montgom. ... ... Montgomeryshire.
M.T. ... ... Mechanical Transport.
Mtd. ... ... Mounted.
Mtn. ... ... Mountain.

N.

N. ... ... North ; or Northern.
Newf'dld. ... ... Newfoundland.
N.F. ... ... Northumberland Fusiliers.
N. Irish H. ... North Irish Horse.
N.M. Fd. Coy. ... North Midland Field Company.
Norf. ... ... Norfolk Regiment.
Northants. Yeo. Northamptonshire Yeomanry.
North'bn. ... ... Northumbrian.
North'd. ... ... Northumberland.
North'n. ... ... Northamptonshire Regiment.
N. Som. ... ... North Somerset.
N. Staff. ... ... North Staffordshire Regiment.
N.S.W. ... ... New South Wales.
N.Z. & A. ... ... New Zealand and Australian.

O.

O. & B.L.I. ... Oxfordshire & Buckinghamshire Light Infantry.
offrs. ... ... officers.
o.r. ... ... other ranks.

P.

(P.) ... ... (Pioneers).
P.E. ... ... Peace Establishment.
Pemb. ... ... Pembrokeshire.
P.P.C.L.I. ... ... Princess Patricia's Canadian Light Infantry.
P.O. Rif. ... ... Post Office Rifles.
Provl. ... ... Provisional.
P.W.O. ... ... Prince of Wales's Own.

Q.

Q.O.O. Hsrs. ... Queen's Own Oxfordshire Hussars.
Q.O.R.R. Staff. Yeo. ... Queen's Own Royal Regiment, Staffordshire Yeomanry.
Queen's ... ... Queen's (Royal West Surrey Regiment.)
Q.V. Rif. ... ... Queen Victoria's Rifles.
Q.W. Rif. ... Queen's Westminster Rifles.

R.

R. ... ... Royal.
R.A.F. ... ... Royal Air Force.
R.A.S.C. ... ... Royal Army Service Corps.
R.B. ... ... Rifle Brigade.
R. Berks. ... Royal Berkshire Regiment.
R. Cdn. H.A. Bde. Royal Canadian Horse Artillery Brigade.
R.D.F. ... ... Royal Dublin Fusiliers.
R.E. ... ... Royal Engineers.
Regt. ... ... Regiment.
R.F. ... ... Royal Fusiliers.
R.F.A. ... ... Royal Field Artillery.
Rfts. ... ... Reinforcements.
R.G.A. ... ... Royal Garrison Artillery.
R. Guern. L.I. ... Royal Guernsey Light Infantry.
R.H.A. ... ... Royal Horse Artillery.
R.H.G. ... ... Royal Horse Guards.
Rid. ... ... Riding.
R. Innis. F. ... Royal Inniskilling Fusiliers.
R. Ir. F. ... ... Royal Irish Fusiliers.
R. Ir. Regt. ... Royal Irish Regiment.
R. Ir. Rif. ... Royal Irish Rifles.
R.M.F. ... ... Royal Munster Fusiliers.
R.M.L.I. ... ... Royal Marine Light Infantry.
R.N.A.C.D. ... Royal Naval Armoured Car Division.
R.N.D. ... ... Royal Naval Division.
R. Scots ... ... Royal Scots (Lothian Regiment).
R. Sec. ... ... Right Section.
R.S.F. ... ... Royal Scots Fusiliers.
R. Suss. ... ... Royal Sussex Regiment.
R.W. ... ... Royal Warrant.
R. War. ... ... Royal Warwickshire Regiment.
R.W.F. ... ... Royal Welsh Fusiliers.
R.W.K. ... ... Queen's Own (Royal West Kent Regiment).

S.

S.	South ; or Southern.
S.A.	South African.
S.A.A. Sec. ...	Small-Arm-Ammunition Section.
S.B.	Siege Battery.
S.B.A.C.	Siege Battery Ammunition Column.
Sco. Rif.	The Cameronians (Scottish Rifles).
Sea. H.	Seaforth Highlanders.
Sec. or Secn. ...	Section.
S.G.	Scots Guards.
Sher. For. ...	Sherwood Foresters (Nottinghamshire & Derbyshire Regiment).
Sig.	Signal.
S. Irish H. ...	South Irish Horse.
S. Lanc.	South Lancashire Regiment.
S. & M.	Sappers & Miners.
S.M. Fd. Coy. ...	South Midland Field Company.
Som. L.I. ...	Somerset Light Infantry.
Sqdn.	Squadron.
S. Staff.	South Staffordshire Regiment.
Suff.	Suffolk Regiment.
S. & T. Coln. ...	Supply & Transport Column.
S.W.B.	South Wales Borderers.

T.

T.A.	Territorial Army.

T—*continued.*

Tempy.	Temporary.
T.F.	Territorial Force.
T.M. Bty.	Trench Mortar Battery.
Trp.	Troop.

U.

U.K.	United Kingdom.

V.

Vety.	Veterinary.

W.

W.	West ; or Western.
w. or wd. ...	wounded.
War.	Warwickshire.
W.E.	War Establishment.
Welsh	Welsh Regiment.
W.G.	Welsh Guards.
Wilts.	Wiltshire Regiment.
Worc....	Worcestershire Regiment.
W. Rid.	West Riding.
W. York. ...	West Yorkshire Regiment.

Y.

Y. & L.	York & Lancaster Regiment.
Yeo.	Yeomanry.

NOTE.—To save space, some place-names have occasionally been shortened, e.g. :—

Burton-on-Trent appears as Burton,
Hebburn-on-Tyne ,, Hebburn,
Newcastle-upon-Tyne ,, Newcastle,
etc.

History teaches everything, even the future.

57TH (2ND/WEST LANCASHIRE) DIVISION

G.O.C.

5 November, 1914 ... ... Br.-Gen. F. A. ADAM (acting).
April, 1915 ... ... Major-General J. B. FORSTER.
20 October, 1916... ... ... Lieut.-General R. G. BROADWOOD (d. of w., 21/6/17).
21 June, 1917 ... ... Br.-Gen. J. C. WRAY (acting).
1 July, 1917 ... ... Major-General R. W. R. BARNES.

G.S.O.1.

10 Dec., 1914...Major G. A. CARLETON (acting).
April, 1915...Major A. H. BARTHORP (acting).
26 Aug., 1915...Lt.-Col. E. B. C. BODDAM.
16 July, 1916...Lt.-Col. C. J. L. ALLANSON.
27 July, 1917...Lt.-Col. J. R. WETHERED.
[12 Nov., 1918...Lt.-Col. C. C. FOSS, V.C.]

A.-A. and Q.-M.-G.

23 Nov., 1914...Major H. W. COBHAM (acting).
April, 1915...Colonel J. G. PANTON.
3 Jan., 1916...Lt.-Col. W. M. STEWART.

B.-G., R.A.

10 Jan., 1915...Colonel G. KYFFIN-TAYLOR (acting).
April, 1915...Br.-Gen. J. J. MACMAHON.
30 Sept., 1915...Colonel G. KYFFIN-TAYLOR (acting).
6 Jan., 1916...Br.-Gen. F. B. ELMSLIE.
17 April, 1916...Br.-Gen. J. C. WRAY.
16 Aug., 1918...Br.-Gen. W. C. E. RUDKIN.

C.R.E.

April, 1915...Lt.-Col. G. E. SAYCE.
9 July, 1916...Lt.-Col. H. LA T. CAMPBELL (wd., 5/10/18).
5 Oct., 1918...Major C. L. FOX (acting).
20 Oct., 1918...Lt.-Col. P.O. L. JORDAN.

170th BDE.

(2nd/1st N. Lancashire)

4 Nov., '14...Col. J. H. CAMPBELL.
April, '15...Colonel S. H. HARRISON.
28 Jan., '16...Br.-Gen. J. J. F. HUME.
28 Aug., '16...Br.-Gen. S. P. ROLT.
15 Dec., '16...Br.-Gen. A. MARTYN.
10 May, '17...Lt.-Col. C. F. HITCHINS (acting).
12 May, '17...Br.-Gen. F. G. GUGGISBERG.
16 July, '18...Br.-Gen. G. F. BOYD.
5 Sept., '18...Br.-Gen. A. L. RANSOME.

171st BDE.

(2nd/1st Liverpool)

4 Nov., '14...Col. S. H. HARRISON.
April, '15...Br.-Gen. A. R. GILBERT.
7 April, '17...Br.-Gen. H. N. BRAY (injured, 21/9/17).
21 Sept., '17...Lt.-Col. O. H. NORTH (acting).
23 Sept., '17...Br.-Gen. F. C. LONGBOURNE (wd., 5/10/18).
5 Oct., '18...Lt.-Col. HON. N. C. GATHORNE-HARDY (acting).
11 Oct., '18...Br.-Gen. G. MEYNELL.

172nd BDE.

(2nd/1st S. Lancashire)

6 Jan., '15...Col. O. J. H. BALL.
April, '15...Br.-Gen. A. L. MACFIE.
25 Aug., '16...Br.-Gen. G. C. B. PAYNTER (wd., 4/10/18).
4 Oct., '18...Lt.-Col. M. E. MAKGILL-CRICHTON-MAITLAND (acting).
25 Oct., '18...Br.-Gen. G. C. B. PAYNTER.

GENERAL NOTES

The following Units also served with the 57th Division :—

1st West Lancashire Division Artillery, from April, 1915–September, 1915.

1st Lancashire Heavy Battery, R.G.A. (4, 4·7" guns), joined the 57th (2nd/West Lancashire) Division in April, 1915, after the West Lancashire Division had been broken up to reinforce the B.E.F. in France. The Heavy Battery served with the 57th (2nd/W. Lanc.) Division until December, 1915. On 28/12/15 the Heavy Battery left the 57th Division for Woolwich, to prepare for service overseas. The Heavy Battery disembarked at le Havre on 26/1/16, and on 1/2/16 it joined XXIX Heavy Brigade, R.G.A., near Bray, on the Somme Front.

2nd/1st Lancashire Heavy Battery, R.G.A., moved from Blackpool on 25/11/15, joined the 57th Division at Canterbury on 26/11/15, and received 4, 4·7" guns from Southampton on 29/12/15. The Heavy Battery did not go to France with the 57th Division, but went independently. The Hy. Bty. disembked. at le Havre on 1/7/16, and on 4/7/16 it was attached to II Anzac Corps, near Erquinghem. On 4/8/16 the Hy. Bty. joined LII H.A.G.

2/4/King's Own served with the 170th Bde. from formation until 20/10/15, when the Bn. left the Bde. and proceeded to Blackpool. The Bn. was replaced in the 170th Bde. by 4/5/L.N.L.

4/5/L.N.L. left Bolton on 21/10/15, and joined 170th Bde. at Ashford on 22/10/15.

1/Lancashire Hussars left the 57th Division on 29/10/15 (1 sqdn.) and 14/11/15 (2 sqdns.) to join 30th, 31st, and 35th Divisions as Divisional Cavalry.

1/Kent Cyclist Bn. raised in 1908 as 6/R.W.K. (Cyclists), the Bn. became 1/Kent Cyclist Bn. in 1910 (headquarters at Tonbridge). At the outbreak of the Great War the Bn. was employed on coast defence and became attached to 57th Div. The Bn. was employed watching the coast between the Swale and Rye, with a detachment in the Medway defences. On 24/11/15 Bn. concentrated at Canterbury. On 2/12/15 Bn. left 57th Div., moved to Chiseldon, and joined a brigade consisting of 2/6/R. Suss., 1/9/Hants., and 1/25/Lond., and the 4 battalions were all converted from cyclists into infantry bns. Mobilized first of all for East Africa and then for Egypt, 1/1/Kent sailed for India on 8/2/16 and disembarked at Bombay on 3/3/16. 1/1/Kent went to Bangalore and was brigaded again with 2/6/R. Suss., 1/9/Hants., and 1/25/Lond. On 10/12/16 the Bde. moved to Burhan, and 1/1/Kent was posted to 44th Ind. Bde., 16th Ind. Div. Between 4/3–15/4/17 Bn. (in 44th Bde.) served with South Waziristan F.F.; from 22/4–23/5/17 the Bn. was at Dalhousie; and from 30/5–18/8/17 the Bn. (in 44th Bde.) formed part of North Waziristan F.F. On 25/8/17 the Bn. returned to Dalhousie and remained there until it mobilized for Baluchistan on 5/3/18. Bn. (in 44th Bde.) was employed in Baluchistan from 11/3–1/5/18, returned to Dalhousie until April, 1919, was engaged in quelling the Punjab riots (12–27/4/19); and between 19/5–17/8/19 took part with 44th Bde., 16th Div., in the 3rd Afghan War, in the neighbourhood of Peshawar. Bn. then served at Dagshai from 21/8–3/11/19; sailed for England on 8/11/19; and disembarked at Plymouth on 6/12/19. Bn. was then demobilized and again became 1/Kent Cyclist Bn. In Feb., 1920, 1/Kent Cyclist Bn. was disbanded.

57th (West Lancashire) Sanitary Section went to France with the Division. The Sanitary Section left the Division on 15/4/17 and was transferred to a Second Army Sanitary Area.

XI Corps Mtd. Troops (1/K.E.H. and 11/Cyclist Bn.) were attached to the 57th Div. from 21/10–9/11/18.

By 6/2/18 the reorganization of the division on a 9-battalion basis was completed; and on 28/2/18 the pioneer battalion was reorganized on a 3-company basis.

57th Division Artillery (H.Q., R.A., and CCLXXXV and CCLXXXVI Brigades), 57th D.A.C., and 505 Coy., A.S.C., were engaged from 9th–29th April, 1918, in the Battles of the Lys, under XV Corps (First Army, until noon, 12/4/18; then in Second Army).

The following **Portuguese** troops were attached to the 57th Division during the Final Advance:

	IV Portuguese Fd. Arty. Bde.	from 17/10/18– 1/11/18;
	1st Portuguese Fd. Coy.	from 17/10/18– 1/11/18;
	14th Portuguese Bn.	from 2/11/18–15/11/18;
	15th Portuguese Bn.	from 29/10/18–15/11/18;
and	5th Portuguese Fd. Amb.	from 1/11/18–15/11/18.

57TH[A] (2ND/WEST LANCASHIRE) DIVISION ORDER OF BATTLE, 1915-1918

Dates	INFANTRY		Mounted Troops	ARTILLERY						Engineers	Signal Service	Pioneers	M.G. Units	Field Ambulances	Mobile Vety. Secn.	Divnl. Emplnt. Coy.	Divnl. Train
	Brigades	Battalions and attached Units		Field Artillery			Trench Mortar Bties.		Divnl. Ammn. Coln.	Field Cos.	Divnl. Signal Coy.						
				Brigades	Batteries	Bde. Ammn. Colns.	Medium	Heavy									
1915 November (England)	170th[A] (2/1/N. Lanc.) 171st[A] (2/1/Liverpool) 172nd[A] (2/1/S.Lanc.)	2/5/K.O., 2/4/L.N.L., 2/5/L.N.L., 4/5/L.N.L. 2/5/King's, 2/6/King's, 2/7/King's, 2/8/King's. 2/9/King's, 2/10/King's, 2/4/S. Lanc., 2/5/S. Lanc.	1st W.[1] Lanc. Div. Cyclist Coy.	2/I W. Lanc.[2] 2/II W. Lanc[2] 2/III W. Lanc.[2] 2/IV W. Lanc.[2] (H.)	2/1/Lanc., 2/2/Lanc., 2/3/Lanc. 2/9/Lanc., 2/10/Lanc., 2/11/Lanc. 2/12/Lanc., 2/13/Lanc., 2/14/Lanc. 2/7/Lanc. (H.), 2/8/Lanc .(H.)	2/I/W. Lanc. 2/II/W. Lanc. 2/III/W.Lanc. 2/IV/W.Lanc. (H.)	...	...	57th (2/1/W. Lanc.) D.A.C.	2/1/W. Lanc.[3] 2/2/W. Lanc.[3] 1/3/W. Lanc.[8]	1st. W. Lanc.[4]	...	...	2/1/W. Lanc.[5] 1/2/W. Lanc.[6] 1/3/W. Lanc.[5]	...	...	57th (1/1/W). Lanc.
1916 September (England)	170th...... 171st ...... 172nd......	2/5/K.O., 2/4/L.N.L., 2/5/L.N.L., 4/5/L.N.L. 2/5/King's, 2/6/King's, 2/7/King's, 2/8/King's. 2/9/King's, 2/10/King's, 2/4/S. Lanc., 2/5/S. Lanc.	A.Sqdn.* 2/1/Bedf. Yeo. 57th* Div. Cyclist Coy.	7; 20 CCLXXXV ... (2/I W. Lanc.) 7; 21 CCLXXXVI... (2/II W. Lanc.) 7; 22 CCLXXXVII (2/III W. Lanc.)	A, B, C; D (H.) A, B, C; D (H.) A, B; C (H.), D (H.)	...	...	...	57th D.A.C.	1/3/W. Lanc.[8] 1/3/ Wessex[9] 2/3/ Wessex[9]	57th[10] (2/1/W. Lanc.)	...	...	2/2/ Wessex[11] 2/3/ Wessex[11] 3/2/ W. Lanc.[11]	57th	...	57th
1917 June (France)	170th...... 171st ...... 172nd......	2/5/K.O., 2/4/L.N.L., 2/5/L.N.L.,[12] 4/5/L.N.L.; [13] 170th M.G. Coy.; [14]; [32] 170th T.M. Bty.[15] 2/5/King's,[16] 2/6/King's, 2/7/King's, 2/8/King's;[17] 171st M.G. Coy.;[14]; [32] 171st T.M. Bty.[15] 2/9/King's,[18] 2/10/King's, 2/4/S. Lanc., 2/5/S. Lanc.;[19] 172nd M.G. Coy; [14]; [32] 172nd T.M. Bty.[15]	...	CCLXXXV[20] CCLXXXVI[21]	A, B, C; D (H.) A, B, C; D (H.)	...	X.57[23] Y.57[23] Z.57[23]	W.57[24]	57th D.A.C.	421[25](1/3/ W. Lanc.) 502[25] (1/3/Wessex) 505[25] (2/3/Wessex)	57th	...	173rd[26] M.-G. Coy.	2/2/ Wessex 2/3/ Wessex 3/2/ W. Lanc.	57th	248th[27]	57th[28]
1918 March (France)	170th...... 171st ...... 172nd......	2/5/K.O., 2/4/L.N.L., 1/5/L.N.L.;[13] 170th T.M. Bty. 2/6/King's, 2/7/King's, 8/King's;[17] 171st T.M. Bty. 9/King's,[18] 2/10/King's,[29] 2/4/S. Lanc.; 172nd T.M. Bty.	...	CCLXXXV ... CCLXXXVI...	A, B, C; D (H.) A, B, C; D (H.)	...	X.57[30] Y.57[30]	...[31]	57th D.A.C.	421st 502nd 505th	57th	2/5/L.N.L.[12] (P.)	No. 57 Bn.,[32] M.G.C.	2/2/ Wessex 2/3/ Wessex 3/2/ W. Lanc.	57th	248th	57th
1918 May (France)	170th...... 171st ...... 172nd......	2/5/K.O., 2/4/L.N.L., 1/5/L.N.L.; 170th T.M. Bty. 2/6/King's, 2/7/King's, 8/King's; 171st T.M. Bty. 9/King's, 2/4/S. Lanc., 1/R.M.F.;[33] 172nd T.M. Bty.	...	CCLXXXV ... CCLXXXVI...	A, B, C; D (H.) A, B, C; D (H.)	...	X.57 Y.57	...	57th D.A.C.	421st 502nd 505th	57th	2/5/ L.N.L. (P.)	No. 57 Bn., M.G.C.	2/2/ Wessex 2/3/ Wessex 3/2/ W. Lanc.	57th	248th	57th

NOTES

A. In August, 1915, the West Lancashire 2nd-line Division and Infantry Brigades were given numbers—Authy., 40/W.O./2609, A.G.1, of 10/8/15.

---

1 Left the Div. on 7/12/15.

2 The 2nd-line Artillery joined the Div. at Canterbury, 16-19/9/15, from Weeton (Lancashire). The 1st-line Artillery left the Div. for France, 27-30/9/15. In July, 1916, 2/IV/W. Lanc.(H.) was broken up and batteries became D(H.)/CCLXXXV and D(H.)/CCLXXXVI.

3 2/1/W. Lanc. and 2/2/W. Lanc. Fd. Cos. left the Div. on 8/12/15; they joined 55th Div. in France on 16 and 17/1/16. In 1917 they were numbered 422nd and 423rd.

4 Left the Div. on 8/12/15.

5 2/1/W. Lanc. and 1/3/W. Lanc. Fd. Ambces. left the Div. on 7/12/15. 1/3/W. Lanc. and 2/1/W. Lanc. joined 55th Div. in France on 16 and 17/1/16.

6 1/2/W. Lanc. Fd. Amb. left the Div. on 22/10/15, and joined 30th Div.

7 18-pdr. equipments were received in Dec., 1915, and 4·5″ (H.) equipments in Jany., 1916.

8 Joined the Div. on 2/11/15.

9 1/3/Wessex joined the Div. on 9/12/15 from Christchurch. 2/3/Wessex joined on 26/2/16 from Taunton.

10 Coy. formed in Septr., 1915.

11 The 3 Fd. Ambces. joined the Div. on 4 and 5/12/15, at Canterbury, Maidstone, and Wye.

12 Became Divnl. Pioneers on 5/2/18.

13 Amalgamated on 4/2/18 with 1/5/L.N.L. from 166th Bde., 55th Div., and Bn. became 1/5/L.N.L.

14 The M.G. Cos. were formed at Grantham and went to France with their respective Brigades in Febry., 1917.

15 Formed in England, complete with mortars and equipment. The T.M. Bties. went to France with their Inf. Bdes. in Febry., 1917.

16 Bn. was broken up on 1/2/18 and distributed among 2/6, 2/7, 11/, and 12/King's.

17 Amalgamated on 31/1/18 with 8/King's from 164th Bde., 55th Div., and Bn. became 8/King's.

18 Amalgamated between 1-6/2/18 with 9/King's from 165th Bde., 55th Div., and Bn. became 9/King's.

19 Bn. was broken up between 1-25/2/18, and drafts were sent to 1/5/S. Lanc., 2/4/S. Lanc., No. 57 M.G. Bn., and No. 2 Entrenching Bn.

20 18-pdr. Bties. were completed to 6 guns each before embarkation in Febry., 1917. On 15/2/17 1 Sec. of D (H.)/CCLXXXVII joined and completed D (H.) to 6, 4·5 Hows.

21 18-pdr. Bties. were completed to 6 guns each before embarkation in Febry., 1917. On 15/2/17 1 Sec. of D (H.)/CCLXXXVII joined and completed D (H.) to 6, 4·5″ Hows.

22 The Bde. (2, 6-gun 18-pdr. Bties., and 2, 4-gun 4·5″ How. Bties.) disembkd. at le Havre on 9/2/17. Between 13-20/2/17 the Bde. was broken up. On 15/2/17 1 sec. of D (H.) joined D (H.)/CCLXXXV and 1 Sec. joined D (H.)/CCLXXXVI. On 20/2/17 Bde. H.Q. joined 57th D. A.C., and A was transferred and became C/CLXXV A.F.A. Bde. B/CCLXXXVII became C/CCXCIII A.F.A. Bde. on 8/3/17; Left Sec. C (H.)/CCLXXXVII joined D (H.)/CCXCV (59th Div.) on 17/3/17; and R. Sec. C (H.)/CCLXXXVII joined D (H.)/CCCXXX (66th Div.) on 7/3/17.

23 The personnel went to France with the Div. in Febry., 1917. After training at Second Army T.M. School, the T.M. Bties. rejoined 57th Div. on 1/3/17.

24 The personnel went to France with the Div. in Febry., 1917. After training at Second Army T.M. School, the Heavy T.M. Bty. rejoined 57th Div. on 1/3/17.

25 The Fd. Cos. were numbered before embkn. in Febry., 1917.

26 Joined by 31/3/17.

27 Formed by 16/6/17, and numbered by 4/8/17.

28 505, 506, 507, and 508 Cos., A.S.C. The Train originally formed part of 1/W. Lanc. Div. [later 55th Div.]. The Train was allotted to 57th Div.

29 On 20/4/18 Bn. was transferred to 55th Div. On 30/4/18 Bn. was broken up, part amalgamated with 1/10/King's, part joined 55th Div. Rft. Camp, and the remainder was drafted.

30 Between 17-28/2/17 Z was absorbed by X and Y.

31 Became XV Corps. H.T.M. Bty. on 17/2/18.

32 Formed 1/3/18. Bn. consisted of 170, 171, 172, and 173 M.G. Cos.

33 Joined on 20/4/18 from 47th Bde., 16th Div.

57TH (2ND/WEST LANCASHIRE) DIVISION

FORMATION, BATTLES, AND ENGAGEMENTS

This 2nd-line (or reserve) Territorial Force division had no existence before the outbreak of the Great War.

On the 15th August, 1914, instructions were issued to separate the home-service men of those T.F. units which had volunteered for service abroad; the home-service men were to be formed into reserve units. On the 31st August the formation of a reserve (or 2nd-line) T.F. unit was authorized for each original (or 1st-line) unit in which 60 per cent. had volunteered for foreign service. The title of the 2nd-line unit would be the same as that of the corresponding 1st-line imperial-service unit, and these reserve units were to be located at the peace headquarters of their 1st-line units. After being clothed, organized, and armed the reserve units would gradually be grouped into larger formations at training centres, war stations, etc. In this way the 2nd-line T.F. divisions came into existence.

On the 24th November, 1914, it was decided to replace each imperial-service unit, which proceeded abroad, by its reserve unit; and, directly this replacement occurred, a second reserve unit (a 3rd-line unit) was to be formed at the peace headquarters of the 1st-line unit. The permissible strength for 2nd-line units was only raised to 50 per cent. on the 29th December; it was not raised to 100 per cent. until early in 1915.

In accordance with the above arrangements, the corresponding 2nd-line units were sent to the West Lancashire Division to replace 1st-line battalions and other units which had left the Division to proceed to France between November, 1914, and March, 1915. In April, 1915, the last three 1st-line battalions left the West Lancashire Division to join the Highland Division.

The remainder of the West Lancashire Division then amalgamated around Canterbury with the 2nd/West Lancashire Division. The G.O.C., G.S.O.1., A.A. & Q.-M.-G., B.-G., R.A., C.R.E., 2 Infantry Brigadiers, the cyclist company, the divisional field artillery, the heavy battery, the signal company, and the train (from the 1st-line division) now became part of the 2nd-line division. In August, 1915, the 2nd/West Lancashire Division received the number 57, and the infantry brigades were numbered 170th, 171st, and 172nd Brigades.

So far the 2nd-line divisional artillery had not joined the 57th Division. The training of the artillery had been seriously delayed by lack of arms and equipment; indeed one field artillery brigade was reduced to obtaining carbines on loan from the Church Lads Brigade at Preston. At last, in the middle of July, each 2nd-line field artillery brigade received two 15-pdr. Mk. I guns (without sights). This issue was followed early in September by complete 15-pdr. B.L.C. and 5" howitzer equipments, which were taken over from the corresponding 1st-line field artillery brigades. Serious training for war could now be carried on. Between the 16th–19th September, 1915, the 2nd-line West Lancashire Division Artillery joined its division at Canterbury, and replaced the 1st-line divisional artillery which went to France with the 2nd Canadian Division, landing on the 1st October.

In the latter half of November the infantry of the division received ·303" rifles; many, however, were not in good condition. With the rifles came bayonets and ammunition. Thereupon the ·256" Japanese rifles (with their bayonets and ammunition) were returned to Weedon.

In December, 1915, the artillery received 18-pdr. Q.F. equipments, and in January, 1916, 4·5" howitzer equipments arrived. Towards the end of February Lewis guns were issued to the battalions which, at this time, were about 800 strong.

Until the middle of 1916 the 57th Division still formed part of the Second Army, Central Force, and was quartered in Canterbury, Maidstone, and Ashford. By July the division was transferred to the Emergency Reserves, and it moved into the Aldershot Command at Rushmore, Bourley, Mytchett, Deepcut, and Blackdown. In October the division's quarters were altered to Blackdown, Woking, Pirbright, Deepcut, and Crookham.

On the 5th January, 1917, the War Office informed G.H.Q., France, that the 57th Division would begin embarkation on the 6th February; and the division crossed to France and disembarked at le Havre between 7th–22nd February. The division completed its concentration in the Merris area by the 23rd February, and joined II Anzac Corps, Second Army; and at noon on the 25th February the 57th Division took over the right sector of II Anzac Corps front (north of le Tilleloy). Throughout the remainder of the Great War the 57th Division served on the Western Front in France and Belgium and was engaged in the following operations:

1917

BATTLES OF YPRES

26 Oct.–7 Nov. ... **Second Battle of Passchendaele** [XIV Corps, until 2 p.m., 29/10; then XIX Corps, Fifth Army].

1918

THE ADVANCE TO VICTORY

SECOND BATTLES OF ARRAS

28–30 August ... ... **Battle of the Scarpe** [XVII Corps, Third Army].
2 and 3 September ... **Battle of the Drocourt-Quéant Line** [XVII Corps, Third Army].

BATTLES OF THE HINDENBURG LINE

27 Sept.–1 Oct. ... **Battle of the Canal du Nord** [XVII Corps, Third Army].
8 and 9 October ... **Battle of Cambrai** [XVII Corps, Third Army].
9 October ... ... **Capture of Cambrai.**

15 Oct.–1 Nov. ... ... **THE FINAL ADVANCE IN ARTOIS AND FLANDERS**
17 October ... ... **Occupation of Lille** [XI Corps, Fifth Army].

On the 1st November 57th Division handed over its sector of the front line on the west bank of the Schelde (north of Tournai) and went into billets in the eastern suburbs of Lille. The division was still resting when the Armistice brought hostilities to a close; and on the 15th November the division found a guard of honour for the official entry into Lille by the Commander-in-Chief of the Allied Forces.

On the 21st November the division was ordered to assist in the collection, sorting, and evacuation of all stores and *matériel* from the Arras area. The move south began on the 30th November and was completed by the 4th December; divisional headquarters shifted from Mons en Barœuil to Duisans. During January, 1919, demobilization proceeded steadily, and the pace increased in February. By the 23rd March divisional headquarters and the division had been reduced to cadre strength, and the G.O.C. handed over the command of the 57th Division Group of Cadres to a brigadier. By the 20th April the strength had shrunk so much that the command devolved on the senior lieutenant-colonel. On the 25th June the last cadre units started for England. On the 4th July the last artillery details embarked at Dunkirk; and, with their departure, the 57th (2nd/West Lancashire) Division passed out of existence.

58TH (2ND/1ST LONDON) DIVISION

G.O.C.

Formation	Major-General W. FRY.
4 May, 1915	Br.-Gen. E. J. COOPER.
5 September, 1916	Major-General H. D. FANSHAWE.
6 October, 1917	Major-General A. B. E. CATOR (sick, 10/5/18).
10 May, 1918	Br.-Gen. C. G. HIGGINS (acting).
21 May, 1918	Major-General N. M. SMYTH, V.C. (sick, 10/6/18).
10 June, 1918	Br.-Gen. C. G. HIGGINS (acting).
13 June, 1918	Major-General F. W. RAMSAY.

G.S.O. 1.

Formation ...Lt.-Col. H. A. BOYCE.
21 Sept., 1915...Col. F. ST. D. SKINNER.
1 June, 1916...Lt.-Col. F. W. RADCLIFFE.
5 Sept., 1916...Lt.-Col. T. H. C. NUNN.
21 Mar., 1917...Lt.-Col. J. E. TURNER.
13 Nov., 1917...Lt.-Col. R. H. MANGLES.
13 July, 1918...Lt.-Col. C. M. DAVIES.

A.-A. and Q.-M.-G.

3 Nov., 1914...Col. ST. G. L. STEELE.
3 May, 1916...Lt.-Col. A. G. P. MCNALTY.

B.-G., R.A.

Formation ...Br.-Gen. G. S. DUFFUS.
11 Feb., 1915...Colonel F. T. M. BEAVER.
13 Jan., 1916...Br.-Gen. E. J. GRANET.
10 May, 1916...Br.-Gen. R. W. FULLER.
25 Aug., 1916 -20 Dec., 1917 } Br.-Gen. E. J. R. PEEL.
15 Jan., 1918...Br.-Gen. J. MCC. MAXWELL.

C.R.E.

Formation ...Lt.-Col. G. W. WALTERS.
13 Mar., 1917...Lt.-Col. E. M. NEWELL.
17 July, 1917...Lt.-Col. W. H. KELLY.
21 Nov., 1917...Lt.-Col. A. J. SAVAGE.

2nd/1st LONDON BDE.

29 Dec., '14...Col. E. Fitz G. M. Wood.
(Bde. was broken up by Feb., 1915).

2nd/2nd LONDON BDE.

Formation ......Col. Sir T. S. Cave.
24 Nov., '14...Br.-Gen. W. C. G. McGrigor.

2nd/3rd LONDON BDE.

19 Jan., '15...Col. G. B. Stevens.
6 Feb., '15...Col. G. Pleydell-Bouverie.

173rd BDE.

(3rd/1st London)

10 May, '15...Col. H. Cholmondley.
9 Jan., '16...Br.-Gen. G. P. S. Hunt.
20 April, '17...Lt.-Col. P. W. Beresford (acting).
21 April, '17...Br.-Gen. B. C. Freyberg, V.C. (wd., 19/9/17).
19 Sept., '17...Lt.-Col. W. R. H. Dann (acting).
3 Oct., '17...Br.-Gen. R. B. Worgan.
22 July, '18...Br.-Gen. C. E. Corkran.

174th BDE.

(2nd/2nd London)

[24 Nov., '14] Br.-Gen. W. C. G. McGrigor.
21 April, '17...Br.-Gen. C. G. Higgins.
10 May, '18...Lt.-Col. C. B. Benson (acting).
21 May, '18...Br.-Gen. C. G. Higgins.
13 June, '18...Lt.-Col. C. B. Benson (acting).
14 June, '18...Br.-Gen. C. G. Higgins.
2 July, '18...Br.-Gen. A. Maxwell.

175th BDE.

(2nd/3rd London)

[6 Feb., '15] Col. G. Pleydell-Bouverie.
17 Jan., '16...Br.-Gen. C. de Winton.
25 Aug., '16...Br.-Gen. H. C. Jackson.
19 Mar., '18...Br.-Gen. M. E. Richardson.
12 July, '18...Lt.-Col. E. G. H. Powell (acting).
2 Aug., '18...Br.-Gen. W. Maxwell-Scott (tempy.).
10 Aug., '18...Br.-Gen. H. W. Cobham (tempy.).
21 Aug., '18...Br.-Gen. H. W. Cobham.

GENERAL NOTES

The following Units also served with the 58th Division :—

1st London Heavy Battery, R.G.A. (T.F.), (4, 4·7" Guns) joined the 2/1st London (58th) Div. after the 1st London Div. had been broken up to reinforce Malta, B.E.F. in France, etc. The Hy. Bty. left the 58th Div. on 11/2/16 and moved to Woolwich to prepare for France. On 3/3/16 the Hy. Bty. disembkd. at le Havre, and on 5/3/16 it joined XXVII H.A. Group.

2/1st London Heavy Battery, R.G.A. (T.F.), joined 58th Div. at Ipswich on 24/9/15. This Hy. Bty. did not accompany the 58th Div. to France. The Hy. Bty. served in England with the 71st Div. from 9/3/17–12/2/18, and with the 67th Div. from 12/2/18 until the end of the War.

1/I Lond. Bde., R.F.A. (T.F.), 1/II Lond. Bde., R.F.A. (T.F.), 1/III Lond. Bde., R.F.A. (T.F.), 1/IV Lond. (How.) Bde., R.F.A. (T.F.) — after the break-up of the 1st Lond. Div., the R.F.A. Bdes. were stationed (in November, 1915) at Newcastle (I), Hull (II), Dover Defences (III), and Edinburgh (IV How.). On the concentration of the 58th Div. in August, 1915, the four R.F.A. Bdes. were attached as its Divisional Arty., and served with the 58th Div. until 21–23/9/15, when the four Bdes. were transferred to the 36th (Ulster) Div. The 4 Brigades disembked. at le Havre on 4 and 5/10/15, served with the 36th Div. until 11 and 12/12/15, and then (after several attachments) the 4 Brigades joined the (reformed) 56th (1st London) Div. on 25 and 26/2/16.

1/Glamorgan Bty., R.H.A. (T.F.)—(4, 18-pdrs. Q.F.)—after the S. Wales Mtd. Bde. (T.F.) went to Egypt in March, 1916, the Bty. was posted (in August, 1916) to CCXCIII Bde. with 58th Div. The Bde. disembkd. at le Havre on 22/1/17, and became CCXCIII A.F.A. Bde. (see note 20).

1/Shropshire Bty., R.H.A. (T.F.)—(4, 18-pdrs. Q.F.)—after the Welsh Border Mtd. Bde. (T.F.) went to Egypt in March, 1916, the Bty. was posted (in August, 1916) to CCXCIII Bde. with 58th Div. The Bde. disembkd. at le Havre on 22/1/17, and became CCXCIII A.F.A. Bde. (see note 20).

10/London Regt. and 11/London Regt. — after the 1st London Div. had been broken up to reinforce the B.E.F., these two battalions joined the 2/1st London Div. until April, 1915. 10/ and 11/London were then transferred to E. Midland (162nd) Bde., E. Anglian (54th) Div., at Norwich, and these two battalions served with the 162nd Bde. for the remainder of the War.

197th M.G. Coy. (from 9th Div.) was attached to 173rd Inf. Bde. from 22/2/17–26/3/17.

44th M.G. Coy. (from 15th Div.) was attached to 175th Inf. Bde. from 23/2/17–22/3/17.

100th (Warwick and S. Notts. Yeo.) Bn., M.G.C., was attached to 58th Div. from 7–25/9/18 (with 2 Cos. under 12th Div. from 16–25/9/18).

58th Sanitary Section accompanied 58th Division to France and embarked on the 25th January, 1917. The Sanitary Section left the Division on 30/3/17 and took over No. 8 Sanitary Area, VIII Corps.

On 2/2/18 the division completed its reorganization on a 9-battalion basis ; and on 4/3/18 the pioneer battalion was reorganized on a 3-company basis.

58TH[1] (2ND/1ST LONDON) DIVISION — ORDER OF BATTLE, 1915-1918

Dates	INFANTRY: Brigades	INFANTRY: Battalions and attached Units	Mounted Troops	ARTILLERY: Field Artillery: Brigades	ARTILLERY: Field Artillery: Batteries	ARTILLERY: Bde. Ammn. Colns.	ARTILLERY: Trench Mortar Bties.: Medium	ARTILLERY: Trench Mortar Bties.: Heavy	ARTILLERY: Divnl. Ammn. Coln.	Engineers: Field Cos.	Signal Service: Divnl. Signal Coy.	Pioneers	M.G. Units	Field Ambulances	Mobile Vety. Secn.	Divnl. Emplnt. Coy.	Divnl. Train
1915 January (England)	2/1st London[2] 2/2nd London 2/3rd London	2/1/Lond.,[3] 2/2/Lond.,[4] 2/3/Lond.,[5] 2/4/Lond.[6] 2/5/Lond., 2/6/Lond., 2/7/Lond., 2/8/Lond. 2/9/Lond., 2/10/Lond., 2/11/Lond., 2/12/Lond.	D. of L. Own Yeo.[7] (less A. Sqdn.)	...	...	...	...	...	...	2/1/London 2/2/London	1/1st London	...	...	2/1/ London 2/2/ London 2/3/ London	...	...	2/1/ London
1915 November (England)	173rd[8] ... (3/1st London) 174th[9] ... (2/2nd London) 175th[9] ... (2/3rd London)	3/1/Lond.,[10] 3/2/Lond.,[10] 3/3/Lond.,[10]; 3/4/Lond.[10] 2/5/Lond., 2/6/Lond., 2/7/Lond., 2/8/Lond. 2/9/Lond., 2/10/Lond., 2/11/Lond., 2/12/Lond.	...	2/I City of London[11] 2/II London[11] 2/III London[11] 2/IV London[11] (H.)	2/1/City of Lond., 2/2/City of Lond., 2/3/City of Lond. 2/4/Lond., 2/5/Lond., 2/6/Lond. 2/7/Lond., 2/8/Lond., 2/9/Lond. 2/10/Lond. (H.), 2/11/Lond. (H.)	2/I City of London 2/II London 2/III London 2/IV London (H.)	...	...	58th (2/1st Lond.) D.A.C.	2/1/ London[12] 2/2/ London[12] 1/5/ London[22]	1/1st Lond.[13]	...	...	2/1 Lond.[14] 2/2/ Lond.[14] 2/3 Lond.[14]	...	...	58th[15] (2/1st Lond.)
1916 October (England)	173rd...... 174th...... 175th......	2/1/Lond.,[10] 2/2/Lond.,[10] 2/3/Lond.,[10] 2/4/Lond.[10] 2/5/Lond., 2/6/Lond., 2/7/Lond., 2/8/Lond. 2/9/Lond., 2/10/Lond., 2/11/Lond., 2/12/Lond.	A Sqn.,[16] 1/Hants. Carabnr. 2/1/ Wessex[17] Div. Cyclist Coy.	CCXC[18]........ (2/I/ Lond.) CCXCI[19] ...... (2/II Lond.) CCXCII[20] ... (2/III Lond.)	A, B, C; D (H.) A, B, C; D (H.) A, B; C (H.), D (H.)	...	...	...	58th D.A.C.	2/1/ Wessex[21] 2/2/ Wessex[21] 1/5/ London[22]	58th[23] (2/1/ Wessex)	...	...	2/1/ Home Cties.[24] 2/2/ Home Cties.[24] 2/3/ Home Cties.[24]	58th[25] (2/1st London)	...	58th
1917 June (France)	173rd...... 174th...... 175th......	2/1/Lond.,[26] 2/2/Lond., 2/3/Lond., 2/4/Lond.; 214th M.G. Coy.;[27]; [46] 173rd T.M. Bty.[28] 2/5/Lond.,[29] 2/6/Lond., 2/7/Lond., 2/8/Lond.; 198th M.G. Coy.; [27]; [46] 174th T.M. Bty.[28] 2/9/Lond., 2/10/Lond., 2/11/Lond.,[30] 2/12/Lond.; 215th M.G. Coy.; [27]; [46] 175th T.M. Bty.[28]	...	CCXC........... CCXCI	A, B, C; D (H.) A, B, C; D (H.)	...	X.58[31] Y.58[31] Z.58[31]	V.58[32]	58th D.A.C.	503rd[33] (2/1/ Wessex) 504th[33] (2/2/ Wessex) 511th[33] (1/5/ London)	58th (2/1 Wessex)	...	206th[34] M.G. Coy.	2/1/ Home Cties. 2/2/ Home Cties. 2/3/ Home Cties.	58th (London)	249th[35]	58th
1918 March (France)	173rd...... 174th...... 175th......	2/2/Lond., 3/Lond.,[36] 2/4 Lond.;[37] 173rd T.M. Bty. 6/Lond.,[38] 7/Lond.,[39] 8/Lond.;[40] 174th T.M. Bty. 9/Lond.,[41] 2/10/Lond., 12/Lond.;[42] 175th T.M. Bty.	...	CCXC........... CCXCI	A, B, C; D (H.) A, B, C; D (H.)	...	X.58[43] Y.58[43]	...[44]	58th D.A.C.	503rd 504th 511th	58th	4/Suff.[45] (P.)	No. 58 Bn.,[46] M.G.C.	2/1/ Home Cties. 2/2/ Home Cties. 2/3/ Home Cties.	58th	249th	58th

1918 September (France)	173rd......	2/2/Lond., 3/Lond., 2/24/ Lond.,[47] 173rd T.M. Bty.	...	CCXC...........	A, B, C; D (H.)	...	X.58	...	58th D.A.C.	503rd	58th	4/Suff. (P.)	No. 58 Bn., M.G.C.	2/1/ Home Cties. 2/2/ Home Cties. 2/3/ Home Cties.	58th	249th	58th
	174th......	6/Lond., 7/Lond., 8/Lond.; 174th T.M. Bty.		CCXCI	A, B, C; D (H.)		Y.58			504th							
	175th......	9/Lond., 2/10/Lond., 12/ Lond.; 175th T.M. Bty.								511th							

NOTES

[1] The division was designated 58th Division in August, 1915. (Authy., 40/W.O./2609, A.G.1, of 10/8/15.)

[2] Bde. H.Q. went to Malta early in 1915 to relieve 1st London Inf. Bde. H.Q. 2/1st Lond. Inf. Bde. H.Q. left for Alexandria on 27/8/15.

[3] The Bn. disembkd. at Malta on 11/2/15; left for Alexandria on 27/8/15; disembkd. at Suvla on 25/9/15, and was attached to 88th Bde., 29th Div. The Bn. arrived back at Alexandria on 13/1/16 and was attached to the 53rd Div. The Bn. disembkd. at Marseille on 24/4/16, and proceeded to Rouen. Between early May and mid-June, 1916, the Bn. was broken up for drafting.

[4] The Bn. disembkd. at Malta on 31/12/14; left for Alexandria on 27/8/15; disembkd. at Helles on 13/10/15, and joined 2nd Bde., R.N. Div., on 14/10/15. The Bn. left Helles between 1-8/9/1/16, arrived Alexandria 21/1/16, and was attached to the 53rd Div. The Bn. disembkd. at Marseille on 24/4/16, and proceeded to Rouen. Between 5/5 and mid-June, 1916, the Bn. was broken up for drafting.

[5] The Bn. disembkd. at Malta on 31/12/14; left for Alexandria on 27/8/15; disembkd. at Suvla on 23/9/15, and joined 86th Bde., 29th Div., on 24/9/15. The Bn. arrived back at Alexandria on 7/1/16, and was attached to the 53rd Div. The Bn. disembkd. at Marseille on 24/4/16, and proceeded to Rouen. Between early May and mid-June, 1916, the Bn. was broken up for drafting.

[6] The Bn. disembkd. at Malta on 31/12/14; left for Alexandria on 21/8/15; disembkd. at Helles and joined 1st Bde., R.N. Div., on 15/10/15. The Bn. arrived back in Alexandria on 21/1/16, and was attached to 53rd Div. The Bn. disembkd. at Marseille on 24/4/16, and proceeded to Rouen. Between early May and mid-June, 1916, the Bn. was broken up for drafting.

[7] Joined as divisional cavalry on the concentration of the division in the Crowborough district. Early in 1915 the Regt. was broken up to form divisional cavalries. D. Sqdn. landed at le Havre on 23/5/15 with the 14th Div.; and Regtl. H.Q., M.G. Sec., and C Sqdn. landed at le Havre on 28/8/15 with the 23rd Div. [A Sqdn. left Southampton with the East Lancashire (later 42nd) Division, and disembkd. at Alexandria on 25/9/14.]

[8] 3/1st London Bde. was formed at Tadworth in April, 1915; it joined the 58th Div. in August, 1915, to replace 2/1st London Bde. In August, 1915, 3/1st London Bde. was numbered 173rd (see note 1).

[9] In August, 1915, 2/2nd and 2/3rd Lond. Bdes. were numbered 174th and 175th (see note 1).

[10] These 3rd-line Bns. were raised in Dec., 1914, to replace their 1st-line battalions, which had gone to Malta in Septr., 1914. The 4 Bns. were brigaded in April, 1915 (see note 8). After the disbandment of the 2nd-line Bns. (see notes 3-6) the four 3rd-line Bns. all became 2nd-line units of the London Regt. (in June, 1916) and henceforward were known as 2nd-line Bns.

[11] The 2nd-line divisional artillery joined as follows: 2/I/London Bde. on 25/9/15, at Ipswich; 2/II/London Bde. on 27/9/15, at Saxmundham; 2/III/London Bde. on 25/9/15, at Framlingham; 2/IV/London Bde. (H.) on 24/9/15, at Ipswich. In July, 1916, 2/IV/London (H.) was broken up and the batteries became D (H.)/CCXC and D (H.)/CCXCI.

[12] These 2 Fd. Cos. left the 58th Div. on 21/2/16, joined the 56th Div. in France on 24/2/16, and served with the 56th Div. for the remainder of the War. In 1917 the Fd. Cos. were numbered 512th and 513th.

[13] Left 58th Div. on 12/2/16, disembkd. at le Havre on 13/2/16, joined 56th Div. on 16/2/16, and served with the 56th Div. for the remainder of the War.

[14] The 3 Fd. Ambces. left 58th Div. on 21/2/16, joined the 56th Div. in France on 24/2/16, and served with the 56th Div. for the remainder of the War.

[15] The Cos. of the Train were numbered 509, 510, 511, and 512 Cos., A.S.C., in November, 1915.

[16] Allotted as divisional cavalry on 24/2/16, and joined at Ipswich on 21/3/16. A Sqdn. went to France on 17/1/17; the Tpt. was rammed outside le Havre and beached; it was only berthed on 20/1/17. A Sqdn. rejoined the Regt. (IX Corps Cavalry) at Bailleul on 25/1/17.

[17] The Cyclist Coy. did not accompany the Division to France.

[18] After arrival in France, D (H.) was made up to 6 hows. on 6/2/17 by 1 Sec. of D/CCXCIII.

[19] After arrival in France, D (H.) was made up to 6 hows. on 6/2/17 by 1 Sec. of D/CCXCIII.

[20] After arrival in France, D (H.) was broken up on 6/2/17 between D/CCXC and D/CCXCI. Remainder of CCXCIII (2, 6-gun 18-pdr. Bties. and 1, 4-gun 4·5" How. Bty.) then formed the nucleus of the CCXCIII A.F.A. Bde.

[21] The 2 Fd. Cos. arrived and joined 58th Div. on 22 and 23/2/16. (Normally the 2 Cos. would have served with 2nd Wessex Div.).

[22] Joined the 58th Div. at Claydon on 16/11/15.

[23] Joined the 58th Div. on 23/2/16. (Normally the Coy. would have served with 2nd Wessex Div.).

[24] The 3 Fd. Ambces. (from 67th Div.) arrived and joined the 58th Div. on 22/2/16; each Ambce. lacked medical equipt. and its 7 motor ambulances.

[25] Joined on 21/11/15, from Tunbridge Wells.

[26] Disbanded on 31/1/18. The Bn. was distributed between 2/2, 2/3, 2/4, and 1/4 London Regt.

[27] The M.G. Cos. joined as follows: 214th formed at Grantham, 10/12/16; disembkd. at le Havre, 17/3/17; and joined 173rd Bde. on 25/3/17. 198th disembkd. at le Havre, 15/12/16; joined 12th Div., 20/12/16; and joined 174th Bde. on 21/2/17. 215th disembkd. at le Havre, 17/3/17; and joined 175th Bde. on 21/3/17.

[28] The Bde. T.M. Bties. went to France in Jany., 1917, with their respective Inf. Bdes.

[29] Disbanded on 31/1/18. The Bn. was distributed between 1/18, 1/28, and 2/10 London Regt.

[30] Disbanded on 31/1/18. The Bn. was distributed between 1/20, 1/21, and 1/22 London Regt.

[31] Personnel of Btics. went to France, in Jany., 1917, with the Div.; the trench mortars were issued in France.

[32] Personnel of Bty. went to France, in Jany., 1917, with the Div.; the trench mortars were issued in France.

[33] The Fd. Cos. were numbered in England, before embkn.

[34] Formed at Grantham, 24/10/16; disembkd. at le Havre, 18/3/17; joined 58th Div. on 24/3/17.

[35] The Coy. was formed by 23/6/17. It was broken up on 22/4/19.

[36] On 31/1/18, 1/3/Lond. (from 167th Bde., 56th Div.) amalgamated with 2/3/Lond., and the Bn. became 3/London.

[37] On 12/9/18, the Bn. was absorbed by 2/2/London.

[38] On 31/1/18, 1/6/Lond. (from 140th Bde., 47th Div.) amalgamated with 2/6/Lond., and the Bn. became 6/London.

[39] On 2/2/18, 1/7/Lond. (from 140th Bde., 47th Div.) amalgamated with 2/7/Lond., and the Bn. became 7/London.

[40] On 2/2/18, 1/8/Lond. (from 140th Bde., 47th Div.) amalgamated with 2/8/Lond., and the Bn. became 8/London.

[41] On 1/2/18, 1/9/Lond. (from 169th Bde., 56th Div.) amalgamated with 2/9/Lond., and the Bn. became 9/London.

[42] On 31/1/18, 1/12/Lond. (from 168th Bde., 56th Div.) amalgamated with 2/12/Lond., and the Bn. became 12/London.

[43] Z was distributed between X and Y on 7 and 8/2/18; most of the personnel of V also joined X and Y.

[44] Most of the personnel of V joined X and Y on 7 and 8/2/18; remdr. of V Bty. joined V/III Corps H.T.M.B. on 18/2/18.

[45] Joined Div. on 15/2/18, from 98th Inf Bde., 33rd Div.

[46] Bn. was formed on 2/3/18; it consisted of 214, 198, 215, and 206 M.G. Cos.

[47] Bn. (formerly in 181st Bde., 60th Div.) embkd. at Alexandria on 3/7/18, disembkd. at Taranto on 8/7/18, reached Serqueux on 15/7/18, moved to Abancourt on 21/7/18; attached to 66th Div. 28/7-10/9/18; left Abancourt on 10/9/18, and joined 173rd Bde., 58th Div., at Guyencourt on 11/9/18.

58TH (2ND/1ST LONDON) DIVISION

FORMATION, BATTLES, AND ENGAGEMENTS

This 2nd-line (or reserve) Territorial Force division had no existence before the outbreak of the Great War.

The formation of reserve (or 2nd-line) T.F. units was authorized on the 31st August, 1914 (see Narrative, 57th Division). After the 1st London Division had transferred the bulk of its infantry—4 battalions to Malta (Septr., 1914), 3 battalions to reinforce the B.E.F. in France (Nov., 1914–Jany., 1915), and 3 battalions to reinforce the 2nd London Division (Nov., 1914)—the G.O.C., G.S.O.1., B.G., R.A., C.R.E., heavy battery, signal company, and the remaining two battalions amalgamated with 2nd-line units of the London Division. In this way the 2nd/1st London Division began its existence; but the field artillery of the 1st London Division did not join the 2nd/1st London Division until August, 1915. Between December, 1914, and February, 1915, the four battalions of the 2nd/1st London Infantry Brigade went to Malta to take the place of the four battalions of the 1st London Infantry Brigade. The 2nd/1st London Infantry Brigade was then replaced in the division by the 3rd/1st London Infantry Brigade.

In August, 1915, the 2nd/1st London Division concentrated in the Eastern Counties around Ipswich. On the 10th August the War Office issued an order that 2nd-line T.F. divisions and infantry brigades would henceforth be designated by numbers. In this order the 2nd/1st London Division was allotted the number 58, and the infantry brigades became 173rd, 174th, and 175th Brigades. Until the spring of 1916 the 58th Division remained in billets around Ipswich, forming part of First Army, Central Force (Home Defence); but, during this period, owing to lack of equipment, serious training for war could not be undertaken. Route marches, physical training, etc., could not replace field training as a rapid means of preparing the division for service in the field. Whilst the division was quartered in the Ipswich area the 1st-line London field artillery brigades left it to join the 36th (Ulster) Division, and the 2nd-line London field artillery brigades then joined the 58th Division.

In the spring of 1916 the division took over a sector of the East Coast defences, trenches were sited and dug, and training was carried on until July. The 58th Division was then transferred to Emergency Reserves, Home Defence Troops, and it concentrated around Sutton Veny, near Warminster (Wilts.). By this time 18-pdr. Q.F. and 4·5″ howitzer equipments had been received, ·303″ rifles had replaced the ·256″ (Japanese) rifles, and ammunition was available. The final training of the division for the field could be undertaken and it was rapidly completed at Sutton Veny.

On the 20th December, 1916, the War Office informed G.H.Q., France, that the 58th Division would embark during the latter half of January, 1917; and on the 1st January the division received orders to prepare for service in France and be ready to embark by the 20th. On the 11th January the War Office informed France that the embarkation of the 58th Division would begin on the 20th January and the move would be completed in about 10 days. On the 13th January the divisional advanced party left Southampton for le Havre, and on the 16th another party left Folkestone for Boulogne. On the 20th January the division began embarkation for France; but not until the 8th February was it concentrated around Lucheux, in XVIII Corps area. The delay was caused by the move to France having been temporarily suspended on the 30th January, before the 175th Brigade had crossed. Throughout the remainder of the Great War the 58th Division served on the Western Front in France and Belgium and was engaged in the following operations:

1917

17–28 March ... ... **German Retreat to the Hindenburg Line** [XVIII Corps, to 19/3; then VII Corps, Third Army].

4–17 May ... ... **Battle of Bullecourt** [175th Bde. with 2nd Aus. Div., I Anzac Corps, 4–12/5; 173rd Bde. with 5th Aus. Div., I Anzac Corps, 12–15/5; and 58th Div., from 16/5, with V Corps, Fifth Army].

20 May–16 June ... **Actions of the Hindenburg Line** [V Corps, Fifth Army, until 10 am., 31/5; then V Corps, Third Army].

BATTLES OF YPRES

20–25 September ... **Battle of Menin Road Ridge** [XVIII Corps, Fifth Army].

26 and 27 September **Battle of Polygon Wood** [XVIII Corps, Fifth Army].

26 Oct.–10 Nov. ... **Second Battle of Passchendaele** [XVIII Corps, Fifth Army, until 10 am., 2/11; then II Corps, Second Army].

1918

21 March–3 April ... **FIRST BATTLES OF THE SOMME** [III Corps, Fifth Army, until 24/3; then I Cav. Corps (Fr.), Sixth Army (Fr.)].

21–23 March ... ... **Battle of St. Quentin** [III Corps, Fifth Army].

4 April ... ... **Battle of the Avre** (6/Lond. and 7/Lond., attd. 18th Div.) [XIX Corps, Fourth Army].

24 and 25 April ... ... **Villers Bretonneux** [III Corps, Fourth Army].

THE ADVANCE TO VICTORY

8–11 August ... ... **Battle of Amiens** [III Corps, Fourth Army].

SECOND BATTLES OF THE SOMME

22 and 23 August ... **Battle of Albert** [III Corps, Fourth Army].
31 Aug. and 1 Septr. ... **Second Battle of Bapaume** [III Corps, Fourth Army].

BATTLES OF THE HINDENBURG LINE

18 September ... ... **Battle of Épéhy** [III Corps, Fourth Army].

---

2 Oct.–11 Nov. ... ... **THE FINAL ADVANCE IN ARTOIS AND FLANDERS** [VIII Corps, First Army, until noon, 14/10; then I Corps, Fifth Army].

On the 4th November the division succeeded in establishing a post on the right bank of the Schelde near Maulde. At 11 a.m. on the 11th November (Armistice) the advanced troops (174th and 175th Bdes.) of the 58th Division were on the Ath–St. Ghislain road about Neufmaison (south of Ath).

After the Armistice the division remained in the Peruwelz area. During December educational training was carried on and refresher courses were arranged; but skilled tradesmen, coal-miners, pivotal men, as well as a few other classes, were gradually sent away for demobilization.

At the beginning of March, 1919, the remainder of the dwindling division concentrated around Leuze. The units were grouped together as the 58th Division Group on the 12th March, and divisional headquarters, divisional artillery headquarters, and the three infantry brigade headquarters were amalgamated under the command of Br.-Gen. J. McC. Maxwell. Units were gradually reduced to cadre. The artillery left for England on the 4th April; and at the end of June, 1919, when the last units left France, the 58th (2nd/1st London) Division ceased to exist.

59TH (2ND/NORTH MIDLAND) DIVISION

G.O.C.

6 January, 1915 ... ... Br.-Gen. H. B. MacCall.
14 November, 1915 ... ... Major-General R. N. R. Reade.
14 February, 1916 ... ... Major-General A. E. Sandbach.
9 April, 1917 ... ... Major-General C. F. Romer.
26 January, 1918 ... ... Br.-Gen. C. H. L. James (acting).
11 February, 1918 ... ... Major-General C. F. Romer.
21 May, 1918 ... ... Br.-Gen. C. H. L. James (acting).
16 June, 1918 ... ... Major-General C. F. Romer.
19 June, 1918 ... ... Major-General Sir R. D. Whigham.
28 August, 1918 ... ... Major-General N. M. Smyth, V.C.

G.S.O. 1.

20 Jan., 1915...Lt.-Col. C. H. Savage.
8 Mar., 1915...Colonel L. R. Carleton.
16 Feb., 1916...Lt.-Col. R. St. G. Gorton.
14 April, 1918...Lt.-Col. G. L. Crossman.
21 Sept., 1918...Lt.-Col. R. S. Follett.

A.-A. and Q.-M.-G.

28 Jan., 1915...Major E. U. Bradbridge.
10 Feb., 1915...Colonel J. A. Fearon.
7 Jan., 1916...Lt.-Col. E. U. Bradbridge.
28 Feb., 1916...Capt. R. W. S. Stanton (acting).
3 Mar., 1916...Lt. Col. E. U. Bradbridge.
3 Sept., 1917...Lt.-Col. R. B. Airey.
4 Sept., 1918...Lt.-Col. J. H. S. Westley.
3 Nov., 1918...Lt.-Col. W. T. Browne (tempy.).
10 Nov., 1918...Lt.-Col. P. F. Fitz-gerald (tempy.).
[17 Nov., 1918...Lt.-Col. J. H. S. Westley].

B.-G., R.A.

3 Feb., 1915...Col. A. H. C. Phillpotts.
31 July, 1915...Col. W. H. Williams (acting).
7 Aug., 1915...Col. A. H. C. Phillpotts.
7 Feb., 1916...Col. L. Graham.
18 April, 1916...Br.-Gen. E. J. R. Peel.
23 Aug., 1916...Lt.-Col. H. V. B. de Satgé (acting).
12 Sept., 1916...Br.-Gen. E. J. Granet.
7 Nov., 1916...Br.-Gen. R. G. Ouseley (injured, 27/3/17).
28 Mar., 1917...Br.-Gen. G. N. Cartwright (tempy.).
13 April, 1917...Br.-Gen. J. W. Stirling.
12 June, 1918...Lt.-Col. V. J. Heather (acting).
9 July, 1918...Br.-Gen. J. F. Laycock.

C.R.E.

Formation ...Major G. B. Roberts (acting).
21 April, 1915...Lt.-Col. W. E. Harrison.
13 Mar., 1916...Lt.-Col. G. B. Roberts.
4 Feb., 1918...Lt.-Col. A. C. Howard.
6 June, 1918...Major H. A. S. Pressey (acting).
13 June, 1918...Lt.-Col. L. J. Coussmaker.

176th BDE.

(2nd/1st Staffordshire)

5 Jan., '15...Col. H. A. CHANDOS-POLE-GELL.
16 Feb., '16...Br.-Gen. L. R. CARLETON.
27 Aug., '16...Br.-Gen. G. M. GLOSTER.
5 Feb., '17...Br.-Gen. C. V. HUMPHREYS.
20 April, '17...Br.-Gen. R. A. M. CURRIE.
14 Aug., '17...Br.-Gen. T. G. COPE.

177th BDE.

(2nd/1st Lincoln and Leicester)

28 Jan., '15...Col. G. M. JACKSON.
5 Jan., '16...Br.-Gen. C. G. BLACKADER.
28 June, '16...Br.-Gen. C. H. L. JAMES.
26 Jan., '18...Lt.-Col. H. B. ROFFEY (acting).
11 Feb., '18...Br.-Gen. C. H. L. JAMES.
21 May, '18...Lt.-Col. G. A. YOOL (acting).
1 June, '18...Lt.-Col. Sir I. COLQUHOUN, BART. (acting).
16 June, '18...Br.-Gen. C. H. L. JAMES.

178th BDE.

(2nd/1st Notts. and Derby)

14 Jan., '15...Col W. W. BEMROSE.
19 July, '15...Col. E. W. S. K. MACONCHY.
6 June, '16...Br.-Gen. E. W. S. K. MACONCHY.
6 April, '17...Lt.-Col. W. C. OATES (acting).
6 April, '17...Br.-Gen, T. W. STANSFELD.

59TH (2ND/NORTH MIDLAND) DIVISION

GENERAL NOTES

The following Units also served with the 59th Division :—

IN ENGLAND

YEOMANRY :

B Sqdn., N. Irish Horse, was attached from 6/8/15 until the Division went to Ireland in April, 1916.

2/2/County of London was attached from 20 Feb. until April, 1916.

ARTILLERY :

1/IV Home Counties (How.) Bde., R.F.A. (T.F.), (8 offrs. and 316 other ranks), served with the Division 10/3–27/6/15.

1/1/Wessex (Hampshire) Hy. Bty., R.G.A. (T.F.), (5 offrs. and 146 other ranks), served with the Division from 13/3/15 until 7/4/15, when it joined 60th Division. The Hy. Bty. went to France on 22/4/16 and joined XLI H.A. Group on 25/4/16.

2/1/Wessex (Hampshire) Hy. Bty., R.G.A. (T.F.), was attached from 20 Feb. until April, 1916. The Hy. Bty. was then used to provide drafts for 1/1/Hants. Hy. Bty. and it was broken up by Oct., 1916.

2/1/N. Midland Hy. Bty., R.G.A. (T.F.), (3 offrs. and 194 other ranks), was attached from 5/2/15 until April, 1916. The Hy. Bty. went to France independently, and landed at le Havre on 30/5/16. On 1/6/16 the Hy. Bty. joined VI Corps Hy Arty. (near Arras), and on 3/6/16 the Hy. Bty. joined VIII H.A.G.

ENGINEERS :

2/1/N. Midland Field Coy. joined 46th (N. Midland) Division in England, and the Fd. Coy. disembarked at le Havre on 1/3/15. The Fd. Coy. served throughout the War, on the Western Front, with the 46th Division. The Fd. Coy. was numbered 468th.

MACHINE GUNS :

200th, 201st, 202nd, and 203rd M.G. Cos. (except 201st formed at Grantham on 25/10/16) were formed on 20/1/17 in the 59th Division ; but the Cos. remained at Fovant when the Div. went to France in Febry., 1917. (200th M.G. Coy. rejoined the Division, in France, in April, 1917, see note 30 ; 201st M.G. Coy. joined 62nd Div. in France on 30/3/17 ; 202nd and 203rd M.G. Cos. joined 66th Div. in England and went to France with 66th Div. in March, 1917.)

OTHER UNITS :

54th Div. Train (483–486 Cos.) was attached from 29/7/15 until Jany., 1916. On 16/1/16 54th Div. Train embkd. for Salonika. On arrival it became 27th Div. Train. (The Cos. were numbered 483, 484, 485, and 486 Cos., A.S.C.)

IN FRANCE

INFANTRY :

1st Provnl. Garr. Gd. Bn. joined 176th Bde. from Reserve Army on 13/5/18 ; and on 25/5/18 Bn. was redesignated 17/Garr. Bn., Worc. Bn. was transferred to 121st Bde., 40th Div., on 18/6/18, absorbed Training Cadre of 12/York, on 29/6/18, and became Divnl. Pioneers.

2/Garr. Gd. Bn., R. Ir. Rgt., embkd. at Dublin on 14/5/18, and joined 178th Bde. at Hurionville on 17/5/18, Bn. was redesignated 8/Garr. Bn., R. Ir. Rgt., on 25/5/18, and on 19/6/18 the Bn. was transferred to 121st Bde., 40th Div., at Tilques.

4th Provl. Garr. Gd. Bn. joined 176th Bde. from Reserve Army on 13/5/18, and on 25/5/18 Bn. was redesignated 23/Garr. Bn., L.F. On 18/6/15 the Bn. was transferred to 121st Bde., 40th Div., at Tilques.

23/Garr. Gd. Bn., Cheshire, embkd. at Dover on 21/5/18, and joined 178th Bde. on 24/5/18. On 19/6/18 the Bn. was transferred to 121st Bde., 40th Div., at Tilques.

NOTE.—In Garrison Guard Battalions, ' Guard ' was dropped on 25/5/18, and ' Garrison ' ceased to be used from 16/7/18.

MACHINE GUNS :

No. 25 Bn., M.G.C. This Bn. was formed in the 25th Div. between 14/2–1/3/18, and consisted of 7th, 74th, 75th, and 195th M.G. Cos. On 23/7/18 the Bn. was transferred to the 59th Div. and served with the Div. until 19/10/18 ; Bn. then rejoined 25th Div.

OTHER UNITS :

59th (North Midland) Sanitary Section went to France on 22/2/17, with the Division. 59th Sanitary Section left the Division and took over C Area in Cavalry Corps, Fourth Army, at m/n. 18/19 May, 1917.

By 31/1/18 the reorganization of the division on a 9-battalion basis was completed ; and on 26/2/18 the pioneer battalion was reorganized on a 3-company basis.

Between 22/3–27/8/18 the **59th Division Artillery** (CCXCV and CCXCVI) served as follows :

22–27/3 under 40th Div. ; 27/3–15/4 under 42nd Div. ; 15–24/4 under 62nd Div. ; 24/4–17/5 under 37th Div.; 17/5–19/6 under 62nd Div. ; 23/6–1/7 under XVIII Corps ; 1/7–8/8 under 5th Div. ; 8/8–26/8 under 61st Div. ; and on 27/8/18 59th Division Artillery rejoined 59th Div. in XI Corps.

During the Final Advance **XI Corps Mtd. Troops** (1/K.E.H. and 11/Cyclist Bn.) were attached to 59th Div. from 17–21/10/18 (then to 57th Div.) and from 9–14/11/18.

The following **Portuguese** troops served with 59th Division during the Final Advance :—

III Artillery Brigade, from 3/10–15/11/18 ;
14th Inf. Bn., from 3/10–2/11/18 (transferred to 57th Div.) ;
15th Inf. Bn., from 3/10–15/11/18.

59TH[1] (2ND/NORTH MIDLAND) DIVISION

ORDER OF BATTLE, 1915-1918

Dates	INFANTRY		Mounted Troops	ARTILLERY						Engineers	Signal Service	Pioneers	M.G. Units	Field Ambu-lances	Mobile Vety. Secn.	Divnl. Emplnt. Coy.	Divnl. Train
	Brigades	Battalions and attached Units		Field Artillery			Trench Mortar Bties.		Divnl. Ammn. Coln.	Field Cos.	Divnl. Signal Coy.						
				Brigades	Batteries	Bde. Ammn. Colns.	Medium	Heavy									
1915 November (England)	176th[1]; [2] (2/1st Staff.) 177th[1]; [2] (2/1st Linc. & Leic.) 178th[1]; [2] (2/1st Notts. & Derby)	2/5/S. Staff., 2/6/S. Staff., 2/5/N. Staff., 2/6/N. Staff. 2/4/Linc., 2/5/Linc., 2/4/Leic., 2/5/Leic. 2/5/Sher. For., 2/6/Sher. For., 2/7/Sher. For., 2/8/Sher. For.	2/1/ North'n[3] Yeo. 59th(2/1st N. Midld.)[4] Div. Cyclist Coy.	2/I N.[5]; [6] Midland 2/II N.[5]; [7] Midland 2/III N.[5]; [8] Midland 2/IV N.[5]; [9] Midland (H.)	2/1/Linc., 2/2/Linc, 2/3/Linc. 2/1/Staff., 2/2/Staff., 2/3/Staff. 2/4/Staff., 2/5/Staff., 2/6/Staff. 2/1/Derby (H.), 2/2/Derby (H.)	2/I N. Midld.[10] 2/II N. Midld.[10] 2/III N. Midld[10] 2/IV N. Midld.(H.)[10]	...	...	59th (N. Midld.)[10] D.A.C.	2/2/N. /Midld.[11] 3/1/N. Midld.[11]	59th[11] (2/1/N. Midld.)	...	...	2/1/N. Midld.[12] 2/2/N. Midld.[12] 2/3/N. Midld.[12]	...	...	59th[13] (2/1/N. Midld.)
1916 September (Ireland)	176th...... 177th...... 178th......	2/5/S. Staff., 2/6/S. Staff., 2/5/N. Staff., 2/6/N. Staff. 2/4/Linc., 2/5/Linc., 2/4/Leic., 2/5/Leic. 2/5/Sher. For., 2/6/Sher. For., 2/7/Sher. For., 2/8/Sher. For.	C.Sqn.,[14] 2/1/ Northbd. Hsrs. 59th Div.[15] Cyclist Coy.	CCXCV[16] ...... (2/I N. Midland) CCXCVI[17]...... (2/II N. Midland) CCXCVII[18] ... (2/III N. Midld.) CCXCVIII[19]... (2/IV N. Midland)	A, B, C; D (H.)[6] A, B, C; D (H.)[7] A, B, C; D (H.)[8] A,[6]; [9] B,[7]; [9] C,[8]; [9]	...	...	...	59th D.A.C.	1/3/N. Midld. 2/2/N. Midld. 3/1/N. Midld.	59th	...	...	2/1/N. Midld. 2/2/N. Midld. 2/3/N. Midld.	59th (2/1/N. Midld.)	...	59th
1917 June (France)	176th...... 177th...... 178th......	2/5/S. Staff.,[20] 2/6/S. Staff., 2/5/N. Staff.,[21] 2/6/N. Staff.; 174th M.G. Coy.; [22]; [44] 176th T.M. Bty.[23]; [35] 2/4/Linc.,[24] 2/5/Linc., 2/4/Leic., 2/5/Leic.;[25] 177th M.G. Coy.;[22]; [44] 177th T.M. Bty.[23]; [35] 2/5/Sher. For., 2/6/Sher. For., 2/7/Sher. For., [26] 2/8/Sher. For.; [27] 175th M.G. Coy.; [22]; [44] 178th T.M. Bty.[23];[35]	...	CCXCV .... CCXCVI	A, B, C; D (H.) A, B, C; D (H.)	...	X.59[28] Y.59[28] Z.59[28]	V.59[28]	59th D.A.C.	467th[29] (1/3/N. Midld.) 469th[29] (2/2/N. Midld.) 470th[29] (3/1/N. Midld.)	59th	...	200th[30] M.G.Coy.	2/1/N. Midld. 2/2/N. Midld. 2/3/N. Midld.	59th	250th[31]	59th
1918 March (France)	176th ...... 177th 178th	2/6/S.Staff.,[32] 5/N.Staff.,[21]; [33] 2/6/N. Staff.;[34] 176th T.M. Bty.[35] 4/Linc.,[24]; [36] 2/5/Linc.,[37] 2/4/Leic.;[38] 177th T.M. Bty.[35] 2/5/Sher. For.,[39] 2/6/Sher. For.,[40] 7/Sher. For.,[26]; [41] 178th T.M. Bty.[35]	...	CCXCV .... CCXCVI........	A, B, C; D (H.) A, B, C; D (H.)	...	X.59[42] Y.59[42]	...[42]	59th D.A.C.	467th 469th 470th	59th	6/7/ R.S.F.[43] (P.)	No. 59 Bn.,[44] M.G.C.	2/1/N. Midld. 2/2/N. Midld. 2/3/N. Midld.	59th	250th	59th
After reconstitution. **1918 Oct. (France)**	176th ...... 177th 178th	25/King's,[45] 26/R.W.F.,[46] 17/R. Suss.[47] 176th T.M. Bty.[48] 11/Som. L.I.,[49] 15/Essex,[50] 2/6/D.L.I.;[51] 177th T.M. Bty.[48] 36/N.F.,[52] 11/R.S.F.,[53] 13/Duke's;[54] 178th T.M. Bty.[48]	...	CCXCV .... CCXCVI	A, B, C; D (H.) A, B, C; D (H.)	...	X.59 Y.59	...	59th D.A.C.	467th 469th 470th	59th	25/ K.R.R.C (P.)[55]	No. 200[56] Bn., M.G.C.	2/1/N. Midld. 2/2/N Midld. 2/3/N. Midld.	59th	250th	59th

1 2nd-line T.F. Divns. and 2nd-line T.F. Inf. Bdes. were designated by numbers in August, 1915. (Authy.—40/W.O./2609, A.G.1, of 10/8/15.)

2 Inf. Bdes. were formed in Jany., 1915; and by 2/2/15 Bns. moved to billets at Luton and Harpenden. The Bns. varied in strength between 17 offrs. and 539 o.r. and 19 offrs. and 1031 o.r.

3 Left when the div. moved to Ireland.

4 Coy. (8 offrs. and 186 o.r.) reached Luton on 17/3/15.

5 Bdes. (varying in strength from 4 offrs. and 215 o.r. to 7 offrs. and 457 o.r.) reached Luton on 5 and 6/2/15.

6 Bties. were lettered A, B, C on 29/4/16, and later the Bde. was numbered CCXCV. At the end of May, 1916, 2/1/Hants. R.H.A. (4, 18-pdrs.) joined and became D/CCXCV. On 10/7/16, D was transferred and became A/CCXCVIII; and A (H.)/CCXCVIII joined and became D (H.)/CCXCV.

7 Bties. were lettered A, B, C on 29/4/16, and later the Bde. was numbered CCXCVI. At the end of May, 1916, 2/1/Essex R.H.A. (4, 18-pdrs.) joined and became D/CCXCVI. On 10/7/16, D was transferred and became B/CCXCVIII; and B (H.)/CCXCVIII joined and became D (H.)/CCXCVI.

8 Bties. were lettered A, B, C on 29/4/16, and later the Bde. was numbered CCXCVII. At the end of May, 1916, 2/1/Glamorgan, R.H.A. (4, 18-pdrs.) joined and became D/CCXCVII. On 10/7/16, D was transferred and became C/CCXCVIII; and C (H.)/CCXCVIII joined and became D (H.)/CCXCVII.

9 Bties. were lettered A (H.) and B (H.) on 29/4/16, and later the Bde. was numbered CCXCVIII. At the end of May, 1916, 3 (H.)/LIX joined and became C (H.)/CCXCVIII. On 10/7/16, A (H.) became D (H.)/CCXCV; B (H.) became D (H.)/CCXCVI; and C (H.) became D (H.)/CCXCVII. On the same day, D/CCXCV, D/CCXCVI, and D/CCXCVII joined and became A, B, and C/CCXCVIII.

10 On 31/7/16 the D.A.C. was reorganised and the B.A.C.s were abolished.

11 Reached Luton on 4/2/15.

12 Arrived Luton on 3/2/15.

13 Arrived at Luton on 22/1/15. On 25/2/16 the Cos. were numbered 513, 514, 515, and 516 Cos., A.S.C.

14 Served with the 59th Div. from 28/3/16—22/1/17. Joined XIX Corps Cav. Regt. in France on 26/3/17.

15 Did not accompany the 59th Div. to France.

16 Before proceeding to France, A, B, and C were made up to 6, 18-pdrs. each by the transfer of 3 sections from CCXCVII. In France, on 17/3/17, D (H.) was made up to 6, 4·5" hows. by L. Sec. of C (H.)/CCLXXXVII (from 57th Div.).

17 Before proceeding to France, A, B, and C were made up to 6, 18-pdrs. each by the transfer of 3 sections from CCXCVII. In France, D (H.) was made up to 6, 4·5" hows. by 1 Sec. of C (H.)/CCXCVIII.

18 Before the division left for France, CCXCVII was broken up: 3 Sections of A, B, and C made up A, B, and C of CCXCV to 6, 18-pdrs. each; the remaining 3 Sections made up A, B, and C of CCXCVI; and D (H.) was transferred and became D (H.)/CCXCVIII.

19 Before leaving Ireland, C was divided and made up A and B to 6, 18-pdrs. each; C (H.) joined; and D (H.)/CCXCVII joined and became D (H.)/CCXCVIII. On 4/4/17, after arrival in France, CCXCVIII became an A.F.A. Bde., and C (H.) was broken up: 1 Sec. went to D (H.)/CCXCVI and 1 Sec. joined D (H.)/CCXII (42nd Div.) on 19/6/17. D (H.)/CCXCVIII was transferred to the Fourth Army on 4/4/17; on 12/4/17 A/CCCXXXII joined and became C/CCXCVIII; and on 1/8/17 D (H.) joined from Third Army and became D (H.)/CCXCVIII.

20 Bn. was drafted and disbanded by 31/1/18.

21 On 30/1/18 Bn. amalgamated with part of 1/5/N. Staff., and was then designated 5/N. Staff.

22 174th joined 59th Div. at Southampton on 24/2/17, was attached to 178th Bde. on 28/2/17, and joined 176th Bde. on 6/3/17. 177th joined 59th Div. at Southampton on 19/2/17, and joined 177th Bde. on 27/2/17. 175th was formed at Grantham on 24/10/16, joined 59th Div. at Southampton on 17/2/17, and joined 178th Bde. on 13/3/17.

23 Formed in England on 20/1/17, and went to France with the Inf. Bdes.

24 On 31/1/18 Bn. amalgamated with part of 1/4/Linc., and was then designated 4/Linc.

25 Bn. was drafted and disbanded by 31/1/18.

26 On 31/1/18 Bn. amalgamated with 1/7/Sher. For., and was then designated 7/Sher. For.

27 Bn. was drafted and disbanded by 30/1/18.

28 Medium and Heavy T.M. Bties. were formed on 20/1/17.

29 Field Cos. were numbered in 1917, before leaving England.

30 Disembkd. at le Havre on 14/4/17, and joined 59th Div. on 18/4/17.

31 Formed by 16/6/17.

32 Bn. reduced to Training Cadre on 9/5/18, transferred to 198th Bde., 66th Div., on 30/5/18; transferred to 199th Bde. on 27/6/18; and Bn. was disbanded on 31/7/18 and absorbed by 1/6/S. Staff. (137th Bde., 46th Div.).

33 Bn. reduced to Training Cadre on 9/5/18 and transferred on 2/6/18 to 49th Bde., 16th Div. When the 16th Div. proceeded to England, the Bn. was transferred on 17/6/18 to 103rd Bde., 34th Div., then on 27/6/18 to 117th Bde., 39th Div., and on 12/8/18 to 116th Bde., 39th Div. On 6/11/18 the Bn. was demobilized to be used for drafting.

34 Bn. reduced to Training Cadre on 9/5/18, and transferred to 66th Div. on 7/6/18; attached to 199th Bde. on 28/6/18, to 198th Bde. on 23/7/18, and Bn. was disbanded on 31/7/18 and absorbed by 1/6/N. Staff. (137th Bde., 46th Div.).

35 Bde. T.M. Bties. were temporarily disbanded: 176th and 177th on 8/5/18; and 178th on 7/5/18. In each case the personnel either returned to their units or went to the Base.

36 Bn. reduced to Training Cadre on 8/5/18, and joined 49th Bde., 16th Div., on 2/6/18; transferred to 102nd Bde., 34th Div., on 17/6/18; to 117th Bde., 39th Div., on 27/6/18; to 118th Bde., on 27/7/18; and on 8/11/18 the Bn. was demobilized for drafting.

37 Bn. reduced to Training Cadre on 8/5/18, and joined 21st Bde., 30th Div., on 29/5/18; transferred to 199th Bde., 66th Div., on 28/6/18; and on 31/7/18 the Bn. was disbanded, the personnel being absorbed by 1/5/Lincoln (138th Bde., 46th Div.).

38 Bn. reduced to Training Cadre on 8/5/18, and joined 47th Bde., 16th Div., on 18/6/18. Bn. went to England with 16th Div. in June, 1918. On 20/6/18 Bn. went to Aldeburgh and joined 14/Leic. On 26/6/18 14/Leic. joined 47th Bde., 16th Div., and served with it for the remainder of the War.

39 Bn. reduced to Training Cadre on 7/5/18, transferred to 49th Bde., 16th Div., on 2/6/18; to 47th Bde. on 10/6/18; to 34th Div. on 17/6/18; and to 117th Bde., 39th Div., on 28/6/18. Bn. was disbanded on 3/8/18.

40 Bn. reduced to Training Cadre on 7/5/18; and on 31/7/18 the Bn. was disbanded and drafted to the 59th Div.

41 Bn. reduced to Training Cadre on 7/5/18, and joined 21st Bde., 30th Div., on 28/5/18; transferred to 198th Bde., 66th Div., 19/6/18; to 199th Bde. on 28/6/18; and to 39th Div. on 15/8/18.

42 In March, 1918, X and Y absorbed Z; and V (H.T.M.B.) left the Div.

43 6/R.S.F. went to France on 12/5/15 in 27th Bde., 9th Div.; on 6/5/16 the Bn. was transferred to 45th Bde., 15th Div., and on 13/5/16 Bn. amalgamated with 7/R.S.F. and became 6/7/R.S.F. On 21/2/18 6/7/R.S.F. joined 59th Div. as Pioneers. Bn. was reduced to Training Cadre, 7-10/5/18 and was then attached to 176th Bde. On 18/6/18 Bn. joined 47th Bde., 16th Div., at Boulogne and went to England. On 20/6/18 the Bn. went to Deal and joined 18/Sco. Rif. On 2/7/18, 18/Sco. Rif. joined 48th Bde., 16th Div., and served with it for the remainder of the War.

44 Bn. formed on 7 and 8/3/18; it contained 174, 175, 177, and 200 M.G. Cos. In May, 1918, the Bn. was reduced to Training Cadre and disappeared.

RECONSTITUTED DIVISION

45 25/Garr. Gd. Bn. King's joined 177th Bde. from England on 12/5/18, and was transferred to 176th Bde. on 16/6/18. (Garr. Gd. was dropped by 16/7/18.)

46 4/Garr. Gd. Bn. R.W.F. joined 176th Bde. from England on 16/5/18. Bn. was redesignated 26/R.W.F. on 16/7/18.

47 5/Prov. Garr. Gd. Bn. joined 176th Bde. from Reserve Army on 13/5/18. Bn. was redesignated 17/Garr. Bn. R. Suss. on 25/5/18, and 17/R. Suss. on 16/7/18.

48 The Bde. Light T.M. Bties. were reformed to replace the previous batteries (note 35) as follows: 176th on 11/7/18; 177th on 17/8/18; and 178th on 24/6/18.

49 11/Garr. Gd. Bn. Som. L. I. joined 177th Bde. from England on 12/5/18. (Garr. Gd. was dropped by 16/7/18.)

50 15/Garr. Gd. Bn. Essex joined 177th Bde. from England on 12/5/18. (Garr. Gd. was dropped by 16/7/18.)

51 2/6/Garr. Gd. Bn., D.L.I. became a Garr. Gd. Bn. at Frinton on 1/5/18; disembkd. at Calais on 6/5/18; and joined 177th Bde., on 10/5/18. Garr. Gd. was dropped by 16/7/18. (2/6/D.L.I. had served in England with 190th Bde., 63rd Div.; 214th Bde., 71st Div.; and 226th Mixed Bde.)

52 36/Garr. Gd. Bn. N.F. joined 178th Bde. from England on 12/5/18. (Garr. Gd. was dropped by 16/7/18.)

53 11/Garr. Gd. Bn. R.S.F. joined 178th Bde. from U.K. on 12/5/18. (Garr. Gd. was dropped by 16/7/18.)

54 3/Prov. Garr. Gd. Bn. joined 176th Bde. from Reserve Army on 13/5/18; transferred to 177th Bde. on 22/5/18; redesignated 13/Garr. Bn. Duke's on 25/5/18; and transferred to 178th Bde. on 16/6/18. (Garr. was dropped on 16/7/18.)

55 2/Prov. Garr. Gd. Bn. joined 176th Bde. from Reserve Army on 13/5/18; transferred to 177th Bde. on 22/5/18; redesignated 25/Garr. Bn. K.R.R.C. on 25/5/18; and became 59th Div. Pioneers on 16/6/18. (Garr. was dropped on 16/7/18.)

56 Bn. formed at Grantham on 1/8/18 (A, B, C, and D Cos.). On 6/9/18, A became 280 M.G. Coy., and left Grantham on 18/9/18 for N. Russia. On 17/9/18 a new A Coy. was formed to replace 280 Coy. Bn. disembarked at le Havre on 28/9/18 and joined 59th Div. on 2/10/18. (Also see No. 25 Bn., M.G.C., under General Notes.)

NOTE—In Garrison Guard Battalions: 'Guard' was dropped on 25/5/18, and 'Garrison' ceased to be used from 16/7/18.

59TH (2ND/NORTH MIDLAND) DIVISION

FORMATION, BATTLES, AND ENGAGEMENTS

This 2nd-line (or reserve) Territorial Force division had no existence before the outbreak of the Great War.

The formation of reserve (or 2nd-line) T.F. units was authorized on the 31st August, 1914 (see Narrative, 57th Division) ; and, in January, 1915, the 2nd/North Midland Division came into existence.

First enlistments for 2nd-line (or reserve) units began in September, 1914. At first the men had to live at home, and they paraded in civilian clothes until the County Associations were able to issue clothing and equipment. Recruits, however, came forward readily.

The numbers also were swelled by transferring from the 1st-line units any men who were unwilling to undertake the imperial service obligation as well as those who were medically unfit. These drafts were of considerable assistance in training the recruits.

In November issues of clothing were received ; and in December equipment arrived, together with 200 rifles per battalion. In February, 1915, Japanese rifles and ammunition were issued ; but it was not until between November, 1915, and March, 1916, that M.L.E. Mk. III rifles were available and the Japanese rifles could be returned. Also in March 4 Lewis guns were issued to each battalion. Analogous difficulties had to be faced in the artillery. Until March, 1915, ' quaker ' guns—logs of wood mounted on any available wheels—had to be constructed and used for training the recruits ; then some 90-mm. guns were obtained on loan from the French, and with some debilitated horses, more realistic gun and driving drill became possible. Later some 15-pdrs. were received and, although they were without dial sights, the arrival of these more modern equipments was much appreciated.

In the meantime, early in January, 1915, the division had concentrated around Luton, its war station, and it now formed part of Third Army, Central Force. In June, 1915, units began to furnish drafts to the 1st-line units in France, and at the same time the home-service men were transferred to provisional battalions. Then in July the division moved to a training area around St. Albans. Here, early in 1916, the batteries were made up to establishment in horses, and 18-pdrs. and 4·5″ howitzers replaced the 15-pdrs. and 5″ howitzers.

In April, 1916, the division was ordered to move to Ireland ; and it moved to Dublin between the 25th April and 17th May. The 59th Division was the first Territorial Force division to serve in Ireland. After the suppression of the trouble in Dublin the division moved out to the Curragh and for the rest of the year was engaged in war training.

In January, 1917, the 59th Division was ordered to move back to England.

The division was relieved in Ireland by the 65th (2nd/Lowland) Division, and by the middle of January 59th Division concentrated at Fovant. Orders were now received that it would be sent to France, and on the 2nd February the advance parties left. On the 13th February H.M. the King inspected the 59th Division, and the division began crossing to France on the 17th February. By the 3rd March it had completed its concentration around Méricourt.

For the remainder of the Great War the 59th Division served on the Western Front in France and Belgium and was engaged in the following operations :

1917

17 March–5 April ... ... **German Retreat to the Hindenburg Line** [III Corps, Fourth Army].

BATTLES OF YPRES

23–25 September ... ... **Battle of Menin Road Ridge** [V Corps, Fifth Army].
26–30 September ... ... **Battle of Polygon Wood** [V Corps, Fifth Army, until 10 a.m. 28/9 ; then II Anzac Corps, Second Army].

BATTLE OF CAMBRAI

28 November ... ... **Capture of Bourlon Wood** [IV Corps, Third Army].
30 Nov.–3 Dec. ... ... **German Counter-Attacks** [IV Corps, until 1/12 ; then V Corps, Third Army].

1918

FIRST BATTLES OF THE SOMME

21 March ... ... **Battle of St. Quentin** [VI Corps, Third Army].

22 and 23 March ... ... **Battle of St. Quentin** [59th Div. Arty. and 177th Bde. remained in action on 22 and 23/3, under 40th Div., VI Corps, Third Army].

24 and 25 March ... ... **Battle of Bapaume** [59th Div. Arty.* and 177th Bde., under 40th Div., VI Corps, Third Army].

BATTLES OF THE LYS

14 and 15 April ... ... **Battle of Bailleul** [IX Corps, Second Army].

17 and 18 April ... ... **First Battle of Kemmel Ridge****[IX Corps, Second Army].

Between the 7th and 10th May the infantry battalions, brigade trench mortar batteries, pioneer battalion, and machine-gun battalion were reduced to training cadre establishment at St. Omer. All surplus men were sent to the Base or drafted. The division then moved to Hestrus, was reconstituted as a 2nd-line division, and made up to strength with Garrison Guard battalions (see Table). Until mid-June the reconstituted division was employed on the construction of rear defences. The division was then reconstituted again, became a Garrison Division, and underwent training to enable it to hold a sector of the line. On the 25th July 59th Division took over the left sector of the line held by VI Corps, Third Army, and on the 21st August the division once more became engaged in active operations :

THE ADVANCE TO VICTORY

SECOND BATTLES OF THE SOMME

21 and 22 August ... ... **Battle of Albert** [VI Corps, Third Army].

2 Oct.–11 Nov. ... ... **THE FINAL ADVANCE IN ARTOIS AND FLANDERS** [XI Corps, Fifth Army].

At Armistice the division was astride the Schelde to the north of Tournai. Between the 15th–21st November the division moved to the south and south-east of Lille and was employed on training and education. On the 4th–7th December the division moved to the Noeux les Mines—Bethune area, and on the 8th–10th December transferred 178th Inf. Bde., 2/2/N.M. Fd. Ambce., and 516 Coy., A.S.C., to Dunkirk, for employment at the dispersal camp for miners returning to England. Between the 13th–15th January, 1919, 177th Bde. moved to Dieppe for demobilization duties, and on the 25th January the pioneer battalion was sent to Dunkirk to assist in the construction of the demobilization camp. On the 8th March divisional headquarters moved to Calais, and during the month other units of the division followed. Between 21st–23rd May the three battalions of 176th Bde. left Calais for Marseille, en route for Egypt. On the 16th June 19th Infantry Brigade (6/Queen's, 5/6/Sco. Rif., and 10/Sco. Rif.) joined 59th Division in the Calais area, on transfer from 33rd Division. In July 176th Bde. H.Q. was reduced to cadre and returned to England. On the 19th July Major-General C. E. D. Budworth took over the command of 59th Division, which at this time was preparing drafts both for Egypt and the Black Sea. By the 8th August the divisional artillery was demobilized and disappeared. On the 29th August orders were received to break up 59th Division. On the 1st September divisional headquarters closed and during the month cadres returned to England. The service of the 59th Division was completed.

---

* 59th Division Artillery was transferred on 27/3 to 42nd Div., IV Corps, Third Army ; and, with 42nd Div., took part in the Battle of Arras (28/3) and the Battle of the Ancre (5/4/18).

** James's Force (about 2,000 of 59th Div.) served from 16–19/4/18 with 49th Div., IX Corps, Second Army.

60TH (2ND/2ND LONDON) DIVISION

G.O.C.

9 October, 1914 ... ... Colonel E. W. D. BAIRD (acting).
24 October, 1914 ... ... Br.-Gen. T. C. P. CALLEY (sick, 26/4/15).
26 April, 1915 ... ... Colonel H. G. WEIR (acting).
29 April, 1915 ... ... Br.-Gen. T. C. P. CALLEY.
20 December, 1915 ... ... Major-General E. S. BULFIN.
6 August, 1917 ... ... Major-General J. S. M. SHEA.
6 January, 1918 ... ... Br.-Gen. F. M. EDWARDS (acting).
13 January, 1918 ... ... Br.-Gen. W. A. ROBINSON (acting).
18 January, 1918 ... ... Major-General J. S. M. SHEA.
15 July, 1918 ... ... Br.-Gen. W. A. ROBINSON (acting).
26 July, 1918 ... ... Major-General J. S. M. SHEA.
13 August, 1918 ... ... Br.-Gen. W. A. ROBINSON (acting).
25 August, 1918 ... ... Major-General J. S. M. SHEA.

G.S.O. 1.

Formation ...Major C. E. SPEARMAN (acting).
16 Mar., 1915...Lt.-Col. A. S. DUNLOP.
21 Jan., 1916...Lt.-Col. E. T. HUMPHREYS.
6 Aug., 1917...Lt.-Col. A. G. C. DAWNAY (sick, 26/8/17).
26 Aug., 1917...Major C. A. BOLTON (acting).
4 Sept., 1917...Lt.-Col. A. C. TEMPERLEY.
10 April, 1918...Lt.-Col. S. B. POPE.

A.-A. & Q.-M.-G.

24 Oct., 1914...Lt.-Col. A. ST. L. GLYN (tempy).
25 Feb., 1915...Major P. MALCOLM (acting).
29 Mar., 1915...Lt.-Col. P. MALCOLM.
13 Nov., 1916...Lt.-Col. H. W. MCCALL.

B.-G., R.A.

16 Jan., 1915...Colonel H. G. WEIR.
22 Nov., 1915...Colonel H. H. BUTLER.
12 April, 1916...Br.-Gen. H. A. D. SIMPSON-BAIKIE.
8 Aug., 1917...Br.-Gen. H. M. DRAKE.
23 Oct., 1917...Lt.-Col. V. M. FERGUSSON (acting).
27 Oct., 1917...Br.-Gen. W. A. ROBINSON.
22 July, 1918...Lt.-Col. E. W. M. CUNINGHAME (acting).
26 July, 1918...Br.-Gen. W. A. ROBINSON.

C.R.E.

29 Jan., 1915...Colonel R. Q. HENRIQUES.
27 Aug., 1917...Lt.-Col. C. B. THOMSON.
5 Jan., 1918...Major D. F. COLSON (acting).
11 Mar., 1918...Lt.-Col. C. B. THOMSON.
20 April, 1918...Major D. F. COLSON (acting).
3 May, 1918...Lt.-Col. C. B. THOMSON.
10 May, 1918...Major D. F. COLSON (acting).
27 May, 1918...Lt.-Col. A. J. G. BIRD.

179th BDE.

(2nd/4th London)

9 Oct., '14...Col. E. W. D. BAIRD.
28 Dec., '15...Lt.-Col. W. R. J. MCLEAN (acting).
5 Jan., '16 Col. E. W. D. BAIRD.
28 May, '16...Br.-Gen. E. W. D. BAIRD.
9 Nov., '16...Br.-Gen. F. M. EDWARDS.
6 Jan., '18...Lt.-Col. C. B. THOMSON (acting).
25 Feb., '18...Lt.-Col. C. M. MACKENZIE (acting).
28 Feb., '18...Br.-Gen. E. T. HUMPHREYS.
10 May, '18...Lt.-Col. R. J. L. OGILBY (acting).
21 May, '18...Br.-Gen. E. T. HUMPHREYS.

180th BDE.

(2nd/5th London)

27 Nov., '14...Col. G. H. TURNER.
28 Dec., '15...Lt.-Col. H. A. CHRISTMAS (acting).
5 Jan., '16...Col. G. H. TURNER.
30 Jan., '16...Br.-Gen. H. W. STUDD.
9 Nov., '16...Br.-Gen. F. M. CARLETON.
29 Aug., '17...Lt.-Col. A. E. NORTON (acting).
30 Aug., '17...Br.-Gen. J. HILL.
11 Sept., '17...Br.-Gen. C. F. WATSON.

181st BDE.

(2nd/6th London)

19 Jan., '15...Col. G. B. STEVENS.
9 Aug., '15...Col. C. N. WATTS.
5 Mar., '16...Br.-Gen. C. Mc N. PARSONS.
15 Oct., '16...Br.-Gen. E. C. DA COSTA.
5–14 June, '18...Lt.-Col. J. A. JERVOIS (acting).
22 June, '18...Lt.-Col. A. D. BORTON, V.C. (acting).
23 Aug., '18...Br.-Gen. E. C. DA COSTA.

GENERAL NOTES

The following Units also served with the 60th Division :—

MOUNTED TROOPS :—B. Sqdn., 1/1/Hants. Carabiniers, joined Div. at Warminster on 26/4/16, disembkd. at le Havre on 25/6/16, and Sqdn. was attached to 1/York. Hsrs. (XVII Corps Cav.) on 8/7/16, and it rejoined Regt. (IX Corps Cavalry) on 19/1/17. **A Sqdn., D. of L. Yeomanry,** attached to 60th Div. in August, 1917 (whilst en route from 53rd Division to XXI Corps Cav. Regt.).

ARTILLERY :—2/2nd London Heavy Battery, served with 60th Div. from 9/4/15 (when it moved to its war station near Hemel Hempstead) until 24/1/16, when the Hy. Bty. was transferred to 61st (2nd/S. Midland) Division. On 9/3/17 the Hy. Bty. joined 71st Div. ; on 12/2/18 the Hy. Bty. (with 226th Mixed Bde.) was transferred from 71st Div. to 67th Div. ; the Hy. Bty. served in England with 67th Div. until Dec., 1918.

1/1/Wessex (Hampshire) Heavy Battery, was attached from 7/4/15. Officers and men of this Heavy Battery had been used in Dec., 1914, to form the greater part of the 28th Division Ammn. Coln. Some offrs. and men eventually rejoined the Bty., but as late as Dec., 1915, the Hy. Bty. had no guns or equipment, and possessed only personnel, horses, and harness. The Hy. Bty. left the 60th Division on 24/1/16, and was attached to 61st Div. The Hy. Bty. embarked for France on 22/4/16, and joined XLI H. A. Group on 25/4/16.

2/1/Wessex (Hampshire) Heavy Battery, joined the 60th Division in April, 1915, and served with the division in England. This Hy. Bty. never went overseas and was used to provide drafts for the 1/1/Hants. Hy. Bty. The Hy. Bty. joined 61st Div. on 24/1/16 ; and the Hy. Bty. was broken up by Oct., 1916.

413 (H.), see note 38.

519 (H.), see note 13.

ENGINEERS :—2/3/London Fd. Coy., formed in Oct., 1914, and joined 2nd/2nd London Div. The Fd. Coy. left Div. and landed at le Havre on 23/6/15. The Fd. Coy. joined 47th Div. on 25/6/15, and for the remainder of the War it served with the 47th Div. In 1917 the Fd. Coy. was numbered 520.

PIONEERS :—2/155 Pioneers, from 28/6/18–19/7/18. The Pioneer Battalion was transferred to the 10th Division.

OTHER UNITS :—60th Sanitary Section, joined 60th Division at Sutton Veny on 29/2/16, and served with the division for the remainder of the War.

60TH[1] (2ND/2ND LONDON) DIVISION — ORDER OF BATTLE, 1915-1918

Dates	INFANTRY		Mounted Troops	ARTILLERY						Engineers	Signal Service	Pioneers	M.G. Units	Field Ambu-lances	Mobile Vety. Secn.	Divnl. Emplnt. Coy.	Divnl. Train
	Brigades	Battalions and attached Units		Field Artillery			Trench Mortar Bties.		Divnl. Ammn. Coln.	Field Cos.	Divnl. Signal Coy.						
				Brigades	Batteries	Bde. Ammn. Colns.	Medium	Heavy									
1915 February (England)	2/4th London 2/5th London 2/6th London	2/13/Lond., 2/14/Lond., 2/15/Lond., 2/16/Lond. 2/17/Lond., 2/18/Lond., 2/19/Lond., 2/20/Lond. 2/21/Lond., 2/22/Lond., 2/23/Lond., 2/24/Lond.	...	...	...	...	...	...	...	2/4/London	2/2nd London	...	...	2/4/London 2/5/London 2/6/London	...	...	2/2nd London
1915 November (England)	179th[1] ... (2/4th London) 180th[1] ... (2/5th London) 181st[1]...... (2/6th London)	2/13/Lond., 2/14/Lond., 2/15/Lond., 2/16/Lond. 2/17/Lond., 2/18/Lond., 2/19/Lond., 2/20/Lond. 2/21/Lond., 2/22/Lond., 2/23/Lond., 2/24/Lond.	2/2nd Cty. of Lond.[2] Yeo. 60th (2/2nd Lond.)[3] Div. Cyclist Coy.	2/V Lond.[4] 2/VI Lond.[5] 2/VII Lond[6] 2/VIII Lond.[7] (H.)	2/12/Lond., 2/13/Lond., 2/14/Lond. 2/15/Lond., 2/16/Lond., 2/17/Lond. 2/18/Lond., 2/19/Lond., 2/20/Lond. 2/21/Lond. (H.), 2/22/Lond. (H.)	2/V Lond.[8] 2/VI Lond.[8] 2/VII Lond.[8] 2/VIII Lond.[8] (H.)	...	...	60th D.A.C.[8] (2/2nd Lond.)	3/3/London 2/4/London 1/6/London	60th (2/2nd Lond.)	...	...	2/4/London 2/5/London 2/6 London	...	...	60th[9] (2/2nd London)
1916 June (France)	179th...... 180th...... 181st	2/13/Lond., 2/14/Lond., 2/15/Lond., 2/16/Lond.; 179th Bde. M.G. Coy.;[10] 179th T.M. Bty.[11] 2/17/Lond., 2/18/Lond., 2/19/Lond., 2/20/Lond.; 180th Bde. M.G. Coy.;[10] 180th T.M. Bty.[11] 2/21/Lond., 2/22/Lond., 2/23/Lond., 2/24/Lond.; 181st Bde. M.G. Coy.;[10] 181st T.M. Bty.[11]	60th Div.[3] Cyclist Coy.	CCC[4]; [12] ...... CCCI[5]; [13] ...... CCCII[6]; [14] ... CCCIII[7]; [15] ...	A, B, C; D (H.) A, B, C A, B, C; D (H.) A, B, C; D (H.)	...[8]	X.60[16] Y.60[16] Z.60[16]	W.60[17]	60th D.A.C.[8]	3/3/London 2/4/London 1/6/London	60th	1/12/L.N.L.[18] (P.)	...	2/4/London 2/5/London 2/6/London	2/2nd London	...	60th
1917 February (Mace-donia)	179th...... 180th...... 181st	2/13/Lond., 2/14/Lond., 2/15/Lond., 2/16/Lond.; 179th M.G. Coy.;[41] 179th T.M. Bty.; S.A.A. Sec. Ammn. Coln.[19] 2/17/Lond., 2/18/Lond., 2/19/Lond., 2/20/Lond.; 180th M.G. Coy.;[41] 180th T.M. Bty.; S.A.A. Sec. Ammn. Coln.[19] 2/21/Lond., 2/22/Lond., 2/23/Lond., 2/24/Lond.; 181st M.G. Coy.;[41] 181st T.M. Bty.; S.A.A. Sec. Ammn. Coln.[19]	...	CCC[20] .... CCCII[21]........ CCCIII[22]	A, B; D (H.)[36] A, B; D (H.)[37] A, B; D (H.)[39]	CCCI B.A.C.[8]; [23] CCCII B.A.C.[8]; [23] CCCIII B.A.C.[8]; [23]	X.60[24] Y.60[24] Z.60[24]	...	60th [8]; [23] D.A.C.	519th[25] (3/3/Lond.) 521st[25] (2/4/Lond.) 522nd[25] (1/6/Lond.)	60th	1/12/L.N.L.[26] (P.)	...	2/4/London 2/5/London 2/6/London	2/2nd London	...	60th[27]

1918 June (Palestine)	179th	2/13/Lond., 2/14/Lond.,[28] 2/15/Lond.,[28] 2/16/Lond.;[28] 179th T.M. Bty.	...	CCCI	A, B ;[36] C (H.)[36]	...[23]	...[24]	...	60th D.A.C.[23]	519th	60th	...	No. 60 Bn.,[41] M.G.C.	2/4/ London [53]	2/2nd London	...	60th[27]
	180th	2/17/Lond.,[29] 2/18/Lond.,[30] 2/19/Lond., 2/20/Lond. ;[31] 180th T.M. Bty.		CCCII	A, B ; C (H.)[38]					521st				2/5/ London [53]			
	181st	2/21/Lond.,[32] 2/22/Lond., 2/23/Lond.,[33] 2/24/Lond. ;[34] 181st T.M. Bty.		CCCIII	A, B ; C (H.)[39]					522nd[40]				2/6/ London [53]			
1918 September (Palestine)	179th	2/13/Lond. ; 2/19/Punjabis,[42] 2/127/Baluchis,[43] 3/151/Inf. ;[44] 179th T.M. Bty.	...	CCCI	A, B ; C (H.)	...	...	...	60th D.A.C.	519th	60th	2/10752 (P.)	No. 60 Bn., M.G.C.	121st C.F.A.[53]	2/2nd London	...	60th
	180th	2/19/Lond. ; 2/Guides,[45] 2/30/Punjabis,[45], 1/50/Kumaon Rif.;[47] 180th T.M. Bty.		CCCII	A, B ; C (H.)[38]					521st				160th C.F.A.[53]			
	181st	2/22/Lond. ; 2/97/Inf.,[48] 130/Baluchis,[49] 2/152/Inf. ;[50] 181st T.M. Bty.		CCCIII	A, B ; C (H.)					No. 1 Coy.,[51] (K.G.O.) S. & M.				179th C.F.A.[53]			

NOTES

[1] 2nd-line T.F. Divisions and 2nd-line T.F. Inf. Bdes. were designated by numbers in August, 1915. (Authy.—40/W.O./2609, A.G.I, of 10/8/15).

[2] Joined Div. at Harlow on 24/6/15, and was transferred to 61st (2/S. Mid.) Div. on 24/1/16.

[3] Cyclist Coy. formed in May, 1915 ; went to France with Div., and on 5/9/16 was transferred to the Cavalry Corps.

[4] Bde. reached its war station on 9/6/15. All Bties. were rearmed in England with 18-pdrs. ; and on 28/4/16 a fourth 18-pdr. Bty. (3/1/Wessex) joined. On 17 and 18/5/16 the Bde. became CCC Bde. and original Bties. were lettered A, B, and C ; the Bde. was then reorganized : 2/21/Lond. (H.) joined and became D (H.) ; 3/1/Wessex was transferred to CCCIII and became A/CCCIII.

[5] Bde. reached its war station on 15/6/15. All Bties. were rearmed in England with 18-pdrs. ; and on 28/4/16 a fourth 18-pdr. Bty. (3/2/Wessex) joined. On 17 and 18/5/16 the Bde. became CCCI Bde. and original Bties. were lettered A, B, and C ; the Bde. was then reorganized : 3/2/Wessex was transferred to CCCIII and became B/CCCIII.

[6] Bde. reached its war station on 9/4/15. All Bties. were rearmed in England with 18-pdrs. ; and on 28/4/16 a fourth 18-pdr. Bty. (3/3/Wessex) joined. On 17 and 18/5/16 the Bde. became CCCII Bde. and original Bties. were lettered A, B, and C ; the Bde. was then reorganized : 3/3/Wessex was transferred to CCCIII and became C/CCCIII ; 2/22 Lond. (H.) joined from CCCIII and became D (H.).

[7] The How. Bde. was formed, at Plumstead, in Oct., 1914. Bde. reached its war station on 9/4/15. Both Bties. were rearmed in England with 4·5" Hows. ; and on 28/4/16 a third 4·5" How. Bty. (4/LX How.) joined. On 17 and 18/5/16 the Bde. was renumbered CCCIII, and the Bde. was reorganized : 2/21 (H.) left and became D (H.)/CCC ; 2/22 (H.) left and became D (H.)/CCCII ; 4/LX became D (H.)/CCCIII ; and 3/1, 3/2 ; and 3/3/Wessex (18-pdr.) Bties. joined and became A, B, and C (see notes 4, 5 and 6).

[8] Before embarkation for France, B.A.C.s were abolished and the D.A.C. was reorganized ; then, between 8-11/11/16 (before embarkation for Macedonia), CCCI, CCCII, and CCCIII B.A.C.s were reformed and the D.A.C. was again reorganized.

[9] The Train consisted of Nos. 517, 518, 519, 520 Cos., A.S.C.

[10] 179 M.G. Coy. was formed at Grantham on 27/3/16, disembkd. at le Havre on 27/6/16, and joined 60th Div. on 29/6/16. 180 and 181 M.G. Cos. went to France with 179, and joined Div. on 29/6/16.

[11] The L.T.M. personnel went to France with 60th Div., then went to the T.M. School, and rejoined the 60th Div. on 4/7/16 (with mortars).

[12] On 30 and 31/8/16 CCC was broken up : D (H.) became D (H.)/CCCI ; A and 1/2 B joined CCCII ; and 1/2 B and C went to CCCIII.

[13] Bde. was reorganized on 30 and 31/8/16 : A was broken up to made B and C up to 6 guns each ; and D (H.)/CCC joined and became D (H.)/CCCI. On 20/10/16, 519 (H.) joined (from England) and became A (H.). On 5/11/16 the Bde. was reorganized for Macedonia in 4-gun Bties. : A was reformed from 1 Sec. B and 1 Sec. C ; and A (H.) became D (H.)/CCC, and was transferred to Lahore Div.

[14] Bde. was reorganized in 6-gun 18-pdr. Bties. on 30 and 31/8/16 : R. Sec. A/CCC joined A/CCCII ; L. Sec. A/CCC joined B ; and 1 Sec. B/CCC made up C/CCCII. On 5/11/16 the Bde. was reorganized for Macedonia in the original 4-gun 18-pdr. Bties. : A/CCC was reformed and made up to 6 18-pdrs. by withdrawing the section of B/CCC from C/CCCII. A/CCC was then transferred to XXVIII (with 5th Div.) ; and, on 21/1/17, A/CCC joined XV (with 5th Div.), and served with XV for the remainder of the War.

[15] Bde. was reorganized in 6-gun 18-pdr. Bties. on 30 and 31/8/16 : 1 Sec. B/CCC joined A/CCCIII ; L. Sec. C/CCC joined B ; and R. Sec. C/CCC made up C/CCCIII. On 5/11/16 the Bde. was reorganized for Macedonia in the original 4-gun 18-pdr. Bties : the sec. of B/CCC and the 2 secs. of C/CCC were withdrawn and made into a 6-gun 18-pdr. Bty., which was designated B/CCC, and became an instructional battery at First Army School.

[16] The Med. T.M. Bties. joined 60th Div. on 6/7/16, from T.M. School.

[17] W.60 was formed in France on 28/7/16 ; and W.60 remained in France when 60th Div. left for Macedonia. [OVER

NOTES (contd.)

18 Joined Div. in England on 1/6/16 and went to France with 60th Div. The Pioneer Bn. was transferred to 32nd Div. on 16/11/16; the Bn. left 32nd Div. on 5/1/17, reached Salonika on 23/1/17, and rejoined 60th Div. on 13/2/17.

19 From arrival in Macedonia in Dec., 1916, and until the departure of the 60th Div. for Egypt in June, 1917, 1 S.A.A. Sec. was attached to each Inf. Bde.

20 On arrival in Macedonia, A was broken up on 20/12/16, to complete B and C to 6 18-pdrs. each; B and C were then redesignated A and B.

21 On arrival in Macedonia, C was broken up on 10/1/17, to complete A and B to 6 18-pdrs. each.

22 On arrival in Macedonia, R. Sec. of C joined A and L. Sec. of C joined B on 22/12/16, to complete A and B to 6 18-pdrs. each.

23 On arrival in Egypt, B.A.C.s were abolished between 11-23/6/17 and the D.A.C. was reorganized.

24 On arrival in Egypt, the Med. T.M. Batteries were disbanded: X on 28/7/17; Y on 29/7/17; and Z on 28 and 29/7/17. Mortars, etc., were returned to Ordnance Stores, and the personnel was drafted to various Batteries in the Divnl. Arty.

25 The Fd. Cos. were numbered: 3/3/Lond. on 5/2/17; 2/4/Lond. on 7/2/17; and 1/6/Lond. on 1/2/17.

26 Pioneer Bn. was transferred to 74th Div., and joined on 10/4/18 at Sarafand.

27 On arrival in Macedonia the Train was reorganized in Dec., 1916, in Pack Echelon (Nos. 861, 862, 863, and 864 Cos., A.S.C.) and Wheeled Echelon (Nos. 517, 518, 519, and 520 Cos.). Between 8-15/6/17, on preparing to move to Egypt, the Train was again reorganized: Pack Echelon ceased to exist; Pack and Wheel Cos. were merged into one, and the Train henceforth consisted of Nos. 517, 518, 519, and 520 Cos., A.S.C.

28 2/14, 2/15, 2/16 Lond. left 179th Bde. on 30/5/18, sailed from Alexandria on 18/6/18, arrived Taranto on 22/6/18, detrained Audruicq on 1 and 2/7/18, and joined 90th Bde., 30th Div., at Serques and Moulle on 1 and 2/7/18.

29 Left Bde. on 27/5/18, sailed from Alexandria on 18/6/18, disembkd. at Taranto on 22/6/18, detrained Audruicq on 30/6/18, and joined 89th Bde., 30th Div., at Ouest Mont.

30 The Bn. was disbanded between 4-7/7/18, and drafts joined 1/R. Ir. Regt., 2/R. Ir. Fus., 1/Leins., and Rft. Camp, Lydda. Horses, mules, saddlery, and stores were handed in at Lydda.

31 Left Bde. 27/5/18, sailed from Alexandria, on 24/6-3/7/18, disembkd. Taranto on 30/6-8/7/18. Bn. concentrated at Abancourt on 16/7/18, and on 19/7/18 was attached to 198th Bde., 66th Div. The Bn. left Abancourt on 9/8/18 and joined 185th Bde., 62nd Div., at Thièvres.

32 The Bn. was disbanded on 8/6/18, and distributed between 2/13, 2/19, and 2/22 Lond. in 60th Div.

33 Left Bde. 26/5/18, sailed from Alexandria on 24/6/18, disembkd. Taranto on 30/6/18, detrained Arques on 8/7/18, and joined 21st Bde., 30th Div., at Clairmarais.

34 Left Bde. 26/5/18, embkd. at Alexandria on 3/7/18, disembkd. Taranto on 8/7/18, arrd. Serqueux on 15/7/18, and on 28/7/18 was attached to 198th Bde., 66th Div. Bn. left Abancourt on 10/9/18 and joined 173rd Bde., 58th Div., at Guyencourt on 11/9/18.

35 B/CCCI was transferred to 74th Div. on 17/6/17, and became A/CCLXVIII. On 25/3/18 A/CCLXVIII rejoined CCCI and became B/CCCI.

36 On 20/6/17 D (H.) was redesignated C (H.).

37 On 19/6/17 D (H.)/CCCII was transferred to 74th Div. and became C (H.)/CCLXVIII. In April, 1918, C (H.)/CCLXVIII became D (H.)/XLIV in 74th Div.

38 On 10/10/17 413 (H.) arrived and joined CCCII. 413 (H.) was then designated C (H.).

39 On 20/6/17 D (H.) was redesignated C (H.).

40 Transferred to 7th (Indian) Div. on 18/7/18.

41 Bn. formed between 14-17/5/18; it consisted of 179th, 180th, and 181st M.G. Cos.

42 Bn. mobd. at Ft. Sandeman, 19/12/17; sailed from Karachi, 11/5/18; disembkd. Suez, 21/5/18, and joined 179th Bde. at 'Ain 'Ariq on 23/6/18.

43 Bn. mobd. at Multan, 19/4/18; sailed from Karachi, 18/5/18; disembkd. Suez, 29/5/18, and joined 179th Bde. at 'Ain 'Ariq on 26/6/18.

44 Bn. was formed at Latrun and 'Ain 'Ariq between 24/5-27/6/18. Bn. consisted of Cos. from 1/Guides, 38/Dogras, 58/Rif., and 59/Rif. Bn. joined 179th Bde. at 'Ain 'Ariq on 4/6/18.

45 Bn. mobd. at Nowshera, 10/2/18; sailed from Bombay, 28/5/18; disembkd. Suez, 9/6/18, and joined 180th Bde. near Deir Ibzia on 13/7/18.

46 Bn. mobd. at Lahore, 24/4-20/5/18; sailed from Karachi, 3/6/18; disembkd. Suez, 18/6/18, and joined 180th Bde. at The Plateau on 1/8/18.

47 Bn. disembkd. Suez on 6/6/18, and joined 180th Bde. near Bir ez Zeit on 23/7/18.

48 Bn. left Sitapur 15/5/18; sailed from Bombay, 18/5/18; disembkd. Suez, 30/5/18, and joined 181st Bde. beyond Beit Nuba on 28/6/18.

49 Bn. left Ferozepore, 12/5/18; sailed from Karachi, 15/5/18; disembkd. Suez, 20/5/18, and joined 181st Bde. at Wadi el Kelb on 26/6/18.

50 Bn. was formed at Hinaidi between 16-19/5/18. Bn. consisted of Cos. from 37/Dogras and 62/, 67/, and 84/Punjabis. Bn. sailed 19/5/18; disembkd. Nahr Umar, 23/5/18; embkd. Nahr Umar, 2/6/18; disembkd. Suez, 20/6/18, and joined 181st Bde. beyond Beit Nuba on 30/6/18.

51 Coy. joined 60th Div. at Bire and 'Ain 'Ariq between 12-16/7/18.

52 Bn. mobd. at Allahabad, between 6-20/6/18; sailed from Bombay, 26/6/18; disembkd. Suez, 8/7/18, and employed on Palestine L. of C. Bn. (less A and D Cos.) joined 60th Div. on the sea-shore north of Arsuf at mn., 16/17/9/18. (A and D Cos. were attached to the 3rd (Lahore) Div. from 15-27/9/18. On 27/9/18 the 2 Cos. rejoined the Bn. at Baqa.)

53 121st, 160th, and 179th C.F.A.s joined 60th Div. at 'Ain 'Ariq on 29/6, 30/6, and 1/7/18; and 2/4/Lond., 2/5/Lond., and 2/6/Lond. Fd. Ambces. were broken up between 30/6-4/7/18, and handed over to 121st, 160th and 179th C.F.A.s.

60TH (2ND/2ND LONDON) DIVISION

FORMATION, BATTLES, AND ENGAGEMENTS

This 2nd-line (or reserve) Territorial Force division had no existence before the outbreak of the Great War.

The formation of reserve (or 2nd-line) T.F. units was authorized on the 31st August, 1914 (see Narrative, 57th Division); and, owing to the large number of recruits who came forward, the 2nd/2nd London Division came into existence soon afterwards. For a few weeks the men lived at home and attended daily for preliminary training at the headquarters of the 1st-line units. The first parades, however, were in civilian clothes and mostly without arms. Uniforms, arms, equipment, and stores only became gradually available. In 1914 no guns or horses could be issued to the artillery; but the batteries improvised dummy wooden guns, equipped them with wooden sights, and mounted them on handcarts. In this way some preliminary training was accomplished; and, by January, 1915, this 2nd-line division was able to send out drafts to 1st-line units which were already in France. On the 26th January Japanese rifles (each with 100 rounds of ammunition) were received; but it was not until February that any 15-pdr. guns reached the batteries, and 5" howitzers did not become available until May, 1915.

In October, 1914, a partial concentration of the infantry of the division was made at the White City (Shepherds Bush). In December, 1914, and January, 1915, the division moved out of London, concentrated in the Dorking–Reigate area, and joined Second Army, Central Force. During January, 1915, the battalions adopted the 4-company organization. On the 21st January Field-Marshal Earl Kitchener, accompanied by the French Minister of War, inspected the division on Epsom Downs, but at this time only one battalion was fully equipped with efficient rifles. In March the division provided heavy drafts to bring its 1st-line division up to establishment before the latter embarked for France. A vigorous recruiting campaign then became essential to restore the depleted strength of the 2nd/2nd London Division.

In March, 1915, the division took the place of the 2nd London Division in Third Army, Central Force, and moved into the St. Albans area. At the end of May it moved into Hertfordshire and Essex (with divisional headquarters at Bishops Stortford).

By the middle of November, 1915, the Japanese ·256" rifles were handed in, and 6,300 ·303" rifles (with 1,890,000 rounds of ammunition) were received by the division. At the end of this month 18-pdr. Q.F. equipments began to arrive, and 4·5" howitzers followed soon after. Progressive training for war was pushed on.

In January 1916, orders were received that the division would move to the Warminster training area (Salisbury Plain), and it moved there towards the end of the month. Divisional headquarters opened at Sutton Veny and the division was attached to the Emergency Reserve. On the 24th April the division was warned that it would shortly proceed to France; and on the 31st May H.M. the King inspected the 60th Division at Sutton Veny.

On the 14th June the division received orders to send advance parties to le Havre (on the 15th) and Boulogne (on the 18th), and the division began to cross to France on the 21st June. By the 29th the move had been completed and the division was concentrated in XVII Corps area. Throughout the remainder of the Great War the 60th Division served firstly on the Western Front in France and Belgium, then in Macedonia, and lastly in Egypt and Palestine. The division was engaged in the following operations:

1916

On the 1st November intimation reached the division that it was to move to Macedonia, and between 4–24 November a certain amount of reorganization was undertaken (see Table). The division entrained at Longpré from 14–25 November and (moving via Marseille and Malta) it assembled at Salonika on Christmas Day.

1917

24 and 25 April; and 8 and 9 May	**Battle of Dojran** [XII Corps].

On the 1st June the division was withdrawn and moved back to Uchantar (7 miles N.W. of Salonika). The division was now destined for Egypt, and on the 4th June reorganization began (to conform with the E.E.F. scale); but the final reorganization of the divisional train (into wheel and camel transport) took place in Alexandria, in July. The division began embarkation at Salonika on the 12th June, and by the 4th July it completed its concentration at Moascar, in the Southern Canal Section. On the next day the division began to move forward, and by the 23rd July it concentrated at Deir el Balah (8 miles S.W. of Gaza). For the rest of the Great War the 60th Division served with the E.E.F. in Palestine and was engaged in the following operations:

30 Oct.–7 Nov. ... ... **THIRD BATTLE OF GAZA** [XX Corps].

31 October ... ... **Capture of Beersheba** [XX Corps].
6 November ... ... **Capture of the Sheria Position** [XX Corps].

---

8 and 9 December ... **Capture of Jerusalem** [XX Corps].
26–30 December ... **Defence of Jerusalem** [XX Corps].

1918

19–21 February ... ... **Capture of Jericho** [XX Corps].
8–12 March ... ... **Tell 'Asur** (181st Bde., in Reserve) [XX Corps].
21 March–2 April ... **First Trans-Jordan Raid** [Shea's Force].
27–30 March ... ... **Attack on 'Amman** (2/17 and 2/18 Lond. (180th Bde.) and 181st Bde.) [Chaytor's Column].
30 April–4 May ... **Second Trans-Jordan Raid** [Desert Mtd. Corps].

Between 26/5–1/8/18 the division (with the exception of the artillery) was changed to the Indian establishment: the infantry brigades were reformed, with one British and three Indian Army battalions each; an Indian S. and M. company and three combined field ambulances joined the division; and, just before the attack, the pioneer battalion arrived. (See Table.)

THE FINAL OFFENSIVE

THE BATTLES OF MEGIDDO

19–21 September ... **Battle of Sharon** [XXI Corps].

After the capture of Tul Karm the pursuit devolved on the mounted troops, and the 60th Division was then employed on salvage work. On the 24th September the division passed directly under army control, and divisional headquarters moved to Mulebbis. Early in October the division moved back to the 'Auja. It was still in this area on the 31st October when the Armistice with Turkey came into force.

On the 3rd November the division moved to Lydda; on the 8th the move back via Qantara to Alexandria was begun, and by the 26th the whole division reached Alexandria. Demobilization gradually took place. In the middle of February, 1919, three Indian battalions left the division to return to India. Nevertheless the shrunken division was always held ready to cope with any local disturbance, and it was employed in collecting contraband arms and ammunition. Gradually units were reduced to cadre, the remaining Indian units left, brigades were disbanded; and by the 31st May, 1919, the 60th Division passed out of existence.

61ST (2ND/SOUTH MIDLAND) DIVISION

G.O.C.

8 January, 1915 ... ... Br.-Gen. MARQUIS OF SALISBURY.
27 August, 1915 ... ... Br.-Gen. E. K. DAUBENEY (acting).
4 September, 1915 ... ... Br.-Gen. MARQUIS OF SALISBURY.
17 September, 1915 ... ... Br.-Gen. E. K. DAUBENEY (acting).
23 September, 1915 ... ... Br.-Gen. MARQUIS OF SALISBURY.
21 December, 1915 ... ... Major-General R. BANNATINE-ALLASON.
4 February, 1916 ... ... Major-General C. J. MACKENZIE (wd., 27/4/18 ; to hospital, 20/5/18).
20 May, 1918 ... ... Br.-Gen. R. G. OUSELEY (acting).
28 May, 1918 ... ... Major-General C. J. MACKENZIE (evacd. sick, 31/5/18).
31 May, 1918 ... ... Br.-Gen. R. G. OUSELEY (acting).
14 June, 1918 ... ... Major-General F. J. DUNCAN.

G.S.O. 1.

8 Jan., 1915...Major R. O. CHESNEY (acting).
9 April, 1915...Colonel E. S. HEARD.
17 July, 1915...Major R. O. CHESNEY (acting).
30 July, 1915...Lt.-Col. A. R. BURROWES.
1 Mar., 1916...Lt.-Col. Sir H. WAKE, Bt.
12 Dec., 1917...Lt.-Col. J. T. WEATHERBY.
16 Mar., 1918...Lt.-Col. R. O'H. LIVESAY.
21 Aug., 1918...Lt.-Col. W. S. WHETHERLY.

A.-A. and Q.-M.-G.

8 Jan., 1915...Captain R. E. SALKELD (acting).
3 April, 1915...Major A. L. LAW (acting).
15 April, 1915...Lt.-Col. A. L. LAW.
19 Mar., 1916...Lt.-Col. C. C. MARINDIN.
20 Sept., 1916...Lt.-Col. H. T. C. SINGLETON.

B.-G., R.A.

22 Jan., 1915...Colonel W. HANNA (sick, 4/11/15).
4 Nov., 1915...Lt.-Col. F. HILDER (acting).
7 Nov., 1915...Lt.-Col. F. K. S. METFORD (acting).
10 Nov., 1915...Colonel R. E. LYON (acting).
18 Nov., 1915...Colonel W. HANNA (sick, 21/11/15).
21 Nov., 1915...Colonel R. E. LYON (acting).
4 Dec., 1915...Colonel W. HANNA (sick, 10/12/15).
10 Dec., 1915...Colonel R. E. LYON (acting).
16 Jan., 1916...Colonel W. HANNA.
11 Feb., 1916...Colonel L. G. F. GORDON.
19 April, 1916...Br.-Gen. R. C. COATES.
21 April, 1917...Br.-Gen. R. G. OUSELEY.

C.R.E.

12 Sept., 1914...Lt.-Col. J. L. V. S. WILLIAMS.
19 Sept., 1916...Major O. S. DAVIES (acting).
2 Oct., 1916...Lt.-Col. G. E. J. DURNFORD.

182nd BDE.

(2nd/1st Warwick)

11 Jan., '15...Colonel H. PALMER.
19 Mar., '15...Br.-Gen. E. K. DAUBENEY (sick, 18/12/15).
18 Dec., '15...Colonel H. J. NUTT (acting).
22 Dec., '15...Br.-Gen. E. K. DAUBENEY.
13 Feb., '16...Br.-Gen. A. F. GORDON (injured, 18/10/16).
18 Oct., '16...Br.-Gen. F. BURNELL-NUGENT (sick, 18/1/17).
18 Jan., '17...Br.-Gen. C. A. BLACKLOCK.
8 Mar., '17...Lt.-Col. J. F. CLYNE (acting).
12 Mar., '17...Br.-Gen. Hon. C. J. SACKVILLE-WEST.
14 Sept., '17...Br.-Gen. W. D. CROFT.
23 Sept., '17...Br.-Gen. W. K. EVANS.

183rd BDE.

(2nd/1st Glouc. and Worc.)

11 Jan., '15...Colonel Sir J. W. BARNSLEY.
3 May, '16...Br.-Gen. C. G. STEWART.
28 July, '16...Major C. L. PORTER (acting).
30 July, '16...Br.-Gen. A. H. SPOONER.
18 Sept., '18...Lt.-Col. N. C. BURNAND (acting).
21 Sept., '18...Br.-Gen. B. D. L. G. ANLEY.

184th BDE.

(2nd/1st S. Midland)

9 Jan., '15...Colonel W. R. LUDLOW.
23 Feb., '16...Br.-Gen. Hon. C. G. FORTESCUE.
7 May, '16...Br.-Gen. C. H. P. CARTER.
31 July, '16...Br.-Gen. W. J. DUGAN (wd., 8/9/16).
8 Sept., '16...Lt.-Col. P. BALFOUR (acting).
12 Sept., '16...Br.-Gen. Hon. R. WHITE (wd., 22/3/18).
23 Mar., '18...Lt.-Col. H. DE R. WETHERALL (acting; wd., 25/3/18).
25 Mar., '18...Lt.-Col. A. B. LAWSON (acting).
26 Mar., '18...Lt.-Col. L. L. BILTON (acting).
28 Mar., '18...Br.-Gen. A. W. PAGAN.
14 Oct., '18...Br.-Gen. A. F. A. N. THORNE.

GENERAL NOTES

The following Units also served with the 61st Division :—

IN ENGLAND

MOUNTED TROOPS :—2/2/County of London Yeo., arrived from the 60th Division on 24/1/16, and served with the 61st Div. until the division moved to Wiltshire in February, 1916.

ARTILLERY :—1/1/Wessex (Hampshire) Heavy Battery, arrived from the 60th Division on 24/1/16 and served with the 61st Div. until the division moved to Wiltshire in February, 1916. This Hy. Bty. embkd. for France on 22/4/16, and joined XLI H.A. Group on 25/4/16.

2/1/Wessex (Hampshire) Heavy Battery, arrived from the 60th Division on 24/1/16 and served with the 61st Div. until the division moved to Wiltshire. This 2nd-line Hy. Bty. remained in England and was used for training drafts. The Hy. Bty. was broken up by Oct., 1916.

2/2/London Heavy Battery, arrived from the 60th Division on 24/1/16 and served with the 61st Div. until 3/2/16. On 9/3/17 the Hy. Bty. joined 71st Div.

2/1/S. Midland (Warwickshire) Heavy Battery, served with the division until 3/2/16. On 4/2/16 this 2nd-line heavy battery took over the guns of 117 Hy. Bty., R.G.A. From Septr., 1916–Aug., 1917 the Hy. Bty. served with 67th (2nd Home Cties.) Div. ; and from January, 1918, until the Armistice it was at Wingham, attached to the Cyclist Div.

ENGINEERS :—2/1/S. Midland Fd. Coy., disembarked at le Havre on 7/6/15, joined 48th (S. Midland) Division on 10/6/15. The Fd. Coy. served for the remainder of the War, in France and Italy, with the 48th Division. The Fd. Coy. was numbered 477th.

IN FRANCE

MOUNTED TROOPS :—C Sqdn., 1/1/Hants. Carabiniers, see note 4.
61st (2/1/S. Midld.) Cyclist Coy., see note 5.

ARTILLERY :—59th Division Artillery (CCXCV and CCXCVI) from 8/8–26/8/18.
520 (H.) Battery, see note 14.

MACHINE-GUN UNIT :—267th Machine-Gun Company, see note 32.

OTHER UNITS :—61st Sanitary Section, went overseas with the division and served with the division until 12/4/17. On 18/4/17 the section was transferred to a IV Corps Sanitary Area.

On 22/2/18 the reorganization of the division on a 9-battalion basis was completed ; and on 27/2/18 the pioneer battalion was reorganized on a 3-company basis.

61ST[1] (2ND/SOUTH MIDLAND) DIVISION

ORDER OF BATTLE, 1915-1918

Dates	INFANTRY		Mounted Troops	ARTILLERY						Engineers	Signal Service	Pioneers	M.G. Units	Field Ambu-lances	Mobile Vety. Secn.	Divnl. Emplnt. Coy.	Divnl. Train
				Field Artillery			Trench Mortar Bties.										
	Brigades	Battalions and attached Units		Brigades	Batteries	Bde. Ammn. Colns.	Medium	Heavy	Divnl. Ammn. Coln.	Field Cos.	Divnl. Signal Coy.						
1915 March (England)	2/1st Warwick 2/1st Glouc. & Worc. 2/1st S. Midland	2/5/R. War., 2/6/R. War., 2/7/R. War., 2/8/R. War. 2/4/Glouc., 2/6/Glouc., 2/7/Worc., 2/8/Worc. 2/5/Glouc., 2/4/O. & B.L.I., 2/1/Bucks., 2/4/R. Berks.	2/1/ Bedford[2] Yeo.; 2/1/S. Midld.[3] Div. Cyclist Coy.	2/I S. Midld. 2/II S. Midld. 2/III S. Midld. 2/IV S. Midld. (H.)	2/1/Glouc., 2/2/Glouc., 2/3/Glouc. 2/1/Worc., 2/2/Worc., 2/3/Worc. 2/1/War., 2/2/ War., 2/3/War. 2/4/War. (H.), 2/5/War. (H.)	2/I S. Midld. 2/II S. Midld. 2/III S. Midld. 2/IV S. Midld. (H.)	...	...	...	2/2/ S. Midld. 3/1/ S. Midld.	2/1/ S. Midld.	...	...	2/1/ S. Midld. 2/2/ S. Midld. 2/3/ S. Midld.	...	...	2/1/ S. Midld.
1916 May (England)	182nd[1] ... (2/1st Warwick) 183rd[1] ... (2/1st Glouc. & Worc.) 184th[1] ... (2/1st S. Midld.)	2/5/R. War., 2/6/R. War., 2/7/R. War., 2/8/R. War. 2/4/Glouc., 2/6/Glouc., 2/7/Worc., 2/8/Worc. 2/5/Glouc., 2/4/O. & B.L.I., 2/1/Bucks., 2/4/R. Berks.	C Sqdn.,[4] 1/1/ Hants. Car-abnrs. 2/1/S. Midld.[5] Div. Cyclist Coy.	CCCV[6] .... (2/I S. Midld.) CCCVI[6] .... (2/II/ S. Midld.) CCCVII[6] ...... (2/III S. Midld.) CCCVIII[6] ...... (2/IV S. Midld.)	A (2/1/Glouc.), B (2/2/Glouc.), C (2/3/Glouc.). A (2/1/Worc.), B (2/2/Worc.), C (2/3/Worc.), D (H.) (2/4/War.). A (2/1/War.), B (2/2/War.), C (2/3/War.), D (H.) (2/5/War.). A, B, C, D (H.)	...	...	...	61st[7] (2/1/S. Midld.) D.A.C.	1/3/ S. Midld. 2/2/ S. Midld. 3/1/ S. Midld.	61st (2/1/ S. Midld.)	1/5/D. C.L.I.[17] (P.)	...	2/1/ S. Midld. 2/2/ S. Midld. 2/3/ S. Midld.	61st (2/1/ S. Midld.)	...	61st (2/1/ S. Midld.)[8]
1916 July (France)	182nd...... 183rd...... 184th......	2/5/R. War., 2/6/R. War., 2/7/R. War., 2/8/R. War.; 182nd Bde. M.G. Coy.;[9] 182nd T.M. Bty.[10] 2/4/Glouc., 2/6/Glouc., 2/7/Worc., 2/8/Worc.; 183rd Bde. M.G. Coy.;[9] 183rd T.M. Bty.[10] 2/5/Glouc., 2/4/O. & B.L.I., 2/1/Bucks., 2/4/R. Berks.; 184th Bde. M.G. Coy.;[9] 184th T.M. Bty.[10]	...	CCCV[11] .... CCCVI[12] ...... CCCVII[13] ...... CCCVIII[14] ...	A, B, C A, B, C; D (H.) A, B, C; D (H.) A, B, C; D (H.)	...	X.61[15] Y.61[15] Z.61[15]	V.61[16]	61st D.A.C.	1/3/ S. Midld. 2/2/ S. Midld. 3/1/ S. Midld.	61st	1/5/D. C.L.I.[17] (P.)	...	2/1/ S. Midld. 2/2/ S. Midld. 2/3/ S. Midld.	61st	...	61st
1917 July (France)	182nd...... 183rd...... 184th......	2/5/R. War.,[18] 2/6/R. War., 2/7/R. War., 2/8/R. War.;[19] 182nd M.G. Coy;[32] 182nd T.M. Bty. 2/4/Glouc.,[20] 2/6/Glouc.,[21] 2/7/Worc.,[22] 2/8/Worc.;[23] 183rd M.G. Coy.;[32] 183rd T.M. Bty. 2/5/Glouc., 2/4/O. & B.L.I., 2/1/Bucks.,[24] 2/4/R. Berks.;	...	CCCVI .... CCCVII	A, B, C; D (H.) A, B, C; D (H.)	...	X.61[25] Y.61[25] Z.61[25]	V.61[26]	61st D.A.C.	476th[27] (1/3/ S. Midld.) 478th[27] (2/2/ S. Midld.) 479th[27] (3/1/ S. Midld.)	61st	1/5/D. C.L.I. (P.)	...	2/1/ S. Midld. 2/2/ S. Midld. 2/3/ S. Midld.	61st	251st[28]	61st

1918 March (France)	182nd......	2/6/R. War., 2/7/R. War., 2/8/Worc.;[23] 182nd T.M. Bty.	...	CCCVI	A, B, C; D (H.)	...	X.61	...	61st D.A.C.	476th	61st	1/5/D.C.L.I. (P.)	No. 61 Bn., M.G.C.[32]	2/1/S. Midld.	61st	251st	61st
	183rd......	1/9/R. Scots,[29] 1/5/Gord. H.,[30] 1/8/A. & S. H.;[31] 183rd T.M. Bty.		CCCVII	A, B, C; D (H.)		Y.61			478th				2/2/S. Midld.			
	184th......	2/5/Glouc., 2/4/O. & B.L.I., 2/4/R. Berks.; 184th T.M. Bty.								479th				2/3/S. Midld.			
1918 June (France)	182nd......	2/6/R. War., 2/7/R. War., 2/8/Worc.; 182nd T.M. Bty.	...	CCCVI	A, B, C; D (H.)	...	X.61	...	61st D.A.C.	476th	61st	1/5/D.C.L.I. (P.)	No. 61 Bn., M.G.C.	2/1/S. Midld.	61st	251st	61st
	183rd......	9/(North'd. Hsrs.) N.F.,[33] 11/Suff.,[34] 1/E. Lanc.;[35] 183rd T.M. Bty.		CCCVII	A, B, C; D (H.)		Y.61			478th				2/2/S. Midld.			
	184th......	2/5/Glouc., 2/4/O. & B.L.I., 2/4/R. Berks.; 184th T.M. Bty.								479th				2/3/S. Midld.			

NOTES

1 2nd-line T.F. Divs. and 2nd-line T.F. Bdes. were designated by numbers in August, 1915. (Authy.—40/W.O./2609, A.G.1, of 10/8/15.)

2 Joined Div. on 26/10/15, and served with it until the Div. moved to Wiltshire in Febry., 1916.

3 Formed on 29/1/15.

4 Joined Div. at Ludgershall on 18/3/16, went to France with Div. on 25/5/16, and joined IX Corps Cav. Regt. on 16 and 17/6/16.

5 Went to France with the Div., and was transferred to the Reserve Army in June, 1916.

6 On 16 and 17/5/16 the designations of Brigades and Batteries were changed as shown, and the Bdes. were re-constituted. CCCVIII (H.) was broken up, and the 2 how. bties. became D(H.)/CCCVI and D(H.)/CCCVII. (2/5/War. (H.) which had been disbanded and distributed on 3/9/15, had been reformed on 9/12/15.) CCCVIII was then reformed with 3, 18-pdr. Bties. and 1, 4·5" How. Bty.

7 Formed in England and went to France with the Div. in May, 1916.

8 Consisted of 521, 522, 523, and 524 Cos., A.S.C.

9 The M.G. Cos. left Grantham on 16/6/16, disembkd. at le Havre on 17/6/16, and joined the Bdes. as follows: 182nd on 19/6/16; 183rd on 19 and 20/6/16; and 184th on 20/6/16.

10 The T.M. Bties. were formed in France: 182nd on 13/6/16; 183rd by 27/6/16; and 184th (formed on 8/6/16 as 184/1 and 184/2) on 27/6/16, when 184/1 and 2 had amalgamated.

11 On 16 and 17/9/16 the Bde. was broken up: 1/2A went to C/CCCVII and 1/2A to A/CCCVI; 1/2B went to C/CCCVI and 1/2B to B/CCCVI; and 1/2C went to A/CCCVII and 1/2C to B/CCCVII.

12 On 17/9/16 A was made up to 6 guns by 1 sec. of A/CCCV, and B and C were each made up by sections of B/CCCV. On 27/1/17 D (H.) was made up to 6 hows. by R. Sec. of D (H.)/CCCVIII.

13 On 16/9/16 A and B were each made up to 6 guns by sections of C/CCCV, and 1 section of A/CCCV made up C. On 27/1/17 D (H.) was made up to 6 hows. by L. Sec. of D (H.)/CCCVIII.

14 On 16/9/16 C was broken up: R. Sec. made up A/CCCVIII to 6 guns and L. Sec. made up B. On 20/10/16 520 (H.) Bty. joined and became C (H.). By 27/1/17 CCCVIII was broken up: A was transferred to CLV A.F.A. Bde.; B was transferred to CCCXI A.F.A. Bde. and became C; R. Sec. C (H.) joined D (H.)/CCCXV A.F.A. Bde.; L. Sec. C (H.) joined D (H.)/LXXXVI A.F.A. Bde.; R. Sec. D (H.) made up D (H.)/CCCVI to 6 hows., and L. Sec. D (H.) made up D (H.)/CCCVII.

15 X and Y were formed in the Div. in June, 1916; and Z was formed on 25/6/16.

16 V was formed in the Div. between 13-16/8/16.

17 Bn. joined the Div. on Salisbury Plain on 17/4/16, and went to France with the Div. on 21/5/16.

18 Bn. broken up and drafted between 15–20/2/18; part went to 2/6/R. War. and remdr. to 24/Entg. Bn.

19 Bn. broken up and drafted between 14-22/2/18; part went to 2/7/R. War. and remdr. to 25/Entg. Bn.

20 Bn. broken up on 20/2/18; part went to No. 55 Inf. Base Depot, and remdr. to 24/Entg. Bn.

21 Bn. broken up and drafted on 20/2/18; surplus joined 24/Entg. Bn.

22 Bn. broken up and drafted on 6/2/18; part went to 2/8/Worc. and remdr. to 24/Entg. Bn.

23 Bn. was transferred to 182nd Bde. on 11/2/18.

24 Bn. was broken up and drafted on 22/2/18; surplus joined 25/Entg. Bn.

25 On 7/2/18 the T.M.B.s were reorganized in 2, 6-mortar batteries; Z was broken up between X and Y, and personnel of Z joined X.

26 V H.T.M.B. left the Div. on 7/2/18.

27 The Fd. Cos. were numbered on 1/2/17.

28 The D.E.C. was formed by 7/7/17.

29 Joined on 6/2/18 from 154th Bde., 51st Div.; on 1/6/18 Bn. left to join 46th Bde., 15th Div.

30 Joined on 2/2/18 from 153rd Bde., 51st Div.; on 1/6/18 Bn. left to join 44th Bde., 15th Div.

31 Joined on 7/2/18 from 152nd Bde., 51st Div.; on 1/6/18 Bn. left to join 45th Bde., 15th Div.

32 Bn. formed on 1/3/18; it consisted on 182nd, 183rd, 184th, and 267th M.G. Cos. (267th M.G. Coy. disembkd. at le Havre on 14/1/18, and joined the Div. on 18/1/18.)

33 Joined on 26/5/18, from 52nd Bde., 17th Div.

34 Joined on 26/5/18, from 101st Bde., 34th Div.

35 Joined on 26/5/18, from 103rd Bde., 34th Div.

61st (2nd/SOUTH MIDLAND) DIVISION

FORMATION, BATTLES, AND ENGAGEMENTS

This 2nd-line (or reserve) Territorial Force division had no existence before the outbreak of the Great War.

The formation of reserve (or 2nd-line) T.F. units was authorized on the 31st August, 1914 (see Narrative, 57th Division); and in January, 1915, the 2nd/South Midland Division came into existence at Northampton, its temporary war-station.

Many of the 2nd-line units were formed in September and October, 1914, at their 1st-line headquarters. At this early period, however, the men all lived at home; and, as no arms and very little uniform or equipment were available, varying degrees of mufti had to be worn on parade. Despite these drawbacks some units soon attained full strength, but thereafter all the units were kept at varying strengths by having to find numerous drafts for their 1st-line units. The battalions were raised under the 8-company system, and further delay was occasioned to training when, early in 1915, the battalions reorganized in 4 companies each.

At first only route marches and elementary training could be undertaken. Some units started with practically no officers or non-commissioned officers and the early parades were a real difficulty. By October, 1914, uniforms began to arrive, but the men continued to live at home until the division concentrated at Northampton in January, 1915. On arrival at the temporary war-station the men were billeted and Japanese rifles were issued, but the only transport for each battalion consisted of 6 untrained mules; and in one battalion, failing a better mount, the C.O. used one of the mules as his charger.

In the divisional artillery both equipment and armament were equally behindhand. Until the end of 1915 the artillery was training with 90-mm. (French) guns and 5" howitzers. In January, 1916, however, each field-gun brigade was issued with 4, 15-pdr. guns for practice; and towards the end of 1915 and early in 1916 18-pdr. Q.F. and 4·5" howitzer equipments at last began to replace the obsolete weapons.

Whilst stationed at Northampton the division formed part of First Army, Central Force; but in April, 1915, after the departure of the 1st South Midland Division from Chelmsford to France, the 2nd/South Midland Division moved from Northampton to the Chelmsford area. The division then became part of Third Army, Central Force, and had a direct interest in the defence of the country. The C.R.E. had 14 miles of defences to look after, as well as supervising the training of his field companies.

After arrival in the Chelmsford area the machine-gun sections were formed in each battalion. The strength of the different battalions varied considerably from time to time: in April one battalion had 27 officers and 927 other ranks; but, in December, another battalion, after supplying several drafts, had shrunk to 508 all ranks. Actually, by the end of January, 1916, the latter battalion had increased in strength to 766. Whilst the 61st Division was in the Chelmsford area it was inspected, on the 6th August, 1915, by Field-Marshal Earl Kitchener.

In February, 1916, the division began to move to Salisbury Plain and the move was completed in March. Final intensive preparation for war now began. ·303" short M.L.E. rifles and 4 Lewis guns were issued to each battalion. The Lewis guns replaced the wooden dummy guns and antique Maxims which had hitherto been the armament of the machine-gun sections. On the 5th May the division, then concentrated in the Tidworth-Bulford area, was inspected on Bulford Fields by H.M. the King.

During April and May final leave was granted preparatory to proceeding overseas. The division was warned that it would move to France, and on the 21st May entrainment began. By the 25th entrainment had been completed, and by the 28th the division (less the divisional ammunition column) had concentrated in the area Merville–Gonnehem–Busnes–Thiennes (XI Corps rest area). On the 31st the D.A.C., which had been detained at le Havre, rejoined the division.

Throughout the remainder of the Great War the 61st Division served on the Western Front in France and Belgium and was engaged in the following operations:

1916

19 July ... ... **Attack at Fromelles** [XI Corps, First Army].

1917

11–15 January ... ... **Operations on the Ancre** [IV Corps, Fifth Army].
14 March–5 April ... **German Retreat to the Hindenburg Line** [IV Corps, Fourth Army].
18 Aug.–15 Sept. ... **BATTLES OF YPRES** [XIX Corps, until noon, 7/9; then V Corps, Fifth Army].
18 August ... ... **Battle of Langemarck** [XIX Corps, Fifth Army].

BATTLE OF CAMBRAI

1–3 December ... ... **German Counter-Attacks** [IV Corps until 2 p.m., 1/12; then III Corps, Third Army].

1918

FIRST BATTLES OF THE SOMME

21 and 22 March ... **Battle of St. Quentin** [XVIII Corps, Fifth Army].
24 and 25 March ... **Actions at the Somme Crossings** [Arty. and Bdes. under 20th and 30th Divs., XVIII Corps, Fifth Army. (Bdes. returned to 61st Div. at 10 p.m., 25/3)].

BATTLES OF THE LYS

11 April ... ... **Battle of Estaires** [XI Corps, First Army].
12–15 April ... ... **Battle of Hazebrouck** [XI Corps, First Army].
18 April ... ... **Battle of Béthune** [XI Corps, First Army].

THE ADVANCE TO VICTORY

THE FINAL ADVANCE IN PICARDY

24 and 25 October ... **Battle of the Selle** [XVII Corps, Third Army].
1 and 2 November ... **Battle of Valenciennes** [XVII Corps, Third Army].

The division was relieved in the front line during the night of the 2nd/3rd November. At Armistice the division was halted to the south of Valenciennes, along the Ecaillon. By the 17th November the division had withdrawn to the Cambrai area, and by the 28th it had moved back behind the Authie, to the west of Doullens. In this area educational and recreational training began.

During January, 1919, demobilization started, and for a time men were leaving the division at the rate of about one thousand a week. On the 31st January two battalions left the division for duty at the Base Ports; on the 2nd February they were followed by two more. On the 13th February the division came under the orders of the G.O.C., L. of C., and thereafter was chiefly employed on guards and working parties. On the 25th, divisional headquarters moved back to le Tréport and the units were employed in working at the ports or in the Abbeville area. On the 18th May trouble broke out between the B.W.I. and Chinese Labour Companies at Abancourt, and a battalion was sent to restore order. On the 27th June the division was informed that it need no longer be held in a state of mobility, and by the end of June several units were reduced to equipment guard. During the middle of July drafts were sent to Egypt and the Black Sea; nine battalions were nominated to go home as cadres, on completion of their present duties; and on the 30th July divisional headquarters closed. The 61st (2nd/South Midland) Division then passed out of existence.

62ND (2ND/WEST RIDING) DIVISION

G.O.C.

17 February, 1915 ... ... Major-General Sir J. K. TROTTER.
23 December, 1915 ... ... Major-General W. P. BRAITHWAITE.
28 August, 1918 ... ... Major-General Sir R. D. WHIGHAM.

G.S.O. 1.

20 Jan., 1915...Captain B. E. CROCKETT (acting).
26 Feb., 1915...Major H. F. LEA (acting).
17 April, 1915...Colonel H. S. SLOMAN.
18 Jan., 1916...Lt.-Col. Hon. A. G. A. HORE-RUTHVEN, V.C.
5 Sept., 1917...Lt.-Col. C. R. NEWMAN.
30 Sept., 1918...Lt.-Col. R. H. JOHNSON.
11 Oct., 1918...Lt.-Col. F. W. GOSSETT.

A.A. and Q.-M.-G.

23 Jan., 1915...Captain F. J. LANGDEN (acting).
13 April, 1915...Lt.-Col. J. D. A. T. LLOYD.
6 Feb., 1916...Captain F. J. LANGDEN (acting).
7 Feb., 1916...Lt.-Col. R. M. FOOT.
3 Nov., 1917...Major H. F. LEA (acting).
7 Nov., 1917...Lt.-Col. J. H. A. ANNESLEY.
29 Dec., 1917...Lt.-Col. H. F. LEA.

B.-G., R.A.

29 Jan., 1915...Colonel J. H. BALGUY.
13 Mar., 1916...Br.-Gen. A. T. ANDERSON.

C.R.E.

12 Jan., 1916...Lt.-Col. R. A. GILLAM.
22 Dec., 1917...Major E. J. WALTHEW (acting).
1 Jan., 1918...Lt.-Col. L. CHENEVIX-TRENCH.

185th BDE.

(2nd/1st West Riding)

11 Feb., '15...Col. H. W. N. GUINNESS.
4 Jan., '16...Br.-Gen. V. W. DE FALBE (invalided, 21/8/17).
21 Aug., '17...Br.-Gen. VISCOUNT HAMPDEN.

186th BDE.

(2nd/2nd West Riding)

2 Mar., '15...Col. H. G. MAINWARING.
9 Dec., '15...Br.-Gen. F. F. HILL.
10 Nov., '17...Br.-Gen. R. B. BRADFORD, V.C. (killed 30/11/17).
30 Nov., '17...Lt.-Col. H. E. P. NASH (acting).
3 Dec., '17...Br.-Gen. J. L. G. BURNETT.

187th BDE.

(2nd/3rd West Riding)

4 Mar., '15...Col. H. B. LASSETER.
22 May, '16...Br.-Gen. R. O'B. TAYLOR (sick, 8/2/18).
8 Feb., '18...Lt.-Col. B. J. BARTON (acting).
28 Mar., '18...Lt.-Col. W. K. JAMES (acting).
3 April, '18...Br.-Gen. A. J. REDDIE.

GENERAL NOTES

INFANTRY :—The 12 Battalions were raised as follows :

2/5/West Yorkshire	... ... at	York	on 28/9/14 ;
2/6/West Yorkshire	... ... ,,	Bradford ...	,, 12/9/14 ;
2/7/West Yorkshire	... ... ,,	Leeds	,, 15/9/14 ;
2/8/West Yorkshire	... ... ,,	Leeds	,, 14/9/14 ;
2/4/Duke of Wellington's	... ... ,,	Halifax	,, 28/9/14 ;
2/5/Duke of Wellington's	... ... ,,	Huddersfield ...	,, 9/10/14 ;
2/6/Duke of Wellington's	... ... ,,	Skipton	,, 17/9/14 ;
2/7/Duke of Wellington's	... ... ,,	Milnsbridge ...	,, 14/10/14 ;
2/4/King's Own Yorkshire Light Infantry	... ,,	Wakefield ...	,, 30/9/14 ;
2/5/King's Own Yorkshire Light Infantry	... ,,	Doncaster ...	,, 16/9/14 ;
2/4/York and Lancaster	... ... ,,	Sheffield ...	,, 21/9/14 ;
2/5/York and Lancaster	... ... ,,	Rotherham ...	,, 3/10/14.

The following also served with the 62nd Division :—

ARTILLERY :—**2/1/West Riding Heavy Battery, R.G.A., T.F.,** served with the division in England, but did not accompany the division to France. The Heavy Battery was then attached to the Tyne Garrison until the end of the War. It was stationed at Blyth and later at Whitburn.

59th Division Artillery (CCXCV and CCXCVI) were attached to 62nd Div. from 15–24/4/18, and from 17/5–19/6/18.

ENGINEERS :—**2/1/W. Riding Field Coy.,** disembarked at le Havre on 21/6/15, and on 23/6/15 the Fd. Coy. joined 49th (West Riding) Division. The Fd. Coy. served for the remainder of the War, on the Western Front, with the 49th Division. (The Fd. Coy. was numbered 458th.)

2/2/W. Riding Field Coy., joined the 6th Division in France on 13/10/15. The Fd. Coy. served for the remainder of the War, on the Western Front, with the 6th Division. (The Field Coy. was numbered 459th.)

OTHER UNIT :—**62nd Sanitary Section,** went to France with the division in January, 1917. The Sanitary Section left the division on 8/4/17 and was transferred to a First Army Sanitary Area.

On 3/2/18 the reorganization of the 62nd Division on a 9-battalion basis was completed ; and on 1/3/18 the pioneer battalion was reorganized on a 3-company basis.

62nd[1] (2nd/WEST RIDING) DIVISION

ORDER OF BATTLE, 1915-1918

Dates	INFANTRY		Mounted Troops	ARTILLERY						Engineers	Signal Service	Pioneers	M.G. Units	Field Ambulances	Mobile Vety. Secn.	Divnl. Emplnt. Coy.	Divnl. Train
	Brigades	Battalions and attached Units		Field Artillery			Trench Mortar Bties.		Divnl. Ammn. Coln.	Field Cos.	Divnl. Signal Coy.						
				Brigades	Batteries	Bde. Ammn. Colns.	Medium	Heavy									
1915 August (England)	185th[1] ... (2/1st W. Riding) 186th[1] ... (2/2nd W. Riding) 187th[1] ... (2/3rd W. Riding)	2/5/W. York., 2/6/W. York., 2/7/W. York., 2/8/W. York. 2/4/Duke's, 2/5/Duke's, 2/6/Duke's, 2/7/Duke's. 2/4/K.O.Y.L.I., 2/5/K.O.Y.L.I., 2/4/Y. & L., 2/5/Y. & L.	62nd[2] (2/1st W. Rid.) Div. Cyclist Coy.	2/I W. Riding[3] 2/II W. Riding[3] 2/III W. Riding[3] 2/IV W. Riding[3] (H.)	2/1/W. Rid., 2/2/W. Rid., 2/3/W. Rid. 2/4/W. Rid., 2/5/W. Rid., 2/6/W. Rid. 2/7/W. Rid., 2/8/W. Rid., 2/9/W. Rid. 2/10/W. Rid. (H.), 2/11/W. Rid. (H.)	2/I W. Riding 2/II W. Riding 2/III W. Riding 2/IV W. Riding (H.)	...	...	...	2/1/W. Riding[4] 2/2/W. Riding[5] 3/1/W. Riding	62nd (2/1/ W. Rid.)	...	...	2/1/ W. Rid. 2/2/ W. Rid. 2/3/ W. Rid.	...	...	62nd[6] (2/1/ W. Rid.)
1916 November (England)	185th ...... 186th 187th	2/5/W. York., 2/6/W. York., 2/7/W. York., 2/8/W. York. 2/4/Duke's, 2/5/Duke's, 2/6/Duke's, 2/7/Duke's. 2/4/K.O.Y.L.I., 2/5/K.O.Y.L.I., 2/4/Y. & L., 2/5/Y. & L.	Hd. Qrs., M.G. Sec. & B Sqdn.,[7] 2/1/ North'd. Hsrs. 62nd Div.[8] Cyclist Coy.	CCCX[3]; [9] ...... (2/1/ W. Rid.) CCCXI[3]; [10] ... (2/II W. Rid.) CCCXII[3]; [11] ... (2/III W. Rid.)	A (2/1/W. Rid.), B (2/2/W. Rid.), C (2/3/W. Rid.), D (H.) A (2/4/W. Rid.), B (2/5/W. Rid.), C (2/6/W. Rid.), D (H.) A (2/7/W. Rid.), B (2/8/W. Rid.), C (2/9/W. Rid.), D (H.)	...[12]	...	...	62nd D.A.C.[12]	1/3/W. Riding 2/3/W. Riding 3/1/W. Riding	62nd	...	...	2/1/ W. Rid. 2/2/ W. Rid. 2/3/ W. Rid.	2/1/ W. Rid.	...	62nd
1917 June (France)	185th ...... 186th 187th	2/5/W. York., 2/6/W. York.,[13] 2/7/W. York., 2/8/W. York.;[14] 212th M.G. Coy.;[15]; [31] 185th T.M. Bty.[16] 2/4/Duke's, 2/5/Duke's,[17] 2/6/Duke's,[18] 2/7/Duke's; 213th M.G. Coy.;[15]; [31] 186th T.M. Bty.[16] 2/4/K.O.Y.L.I., 2/5/K.O.Y.L.I.,[19] 2/4/Y. & L., 2/5/Y. & L.;[20] 208th M.G. Coy.;[15]; [31] 187th T.M. Bty.[16]	...	CCCX[9] .... CCCXII[11]	A, B, C; D (H.) A, B, C; D (H.)	...	X.62[21] Y.62[21] Z.62[21]	V.62[21]	62nd D.A.C.[12]	457th[22] (1/3/ W. Rid.) 460th[22] (2/3/ W. Rid.) 461st[22] (3/1/ W. Rid.)	62nd	...	201st[23] M.G. Coy.	2/1/ W. Rid. 2/2/ W. Rid. 2/3/ W. Rid.	2/1/ W. Rid.	252nd[24]	62nd
1918 March (France)	185th ...... 186th 187th	2/5/W. York.,[25] 2/7/W. York.,[26] 8/W. York.;[14] 185th T.M. Bty. 2/4/Duke's, 5/Duke's,[17] 2/7/Duke's;[27] 186th T.M. Bty. 2/4/K.O.Y.L.I., 5/K.O.Y.L.I.,[19] 2/4/Y. & L.; 187th T.M. Bty.	...	CCCX............ CCCXII.........	A, B, C; D (H.) A, B, C; D (H.)	...	X.62[28] Y.62[28]	...[29]	62nd D.A.C.	457th 460th 461st	62nd	1/9/ D.L.I.[30] (P.)	No. 62 Bn., M.G.C.[31]	2/1/ W. Rid. 2/2/ W. Rid. 2/3/ W. Rid.	2/1/ W. Rid.	252nd	62nd
1918 August (France)	185th 186th	1/5/Devon.,[32] 8/W. York., 2/20/Lond.;[33] 185th T.M. Bty. 2/4/Duke's, 5/Duke's, 2/4/ Hants.;[34] 186th T.M. Bty.	...	CCCX............ CCCXII.........	A, B, C; D (H.) A, B, C; D (H.)	...	X.62 Y.62	...	62nd D.A.C.	457th 460th 461st	62nd	1/9/ D.L.I. (P.)	No. 62 Bn., M.G.C.	2/1/ W. Rid. 2/2/ W. Rid. 2/3/	2/1/ W. Rid.	252nd	62nd

NOTES

1 The Division and the Inf. Bdes. were designated by numbers between 17-24/8/15. (Authy.—40/W.O./2609, A.G. 1, of 10/8/15.)

2 The Cyclist Coy. was formed on 23/3/15.

3 In May, 1916, the designations of the Brigades and Batteries were changed as shown, and the Bdes. were re-constituted: 2/IV/W. Riding (H.) Bde. was broken up, and each of the other Bdes. had a howitzer battery added to it.

4 2/1/W. Rid. Fd. Coy. joined 49th Div. in France on 23/6/15; and in 1917 the Fd. Coy. was numbered 458th.

5 2/2/W. Rid. Fd. Coy. joined 6th Div. in France on 13/10/15; and in 1917 the Fd. Coy. was numbered 459th.

6 525, 526, 527, and 528 Cos., A.S.C.

7 Hd. Qrs., M.G. Sec., and B Sqdn., served with the division from 18/4/16 until the division embkd. for France. The Regt. went to France in March, 1917, and formed XIX Corps Cav. Regt. on 26/3/17.

8 Went to France with the Division, and on 19/1/17 the Cyclist Coy. was posted to XVIII Corps Cyclist Bn.

9 Bde. was re-armed with 18-pdrs. and 4.5" hows. (4 per battery) at the end of 1915. 18-pdr. batteries were made up to 6, 18-pdrs., each before embkn.; and, on 19/1/17, R. Sec. of D (H.)/CCCXI joined and made up D (H.)/CCCX to 6 hows.

10 Bde. was re-armed with 18-pdrs. and 4.5" hows. (4 per battery) at the end of 1915. 18-pdr. batteries were made up to 6, 18-pdrs., each before embkn.; and C (H.) joined (4, 4.5" hows.). On 18/1/17, CCCXI became an A.F.A. Bde.; on 19/1/17 R. Sec. D (H.) made up D/CCCX to 6 hows., and on 18/1/17 L. Sec. D (H.) made up D/CCCXII. On 18/1/17 C (H.)/CCCXI became D (H.)/CCCXI, and on 25/1/17 D (H.) was made up to 6 hows. by 1/2 517 (H.) from 31st Div. Arty.; and on 27/1/17 B/CCCVIII joined from 61st Div. Arty. and became C/CCCXI. On 19/1/17 a proportion of the D.A.C. joined CCCXI A.F.A. Bde.

11 Bde. was re-armed with 18-pdrs. and 4.5" hows. (4 per battery) at the end of 1915. 18-pdr. batteries were made up to 6, 18-pdrs., each before embkn.; and, on 18/1/17, L. Sec. of D (H.)/CCCXI joined and made up D (H.)/CCCXII to 6 hows.

12 Before leaving England the B.A.C.s were abolished and the D.A.C. was reorganized. On 19/1/17 A Echelon was re-arranged in 2 enlarged sections, and a proportion of B Echelon was handed over to CCCXI A.F.A. Bde. (note 10). On 4-13/4/17 the D.A.C. was again reorganized owing to the shortage of horses, all horses from B Echelon were transferred to batteries, B Echelon wagons were parked, and loads were to be carried by M.T. A further reorganization took place on 29/8/17; the D.A.C. then consisted of 2 sections carrying gun ammunition and 1 section carrying S.A.A. and grenades; a reduction of 155 horses was effected.

13 Bn. was broken up and drafted on 31/1/18.

14 Bn. amalgamated with 1/8/W. York. (from 146th Bde., 49th Div.) and became 8/W. York. on 1/2/18.

15 212th M.G. Coy. arrived le Havre on 28/2/17, and joined 185th Bde. on 9/3/17; 213th M.G. Coy. arrived le Havre on 2/3/17, and joined 186th Bde. on 9/3/17; 208th M.G. Coy. arrived le Havre on 26 and 27/2/17, and joined 187th Bde. on 4/3/17.

16 The Bde. T.M. Bties. went to France with the Bdes. in Jany., 1917.

17 Bn. amalgamated on 31/1 and 1/2/18 with 1/5/Duke's (from 147th Bde., 49th Div.) and became 5/Duke's.

18 Bn. was broken up on 31/1/18, and drafted to 5/, 2/4, and 2/7 Duke's.

19 Bn. amalgamated on 2/2/18 with 1/5/K.O.Y.L.I. (from 148th Bde., 49th Div.) and became 5/K.O.Y.L.I.

20 Bn was broken up on 3/2/18, and drafted to 1/4, 1/5, and 2/4/ Y. & L.

21 Medium and Heavy T.M. Bties. went to France with the Div. in Jany., 1917.

22 The Fd. Cos. were numbered: 457th on 31/1/17; and 460th and 461st on 1/2/17.

23 Formed at Grantham on 25/10/16; served with 177th Bde., 59th Div., at Fovant, from 10/2-17/2/17; Coy. disembkd. at le Havre on 28/3/17, and joined 62nd Div. on 30/3/17.

24 Formed by 14/7/17.

25 Bn. was broken up and drafted between 13-18/8/18.

26 Bn. was broken up between 16-19/6/18, and drafted to 8/W. York., 2/5/W. York., Base, and Training Staff.

27 Bn. was broken up on 17 and 18/6/18, and drafted to 5/ and 2/4/Duke's, and Base.

28 Med. T.M. Bties. were reorganized on 11/2/18, and Z was absorbed in X and Y.

29 V H.T.M.B was broken up on 11/2/18.

30 Bn. was transferred, as Pioneers, from 151st Bde., 50th Div., and joined 62nd Div. on 12/2/18.

31 Bn. was formed on 9/3/18; it consisted of 201st, 208th, 212th, and 213th M.G. Cos.

32 Bn. went to India with 43rd (Wessex) Div. on 9/10/14; transferred to 232nd Bde. and joined in Palestine on 14/4/17; Bde. joined 75th Div. (on formation) on 20/8/17. Bn. left 75th Div. on 4/5/18, disembkd. Marseille on 1/6/18, and joined 185th Bde. on 6/6/18.

33 Bn. went to France with 180th Bde., 60th Div., in June, 1916. Bn. left 60th Div. in Palestine on 27/5/18, disembkd. at Taranto 30/6-8/7/18, attached 198th Bde., 66th Div., from 19/7-9/8/18, and joined 185th Bde. on 9/8/18.

34 Bn. went to India with 45th (2/Wessex) Div. on 12/12/14; transferred to 233rd Bde. and joined in Palestine on 25/5/17; Bde. joined 75th Div. (on formation) 18/8/17. Bn. left 75th Div. on 2/5/18, disembkd. at Marseille on 1/6/18, joined 62nd Div. on 6/6/18, and joined 186th Bde. on 14/6/18.

62ND (2ND/WEST RIDING) DIVISION

FORMATION, BATTLES, AND ENGAGEMENTS

This 2nd-line (or reserve) Territorial Force division had no existence before the outbreak of the Great War.

The formation of reserve (or 2nd-line) T.F. units was authorized on the 31st August, 1914 (see Narrative, 57th Division). The twelve reserve (or 2nd-line) West Riding battalions came into existence between the 12th September and the middle of October (see General Notes); but the headquarters of the 2nd/West Riding Division only began to assemble at Doncaster early in 1915. In March divisional headquarters moved to Matlock Bath, and brigades and units gradually left their regimental stations and moved into billets at Matlock, Derby, Belper, Nottingham, and Bakewell.

In raising and training the units the usual difficulties were encountered. Nevertheless by the end of November, 1914, battalions were able to furnish drafts to their first-line formations. Although the units were first of all designated 'home-service' yet this was a misnomer, as recruits were only accepted for general service. Later on the designation was changed to 'reserve,' and in February, 1915, it was altered to '2nd-line'. The battalions, as well as supplying drafts, received from their 1st-line battalions any home-service men and all those who were medically unfit for the field. On the formation of 3rd-line units, these units undertook the provision of all necessary drafts; and, in May, 1915, all home-service officers and men, and those who were medically unfit for the field, were transferred to provisional battalions for home service and for coast defence.

Up to the end of 1914 clothing and equipment arrived slowly. In some cases this delay in delivery did prejudice recruiting; but, despite this, 2/6/West Yorkshire recruited 1,500 men by November, 1914. Arms—drill-pattern rifles and charger-loading Lee-Enfields—were first received in April. This first issue, however, was withdrawn in the following month, and it was replaced by Japanese rifles and bayonets, with 200 rounds of ammunition for each rifle; but, until the 1914-pattern equipment was received, the men had to carry the ammunition in their coat pockets. In April, 1915, horses began to reach the battalions. In January, 1916, ·303″ short M.L.E. Mk.III rifles became available, and by March each battalion also received 4 Lewis guns.

The training of the divisional artillery for war was carried on under great difficulties. After the 1st-line division left for France in April, 1915, the 2nd-line artillery received some French guns (90-mm.), with 20 rounds of ammunition for each gun. The ammunition, however, had lain in store for many years, the sights were graduated in such a way that they were very little use, and no one could interpret the markings on the fuzes. At this time the division was under orders to entrain at the shortest notice to assist in repelling any raid on the east coast, and trains, to move the troops were held in readiness day and night; but this antiquated armament was all that was available. It was only at the beginning of 1916 that the 62nd Division artillery received 18-pdr. and 4·5″ howitzer equipments.

In the meantime (in May, 1915) the division moved to Thoresby Park, Babworth Park, Welbeck Park, Southwell, and Beverley. It remained here until mid-October, and then it concentrated around Retford until November. The division then moved to Newcastle, and during December it dug an entrenched line of defence. Early in 1916 the division moved to Salisbury Plain. At last the end of the long period of training seemed to be in sight, but all ranks were destined to be disappointed. There was a definite shortage of men available in the West Riding of Yorkshire, which had to maintain at war establishment eight regular battalions and four special reserve battalions, as well as the 49th Division and the 62nd Division. Orders were therefore issued to the 62nd Division that on the arrival of each draft in the division a corresponding number of men were to be sent to 3rd-line units for drafting to 1st-line battalions overseas. A divisional order to this effect was issued on the 14th March, 1916. This arrangement considerably delayed the despatch of the 62nd Division to a theatre of war.

In June, 1916, the division moved to Lowestoft, Wangford, Flixton Park, Bungay, and Somerleytown; and, on the 26th July, while it was in Norfolk, the division was inspected by H.M. the King. In October, 1916, the division moved inland to Bedford, Wellingborough, and Northampton; and on the 23rd December orders were received that the division was to be ready to embark for France on the 5th January, 1917.

The divisional ammunition column left Avonmouth (for Rouen) on the 30th December, 1916; and entrainment for the remainder of the division began on the 5th January, 1917. The division crossed from Southampton to le Havre. By the 18th the last units of the division had arrived, and the concentration of the division was completed between the Canche and Authie, in the Third Army area.*

Throughout the remainder of the Great War the 62nd Division served on the Western Front in France and Belgium and was engaged in the following operations :—

1917

15 Feb.–13 Mar. ... ... **Operations on the Ancre** [V Corps, Fifth Army].
14 Mar.–19 Mar. ... ... **German Retreat to the Hindenburg Line** (V Corps, Fifth Army].
11 April ... ... **First attack on Bullecourt** [V Corps, Fifth Army].
15 April ... ... **German Attack on Lagnicourt** (186th Bde.), [V Corps, Fifth Army].
3–17 May ... ... **Battle of Bullecourt** [V Corps, Fifth Army].
20–28 May ... ... **Actions on the Hindenburg Line** [V Corps, Fifth Army].

BATTLE OF CAMBRAI

20 and 21 Nov. ... ... **The Tank Attack** [IV Corps, Third Army].
27 and 28 Nov. ... ... **Capture of Bourlon Wood** [IV Corps, Third Army].

1918

FIRST BATTLES OF THE SOMME

25 March ... ... **Battle of Bapaume** [IV Corps, Third Army].
28 March ... ... **Battle of Arras** [IV Corps, Third Army].

THE ADVANCE TO VICTORY

BATTLES OF THE MARNE

20–30 July ... ... **Battle of Tardenois** [XXII Corps, Fifth (Fr.) Army].

SECOND BATTLE OF ARRAS

26–30 August ... ... **Battle of the Scarpe** [VI Corps,** Third Army].
2 September ... ... **Battle of the Drocourt–Quéant Line** [VI Corps, Third Army].

BATTLES OF THE HINDENBURG LINE

12 September ... ... **Battle of Havrincourt** [VI Corps, Third Army].
27–30 September ... **Battle of the Canal du Nord** [VI Corps, Third Army].

THE FINAL ADVANCE IN PICARDY

17–23 October ... ... **Battle of the Selle** [VI Corps, Third Army].
20 October ... ... **Capture of Solesmes.**
4 November ... ... **Battle of the Sambre** [VI Corps, Third Army].

After the Battle of the Sambre, the division remained in the front line and fought its way forward towards Maubeuge, advancing past Mecouignies and Neuf Mesnil (8th Nov.). On the 9th the southern outskirts of Maubeuge were entered, the Sambre was crossed, Louvroil and St. Lazare were captured, and the line of the Maubeuge–Avesnes road was reached. On the 11th November an outpost line was established along the R. Solre with picquets to the east of the river, but no signs of the enemy were encountered by cyclist patrols who pushed on as far as Cerfontaine and Recquignies (3 miles east of Maubeuge). At 11 a.m. the Armistice came into force and hostilities ceased.

On Armistice Day the 62nd Division was informed that it had been selected to accompany the Army which was to move into Germany and occupy the Rhine bridgeheads. On the 13th November preliminary instructions were issued and, on the 18th, the

* Except 2/6/Duke's which was detained in England by an outbreak of scarlet fever. This battalion rejoined 62nd Division in France on the 8th and 9th February, 1917.

**During the Advance to Victory the composition of VI Corps was: Guards, 2nd, 3rd, and 62nd Divisions.

advance began. On the 28th November the division was transferred from VI Corps to IX Corps. The division halted from the 1st to the 9th December between Ciney and Rochefort (to the west of Marche). On the 10th the advance was resumed, on the 15th the German frontier was crossed, and on Christmas Day the last units of the division reached the allotted area around Schleiden. The 62nd Division was the only division of the Territorial Force to enter Germany.

On the 17th February, 1919, orders were received that the infantry battalions would be replaced by Highland battalions, and on the 21st February the Highland battalions began to arrive. On the 12th March the 62nd Division was transferred from IX Corps to VI Corps, and on the 15th March the division became the Highland Division in Second Army, Army of Occupation. With this change the war story of the 62nd (2nd/West Riding) Division came to an end.

63RD (2ND/NORTHUMBRIAN) DIVISION

G.O.C.

17 February, 1915 ... ... Br.-Gen. A. C. BECHER.
3 February, 1916 –21 July, 1916 ... ... Major-General G. T. FORESTIER-WALKER.

G.S.O. 1.

13 Jan., 1915...Lt.-Col. W. H. F. BASEVI.
20 Feb., 1915...Capt. H. C. W. H. WORTHAM (acting).
9 Mar., 1915...Capt. S. C. G. F. ASTELL (acting).
19 April, 1915 –21 July, 1916 Lt.-Col. A. F. MOCKLER-FERRYMAN.

A.-A. and Q.-M.-G.

8 Feb., 1915...Capt. H. C. W. H. WORTHAM (acting).
29 April, 1915...Lt.-Col. F. R. P. KANE.
4 May, 1916 –21 July, 1916 Lt.-Col. A. G. P. MCNALTY.

B.-G., R.A.

16 Feb., 1915...Colonel E. GUNNER.
23 Oct., 1915...Lt.-Col. H. B. ALLEN (acting).
7 Nov., 1915...Colonel E. GUNNER.
16 Jan., 1916...Colonel A. J. ABDY.
16 April, 1916...Br.-Gen. R. W. FULLER.
10 May, 1916...Br.-Gen. E. J. GRANET.

---

20 June, 1916...Br.-Gen. C. H. DE ROUGEMONT [Transferred, with 63rd Div. Arty., to R.N. Division.]

C.R.E.

18 Nov., 1915...Lt.-Col. J. E. MCPHERSON.

188th BDE.

(2nd/1st Northumberland)

5 Jan., '15...Colonel F. W. ROBINSON.
27 June, '15...Colonel O. J. H. BALL.
15 Mar., '16 –14 Nov., '16 } Br.-Gen. R. BAYARD.

189th BDE.

(2nd/1st York and Durham)

5 Jan., '15...Colonel R. L. A. PENNINGTON.
18 Mar., '16...Br.-Gen. P. J. MILES.
14 Oct., '16 –11 Nov., '16 } Br.-Gen. E. T. LE MARCHANT (of 190th Bde.).

190th BDE.

(2nd/1st Durham Light Infantry)

18 Jan., '15...Colonel E. T. LE MARCHANT.
1 Sept., '16 –2 Dec., '16 } Br.-Gen. E. T. LE MARCHANT.

GENERAL NOTES

The following Units of the 63rd Division served in the field with other formations :—

ENGINEERS :—2/1/Northumbrian Field Coy., went to France and joined the 28th Division on 10/7/15. For the remainder of the Great War the Fd. Coy. served in France and Macedonia with the 28th Division. In 1917 the Fd. Coy. was numbered **449th.** The Fd. Coy. remained with the 28th Division after the Armistice with Bulgaria (30/9/18), and in November, 1918, it moved to the Dardanelles, with the Division. During 1919 the Fd. Coy. remained in Turkey with the 28th Division.

MEDICAL :—2/2/Northumbrian Field Ambce., joined 50th (Northumbrian) Division in England and went to France with the 50th Division, disembarking at le Havre on 20/4/15. For the remainder of the Great War the Field Ambulance served with the 50th Division on the Western Front.

The following formations and units also served with, or were attached to, the 63rd Division :—

1/1/Scottish Horse Mounted Brigade (Br.-Gen. Marquis of Tullibardine), until August, 1915 ;

2/1/Welsh Border Mounted Brigade (Br.-Gen. M. D. Little), until April, 1916 ;

1/1/East Riding of Yorkshire Yeomanry, until 21/5/15 ;

2/1/North Riding (Northumbrian) Hy. Bty., R.G.A., until 9/11/15 ; this Heavy Battery was thereafter part of the Tyne Garrison until it disappeared between 28/11–30/12/18 ;

63rd (2/1/Northumbrian) Sanitary Section, from formation until disbandment ; and

63rd (2/1/Northumbrian) Motor Ambulance Workshop, until it was absorbed by the Train in 1916.

In January, 1915, the battalions adopted the 4-company organization.

63RD[1] (2ND/NORTHUMBRIAN) DIVISION ORDER OF BATTLE, 1915-1916

Dates	INFANTRY		Mounted Troops	ARTILLERY						Engineers	Signal Service	Pioneers	M.G. Units	Field Ambulances	Mobile Vety. Secn.	Divnl. Emplnt. Coy.	Divnl. Train
	Brigades	Battalions and attached Units		Field Artillery			Trench Mortar Bties.		Divnl. Ammn. Coln.	Field Cos.	Divnl. Signal Coy.						
				Brigades	Batteries	Bde. Ammn. Colns.	Medium	Heavy									
1915 August (England)	188th[1]; [2] (2nd/1st/ North'd.) 189th[1]; [7] (2nd/1st/ Y. & D.) 190th[1]; [12] (2nd/1st/ D.L.I.)	2/4/N.F.,[3] 2/5/N.F.,[4] 2/6/N.F.,[5] 2/7/N.F.[6] 2/4/E. York.,[8] 2/4/Gr. How.,[9] 2/5/Gr. How.,[10] 2/5/D.L.I.[11] 2/6/D.L.I.,[13] 2/7/D.L.I.,[14] 2/8/D.L.I.,[15] 2/9/D.L.I.[16]	63rd (2nd/1st/ N'thbn.) Div. Cyclist Coy.[17]	2nd/I North'bn. 2nd/II North'bn. 2nd III North'bn. 2nd/IV North'bn. (H.)	2/1/North'd., 2/2/North'd., 2/3/North'd. 2/1/E. Riding, 2/2/E. Riding, 2/3/E. Riding. 2/1/Durham, 2/2/Durham, 2/3/Durham. 2/4/Durham (H.), 2/5/Durham (H.)	2nd/I North'bn. 2nd/II North'bn. 2nd/III North'bn. 2nd/IV North'bn (H.)	...	...	...	2/2/ North'bn. 3/1/ North'bn.	63rd (2nd/1/ N'thbn.)	...	...	2/1/ North'bn 3/2/ North'bn 2/3/ North'bn	2/1/18 North'bn	...	63rd[19] (2nd/1/ N'thbn.)
1916 January (England)	188th...... 189th...... 190th......	2/4/N.F., 2/5/N.F., 2/6/N.F., 2/7/N.F. 2/4/E. York., 2/4/Gr. How., 2/5/Gr. How., 2/5/D.L.I. 2/6/D.L.I., 2/7/D.L.I., 2/8/D.L.I., 2/9/D.L.I.	63rd Div. Cyclist Coy.	2nd/I North'bn. 2nd/II North'bn. 2nd/III North'bn. 2nd/IV North'bn. (H.)	2/1/North'd., 2/2/North'd., 2/3/North'd. 2/1/E. Riding, 2/2/E. Riding, 2/3/E. Riding. 2/1/Durham, 2/2/Durham, 2/3/Durham. 2/4/Durham (H.), 2/5/Durham (H.)	2nd/I North'bn. 2nd/II North'bn. 2nd/III North'bn. 2nd/IV North'bn.(H.)	...	...	63rd D.A.C. (2nd/1/ N'thbn.)	1/3/ North'bn. 2/2/ North'bn. 3/1/ North'bn.	63rd	...	...	2/1/ North'bn 3/2/ North'bn 2/3/ North'bn	...	...	63rd
1916 June (England)	188th[20] ... 189th[24] ... 190th[28] ...	2/4/N.F.,[21] 2/5/N.F.,[21] 2/6/N.F.,[22] 2/7/N.F.[23] 2/4/E. York.,[25] 2/4/Gr. How.,[26] 2/5/Gr. How.,[26] 2/5/D.L.I.[27] 2/6/D.L.I.,[29] 2/7/D.L.I.,[30] 2/8/D.L.I.,[29] 2/9/D.L.I.[31]	63rd Div. Cyclist Coy.	CCCXV[32]; [33] (2/I North'bn.) CCCXVI[32]; [34] (2/II North'bn.) CCCXVII[32]; [35] (2/III North'bn.) CCCXVIII[32]; [36] (2/IV North'bn.)	A, B, C; D (H.) A, B, C; D (H.) A, B, C A, B, C	CCCXV B.A.C. CCCXVI B.A.C. CCCXVII B.A.C. CCCXVIII B.A.C.	...	...	63rd D.A.C.[37]	1/3/ North'bn[38] 2/2/ North'bn[39] 3/1/ North'bn[40]	63rd	...	...	2/1/[41] North'bn 3/2/ North'bn 2/3/[42] North'bn	...	...	63rd[43]

NOTES

1 On the 16th Aug., 1915, the Northumbrian 2nd-line Division and Infantry Brigades were given numbers. (Authy., 40/W.O./2609, A.G.I, of 10/8/15.)

2 The Bde. was formed in Jany., 1915, at Newcastle.

3 Bn. was formed at Blyth on 23/11/14.

4 Bn. was formed at Blyth on 22/11/14.

5 Bn. was formed at Newcastle on 28/12/14.

6 Bn. was formed at Alnwick on 26/9/14.

7 The Bde. was formed on 5/1/15 at Malton.

8 Bn. was formed at Hull in Septr., 1914.

9 Bn. was formed at Northallerton on 4/9/14.

10 Bn. was formed at Scarborough in Septr., 1914.

11 Bn. was formed at Stockton in Septr., 1914.

12 The Bde. was formed at Durham on 18/1/15.

13 Bn. was formed at Ravensworth on 26/9/14.

14 Bn. was formed at Sunderland on 16/9/14.

15 Bn. was formed at Durham in Septr., 1914.

16 Bn. was formed at Ravensworth Park (near Gateshead) on 11/9/14.

17 Coy. formed at Whitburn Hall (near Sunderland) between 13/2-19/4/15 (strength 8 offrs. and 210 o.r.).

18 On 11/8/15 the Mobile Vety. Sec. ceased to form part of the Division.

19 The Train was formed in November, 1914; and it consisted of 529, 530, 531, and 532 Cos., A.S.C.

20 The Bde. was broken up on 14/11/16 at York.

21 2/4/ and 2/5N.F. joined 217th Bde., 72nd Div., in Nov., 1916.

22 Bn. joined 217th Bde., 72nd Div., at Clevedon (Somerset) on 27/11/16.

23 Bn. embkd. on 20/1/17 for service with E.E.F. as a Garr. Bn.; it served in the Delta.

24 The Bde. was broken up on 11/11/16 at Catterick.

25 Bn. left Bde. on 4/11/16 and arrived in Bermuda by 1/12/16.

26 2/4/ and 2/5/ Gr. How. left Bde. on 9/11/16, and joined 220th Bde., 73rd Div., at Blackpool. (2/4/Gr. How. was disbanded on 21/12/17.)

27 Bn. left Bde. on 31/10/16 and went out to Salonika as a Garr. Bn.; it arrived on 15/11/16, joined XVI Corps Troops, and on 1/3/17 Bn. joined 228th Inf. Bde. (served with 28th Div.).

28 The Bde. was broken up on 4/12/16 at Catterick.

29 2/6/ and 2/8/D.L.I. left Bde. on 29/11/16 and joined 214th Bde., 71st Div., at Andover and Basingstoke.

30 Bn. left Bde. on 29/11/16 and joined 214th Bde., 71st Div., at Andover. On 7/10/18 Bn. went to N. Russia as a Garr. Bn. and joined the Archangel Force on 24/10/18.

31 Bn. left Bde. on 1/11/16 for Salonika, as a Garr. Bn., and embkd. at Southampton on 4/11/16. Bn. reached Salonika on 15/11/16 (via le Havre and Marseille), and joined Army Troops.

32 Bdes. were numbered and batteries lettered between 8-22/5/16. 2/4/Durh., and 2/5 Durh./CCCXVIII (H.) became D (H.)/CCCXV and D (H.)/CCCXVI.

33 Bde. arrived le Havre on 3/7/16, and joined R.N. Div. on 5/7/16. On 31/8/16 Bde. was reorganized: 1 sec. C joined A, and 1 sec. C joined B, making A and B up to six 18-pdrs. each. On 18/11/16 525 (H.) joined and became C (H.). On 24/1/17 D (H.) was broken up: R. Sec. joined D (H.)/CCCXVII; and L. Sec. joined D (H.)/CCXXIII. On 11/2/17 one sec. of C (H.)/CCCVIII joined C (H.)/CCCXV, and on the same day C (H.) became D (H.); and on 11/2/17 A/CCLX joined and become C/CCCXV. On 1/3/17 the Bde. became an A.F.A. Bde.

34 Bde. arrived le Havre on 3/7/16, and joined R.N. Div. on 5/7/16. On 31/8/16 the Bde was broken up: R. Sec. A joined A/CCXXIII, L. Sec. A joined B/CCXXIII; R. Sec. B joined C, and C then became C/CCCXVII; L. Sec. B joined C/CCXXIII; and D (H.) became D (H.)/CCCXVII.

35 Bde. arrived le Havre on 3/7/16, and joined R.N. Div. on 5/7/16. Bde. was reorganized 31/8-1/9/16: R. Sec. of C joined A; L. Sec. of C joined B; C/CCCXVI with R. Sec., B/CCCXVI joined Bde. and became C/CCCXVII; and D (H.)/CCCXVI joined and became D (H.)/CCCXVII. On 24/1/17 R. Sec., D (H.) CCCXV joined D (H.)/CCCXVII, and made Bty. up to six hows.

36 Bde. arrived le Havre on 3/7/16, and joined R.N. Div. on 5/7/16. On 18/7/16 A (H.)/CCXXIII joined and became D (H.)/CCCXVIII. On 19/7/16 CCCXVIII was designated CCXXV, and on 31/7/16 the Bde. was re-designated CCXXIII. On 31/8/16 Bde. was reorganized: R. Sec., A/CCCXVI joined A, and L. Sec., A/CCCXVI joined B, and L. Sec., B/CCCXVI joined C. On 24/1/17 L. Sec., D (H.)/CCCXV joined D (H.)/CCXXIII and made Bty. up to 6 hows.

37 D.A.C. arrived le Havre on 4/7/16 and joined R.N. Div. on 12/7/16.

38 Fd. Coy. went to Mesopotamia and joined 15th (Indian) Div. at Nasiriya on 30/11-1/12/16. Fd. Coy. was numbered 448th on 6/3/17.

39 Fd. Coy. went to Mesopotamia and joined 15th (Indian) Div. at Nasiriya on 10/3/17. Fd. Coy. was numbered 450th on 6/3/17.

40 Fd. Coy. went to Mesopotamia and joined 15th (Indian) Div. at Nasiriya on 10/1/17. Fd. Coy. was numbered 451st on 6/3/17.

41 Fd. Ambce. went to Salonika and arrived in Sept., 1916; it joined Army Troops.

42 Fd. Ambc. embkd. Southampton on 10/9/16 and disembkd. at Salonika on 22/9/16; it was posted to XVI Corps Troops on 27/9/16.

43 The H.Q. of the Train was disbanded in July, 1916. The four Companies went on until 1919: 529 at Grantham; 530 at Newcastle; 531 at York; and 532 at York and Grimsby.

63RD (2ND/NORTHUMBRIAN) DIVISION

FORMATION AND NARRATIVE

This 2nd-line (or reserve) Territorial Force division had no existence before the outbreak of the Great War.

The formation of reserve (or 2nd-line) T.F. units was authorized on the 31st August, 1914 (see Narrative, 57th Division); and the twelve reserve (or 2nd-line) Northumbrian battalions were raised at their respective regimental headquarters between the 4th September and the 28th December, 1914. The reserve battalions were originally raised for home defence, but individual recruits were to be encouraged to volunteer for imperial service. It was not until late in May, 1915, that all the home-service men were drafted to home-service units and the 2nd-line battalions were organized with only foreign-service men. Nevertheless, beginning in January, 1915, drafts had been continually supplied to the 1st-line battalions. Naturally the progressive training of the recruits was considerably delayed by this constant provision of drafts, as well as by the fact that some of the few available arms, as well as equipment and greatcoats, had on more than one occasion to be withdrawn from the men and handed over to the sister 1st-line battalions.

Infantry brigades were formed in January, 1915, and shortly afterwards divisional headquarters opened at Newcastle. Gradually the division was assembled at and around Newcastle in the Northern Command: 188th Brigade at Swallwell Camp, 189th at Cramlington Camp, 190th at Heworth, divisional artillery at Newcastle, Gosforth Park, and Gateshead, and engineers at Newcastle. On the 20th May, whilst it was still around Newcastle, the division was inspected by His Majesty the King.

During the time it was quartered around Newcastle, and practically until its dissolution, the division was responsible for the defence of the North-East Coast in the Seaham Harbour–Sunderland–Newcastle area. Until the end of May the 190th Brigade manned trenches on the coast between Seaham and Roker.

On the 26th July, 1915, instructions were received that 600 was the minimum strength for any 2nd-line battalion, and any men in excess of 600 could be taken for overseas reinforcements.

On the 30th November divisional headquarters opened at Retford and the division then moved into the following quarters: 188th Brigade in York, 189th in Retford and Gainsborough, 190th in Doncaster, with divisional artillery in Retford, York, and Doncaster, heavy battery (2/1/N. Riding) at Hedon, and engineers in Worksop. These quarters were retained for the remainder of the division's brief existence, and during this period the division formed part of the Eighth New Army.

At the end of March, 1916, the strength of the 63rd Division was only 12,867, out of an establishment of 17,243. In the latter half of May the divisional artillery left and moved to Heytesbury, and then began to prepare for service overseas. On the 2nd July the artillery left for France and joined the Royal Naval Division* (see Table and notes). By this time the strength of the 63rd (2nd/Northumbrian) Division was reduced to 9,135 all ranks; and on the 16th July the 189th Brigade furnished a draft of 621 other ranks for 1st-line units overseas, thus further depleting the strength. The decision to break up the 63rd Division, however, had already been reached, and an order to this effect was issued.

In accordance with this order, on the 20th July, divisional headquarters issued a special farwell order 'on the eve of the final dissolution of the division,' and on the 21st July, 1916, the 63rd (2nd/Northumbrian) Division ceased to exist.

The three infantry brigades remained in existence until late in 1916 (see Table and notes), and, as heretofore, the infantry continued to supply drafts. The 188th Brigade remained at York; but, on the 22nd July, the 189th and 190th Brigades both moved to Catterick. Gradually all the units (which had originally belonged to the division) were either transferred to other formations or to various theatres of war, or drafted, or broken up. The last unit disappeared on the 29th January, 1917.

* On 19/7/16 the Royal Naval Division became 63rd (Royal Naval) Division (see Part 3B, pp. 117–128).

64TH (2ND/HIGHLAND) DIVISION

G.O.C.

25 January, 1915 ... ... Br.-Gen. G. C. I. STOCKWELL.
8 February, 1916 ... ... Major-General R. BANNATINE-ALLASON.
14 August, 1917 ... ... Major-General H. J. S. LANDON.
28 March, 1918 ... ... Major-General Sir H. T. LUKIN.
4 November, 1918 ... ... Major-General Sir J. E. CAPPER.

G.S.O. 1.

25 Jan., 1915...Capt. J. B. L. MONTEITH (acting).
6 Feb., 1915...Major W. S. BANKS (acting).
18 Mar., 1915...Colonel H. W. G. GRAHAM.
6 April, 1916...Lt.-Col. H. ST. C. WILKINS.
16 Dec., 1916...Lt.-Col. W. E. DAVIES.
8 Jan., 1918...Lt.-Col. T. E. L. HILL-WHITSON.
18 July, 1918...Lt.-Col. P. S. ROWAN.

A.-A. and Q.-M.-G.

25 Jan., 1915...Capt. J. B. L. MONTEITH (acting).
17 Mar., 1915...Major J. R. FRASER (acting).
15 June, 1915...Lt.-Col. J. R. FRASER.
4 July, 1916...Lt.-Col. A. L. LAW.
11 Sept., 1918...Lt.-Col. C. T. M. HARE.

B.-G., R.A.

25 Jan., 1915...Colonel D. E. DEWAR.
19 Jan., 1916...Colonel H. A. BRENDON.
26 April, 1916...Colonel L. G. F. GORDON.
29 May, 1916...Br.-Gen. H. G. SANDILANDS.
22 Oct., 1916...Br.-Gen. G. W. BIDDULPH.
18 May, 1918...Br.-Gen. H. G. LLOYD.
30 Oct., 1918...Br.-Gen. J. C. WRAY.

C.R.E.

19 May, 1915...Lt.-Col. G. A. CORNWALL.
6 May, 1916...Major G. A. LEDINGHAM (acting).
15 May, 1916...Lt.-Col. H. J. KINGHORN.

191st BDE.

(2nd/1st Sea. and Cam.)

16 Jan., '15...Col. J. H. EWART (sick, 19/11/15).
19 Nov., '15...Col. E. G. BUIK (acting).
8 Dec., '15...Br.-Gen. R. SCOTT-KERR.
15 Jan., '18...Br.-Gen. T. H. F. PEARSE.

192nd BDE.

(2nd/1st Gordon)

20 Jan., '15...Col. A. M. CARTHEW-YORSTOUN.
1 June, '16...Br.-Gen. R. W. H. RONALDSON.
5 Dec., '17...Br.-Gen. W. L. OSBORNE.
10 April, '18...Br.-Gen. W. MARRIOTT-DODINGTON.

193rd BDE.

(2nd/1st A. and S.)

29 Jan., '15...Col. A. C. D. DICK.
1 June, '16...Br.-Gen. D. L. MACEWEN.
19 June, '16...Lt.-Col. Sir A. W. G. T. LEITH-BUCHANAN (acting).
26 June, '16...Br.-Gen. J. D. MCLACHLAN.
20 Aug., '17...Br.-Gen. C. T. SHIPLEY.

64TH[1] (2ND/HIGHLAND) DIVISION — ORDER OF BATTLE, 1915-1918

Dates	INFANTRY: Brigades	INFANTRY: Battalions and attached Units	Mounted Troops	ARTILLERY: Field Artillery: Brigades	ARTILLERY: Field Artillery: Batteries	ARTILLERY: Field Artillery: Bde. Ammn. Colns.	ARTILLERY: Trench Mortar Bties.: Medium	ARTILLERY: Trench Mortar Bties.: Heavy	ARTILLERY: Divnl. Ammn. Coln.	Engineers: Field Cos.	Signal Service: Divnl. Signal Coy.	Pioneers	M.G. Units	Field Ambu-lances	Mobile Vety. Secn.	Divnl. Emplnt. Coy.	Divnl. Train
1915 August (Scotland)	191st[1]; [2] (2nd/1st Sea. & Cam.) 192nd[1]; [3] (2nd/1st Gord.) 193rd[1]; [4] (2nd/1st A. & S.)	2/4/Sea. H., 2/5/Sea. H., 2/6/ Sea. H., 2/4/Cam. H. 2/4/Gord. H., 2/5/Gord. H., 2/6/Gord. H., 2/7/Gord. H. 2/6/A. & S. H., 2/7/A. & S. H., 2/8/A. & S. H., 2/9/ A. & S. H.	64th (2/1/ High-land) Div. Cyclist Coy.	2nd/I Highl'd. 2nd/II Highl'd. 2nd/III Highl'd. (H.)	2/1/Aberdeen, 2/2/Aberdeen, 2/3/Aberdeen. 2/1/Forfarshire, 2/1/Fifeshire, 2/1/Dundee. 2/1/Renfrew (H.), 2/2/Renfrew (H.)	2nd/I Highl'd. 2nd/II Highl'd. 2nd/III Highl'd (H.)	...	...	...	2/1/ Highland 3/2/ Highland	64th (2/1/ High-land)	...	...	2/2/ Highland 2/3/ Highland	64th (2/1/ High land)	...	64th[5] (2/1/ High-land)
1915 November (Scotland)	191st[6] ... 192nd[6] ... 193rd[6] ...	No. 1 Bn. (2/4/Sea. H.), No. 2 Bn. (2/5/6/Sea. H.), No. 3 Bn. (2/4/Cam. H.), No. 4 Bn. (2/4/5/B.W.) No. 5 Bn. (2/4/5/Gord. H.), No. 6 Bn. (2/6/7/Gord. H.), No. 7 Bn. (2/6/B.W.), No. 8 Bn. (2/7/B.W.) No. 9 Bn. (2/5/8/A. & S. H.), No. 10 Bn. (2/6/A. & S. H.), No. 11 Bn. (2/7/A. & S. H.), No. 12 Bn. (2/9/A. & S. H.)	64th Div. Cyclist Coy.	2nd/I Highl'd. 2nd/II Highl'd. 2nd/III Highl'd (H.)	2/1/Aberdeen, 2/2/Aberdeen, 2/3/Aberdeen. 2/1/Forfarshire, 2/1/Fifeshire, 2/1/Dundee. 2/1/Renfrew (H.), 2/2/Renfrew (H.)	2nd/I Highl'd. 2nd/II Highl'd. 2nd/III Highl'd. (H.)	...	...	64th D.A.C. (2nd/1/ High-land)	1/3/ Highland 2/1/ Highland 3/2/ Highland	64th	...	...	3/1/ Highland 2/2/ Highland 2/3/ Highland	64th	...	64th
1916 April (England)	191st[7] ... 192nd[7] ... 193rd[7] ...	2/4/B.W., 2/4/Sea. H., 2/6/ Sea. H., 2/4/Cam. H. 2/6/B.W., 2/7/B.W., 2/5/Gord. H., 2/7/Gord. H. 2/6/A. & S.H., 2/7/A. & S. H., 2/8/A. & S. H., 2/9/A. & S.H.	64th Div. Cyclist Coy.	CCCXX[8] ...... (2nd/I Highl'd.) CCCXXI[8] ...... (2nd/II Highl'd.) CCCXXIII (H.)[8] (2nd/III Highl'd.)	A, B, C A, B, C A (H.), B (H.)	CCCXX B.A.C. CCCXXI B.A.C. CCCXXIII B.A.C. (H.)	...	...	64th D.A.C.	1/3/ Highland 2/1/ Highland 3/2/ Highland	64th	...	...	3/1/ Highland 2/2/ Highland 2/3/ Highland	64th	...	64th
1916 October (England)	191st ...... 192nd...... 193rd	2/4/B.W., 2/4/Sea. H., 2/6/ Sea. H., 2/4/Cam. H. 2/6/B.W., 2/7/B.W., 2/5/Gord. H., 2/7/Gord. H. 2/6/A. & S. H., 2/7/A. & S. H., 2/8/A. & S. H., 2/9/A. & S. H.	C Sqdn., 2/1/ Glasgow Yeo. 64th Div. Cyclist Coy.	CCCXX .... CCCXXI .... CCCXXII[10] ...	A, B, C; D (H.); A/CCXCIII[9] A, B, C; D (H.); B/CCXCIII[9] A, B. C	...	...	...	64th D.A.C.	1/3/ Highland 2/1/ Highland 3/2/ Highland	64th	...	...	3/1/ Highland 2/2/ Highland 2/3/ Highland	64th	...	64th

1917 June (England)	191st ...... 192nd...... 193rd......	2/4/B.W., 2/4/Sea. H., 2/6/Sea. H., 2/4/Cam. H. 2/6/B.W., 2/7/B.W., 2/5/Gord. H., 2/7/Gord. H. 2/6/A. & S. H., 2/7/A. & S. H., 2/8/A. & S. H., 2/9/ A. & S. H.	64th Div. Cyclist Coy.	CCCXX ...... CCCXXI	A, B, C; D (H.) A, B, C; D (H.)	...	...	...	64th D.A.C.	402nd (1/3/ Highl'd.) 403rd (2/1/ Highl'd.) 405th (3/2/ Highl'd.)	64th	...	...	310th (3/1/ Highland) 311th (2/2/ Highland) 312th (2/3/ Highland.)	64th	...	64th
1917 September (England)	191st ...... 192nd...... 193rd......	2/4/B.W., 2/4/Sea. H., 2/4/Cam. H., 201st Bn.,[11]; [12] 202nd Bn.[11]; [12] 2/7/B.W., 2/5/Gord. H., 205th Bn.,[11]; [12] 206th Bn.[11]; [12] 2/6/A. & S. H., 2/8/A. & S. H., 209th Bn.,[11]; [12] 210th Bn.[11]; [12]	64th Coy., A.C.C.	CCCXX......... CCCXXI	A, B, C; D (H.) A, B, C; D (H.)	...	...	...	64th D.A.C.	402nd 403rd 405th	64th	...	...	310th 311th 312th	64th	...	64th
1917 December (England)	191st ...... 192nd...... 193rd......	2/4/B.W., 51/H.L.I. (G.),[12] 2/4/Sea. H., 51/Gord. H. (G.),[12] 2/4/Cam. H. 51/Devon. (G.),[12] 2/7/B.W., 52/H.L.I. (G.),[12] 2/5/Gord. H. 52/Devon. (G.),[12]; [16] 51/Midd'x. (G.)[13] 2/6/A. & S. H., 2/8/A. & S. H.	64th Coy., A.C.C.	CCCXX......... CCCXXI	A, B, C; D (H.) A, B, C; D (H.)	...	...	...	64th D.A.C.	402nd 403rd 405th	64th	...	...	310th 311th 312th	64th	...	64th
1918 April (England)	191st ...... 192nd...... 193rd......	51/R. Suss. (G.),[13] 52/R. Suss. (G.),[14] 51/H.L.I. (G.), 51/Gord. H. (G.) 52/Queen's (G.),[15] 51/Devon. (G.), 52/Devon. (G.),[16] 52/H.L.I. (G.). 51/Bedf. (G.),[17] 52/Bedf.(G.),[18] 51/Midd'x. (G.), 52/Midd'x. (G.)[19]	64th Coy., A.C.C.	CCCXX......... CCCXXI	A, B, C; D (H.) A, B, C; D (H.)	...	...	...	64th D.A.C.	402nd 403rd 405th	64th	...	...	310th 311th 312th	64th	...	64th
1918 October (England)	191st ...... 192nd...... 193rd......	51/R. Suss. (G.), 52/R. Suss. (G.), 51/H.L.I. (G.), 51/Gord. H. (G.) 52/Queen's (G.), 51/Devon. (G.), 52/Devon. (G.), 52/H.L.I. (G.) 51/Bedf. (G.), 52/Bedf. (G.), 51/Midd'x. (G.), 52/Midd'x. (G.)	64th Coy., A.C.C.	CCCXX......... CCCXXI	A, B, C; D (H.) A, B, C; D (H.)	...	...	...	64th D.A.C.	402nd 403rd 405th	64th	...	...	310th 311th 312th	64th	...	64th

NOTES

1 On the 17th Aug., 1915, the Highland 2nd-line Division and Infantry Brigades were given numbers. (Authy., 40/W.O./2609, A.G.1, of 10/8/15.)

2 The Bde. was formed in January, 1915.

3 The Bde. was formed in January, 1915.

4 The Bde. was formed in January, 1915.

5 The Train consisted of 533, 534, 535, and 536 Cos., A.S.C. The 4 Companies received the numbers on 14/2/16.

6 The Inf. Bdes. were reorganized on 8/11/15, and the numbering of the battalions was altered. (Authy. Div. R.O., No. 173/4.)

7 On 11/1/16 titles were given to the composite battalions in the Inf. Bdes. (Authy. W.O. letter No. 9/Gen./No. 5510, A.G.1, of 4/1/16.)

8 Numbers were allotted to the Artillery Bdes. and the batteries were lettered on 18/5/16. (Authy., W.O. letter No. 9/Gen./No. 6051 (S.D. 2.), of 6/5/16.) By this date 18-pdrs. had been received by CCCXX and CCCXXI Bdes., and 4.5" hows. by CCCXXIII Bde. CCCXXIII was broken up in May.

9 These batteries were attached from 58th (2/1st London) Div. Arty., as a temporary measure.

10 3 18-pdr. batteries were formed at Catterick by V Res. Bde., R.F.A. (T.F.), and joined 64th Div. on 3/11/16. The 3 batteries then formed CCCXXII Bde. By 29/1/17 CCCXXII was broken up and the batteries were used to complete the other 18-pdr. batteries of the 64th Div. to 6 guns each.

11 These 6 Graduated Battalions of the Training Reserve served with the division from 16/7/17.

12 The 6 Graduated Bns. of the Training Reserve were affiliated to line regiments and adopted territorial designations from 27/10/17.

13 Transferred on 25/2/18 from 213th Bde., 71st Div. (disbanded).

14 Transferred on 18/2/18 from 212th Bde., 71st Div. (disbanded).

15 Transferred on 18/2/18 from 213th Bde., 71st Div. (disbanded).

16 Transferred on 26/2/18 from 193rd Bde. to 192nd Bde.

17 Transferred on 19/2/18 from 212th Bde., 71st Div. (disbanded).

18 Transferred on 25/2/18 from 213th Bde., 71st Div. (disbanded).

19 Transferred on 26/2/18 from 212th Bde., 71st Div. (disbanded).

GENERAL NOTES

The following Units of the 64th Div. served with the 51st Div. :—

2/2/Highland Field Coy., joined 51st (Highland) Division, and served on the Western Front, throughout the War, with the 51st Division. The Fd. Coy. was numbered 404th.

2/1/Highland Fd. Ambce., joined 51st Highland Division, and served on the Western Front with the 51st Division throughout the War.

The following Units also served with, or were attached to, the 64th Division :—

ARTILLERY :—1129 Bty., R.F.A., attached in May, 1917.

Bute Mountain Bty. (IV Highland Mtn. Arty. Bde.)—from April, 1915–Septr., 1916. (The Bty. went to Salonika on 6/9/16 and disembkd. there on 20/9/16.)

2/1/Highland (Fifeshire) Heavy Battery, R.G.A. (T.F.), served with the Division until Septr., 1916, when the Hy. Bty. was attached to the 3rd Provisional Bde. at Sheringham. By August, 1917, the Hy. Bty. was attached to the 223rd Mixed Brigade at Sheringham ; and the Hy. Bty. remained with this Bde. until the end of the War.

OTHER UNITS :—2/1/Highland Sanitary Section, until the end of 1917 ; and

64th Motor Ambulance Workshop, until it was absorbed by the Train in 1916.

64TH (2ND/HIGHLAND) DIVISION

FORMATION AND NARRATIVE

This 2nd-line (or reserve) Territorial Force division had no existence before the outbreak of the Great War.

The formation of reserve (or 2nd-line) T.F. units was authorized on the 31st August, 1914 (see Narrative, 57th Division); and during 1914 the twelve reserve (or 2nd-line) Highland battalions, as well as the 2nd-line Highland batteries, field companies, train, and field ambulances, were raised at their respective headquarters. The infantry brigades were formed in January, 1915; but progressive training was delayed and complicated by the frequent provision of drafts to the 1st-line battalions and by the lack of up-to-date arms and equipment.

Divisional headquarters opened at Perth in January, 1915; but some time elapsed before the various units were sufficiently assembled for the division to be considered more or less complete. By August, however, the three infantry brigades were around Blair Athol, Scone, and Falkirk, the artillery was at Edzell, Forfar, Brechin, and Rothesay, with the heavy battery at Dunfermline, and the engineers, field ambulances, and the train were at Blair Athol, Perth, and Scone. Winter stations were occupied in November, and the division then billetted as follows: divisional headquarters in Perth; 191st Brigade at Pitlochry, Crieff, Aberfeldy, and Auchterarder; 192nd Brigade at Blairgowrie and Forfar; and 193rd Brigade at Montrose and Arbroath. The artillery was at Perth, Forfar, Brechin, and Rothesay; the engineers at Perth, Alyth, Dundee, and Coupar; the field ambulances at Comrie, Alyth, and Forfar; and the train at Kirriemuir, Montrose, Blairgowrie, and Crieff.

By January, 1916, 64th Division had been allotted to the Eighth New Army; in March the division moved southward into England, and, by the 31st, divisional headquarters opened at Norwich. In this city the divisional headquarters remained for the rest of the War, and during this period the division was employed on home defence. In March, however, the organization of Home Defence Troops was altered and the division came under Northern Army; and, in October, army headquarters also moved to Norwich.

The division was now quartered as follows: 191st Brigade at Kelling, 192nd Brigade at Taverham, and 193rd Brigade at North Walsham; mounted troops were at Taverham; artillery at Blickling and Worstead; and engineers at Norwich, Taverham, North Walsham, and Kelling. These stations were maintained until the winter of 1917; but, during this year the composition of the infantry of the division gradually changed: the 2nd-line battalions were withdrawn; and, as a first step in reorganization, two graduated battalions of the Training Reserve were posted to each infantry brigade. At this time the division took up the following winter quarters: 191st Brigade at Cromer, 192nd Brigade at Norwich, and 193rd Brigade at Norwich and Sheringham; the cyclists were in Norwich; the artillery at Norwich, Aylsham, and Haveringland; and the engineers at Norwich, Holt, Taverham, and Witton. Whilst occupying these winter quarters the final reorganization of the division took place and the remaining 2nd-line battalions were replaced by graduated battalions of the Training Reserve. By the end of October all the graduated battalions of the Training Reserve were affiliated to line regiments and adopted territorial designations. In this way the division lost its original territorial association.

By the end of February, 1918, the change over was completed (see Table); and, in April, the division (now in XXIII Corps) occupied the following summer stations: 191st Brigade at Thetford, 192nd Brigade at Kelling, Holt, and Metton, and 193rd Brigade at Taverham; the cyclists were at Costessey, the artillery at Norwich, Aylsham, and Westwick Park, and the engineers at Norwich, West Runton, and Taverham. At the end of the War the division, still in the XXIII Corps, was again in winter quarters: 191st Brigade at Thetford and Fakenham, 192nd Brigade at Cromer and Sheringham, and 193rd Brigade at Norwich; the cyclists were at Oulton Broad, the artillery at Norwich, Reepham, and Aylsham, and the engineers at Norwich, West Runton, Burlingham, and Taverham.

After the Armistice the division remained in Norfolk, and there it received orders for its demobilization and disbandment. Early in January, 1919, the cyclist company began to demobilize. Thereafter the strength gradually dwindled. By the 10th March the division had shrunk to 11,969 all ranks; and on the 15th April, 1919, the 64th Division ceased to exist.

65TH (2ND/LOWLAND) DIVISION

G.O.C.

12 April, 1915 ... ... Br.-Gen. EARL OF ERROLL.
12 February, 1916... ... ... Major-General T. E. STEPHENSON (sick, 15/8/16).
15 August, 1916 ... ... Br.-Gen. D. G. PRINSEP (acting).
19 August, 1916 ... ... Major-General T. E. STEPHENSON.
9 September, 1916 ... ... Major-General G. T. FORESTIER-WALKER.
11 December, 1916 ... ... Br.-Gen. D. G. PRINSEP (acting).
23 December, 1916 –18 March, 1918 ... ... Major-General Hon. E. J. MONTAGU-STUART-WORTLEY.

G.S.O. 1.

20 Jan., 1915...Colonel F. G. BLAIR.
14 Mar., 1915...Major W. J. ANDERSON (acting).
6 May, 1915...Lt.-Col. T. E. L. HILL-WHITSON.
6 Nov., 1915...Lt.-Col. J. M. HOME.
26 Sept., 1916...Lt.-Col. B. J. CURLING.
21 April, 1917...Lt.-Col. H. A. WALKER.
7 Oct., 1917...Lt.-Col. E. A. BRADFORD.

A.-A. and Q.-M.-G.

22 Jan., 1915...Captain A. LYON (acting).
17 May, 1915...Colonel J. R. MATHEWES (sick, 24/8/16).
24 Aug., 1916...Major E. MOLYNEUX-SEEL (acting).
8 Sept., 1916 –5 Feb., 1918 Colonel J. R. MATHEWES.

B.-G., R.A.

25 Jan., 1915...Colonel H. C. DUNLOP.
30 Nov., 1915...Colonel D. G. PRINSEP.
7 July, 1916...Br.-Gen. D. G. PRINSEP.
21 April, 1917...Br.-Gen. F. A. G. Y. ELTON.

C.R.E.

8 Nov., 1915...Lt.-Col. J. M. ARTHUR.

194th BDE.

(2nd/1st South Scottish)

15 Jan., '15...Colonel W. C. DOUGLAS
17 Mar., '16 –15 Mar., '18 Br.-Gen. F. A. MACFARLAN.

195th BDE.

(2nd/1st Scottish Rifle)

21 Jan., '15...Colonel J. C. L. CAMPBELL.
10 Dec., '15 –15 Mar., '18 Br.-Gen. P. A. TURNER.

196th BDE.

(2nd/1st Highland Lt. Inf.)

18 Jan., '15...Colonel LORD SALTOUN.
15 Mar., '16...Br.-Gen. H. F. KAYS (sick, 1/6/16).
1 June, '16...Lt.-Col. G. McNISH (acting).
18 Aug., '16 –16 Mar., '18 Br.-Gen. H. F. KAYS.

65TH[1] (2ND/LOWLAND) DIVISION — ORDER OF BATTLE, 1915-1918

Dates	INFANTRY: Brigades	INFANTRY: Battalions and attached Units	Mounted Troops	ARTILLERY: Field Artillery: Brigades	ARTILLERY: Field Artillery: Batteries	ARTILLERY: Field Artillery: Bde. Ammn. Colns.	ARTILLERY: Trench Mortar Bties.: Medium	ARTILLERY: Trench Mortar Bties.: Heavy	ARTILLERY: Divnl. Ammn. Coln.	Engineers: Field Cos.	Signal Service: Divnl. Signal Coy.	Pioneers	M.G. Units	Field Ambu-lances	Mobile Vety. Secn.	Divnl. Emplnt. Coy.	Divnl. Train
1915 August (Scotland)	194th[1]; [2] (2nd/1st S. Scottish) 195th[1]; [3] (2nd/1st Sco. Rif.) 196th[1]; [4] (2nd/1st H.L.I.)	2/4/R.S.F., 2/5/R.S.F., 2/4/K.O.S.B., 2/5/K.O.S.B. 2/5/Sco. Rif., 2/6/Sco. Rif., 2/7/Sco. Rif., 2/8/Sco. Rif. 2/5/H.L.I., 2/6/H.L.I., 2/7/H.L.I., 2/9/H.L.I.	...	2nd/I Lowland. 2nd/II Lowland 2nd/III Lowland 2nd/IV Lowland (H.)	2/1/Edinburgh, 2/2/Edinburgh, 2/1/Midlothian. 2/1/Ayr, 2/2/Ayr, 2/1/Kirkcudbright. 2/1/Glasgow, 2/2/Glasgow, 2/3/Glasgow. 2/4/Glasgow (H.), 2/5/Glasgow (H.)	2nd/I Lowland 2nd/II Lowland 2nd/III Lowland 2nd/IV Lowland (H.)	...	...	...	3/1/ Lowland 3/2/ Lowland	65th (2nd/1/ Lowland)	...	...	2/1/ Lowland 2/2/ Lowland 2/3/ Lowland	65th (2/1/ Lowland)	...	65th[5] (2nd/1/ Lowland)
1915 November (Scotland)	194th[6] ... 195th[6] ... 196th[6] ...	No. 13 Bn. (2/4/5/R.S.F., 2/5/Bord.), No. 14 Bn. (2/4/5/K.O.S.B.), No. 15 Bn. (2/7/R. Scots), No. 16 Bn. (2/8/R. Scots) No. 17 Bn. (2/5/8/Sco. Rif.), No. 18 Bn. (2/6/7/Sco. Rif.), No. 19 Bn. (2/4/5/6/R. Scots), No. 20 Bn. (2/9/R. Scots) No. 21 Bn. (2/5/H.L.I.), No. 22 Bn. (2/6/H.L.I.), No. 23 Bn. (2/7/H.L.I.), No. 24 Bn. (2/9/H.L.I.)	65th (2nd/1/ Lowland) Div. Cyclist Coy.	2nd/I Lowland 2nd/II Lowland 2nd/III Lowland 2nd/IV Lowland (H.)	2/1/Edinburgh, 2/2/Edinburgh, 2/1/Midlothian. 2/1/Ayr, 2/2/Ayr, 2/1/Kirkcudbright. 2/1/Glasgow, 2/2/Glasgow, 2/3/Glasgow. 2/4/Glasgow (H.), 2/5/Glasgow (H.)	2nd/I Lowland 2nd/II Lowland 2nd/III Lowland 2nd/IV Lowland (H.)	...	...	65th D.A.C. (2nd/1/ Lowland)	1/3/ Lowland 3/1/ Lowland 3/2/ Lowland	65th	...	...	2/1/ Lowland 2/2/ Lowland 2/3/ Lowland	65th	...	65th
1916 May (England)	194th[7] ... 195th[7] ... 196th[7] ...	2/7/R. Scots, 2/8/R. Scots, 2/4/R.S.F., 2/5/K.O.S.B. 2/4/R. Scots, 2/9/R. Scots, 2/5/Sco. Rif., 2/6/Sco. Rif. 2/5/H.L.I., 2/6/H.L.I., 2/7/H.L.I., 2/9/H.L.I.	65th Div. Cyclist Coy.	CCCXXV[8]...... (2nd/I Lowland) CCCXXVI[8] (2nd/II Lowland) CCCXXVII[8]... (2nd/III Lowland) CCCXXVIII... (H.)[8] (2nd/IV Lowland)	A, B, C A, B, C A, B, C A (H.), B (H.)	CCCXXV B.A.C. CCCXXVI B.A.C. CCCXXVII B.A.C. CCCXXVIII (H.) B.A.C.	...	...	65th D.A.C.	1/3/ Lowland 3/1/ Lowland 3/2/ Lowland	65th	...	...	2/1/ Lowland 2/2/ Lowland 2/3/ Lowland	65th	...	65th
1916 October (England)	194th...... 195th...... 196th......	2/7/R. Scots, 2/8/R. Scots, 2/4/R.S.F., 2/5/K.O.S.B. 2/4/R. Scots, 2/9/R. Scots, 2/5/Sco. Rif., 2/6/Sco. Rif. 2/5/H.L.I., 2/6/H.L.I., 2/7/H.L.I, 2/9/H.L.I.	1 Sqdn., 2/1/ Glasgow Yeo. 65th Div. Cyclist Coy.	CCCXXV ...... CCCXXVI...... CCCXXVII ...	A, B, C; D (H.) A, B, C; D (H.) A, B, C	...	...	...	65th D.A.C.	1/3/ Lowland 3/1/ Lowland 3/2/ Lowland	65th	...	...	2/1/ Lowland 2/2/ Lowland 2/3/ Lowland	65th	...	65th

1917 February (Ireland)	194th...... 195th...... 196th......	2/7/R. Scots, 2/8/R. Scots, 2/4/R.S.F., 2/5/K.O.S.B. 2/4/R. Scots, 2/9/R. Scots, 2/5/Sco. Rif., 2/6/Sco. Rif. 2/5/H.L.I., 2/6/H.L.I., 2/7/H.L.I., 2/9/H.L.I.	1 Sqdn. 2/1/ Glasgow Yeo. 65th Div. Cyclist Coy.	CCCXXV ...... CCCXXVI......	A, B, C; D (H.) A, B, C; D (H.)	...	...	...	65th D.A.C.	411th (1/3/ Lowland) 414th (3/1/ Lowland) 415th (3/2/ Lowland)	65th	...	...	313th (2/1/ Lowland) 314th (2/2/ Lowland) 315th (2/3/ Lowland)	65th	...	65th
1917 August (Ireland)	194th...... 195th...... 196th......	2/7/R. Scots, 2/4/R.S.F., 2/5/K.O.S.B., 213th Bn.[9]; [10] 2/9/R. Scots, 2/5/Sco. Rif., 2/6/Sco. Rif., 217th Bn.[9]; [10] 2/5/H.L.I., 2/6/H.L.I., 2/9/H.L.I., 221st Bn.[9]; [10]	65th Coy., A.C.C.	CCCXXV ...... CCCXXVI......	A, B, C; D (H.) A, B, C; D (H.)	...	...	...	65th D.A.C.	411th 414th 415th	65th	...	...	313th 314th 315th	65th	...	65th
1917 December (Ireland)	194th...... 195th...... 196th......	2/7/R. Scots, 2/4/R.S.F., 51/Ches. (G.),[10] 2/5/K.O.S.B. 2/9/R. Scots, 51/King's (G.),[10] 2/5/Sco. Rif., 2/6/Sco. Rif. 52/Ches. (G.),[10] 2/5/H.L.I., 2/6/H.L.I., 2/9/H.L.I.	65th Coy., A.C.C.	CCCXXV ...... CCCXXVI......	A, B, C; D (H.) A, B, C; D (H.)	...	...	...	65th D.A.C.	411th 414th 415th	65th	...	...	313th 314th 315th	65th	...	65th
1918 February (Ireland)	194th...... 195th...... 196th......	2/7/R. Scots, 2/4/R.S.F., 51/Ches. (G.),[11] 2/5/K.O.S.B. 2/9/R. Scots, 51/King's (G.),[12] 2/5/Sco. Rif., 2/6/Sco. Rif. 52/Ches. (G.),[13] 2/5/H.L.I., 2/6/H.L.I., 2/9/H.L.I.	65th Coy., A.C.C.	CCCXXV[14] ... CCCXXVI[15]...	A, B, C; D (H.) A, B, C; D (H.)	...	...	...	65th D.A.C.	411th[16] 414th[17] 415th[18]	65th[19]	...	...	313th[20] 314th[21] 315th[22]	65th[23]	...	65th[24]

On the 18th March, 1918, the 65th Division was broken up.

NOTES

1 In the middle of August, 1915, the Lowland 2nd-line Division and Infantry Brigades were given numbers. (Authy., 40/W.O./2609, A.G.1, of 10/8/15.)

2 The Bde. was formed in January, 1915.

3 The Bde. was formed in January, 1915.

4 The Bde. was formed in January, 1915.

5 The Train consisted of 537, 538, 539, and 540 Cos., A.S.C. The Cos. received numbers in February, 1916.

6 In Nov., 1915, the Inf. Bdes. were reorganized, and the numbering of the battalions was altered.

7 In January, 1916, titles were given to the composite battalions in the Inf. Bdes.

8 In May, 1916, numbers were allotted to the Artillery Bdes., and the batteries were lettered. By this time 18-pdrs. had also been received as well as 4.5" hows. In 1916 CCCXXVIII was broken up and the batteries joined CCCXXV and CCCXXVI.

9 These 3 battalions were Graduated Battalions of the Training Reserve; they served with the Division: 213th and 217th from 23/7/17; and 221st from 30/7/17.

10 The Graduated Battalions of the Training Reserve were affiliated to line regiments and adopted territorial designations from 27/10/17.

11 Bn. remained at the Curragh until 25/11/18; and by 2/12/18 it had joined 214th Bde., 67th Div., near Colchester.

12 By 11/3/18 the Bn. joined 203rd Bde., 68th Div., near Lowestoft.

13 Bn. remained at the Curragh until 25/11/18; and by 2/12/18 it had joined 214th Bde., 67th Div., near Colchester.

14 Bde. remained at Fermoy until 29/12/19, when it completed disbandment.

15 Bde. remained at Kildare until 27/10/19, when it completed disbandment.

16 By 24/6/18 the Coy. had left Balbriggan for Sandling. The Coy. went to France, disembkd. at le Havre on 16/7/18, left le Havre on 19/7/18, and joined Army Troops, Second Army, on 20/7/18.

17 The Coy. remained at the Curragh until it was disbanded on 6/10/19.

18 By 7/10/18 the Coy. had moved from the Curragh to Ballinrobe. The Coy. remained at Ballinrobe until it was disbanded on 6/10/19.

19 Disbanded by 25/3/18.

20 Remained at the Curragh. It was disbanded by 3/3/19.

21 Remained at Fermoy and then moved to Randalstown. It was disbanded by 21/4/19.

22 Disbanded by 25/2/18.

23 Disbanded by 18/3/18.

24 H.Q. of the Train remained at the Curragh and was disbanded by 12/8/18; 537 Coy. remained at Fermoy until the end of 1919; 538, at the Curragh, was disbanded by 21/4/19; 539 remained at the Curragh until the end of 1919; and 540, at Dublin, was disbanded by 10/3/19.

GENERAL NOTES

The following Units of the 65th Div. served in the field with the 52nd Div.:—

2/1/Lowland Fd. Coy. and **2/2/Lowland Fd. Coy.** } joined 52nd (Lowland) Division in 1915, and served with the 52nd Division in Gallipoli, Egypt, Palestine, and France. The Fd. Cos. were numbered 412th and 413th.

The following Units also served with the 65th Division:—

ARTILLERY:—2/1/Lowland (City of Edinburgh) Heavy Battery, R.G.A. (T.F.), served with the Division until May, 1916, when the Heavy Battery went to France; it disembarked at le Havre on 30/5/16. The Heavy Battery served on the Western Front for the remainder of the Great War; it joined VI Corps Hy. Arty. (near Arras) on 1/6/16, and joined VIII H.A.G. on 10/6/16.

OTHER UNITS:—2/1/Lowland Sanitary Section, until 7 May, 1917; and **65th Motor Ambulance Workshop,** until it was absorbed by the Train in 1916.

65TH (2ND/LOWLAND) DIVISION

FORMATION AND NARRATIVE

This 2nd-line (or reserve) Territorial Force division had no existence before the outbreak of the Great War.

The formation of reserve (or 2nd-line) T.F. units was authorized on the 31st August, 1914 (see Narrative, 57th Division); and before the end of 1914 the twelve reserve (or 2nd-line) Lowland battalions, as well as the 2nd-line Lowland batteries, field companies, train, and field ambulances, were raised at the headquarters of their 1st-line units.

In January, 1915, the Lowland infantry brigades were formed. Progressive training for war was delayed by the provision of frequent drafts for the 1st-line units. In addition training was complicated by the lack of up-to-date arms and equipment and by the necessary reorganization of the units, when the home-service men were drafted to home-service units.

Divisional headquarters began to form in January, 1915, but some time elapsed before the various formations and units were sufficiently assembled for the division to be considered more or less complete. By August, however, the division had its headquarters at Bridge of Allan (north of Stirling), and the three infantry brigades were then around Rumbling Bridge, Cambusbarron, and Dunfermline, with one battalion in the Cheviots. The field artillery brigades were at Edinburgh, Larbert, and Tillicoultry, with the heavy battery in Stirling; the field companies were at Bridge of Allan; the field ambulances at Dunfermline, Rumbling Bridge, and Stirling; and the train at Bridge of Allan, Rumbling Bridge, Stirling, and Dunfermline.

In November, 1915, after the reorganization of the battalions, the infantry was quartered, for the winter, as follows: 194th Brigade at Falkirk, Grangemouth, Milnathort, and Larbert; 195th Brigade at Cambusbarron, with one battalion at Tillicoultry; and 196th Brigade at Dunfermline, with one battalion in the Cheviots. The cyclist company was at Markinch; the field artillery brigades were at Edinburgh, Larbert, Callander, and Tillicoultry; the heavy battery was at Buddon; and the engineers were at Bridge of Allan and Alloa. The 65th Division was still serving in the Scottish Command.

In March, 1916, the 65th Division moved into England and joined Southern Army, Home Forces (Army Headquarters at Brentwood). By the 26th March divisional headquarters opened at Chelmsford, and the infantry brigades were near Chelmsford, Billericay, and Danbury. Before the end of the year, however, the dispositions underwent some alteration, and in October the division was disposed as follows: 194th Brigade at Chelmsford, 195th Brigade at Witham and Terling, 196th Brigade at Danbury and Wyndham Mortimer; mounted troops at Danbury and Maldon; artillery at Chelmsford, Great Leighs, Great Baddow, and Little Grange; and engineers at Witham, Bourne End, and Springfield Camp. These dispositions were maintained for the rest of the year.

In the meantime it had been decided that the 65th Division should move to Ireland and relieve the 59th Division. Early in 1917 the move began, and by the 10th January divisional headquarters opened at the Curragh. The 65th Division, now in the Irish Command, was the second Territorial Force division to serve in Ireland. On arrival in Ireland the troops of the division were quartered as follows: 194th Brigade at Dublin and the Curragh, 195th Brigade at Fermoy, Tralee, Limerick, Moore Park, and Kilworth, 196th Brigade at the Curragh, Galway, and Naas; mounted troops at Newbridge and the Curragh; artillery at Kildare and Limerick; and engineers at the Curragh. By August 194th Brigade moved to Oughterard and Moycullen, and 196th Brigade moved into Dublin; otherwise the troops occupied substantially the same quarters as before.

Before the end of 1917 it had been decided to break up the 65th Division; and on the 8th January, 1918, a notification was sent to Home Forces that the division was to be disbanded. On the 11th this was followed by an order to disband the division forthwith. Thereafter the division began to dwindle: 12,036 strong on the 18th February, it had shrunk to 5,874 by the 25th. In the middle of March the three brigade headquarters disappeared; and on the 18th March, with the closing of divisional headquarters, the 65th (2nd/Lowland) Division ceased to exist. On this date the strength of the division was only 3,887 all ranks; and by the 15th May, 1918, a report was rendered that all the remaining units of the division had been transferred, drafted, or disbanded.

66TH (2ND/EAST LANCASHIRE) DIVISION

G.O.C.

6 November, 1914	Br.-Gen. C. E. BECKETT.
14 November, 1915	Major-General C. J. BLOMFIELD.
10 February, 1916	Colonel C. S. GORDON STEWARD (acting).
1 March, 1916	Major-General C. J. BLOMFIELD.
12 February, 1917	Major-General Hon. H. A. LAWRENCE.
22 December, 1917	Major-General N. MALCOLM (wd., 29/3/18).
29 March, 1918	Br.-Gen. A. J. HUNTER (acting).
31 March, 1918	Major-General H. K. BETHELL.

G.S.O. 1.

11 Nov., 1914...Major E. M. LANG (acting).
12 April, 1915...Lt.-Col. L. W. G. BUTLER.
2 Mar., 1916...Lt.-Col. A. R. BURROWES.
29 Mar., 1918...Lt.-Col. F. P. NOSWORTHY.

A.-A. and Q.-M.-G.

6 Nov., 1914...Lt.-Col. W. S. FRANCE.
1 Feb., 1917...Lt.-Col. R. LUKER.
26 Nov., 1917...Lt.-Col. G. N. MACREADY.
24 April, 1918...Lt.-Col. F. J. LEMON.

B.-G., R.A.

Nov., 1914...Lt.-Col. J. MAGNUS (acting).
1 Feb., 1915...Col. C. B. WATKINS.
30 Mar., 1916...Col. E. H. ARMITAGE.
7 July, 1916...Br.-Gen. E. H. ARMITAGE.
17 Feb., 1917...Br.-Gen. J. J. MACMAHON.
3 July, 1917...Lt.-Col. J. LAIRD (acting).
13 July, 1917...Br.-Gen. D. B. STEWART (wd., 28/8/17).
28 Aug., 1917...Lt.-Col. H. E. O'B. TRAILL (acting).
12 Sept., 1917...Br.-Gen. A. C. LOWE (killed, 24/11/17).
24 Nov., 1917...Br.-Gen. A. B. FORMAN (tempy.).
25 Nov., 1917...Lt.-Col. J. LAIRD (acting).
1 Dec., 1917...Br.-Gen. A. BIRTWISTLE.

C.R.E.

9 Nov., 1914...Lt.-Col. H. A. FIELDING.
20 Nov., 1916...Lt.-Col. F. G. GUGGISBERG.
10 May, 1917...Major G. S. KNOX (acting).
12 June, 1917...Lt.-Col. G. C. WILLIAMS (to 199th Bde.).
15 Mar., 1918...Captain C. A. WEST (acting).
2 April, 1918...Lt.-Col. G. J. P. GOODWIN.
11 Aug., 1918...Major S. H. MORGAN (acting).
19 Aug., 1918...Lt.-Col. G. J. P. GOODWIN.
1 Sept., 1918...MAJOR S. H. MORGAN (acting).
30 Sept., 1918...Lt.-Col. O. S. DAVIES.

197th BDE.

(2nd/1st Lanc. Fus.)

5 Nov., '14...Colonel A. A. GARSTIN.
19 May, '16...Br.-Gen. F. L. BANON.
13 July, '17...Br.-Gen. O. C. BORRETT (wd., 30/3/18).
30 Mar., '18...Lt.-Col. G. P. NORTON (acting).
3 April, '18...Br.-Gen. L. L. WHEATLEY.

(On 20/9/18 197th Bde. left 66th Division for L. of C.*)

198th BDE.

(2nd/1st E. Lanc.)

5 Nov., '14...Colonel C. S. GORDON STEWARD.
10 Feb., '16...Lt.-Col. W. PATTERSON (acting).
1 Mar., '16...Colonel C. S. GORDON STEWARD.
8 June, '16...Br.-Gen. G. E. MATTHEWS (wd., 12/4/17; d. of w. 13/4/17).
12 April, '17...Lt.-Col. G. T. B. WILSON (acting).
17 April, '17...Br.-Gen. A. J. HUNTER.

199th BDE.

(2nd/1st Manch.)

16 Nov., '14...Colonel B. N. NORTH.
20 May, '16...Br.-Gen. J. O. TRAVERS.
16 Mar., '18...Br.-Gen. G. C. WILLIAMS.

SOUTH AFRICAN BDE.

(Transferred from 9th Division, and joined 66th Division on 23/9/18).
[1 April, '18]...Br.-Gen. W. E. C. TANNER.

* On 22/9/18 Br.-Gen. L. L. Wheatley left 197th Bde. and assumed the command of 1st Bde., 1st Division. Thereafter, until Armistice, 197th Bde. was commanded by the following officers:—
22 Sept., 1918...Lt.-Col. A. W. BLOCKLEY (acting).
1 Oct., 1918...Lt.-Col. G. V. W. HILL (acting).
6 Oct., 1918...Br.-Gen. J. HAMILTON HALL.

66TH (2ND/EAST LANCASHIRE) DIVISION

GENERAL NOTES

The following Units also served with the 66th Division :—

IN ENGLAND

1/2/Lancashire Heavy Battery—(4, 4·7" Guns)—On 16/9/15 the Right Section from Sunderland rejoined the Hy. Bty., which was then with the 66th Div. The Hy. Bty. left the 66th Div. on 5/1/16 and went to Woolwich. The Hy. Bty. (with 4·7" guns) disembkd. at le Havre on 9/2/16 ; joined XVI Hy. Bde., R.G.A., on 15/2/16 ; and was transferred to XVII Hy. Arty. Group on 23/10/17. By 1917 the Hy. Bty. was rearmed with 6, 60-pdrs.

2/1/Lancashire Heavy Battery, transferred from 57th Div. in 1916, served with 66th Div. in England. Before going to France the Hy. Bty. was rearmed with 6, 60-pdrs. On 1/7/16 the Hy. Bty. disembkd. at le Havre, and on 4/7/16 it was attached to II Anzac Corps ; on 4/8/16 the Hy. Bty. joined LII H.A.G.

2/2/Lancashire Heavy Battery, joined the 66th Div. after concentration. On 7/1/16 the Hy. Bty received 4, 4·7" Guns—incomplete and worn out, but useful for drill and gun-laying. After the embkn. of the 66th Div. in Febry., 1917, the Hy. Bty. remained in England ; it was attached to the 67th Div. from Septr., 1916–Aug., 1917. From Jany., 1918, the Hy. Bty. was stationed at Minster under the Kent Force, Eastern Command, with which it served at Minster until the end of the Great War. Towards the end of the War, the Hy. Bty. was attached to the Cyclist Division.

2/5/Lancashire Fusiliers, raised at Bury in 1914, the Bn. joined 197th (2/1/Lanc. Fus.) Bde. on its formation. In April, 1915, the Bn. was transferred to 154th (3rd Highland) Bde., 51st (Highland) Div., and joined the Bde. at Bedford by 18/4/15. Bn. went to France with 51st Div. in May, 1915. On 7/1/16 the Bn. was transferred to 55th Div., with 154th Bde. (which then became 164th Bde.). 2/5/L.F. served with 164th Bde., 55th Div., for the remainder of the Great War.

3/1/London Sanitary Section, left before embkn. of Div. in 1917.

The following Unit also served in FRANCE with the 66th Div. :—

66th Sanitary Section. This Section went to France independently. It disembkd. at le Havre on 2/3/17 ; joined 66th Div., near St. Venant, on 5/3/17 ; and, leaving the Division on 8 and 9/4/17, the Section became XI Corps Sanitary Section.

On 20/2/18 the reorganization of the 66th Division on a 9-battalion basis was completed ; and the pioneer battalion was reorganized on 21/2/18 on a 3-company basis.

66th Division Artillery (21 March–11 November, 1918).

From 21/3/18 the 66th D.A. took part in the First Battles of the Somme, 1918, and was engaged in covering the 66th Div. until 28/3/18. On 29/3/18 66th D.A. (east of Villers Bretonneux) was covering Carey's Force, the remaining divisional infantry having been withdrawn from the line. The Artillery remained in action until the end of the Somme Battles, and took part in the Battle of the Avre (4/4/18) when it was engaged in covering the 18th Div. By this time 66th D.A. had been re-organized on a 4-gun battery basis ; the D.A. was then 21 guns and 4 hows. short of a 6-gun establishment. On 7/4/18, B.-G., R.A., 66th Div., had 106 guns in action under his command and his S.O.S. frontage was 6,800 yards. 66th D.A. was relieved on the night of 7/8/4/18. On 11/4/18, 4, 4·5" hows. and 1, 18-pdr. were drawn from No. 5 Park. (By the end of May all the guns had been completed and the batteries had been organized once more on a 6-gun basis.) On 16/4/18, 66th D.A. (with 541 Coy., A.S.C., of the 66th Div. Train) came under VIII Corps, Second Army, and on 20/4/18 CCCXXX (Comp.) Bde. was attached to 36th Div., II Corps. The Comp. Bde. was in action 21–26/4/18 (Battles of the Lys). On 28/4/18 the 66th D.A. concentrated in the Proven area and batteries returned to their own brigades. From 14 and 15/5–22/5/18 the 66th D.A. was in action near Busseboom covering the French 14th Div. From 13–17/6/18 the 66th D.A. was covering 3rd Div., XIII Corps. From 21 and 22/6/18 the 66th D.A. was under the 61st Div. until 14/7/18, when it was transferred in the line to the 74th Div. On 15/7/18 66th D.A. was relieved. On 20/7/18 66th D.A. was detailed by XIX Corps to co-operate with the American 27th Div. in the defence of the E. Poperinghe Line (or 2nd Position). On 17 and 18/8/18 the 66th D.A. came into action in the front line until 26/8/18, under 41st Div. On 30/8/18, 66th D.A. went into action near Poperinghe to cover the American 30th Div. ; and on 1/9/18 the batteries began to move forward. From 4–6/9/18 66th D.A. was under 35th Div. ; and from 7/9/18 66th D.A. was attached to the 40th Div. (in the front line along the R. Lys). From 12/9–1/10/18 CCCXXX was lent to the 31st Div. ; and 66th D.A. took part in the Battle of Ypres, 28/9–2/10/18. On 5/10/18 the batteries began to move across the R. Lys and on 18/10/18 66th D.A. was relieved near Armentières. On 26 and 27/10/18 66th D.A. went into the line, near Fontaine au Bois, under 25th Div., XIII Corps, and took part in the Battle of the Sambre (4/11/18). On 8/11/18, whilst still in the line, 66th D.A. was at last transferred back to the 66th Div., then in XIII Corps, Fourth Army. 66th D.A. then remained covering the 66th Div. until the Armistice on 11/11/18, by which time batteries had advanced as far as Solre le Château.

BETHELL'S FORCE was formed on 9/11/1918, it was composed as follows :—G.O.C., Major-General H. K. Bethell (Comdg. 66th Divn.). 2 Sqdns., R.A.F., 5th Cav. Bde., A, B, and 2 secs., D (H.)/CCCXXXI, 1 Sec., A.–A., 430th, 431st, 432nd, Fd. Cos., 66th Div. Sig. Coy., No. 17 Armoured Car Bn., IX Corps and XIII Corps Cyclist Bns., 1 Coy., 9/Glouc. (P.), 1 Coy., 100th Bn., M.G.C., S. African Infantry Bde. Group, 1st S.A. Fd. Amb., and Detnts. from 2/2 and 2/3/E. Lanc. Fd. Amb.

Bethell's Force was dissolved after the Armistice. The troops then returned to their own formations.

66TH[1] (2ND/EAST LANCASHIRE) DIVISION

ORDER OF BATTLE, 1915-1918

Dates	INFANTRY		Mounted Troops	ARTILLERY						Engineers	Signal Service	Pioneers	M.G. Units	Field Ambu-lances	Mobile Vety. Secn.	Divnl. Emplnt. Coy.	Divnl. Train
				Field Artillery			Trench Mortar Bties.										
	Brigades	Battalions and attached Units		Brigades	Batteries	Bde. Ammn. Colns.	Medium	Heavy	Divnl. Ammn. Coln.	Field Cos.	Divnl. Signal Coy.						
1915 November (England)	197th[1] ... (2/1/ Lanc. Fus.) 198th[1] ... (2/1/E. Lanc.) 199th[1] ... (2/1/Manch.)	3/5/L.F.,[2] 2/6/L.F., 2/7/L.F., 2/8/L.F. 2/4/E. Lanc., 2/5/E. Lanc., 2/9/Manch., 2/10/Manch. 2/5/Manch., 2/6/Manch., 2/7/ Manch., 2/8/Manch.	66th (2/1/E. Lanc.) Div. Cyclist Coy.	2/I E. Lanc.[3] 2/II E. Lanc.[3] 2/III E. Lanc.[3] 2/IV E. Lanc.[4] (H.)	2/4/Lanc., 2/5/Lanc., 2/6/Lanc. 2/15/Lanc., 2/16/ Lanc., 2/17/Lanc. 2/18/Lanc., 2/19/ Lanc., 2/20/Lanc. 2/1/Cumbd. (H.), 2/2/Cumbd. (H.)	2/I E. Lanc. 2/II E. Lanc. 2/III E. Lanc. 2/IV E. Lanc. (H.)	...	...	66th (2/1/E. Lanc.) D.A.C.	2/1/ E. Lanc. 2/2/ E. Lanc.	66th (2/1/E. Lanc.)	...	...	2/1/ E. Lanc. 2/2/ E. Lanc. 2/3/ E. Lanc.	...	...	66th[5] (2/1/ E. Lanc.)
1916 September (England)	197th ...... 198th 199th	3/5/L.F., 2/6/L.F., 2/7/L.F., 2/8/L.F. 2/4/E. Lanc., 2/5/E. Lanc., 2/9/Manch., 2/10/Manch. 2/5/Manch., 2/6/Manch., 2/7/ Manch., 2/8/Manch.	BSqdn.,[6] 2/1/ Bedf. Yeo. 66th Div. Cyclist Coy.[6]	CCCXXX[5; 7] (2/I E. Lanc.) [5; 4; 9] CCCXXXI ... (2/II E. Lanc.) [5; 4; 10] CCCXXXII ... (2/III E. Lanc.)	A (2/4/Lanc.), B (2/5/Lanc.), C (2/6/Lanc.), D (H.)[8] A (2/15/Lanc.), B (2/16/Lanc.), C (2/17/Lanc.), D (H.) (2/1/Cumbd.) A (2/18/Lanc.), B (2/19/Lanc.), C (2/20/Lanc.), D (H.) (2/2/Cumbd.)	...[11]	...	...	66th D.A.C.[11]	2/1/ E. Lanc. 2/2/ E. Lanc. 2/3/ E. Lanc.	66th	...	...	2/1/ E. Lanc. 2/2/ E. Lanc. 2/3/ E. Lanc.	1/1/[12] E. Lanc.	...	66th
1917 June (France)	197th ...... 198th 199th	3/5/L.F.,[13] 2/6/L.F.,[14] 2/7/ L.F., 2/8/L.F.; 202nd M.G. Coy.;[15; 58] 197th T.M. Bty.[16] 2/4/E. Lanc.,[17] 2/5/E. Lanc., 2/9/Manch., 2/10/Manch.;[18] 203rd M.G. Coy.;[15; 58] 198th T.M. Bty.[16] 2/5/Manch., 2/6/Manch., 2/7/ Manch., 2/8/Manch.;[19] 204th M.G. Coy.;[15; 58] 199th T.M. Bty.[16]	...	CCCXXX ...... CCCXXXI ...	A, B, C; D (H.) A, B, C; D (H.)	...	X.66[20] Y.66[20] Z.66[20]	V.66[20]	66th D.A.C.[11]	430th[21] (2/1/ E. Lanc.) 431st[21] (2/2/ E. Lanc.) 432nd[21] (2/3/ E. Lanc.)	66th	10/D. C.L.I.[22] (P.)	...	2/1/ E. Lanc. 2/2/ E. Lanc. 2/3/ E. Lanc.	1/1/ E. Lanc.	254th[23]	66th
1918 March (France)	197th[24] ... 198th 199th	6/L.F.,[14]; [25] 2/7/L.F.,[26] 2/8/ L.F.;[27] 197th T.M. Bty.[28] 4/E. Lanc.,[17; 29] 2/5/E. Lanc.,[30] 9/Manch.[31]; 198th T.M. Bty. 2/5/Manch.,[32] 2/6/Manch.,[33] 2/7/Manch.;[34] 199th T.M. Bty.	...	CCCXXX ...... CCCXXXI ...	A, B, C; D (H.) A, B, C; D (H.)	...	X.66[35] Y.66[35]	...[36]	66th D.A.C.	430th 431st 432nd	66th	1/5/ Bord.[37] (P.)	No. 66 Bn., M.G.C.[38]	2/1/E. Lanc.[39] 2/2/ E. Lanc. 2/3/ E. Lanc.	1/1/ E. Lanc.	254th	66th
[...] reconstitution { **1918 Sept. (France)**	198th ...... 199th ...... South[45]	6/L.F.,[25] 5/R. Innis F.,[40] 6/ R.D.F.;[41] 198th T.M. Bty.[42] 18/King's (Lanc. Hsrs.),[43] 9/ Manch.,[31] 5/Conn. Rang.;[44] 199th T.M. Bty.[42] 1/S.A. Inf.,[45] 2/S.A. Inf.,[45] 4/	...	CCCXXX[46] ... CCCXXXI[46] ...	A, B, C; D (H.) A, B, C; D (H.)	...	...[47]	...	66th [46; 48] D.A.C.	430th 431st 432nd	66th	9/Glouc. (P.)[49]	100th[50] (War. & S. Notts. Yeo.) Bn., M.G.C.	2/2/ E. Lanc. 2/3/ E. Lanc. S.A.Fd. Amb.[45]	1/1/ E. Lanc.	254th	66th[51]

NOTES

1 The Division and the Inf. Bdes. were designated by numbers in August, 1915. (Authy., 40/W.O./2609, A.G.1, of 10/8/15.)

2 In April, 1915, 3/5/L.F. replaced 2/5/L.F. in the 2/1/L.F. Bde. (2/5/L.F. was transferred in April, 1915, to 154th (3rd Highld.) Bde., 51st (Highld.) Div. at Bedford, see General Notes).

3 In May, 1916, the designations of the 18-pdr. Bdes. and Bties. were changed, Bdes. were numbered and Bties. lettered; and Bdes. were reconstituted. (18-pdrs. were received in Nov. and Dec., 1915.)

4 On 1/9/15 2/IV (How.) Bde. was reduced to 1 Bty. of 2 guns and an ammn. coln.; but in Dec., 1915, it was again brought up to full establishment of 2 How. Bties. and an Ammn. Coln., and 4.5" hows. arrived. In May, 1916, the How. Bde. was broken up, and the batteries joined CCCXXXI(2/IIE. Lanc.) and CCCXXXII (2/III E. Lanc.) Bdes.

5 In Dec., 1915, the Cos. of the Train were numbered 541, 542, 543, and 544.

6 The Bedford Yeo. and the Cyclist Coy. remained in England.

7 Before leaving England the 18-pdr. Bties. were made up to 6 guns each; and 550(H.)—4, 4.5" hows.—joined and became D (H.). On 7/3/17, R. Sec. of C (H.)/CCLXXXVII arrived from 57th Div. and made D (H.) up to 6 hows.

8 550 (H.)—4, 4.5" hows.—joined CCCXXX in England and became D (H.).

9 Before leaving England the 18-pdr. Bties. were made up to 6 guns each. On 17/3/17 1 sec. of D (H.)/CCCXXXII joined and made D (H.)/CCCXXXI up to 6 hows.

10 Before leaving England C was split up between A and B, to make the 2 batteries up to 6 18-pdrs. each; and C (H.)—4, 4.5" hows.—joined the Bde. On 17/3/17 D (H.) was broken up: 1 sec. joined D (H.)/CCCXXXI, and 1 sec. joined C (H.)/CCCXXXII. In April, 1917, CCCXXXII was broken up: A was transferred to CCXCVIII A.F.A. Bde. on 11/4/17, joined on 12/4/17 and became C/CCXCVIII; B was transferred on 30/4/17 to complete the Composite Bty. with the 1st. Cdn. Div.; C (H.) joined First Army Artillery School, and on 30/5/17 C (H.) joined 49th Div. Arty. (temporarily). Later on the battery was broken up (after 5/6/17).

11 B.A.C.s were abolished and the D.A.C. was reorganized in England. On 15/3/17, after arrival in France, the D.A.C. was reorganized in 2 Sections and B Echelon.

12 Joined in England and went to France with the division.

13 Bn. was broken up on 13/2/18, and drafted to 2/7/L.F. and 2/8/L.F., as well as 19/L.F. (P.) in 49th Div.

14 On 20/2/18 the Bn. amalgamated with 1/6/L.F. from 125th Bde., 42nd Div., and became 6/L.F.

15 202nd joined 66th Div. in England (from 59th Div.) and went to France in March, 1917, with the Div. 203rd left Grantham (for 59th Div.) on 10/3/17; transferred at Fovant on 12/3/17 to 66th Div., and went to France with 66th Div. 204th joined 66th Div. in England and went to France in March, 1917, with the Div.

16 The T.M. Bties. all joined the 66th Div. in England, and went to France with the Div. in Febry. and March, 1917.

17 On 19/2/18 the Bn. amalgamated with 1/4/E. Lanc. from 126th Bde., 42nd Div., and became 4/E. Lanc.

18 Bn. was broken up on 15/2/18, and drafted to 42nd Div.

19 Bn. was broken up on 13/2/18, and drafted to 2/5, 2/6, and 2/7/Manch.

20 The Medium and Heavy T.M. Bties. were formed in Febry., 1917, and went to France in March, 1917, with 66th Div.

21 The Fd. Cos. were numbered in Febry., 1917, before leaving England.

22 The pioneer bn. of the 2nd Div. was attached to 66th Div. from 16/7/17-7/11/17; 10/D.C.L.I.(P.) then rejoined 2nd Div.

23 Formed by 14/7/17.

24 From 9/4/18 the Bde. was reduced to Training Cadre. The 66th Division was reconstituted from 18/9/18, but the 197th Bde. was then left out of the division. Thereafter 197th Bde. was employed until Dec., 1918, in training drafts and reinforcements. (197th Bde. left 66th Div. on 20/9/18.)

25 Bn. was transferred on 22/7/18 to 199th Bde.; on 13/8/18 6/L.F. absorbed 12/L.F. (from 65th Bde., 22nd Div., at Salonika); and on 22/9/18 6/L.F. joined 198th Bde.

26 Bn. left Bde. and moved to England, disembkg. at Folkestone on 30/6/18. Bn. then moved to Aldershot and was attached temporarily to 74th Bde., 25th Div. On 3/7/18 Bn. became 24/L.F., and later on the Bn. was broken up.

27 Bn. was reduced to cadre on 22/4/18; and the Bn. cadre was disbanded and drafted on 31/7/18 to 1/8/L.F. (125th Bde., 42nd Div.).

28 Bty. was broken up in mid-April, 1918; it was reformed on 19/8/18.

29 Bn. was reduced to cadre in April, 1918. Bn. cadre was transferred to 39th Div. Offrs. Training Depot, joined at Calais on 16/8/18, and was posted to 118th Bde. On 16/11/18 Bn. was transferred to 116th Bde.

30 Bn. was reduced to Training Cadre in April, 1918; Bn. cadre was disbanded on 31/7/18, and personnel joined 1/5/E. Lanc. (126th Bde., 42nd Div.).

31 Bn. was reduced to Training Cadre in April, 1918. On 22/7/18 Bn. cadre was transferred to 199th Bde., and on 13/8/18 9/Manch. absorbed 13/Manch. (from 66th Bde., 22nd Div., at Salonika).

32 Bn. was reduced to cadre in April, 1918; Bn. was disbanded on 31/7/18, and cadre joined 1/5/Manch. (127th Bde., 42nd Div.).

33 Bn. was reduced to cadre in April, 1918; Bn. was disbanded on 31/7/18; personnel left for Base and was drafted to 1/6/Manch. (127th Bde., 42nd Div.).

34 Bn. was reduced to cadre in April, 1918; Bn. was disbanded on 31/7/18, and personnel joined 1/7/Manch. (127th Bde., 42nd Div.).

35 The Medium T.M. Bties. were reorganized on 6/2/18: Y was broken up between X and Z, and then Z became Y.

36 On 3/2/18 V was transferred complete to XXII Corps, and was absorbed in XXII Corps H.T.M. Bty.

37 On 12/2/18 the Bn. was transferred as Pioneers to 66th Div. from 151st Bde., 50th Div.; Bn. joined 66th Div. on 13/2/18. On 7/5/18 the Bn. was transferred to 97th Bde., 32nd Div.

38 Bn. was formed on 11/3/18, and consisted of 202nd, 203rd, and 204th M.G. Cos. The Bn. was broken up by 15/4/18.

39 From 22/6/18 the Fd. Amb. was attached to the 27th (Am.) Div., and from 26/9/18 to the 9th Div.

RECONSTITUTED DIVISION

40 Bn. (from 31st Bde., 10th Div., Palestine) left 10th Div. on 28/5/18; left Alexandria on 18/6/18; disembkd. Taranto on 22/6/18; reached Serqueux on 29/6/18; and joined 198th Bde. at Abancourt on 19/7/18.

41 Bn. (from 30th Bde., 10th Div.—Palestine) left 10th Div. on 27/5/18; embkd. Alexandria on 3/7/18; disembkd. Taranto on 8/7/18; reached Serqueux on 15/7/18; and Bn. came under 50th Div. for administration on 18/7/18. Bn. joined 197th Bde., 66th Div., on 21/7/18, and was transferred to 198th Bde. on 10/9/18.

42 The Bde. T.M. Bties. were reformed: 198th by 21/9/18; and 199th on 21/8/18. [197th T.M. Bty., reformed on 19/8/18, went to L. of C. with 197th Bde. on 20/9/18—see note 24.]

43 Bn. (from 89th Bde., 30th Div.) was reduced to training cadre on 14/5/18. Bn. left 30th Div. on 19/6/18 and joined 66th Div.; Bn. joined 197th Bde. on 8/8/18; absorbed 14/King's (from 65th Bde., 22nd Div.—Salonika) on 13/8/18; and, on 19/9/18, 18/King's was transferred to 199th Bde.

44 Bn. (from 29th Bde., 10th Div.—Palestine) left 10th Div. on 29/4/18; embkd. at Port Said on 23/5/18; sailed, 25/5/18; disembkd. Marseille on 1/6/18; reached Aire on 7/6/18, and Bn. was attached to 14th Div., 7/6/18-28/6/18. Bn. moved to Serqueux on 28/6/18, and joined 199th Bde. on 25/8/18.

45 Bde. (complete) left 9th Div. on 13/9/18, and came under VII Corps until 22/9/18. Bde. joined 66th Div. on 23/9/18.

46 66th Div. Arty. only rejoined 66th Div. on 8/11/18 (see General Notes).

47 X and Y (Medium) T.M. Bties. were broken up on 28/4/18, and the mortars were returned to Ordnance Base Depot. The 2 Bties. were not reformed.

48 S.A.A. Sec. of D.A.C. was disbanded on 22/4/18. The S.A.A. Sec. was reformed early in October, 1918.

49 Bn. (from 78th Bde., 26th Div., Salonika) left 26th Div. on 4/7/18, embkd. at Itea on 9/7/18, disembkd. at Taranto on 10/7/18, reached Serqueux on 17/7/18. From 17-21/7/18 the Bn. was administered by 50th Div.; on 21 and 22/7/18 Bn. was transferred to 198th Bde., 66th Div.; and on 22/9/18 Bn. became Pioneer Bn., 66th Div.

50 The War. Yeo. and S. Notts. Hsrs. were amalgamated from 3/4/18 to form a machine-gun Bn. at Bela. The Bn. embkd. at Alexandria on 17/6/18, disembkd. at Taranto on 21/6/18, and reached Etaples on 29/6/18. On 1/7/18 the Bn. was designated B Bn., M.G.C.; and on 19/8/18 B Bn. became 100th (War. and S. Notts. Yeo.) Bn., M.G.C. 100th Bn. was under 12th and 47th Divs. on 5 and 6/9/18; under 58th Div., 7-25/9/18 (with 2 Cos. under 12th Div., 16-25/9/18); under 46th Div., 26/9-1/10/18; under 25th Div., 2-19/10/18; and on 19/10/18 100th Bn. joined 66th Div.

51 541-544 Cos. A.S.C. (541 Coy. rejoined with 66th Div. Arty.—see note 46.)

IN FRANCE

The following Units and Training Cadres served with the 66th Division :—

Unit	From	Reduced to Training Cadre	Served with 66th Div. From	To	Transferred to, Absorbed by, or Disbanded	Notes
18/N.F.	Pioneers, 34th Div.	18/5/18	16/8	20/9/18	To L. of C. with 197th Bde.	
23/N.F.	102nd Bde., 34th Div.	17/5/18	16/8	20/9/18	To L. of C. with 197th Bde.	
25/N.F.	102nd Bde., 34th Div.	15 & 16/5/18	16/8	20/9/18	To L. of C. with 197th Bde.	
14/King's	65th Bde., 22nd Div. (Salonika).	—	23/7	13/8/18	Absorbed by 18/King's (199th Bde.—see note 43).	
17/King's	89th Bde., 30th Div.	14/5/18	19/6	30/6/18	To England, with 75th Bde., 25th Div.	Transferred on 9/9/18 to 236th Bde. (for N. Russia).
19/King's	89th Bde., 30th Div.	14/5/18	19/6	1/8/18	Absorbed by 14/King's (see above).	
2/5/Lincoln	177th Bde., 59th Div.	8/5/18	28/6	31/7/18	Absorbed by 1/5/Lincoln (138th Bde., 46th Div).	
10/Lincoln	101st Bde., 34th Div.	18/5/18	16/8	20/9/18	To L. of C. with 197th Bde.	
7/Suffolk	35th Bde., 12th Div.	19/5/18	16/8	20/9/18	To L. of C. with 197th Bde.	
7/Bedford	54th Bde., 18th Div.	27/5/18	19/6	31/7/18	Absorbed by 2/Bedford (54th Bde., 18th Div.).	
6/York.	32nd Bde., 11th Div.	14/5/18	19/6	30/6/18	To England with 75th Bde., 25th Div.	Transferred on 9/9/18 to 236th Bde. (for N. Russia).
12/L.F.	65th Bde., 22nd Div. (Salonika).	—	22/7	13/8/18	Absorbed by 6/L.F. (198th Bde.—see note 25).	
13/Glouc.	Pioneers, 39th Div.	5 & 6/5/18	16/8	20/9/18	To L. of C. with 197th Bde.	
11/Border	97th Bde., 32nd Div.	10/5/18	13/5	31/7/18	Absorbed by 1/5/Border (97th Bde., 32nd Div.).	
2/6/S. Staff.	176th Bde., 59th Div.	9/5/18	30/5	31/7/18	Absorbed by 1/6/S. Staff. (137th Bde., 46th Div.).	
11/S. Lanc.	Pioneers, 30th Div.	15/5/18	19/6	30/6/18	To England with 25th Div.	Bn. returned to France on 7 and 8/10/18, and became Pioneer Bn., 25th Division, on 13/10/18.
10/B.W.	77th Bde., 26th Div. (Salonika).	—	21/7	20/9/18	To L. of C. with 197th Bde.	Disbanded on 15/10/18, and drafted.
7/Sher. For.	178th Bde., 59th Div.	7/5/18	[illegible]/6	15/8/18	To 39th Div.	
16/Sher. For.	117th Bde., 39th Div.	8/5/18	16/8	20/9/18	To L. of C. with 197th Bde.	
17/K.R.R.C.	117th Bde., 39th Div.	13/5/18	16/8	20/9/18	To L. of C. with 197th Bde.	
13/Manch.	66th Bde., 22nd Div. (Salonika).	—	21/7	13/8/18	Absorbed by 9/Manch. (199th Bde.—see note 31).	
17/Manch.	90th Bde., 30th Div.	15/5/18	19/6	30/7/18	Absorbed by 13/Manch. (see above).	
2/6/N. Staff.	176th Bde., 59th Div.	9/5/18	7/6	31/7/18	Absorbed by 1/6/N. Staff. (137th Bde., 46th Div.).	
14/H.L.I.	120th Bde., 40th Div.	6/5/18	16/8	20/9/18	To L. of C. with 197th Bde.	
5/R. Ir. Fus.	31st Bde., 10th Div. (Palestine).	—	23/7	24/8/18	To 16th Div.	Absorbed 11/R. Ir. Fus. on 27/8/18, and posted to 48th Bde., 16th Div.
16/R.B.	117th Bde., 39th Div.	13/5/18	16/8	20/9/18	To L. of C. with 197th Bde.	
6/Leinster	29th Bde., 10th Div. (Palestine).	—	20/7	12/9/18	Disbanded and drafted.	
2/20/London	180th Bde., 60th Div. (Palestine).	—	19/7	9/8/18	To 185th Bde., 62nd Div.	
2/24/London	181st Bde., 60th Div. (Palestine).	—	28/7	10/9/18	To 173rd Bde., 58th Div.	

66TH (2ND/EAST LANCASHIRE) DIVISION

FORMATION, BATTLES, AND ENGAGEMENTS

This 2nd-line (or reserve) Territorial Force division had no existence before the outbreak of the Great War.

The formation of reserve (or 2nd-line) T. F. units was authorized on the 31st August, 1914 (see Narrative, 57th Division). During September and October the artillery, engineers, and infantry (required to form the 2nd/East Lancashire Division) were raised in Manchester and district and in the cotton and colliery towns of Lancashire. In November the brigade and divisional headquarters began to assemble.

After the 1st/East Lancashire Division [42nd Division] embarked for Egypt on the 10th September, 1914, the formation of its 2nd-line division was hurried on despite the small available nucleus, the large number of recruits which were required, and the dearth of trained instructors. Gradually these difficulties were surmounted. The battalions eventually received Japanese rifles, bayonets, and ammunition (600–700 rifles and bayonets, and 180,000 rounds, per battalion). The Japanese rifles were retained until the end of 1915, and then they were replaced by charger-loading Lee-Enfield rifles, together with bayonets and ·303" ammunition. Shortage of technical equipment was not confined to the infantry. The artillery lacked guns, with modern sights and gears, ammunition wagons, directors, telephones, and harness. Even in August, 1915, no veterinary officer was attached to any of the artillery brigades, and at this time the artillery had 1,373 horses.

On the 10th October, 1914, 2/IV/E. Lanc. (How.) Bde. accompanied 1/IV/E. Lanc. (H.) to Crown Hill (Devon) and 2/IV remained there. (I/IV left on the 17th November, for Newcastle.) On the 10th February, 1915, 2/IV/E. Lanc. (How.) Bde., moved to Southport, on the 23rd May it went to East Grinstead, on the 3rd June the brigade received two 5" B.L. howitzers and limbers, and on the 5th August the howitzer brigade reached its war station at Plow Hatch (Forest Row).

The preliminary training of the division had been delayed and made more difficult by furnishing drafts of its best men to reinforce its 1st-line division (the 42nd) in Gallipoli, and it was August before the 66th Division effected its concentration at its war stations in Kent and Sussex. The division now formed part of Second Army, Central Force. At this time divisional headquarters, three infantry brigades, and the engineers were at Crowborough, three of the artillery brigades were at Forest Row, and the howitzer brigade and the heavy battery were at Plow Hatch. By the end of this month all the home-service men left the various units, and only those men were retained who had Imperial Service obligations. In October 197th Brigade moved to Tunbridge Wells.

During August, 1915, the three field artillery brigades each received four French 90-m./m. equipments; however, before the end of the year 18-pdr. Q.F. equipments began to arrive, and shortly afterwards the howitzer brigade was issued with 4·5" howitzers.

In 1916 the 66th Division was transferred to Southern Army, Home Defence Force, and was entrusted with the defence of part of the East Coast. At this time, divisional headquarters, divisional mounted troops, two infantry brigades, the artillery, and the engineers were at Colchester, one infantry brigade was at Wivenhoe, and the heavy batteries (2/1/London and 2/2/London) were at Thorpe le Soken and St. Osyth. Now that it was compactly quartered, the division could soon have been brought to a high state of efficiency had it not been for the provision of large drafts for overseas. To provide even one draft of 250 trained gunners considerably delayed the preparation of the division for war. Consequently it was the 18th January, 1917, before the War Office was able to notify G.H.Q., France, that the 66th Division would embark about the 1st March.

On the 11th February, 1917, embarkation orders were received; and on the 22nd February the 66th Division was inspected at Colchester by H.M. the King. Entrainment began on the 25th, divisional headquarters started on the 28th February, and on the 1st March the division began detraining at Berguette and Thiennes. On the 16th March the move to France was completed, and the division concentrated under XI Corps, First Army.

Throughout the remainder of the Great War the 66th Division served on the Western Front in France and Belgium and was engaged in the following operations :—

1917

26 June–25 Sept. ... ... **Operations on the Flanders Coast** [XV Corps, Fourth Army].
6–10 October ... ... **BATTLES OF YPRES.**
9 October ... ... **Battle of Poelcappelle** [II Anzac Corps, Second Army].

1918

21–night 30/31 March ... **FIRST BATTLES OF THE SOMME.**
21–23 March ... ... **Battle of St. Quentin** [XIX Corps, Fifth Army].
24 and 25 March ... ... **Actions at the Somme Crossings** [XIX Corps, Fifth Army].
26 and 27 March ... ... **Battle of Rosières** [XIX Corps, Fifth Army].

When the 66th Division was withdrawn from the front line, 66th Division Artillery remained in action. The artillery did not rejoin 66th Division until the 8th November, during the last days of the Final Advance (see General Notes). Owing to the losses which it had suffered during the Battles of the Somme, the division (less its artillery) was reduced to Training Cadre from the 9th April until the 18th September.

66th Division was then re-formed and reconstituted (see General Notes and Table). On the 20th and 21st September the re-formed division was placed under VIII Corps, First Army, and on the 23rd the South African Infantry Brigade joined the division. Thereafter the reconstituted 66th Division was engaged in the following operations :—

THE ADVANCE TO VICTORY

BATTLES OF THE HINDENBURG LINE

8 and 9 October ... ... **Battle of Cambrai** [XIII Corps, Fourth Army].
9–12 October ... ... **Pursuit to the Selle** [XIII Corps, Fourth Army].

THE FINAL ADVANCE IN PICARDY

17–20 October ... ... **Battle of the Selle** [XIII Corps, Fourth Army].

On the night of 20th/21st October the 66th Division was relieved in the front line, and until the 1st November the division rested in the Serain area. On the 2nd November the division began to move forward. The division advanced through le Cateau, and on the 6th it was placed in close support to the 25th Division. On the 7th November 66th Division relieved 25th Division (in the front line of the XIII Corps) and continued the advance on the 8th. For the further pursuit Bethell's Force was formed on the 9th (for composition see General Notes). On the 10th November, after a sharp fight, the South African Infantry Brigade entered Hestrud (on the Belgian Frontier). On the same day 199th Infantry Brigade reached Solre le Château, and on the 11th Bethell's Force continued to advance in Belgium. By 11 a.m. (Armistice) the leading troops of Bethell's Force held a line running from Pont de la République–Grandrieu–east of Sivry–Montbliart. On the right the Force was in touch with French troops at Eppé Sauvage.

On the 14th November 66th Division was transferred from XIII Corps to IX Corps, on the 15th the division was informed that it had been selected to advance to the Rhine, and on the 18th November the march to the Rhine began. The division moved via Philippeville, and Waulsort and Dinant on the Meuse. On the 14th December divisional headquarters reached Ciney, and the division billetted in the area Dinant–Huy–Marche–Rochefort. The advance of the 66th Division then came to an end, and it was still halted in this district when its demobilization began. On the 13th February, 1919, General Botha visited the South African Infantry Brigade at Huy. Demobilization, however, continued daily and gradually the division dwindled. On the 16th March the last unit of the South African Brigade left the division for England ; and at mn. 24th/25th March, 1919, the 66th Division ceased to exist.

67TH (2ND/HOME COUNTIES) DIVISION

G.O.C.

14 November, 1914 ... ... Br.-Gen. C. T. CAULFEILD (acting).
3 January, 1915 ... ... Br.-Gen. W. R. CLIFFORD (acting).
20 January, 1915 ... ... Major-General J. C. YOUNG.
4 April, 1917 –6 June, 1919 ... ... Major-General Hon. C. E. BINGHAM.

G.S.O. 1.

14 Nov., 1914...Major F. M. CARLETON (acting).
4 May, 1915...Colonel P. S. MARLING, V.C.
3 Sept., 1915...Lt.-Col. C. P. HIGGINSON.
28 May, 1916...Lt.-Col. H. D. FARQUHARSON.
22 June, 1916...Lt.-Col. H. I. NICHOLL.
6 Mar., 1918...Lt.-Col. W. S. WHETHERLY.
9 July, 1918...Lt.-Col. P. S. ALLAN.

A.-A. and Q.-M.-G.

14 Nov., 1914...Lt.-Col. R. H. L. WARNER.
20 Jan., 1915...Captain H. W. GRUBB (acting).
11 June, 1915...Colonel S. D. GORDON.
5 Aug., 1916...Lt.-Col. C. J. PICKERING.
11 July, 1918...Lt.-Col. K. H. BRUCE.

B.-G., R.A.

14 Nov., 1914...Br.-Gen. C. T. CAULFEILD.
7 Jan., 1915...Major J. W. M. NEWTON (acting).
21 April, 1915...Colonel J. W. M. NEWTON.
14 Jan., 1916...Br.-Gen. W. H. SUART.
18 April, 1916...Colonel L. GRAHAM.
25 May, 1916...Colonel H. E. STOCKDALE.
7 July, 1916...Br.-Gen. H. E. STOCKDALE.
7 Nov., 1917...Br.-Gen. R. F. FOX.
16 June, 1918 –8 Jan., 1919 Br.-Gen. W. A. M. THOMPSON.

C.R.E.

12 Dec., 1914...Lt.-Col. E. G. HALES.
23 April, 1917...Lt.-Col. R. H. MACKENZIE.

200th BDE.

(2nd/1st Surrey)

12 Nov., '14...Br.-Gen. J. MARRIOTT.
27 June, '15...Br.-Gen. J. H. CAMPBELL.
5 Jan., '16...Lt.-Col. W. A. GILLETT (acting).
12 Jan., '16...Br.-Gen. J. MARRIOTT.
17 April, '17 – 24 Feb., '18 } Br.-Gen. E. H. GORGES.

(The 200th Inf. Bde. was demobilized in Feb., 1918.)

201st BDE.

(2nd/1st Middlesex)

30 Oct., '14...Br.-Gen. W. R. CLIFFORD.
22 Feb., '15...Br.-Gen. A. W. TAYLOR.
18 Oct., '15...Lt.-Col. E. O. EATON (acting).
24 Oct., '15...Lt.-Col. J. C. WORTHINGTON (acting).
25 Nov., '15...Br.-Gen. E. H. MOLESWORTH (sick, 23/2/16).
23 Feb., '16...Lt.-Col. J. C. WORTHINGTON (acting).
14 April, '16...Br.-Gen. C. L. MACNAB.
28 May, '16...Colonel C. P. HIGGINSON.
7 July, '16...Br.-Gen. C. P. HIGGINSON.
27 Oct., '16...Br.-Gen. A. BLAIR.
26 Feb., '17...Br.-Gen. M. L. MACEWEN.
18 April, '17...Br.-Gen. E. D. WHITE.
22 May, '18 – 31 Mar., '19 } Br.-Gen. R. K. WALSH.

214th BDE.

(On 12/2/18 the 214th Inf. Bde. was transferred from the 71st Div. to the 67th Div.).
[8 Nov., '17] Br.-Gen. L. A. E. PRICE-DAVIES, V.C.
8 April, '18...Br.-Gen. A. G. PRITCHARD.
5 July, '18...Br.-Gen. F. W. TOWSEY.

202nd BDE.

(2nd/1st Kent)

30 Oct., '14...Br.-Gen. L. COMBE.
25 Feb., '18...Br.-Gen. E. H. GORGES.

67th (2ND/HOME COUNTIES) DIVISION

GENERAL NOTES

The following Units belonged to the 2nd/Home Counties Division, but they served in the field with other divisions or garrisons :—

INFANTRY :—2/4/Queen's, joined 160th (Welsh Border) Inf. Bde., 53rd (Welsh) Division, on 24/4/15. The Bn. served with the Div. in Gallipoli, Egypt, and Palestine. On 31/5/18 the Bn. left 160th Bde., embkd. at Alexandria on 15/6/18, disembkd. at Taranto on 21/6/18, arrived at Proven on 29/6/18, and joined 101st Bde., 34th Division, on 30/6/18. The Bn. served on the Western Front with the 34th Division for the remainder of the Great War.

2/4/Q.O.R.W.K., joined 160th (Welsh Border) Inf. Bde., 53rd (Welsh) Division, on 24/4/15. The Bn. served with the Div. in Gallipoli, Egypt, and Palestine. The Bn. left 160th Bde. on 25/8/18, and thereafter was employed on repair of roads, etc.

2/7/Midd'x., raised in Aug., 1914, and recruited up to strength in a few weeks. Bn. went to Gibraltar on 1/2/15, and arrived on 7/2/15. Bn. left Gibraltar on 23/8/15 and joined the garrison in Egypt. Bn. left Alexandria on 9/5/16 for France, disembkd. at Marseille on 15/5/16, and left Marseille on 13/6/16. Bn. was disbanded. (After Bn. was disbanded, 3/7/Middx. (in 201st Bde.) became 2/7/Middx.—see Table).

2/8/Midd'x., raised in Aug., 1914, and recruited up to strength in a few weeks. Bn. went to Gibraltar on 1/2/15, and arrived on 7/2/15. Bn. left Gibraltar on 23/8/15 and joined the garrison in Egypt. Bn. left Alexandria on 9/5/16 for France, disembkd. at Marseille on 15/5/16, and left Marseille on 13/6/16. Bn. was disbanded. (After Bn. was disbanded, 3/8/Middx. (in 201st Bde.) became 2/8/Middx.—see Table).

2/10/Midd'x., joined 160th (Welsh Border) Inf. Bde., 53rd (Welsh) Division, on 24/4/15. The Bn. served with the Div. in Gallipoli, Egypt, and Palestine. On 19/8/18 the Bn. left 160th Bde., and the Bn. moved back to El Qantara. The Bn. was then broken up for drafts.

The following also served with the 67th Division :—

226th Mixed Brigade (Br.-Gen. Hon. C. G. Fortescue, until 11/3/18, then Br.-Gen, B. C. M. Carter) from 12/2/18 (transferred from 71st Div.).

ARTILLERY :—XLIX Bde., R.F.A. (2 batteries) joined with 214th Inf. Bde. on 12/2/18. XLIX was disbanded by 25/3/18.

1/1/Home Counties (Kent) Hy. Bty. (4, 4·7″ guns), from 30/10/14–17/11/15. Bty. left to equip for overseas. Bty. disembkd. at le Havre on 29/12/15, and joined XVI H.A. Bde. on 31/12/15.

2/1/Home Counties (Kent) Hy. Bty., became a separate unit from 26/12/14. On 10/1/16 Bty. received 4, 4·7″ guns, and on 7/2/16 passed on 2 to 2/1/London Hy. Bty. In Septr., 1916, 2/1/Kent Hy. Bty., at Mundesley, was attached to 4th Provisional Bde. In Nov., 1918, the Hy. Bty., still at Mundesley, was attached to 224th Mixed Bde. (H.Q., North Walsham).

2/2/Lancashire Hy. Bty., at Upstreet Camp and Minster, from Septr., 1916–Aug., 1917. From Jany., 1918, the Hy. Bty. was at Minster, attached to the Kent Force.

2/1/London Hy. Bty., at Great Bentley, was transferred on 12/2/18 from 71st Div. to 67th Div., and served with 67th Div. until Dec., 1918.

2/2/London Hy. Bty., at Great Bentley, was transferred on 12/2/18 from 71st Div. to 67th Div., and served with 67th Div. until Dec., 1918.

2/1/South Midland (Warwickshire) Hy. Bty., at Ramsgate and Sandwich, from Septr., 1916–Aug., 1917. In Nov., 1918, the Hy. Bty. was at Wingham, attached to the Kent Force.

130 Heavy Battery, R.G.A., (4, 60-pdrs.), was attached, to 67th Div., from 19/11/15–7/2/16. 130 Hy. Bty. then went to Egypt and disembkd. at Alexandria on 20/2/16. 130 Hy. Bty. embkd. at Alexandria (for France) on 8/4/16, disembkd. at Marseille on 15/4/16, and 130 Hy. Bty. came into action in the Fourth Army Area, at Meaulte, on 25/5/16.

CYCLISTS :—2/1/Kent Cyclist Bn., at Folkestone, from May–Aug., 1917. During the Great War 2/1/Kent Cyclist Bn. remained in England. In March, 1918, the Bn. was attached to the Cyclist Division, and the Bn. served with this division until the Armistice. In Nov., 1918, 2/1/Kent was stationed at Folkestone.

GRADUATED BATTALIONS OF THE TRAINING RESERVE :—

280 Bn., from 1/10/17, in 201st Bde. ;
285 Bn., from 1/10/17, in 202nd Bde.
} On 27/10/17 these 2 Graduated Bns. of the Training Reserve were affiliated to line regiments and adopted territorial designations (see note 24).

OTHER UNITS :—67th Sanitary Section, from 5/6/16–end of 1918; and
67th Motor Ambulance Workshop, until it was absorbed by the Train in 1916.

67TH[1] (2ND/HOME COUNTIES) DIVISION — ORDER OF BATTLE, 1915-1918

Dates	INFANTRY		Mounted Troops	ARTILLERY						Engineers	Signal Service	Pioneers	M.G. Units	Field Ambu-lances	Mobile Vety. Secn.	Divnl. Emplnt. Coy.	Divnl. Train
	Brigades	Battalions and attached Units		Field Artillery			Trench Mortar Bties.		Divnl. Ammn. Coln.	Field Cos.	Divnl. Signal Coy.						
				Brigades	Batteries	Bde. Ammn. Colns.	Medium	Heavy									
1915 November (England)	200th[1]; [2] (2nd/1st Surrey) 201st[1]; [2] (2nd/1st Midd'x.) 202nd[1]; [2] (2nd/1st Kent)	3/4/Queen's, 2/5/Queen's, 2/5/E. Surr., 2/6/E. Surr. 3/7/Midd'x., 3/8/Midd'x., 2/9/Midd'x., 3/10/Midd'x. 2/4/Buffs, 2/5/Buffs, 3/4/Q.O. R.W.K., 2/5/Q.O.R.W.K.	67th (2nd/1st/Home Cties.) Div. Cyclist Coy.[3]	2nd/I Home Counties 2nd/II Home Counties 2nd/III Home Counties 1st/IV Home[4] Counties (H.)	2/1/Sussex, 2/2/Sussex, 2/3/Sussex. 2/4/Sussex, 2/5/Sussex, 2/6/Sussex. 2/1/Kent, 2/2/Kent, 2/3/Kent. 1/4/Kent (H.), 1/5/Kent (H.)	2nd/I Home Counties 2nd/II Home Counties 2nd/III Home Counties 1st/IV Home Counties (H.)	...	...	...	1/3/ Home[5] Counties 2/1/ Home[6] Counties 2/2/ Home[7] Counties	67th[8] (2nd/1/ Home Counties)	...	...	2/1/ Home[12] Counties 2/2/ Home[12] Counties 2/3/ Home[12] Counties	67th (2/1/ Home Counties)	...	67th[9] (2nd/1/ Home Counties)
1916 May (England)	200th ...... 201st ...... 202nd......	3/4/Queen's, 2/5/Queen's, 2/5/E. Surr., 2/6/E. Surr. 3/7/Midd'x., 3/8/Midd'x., 2/9/Midd'x., 3/10/Midd'x. 2/4/Buffs, 2/5/Buffs, 3/4/Q.O. R.W.K., 2/5/Q.O.R.W.K.	67th Div. Cyclist Coy.	CCCXXXV[10] (2nd/I Home Counties) CCCXXXVI[10] (2nd/II Home Counties) CCCXXXVII[10] (2nd/III Home Counties) CCCXXXVIII (H.)[11] (2nd/IV Home Counties)	A, B, C A, B, C A, B, C A (H.), B (H.)	CCCXXXV B.A.C. CCCXXXVI B.A.C. CCCXXXVII B.A.C. CCCXXXVIII (H.) B.A.C.	...	...	67th D.A.C. (2nd/1/ Home Cties.)	1/3/ Home Counties 2/1/ Home Counties 2/2/ Home Counties	67th	...	...	3/1/ Home[12] Counties 3/2/ Home[12] Counties 3/3/ Home[12] Counties	67th	...	67th
1916 October (England)	200th ...... 201st ...... 202nd......	3/4/Queen's,[13] 2/5/Queen's, 2/5/E. Surr., 2/6/E. Surr. 2/7/Midd'x., 2/8/Midd'x., 2/9/Midd'x., 3/10/Midd'x.[14] 2/4/Buffs, 2/5/Buffs, 3/4/Q.O. R.W.K.,[15] 2/5/Q.O.R.W.K.	1 Sqdn., 2/1/ North'ts. Yeo. 67th Div. Cyclist Coy.	CCCXXXV[18] CCCXXXVI CCCXXXVII	A, B, C; D (H.)[11] A, B, C; D (H.)[11] A, B, C	...	...	...	67th D.A.C.	1/3/ Home Counties 2/1/ Home Counties 2/2/ Home Counties	67th	...	...	3/1/ Home Counties 3/2/ Home Counties 3/3/ Home Counties	67th	...	67th
1917 June (England)	200th ...... 201st ...... 202nd......	2/5/Queen's, 2/5/E. Surr., 2/6/E. Surr., 1/4/N. Staff.;[17] 200th T.M. Bty. 2/7/Midd'x., 2/8/Midd'x., 2/9/Midd'x., 1/4/S. Staff.;[17] 201st T.M. Bty. 2/4/Buffs, 2/5/Buffs, 2/5/Q.O. R.W.K., 1/1/R. Guern. L.I.[18]	1 Sqdn., 2/1/ North'ts. Yeo. 67th Div. Cyclist Coy.	CCCXXXVI... CCCXXXVII	A, B, C; D (H.) A, B, C; D (H.)	...	...	...	67th D.A.C.	492nd (1/3/ Home Counties) 493rd (2/1/ Home Counties) 494th (2/2/ Home Counties)	67th	...	...	3/1/ Home Counties 3/2/ Home Counties 3/3/ Home Counties	67th	...	67th

1917 September (England)	200th...... 201st...... 202nd......	2/5/Queen's, 2/5/E. Surr., 2/6/E. Surr., 1/4/N. Staff.,[19] 276th Bn.,[20]; [24] 277th Bn.,[20]; [24] 278th Bn.[20]; [24] 2/7/Midd'x., 2/9/Midd'x., 1/4/S. Staff.,[21] 281st Bn.,[20]; [24] 282nd Bn.[20]; [24] 2/4/Buffs, 2/5/Buffs, 2/5/Q.O. R.W.K., 1/1/R. Guern. L.I.,[22] 284th Bn.,[20]; [24] 286th Bn.[20]; [24]	67th Coy., A.C.C.	CCCXXXVI[23] CCCXXXVII[23]	A, B, C; D (H.) A, B, C; D (H.)	...	...	...	67th D.A.C.	492nd 493rd 494th	67th	...	...	3/1/ Home Counties 3/2/ Home Counties 3/3/ Home Counties	67th	...	67th
1917 December (England)	200th[31] ... 201st...... 202nd......	52/N.F. (G.),[24] 52/W. York. (G.),[24] 52/Sher. For. (G.),[24] 2/1/Camb.[25] 52/S.W.B. (G.),[24] 51/Hants. (G.),[24] 52/Hants. (G.),[24] 2/7/Essex[26] 2/5/Suff.,[27] 51/K.R.R.C. (G.),[24] 52/K.R.R.C. (G.),[24] 52/Gord. H. (G.)[24]	67th Coy., A.C.C.	XII[28]........... XLIII[28]	1203, 1204, 1207; D (H.) 1212, A, B; D (H.)	...	...	...	67th D.A.C.	492nd[29] 493rd 494th 645th[30] (W. Lanc.)	67th	...	...	316th (3/1/ Home Counties) 317th (3/2/ Home Counties) 318th (3/3/ Home Counties)	67th	...	67th
1918 April (England)	201st...... 202nd...... 214th[31] ...	52/S.W.B. (G.), 51/Hants. (G.), 52/Hants. (G.), 51/R.B. (G.)[32] 51/K.R.R.C. (G.), 52/K.R.R.C. (G.), 52/Gord. H. (G.), 52/R.B.(G.)[33] 2/1/War. Yeo. (Cyclists),[34] 2/1/Herts. Yeo. (Cyclists),[34] 16/Queen's,[34] 2/7/D.L.I.,[34] 252nd M.G. Coy.,[35] 253rd M.G. Coy.[35]	67th Coy., A.C.C.	XII .... XLIII	1203, 1204, 1207; D (H) 1212, A, B; D (H.)	...	...	...	67th D.A.C.	493rd 494th 645th	67th	...	...	302nd[36] 316th 317th 318th	67th	...	67th
1918 August (England)	201st...... 202nd...... 214th......	52/S.W.B. (G.), 51/Hants. (G.), 52/Hants. (G.), 51/R.B. (G.) 51/K.R.R.C. (G.), 52/K.R.R.C. (G.), 52/Gord. H. (G.), 52/R.B. (G.) 2/1/War. Yeo. (Cyclists),[37] 2/1/Herts. Yeo. (Cyclists),[37] 16/Queen's,[38] 2/7/D.L.I.[39]	67th Coy., A.C.C.	XII .... XLIII	1203, 1204, 1207; D (H.) 1212, A, B; D (H.)	...	...	...	67th D.A.C.	493rd 494th 645th	67th	...	...	316th 317th 318th	67th	...	67th
1918 December (England)	201st...... 202nd...... 214th......	52/S.W.B. (G.), 51/Hants. (G.), 52/Hants. (G.), 51/R.B. (G.) 51/K.R.R.C. (G.), 52/K.R.R.C. (G.), 52/Gord. H. (G.), 52/R.B. (G.) 1/4/Buffs,[40] 51/Ches. (G.),[41] 52/Ches. (G.),[41] 1/4/R. W.F.[40]	67th Coy., A.C.C.	XII .... XLIII	1203, 1204, 1207; D (H.) 1212, A, B; D (H.)	...	...	...	67th D.A.C.	493rd 494th 645th	67th	...	...	316th 317th 318th	67th	...	67th

67TH (2ND/HOME COUNTIES) DIVISION

NOTES

1 In the middle of August, 1915, the Home Counties 2nd-line Division and Infantry Brigades were given numbers. (Authy., 40/W.O./2609, A.G.1., of 10/8/15.)

2 The Bdes. were formed late in October, 1914, after the 1st-line Bdes. left for India. The Bdes. concentrated in Nov., 1914.

3 Formation of Coy. was ordered on 30/7/15. The Coy. formed at Brighton in Septr., 1915, and by 8/11/15 it had recruited up to full strength. From 27/11-16/12/15 the Coy. was employed on Coast Defence; and on 20/12/15 the Coy. joined 67th Div. at Hildenborough.

4 The Bde. remained in England when the 44th (Home Counties) Div. went to India in Oct., 1914; and the Bde. assisted in the formation of the 27th D.A.C., which went to France on 21/12/14. In June, 1915, the Bde. joined 67th Div. On 22/12/15 the Bde. left the 67th Div., to prepare for overseas, and on 10/3/16 1/IV Home Counties (H.) Bde. (2 Bties., 8, 4·5" hows.) disembkd. at le Havre, and it was attached to the Fourth Army. On 18/7/16 the Bde. joined R.N. Div., and on 31/7/16 was numbered CCXXIII.

5 Coy. formed at Newhaven on 21/8/15; it joined 67th Div. at Southborough on 6/11/15.

6 Coy. was formed at Brighton and Eastbourne.

7 Coy. was formed at Hastings in Oct., 1914.

8 Coy. was formed at Brighton; and on 19/1/16 Nos. 2, 3, and 4 Bde. Secs. were detached and joined their Inf. Bdes.

9 The Cos. of the Train came into existence as separate units between late in Septr. and late in Nov., 1914. By 10/11/15 the Cos. had been numbered 545, 546, 547, and 548 Cos., A.S.C.

10 12, 18-pdr. Q.F. were received by each Bde. between 11-13/1/16. In May, 1916, the Bdes. were numbered and the batteries were lettered A, B, and C in each brigade.

11 The 2nd-line howitzer brigade joined the 67th Div. on 23/12/15 at Seal. On 28/1/16 the Bde. received 8, 5" B.L. Hows. from I/IV Home Cties. (H.) Bde. In May, 1916, the Bde. was numbered and the batteries were lettered A (H.) and B (H.). The Bde. was broken up in 1916, and the two batteries were transferred to CCCXXXV and CCCXXXVI.

12 The 3 2nd-line Fd. Ambces. left the Div. and joined the 58th Div. in England on 22/2/16, went to France in Jany., 1917, with the 58th Div., and served with the 58th Div. on the Western Front for the remainder of the War. After the departure of the 2nd-line Fd. Ambces., the 3rd-line Fd. Ambces. joined the 67th Div.

13 Bn. went to France and disembkd. at le Havre on 1/6/17. Bn. was attached to 1st S.A. Bde., 9th Div., 6/6-23/7/17; then served with the 12th Div., 23/7-8/8/17; and joined 62nd Bde., 21st Div. on 9/8/17. Bn. was disbanded between 2-11/2/18.

14 Bn. went to France and disembkd. at le Havre on 1/6/17. Bn. joined 1st S.A. Bde., 9th Div., on 6/6/17; was transferred to 4th Div. on 23/7/17; and joined 10th Bde., 4th Div., on 2/8/17. Left 4th Div. on 8/2/18 to be broken up, but Bn. became 11th Entrenching Bn. on 20/2/18.

15 Bn. went to France and disembkd. at le Havre on 1/6/17. Bn. was attached to 1st S.A. Bde., 9th Div., on 7/6/17, and to 103rd Bde., 34th Div., on 18/6/17, Bn. was transferred to 51st Bde., 17th Div., on 22/6/17. Bn. became Pioneers 9/7-3/8/17, and then joined 52nd Bde., 17th Div., Bn. was disbanded between 1-28/2/18.

16 In 1917 the Bde. was broken up to complete CCCXXXVI and CCCXXXVII.

17 These 2 Special Reserve Bns. had previously been in a Composite Inf. Bde. in the Northern Command.

18 This Channel Islands Militia Bn. joined by May, 1917.

19 Bn. disembkd. at le Havre on 7/10/17, and was attached to 56th Div., 11/10-9/11/17. On 15/11/17 Bn. joined 106th Bde., 35th Div.; and on 3/2/18 Bn. was transferred to 105th Bde., 35th Div.

20 These 7 battalions were Graduated Battalions of the Training Reserve. They served with the Div.: 284th and 286th from 17/9/17; and the others from 24/9/17.

21 Bn. disembkd. at le Havre on 10/10/17, and joined 7th Bde., 25th Div., on 13/10/17. Bn. joined Composite Bde., 25th Div., on 22/6/18, and was transferred on 25/6/18 (with Comp. Bde.) to 50th Div. Bn. left 50th Div. on 7/7/18; and on 11/7/18 Bn. was reduced to Training Cadre. Bn. reached Etaples on 16/8/18, and joined 116th Bde., 39th Div., on 16/8/18. Bn. was demobilized, 6-8/11/18.

22 Bn. disembkd. at le Havre on 27/9/17, and joined 86th Bde., 29th Div., on 2/10/17. Bn. was transferred on 27/4/18 to G.H.Q. Troops.

23 The Bdes. ceased to belong to 67th Div. after 19/11/17.

24 The 7 Graduated Bns. of the Training Reserve (see note 20) were affiliated to line regiments and adopted territorial designations from 27/10/17. The other 2 Graduated Bns. joined by 1/10/17 (see General Notes).

25 Transferred from 207th Bde., 69th Div., on 8/10/17.

26 Transferred from 206th Bde., 69th Div., on 10/10/17.

27 Transferred from 208th Bde., 69th Div., on 28/9/17.

28 These 2 Bdes. served with the Div. from 26/11/17. (XII(How.) Bde. had served with the 6th Div.; this How. Bde. was broken up in France on 12/5/16. XLIII(How.) Bde. had served with the 1st Div.; this How. Bde. was broken up in France on 22/5/16.) 1203, 1204, 1207, and 1212 Bties. had been, until 1/1/17, 1st, 2nd, 5th, and 10th Provl. Fd. Bties.

29 Left the Div. on 26/10/17 and joined 71st Div.

30 Joined on 26/10/17 from 71st Div.

31 214th Bde. (from 71st Div.) joined on 12/2/18, and took the place of the 200th Bde. The 200th Bde. was then demobilized.

32 Transferred from 206th Bde., 69th Div., in Febry., 1918.

33 Transferred from 207th Bde., 69th Div., on 22/2/18.

34 These 2 Bns. and the 2 Cyclist Bns. joined with 214th Bde. (from 71st Div.) on 12/2/18.

35 These 2 Home-Service M.G. Cos. joined with 214th Bde. (from 71st Div.) on 12/2/18.

36 This Fd. Ambce. was transferred from 71st Div., (with 214th Bde.), and it was then broken up.

37 The 2 Cyclist Bns. left the Div. by 2/9/18.

38 Bn. left the Div. by 28/10/18.

39 Bn. left the Div. by 23/9/18. On 7/10/18 Bn. went to N. Russia as a Garr. Bn., and joined the Archangel Force.

40 These 2 Special Reserve Bns. joined the Div. by 28/10/18.

41 These 2 Graduated Bns. had previously served in the 194th and 196th Bdes., 65th Div. After the 65th Div. was disbanded in March, 1918, these 2 Bns. remained at the Curragh until 25/11/18; they then came to England and joined 214th Bde. by 2/12/18.

67TH (2ND/HOME COUNTIES) DIVISION

FORMATION AND NARRATIVE

This 2nd-line (or reserve) Territorial Force division had no existence before the outbreak of the Great War.

The formation of reserve (or 2nd-line) T.F. units was authorized on the 31st August, 1914 (see Narrative, 57th Division). In most cases 2nd-line divisions and brigades were not given staffs, or formed, until early in 1915. The formation, however, of the 2nd-line Home Counties Division was expedited, on account of the 1st-line Home Counties Division having embarked for India on the 30th October, 1914.

Whereas some of the 2nd-line Home Counties units did not begin to form until immediately after the departure of the 1st-line units for India, other units were raised in September, 1914. In fact on the 22nd October (8 days before the 1st-line division sailed) the parade state of the 2nd/1st Middlesex Infantry Brigade showed a strength of 114 officers and 4,038 other ranks. Officers and men of the 1st-line artillery brigades and infantry battalions, who remained at home, joined the sister 2nd-line unit which was forming in England. The 1st-line infantry brigade staffs remained in being, pending the formation of the 2nd-line division.

On the 14th November Br.-Gen. C. T. Caulfeild received orders to report at Eastern Command Headquarters (Horse Guards, Whitehall), and he was then directed to form the 2nd/Home Counties Division and concentrate it in the country round Windsor. In pursuance of these orders, Br.-Gen. Caulfeild sent Br.-Gen. J. Marriott to arrange the billeting areas—one brigade was placed at Staines, and another at Ascot and Sunninghill. By the 20th November all moves were completed and the division was settled in billets in the Windsor area. On the 27th November the division was inspected and was reported fit to receive rifles.

Major-General J. C. Young (accompanied by Captain H. W. Grubb) went out in command of the 1st Home Counties Division during the voyage to India. On arrival in India Major-General Young handed over the Home Counties units and then (accompanied by Captain Grubb) returned to England. Major-General Young and Captain Grubb reached England on the 22nd December, 1914, and on the 20th January, 1915, General Young assumed command of the 2nd/Home Counties Division.

Training for war was hampered and complicated by the lack of up-to-date arms and equipment. In addition, in July, 1915, the units had to be re-organized, as the home-service men were drafted to home-service units, since all the 2nd-line units were liable for service overseas. Further the system of relying on local tradesmen to hold sufficient stocks of essential stores naturally broke down in the emergency of a general mobilization. To give a common example: there was at first a general shortage of blankets. The shortage caused a good deal of discomfort, as many men had to be billeted in halls and unoccupied buildings. This particular deficiency would have been overcome at once, had an arrangement been in force for each man to bring 2 blankets with him on joining.

The earliest rifles, obtainable in any numbers by the infantry, were the Japanese ·256″ rifles; at the same time the artillery had to rely on the 90-mm. French guns. It is true that a few 15-pdrs. were on charge, but there was no ammunition for them. Even as late as September, 1915, the B.-G., R.A. had to report that, on an emergency, he could only turn out one 90-mm. battery in each field-gun brigade, the howitzer brigade had neither howitzers nor ammunition, and the 2nd-line heavy battery was without guns. Up to the end of June, 1915, the divisional train was short of horses and transport, and it possessed no rifles. At the end of November, however, the infantry received ·303″ Mk. I Lee-Enfield rifles (pattern 1890) and a half-issue of bayonets.

With the opening of 1916 things slowly began to mend. Before the middle of January, 36, 18-pdrs. (each with 100 rounds of ammunition) arrived for the three gun-brigades, although some time elapsed before telescopic sights were received. By the end of the month 8, 5″ howitzers were issued to the howitzer brigade; no sights, however, could be provided. At about the same time the heavy battery obtained 2, 4·7″ guns, but dial sights, aiming posts, handspikes, and drag-ropes were still lacking; and in February the artillery was 817 men and 716 horses below establishment. It was still difficult to carry out the serious training of the division for war.

In the meantime the division had been assembled. In November, 1915, it formed part of Second Army, Central Force, and was quartered as follows: Divisional headquarters and 201st Brigade at Sevenoaks, 200th Brigade at Reigate and Redhill, 202nd Brigade and two field companies at Tonbridge; cyclist company at Brighton; artillery brigades at Westerham, Brasted, Riverhead, and Seal; heavy battery (2/1st Kent) at Ightham; and the remaining field company at Southborough.

During 1915, 1916, and 1917 the division was occupied in recruiting, training, supplying drafts to oversea units, and in addition it formed part of the mobile force responsible for Home Defence. Twice the division was ordered to be ready to proceed to Ireland, and in April, 1917, it was ordered to prepare for service in France. However, neither move materialized, and for the whole of the Great War the division served in various stations in England.

In September, 1916, the division (then in the Southern Army) had its headquarters at Canterbury, with the infantry brigades in camps: 200th at Westbere and Gore Street, 201st at Bourne Park and Barham, and 202nd at Scotland Hills and Old Park. Mounted troops were at Canterbury, field artillery at Canterbury, Patrixbourne, and Wingham, the two heavy batteries (2/1st Warwickshire and 2/2nd Lancashire) at Northbourne and Upstreet, and the engineers at Broomfield, Preston, and Northbourne. Throughout the summer of 1917 much the same distribution was maintained; but the field artillery was now concentrated at Canterbury, and the two attached heavy batteries were at Eastry and Minster.

Between September and the end of 1917 the infantry of the Division was completely reorganized (see Table), and in February, 1918, 200th Infantry Brigade was replaced by 214th Brigade (from the 71st Division).* In this way the division lost its territorial association, and thenceforward it was known as 67th Division. During the winter the division joined XXIII Corps (headquarters at Brentwood) and was quartered as follows: Headquarters and two infantry brigades at Colchester, with the other brigade at Ipswich; cyclists and two attached heavy batteries at Great Bentley; field artillery brigades at Colchester and Ipswich; and engineers at Colchester and Driffield. Until the end of the War the 67th Division maintained the same stations, and the division remained in XXIII Corps. Corps headquarters shifted to Bury St. Edmunds before the end of September, 1918.

In December, 1918, 214th Brigade was reorganized (see Table). The division still occupied the same stations around Colchester and continued to do so for the remainder of its existence. By the end of February, 1919, the strength of the division had shrunk to 14,095 (nearly 2,500 below establishment), and in March the artillery and engineers began disbandment. By the 10th the strength of the division had decreased to 9,168; and by the 17th March, 1919, the 67th Division disappeared from the Weekly Return of the Army at Home.

* In Oct., 1917, 214th Bde. had been formed into a Special Bde. so as to be available for service in Murmansk. For this purpose the Bde. had been filled up with A.1 men, and an artillery brigade (XLIX), signal section, two cyclist battalions, and two machine-gun companies had also been attached to it. Actually 214th Bde. never went to Murmansk, and the A.1 men were all drafted to the Western Front in March, 1918, to assist in replacing the casualties incurred during that month's fighting.

68TH (2ND/WELSH) DIVISION

G.O.C.

23 January, 1915	Br.-Gen. R. B. MAINWARING.
15 November, 1915	Major-General A. E. SANDBACH.
14 February, 1916	Major-General R. N. R. READE.
1 December, 1917 –15 April, 1919	Major-General E. M. PERCEVAL.

G.S.O. 1.

26 Mar., 1915	...Captain G. G. WHIFFIN (acting).
25 Sept., 1915	...Lt.-Col. F. J. MOBERLY.
17 May, 1916	...Lt.-Col. Sir T. A. A. M. CUNINGHAME, BT.
20 Oct., 1917	...Lt.-Col. A. W. TUFNELL.
15 Oct., 1918 –4 Feb., 1919	Lt.-Col. K. M. LAIRD.

A.-A. and Q.-M.-G.

25 Jan., 1915	...Major W. R. B. PEYTON (acting.)
20 Sept., 1915	...Lt.-Col. S. FREWEN.
19 April, 1917	...Lt.-Col. R. Q. CRAUFURD.
15 Nov., 1917 –30 April, 1919	Lt.-Col. H. B. DES V. WILKINSON.

B.-G., R.A.

23 Jan., 1915	...Colonel R. A. G. HARRISON.
14 Jan., 1916	...Colonel Sir G. V. THOMAS, BT.
17 April, 1916	...Colonel F. A. G. Y. ELTON.
7 July, 1916	...Br.-Gen. F. A. G. Y. ELTON.
21 April, 1917	...Br.-Gen. D. G. PRINSEP.
21 Dec., 1917	...Br.-Gen. W. H. KAY.
23 May, 1918	...Br.-Gen. S. LUSHINGTON.

C.R.E.

9 April, 1915	...Lt.-Col. W. H. FORDE.
Nov., 1917	...Major E. H. FAWCKNER (acting).
16 May, 1918 –6 Feb., 1919	Lt.-Col. E. H. FAWCKNER.

203rd BDE.

(2nd/1st N. Wales)

29 Jan., '15...Col. J. H. A. ANDERSON.
23 Feb., '16...Col. H. L. RICHARDSON.
7 July, '16...Br.-Gen. H. L. RICHARDSON.
14 May, '18...Br.-Gen. T. N. S. M. HOWARD.

204th BDE.

(2nd/1st Cheshire)

6 Jan., '15...Col. HERVEY TALBOT.
19 Feb., '16...Col. H. S. SLOMAN.
7 July, '16...Br.-Gen. H. S. SLOMAN.
2 Sept., '18 – 1 April, '19 } Br.-Gen. W. W. SEYMOUR.

205th BDE.

(2nd/1st Welsh Border)

6 Jan., '15...Col. C. E. CURLL (invalided, 16/9/15).
16 Sept., '15...Lt.-Col. A. B. HOPPS (acting).
11 Oct., '15...Col. C. J. MARKHAM.
7 July, '16...Br.-Gen. C. J. MARKHAM.
15 Mar., '17...Br.-Gen. G. H. NICHOLSON.

GENERAL NOTES

The following Units belonged to the 2nd/Welsh Division, but they served with other divisions in the field :—

2/1/Welsh Fd. Coy. The Fd. Coy. was raised at Carmarthen and Llanelly between 21/9–4/11/14, and joined the 2nd/Welsh Div. The Fd. Coy. left England on 4/10/15, disembarked at Suvla on 24/10/15, and was attached to IX Corps. On 2/12/15 the Fd. Coy. joined 53rd (Welsh) Div. at Lala Baba. The Fd. Coy. served with the 53rd Div. for the remainder of the War, and in 1917 it was numbered 437th Fd. Coy.

2/1/Cheshire Fd. Coy. The Fd. Coy. was raised at Birkenhead in 1914, and joined the 2nd/Welsh Div. In July, 1915, the Fd. Coy. joined the 53rd (Welsh) Div. at Bedford, and it embarked with the division for Gallipoli. The Fd. Coy. landed at Suvla on 9/8/15. In 1917 the Fd. Coy. was numbered 439th Fd. Coy., and it served with the 53rd Div. until, at Ramle, on 9/4/18, the Fd. Coy. was transferred to the 74th (Yeomanry) Division. The 439th Fd. Coy. then served with the 74th Div. for the remainder of the War.

The following Units also served with the 68th Division :—

ARTILLERY :—53rd Div. Artillery—Br.-Gen. W. A. Macbean—**(I Welsh (How.) Bde., II Welsh Bde., Cheshire Bde., IV Welsh Bde., and 53rd D.A.C.).** After the 53rd Div. left for Gallipoli in July, 1915, the 53rd Div. Artillery remained at Bedford and was attached to the 2nd/Welsh Div. from 14/7–19/10/15. In Oct., 1915, the batteries were rearmed with 4·5" hows. and 18-pdrs. On 20/11/15 the 53rd Div. Arty. proceeded overseas (via France) to rejoin its own Division ; and it rejoined 53rd Div., in Egypt, between 11–22/2/16. (On 24/11/15 Br.-Gen. A. H. Short became B.-G., R.A., 53rd D.A.).

1128 Battery, R.F.A., was attached to the 68th Div. in May, 1917, and it remained until after August, 1917.

1/1/Welsh (Caernarvonshire) Hy. Bty., R.G.A., T.F. This Hy. Bty. was left behind by the 53rd Div. at Bedford in July, 1915, and it was then attached to the 2nd/Welsh Div. until 16/2/16, when it left for Woolwich to prepare for overseas. The Hy. Bty. (4, 4·7" guns) disembkd. at le Havre on 3/3/16 and joined XXIII H.A. Group. The Hy. Bty. was in action by 17/3/16.

2/1/Welsh (Caernarvonshire) Hy. Bty., R.G.A., T.F. This 2nd-line Heavy Battery was raised in 1914, and it remained with the 68th Division until May, 1918. Thereafter, and until the end of the War, the Heavy Battery was attached to the 227th Mixed Brigade (H.Q., Saxmundham), and the Heavy Battery was stationed at Blythburgh.

CYCLIST BATTALIONS :—1/6/Suffolk, was attached to 68th Div. in May, 1917, and the Bn. remained with the Division until March, 1918.

2/6/R. Sussex, was raised at Brighton, and was attached to 68th Division in Aug. and Septr., 1915.

2/25/London, was attached to the 68th Div. in May, 1917, and the Bn. remained with the Division until March, 1918.

OTHER UNITS :—2/1/Welsh Sanitary Section, was raised in 1914 and served with 68th Division from 1916.

1/1/Welsh Mobile Vety. Section, was left behind at Bedford in July, 1915, when the 53rd Div. embarked for Gallipoli. The Section then joined Welsh Div. Vety. Hospital at Luton until 7/1/16, when it was attached to 68th Div. until 21/3/16. On 21/3/16 the Section left for Egypt, and it rejoined 53rd Div., in Egypt, on 11/4/16.

2/1/Welsh Motor Ambulance Workshop, from 1915, until absorbed in 1916 by the Divisional Train.

68TH[1] (2ND/WELSH) DIVISION

ORDER OF BATTLE, 1915-1918

Dates	INFANTRY		Mounted Troops	ARTILLERY						Engineers	Signal Service	Pioneers	M.G. Units	Field Ambu-lances	Mobile Vety. Secn.	Divnl. Emplnt. Coy.	Divnl. Train
	Brigades	Battalions and attached Units		Field Artillery			Trench Mortar Bties.		Divnl. Ammn. Coln.	Field Cos.	Divnl. Signal Coy.						
				Brigades	Batteries	Bde. Ammn. Colns.	Medium	Heavy									
1915 November (England)	203rd[1; 2] (2nd/1st N. Wales) 204th[1; 3] (2nd/1st Cheshire) 205th[1; 5] (2nd/1st Welsh Border)	2/4/R.W.F., 2/5/R.W.F., 2/6/R.W.F., 2/7/R.W.F. 2/4/Ches.,[4] 2/5/Ches., 2/6/Ches., 2/7/Ches.[4] 2/1/Mon., 2/2/Mon., 2/3/Mon., 2/1/Hereford[6]	68th (2nd/1st/Welsh) Div. Cyclist Coy[7].	2nd/I Welsh[8] (H.) 2nd/II Welsh[9] 2nd/I Cheshire[10] 2nd/IV Welsh[11]	2/1/Glamorgan (H.), 2/2/Glamorgan (H.) 2/3/Glamorgan, 2/4/Glamorgan, 2/1/Cardigan. 2/1/Cheshire, 2/2/Cheshire, 2/3/Cheshire. 2/1/Monmouth, 2/2/Monmouth, 2/3/Monmouth.	2nd/I Welsh (H.) 2nd/II Welsh 2nd/I Cheshire 2nd/IV Welsh	...	...	2nd/1/Welsh[12]	3/1/Cheshire[13]	68th[14] (2nd/1/Welsh)	...	...	2/1/Welsh[15] 2/2/Welsh[15] 2/3/Welsh[15]	...	...	68th[16] (2nd/1/Welsh)
1916 May (England)	203rd ...... 204th 205th	2/4/R.W.F., 2/5/R.W.F., 2/6/R.W.F., 2/7/R.W.F. 2/5/Ches., 2/6/Ches., 2/7/Ches.,[4] 2/4/K.S.L.I.[17] 2/1/Mon., 2/2/Mon., 2/3/Mon., 2/1/Hereford.	68th Div. Cyclist Coy.	CCCXL (H.)[18] (2nd/I Welsh) CCCXLI[19]...... (2nd/II Welsh) CCCXLII[19] ... (2nd/I Ches.) CCCXLIII[19]... (2nd/IV Welsh)	A (H.), B (H.) A, B, C A, B, C A, B, C	CCCXL (H.) B.A.C. CCCXLI B.A.C. CCCXLII B.A.C. CCCXLIII B.A.C.	...	...	68th D.A.C. (2nd/1/Welsh)	3/1/Cheshire 1/1/[20] Glamorgan 2/1/[21] Glamorgan	68th	...	...	2/1/Welsh 2/2/Welsh 2/3/Welsh	68th (2/1/Welsh)	...	68th
1916 October (England)	203rd ...... 204th 205th	2/4/R.W.F., 2/5/R.W.F., 2/6/R.W.F., 2/7/R.W.F. 2/5/Ches., 2/6/Ches., 2/7/Ches., 2/4/K.S.L.I. 2/1/Mon., 2/2/Mon., 2/3/Mon., 2/1/Hereford.	C Sqdn., 2/1/Bedf. Yeo. 68th Div. Cyclist Coy.	CCCXLI ...... CCCXLII ...... CCCXLIII......	A, B, C A, B, C; D (H.)[18] A, B, C; D (H.)[18]	...	...	...	68th D.A.C.	3/1/Cheshire 1/1/Glamorgan 2/1/Glamorgan	68th	...	...	2/1/Welsh 2/2/Welsh 2/3/Welsh	68th	...	68th
1917 June (England)	203rd ...... 204th 205th	2/4/R.W.F., 2/5/R.W.F., 2/6/R.W.F., 2/7/R.W.F. 2/5/Ches., 2/6/Ches., 2/7/Ches., 2/4/K.S.L.I. 2/1/Mon., 2/2/Mon., 2/3/Mon., 2/1/Hereford.	68th Div. Cyclist Coy.	CCCXLII ...... CCCXLIII......	A, B, C; D (H.) A, B, C; D (H.)	...	...	...	68th D.A.C.	440th (3/1/Cheshire) 441st (1/1/Glamorgan) 442nd (2/1/Glamorgan)	68th	...	...	319th (2/1/Welsh) 320th (2/2/Welsh) 321st (2/3/Welsh)	68th	...	68th

1917 September (England)	203rd...... 204th...... 205th......	2/4/R.W.F., 2/5/R.W.F., 225th Bn.,22 ; 23 226th Bn.22 ; 23 2/5/Ches., 2/7/Ches., 2/4/K.S.L.I., 229th Bn.,22 ; 23 230th Bn.22 ; 23 2/1/Mon., 2/2/Mon., 233rd Bn.,22 ; 23 234th Bn.22 ; 23	68th Coy., A.C.C.	CCCXLII ...... CCCXLIII......	A, B, C ; D (H.) A, B, C ; D (H.)	...	...	...	68th D.A.C.	440th 441st 442nd	68th	...	...	319th 320th 321st	68th	...	68th
1917 December (England)	203rd...... 204th...... 205th......	2/4/R.W.F., 51/Welsh (G.),23 51/Manch. (G.),23 52/Manch. (G.),23 2/5/Ches., 2/7/Ches., 2/5/R.W.F.,24 2/2/Mon.25 52/King's (G.),23 51/S.W.B. (G.),23 52/Welsh (G.),23 2/1/Mon.	68th Coy., A.C.C.	CCCXLII ...... CCCXLIII......	A, B, C ; D (H.) A, B, C ; D (H.)	...	...	...	68th D.A.C.	440th 441st 442nd	68th	...	...	319th 320th 321st	68th	...	68th
1918 April (England)	203rd...... 204th...... 205th......	51/King's (G.),26 2/4/R.W.F., 51/Welsh (G.), 51/Manch. (G.), 52/Manch. (G.) 51/R.F. (G.),27 52/R.F. (G.),28 2/5/Ches., 2/7/Ches., 51/S.W.B. (G.) 51/R. War. (G.),29 52/R. War. (G.),30 52/King's (G.), 52/Welsh (G.), 2/1/Mon., 2/2/Mon.	68th Coy., A.C.C.	CCCXLII ...... CCCXLIII......	A, B, C ; D (H.) A, B, C D (H.)	...	...	...	68th D.A.C.	440th 441st 442nd	68th	...	...	319th 320th 321st	68th	...	68th
1918 October (England)	203rd...... 204th...... 205th......	51/King's (G.), 51/Welsh (G.), 51/Manch. (G.), 52/Manch. (G.) 51/Queen's (G.),31 51/R.F. (G.), 52/R.F. (G.), 51/S.W.B. (G.) 51/R. War. (G.), 52/R. War. (G.), 52/King's (G.), 52/Welsh (G.)	68th Coy., A.C.C.	CCCXLII ...... CCCXLIII......	A, B, C ; D (H.) A, B, C ; D (H.)	...	...	...	68th D.A.C.	440th 441st 442nd	68th	...	...	319th 320th 321st	68th	...	68th

NOTES

1 In the middle of August, 1915, the Welsh 2nd-line Division and Infantry Brigades were given numbers. (Authy., 40/W.O./2609, A.G.1, of 10/8/15.)

2 Between Septr. and the end of 1914 the 4 battalions were raised at Wrexham, Flint, Caernarvon, and Newtown.

3 In Septr., 1914, the 4 battalions were raised at Birkenhead, Chester, Stockport, and Macclesfield.

4 On 13/11/15 2/4/Ches. and 2/7/Ches. were amalgamated and designated 1st Bn., 204th Bde. On 8/12/15 Bn. was re-designated 2/7/Ches. Strength of composite Bn. was 29 offrs. and 600 o.r.; all numbers in excess of 600 were drafted to the 3rd-line battalions.

5 In Septr., 1914, the 4 battalions were raised at Newport, Pontypool, Abergavenny, and Hereford.

6 The Bn. moved to Aberystwith on 11/12/14 and joined 2/1/Welsh Border Bde. Bn. moved to Northampton on 27/4/15, was employed on N. London Defences (near Billericay) 30/5-17/6/15, and moved with Bde. to Bedford on 22/7/15.

7 Coy. was raised at Stockport in 1915; it reached Bedford on 22/10/15 and joined 68th Div.

8 Bde. was raised in 1914, moved to Northampton in April, 1915, to Reigate in August, 1915, and to St. Neots on 2/11/15. On 7/11/15 Bde. took over 8, 5" Hows. from 1/I Welsh (How.) Bde.

9 Bde. was raised at Cardiff on 14/9/14, reached Northampton on 29/4/15, moved to Earlswood on 4/8/15, and arrived at Bedford on 2/11/15, and took over 12, 15-pdr. B.L.C. guns. Between 4-21/12/15 the Bde. drew 12, 18-pdr. Q.F. guns, 18 wagons, and ammunition, and returned the 15-pdr. equipments.

10 Bde. was raised at Chester in Septr., 1914; moved to Northampton on 29/4/15; to Redhill on 4/8/15; and reached Bedford on 3/11/15. On 8/11/15 Bde. took over 12, 15-pdr. B.L.C. guns and wagons, with limbers, from 2/I Ches. Bde. On 21/11/15 the Bde. moved to Elstow; and between 11-15/12/15 the Bde. was re-armed with 12, 18-pdr. Q.F. guns and 36 ammn. wagons.

11 Bde. was raised in 1914, moved to Northampton in April, 1915, to Redhill in August, 1915, and reached Bedford on 3/11/15. Between 6-22/11/15 the Bde. took over 12, 15-pdr. B.L.C. guns from 1/IV Welsh Bde. By 20/12/15 the Bde. had been re-armed with 18-pdr. Q.F. equipts.

12 D.A.C. began to form at Turvey on 8/1/15.

13 Coy. was formed at Birkenhead in Dec., 1914; it joined 68th Div. at Northampton on 22/7/15, and moved to Bedford on 22/8/15.

14 Coy. was raised at Cardiff in Septr., 1914; moved to Northampton on 22/4/15, and to Bedford on 24/7/15.

15 The Fd. Ambces. were raised in 1914 at Ebbw Vale, Cardiff, and Swansea; they moved to Northampton in April, 1915, and to Bedford in July, 1915.

16 The Train was raised in 1914 at Leominster, Pentre (Rhondda), Birkenhead, and Ruthin; it concentrated at Aberystwith; moved to Northampton in April, 1915, and to Bedford in July, 1915, where it took over the supply work of the 68th Div. The Cos. became 549, 550, 551, and 552 Cos., A.S.C.

17 Bn. was raised at Shrewsbury in 1914. Bn. was employed on garrison duty at Ramsay (Isle of Man) from 17/7-25/11/15. Bn. reached Bedford on 26/11/15 and joined 204th Bde. On arrival at Bedford Bn. was issued with 525 Lee-Enfield ·303" rifles.

18 In May, 1916, the Bde. was numbered and the batteries were lettered A (H.) and B (H.). In 1916 the Bde. was broken up and the 2 batteries were transferred as D (H.) to CCCXLII and CCCXLIII Bdes.

19 In May, 1916, the Bdes. were numbered and the batteries lettered A, B, and C in each Brigade.

20 Joined 68th Div. at Bedford (from Cardiff) on 29/11/15.

21 Joined 68th Div. at Bedford by 1/1/16.

22 These 6 battalions were Graduated Battalions of the Training Reserve; they served with the 68th Div.: 225, 226, 229, 233, and 234 from 23/7/17; and 230 from 24/9/17.

23 The 6 Graduated Bns. of the Training Reserve were affiliated to line regiments and adopted territorial designations from 27/10/17.

24 From 203rd Bde.

25 From 205th Bde.

26 By 11/3/18 Bn. joined from 195th Bde., 65th Div. (disbanded).

27 By 11/3/18 Bn. joined from 215th Bde., 72nd Div. (disbanded).

28 By 11/3/18 Bn. joined from 217th Bde., 72nd Div. (disbanded).

29 By 11/3/18 Bn. joined from 216th Bde., 72nd Div. (disbanded).

30 By 11/3/18 Bn. joined from 220th Bde., 73rd Div. (disbanded).

31 Bn. served in 208th Bde., 69th Div., until 20/4/18; and Bn. joined 204th Bde., 68th Div., by 22/7/18, from Bury St. Edmunds.

68TH (2ND/WELSH) DIVISION

FORMATION AND NARRATIVE

This 2nd-line (or reserve) Territorial Force division had no existence before the outbreak of the Great War.

The formation of reserve (or 2nd-line) T.F. units was authorized on the 31st August, 1914 (see Narrative, 57th Division); but the 2nd/Welsh Division only came into existence in January, 1915, and it was April before the division concentrated at Northampton, its war station.

In July and August 2nd/Welsh Division moved to Bedford to replace its 1st-line division, when the latter left Bedford for the Dardanelles in mid-July.

Meanwhile the training of all the units was made difficult by the lack of arms and equipment, as well as by the necessity of providing drafts for the 1st-line units, and by the reorganization (in July) of the infantry battalions, after the home-service men had been drafted to home-service units. By the end of August, 1915, one battalion (2/7/Cheshire) had sent no fewer than 800 N.C.O.s and men to its 1st-line battalion; but, even so, this 2nd-line battalion still had 35 officers and 809 N.C.O.s and men. Other battalions, however, had more difficulty in keeping up to strength, and by the end of October one battalion only numbered 317 all ranks. In November the strength of a 2nd line battalion was reduced to 600, and again the battalions had to be reorganized. The men had been armed with the ·256" Japanese rifles, but, late in 1915, these rifles were withdrawn (for re-issue to provisional battalions) and 2nd-line battalions each received 525 converted charger-loading Lee-Enfield rifles.

The artillery also had to overcome difficulties in training for war. Up to the end of May the batteries had not received any guns, horses, or saddlery, nevertheless drafts had been called for, and at the end of May 2/I Cheshire Bde. sent 2 officers and 106 men to the newly-formed 53rd (1st Welsh) Division Ammunition Column. In June equipment at last began to arrive, some saddlery was received (19 sets in one brigade), and this issue was followed in July by the horses (in one brigade, 278). So far no guns had been issued. In one report the situation is summed up very fairly: " the preparation for Imperial Service is the best that is possible in the circumstances." In August the issue of harness was completed, and four 90-mm. guns were received by each brigade; one brigade, however, was still over 200 below establishment. In September some ammunition wagons arrived, and in October eight more 90-mm. guns with wagons, reached each brigade. Progress became rapid in driving drill, field movements, and gunnery; and, as far as possible, the 90-mm. guns were used as 15-pdrs. In November the 90-mm. guns were returned. The batteries then moved to Bedford and were rearmed with 15-pdr. equipments, handed over by the 1st-line Welsh units, and the howitzer batteries took over 5" howitzer equipments. All units were now able to report that they were fairly well up to strength in personnel, horses, and equipment. In December, 1915, each field-gun brigade received 12, 18-pdr. Q.F. guns, limbers, ammunition wagons, and ammunition, and the 15-pdr. equipments were transferred.

In the meantime the division had been allotted a position in the scheme for Home Defence, and in November, 1915, it joined First Army, Central Force. At this time the 68th Division was concentrated at Bedford with the howitzer brigade at St. Neots. By September, 1916, the division had moved into General Reserve, Home Forces, and was quartered as follows: Divisional headquarters and 203rd Brigade at Bedford, 204th Brigade at Old Warden and Lowestoft, 205th Brigade at Howbury and Orford; mounted troops at Turvey; artillery brigades at Austin Cannon, Old Warden, and Howbury; and field companies at Orford, Yatesbury, and Bungay.

By May, 1917, 68th Division had been transferred to Northern Army, Home Forces (Army Headquarters at Norwich), and the summer stations of the division were as follows: Divisional headquarters at Bungay; 203rd Brigade at Halesworth, 204th Brigade at Westleton, Southwold, Wrentham, and Aldeburgh, and 205th Brigade at Lowestoft. The cyclists were at Great Yarmouth and Saxmundham; the artillery brigades at

Huntingdon and Flixton, with the attached field battery and the heavy battery at Leiston; the field companies were at Halesworth, Yarmouth, and Southwold. By August 205th Brigade, the cyclist company, an artillery brigade, and a field company had moved to Herringfleet, and the other field artillery brigade to Halesworth. These stations were occupied until the division (now in XXIII Corps, with Corps Headquarters at Brentwood) took up its winter quarters, and the troops were billeted as follows: 203rd Brigade at Yarmouth, 204th Brigade at Bury St. Edmunds, Newmarket, and Stowlangtoft, and 205th Brigade at Lowestoft. The cyclists were at Lowestoft, Peasenhall, and Wickham Market; the field artillery brigades were at Langley and Harleston, with the heavy battery at Blythburgh; and the field companies were at Lowestoft, Yarmouth, and Heydon.

During the winter the infantry brigades were extensively remodelled, the 2nd-line T.F. battalions being gradually replaced by graduated battalions (see Table). In this way the division lost its territorial association, and henceforth was known as 68th Division. With the arrival of spring the division took up its summer stations for 1918: Divisional headquarters at Bungay, 203rd Brigade at Benacre Park and Herringfleet, 204th Brigade at Bury St. Edmunds, Newmarket, and Stowlangtoft, and 205th Brigade at Saxmundham. The cyclist company was at Henham; the field artillery brigades were at Herringfleet and Henham; and the field companies were at Henham, Herringfleet, and Southwold. Until the end of the War the 68th Division remained in XXIII Corps (Corps Headquarters now at Bury St. Edmunds), and, in November, 1918, the division was disposed as follows: Headquarters at Bungay; 203rd Brigade at Herringfleet, 204th Brigade at Bury St. Edmunds, Newmarket, and Stowlangtoft, and 205th Brigade at Henham. The cyclist company was at Oulton; the field artillery brigades were at Herringfleet and Harleston; and the field companies were at Diss, Yarmouth, and Southwold.

For the remainder of its existence the division continued to occupy the same stations in Norfolk and Suffolk, but the need for the division had passed away. The disbandment of the artillery began by the 6th January, 1919, and on the same date the strength of the engineers had fallen to 472, from the establishment strength of 844. A month later found the strength of the artillery reduced to 322 (establishment, 1,774), and the engineers only numbered 339. The strength of the infantry was maintained longer; at the beginning of March it was 11,821, but of this number only 9,374 were returned as trained. The end, however, was near; and by the 17th March, 1919, the 68th Division disappeared from the Weekly Return of the Army at Home.

69TH (2ND/EAST ANGLIAN) DIVISION

G.O.C.

24 November, 1914	... ...	Br.-Gen. W. F. CAVAYE.
14 November, 1915	... ...	Major-General F. H. KELLY.
3 February, 1917	... ...	Br.-Gen. F. A. FORTESCUE (acting).
18 February, 1917	... ...	Major-General F. H. KELLY.
8 September, 1917	... ...	Major-General C. ROSS.
4 November, 1918	... ...	Major-General Sir R. FANSHAWE.

G.S.O. 1.

Formation ...Major G. WILKS (acting).
15 Jan., 1915...Captain G. E. B. STEPHENS (acting).
3 Mar., 1915...Major D. D. BAYNES (acting).
15 June, 1915...Lt.-Col. H. M. BIDDULPH.
8 May, 1916...Major D. D. BAYNES (acting).
13 May, 1916...Lt.-Col. H. M. BIDDULPH (sick, 5/6/16).
5 June, 1916...Lt.-Col. C. H. D. LYON-CAMPBELL (acting).
20 June, 1916...Lt.-Col. H. M. BIDDULPH.
3 Dec., 1916...Major D. D. BAYNES (acting).
4 Dec., 1916...Lt.-Col. A. L. C. CLARKE.

A.-A. and Q.-M.-G.

25 Jan., 1915...Lt.-Col. T. M. M. BERKELEY.
12 June, 1915...Lt.-Col. P. W. DRAKE-BROCKMAN.
15 May, 1916...Major G. WILKS (acting).
20 May, 1916...Lt.-Col. P. W. DRAKE-BROCKMAN.
21 Feb., 1918...Lt.-Col. A. W. B. WALLACE.

B.-G., R.A.

20 Jan., 1915...Colonel A. C. BAILWARD.
12 Jan., 1916...Colonel C. H. ALEXANDER.
18 April, 1916...Colonel H. H. BUTLER.
7 July, 1916...Br.-Gen. H. H. BUTLER.
8 Jan., 1918 –12 Jan., 1918 } Br.-Gen. J. McC. MAXWELL.
5 Feb., 1918 –31 Dec., 1918 } Br.-Gen. L. A. C. GORDON.

C.R.E.

6 Nov., 1914...Lt.-Col. M. MOWAT.
25 Nov., 1916...Lt.-Col. F. WILSON.

206th BDE.

(2nd/1st Essex)

9 Jan., '15...Col. A. G. WATSON.
18 Mar., '16...Lt.-Col. G. DOWNING.
7 July, '16...Br.-Gen. G. DOWNING.
7 Nov., '17...Br.-Gen. C. CUNLIFFE-OWEN.

207th BDE.

(2nd/1st East Midland)

18 Jan., '15..Col. Hon. A. E. DALZELL.
21 May, '16..Col. M. L. MACEWEN.
7 July, '16...Br.-Gen. M. L. MACEWEN.
20 Feb., '17...Br.-Gen. H. HAGGARD.
7 Aug., '18...Lt.-Col. W. H. YOUNG (acting).
10 Aug., '18...Lt.-Col. V. R. PIGOTT (acting).
29 Aug., '18...Br.-Gen. R. M. OVENS.

208th BDE.

(2nd/1st Norfolk and Suffolk)

9 Jan., '15...Col. W. BODLE.
17 Mar., '16...Col. F. A. FORTESCUE.
29 July, '16...Br.-Gen. F. A. FORTESCUE.
6 Jan., '18...Br.-Gen. A. G. PRITCHARD.
8 April, '18...Br.-Gen. F. F. W. DANIELL.
[7 Feb., '19 –20 Mar., '19 Br.-Gen. C. R. P. WINSER.]

GENERAL NOTES

The following Units belonged to the 2nd/East Anglian Division, but they served with the 54th (East Anglian) Division :—

2/1/East Anglian Fd. Coy., left the 2nd/East Anglian Division in July, 1915, and joined the 54th Division before embarkation. The Fd. Coy. embarked on 28/7/15, and it served with the 54th Division throughout the remainder of the War. In 1917, the Fd. Coy. was numbered 486th.

2/1/East Anglian Fd. Ambce., left the 2nd East Anglian Division in July, 1915, and joined the 54th Division before embarkation. The Fd. Ambce. embarked on 22/7/15, and it served with the 54th Division throughout the remainder of the War.

The following Units also served with the 69th Division :—

ARTILLERY :—54th Division Artillery, (Br.-Gen. G. W. Biddulp)—I, II, III (How.), and IV E. Anglian Bdes., and D.A.C.—was attached to 69th Div. at Thetford, from 8/8–15/11/15, when 54th Div. Artillery went to France. On 21/11/15 54th Div. Artillery was attached, in France, to 33rd Division.

2/1/Shropshire Bty., R.H.A., T.F., was attached from 14/3–2/4/1917. The Battery had previously served with the 1st Mtd. Div. On leaving the 69th Div., 2/1/Shropshire Bty. joined CLVIII, then forming at Heytesbury, and the Bty. was rearmed with 18-pdrs. The Bde. (CLVIII) disembkd. at Boulogne on 24/5/17 and became an A.F.A. Bde. On 6/7/17, 2/1/Shropshire Bty. was redesignated A/CLVIII.

533, 536, 384, 385, 386, 387, and 388 Batteries, see notes, 15, 16, 18, and 19.

1/1/East Anglian (Essex) Hy. Bty., R.G.A., T.F. (4, 4·7″ guns), was attached to the Div. in July, 1915, after the 54th Div. embkd. for Gallipoli. The Hy. Bty. left the 69th Div. on 1/3/16 and went to Woolwich. The Hy. Bty. disembkd. at le Havre on 14/3/16 ; and, on 16/3/16, the Hy. Bty. joined XXIII H.A.G. In 1917 the Hy. Bty. was rearmed with 6, 60-pdr. guns.

2/1/East Anglian (Essex) Hy. Bty., R.G.A., T.F., served with the 69th Div. from 6/11/15–26/4/16. In April, 1916, the Hy. Bty. joined the 5th Provisional Bde. at Lowestoft, and served with the 5th Provl. Bde. until the end of the year. In 1917 the Hy. Bty., still at Lowestoft, was attached to the 225th Mixed Brigade, and the Hy. Bty. served with the 225th Mixed Bde. (XXIII Corps) until the end of 1918.

ENGINEERS :—1/1/City of Edinburgh Fd. Coy., served with the 69th Div. from 16/11/15–19/12/15. Formerly a T.F. fortress coy., it became a field coy. after mobilization. On leaving the 69th Div. the Fd. Coy. embarked at Plymouth, and on 3–5/1/16 it disembkd. at Port Said. The Fd. Coy. joined Army Troops and was employed on the Suez Canal Defences. On 17/4/16 the Fd. Coy. embkd. at Alexandria, disembkd. at Marseille on 24/4/16, and joined 56th Div. on 27/4–4/5/16. The Fd. Coy. served with the 56th Div. for the remainder of the War, and in 1917 it was numbered 416th Fd. Coy.

1/1/Renfrewshire Fd. Coy., served with the 69th Div. from 16/11/15–19/12/15. Formerly a T.F. fortress coy., it became a field coy. after mobilization. On leaving the 69th Div. the Fd. Coy. embarked at Plymouth, and on 3–5/1/16 it disembkd. at Port Said. The Fd. Coy. joined Army Troops and was employed on the Suez Canal Defences. On 17/4/16 the Fd. Coy. embkd. at Alexandria, disembkd. at Marseille on 24/4/16, and joined 4th Div. on 2/5/16. The Fd. Coy. served with the 4th Div. for the remainder of the War, and in 1917 it was numbered 406th Fd. Coy.

INFANTRY :—3rd Provisional Bde. (43rd, 62nd, 64th, 66th, and 67th Provl. Bns.) (Br.-Gen. H. J. Archdale), was attached to the 69th Div. from 18/9–16/10/15. On 15/10/15 117 Hy. Bty., 1/2 1/1/Devon. Hy. Bty., No. 2 Armoured Train, 1/6/Norf. (Cyclists), and 2/25/Lond. (Cyclists) were attached to 3rd Provl. Bde. ; they all left 69th Div. on 16/10/15, with the 3rd Provl. Bde. (In Dec., 1916, 3rd Provl. Bde. became 223rd Mixed Bde. ; and 43rd Bn. became 25/King's, 62nd Bn. became 9/North'n, 64th Bn. became 14/Suff., 66th Bn. became 16/Essex, and 67th Bn. became 17/Essex.)

23/Welsh (P.), attached from 13/5–22/6/16. **26/Middx.(P.)**, attached from 1/6–22/6/16.

Comp. Bn. (2/7/R.W.F. and 2/1/S.W.B.) attached from 25/5–22/6/16.

1/12/L.N.L.(P.), was attached from 13/5–1/6/16. The Bn. then joined 60th (2nd/2nd London) Div. and it served with 60th Div. until 10/4/18, when the Pioneer Bn. was transferred to 74th Division.

OTHER UNITS :—1/1/East Anglian Mobile Vety. Sec., was attached from July, 1915, until it left in March, 1916, to rejoin 54th Div. in Egypt. It rejoined on 11/4/16.

1/1/London Sanitary Sec., joined 69th Div. on 15/6/16 and served with 69th Div. for the remainder of the War.

69th Motor Amb. Workshop, served with the Div., until absorbed by the Train in 1916.

69TH[1] (2ND/EAST ANGLIAN) DIVISION

ORDER OF BATTLE, 1915-1918

Dates	INFANTRY		Mounted Troops	ARTILLERY						Engineers	Signal Service	Pioneers	M.G. Units	Field Ambu-lances	Mobile Vety. Secn.	Divnl. Emplnt. Coy.	Divnl. Train
				Field Artillery			Trench Mortar Bties.		Divnl. Ammn. Coln.								
	Brigades	Battalions and attached Units		Brigades	Batteries	Bde. Ammn. Colns.	Medium	Heavy		Field Cos.	Divnl. Signal Coy.						
1915 November (England)	206th[1] ... (2nd/1st Essex) 207th[1] ... (2nd/1st E. Midland) 208th[1] ... (2nd/1st Norfolk and Suffolk).	2/4/Essex,[2] 2/5/Essex, 2/6/Essex, 2/7/Essex. 2/5/Bedf., 2/4/Northn., 2/1 Herts.,[7] 2/1/Camb.[8] 2/4/Norf., 2/5/Norf., 2/4/Suff.,[3] 2/5/Suff.	2/1/ Herts. Yeo.[4] 69th (2nd/1/E. Anglian) Div. Cyclist Coy.	2nd/I E. Anglian 2nd/II E. Anglian 2nd/III E. Anglian (H.) 2nd/IV E. Anglian	2/1/Norfolk, 2/2/Norfolk, 2/3/Norfolk. 2/1/Essex, 2/2/Essex, 2/3/Essex. 2/1/Suffolk (H.), 2/2/Suffolk (H.) 2/1/Herts., 2/2/Herts., 2/1/Northn.	2nd/I E. Anglian 2nd/II E. Anglian 2nd/III E. Anglian (H.) 2nd/IV E. Anglian	...	...	...	3/1/E. Anglian 2/2/E. Anglian 1/3/E. Anglian[5]	69th (2nd/1/E. Anglian)	...	...	2/2/E. Anglian 2/3/E. Anglian	...	...	69th[6] (2nd/1/E. Anglian)
1916 May (England)	206th ...... 207th 208th	2/5/Essex, 2/6/Essex, 2/7/Essex, 4/1/Herts.[7] 2/5/Bedf., 2/4/Northn., 2/1/Herts.,[7] 2/1/Camb.[8] 2/4/Norf., 2/5/Norf., 2/5/Suff., 4/1/Camb.[8]	H.Q.,[9] M.-G. Sec., & A Sqdn., 2/1/ North-ants. Yeo. 69th Div. Cyclist Coy.	CCCXLV[10] ... (2nd/I E. Anglian) CCCXLVI[10] ... (2nd/II E. Anglian) CCCXLVII (H.)[11] (2nd/III E. Anglian) CCCXLVIII[10] (2nd/IV E. Anglian)	A, B, C A, B, C A (H.), B (H.) A, B, C	CCCXLV B.A.C. CCCXLVI B.A.C. CCCXLVII (H.) B.A.C. CCCXLVIII B.A.C.	...	...	69th D.A.C.	3/1/E. Anglian 2/2/E. Anglian 1/3/E. Anglian	69th	...	...	3/1/E.[12] Anglian 2/2/E. Anglian 2/3/E. Anglian	69th[13] (2/1/E. Anglian)	...	69th
1916 October (England)	206th ...... 207th 208th	2/5/Essex, 2/6/Essex, 2/7/Essex, 4/1/Herts. 2/5/Bedf., 2/4/Northn., 2/1/Herts., 2/1/Camb. 2/4/Norf., 2/5/Norf., 2/5/Suff., 4/1/Camb.	A Sqdn.,[9] 2/1/ North-ants Yeo. 69th Div. Cyclist Coy.	CCCXLV[17] ... CCCXLVI ...... CCCXLVIII ...	A, B,[14] C; [15] D (H.)[11] A, B,[14] C; D (H.)[11]; [16] A, B,[14] C	...	...	...	69th D.A.C.	3/1/E. Anglian 2/2/E. Anglian 1/3/E. Anglian	69th	...	...	3/1/E. Anglian 2/2/E. Anglian 2/3/E. Anglian	69th	...	69th
1917 June (England)	206th ...... 207th 208th	2/5/Essex, 2/6/Essex, 2/7/Essex, 4/1/Herts. 2/5/Bedf., 2/4/Northn., 2/1/Herts., 2/1/Camb. 2/4/Norf., 2/5/Norf., 2/5/Suff.,[20] 4/1/Camb.	69th Div. Cyclist Coy.	CCCXLVI[18] ... CCCXLVIII[19]	A, B,[17] C; D (H.) A, B,[17] C; D (H.)[17]	...	...	...	69th D.A.C.	485th (3/1/E. Anglian) 487th (2/2/E. Anglian) 488th (1/3/E. Anglian)	69th	...	...	322nd (3/1/E. Anglian) 323rd (2/2/E. Anglian) 324th (2/3/E. Anglian)	69th	...	69th

1917 October (England)	206th ...... 207th 208th	2/5/Essex, 2/6/Essex, 2/7/Essex,[21] 237th Bn.,[22]; [24] 238th Bn. [22]; [24] 2/5/Bedf., 2/4/Northn., 2/1/Camb.,[23] 241st Bn.,[22]; [24] 242nd Bn.[22]; [24] 2/4/Norf., 2/5/Norf., 4/1/Camb.,[23] 245th Bn.,[22]; [24] 246th Bn.[22]; [24]	69th Coy., A.C.C.	CCCXLVI ...... CCCXLVIII ...	A, B, C; D (H. A, B, C; D (H.)	...	...	...	69th D.A.C.	485th 487th 488th	69th	...	...	322nd 323rd 324th	69th	...	69th
1917 December (England)	206th ...... 207th 208th	51/N.F. (G.),[24] 2/5/Essex, 2/6/Essex, 51/R.B. (G.)[24] 51/W. York. (G.),[24] 2/5/Bedf., 2/4/Northn., 52/R.B. (G.)[24] 51/Queen's (G.),[24] 2/4/Norf., 2/5/Norf., 51/Sher. For. (G.)[24]	69th Coy., A.C.C.	CCCXLVI ...... CCCXLVIII ...	A, B, C; D (H.) A, B, C; D (H.)	...	...	...	69th D.A.C.	485th 487th 488th	69th	...	...	322nd 323rd 324th	69th	...	69th
1918 April (England)	206th ...... 207th 208th	51/N.F. (G.), 52/N.F. (G.),[25] 2/5/Essex, 51/D.L.I. (G.),[26] 52/D.L.I. (G.)[27] 51/W. York. (G.), 52/W. York. (G.),[28] 51/Leic. (G.),[29] 52/Leic. (G.),[30] 52/Sher. For. (G.)[31] 51/Queen's (G.),[32] 2/4/Norf., 2/5/Norf., 51/Sher. For. (G.), 51/K.O.Y.L.I. (G.),[33] 52/K.O.Y.L.I. (G.)[34]	69th Coy., A.C.C.	CCCXLVI ...... CCCXLVIII ...	A, B, C; D (H.) A, B, C; D (H.)	...	...	...	69th D.A.C.	485th 487th 488th	69th	...	...	322nd 323rd 324th	69th	...	69th
1918 October (England)	206th ...... 207th 208th	51/N.F. (G.), 52/N.F. (G.), 51/D.L.I. (G.), 52/D.L.I. (G.) 51/W. York. (G.), 52/W. York. (G.), 51/K.O.Y.L.I. (G.),[35] 52/K.O.Y.L.I. (G.)[35] 51/Leic. (G.),[36] 52/Leic. (G.),[36] 51/Sher. For. (G.), 52/Sher. For. (G.)[37]	69th Coy., A.C.C.	CCCXLVI ...... CCCXLVIII ...	A, B, C; D (H.) A, B, C; D (H.)	...	...	...	69th D.A.C.	485th 487th 488th	69th	...	...	322nd 323rd 324th	69th	...	69th

NOTES

1 On 15/8/1915 the E. Anglian 2nd-line Division and Infantry Brigades were given numbers. (Divnl. Order No. 788 of 15/8/15.) Authy., 40/W.O./2609, A.G.1, of 10/8/15.

2 Bn. was abolished on 6/12/15; personnel left the Div. to join 3/4/Essex.

3 Bn. was abolished on 6/12/15; personnel (9 offrs. and 282 o.r.) left the Div. to join 3/4/Suff.

4 Regt. served with the Div. until 28/4/16.

5 Fd. Coy. was raised at Northampton and joined the Div. at Thetford on 4/10/15.

6 The Cos. were numbered 553, 554, 555, and 556 Cos., A.S.C.

7 4/1/Herts. began to form on 6/11/15. 2/1/Herts. was divided into 2 battalions on 17/11/15, each of 200 o.r. Each battalion was brought up to 400 o.r. by drafts from 3rd-line. One battalion remained in 207th Bde. (2/1/Herts.); the other battalion (4/1/Herts.) joined 206th Bde. on 8/12/15, to replace 2/4/Essex.

8 4/1/Camb. began to form in Nov., 1915. On 30/11/15 2/1/Camb. was divided into 2 battalions, each of 200 o.r. Each battalion was brought up to 400 o.r. by drafts from 3rd-line. One battalion remained in 207th Bde. (2/1/Camb.); the other battalion (4/1/Camb.) joined 208th Bde. on 12/12/15, to replace 2/4/Suff.

9 Served with the Div. from 17/4/16-15/6/17.

10 In May, 1916, the Bdes. were numbered and the batteries were lettered—A, B, and C—in each Brigade.

11 In May, 1916, the Bde. was numbered and the batteries were lettered A (H.) and B (H.). In 1916 the Bde. was broken up and the 2 batteries were transferred and became D (H.) in CCCXLV and CCCXLVI.

12 Arrived at Newmarket on 6/3/16, and joined the Division.

13 Arrived at Thetford on 22/12/15, and joined the Division.

14 B/CCCXLV was broken up on 7/11/16; and B/CCCXLVI and B/CCCXLVIII were broken up on 10/11/16.

15 C left for Cowshott on 1/9/16 and became 533 (H.) Bty., and original 533 (H.) joined from Cowshott and became C/CCCXLV.

16 D (H.) left for Cowshott on 1/9/16 and became 536 (H.) Bty.; and original 536 (H.) joined from Cowshott and became D (H.)/CCCXLV.

17 On 26/12/16 CCCXLV was broken up and A became B/CCCXLVIII, D (H.) became D (H.)/CCCXLVIII, and C became B/CCCXLVI.

18 On 30/12/16 two new 6-gun 18-pdr. batteries joined, and 384 was affiliated to A and 385 to B.

19 On 30/12/16 three new 6-gun 18-pdr. batteries joined, and 386 was affiliated to A, 387 to B, and 388 to C.

20 Bn. left the Div. on 28/9/17, and was broken up in 67th Div.

21 Bn. left the Div. on 10/10/17, and was broken up in 67th Div.

22 The 6 Graduated Bns. of the Training Reserve joined the Div. between 21/7/17-11/10/17.

23 2/1/Camb. left 69th Div. and joined 200th Bde., 67th Div., on 8/10/17 and was broken up. 4/1/Camb. was broken up at Thoresby (in 69th Div.) between July, 1917, and 8/10/17.

24 The 6 Graduated Bns. of the Training Reserve (see note 22) were affiliated to line regts. and adopted territorial designations from 27/10/17. In Febry., 1918, 51/R.B. and 52/R.B. were transferred to 67th Div.

25 Bn. joined on 5/3/18.

26 Bn. joined on 15/1/18, from 215th Bde., 72nd Div. (disbanded).

27 Bn. joined on 15/1/18, from 220th Bde., 73rd Div. (disbanded).

28 Bn. joined on 23/2/18.

29 Bn. joined on 15/1/18, from 216th Bde., 72nd Div. (disbanded).

30 Bn. joined on 17/1/18, from 218th Bde., 73rd Div. (disbanded).

31 Bn. joined on 23/2/18.

32 Bn. left the Div. on 20/4/18, and by 22/7/18 joined 204th Bde., 68th Div.

33 Bn. joined on 15/1/18, from 217th Bde., 72nd Div. (disbanded).

34 Bn. joined in Jany., 1918, from 219th Bde., 73rd Div. (disbanded).

35 Bns. were transferred from 208th Bde.

36 Bns. were transferred from 207th Bde.

37 Bn. was transferred in April, 1918, from 207th Bde.

69TH (2ND/EAST ANGLIAN) DIVISION

FORMATION AND NARRATIVE

This 2nd-line (or reserve) Territorial Force division had no existence before the outbreak of the Great War.

The formation of reserve (or 2nd-line) T.F. units was authorized on the 31st August, 1914 (see Narrative, 57th Division); but it was not until towards the end of 1914 that the 2nd/East Anglian Division actually came into existence at Peterborough. The training of all the units was impeded by the lack of arms and equipment, by the constant provision of drafts for the 1st-line units, and by the necessary reorganization of the units after the home-service men had been transferred to home-service units.

The 2nd/East Anglian Division concentrated around Thetford early in 1915. On the 17th August the 206th Brigade was detached for work on the London Defences at Rayleigh, Billericay, Hadleigh, and Brentwood. On the 7th September 208th Brigade relieved 206th Brigade; and 208th Brigade then worked on the London Defences until the 28th September, the brigade then rejoined the 69th Division.

In October, 1915, the strength of a battalion was fixed at 23 officers and 600 other ranks. Once more the battalions had to be reorganized and surplus personnel was transferred to 3rd-line battalions. In November, the infantry received charger-loading Lee-Enfield rifles and ammunition and the Japanese rifles were returned to Weedon.

At the outset, training the batteries for war was made difficult by the lack of *matériel*. Some months passed before guns, horses, and harness were received, and even then only French 90-mm. guns were available. It was not until November, 1915, that 15-pdr. equipments and 5″ howitzers were taken over from the 1st-line batteries, and the 90-mm. guns were transferred to various stations. Then in January, 1916, 12, 18-pdr. Q.F. equipments (with 36 wagons) were received by each of the field-gun brigades.

Whilst at Thetford the division formed part of First Army, Central Force, and was quartered as follows: 206th Brigade at Thetford, 207th Brigade at Newmarket, and 208th Brigade at Bury St. Edmunds and Stowlangtoft; the mounted troops were at Huntingdon and Ingham; the artillery was at Cambridge, Tuddenham, and Brandon, with the heavy batteries at Cavenham and Cambridge; and the field companies were at Norwich and Attleborough.

Between 22nd–25th June, 1916, the division moved to Harrogate and it then formed part of Local Forces, Northern Command. The three infantry brigades were all concentrated around Harrogate; the mounted troops were at Mablethorpe and Anderby Creek; the artillery had two brigades at Harrogate and the third at Laceby; and the field companies were at Thirklebridge and Millington, Saltfleetby, and Sutton-on-Sea. The camps around Harrogate were all broken up in October; and from the middle of October, 1916, until the end of April, 1917, the division went into winter quarters, billeting in Harrogate, Catterick, and Doncaster.

Between 30th April and 7th May, 1917, the division moved to Retford, but still remained part of Local Forces, Northern Command. The stations occupied by the 69th Division were now as follows: 206th Brigade at Welbeck Camp, 207th Brigade at Carburton Camp, and 208th Brigade at Thoresby Camp; the mounted troops at Scarborough and Skipsea; the artillery at Welbeck Camp; and the engineers at Thoresby, Carburton, and Welbeck Camps. These stations were maintained until winter set in, and the division moved into winter quarters: Divisional Headquarters in Retford; 206th Brigade in Middlesborough, Barnard Castle, Durham, and Stockton, 207th Brigade in Clipstone, and 208th Brigade in Doncaster and Radmires. The cyclists were in Skipsea; the artillery in Doncaster and Darlington; and the field companies in Doncaster, Mablethorpe, and Darlington.

Whilst the division occupied its winter stations the infantry brigades were extensively remodelled: the 2nd-line T.F. battalions were all replaced by graduated battalions (see Table). In this way the Division lost its territorial association, and from the 1st January, 1918, the Division was designated 69th Division, and 'East Anglian' was dropped.

At the end of the winter the division moved out to its summer stations, and by May, 1918, it was thus disposed: Headquarters at Retford, 206th Brigade at Guisborough, 207th Brigade at Thoresby, and 208th Brigade at Welbeck. The cyclists were at Skipsea; the artillery at Doncaster and Darlington; and the engineers at Doncaster, Mablethorpe, and Darlington. Later, during 1918, the 206th Brigade was stationed at Guisborough and Catterick, the 207th Brigade moved to Clipstone, and the artillery brigades to Middlesborough and Doncaster; and, on the 18th October, Divisional Headquarters left Retford and opened at Sherwood Hall, Mansfield. No further changes were made before the end of 1918, and during the whole of the year 69th Division remained under Northern Command.

From the end of 1917 the engineers were mainly employed on building aerodromes. In this work they were assisted by two Welsh field companies as well as by two American bricklayer companies. For this purpose these four extra companies served, until demobilization, under the C.R.E., 69th Division.

For the rest of its short life the division continued to occupy the same stations. Early in 1919, however, the cyclists disappeared. The disbandment of the artillery also began; and by the 27th January the strength of the divisional artillery had shrunk to 79, out of an establishment of 1,774; at the same date the strength of the engineers had fallen to 87. The infantry maintained its strength rather longer; and as late as the 24th February it still mustered 10,014 (with 3,168 returned as trained) out of an establishment strength of 12,075. The end, however, was drawing near; and by the 17th March, 1919, the 69th Division ceased to appear in the Weekly Return of the Army at Home.

70TH DIVISION

(209TH, 210TH, & 211TH INFANTRY BRIGADES)

THIS DIVISION WAS NEVER FORMED

71st DIVISION

G.O.C.

3 November, 1916 ... ... Br.-Gen. C. T. Caulfeild (acting).
6 November, 1916 ... ... Major-General Hon. H. A. Lawrence.
12 February, 1917 ... ... Major-General C. J. Blomfield.
17 July, 1917 ... ... } Major-General A. G. Dallas.
–1 March, 1918 ... ... }

G.S.O. 1.

30 Oct., 1916...Lt.-Col. H. R. Blore.
31 Mar., 1917...Lt.-Col. R. M. Johnson.
10 Oct., 1917 } Lt.-Col. W. S. Whetherly.
–6 Mar., 1918 }

A.-A. and Q.-M.-G.

27 Oct., 1916 } Lt.-Col. J. M. Home.
–10 April, 1918 }

B.-G., R.A.

3 Nov., 1916...Br.-Gen. C. T. Caulfeild.
21 Nov., 1917...Lt.-Col. S. H. Gosling (acting).
28 Nov., 1917 } Br.-Gen. W. B. Browell.
–25 Feb., 1918 }

C.R.E.

11 Nov., 1916 } Lt.-Col. J. L. V. S. Williams.
–30 Mar., 1918 }

212th BDE.

29 Nov., '16...Br.-Gen. Hon. C. G. Fortescue.
24 Nov., '17 } Br.-Gen. H. W. Cobham.
–12 Feb., '18 }

213th BDE.

2 Nov., '16 } Br.-Gen. W. MacL. Campbell.
–1 Mar., '18 }

214th BDE.

1 Nov., '16...Br.-Gen. W. C. Ross.
11 Dec., '16...Br.-Gen. C. H. T. Lucas.
14 April, '17...Br.-Gen. F. J. Duncan.
8 Nov., '17...Br.-Gen. L. A. E. Price-Davies, V.C.

[On 12/2/18 214th Bde. was transferred to 67th Division.]

71st DIVISION

ORDER OF BATTLE, 1916-1917

Dates	INFANTRY		Mounted Troops	ARTILLERY						Engineers	Signal Service	Pioneers	M.G. Units	Field Ambu-lances	Mobile Vety. Secn.	Divnl. Emplnt. Coy.	Divnl. Train
	Brigades	Battalions and attached Units		Field Artillery			Trench Mortar Bties.		Divnl. Ammn. Coln.	Field Cos.	Divnl. Signal Coy.						
				Brigades	Batteries	Bde. Ammn. Colns.	Medium	Heavy									
1916 November (England)	212th...... 213th...... 214th......	61/Provl. Bn.,[1] 100/Provl. Bn.,[2] 101/Provl. Bn.[3] 16/Queen's,[4] 25/Middx.,[5] 66/Provl. Bn.[6] 2/6/D.L.I.,[7] 2/7/D.L.I.,[7] 2/8/D.L.I.[7]	...	CCCL[8] .... CCCLI[8]	A,[9] B ;[10] C (H.)[11] A,[12] B ;[13] C (H.)[14]	...	...	...	71st[15] D.A.C.	2/1/ Dundee[16] 2/3/ Lanc.[17] 6/Provl.[18] Fd. Coy.	71st[19]	...	...	301st[20] (Welsh) 302nd[20] (Welsh) 303rd[20] (Welsh)	...	...	71st[21]
1917 May (England)	212th...... 213th...... 214th......	11/Norf.,[1] 29/Lond.,[2] 30/Lond.[3] 16/Queen's, 18/Hants.,[22] 16/Essex[6] 2/6/D.L.I., 2/7/D.L.I., 2/8/D.L.I.	71st[23] Div. Cyclist Coy.	CCCL............ CCCLI	1208,[9] B ; C (H.) A, B ; C (H.)	...	...	...	71st D.A.C.	548th[15] (2/1/Dundee) 549th[17] (2/3/Lanc.) 645th[18] (W. Lanc.)	71st	...	...	301st 302nd 303rd	56th[24]	...	71st
1917 August (England)	212th...... 213th...... 214th......	11/Norf., 29/Lond.,[25] 30/Lond., 249th Bn.,[26]; [32] 250th Bn.[26]; [32] 16/Queen's, 18/Hants., 16/Essex, 252nd Bn.[26]; [32] 2/6/D.L.I.,[27] 2/7/D.L.I., 2/8/D.L.I.,[28] 255th Bn.[26]; [32]	71st Div. Cyclist Coy.	CCCL............ CCCLI	1208, B ; C (H.) A, B ; C (H.)	...	...	...	71st D.A.C.	548th 549th 645th	71st	...	...	301st 302nd 303rd	56th	...	71st
1917 October (England)	212th...... 213th...... 214th......	11/Norf.,[29] 30/Lond., 249th Bn., 250th Bn. 16/Queen's, 18/Hants., 16/Essex, 252nd Bn., 253rd Bn.[30]; [32] 2/7/D.L.I., 255th Bn., 256th Bn.[30]; [32]	71st Coy., A.C.C.	CCCL............ CCCLI	1208, B ; C (H.)[37] A, B ; C (H.)[37]	...	...	...	71st D.A.C.	548th 549th 645th[31]	71st	...	...	301st 302nd 303rd	56th	...	71st
1917 November (England)	212th...... 213th...... 214th......	51/Bedf. (G.),[32] 52/Middx. (G.),[32] 30/Lond. 16/Queen's,[35] 18/Hants.,[36] 16/Essex,[36] 52/Bedf. (G.),[32] 51/R. Suss. (G.)[32] 52/Queen's (G.),[32]; [33] 52/R. Suss. (G.),[32]; [34] 2/7/D.L.I.	71st Coy., A.C.C.	XLIX[37]......... CCCL............ CCCLI	A (H.),[37] B (H.)[37] 1208, B A, B	...	...	...	71st D.A.C.	492nd[38] 548th 549th	71st	...	...	301st 302nd 303rd	56th	...	71st
1917 December (England)	212th[39] ... 213th[44] ... 214th[48] ...	51/Bedf. (G.),[40] 52/R. Suss. (G.),[34]; [41] 52/Middx. (G.),[42] 30/Lond.[43] 52/Queen's (G.),[33]; [45] 52/Bedf. (G.),[46] 51/R. Suss.[47] 16/Queen's,[48] 2/7/D.L.I.[48]; [49]	71st[50] Coy., A.C.C.	XLIX[48]; [51] ... CCCL[52] .... CCCLI[53]	A (H.), B (H.) 1208, B A, B	...	...	...	71st[54] D.A.C.	492nd[55] 548th[56] 549th[57]	71st[48]	...	...	301st[58] 302nd[59] 303rd[58]	56th[60]	...	71st[61]

NOTES

1 Bn. (at Wrentham) was transferred from 6th Provl. Bde., and joined at Guildford on 28/11/16. On 1/1/17 Bn. became 11/Norf. (T.F.).

2 Bn. (at Aldeburgh) was transferred from 6th Provl. Bde., and joined at Guildford on 24/11/16. On 1/1/17 Bn. became 29/Lond. (T.F.).

3 Bn. (at Southwold) was transferred from 6th Provl. Bde., and joined at Guildford on 26/11/16. On 1/1/17 Bn. became 30/Lond. (T.F.).

4 Formed at Farnham on 11/11/16.

5 Formerly 25/Garr. Bn., Middx.; became 25/Middx. on 1/11/16, and joined on 3/11/16. Bn. left Bde. and embkd. at Devonport on 22/12/16. Bn. reached Hong Kong on 1/4/17 and left Hong Kong on 27/7/18. Bn. disembkd. Vladivostock on 3/8/18 and reached Omsk on 26/10/18. Bn. left Omsk on 21/5/19, embkd. Vladivostock on 7/9/19, and disembkd. at Glasgow in Nov., 1919. Bn. then returned to London and was disbanded.

6 Bn. (at Dunwich) was transferred from 6th Provl. Bde., and joined at Fleet on 30/11/16. On 1/1/17 Bn. became 16/Essex (T.F.).

7 Bns. formerly in 190th Bde., 63rd Div., were transferred and joined at Andover and Basingstoke on 29/11/16.

8 Bdes. formed on 13/11/16.

9 6th Provl. Bde. Fd. Bty. joined on 27/11/16 and became A/CCCL. On 1/1/17 A became 1208 Fd. Bty. (6, 18-pdr. Q.F.).

10 Formerly A/CCCXXI; joined on 29/11/16 and became B/CCCL (6, 18-pdr. Q.F.).

11 Formerly A/CCCXX; joined on 27/11/16 and became C (H.)/CCCL (4, 4·5" Hows.).

12 Formerly A/CCCXXII; joined on 29/11/16 and became A/CCCLI (6, 18-pdr. Q.F.).

13 6, 18-pdr. Q.F.

14 4, 4·5" Hows.

15 6th Provl. Bde. Ammn. Coln. joined on 27/11/16 and became 71st D.A.C.

16 2/1/Dundee Fortress Coy. joined on 27/11/16 and became a Fd. Coy. On 3/2/17 the Fd. Coy. was numbered 548th.

17 2/3/Lanc. Fortress Coy. joined on 12/12/16 and became a Fd. Coy. On 3/2/17 the Fd. Coy. was numbered 549th.

18 6/Provl. Fd. Coy. joined on 14/11/16. Later the Fd. Coy. was made W. Lanc. Fd. Coy., and on 3/2/17 was numbered 645th.

19 6th Provl. Bde. Sig. Sec. joined on 7/11/16, and on 13/11/16 became Div. Sig. Coy.

20 6th Provl. Bde. Fd. Amb. joined on 26/11/16: A Sec. formed 301st Fd. Amb., C Sec. formed 302nd Fd. Amb., and B. Sec. formed 303rd Fd. Amb.

21 Train was composed of 821, 822, 823, and 824 Cos., A.S.C. 6th Provl. Bde. Coy., A.S.C. joined on 28/11/16 and formed 821 Coy.; 822 Coy. joined on 13/12/16, 823 Coy. on 18/12/16, and 824 Coy. on 30/12/16.

22 Bn. was formed at Alton and joined on 26/12/16.

23 Coy. joined on 11/1/17.

24 Sec. joined on 8/1/17.

25 Bn. was transferred to 226th Mixed Bde.

26 These 4 Graduated Bns. of the Training Reserve joined by 9/7/17.

27 Bn. was transferred to 226th Mixed Bde. On 1/5/18 Bn. became a Garr. Gd. Bn. at Frinton. Bn. went to France and disembkd. at Calais on 6/5/18. Bn. joined 177th Bde., 59th Div., on 10/5/18.

28 Bn. left Bde. by 9/7/17.

29 Bn. left Bde. by 29/10/17.

30 These 2 Graduated Bns. of the Training Reserve joined by 17/9/17.

31 Left the Div. on 26/10/17 and joined 67th Div.

32 The 6 Graduated Bns. of the Training Reserve (see notes 26 and 30) were affiliated to line regiments and adopted territorial designations from 27/10/17.

33 Bn. transferred to 213th Bde. by 12/11/17.

34 Bn. transferred to 212th Bde. by 12/11/17.

35 Bn. transferred to 214th Bde. by 12/11/17.

36 Bns. had left Div. by 24/12/17.

37 Bde. formed on 22/10/17 at Colchester: C (H.)/CCCL joined and became A; C (H.)/CCCLI joined and became B.

38 Fd. Coy. joined on 26/10/17, from 67th Div.

39 Bde. broken up by 7/3/18.

40 Bn. transferred to 193rd Bde., 64th Div., on 19/2/18.

41 Bn. transferred to 191st Bde., 64th Div., on 18/2/18.

42 Bn. transferred to 193rd Bde., 64th Div., on 26/2/18.

43 Bn. transferred to 226th Mixed Bde. on 5/2/18.

44 Bde. broken up by 11/3/18.

45 Bn. transferred to 192nd Bde., 64th Div., on 18/2/18.

46 Bn. transferred to 193rd Bde., 64th Div., on 25/2/18.

47 Bn. transferred to 191st Bde., 64th Div., on 25/2/18.

48 214th Special Bde. (with XLIX Bde. and 71st Div. Sig. Coy.) left the Div. on 12/2/18 and joined 67th Div.

49 Bn. left 67th Div. on 7/10/18 to join the Archangel Force as a Garr. Bn. Bn. reached Archangel on 23/10/18, and disembkd. on 24/10/18 at Bakaritza.

50 Cyclist Coy. was disbanded on 3/2/18.

51 Bde. left Div. with 214th Bde. and joined 67th Div. Bde. was disbanded by 25/3/18.

52 Bde. was disbanded on 25/2/18.

53 Bde. left the Div. on 29/1/18 and moved to Larkhill; and Bde. served at Larkhill for the remainder of the War.

54 D.A.C. was disbanded on 25/2/18.

55 Fd. Coy. left Div. by 12/2/18. Late in 1918 the Fd. Coy. went to N. Russia and joined N.R.E.F. The Fd. Coy. reached Murmansk on 27/9/18.

56 Fd. Coy. left Div. on 30/3/18. Fd. Coy. went to Murmansk and joined N.R.E.F.: advd. party disembkd. on 20/6/18 and the main body on 23/6/18.

57 Fd. Coy. left Div. on 30/3/18. Fd. Coy. went to France and disembkd. at le Havre on 23/6/18. Fd. Coy. then served on the Western Front with First, Fifth, and Third Armies.

58 Both Fd. Ambces. were disbanded on 31/1/18.

59 On 12/2/18 Fd. Ambce. was transferred (with 214th Bde.) to 67th Div. The Fd. Ambce. was then broken up.

60 Left Div. on 7/3/18.

61 824 Coy. was disbanded on 30/1/18; 823 Coy. on 13/2/18; 822 Coy. on 16/2/18; and 821 Coy. on 23/2/18.

GENERAL NOTES

The following were attached to, or served with, the 71st Division :—

226th Mixed Brigade:—Hd. Qrs., Great Clacton—Br.-Gen. J. F. Erskine (until 24/10/17), then Br.-Gen. Hon. C. G. Fortescue (from 21/11/17), was attached to 71st Division from 13/4/17–12/2/18, when the Brigade was transferred to 67th Division.

MOUNTED TROOPS :—

2/1/Warwickshire Yeo. (Cyclists),
2/1/Herts. Yeo. (Cyclists), } joined on 26/10/17 and were attached to the 214th Bde.; transferred (with 214th Bde.) on 12/2/18 to 67th Division.

C Sqdn., 2/1/Bedfordshire Yeo., served with 71st Division from 6/3/17.

ARTILLERY :—

2/1/London Heavy Battery,
2/2/London Heavy Battery, } joined on 9/3/17. The two heavy batteries were transferred (with 226th Mixed Brigade) on 12/2/18 to 67th Division.

MACHINE-GUN COMPANIES :—

252nd Machine-Gun Company,
253rd Machine-Gun Company, } joined on 9/11/17 and were attached to 214th Bde.; transferred (with 214th Bde.) on 12/2/18 to 67th Division.

OTHER UNIT :—104th Sanitary Section, served with the 71st Division from formation to disbandment.

71st DIVISION

FORMATION AND NARRATIVE

This home-service division had no existence before the outbreak of the Great War.

Late in 1916 it was decided to form three additional home-service divisions, and in November the 71st Division was formed in Hampshire and Surrey. Divisional Headquarters opened at Gostrey House, Farnham, but moved to Elmer House, Farnham, on the 11th November. The three infantry brigades assembled at Guildford, Aldershot, and Whitchurch, and the artillery concentrated at Basingstoke. To form the division the 6th Provisional Brigade (Saxmundham) was broken up. This brigade then provided four battalions, a battery, the ammunition column, a field company, signal company, field ambulances, and a company of the divisional train (see Table). The 190th Brigade (formerly part of the 63rd Division, which had been broken up) provided three more battalions; and another division found three batteries. The other units were new formations. The divisional artillery was armed with 18-pdr. Q.F. guns (6-gun batteries) and 4·5" howitzers (4-gun batteries).

On the 1st January, 1917, all the provisional units received new designations; the four battalions were affiliated to regiments of the line, and the battery and field company were numbered. In the first week of March the division moved into the eastern counties, and concentrated at Colchester by the 8th March. Henceforward the 71st Division formed part of Southern Army, Home Forces, and was responsible for the defence of the East Coast from Mersea Island to Walton on the Naze.

For the remainder of 1917 the division remained at Colchester; but, as the Table shows, the infantry underwent some reorganization. Between July and the middle of September six graduated battalions of the Training Reserve joined the brigades. In October these six battalions were affiliated to line regiments and adopted territorial designations. In the same month the 214th Brigade was formed into a Special Brigade for possible service in Murmansk; and, for this purpose, it was filled up with A.1 men, and had attached to it a brigade of artillery (XLIX), as well as two battalions of cyclists and two machine-gun companies (see General Notes).

About this time the fate of the three home-service divisions came under consideration, and towards the end of December it was decided to break them up. On the 10th January, 1918, instructions were issued to break up the 71st Division; and, on the 12th, orders were given to Commander-in-Chief, Home Forces, to break up the division with the least possible delay. Shortly afterwards the disbandment of the division was begun. On the 12th February the 214th Special Brigade (with attached troops) was transferred to the 67th Division, and this date marks the disappearance of the 71st Division as an effective unit in the scheme of Home Defence. On the 24th February G.O.C., 71st Division, reported that demobilization of the division should be completed by the 15th March. On the 1st March Major-General Dallas left the division and the command of the divisional details thereafter devolved on Colonel J. M. Home.

Gradually, as units were transferred, drafted, or broken up, the strength dwindled. On the 25th February it had been 10,931 (out of an establishment of 13,306), but by the 11th March it had shrunk to 768; and by the 8th April, 1918, the 71st Division finally disappeared from the Weekly Return of the Army at Home.

72ND DIVISION

G.O.C.

3 November, 1916 ... ... Major-General F. S. INGLEFIELD.
6 September, 1917 ... ... }
–31 January, 1918 ... ... } Major-General G. J. CUTHBERT.

G.S.O. 1.

1 Nov., 1916 }
–8 Jan., 1918 } Lt.-Col. T. E. L. HILL-WHITSON.

A.-A. and Q.-M.-G.

1 Nov., 1916 }
–20 Feb., 1918 } Lt.-Col. A. W. B. WALLACE.

B.-G., R.A.

2 Nov., 1916 }
–9 Mar., 1918 } Br.-Gen. F. B. JOHNSTONE.

C.R.E.

27 Nov., 1916 }
–18 Oct., 1918 } Lt.-Col. A. O. EVANS.

215th BDE.

1 Nov., '16 }
–17 Jan., '18 } Br.-Gen. P. W. HENDRY.

216th BDE.

2 Nov., '16 ...Br.-Gen. C. V. HUMPHRYS.
5 Feb., '17 }
–10 Mar., '18 } Br.-Gen. G. M. GLOSTER.

217th BDE.

1 Nov., '16...Br.-Gen. A. L. MACFIE.
16 June, '17 }
–2 Feb., '18 } Br.-Gen. DOUGLAS CAMPBELL.

72ND DIVISION — ORDER OF BATTLE, 1916-1917

Dates	INFANTRY		Mounted Troops	ARTILLERY						Engineers	Signal Service	Pioneers	M.G. Units	Field Ambu-lances	Mobile Vety. Secn.	Divnl. Emplnt. Coy.	Divnl. Train
				Field Artillery			Trench Mortar Bties.										
	Brigades	Battalions and attached Units		Brigades	Batteries	Bde. Ammn. Colns.	Medium	Heavy	Divnl. Ammn. Coln.	Field Cos.	Divnl. Signal Coy.						
1916 November (England)	215th ...... 216th 217th	28/Provl. Bn.,[1] 70/Provl. Bn.,[2] 81/Provl. Bn.[3] 10/Som. L.I.,[4] 14/K.O.Y.L.I.,[4] 83/Provl. Bn.[5] 2/4/N.F.,[6] 2/5/N.F.,[6] 2/6/N.F.[6]	72nd[7] Div. Cyclist Coy.	CCCLII[8] ...... CCCLIII[8]	A,[9] B; C (H.) A, B; C (H.)	...	...	...	72nd D.A.C.[10]	3/1/[11] Glamorgan 2/2/[11] Glamorgan 8/Provl. Fd. Coy.[12]	72nd[13]	...	...	304th[14] (S. Midland) 305th[14] (S. Midland) 306th[14] (S. Midland)	...	...	72nd[15]
1917 May (England)	215th ...... 216th 217th	18/R. War.,[3] 13/Linc.,[1]; [16] 15/R. Suss.[2] 10/Som. L.I.,[17] 10/O. & B.L. I.,[5]; [18] 14/K.O.Y.L.I. 2/4/N.F., 2/5/N.F.,[19] 2/6/N.F.	72nd Div. Cyclist Coy.	CCCLII .... CCCLIII	1210,[9] B; C (H.) A, B; C (H.)	...	...	...	72nd D.A.C.	550th[11] (3/1/Glam.) 551st[11] (2/2/Glam.) 647th[12] (S. Midld.)	72nd	...	...	304th 305th 306th	57th[20]	...	72nd
1917 August (England)	215th ...... 216th 217th	18/R. War., 15/R. Suss., 258th Bn.[22] 14/K.O.Y.L.I., 261st Bn.,[22] 262nd Bn.[21] 2/4/N.F., 2/6/N.F., 264th Bn.[21]	72nd Div. Cyclist Coy.	CCCLII .... CCCLIII	1210, B; C (H.) A, B; C (H.)	...	...	...	72nd D.A.C.	550th 551st 647th	72nd	...	...	304th 305th 306th	57th	...	72nd
1917 October (England)	215th ...... 216th 217th	18/R. War., 15/R. Suss., 258th Bn.,[25] 259th Bn.[23]; [25] 14/K.O.Y.L.I., 261st Bn.,[25] 262nd Bn.[25] 2/4/N.F., 2/6/N.F., 264th Bn.,[25] 265th Bn.[23]; [25]	72nd Coy., A.C.C.	CCCLII .... CCCLIII	1210, B; C (H.) A, B; C (H.)	...	...	...	72nd D.A.C.	550th 551st 647th	72nd	...	...	304th 305th 306th	57th	...	72nd
1917 November (England)	215th...... 216th 217th	18/R. War.,[24] 51/R.F. (G.),[25] 15/R. Suss., 51/D.L.I. (G.)[25] 51/R. War. (G.),[25] 51/Leic. (G.),[25] 14/K.O.Y.L.I. 2/4/N.F., 2/6/N.F.,[26] 52/R.F. (G.),[25] 51/K.O.Y.L.I. (G.)[25]	72nd Coy., A.C.C.	CCCLII .... CCCLIII	1210, B; C (H.) A, B; C (H.)	...	...	...	72nd D.A.C.	550th 551st 647th	72nd	...	...	304th 305th 306th	57th	...	72nd
1917 December (England)	215th ...... 216th 217th	51/R.F. (G.),[27] 15/R. Suss.,[28] 51/D.L.I. (G.)[29] 51/R. War. (G.),[30] 51/Leic. (G.),[31] 14/K.O.Y.L.I.[32] 2/4/N.F.,[33] 52/R.F. (G.),[27] 51/K.O.Y.L.I. (G.)[34]	72nd[35] Coy., A.C.C.	CCCLII[36] ...... CCCLIII[36] ...	1210, B; C (H.) A, B; C (H.)	...	...	...	72nd D.A.C.[36]	550th[37] 551st[38] 647th[38]	72nd[39]	...	...	304th[40] 305th[40] 306th[41]	57th[42]	...	72nd[43]

NOTES

1 Bn. (at Tillingham) was transferred in Nov., 1916, from 8th Provl. Bde. On 1/1/17 Bn. became 13/Linc. (T.F.).

2 Bn. (at Burnham) was transferred in Nov., 1916, from 8th Provl. Bde. On 1/1/17 Bn. became 15/R. Suss. (T.F.).

3 Bn. (at Southminster) was transferred in Nov., 1916, from 8th Provl. Bde. On 1/1/17 Bn. became 18/R. War. (T.F.).

4 Bns. joined by 20/11/16.

5 Bn. (at West Mersea) was transferred in Nov., 1916, from 8th Provl. Bde. On 1/1/17 Bn. became 10/O. and B.L.I. (T.F.).

6 The 3 Bns. were transferred from 188th Bde. (formerly in 63rd Div.) and joined by 27/11/16.

7 Joined by 4/12/16.

8 Both Bdes. had begun to form by 20/11/16. The personnel to form 3, 18-pdr. bties. and 2, 4·5" howitzer batteries were transferred from A/CCCXXVII (65th Div.), C/CCCXXXVII, C/CCCXXXVI, and A/CCCXXXV (67th Div.), and B/CCCXLII (68th Div.).

9 8th Provl. Bde. Fd. Bty. (at Southminster) joined by 20/11/16 and became A/CCCLII. On 1/1/17 A/CCCLII became 1210 Bty. (6, 18-pdr. Q.F.).

10 6th Provl. Bde. Ammn. Coln. joined by 20/11/16 and became D.A.C.

11 These 2 Fortress Cos. joined by 20/11/16 and became Fd. Cos. In Feb., 1917, they were numbered 550th and 551st.

12 8/Provl. Fd. Coy. (at Southminster) joined by 20/11/16. Later the Coy. became S. Midland Fd. Coy., and in February, 1917, it was numbered 647th.

13 8th Provl. Bde. Sig. Sec. (at Maldon) joined by 20/11/16 and became 72nd Div. Sig. Coy.

14 8th Provl. Bde. Fd. Ambce. (at Burnham) joined by 4/12/16 and formed the 3 Fd. Ambces.

15 Train was composed of 825, 826, 827, and 828 Cos., A.S.C. 8th Provl. Bde. Coy., A.S.C. (at Southminster) joined by 4/12/16 and formed 825 Coy. The other 3 Cos. were new formations.

16 Bn. left by July, 1917.

17 Bn. left by July, 1917.

18 Bn. left by July, 1917; it was disbanded by Jany., 1918.

19 Bn. left by July, 1917; it was disbanded by Jany., 1918.

20 Sec. joined in Jany., 1917.

21 These 2 Graduated Bns. of the Training Reserve joined by 9/7/17.

22 These 2 Graduated Bns. of the Training Reserve joined by 23/7/17.

23 These 2 Graduated Bns. of the Training Reserve joined by 24/9/17.

24 Bn. left the Div. by 24/12/17, and it was disbanded on 17/1/18.

25 The 6 Graduated Bns. of the Training Reserve (see notes 21, 22, and 23) were affiliated to line regiments and adopted territorial designations from 27/10/17.

26 Bn. left the Div. by 10/12/17.

27 These 2 Bns. were transferred to 204th Bde., 68th Div., by 11/3/18.

28 Bn. was disbanded by 25/3/18.

29 Bn. was transferred to 206th Bde., 69th Div., on 15/1/18.

30 Bn. was transferred to 205th Bde., 68th Div., by 11/3/18.

31 Bn. was transferred to 207th Bde., 69th Div., on 15/1/18.

32 Bn. was disbanded by 8/4/18.

33 Bn. was disbanded by 8/4/18.

34 Bn. was transferred to 208th Bde., 69th Div., on 15/1/18.

35 Coy. was broken up by 25/2/18.

36 Both Bdes. and the D.A.C. were broken up by 25/2/18.

37 Fd. Coy. left the Div. by 8/4/18; on 23/6/18 it disembkd. at le Havre, and on 7/7/18 it joined Second Army. On 11/11/18 the Fd. Coy. was transferred to First Army.

38 Both Fd. Cos. were broken up by 8/4/18.

39 Broken up by 4/2/18.

40 Both Fd. Ambces. were broken up by 18/3/18.

41 Broken up by 11/3/18.

42 Broken up by 4/3/18.

43 Train was broken up by 8/4/18.

GENERAL NOTES

The following also served with the 72nd Division :—

105th Sanitary Section, from January, 1917–January, 1918.

72ND DIVISION

FORMATION AND NARRATIVE

This home-service division had no existence before the outbreak of the Great War.

Late in 1916 it was decided to form three additional home-service divisions, and in November the 72nd Division was formed in Somersetshire. Divisional Headquarters opened at Weston and then moved to Bath. The three infantry brigades concentrated at Bath, Weston, and Clevedon, and the artillery collected at Bridgwater, with the ammunition column at Taunton. To form the division the 8th Provisional Brigade (Maldon) was broken up. This brigade then provided four battalions, a battery, the ammunition column, a field company, signal company, field ambulances, and a company of the divisional train (see Table). The 188th Brigade (formerly part of the 63rd Division which had been broken up) provided three more battalions; and 65th, 67th, and 68th Divisions transferred sufficient personnel to form five batteries. Each artillery brigade was to consist of two 6-gun 18-pdr. Q.F. batteries and one 4-gun 4·5" howitzer battery. Until the equipments were issued, Northern Command and Northern and Southern Armies loaned a section of 18-pdr. guns, or 4·5" howitzers, to each of the batteries of the 72nd Division Artillery. The other units of the division were new formations.

On the 1st January, 1917, all the provisional units received new designations: the four battalions were affiliated to regiments of the line, and the battery and field company were numbered. The division, having completed its assembly in Somersetshire, moved in January to Bedford, Wellingborough, and Northampton to replace the 62nd Division, which had gone to France. In this area the division remained until May, when it moved to Ipswich, with two of the field companies (550th and 551st) for a time at Yatesbury. The 72nd Division now formed part of Southern Army, Home Forces, and the division was responsible for the defence of the East Coast from the River Deben to Orfordness.

For the remainder of 1917 the division continued at Ipswich; but, as the Table shows, the infantry underwent some reorganization. Between July and the end of September six graduated battalions of the Training Reserve joined the brigades. In October these six battalions were affiliated to line regiments and adopted territorial designations. Very shortly after this the fate of the three home-service divisions came under consideration, and on the 21st December instructions were issued to break up the 72nd Division. On the next day orders were given to Commander-in-Chief, Home Forces, to break up the division as soon as possible.

The disbandment of the division began early in 1918. Three battalions left on the 15th January, and the effective life of the division, as a unit in Home Defence, came to an end with the disappearance of the G.O.C. at the end of the month. Gradually the strength of the division dwindled as units were transferred, drafted, or broken up. By the 11th February the strength was only 8,779 (out of an establishment of 13,306). A month later the division had shrunk to 550; and by the 8th April, 1918, the 72nd Division ceased to appear in the Weekly Return of the Army at Home.

73RD DIVISION

G.O.C.

2 November, 1916	Major-General Hon. C. E. BINGHAM.
28 December, 1916	Br.-Gen. R. DAWSON (acting).
3 January, 1917	Major-General Hon. C. E. BINGHAM.
4 April, 1917	Major-General J. C. YOUNG.
6 September, 1917	Major-General H. G. RUGGLES-BRISE.
12 January, 1918	Br.-Gen. F. L. BANON (acting).
20 January, 1918 ... ... –4 March, 1918	Major-General H. G. RUGGLES-BRISE.

G.S.O. 1.

1 Nov.,	1916...	Lt.-Col. E. B. C. BODDAM.
14 Dec.,	1916...	Major T. A. POLLOK-MORRIS (acting).
12 Jan.,	1917...	Major C. M. DAVIES (acting).
16 Jan.,	1917...	Lt.-Col. C. M. DAVIES.
1 Jan., –4 Mar.,	1918 1918	Major K. HENDERSON (acting).

A.-A. and Q.-M.-G.

1 Nov.,	1916...	Colonel C. L. MACNAB.
17 April,	1917...	Major C. G. WICKHAM (acting).
24 April,	1917...	Lt.-Col. F. C. DUNDAS.
1 Mar., –4 Mar.,	1918 1918	Major H. J. MACKENZIE (acting).

B.-G., R.A.

8 Nov.,	1916...	Br.-Gen. J. J. MACMAHON.
12 Mar.,	1917...	Br.-Gen. W. A. ROBINSON.
19 Nov., –4 Feb.,	1917 1918	Br.-Gen. L. A. C. GORDON.

C.R.E.

17 Nov.,	1916...	Lt.-Col. H. W. SANDERS.
[22 June,	1918......	Lt.-Col. B. R. LAMBERT.
2 July,	1918......	Lt.-Col. O. S. DAVIES.
1 Oct.,	1918......	Lt.-Col. R. A. NEVILL.
7 Oct.,	1918......	Lt.-Col. M. WHITWILL.
8 Nov.,	1918......	Major J. LL. LEWIS (acting).
22 Nov.,	1918......	Lt.-Col. G. F. EVANS.]*

* On 22/6/18 73rd Div. R.E. (Hd. Qrs., and 546th, 547th, and 648th Fd. Cos.), went to France and disembarked at le Havre on 23/6/18 (see notes 37, 38, and 39).

218th BDE.

1 Nov., '16...Br.-Gen. H. MARTIN.
17 Mar., '17...Br.-Gen. W. M. WITHYCOMBE.
10 July, '17 –31 Jan., '18 } Br.-Gen. A. MARTYN.

219th BDE.

1 Nov., '16...Br.-Gen. R. DAWSON.
7 Sept., '17 –22 Feb., '18 } Br.-Gen. F. L. BANON.

220th BDE.

1 Nov., '16 –27 Feb., '18 } Br.-Gen. F. F. W. DANIELL.

GENERAL NOTES

The following Units also were attached to, or served with, the 73rd Division :—

CYCLIST BATTALIONS :—1/8/Essex (Cyclist), from January–October, 1917 ; and **2/7/Devon (Cyclist),** from October, 1917–January, 1918.

OTHER UNIT :—106th Sanitary Section, served with the Division from formation to disbandment.

73RD DIVISION — ORDER OF BATTLE, 1916-1917

Dates	INFANTRY		Mounted Troops	ARTILLERY						Engineers	Signal Service	Pioneers	M.G. Units	Field Ambulances	Mobile Vety. Secn.	Divnl. Emplnt. Coy.	Divnl. Train
	Brigades	Battalions and attached Units		Field Artillery			Trench Mortar Btties.		Divnl. Ammn. Coln.	Field Cos.	Divnl. Signal Coy.						
				Brigades	Batteries	Bde. Ammn. Colns.	Medium	Heavy									
1916 November (England)	218th ...... 219th 220th	41/Provl. Bn.,[1] 42/Provl. Bn.,[2] 44/Provl. Bn.[3] 8/Dorset.,[4] 13/L.N.L.,[5] 45/Provl. Bn.[6] 2/4/Gr. How.[7] 2/5/Gr. How.,[7] 17/Gr. How.[8]	73rd Div. Cyclist Coy.[9]	CCCLIV[10] ...... CCCLV[10]	A[11] B ; C (H.) A, B ; C (H.)	...	...	...	73rd D.A.C.[12]	1/6/ Kent[13] 1/7/ Kent[13] 9/Provl. Fd. Coy.[14]	73rd[15]	...	...	307th[16] (Home Counties) 308th[16] (Home Counties) 309th[16] (Home Counties)	...	...	73rd[17]
1917 May (England)	218th ...... 219th 220th	12/K.O.,[1] 26/King's,[3] 14/L.N.L.[2] 8/Dorset., 13/L.N.L., 28/Manch.[6] 2/4/Gr. How., 2/5/Gr. How., 17/Gr. How.	73rd Div. Cyclist Coy.	CCCLIV......... CCCLV	1211,[11] B ; C (H.) A, B ; C (H.)	...	...	...	73rd D.A.C.	546th[13] (1/6/ Kent) 547th[13] (1/7/ Kent) 648th[14] (E. Lanc.)	73rd	...	...	307th 308th 309th	58th[18]	...	73rd
1917 August (England)	218th ...... 219th 220th	12/K.O., 26/King's, 14/L.N.L., 267th Bn.[20] 8/Dorset., 13/L.N.L., 28/Manch., 270th Bn.[19] 2/4/Gr. How., 2/5/Gr. How., 17/Gr. How., 273rd Bn.,[20] 274th Bn.[19]	73rd Div. Cyclist Coy.	CCCLIV......... CCCLV	1211, B ; C (H.) A, B ; C (H.)	...	...	...	73rd D.A.C.	546th 547th 648th	73rd	...	...	307th 308th 309th	58th	...	73rd
1917 October (England)	218th ...... 219th 220th	12/K.O., 26/King's, 14/L.N.L., 267th Bn.[22] 8/Dorset., 13/L.N.L., 28/Manch., 270th Bn.[22] 2/4/Gr. How., 2/5/Gr. How., 17/Gr. How.,[21] 273rd Bn.,[22] 274th Bn.[22]	73rd Coy., A.C.C.	CCCLIV......... CCCLV	1211, B ;C (H.) A, B ; C (H.)	...	...	...	73rd D.A.C.	546th 547th 648th	73rd	...	...	307th 308th 309th	58th	...	73rd
1917 November (England)	218th ...... 219th 220th	12/K.O., 26/King's, 52/Leic. (G.),[22] 14/L.N.L.[23] 8/Dorset.,[24] 13/L.N.L., 52/K.O.Y.L.I. (G.),[22] 28/Manch. 52/R. War. (G.),[22] 2/4/Gr. How.,[25] 2/5/Gr. How., 52/D.L.I. (G.)[22]	73rd Coy., A.C.C.	CCCLIV......... CCCLV	1211, B ; C (H.) A, B ; C (H.)	...	...	...	73rd D.A.C.	546th 547th 648th	73rd	...	...	307th 308th 309th	58th	...	73rd

1917 December (England)	218th......	12/K.O.,[26] 26/King's,[27] 52/Leic. (G.)[28]	73rd Coy.,[35] A.C.C.	CCCLIV[36]......	1211, B; C (H.)	...	...	...	73rd D.A.C.[36]	546th[37]	73rd[40]	...	...	307th[41]	58th[43]	...	73rd[44]
	219th......	13/L.N.L.,[29] 52/K.O.Y.L.I. (G.),[30] 28/Manch.[31]		CCCLV[36]	A, B; C (H.)					547th[38]				308th[41]			
	220th......	52/R. War. (G.),[32] 2/5/Gr. How.,[33] 52/D.L.I. (G.)[34]								648th[39]				309th[42]			

On the 4th March, 1918, the 73rd Division was broken up.

NOTES

1 Bn. (at Westgate) was transferred in Nov., 1916, from 9th Provl. Bde. On 1/1/17 Bn. became 12/K.O. (T.F.).

2 Bn. (at Broadstairs) was transferred in Nov., 1916, from 9th Provl. Bde. On 1/1/17 Bn. became 14/L.N.L. (T.F.).

3 Bn. (at Ramsgate) was transferred in Nov., 1916, from 9th Provl. Bde. On 1/1/17 Bn. became 26/King's (T.F.).

4 Bn. raised on 1/9/16 at Wool as 2/Garr. Bn., Dorset. On 1/11/16 Bn. became 8/Dorset., and on 7/11/16 Bn. joined 219th Bde. at Blackpool.

5 By 4/12/16 the Bn. had begun to form in the Bde. area.

6 Bn. (at Margate) was transferred in Nov., 1916, from 9th Provl. Bde. On 1/1/17 Bn. became 28/Manch. (T.F.).

7 The 2 Bns. were transferred from 189th Bde. (formerly in 63rd Div.) at Catterick, and they joined 220th Bde. on 9/11/16.

8 Bn. joined by 4/12/16.

9 Coy. joined by 18/12/16.

10 Both Bdes. had begun to form by 20/11/16. To assist in forming the batteries, personnel was transferred from other divisions.

11 9th Provl. Bde. Fd. Bty. (at Minster) joined by 4/12/16 and became A/CCCLIV. On 1/1/17 A/CCCLIV became 1211 Bty. (6, 18-pdr. Q.F.).

12 9th Provl. Bde. Ammn. Col. joined by 20/11/16 and became D.A.C.

13 These 2 Fortress Cos. joined by 20/11/16 and became Fd. Cos. In Feb., 1917, they were numbered 546th and 547th.

14 9th Provl. Fd. Coy. (at Margate) joined by 20/11/16. Later the Coy. became E. Lanc. Fd. Coy., and in Feb., 1917, it was numbered 648th.

15 9th Provl. Bde. Sig. Sec. (at Margate) joined by 20/11/16 and became Div. Sig. Coy.

16 9th Provl. Fd. Ambce. (at Margate) joined on 23/11/16 and formed the 3 Fd. Ambces.

17 Train was composed of 829, 830, 831, and 832 Cos., A.S.C. 9th Provl. Bde. Coy., A.S.C. (at Margate) joined by 20/11/16 and formed 829 Coy. The other 3 Cos. were new formations.

18 Joined on 24/1/17.

19 These 2 Graduated Bns. of the Training Reserve joined by 9/7/17.

20 These 2 Graduated Bns. of the Training Reserve joined by 23/7/17.

21 Bn. was disbanded by 5/11/17.

22 The 4 Graduated Bns. of the Training Reserve (see notes 19 and 20) were affiliated to line regiments and adopted territorial designations from 27/10/17.

23 Bn. was gradually drafted, and finally disappeared by 17/12/17.

24 Bn. was gradually drafted, and finally disappeared by 3/12/17.

25 On 16/7/17 2/4/Gr. How. began to be drafted at Chelmsford, and by 31/7/17 the strength was reduced to 12 offrs. and 174 o.r. On 21/12/17 Bn. completed disbandment at Chelmsford.

26 Bn. was disbanded by July, 1918.

27 Bn. was disbanded in 1919.

28 Bn. was transferred on 17/1/18 to 207th Bde., 69th Div.

29 Bn. was disbanded by August, 1918.

30 Bn. was transferred in January, 1918, to 208th Bde., 69th Div.

31 Bn. was disbanded by November, 1918.

32 Bn. was transferred by 11/3/18 to 205th Bde., 68th Div.

33 Bn. was disbanded at Chelmsford in March, 1918.

34 Bn. was transferred on 15/1/18 to 206th Bde., 69th Div.

35 Coy. was broken up by 1/4/18.

36 Both Bdes. and the D.A.C. were broken up by 25/2/18.

37 Fd. Coy. went to France. It disembkd. at le Havre on 23/6/18, and it worked in Third Army Area from 7/7/18. Fd. Coy. was transferred to Fourth Army on 11/11/18; and on 4/6/19 it was disbanded at Candas.

38 Fd. Coy. went to France. It disembkd. at le Havre on 23/6/18, and it worked in Third Army Area from 7/7/18. On 4/6/19 it was disbanded at Candas.

39 Fd. Coy. went to France. It disembkd. at le Havre on 23/6/18, and it worked in Fourth Army Area from 7/7/18. On 1/5/19 it was disbanded at Candas.

40 Sig. Coy. was disbanded by 25/3/18.

41 Both Fd. Ambces. were disbanded by 18/3/18.

42 Disbanded by 1/4/18.

43 Disbanded by 4/3/18.

44 Train was disbanded by 8/4/18.

73RD DIVISION

FORMATION AND NARRATIVE

This home-service division had no existence before the outbreak of the Great War.

Late in 1916 it was decided to form three additional home-service divisions, and in November the 73rd Division was formed at Blackpool. Divisional Headquarters opened at Blackpool, and the three infantry brigades and the divisional troops gradually assembled there. To form the division the 9th Provisional Brigade (Margate) was broken up. This brigade then provided four battalions, a battery, the ammunition column, a field company, signal company, field ambulances, and a company of the divisional train (see Table). The 189th Brigade (formerly part of the 63rd Division which had been broken up) provided two more battalions; and personnel to assist in forming five batteries was transferred from other home-service divisions. Each artillery brigade was to consist of two 6-gun 18-pdr. Q.F. batteries and one 4-gun 4·5″ howitzer battery. The other units of the division were new formations.

On the 1st January, 1917, all the provisional units received new designations: the four battalions were affiliated to regiments of the line, and the battery and field company were numbered. Having completed its assembly at Blackpool, the division moved, between the 5th–18th January, into Essex and Hertfordshire. It was then quartered as follows: Divisional Headquarters at Boreham House, near Chelmsford; 218th Brigade at Witham, Terling, and Kelvedon; 219th Brigade at Danbury and Maldon; 220th Brigade at Chelmsford, Widford, and Arbour Lane; mounted troops at Wickford and Southminster; artillery headquarters at Chelmsford, with the brigades at Danbury and Great Leighs; engineers at Witham and Chelmsford; and the signal company at Hitchin. The 73rd Division now formed part of Southern Army, Home Forces.

Except that the 219th Brigade moved to Southend in October, the stations named above were maintained during 1917. The time was occupied in training, particularly with regard to improving the physique of the men; and in this latter respect it was successful. During the year, as the Table shows, the infantry underwent some reorganization. During July four graduated battalions of the Training Reserve joined the brigades; and in October these four battalions were affiliated to line regiments and adopted territorial designations.

Towards the end of the year, however, the fate of the three home-service divisions came under consideration, and on the 21st December instructions were issued to break up the 73rd Division. On the following day orders were given to Commander-in-Chief, Home Forces, to break up the division as soon as possible.

The disbandment of the division began early in 1918. In January three battalions left, in February the artillery was broken up; and with the disappearance of the G.O.C., early in March, the life of the division came to an end as an effective unit in Home Defence. Gradually, as units were transferred, drafted, or broken up, the strength dwindled. By the end of February the division was reduced to 6,769 (out of an establishment of 13,306), and by the 25th March it had shrunk to 573. Finally on the 8th April, 1918, the 73rd Division ceased to appear in the Weekly Return of the Army at Home.

74TH (YEOMANRY) DIVISION

G.O.C.

4 March, 1917 ... ... Major-General E. S. GIRDWOOD.

G.S.O. 1.

10 Mar., 1917...Major C. R. ROBERTS-WEST (acting).
12 Mar., 1917...Lt.-Col. P. S. ALLAN.
7 April, 1918...Major C. R. ROBERTS-WEST (acting).
10 April, 1918...Lt.-Col. A. C. TEMPERLEY.
[12 Nov., 1918...Lt.-Col. C. N. F. BROAD.]

A.-A. and Q.-M.-G.

9 Mar., 1917...Captain H. J. BUTCHART (acting).
11 Mar., 1917...Lt.-Col. R. B. COUSENS.

B.-G., R.A.

11 July, 1917...Br.-Gen. L. J. HEXT.*

C.R.E.

24 Mar., 1917...Lt.-Col. R. P. T. HAWKSLEY.
11 Aug., 1917...Major A. GLEN (acting).
24 Sept., 1917...Lt.-Col. W. R. IZAT.

229th BDE.

[1 April, '12]...Br.-Gen. R. HOARE** (wounded, 9/9/18).
9 Sept., '18 ...Lt.-Col. C. J. H. SPENCE-JONES (acting).
11 Sept., '18 ...Br.-Gen. F. S. THACKERAY.

230th BDE.

[18 Feb., '17]...Br.-Gen. A. J. MCNEILL (sick, 12/12/17).
12 Dec., '17 ...Lt.-Col. F. W. JARVIS (acting).
21 Dec., '17 ...Br.-Gen. H. B. ORPEN-PALMER.
12 Feb., '18 ...Br.-Gen. W. J. BOWKER.
1 July, '18 ...Br.-Gen. A. A. KENNEDY.

231st BDE.

[4 April, '12]...Br.-Gen. E. A. HERBERT.***
28 April, '17 ...Lt.-Col. LORD KENSINGTON (acting).
5 May, '17 ...Br.-Gen. W. J. BOWKER (sick, 21/7/17).
21 July, '17 ...Lt.-Col. LORD KENSINGTON (acting).
2 Sept., '17 ...Br.-Gen. C. E. HEATHCOTE.

---

* Reached 74th Div. area on 25/7/17.

** Commanded 2/South-Western Mtd. Bde. from 1/4/1912. Col. Hoare became Br.-Gen. on 5/8/14. 2/S.-Wn. Mtd. Bde. became 2nd Dismtd. Bde.; and 2nd Dismtd. Bde. on 15/1/17 became 229th Bde.

***Commanded Welsh Border Mtd. Bde. from 4/4/1912. Col. Herbert became Br.-Gen. on 5/8/14. Welsh Border Mtd. Bde. became 4th Dismtd. Bde.; and 4th Dismtd. Bde. on 14/1/17 became 231st Bde.

74TH[1] (YEOMANRY) DIVISION ORDER OF BATTLE, 1917-1918

Dates	INFANTRY		Mounted Troops	ARTILLERY						Engineers	Signal Service	Pioneers	M.G. Units	Field Ambulances	Mobile Vety. Secn.	Divnl. Emplnt. Coy.	Divnl. Train
				Field Artillery			Trench Mortar Bties.		Divnl. Ammn. Coln.								
	Brigades	Battalions and attached Units		Brigades	Batteries	Bde. Ammn. Colns.	Medium	Heavy		Field Cos.	Divnl. Signal Coy.						
1917 April (Palestine)	229th[2] ...	16 (R. 1st Dev. & R.N. Dev. Yeo. Bn.) Devon.,[3] 12 (W. Som. Yeo. Bn.) Som. L.I.,[4] 12 (Ayr. & Lanark. Yeo. Bn.) R.S.F.,[5] 14 (Fife & Forfar. Yeo. Bn.) B.W.;[6] 4th M.G Coy.;[7] 229th T.M. Bty.[8]	ASqdn.[23] 1/2/ Lond. Yeo.	XLIV[24]; [39] ...	A [340], B [382]	...	...	...	74th D.A.C.[27]	5/R.[28] Monmouth	74th[30]	...	...	229th[31]	59th[34]	...	74th[35]
	230th[9] ...	10 (R.E.Kent & W. Kent Yeo. Bn.) Buffs,[10] 12 (Norf. Yeo. Bn.) Norf.,[11] 15 (Suff. Yeo. Bn.) Suff.,[12] 16 (Sussex Yeo. Bn.) R. Suss.;[13] 209th M.G. Coy.;[14] 230th T.M. Bty.[15]		CXVII[25]; [40]	A, B; C (H.)					5/R.[29] Anglesey				230th[32]			
	231st[16] ...	24 (Denbigh. Yeo. Bn.) R.W.F.,[17] 25 (Montgomy. & Welsh Horse Yeo. Bn.) R.W.F.,[18] 24 (Pemb. & Glam. Yeo. Bn.) Welsh,[19] 10 (Shrop. & Ches. Yeo. Bn.) K.S.L.I.;[20] 210th M.G. Coy.;[21] 231st T.M. Bty.[22]		CCLXVIII[26]; [41]	A, B[366]; C (H.)									231st[33]			
1918 April (Palestine)	229th......	16/Devon., 12/Som. L.I., 12/R.S.F.,[36] 14/B.W.; 4th M.G. Coy.;[45] 229th T.M. Bty.	...	XLIV[39].........	340, 382, 425; D (H.)	...	...	...	74th D.A.C.	5/R. Monmouth	74th	1/12/ L.N.L.[43] (P.)	...	229th	59th	...	74th
	230th......	10/Buffs, 12/Norf.,[37] 15/Suff., 16/R. Suss.; 209th M.G. Coy.;[45] 230th T.M. Bty.		CXVII[40]	366, A, B; D (H.)					5/R. Anglesey				230th			
	231st	24/R.W.F.,[38] 25/R.W.F., 24/Welsh, 10/K.S.L.I.; 210th M.G. Coy.;[45] 231st T.M. Bty.								439th[42] (2/1/ Cheshire)				231st			
1918 June (France)	229th......	16/Devon., 12/Som. L.I., 14/B.W.; 229th T.M. Bty.	...	XLIV............	340, 382, 425; D (H.)	...	X.74[44]	...	74th D.A.C.	5/R. Monmouth	74th	1/12/ L.N.L. (P.)	No. 74 Bn.,[45] M.G.C.	229th	59th	985th[46]	74th
	230th......	10/Buffs, 15/Suff., 16/R. Suss.; 230th T.M. Bty.		CXVII	366, A, B; D (H.)		Y.74[44]			5/R. Anglesey				230th			
	231st	25/R.W.F., 24/Welsh, 10/K.S.L.I.; 231st T.M. Bty.								439th (2/1/ Cheshire)				231st			

NOTES

The formation of the division, recommended on 23/2/17, was approved on 25/2/17. The number 74 was then allotted to the new division. On 4/3/17, 74th Division began to form at el'Arish.

2 2nd Dismtd. Bde. (formerly 1/2/South-Western Mtd. Bde. and parts of Highld. and Lowland Mtd. Bdes.) was re-designated 229th Inf. Bde. at el Ferdan on 15/1/17. Bde. joined 74th Div. at el'Arish, 7-9/3/17.

3 Regts. served in 2nd Dismtd. Bde.; amalgamated on 4/1/17 (antedated, 21/12/16); designated 16/Devon. in Febry., 1917; joined 74th Div., with 229th Bde., on 7/3/17.

4 Regt. served in 2nd Dismtd. Bde.; reorganized 4/1/17; designated 12/Som. L.I. on 8/2/17; joined 74th Div., with 229th Bde., on 8/3/17.

5 Regts. served in 2nd Dismtd. Bde.; amalgamated on 4/1/17; designated 12/R.S.F. in Febry., 1917; joined 74th Div., with 229th Bde., on 9/3/17.

6 Regt. served in 2nd Dismtd. Bde.; reorganized on 14/1/17 (antedated, 21/12/16); designated 14/B.W. in Jany., 1917; and joined 74th Div., with 229th Bde., on 8/3/17.

7 Formerly 2nd Dismtd. Bde. M.G. Coy.; became 4th M.G. Coy. on 14/1/17; joined 74th Div., with 229th Bde., 8-17/3/17.

8 Formed in 229th Bde. on 22/5/17. 3·7" T.Ms. replaced by Stokes T.Ms. on 24/8/17.

9 3rd Dismtd. Bde. (formerly Eastern and South-Eastern Mtd. Bdes.) was re-designated 230th Inf. Bde. on 14/1/17. Bde. joined 74th Div. at Deir el Balah, 9-13/4/17.

10 Regts. served in 3rd Dismtd. Bde.; amalgamated on 1/2/17 and designated 10/Buffs; joined 74th Div., with 230th Bde., on 13/4/17.

11 Regt. served in 3rd Dismtd. Bde.; reorganized on 7/2/17; designated 12/Norf. on 11/2/17; joined 74th Div., with 230th Bde., 12/4/17.

12 Regt. served in 3rd Dismtd. Bde.; reorganized on 5/1/17; designated 15/Suff. on 19/2/17; joined 74th Div., with 230th Bde., on 9/4/17.

13 Regt. served in 3rd Dismtd. Bde.; reorganized on 3/1/17; designated 16/R. Suss. on 28/2/17; joined 74th Div., with 230th Bde., on 10/4/17.

14 Formerly 3rd Dismtd. Bde. M.G. Coy.; became 209th M.G. Coy. on 14/1/17; joined 74th Div., with 230th Bde., on 9 and 10/4/17.

15 Formed in 230th Bde. on 27/5/17.

16 4th Dismtd. Bde. (formerly Welsh Border and S. Wales Mtd. Bdes.) was re-designated 231st Inf. Bde. on 14/1/17. Bde. joined 74th Div. at Khan Yunis, 1-6/4/17.

17 Regt. served in 4th Dismtd. Bde.; reorganized on 23/12/16; designated 24/R.W.F. in Febry., 1917; joined 74th Div., with 231st Bde., on 4/4/17.

18 Regts. (Montgomy., from 4th Dismtd. Bde., and Welsh Horse, from 3rd Dismtd. Bde.) amalgamated at Helmie on 4/3/17 and designated 25/R.W.F.; joined 74th Div., with 231st Bde., on 5/4/17.

19 Regts. served in 4th Dismtd. Bde.; amalgamated on 2/2/17 and designated 24/Welsh; joined 74th Div., with 231st Bde., on 1/4/17.

20 Regts. served in 4th Dismtd. Bde.; amalgamated on 2/3/17 and designated 10/K.S.L.I.; joined 74th Div., with 231st Bde., on 3/4/17.

21 Formerly 4th Dismtd. Bde. M.G. Coy.; became 210th M.G. Coy. on 21/1/17; joined 74th Div., with 231st Bde., on 6/4/17.

22 Formed in 231st Bde. by 15/5/17.

23 Sqdn. joined 74th Div. at Khan Yunis on 5/4/17. Sqdn. left 74th Div. on 23/8/17; Sqdn. joined up on 28/8/17 with 1/2/County of Lond. Yeo. (XX Corps Cav. Regt.).

24 XLIV(H.) went to France in Aug., 1914, with 2nd Div.; and, on 26/5/16, the Bde. was broken up in France. XLIV was reformed in England with 340, 382, and 399 Btics. XLIV disembkd. at Alexandria on 27/5/17, and reached Sidi Bishr on 2/6/17. At Sidi Bishr XLIV reorganized from 3 (13-pdr. 4-gun) Bties. into 2 (18-pdr. 6-gun) Bties.—399 was broken up and completed 340 and 382. 340 and 382 were then lettered A and B. XLIV joined 74th Div. at Rafa on 3/7/17.

25 CXVII (from 26th Div.) disembkd. (from Salonika) at Alexandria on 5/7/17, with A, B, C, and D (H.) Bties.—12, 18-pdrs. and 4, 4·5" hows. Bde. reached el Ferdan on 6/7/17 and reorganized—C was broken up to complete A and B to 6, 18-pdrs. each, and D (H.) was designated C (H.). CXVII joined 74th Div. at Deir el Balah on 9/8/17.

26 CCLXVIII was formed at el Ferdan on 17/6/17. B/CCCI (from 60th Div. in Macedonia) joined at el Ferdan on 17/6/17 and became A/CCLXVIII; D (H.)/CCCII (from 60th Div. in Macedonia) joined at el Ferdan on 19/6/17 and became C (H.)/CCLXVIII. CCLXVIII joined 74th Div. on 23/7/17 at Deir el Balah. On 11/9/17, 366/CXLVI (from 28th Div. in Macedonia) joined and became B/CCLXVIII. [The original CCLXVIII (IV Welsh) in 53rd Div. had been renumbered CCLXVI on 25/12/16.]

27 Formed between 21/6-10/7/17 from portions of ammn. colns. of XLIV and CXVII, and draft from General Base Depôt; on 22/8/17 horses and mules began to join from Remount Depôt, Alexandria. In Aug., 1917, the D.A.C. joined 74th Div. On 13/4/18 the D.A.C. was reorganized at Sarafand.

28 Coy. reached divnl. area between 12-19/4/17, and joined 74th Div. at Deir el Balah.

29 Coy. joined 74th Div. on 14/4/17 at Deir el Balah.

30 On 2/3/17 H.Q. and No. 1 Sec. began to form in Alexandria; and on 26/3/17 H.Q. and No. 1 Sec. reported, at Rafa, to H.Q., 74th Div.

31 By E.E.F. Order No. 26, of 14/1/17, Highland Mtd. Bde. Fd. Amb. and Lowland Mtd. Bde. Fd. Amb. formed and became 229th Fd. Amb.

32 By E.E.F. Order No. 26, of 14/1/17, Eastern Mtd. Bde. Fd. Amb. and South-Eastern Mtd. Bde. Fd. Amb. formed and became 230th Fd. Amb.

33 By E.E.F. Order No. 26, of 14/1/17, South-Western Mtd. Bde. Fd. Amb. and Welsh Border Mtd. Bde. Fd. Amb. formed and became 231st Fd. Amb.

34 Joined on 13/4/17 at Deir el Balah.

35 When 42nd Div. left Egypt for France, in Feb., 1917, the 42nd Div. Train (447, 448, 449, 450 Cos., A.S.C.) was left behind in Egypt. On 20/3/17 the Train was attached to the 53rd Div., for the Gaza operations. On 1/4/17 the Train joined 74th Div.; and, on 13/4/17, it was re-designated 74th Div. Train.

36 Bn. left 74th Div. (in France) on 21/6/18, and joined 94th Bde., 31st Div., on 21/6/18.

37 Bn. left 74th Div. (in France) on 21/6/18, and joined 94th Bde., 31st Div., on 21/6/18.

38 Bn. left 74th Div. (in France) on 21/6/18, and joined 94th Bde., 31st Div., on 21/6/18.

39 Between 11-17/4/18 XLIV was reorganized at Sarafand: A was again designated 340, and B resumed 382; A/CCLXVIII joined and became C, and then resumed its old number—425 (see note 41); and C (H.)/CCLXVIII joined and became D (H.). In May, 1918 (after arrival in France), D (H.) was made up to 6 hows.

40 On 13/4/18, CXVII was reorganized at Lydda: B/CCLXVIII joined and then resumed its old number—366; and C (H.) became D (H.). On 21/5/17, at Noulette, D (H.) was made up to 6 hows.

41 On 21/3/18, A/CCLXVIII left to rejoin 60th Div.; the Bty. rejoined CCCI and again became B/CCCI. On 20/3/18 425 arrived, and, on 21/3/18, 425 became A/CCLXVIII. Between 13-21/4/18 CCLXVIII was broken up at Lydda; A [425] joined XLIV, and resumed its old number—425; B [366] joined CXVII, and resumed its old number—366; and C (H.) joined XLIV, and became D (H.)/XLIV.

42 On 9/4/18 the Fd. Coy. (from 53rd Div.) joined 74th Div. at Ramle.

43 Bn was transferred from 60th Div., and on 10/4/18 Bn. joined 74th Div. at Sarafand.

44 In May, 1918, D.T.M.O. came from Egypt to France with 74th Div., and went to Fifth Army T.M. School on 28/5/18. On 1/6/18 X and Y were formed at Fifth Army T.M. School; on 12/6/18 X and Y joined 74th Div. at Houvin Houvigneul; and on 14/6/18 X and Y received 12, 6" (Newton) T.Ms.

45 On 11/4/18 Bn. was formed at Qantara; and between 17-30/4/18 the Bn. concentrated at Alexandria for embarkation for France. The Bn. (consisting of 4th, 209th, 210th, and 261st M.G. Cos.) embkd. at Alexandria on 30/4/18.

261st M.G. Coy. began to mobilize at Quetta on 20/12/17, and on 15/2/18 Vickers Light Automatic M.Gs. were issued to replace the Maxim M.Gs. On 21/2/18, 261st embkd. at Karachi; disembkd. at Suez on 5/3/18; and reached Tell el Kebir on 5/3/18. 261st M.G. Coy. joined No. 74 Bn., M.G.C., at Alexandria on 22/4/18.

46 Coy. was formed in the Div. by 18/5/18.

GENERAL NOTES

The following Units also served with the 74th Division :—

ARTILLERY :—527 (How.) Bty., R.F.A., from 7–24/3/18 (from 7th Indian Division).
16th Mountain Bty., R.G.A., from 7–9/3/18.
Hong Kong and Singapore Mountain Bty., R.G.A., from 31/10–4/11/17.

ENGINEERS :—496th (2/Kent) Field Coy., R.E., between 24/3–12/4/17 the Fd. Coy. reached Rafa (from Suez Canal Defences), and was attached to 74th Division until 25/5/17, when the Fd. Coy. was transferred to the 53rd Division. On 4/7/17 the Fd. Coy. joined 75th Division at el 'Arish.

MACHINE-GUN COMPANIES :—221st, 262nd, 264th, 271st, and 272nd Machine-Gun Companies, came from Egypt, in May, 1917, with 74th Division. On arrival in France, these companies were formed into Army Troops M.G. Bn., Fourth Army.

OTHER UNITS :—87th Sanitary Section, joined 74th Division on 22/4/17 at Deir el Balah. The Section embarked for France with the Division, on 30/4/18, at Alexandria. On 21/5/18 the Section left 74th Division and came under Fourth Army ; on 25/5/18 the Section came under XIX Corps ; on 26/6/18 under XXII Corps ; on 3/8/18 under G.H.Q. (South) ; on 8/8/18 under Fifth Army ; on 21/8/18 under XIII Corps ; and on 9/10/18 the Sanitary Section came under III Corps and served with III Corps until the end of the War.

On 21/6/18 the division was reorganized (in France) on a 9-battalion basis. On 16/5/18 the pioneer battalion had been reorganized on a 3-company basis.

74TH (YEOMANRY) DIVISION

FORMATION, BATTLES, AND ENGAGEMENTS

The division was formed in the field in 1917 ; it had no existence before the Great War.

On the 14th January, 1917, Egyptian Expeditionary Force Order No. 26 gave directions for the reorganization of the 2nd, 3rd, and 4th Dismounted Brigades of Yeomanry (then in the area of the Suez Canal Defences) and their reappearance (after reorganization) as the 229th, 230th, and 231st Infantry Brigades (see Table and Notes). Then on the 23rd February, as a result of the growing strength of the enemy, the G.O.C., E.E.F., cabled to the War Office for permission to organize the 229th, 230th, and 231st Infantry Brigades into a new division for employment in the forthcoming operations. On the 25th February the War Office approved the formation of this new division, which was to be numbered 74.

On the 4th March the 74th Division began to form at el'Arish. By the 9th March the 229th Brigade joined at el'Arish ; by the 6th April the 231st Brigade reached the division at Khan Yunis ; and by the 13th April the 230th Brigade joined at Deir el Balah. The field ambulances came with the infantry brigades ; the cavalry squadron, field companies, veterinary section, and the divisional train all reached the division in April. The artillery, however, did not arrive in the divisional area until July and August (see Table and Notes), and only then was the 74th Division completely assembled. But, before receiving its artillery, the rest of the 74th Division took part in the Second Battle of Gaza.

During the two years of its existence the 74th Division served at first in Sinai and Palestine and then on the Western Front in France and Belgium. The 74th Division was engaged in the following operations :—

1917

INVASION OF PALESTINE

17–19 April ... ... **Second Battle of Gaza** [In Reserve, Eastern Force].
27 Oct.–7 Nov. ... ... **THIRD BATTLE OF GAZA** [XX Corps].
31 October ... ... **Capture of Beersheba** [XX Corps].
6 November ... ... **Capture of the Sheria Position** [XX Corps].

---

8 and 9 December ... **Capture of Jerusalem** [XX Corps].
27–30 December ... ... **Defence of Jerusalem** [XX Corps].

1918

8–12 March ... ... **Tell 'Asur** [XX Corps].

On the 3rd April the 74th Division was warned that it would move to France in the near future. Between the 7th and 9th the division was relieved and withdrawn from the front line, and by the 13th April 74th Division had marched back and concentrated at Lydda. The divisional artillery was now reorganized, the pioneer battalion joined, and the machine-gun battalion was formed (see Table and Notes).

On the 14th April divisional headquarters moved to Qantara, and by the 20th the division completed its concentration at Qantara. On the 29th April the division began to embark at Alexandria, and it completed embarkation on the next day—except the artillery which embarked at Alexandria on the 3rd May.

The division began to arrive at Marseille on the 7th May, 1918, and entrained for Noyelles.

By the 18th May 74th Division concentrated around Rue (in the Abbeville district). The principal training was devoted to gas defence. Towards the end of the month the division moved forward between Doullens and St. Pol, and on the 31st May 74th Division was placed in G.H.Q. Reserve. In June, whilst it was still engaged in training around le Cauroy, the division was reduced to a 9-battalion basis (see Table and Notes). Then, on the 14th July, 74th Division went into the line near Merville, on the right of XI Corps front, and took part in the following operations :—

THE ADVANCE TO VICTORY

SECOND BATTLES OF THE SOMME

2 and 3 September ...	**Second Battle of Bapaume** [III Corps, Fourth Army].
12–24 September	**BATTLES OF THE HINDENBURG LINE.**
18 September	**Battle of Épehy** [III Corps, Fourth Army].
3 October–11 November	**THE FINAL ADVANCE IN ARTOIS AND FLANDERS** [XI Corps, until 10 a.m. 8/10; then III Corps, Fifth Army].

On the 9th November 74th Division crossed the Schelde, to the north of Tournai, and reached Thimougies. By 8.30 a.m. on the 11th the advanced troops of the division crossed the Dendre Canal and occupied Ath ; and here the advance was brought to an end by the Armistice.

On the 16th November the division shifted into the area Rebaix–Herinnes–Tournai, with divisional headquarters at Frasnes lez Buissenal. The division was employed on the repair of the Tournai–Leuze railway, and at the same time the organization of education was undertaken. On the 7th December the 74th Division was visited by H.M. the King. Between the 15th and the 18th December the division moved into the Lessines–Grammont–Herinnes area, with divisional headquarters at les deux Acren, near Lessines.

On the 26th January, 1919, 74th Division was represented by a composite brigade group at a ceremonial parade held at Brussels by H.M. the King of the Belgians. Throughout February drafting and demobilization progressed steadily and the division gradually dwindled. On the 16th March Major-General Girdwood left the division. By the 29th the strength of the division was only 291 officers and 3,525 other ranks. Divisional headquarters, however, remained near Lessines until the 10th July, 1919, when the 74th Division, whose very appropriate badge had been a ' Broken Spur,' passed out of existence.

75TH DIVISION

G.O.C.

25 June, 1917	Major-General P. C. PALIN (sick, 10/12/17).
10 December, 1917	Br.-Gen. Hon. E. M. COLSTON (acting).
29 December, 1917	Major-General P. C. PALIN.

G.S.O. 1.

25 June, 1917...Lt.-Col. J. SPENCER.
6 Dec., 1917...Lt.-Col. S. H. KERSHAW.
20 May, 1918...Major G. M. GLYNTON (acting).
14 Aug., 1918...Lt.-Col. S. H. KERSHAW.
30 Aug., 1918...Lt.-Col. G. B. ROWAN-HAMILTON (sick, 18/10/18).
18 Oct., 1918...Captain W. BECKETT (acting).
29 Oct., 1918...Lt.-Col. D. OVEY.

A.-A. and Q.-M.-G.

25 June, 1917...Lt.-Col. R. L. MACALPINE-LENY.
1 Feb., 1918...Major H. N. BRIDGWATER (acting).
2 May, 1918...Lt.-Col. R. L. MACALPINE-LENY.

B.-G., R.A.

13 July, 1917...Br.-Gen. H. A. BOYCE.
25 Oct., 1918...Lt.-Col. G. N. WYATT (acting).
11 Nov., 1918...Lt.-Col. L. H. D. BROUGHTON (acting).
[7 Dec., 1918...Lt.-Col. S. S. TAYLOR (acting).]

C.R.E.

27 June, 1917...Lt.-Col. G. S. C. COOKE (sick, 18/11/17).
18 Nov., 1917...Major A. H. B. PAPILLON (acting).
30 Nov., 1917...Major C. E. WILSON (acting).
4 Jan., 1918...Lt.-Col. G. S. C. COOKE.
1 Sept., 1918...Lt.-Col. A. G. TURNER.

232nd BDE.

15 April, '17...Br.-Gen. H. J. HUDDLESTON.

233rd BDE.

25 May, '17...Br.-Gen. Hon. E. M. COLSTON.
10 Dec., '17...Lt.-Col. E. F. COOKE-HURLE (acting).
30 Dec., '17...Br.-Gen. Hon. E. M. COLSTON.
21 June, '18...Lt.-Col. H. B. FORD (acting).
25 Aug., '18...Br.-Gen. Hon. E. M. COLSTON.

234th BDE.

26 June., '17...Br.-Gen. F. G. ANLEY (sick, 19/11/17).
19 Nov., '17...Br.-Gen. C. A. H. MACLEAN (sick, 8/4/18).
8 April, '18...Lt.-Col. G. R. CASSELS (acting).
23 April, '18...Br.-Gen. C. A. H. MACLEAN.
25 April, '18...Lt.-Col. G. R. CASSELS (acting).
7 May, '18...Br.-Gen. C. A. H. MACLEAN.
12 July, '18...Lt.-Col. G. E. S. SMITH (acting).
17 July, '18...Lt.-Col. J. N. MACRAE (acting).
21 July, '18...Lt.-Col. G. R. CASSELS (acting).
16 Aug., '18...Br.-Gen. C. A. H. MACLEAN.
2 Oct., '18...Lt.-Col. G. R. CASSELS (acting).
3 Oct., '18...Br.-Gen. F. P. C. KEILY.

GENERAL NOTES

The following Units also served with the 75th Division :—

ARTILLERY :—VIII Mountain Bde., R.G.A. (11th Bty.—3·7″ hows. ; 13th Bty.—3·7″ hows.; and 17th Bty.—2·75″ guns), was attached to the division from 25/3–15/9/18. The Bde. was then transferred to co-operate with the 54th Division on 19/9/18 in the Final Offensive.

NOTE.—VIII Mountain Bde. (10th, 11th, 12th, and 13th Mtn. Bties.—all 3·7″ hows.) was formed at Catterick on 11/7/17. On 22/8/17 the Bde. began to move to Egypt, and began embkn. at Southampton on 23/8/17. Moving via Cherbourg and Taranto, VIII Mtn. Bde. began disembkg. at Alexandria on 12/9/17, and on 27/9/17 the Bde. began to concentrate at Sidi Bishr. The Bties. reached Egypt as follows : 10th Bty. on 12/9/17 ; 11th Bty. on 27/9/17 ; 12th Bty. on 15/2/18 ; and 13th Bty. on 29/1/18.
On 26/1/18, VIII Mtn. Bde. was reformed at Deir el Bela, and it then comprised 11th Bty. (3·7″ hows.), 13th Bty. (3·7″ hows.), and 17th Bty. (formerly A Battery, IX Mtn. Bde.—2·75″ guns). IX Mtn. Bde. was reformed at the same time as VIII ; and IX included: 10th Bty. (3·7″ hows.—transferred from VIII), 12th Bty. (3·7″ hows.—transferred from VIII), and 16th Bty. (2·75″ guns—formerly B/IX).

PIONEERS :—1/23/Sikh (P.). Bn. was attached to the division from 10/5/18–24/7/18. Bn. (less 1 Coy.) left the division on 12/7/18, and the remaining Coy. left on 24/7/18.

OTHER UNITS :—107th Sanitary Section. The Section arrived at Alexandria on 31/5/17 (from Marseille) ; and the Sanitary Section joined the division at el 'Arish on 14/7/17.

75TH[1] DIVISION

ORDER OF BATTLE, 1917-1918

Dates	INFANTRY: Brigades	INFANTRY: Battalions and attached Units	Mounted Troops	ARTILLERY: Field Artillery: Brigades	ARTILLERY: Field Artillery: Batteries	ARTILLERY: Field Artillery: Bde. Ammn. Colns.	ARTILLERY: Trench Mortar Bties.: Medium	ARTILLERY: Trench Mortar Bties.: Heavy	ARTILLERY: Divnl. Ammn. Coln.	Engineers: Field Cos.	Signal Service: Divnl. Signal Coy.	Pioneers	M.G. Units	Field Ambu-lances	Mobile Vety. Secn.	Divnl. Emplnt. Coy.	Divnl. Train
1917 June (Palestine)	232nd[2] ... 233rd[8] ... 234th[14] ...	1/5/Devon.,[3] 2/5/Hants.,[4] 2/3/Gurkha Rif.;[5] 229th M.G. Coy.;[6] 232nd T.M. Bty.[7] 1/5/Som. L.I.,[9] 2/4/Hants.,[10] 3/3/Gurkha Rif.;[11] 230th M.G. Coy.;[12] 233rd T.M. Bty.[13] 2/L.N.L.,[15] 1/4/D.C.L.I.,[16] 123/Outram's Rif.;[17] 231st M.G. Coy.;[18] 234th T.M. Bty.[19]	...	...	...	...	...	...	...	496th[20] (2/Kent)	75th[21]	...	...	145th[22] 146th[23] 147th[24] 123rd[25] Ind.	60th[26]	...	75th[27]
1917 October (Palestine)	232nd...... 233rd...... 234th......	1/5/Devon.,[28] 2/4/Som. L.I.,[29] 2/5/Hants., 2/3/Gurkha Rif.; 229th M.G. Coy.;[51] 232nd T.M. Bty. 1/5/Som. L.I., 2/4/Hants.,[30] 1/4/Wilts.,[31]; [45] 3/3/Gurkha Rif.; 230th M.G. Coy.;[51] 233rd T.M. Bty. 1/4/D.C.L.I., 2/4/Dorset.,[32];[47] 58/Rif.,[33] 123/Outram's Rif.; 231st M.G. Coy.;[51] 234th T.M. Bty.[19]	...	XXXVII[34] ... CLXXII[35] ... I S. African[36]	389, 390; 405 (H.) 391, 392; 406 (H.) A, B; C (H.)[37]	...	X.75[38] Y.75[38] Z.75[38]	...	75th D.A.C.[39]	495th[40] (1/Kent) 496th (2/Kent) 10/2nd Q.V.O. S. & M.[41]	75th	...	...	145th[42] 146th[42] 147th[42] 123rd[43] Ind.	60th	...	75th
1918 June (Palestine)	232nd...... 233rd...... 234th......	2/5/Hants.,[44] 1/4/Wilts.,[45] 72/Punjabis,[46] 2/3/Gurkha Rif.; 232nd T.M. Bty. 1/5/Som. L. I., 2/4/ Dorset.,[47] 29/Punjabis,[48] 3/3/Gurkha Rif.; 233rd T.M. Bty. 2/4/Devon.,[49] 1/4/D.C.L.I., 58/Rif., 123/Outram's Rif.; 234th T.M. Bty.	...	XXXVII ...... CLXXII ...... I S. African	389, 390; 405 (H.) 391, 392; 406 (H.) A, B; C (H.)	...	...	...	75th D.A.C.	496th (2/Kent) 10/2nd Q.V.O. S. & M. 16/2nd Q.V.O. S. & M.[50]	75th	...	75th Bn.,[51] M.G.C.	123rd[43] C.F.A. 127th[52] C.F.A. 163rd[53] C.F.A.	60th	...	75th
1918 September (Palestine)	232nd...... 233rd...... 234th......	1/4/Wilts., 72/Punjabis, 2/3/Gurkha Rif., 3/Kashmir Rif.;[54] 232nd T. M. Bty. 1/5/Som. L.I., 29/Punjabis, 3/3/Gurkha Rif., 2/154/Inf.;[55] 233rd T.M. Bty. 1/4/D.C.L.I., 58/Rif., 123/Outram's Rif., 1/152/Inf.;[56] 234th T.M. Bty.	...	XXXVII ...... CLXXII ...... I S. African	389, 390; 405 (H.) 391, 392; 406 (H.) A, B; C (H.)	...	...	...	75th D.A.C.	496th (2/Kent) 10/2nd Q.V.O. S. & M. 16/2nd Q.V.O. S. & M.	75th	2/32/Sikh (P.)[57]	75th Bn., M.G.C.	123rd C.F.A. 127th C.F.A. 163rd C.F.A.	60th	...	75th

NOTES

1 The formation of the division was approved on 16/3/17, and the number 75 was allotted to it on 7/4/17. On 25/6/17 the 75th Div. began to form at el 'Arish.

2 Bde. was formed at Moascar on 14/4/17. From 5/6-20/8/17 the Bde. was attached to 54th Div., and on 20/8/17 the Bde. joined 75th Div. at Deir el Balah.

3 Bn. went to India with 43rd (Wessex) Div. in Oct., 1914. Bn. landed at Suez on 4/4/17, and joined 232nd Bde. on 14/4/17.

4 Bn. went to India with 45th (2nd Wessex) Div. in Dec., 1914. Bn. landed at Suez on 5/4/17, and joined 232nd Bde. on 14/4/17.

5 On 24/6/17 Bn. was transferred from 29th Ind. Bde. (Canal Defences); and from 29/6-16/7/17 the Bn. was attached to 233rd Bde. On 22/7/17 the Bn. joined 232nd Bde. near Deir el Balah.

6 Coy. left Grantham on 24/4/17 and disembkd. at Alexandria on 1/6/17. Coy. joined 232nd Bde. on 18/6/17 at Deir el Balah.

7 Formed by 26/7/17.

8 Bde. was formed at Zeitun (N.-E. of Cairo) on 25/5/17. Bde. took over Rafa Defences from 21/6-18/8/17. On 18/8/17 Bde. joined 75th Div.

9 Bn. went to India with 43rd (Wessex) Div. in Oct., 1914. Bn. landed at Suez on 11/5/17, and joined 233rd Bde. on 25/5/17.

10 Bn. went to India with 45th (2nd Wessex) Div. in Dec., 1914. Bn. landed at Suez on 15/5/17, and joined 233rd Bde. on 25/5/17.

11 Bn. was transferred from 29th Ind. Bde. (Canal Defences) and joined 233rd Bde. at Rafa on 30/6/17.

12 Coy. left Alexandria on 13/7/17 and joined 233rd Bde. at Rafa on 15/7/17.

13 Joined 233rd Bde near Gaza on 1/9/17.

14 Bde. was formed at el 'Arish on 25/6/17 and joined 75th Div. on that day.

15 Bn. served in East Africa with 27th (Bangalore) Bde. from 30/10/14-18/1/17 (including 21/5-18/8/16, spent in S. Africa). From E. Africa Bn. was transferred to L. of C., Egypt. Bn. was attached to 232nd Bde. on 14/4/17, to 233rd Bde. on 4/6/17, and joined 234th Bde. on 25/6/17. On 9/8/17 Bn. (as a result of a medical board) left 234th Bde. and went to Sidi Bishr. Bn. returned to L. of C. at Gaza on 17/12/17. In May, 1918, the Bn. was ordered to France; it left Port Said on 18/5/18, disembkd. at Marseille on 27/5/18, reached Racquinghem on 4/6/18, and was attached to 94th Bde., 31st Div. On 24/6/18 Bn. was attached to 103rd Bde., 34th Div., and on 28/6/18 Bn. joined 101st Bde., 34th Div.

16 Bn. went to India with 43rd (Wessex) Div. in Oct., 1914. Bn. served at Aden from 28/1/16-8/2/17. Bn. embkd. at Aden on 8/2/17, disembkd. at Suez on 13/2/17 and was employed on L. of C. On 14/4/17 Bn. was attached to 232nd Bde., on 4/6/17 to 233rd Bde., and Bn. joined 234th Bde. on 25/6/17.

17 Bn. was transferred from 29th Ind. Bde. (Canal Defences) and joined 234th Bde. at el 'Arish on 1/7/17.

18 Coy. left Grantham on 24/4/17, embkd. at Southampton on 25/4/17, disembkd. at le Havre on 26/4/17, embkd. at Marseille on 21/5/17, disembkd. at Alexandria on 1/6/17, and joined 234th Bde. at el 'Arish on 13/8/17.

19 Formed, near Qubeibe, on 7/12/17.

20 Fd. Coy. was attached to 74th Div. from 12/4-25/5/17; Coy. was transferred to 53rd Div. on 25/5/17, and on 4/7/17 Coy. joined 75th Div. at el 'Arish.

21 Coy. joined at el 'Arish (from Ismailia) on 29/7/17.

22 Joined at Deir el Balah (from Abasiya) on 14/8/17.

23 Joined at Rafa (from Abasiya) on 14/8/17.

24 Joined at el 'Arish (from Abasiya) on 14/8/17.

25 Joined at el 'Arish (from 29th Ind. Bde., Canal Defences) on 30/6/17. One section was attached to each Fd. Amb.

26 Formed at Mustafa on 11/5/17; joined 75th Div. at el 'Arish on 3/7/17.

27 Originally formed at Alexandria in March, 1917, as "X" Div. Train; it became 75th Div. Train and joined 75th Div. at el 'Arish (from Qantara) on 4/7/17. The Cos. were numbered 925, 926, 927, and 928.

28 Bn. left Bde. on 4/5/18, embkd. at Alexandria on 24/5/18, disembkd. at Marseille on 1/6/18, reached Famechon and joined 185th Bde., 62nd Div., on 6/6/18.

29 Bn. went to India with 45th (2nd Wessex) Div. in Dec., 1914. Bn. landed at Suez on 25/9/17, and on 16/10/17 joined 232nd Bde. near Deir el Balah. On 2/5/18 Bn. left 232nd Bde., embkd. at Port Said on 23/5/18, disembkd. at Marseille on 1/6/18, reached Berguette on 7/6/18, joined 34th Div. at Berthen on 19/6/18; and at Proven, on 5/7/18, became Pioneer Bn. of 34th Div., and was reorganized in 3 companies.

30 Bn. left 233rd Bde. on 2/5/18, disembkd. at Marseille on 1/6/18, joined 62nd Div. at Doullens on 6/6/18, and Bn. was posted to 186th Bde. on 14/6/18.

31 Bn. went to India with 43rd (Wessex) Div. in Oct., 1914. Bn. landed at Suez on 25/9/17, and on 15/10/17 joined 233rd Bde. near Deir el Balah.

32 Bn. went to India with 45th (2nd Wessex) Div. in Dec., 1914. Bn. landed at Suez on 29/8/17, and on 19/9/17 joined 234th Bde. near Deir el Balah. On 25/4/18 the Bn. was attached to 233rd Bde., on 1/5/18 it was lent to 232nd Bde., and on 2/5/18 it returned to 233rd Bde. The Bn. was disbanded between 3-10/8/18.

33 Bn. (from Canal Defences) joined 75th Div. on 14/9/17, near Deir el Balah. On 16/9/17 Bn. was posted to 234th Bde.

[TURN OVER.

NOTES—*contd.*

34 CXLVI H.Q. (from 28th Div. in Macedonia) took over A [389] and B [390] from CLXXVII at Qantara on 2/9/17, and then became XXXVII Bde. On 4/9/17, XXXVII joined 75th Div. near Deir el Balah. On 16/9/17, 405 (H.) landed at le Havre from England, and on 23/9/17 the Bty. disembkd. at Alexandria from Marseille. On 9/10/17, 405 (H.)-4, 4·5" hows.—reached Deir el Balah and became C (H.)/XXXVII. During October, 1917, the Bties. resumed their original numbers—389, 390, and 405 (H.) [Original XXXVII (H.) went to France in Aug., 1914, with 4th Div. Bde. joined 7th Div. on 24/6/15, and on 17/5/16 XXXVII (H.) was broken up.]

35 Bde. was formed in England with H.Q., 389, 390, 391, and 392 Bties. (each 6, 18-pdrs.), and B.A.C. Between 9-11/7/17 CLXXII reached le Havre from England, and on 23/7/17, the Bde. disembkd. at Alexandria from Marseille. On 29/8/17, at Alexandria, 389 and 390 Bties. became A and B/XXXVII; and 391 and 392 became A and B/CLXXII; and the B.A.C. became No. 3 Sec., 75th D.A.C. At Qantara on 2/9/17, A[389] and B [390] were handed over to XXXVII. On 5 and 6/9/17, CLXXII joined 75th Div. near Deir el Balah. On 16/9/17, 406 (H.) landed at le Havre from England, and on 23/9/17 the Bty. disembkd. at Alexandria from Marseille. On 12/10/17, 406 (H.)—4, 4·5" hows.—reached Deir el Balah and became C (H.)/CLXXII. Durng October, 1917, the Bties. resumed their original numbers—391, 392, and 406 (H.).

36 H.Q., 3, 4-gun, 13-pdr. Bties., and B.A.C. embkd. at Durban on 8/7/17, disembkd. at Suez on 21/7/17, and reached Moascar on 27/7/17. On 14/8/17 the 2nd Bty. was broken up and completed the 1st and 4th Bties. to 6 guns each; 1st Bty. was then designated A, and 4th Bty. became B. On 29/8/17 the B.A.C. became No. 2 Sec., 75th D.A.C. On 6/9/17 Bde. left Qantara and reached Khan Yunis on 7/9/17. At Khan Yunis, on 9/9/17, the Bde. exchanged its 12, 13-pdr., equipments for the 12, 18-pdr. equipments of XVIII Bde., R.H.A. (of A. and N.Z. Mtd. Div.). On 12/9/17, I S. African Bde. joined 75th Div. near Deir el Balah.

37 On 11/4/18, C (H.)—4, 4·5" hows.—from Alexandria, joined I S. African Bde. near Wadi Ballut.

38 Bties. entrained at Sidi Bishr on 1/10/17; detraining on 2/10/17, at Qantara, mortars and equipt. were handed over at the School of Mortars, E.E.F. Personnel then entrained at Qantara, detrained on 3/10/17 at Deir el Balah and took over mortars and equipt. X, Y, and Z then joined 75th Div. On 22/2/18, X, Y, and Z were disbanded; mortars and equipt. were handed in to Ordnance Stores, officers went to School of Mortars, E.E.F., and remainder of personnel went to Qantara to form 6" batteries.

39 On 29/8/17 the D.A.C. was formed at el Ferdan, as follows: H.Q. from General Base Depôt; B Echelon from Divnl. Arty.; No. 1 Sec. from XXXVII B.A.C.; No. 2 Sec. from S. African B.A.C.; and No. 3 Sec. from CLXXII B.A.C. Vehicles, horses, and mules arrived between 29/8-19/9/17. On 3/10/17 D.A.C. marched via Pelusium–Romani–Bardawil–el 'Arish and joined 75th Div. at Sheikh Nabhan on 19/10/17 (158¾ miles in 15 marching days).

40 On 26/8/17 the Fd. Coy. was transferred from 54th Div. and joined 75th Div. near Sheikh Abbas. On 26/5/18 the Fd. Coy. rejoined 54th Div. near Wilhelma.

41 Coy. joined 75th Div. near Ramle on 7/12/17 (from Palestine L. of C.).

42 On 16/5/18, 145th, 146th, and 147th began handing over personnel, equipt., and transport to 123rd, 127th, and 163rd C.F.A.s; the surplus personnel was sent to R.A.M.C. Base Depôt, Qantara. On 19/5/18, 145th, 146th, and 147th Fd. Ambces. ceased to exist.

43 123rd Ind. F.A. became 123rd C.F.A. between 16-21/5/18 (see note 42).

44 Bn. was disbanded between 3-13/8/18.

45 Bn. was transferred from 233rd Bde. to 232nd Bde. on 3/5/18.

46 Bn. left Karachi on 1/3/18, disembkd. at Suez on 10/3/18, and went to Tell el Kebir until 25/4/18. Bn. reached Lydda on 26/4/18, and on 28/4/18 joined 232nd Bde. near Wadi Ballut.

47 Bn. was transferred from 234th Bde. to 233rd Bde. on 2/5/18; and the Bn. was disbanded between 3-10/8/18.

48 Bn. left Peshawar on 19/3/18, embkd. at Karachi on 26/3/18, disembkd. at Suez on 5/4/18, and went to Tell el Kebir until 25/4/18. Bn. reached Lydda on 26/4/18 and joined 233rd Bde. on 28/4/18.

49 Bn. went to India with 45th (2nd Wessex) Div. in Dec., 1914. Bn. disembkd. at Qantara on 26/10/17 and was employed on L. of C. On 13/12/17 Bn. joined 234th Bde. at Ramle; and on 17/8/18 the Bn. was disbanded at Wadi Ballut.

50 Coy. mobilized at Rawal Pindi between 15-28/2/18; embkd. at Karachi on 27/4/18, disembkd. at Qantara on 9/5/18, and reached Lydda on 21/5/18. Coy. joined 75th Div. at Wadi Ballut on 23/5/18.

51 Bn. was formed on 3/5/18. It consisted of 229th, 230th, and 231st M.G. Cos.

52 The Fd. Amb. came from 7th (Meerut) Div. in Mesopotamia. The Fd. Amb. disembkd. at Suez on 13/1/18 and went to Moascar. On 24/3/18 the Fd. Amb. was demobilized at Moascar and on 26/4/18 it re-mobilized at Qantara. The Fd. Amb. left Qantara on 7/5/18, detrained at Lydda on 8/5/18, and on 14/5/18 the Fd. Amb. reached Wilhelma and joined 75th Div. (Also see note 42.)

53 The Fd. Amb. came from Secunderabad; it embkd. at Bombay on 18/4/18, disembkd. at Suez on 28/4/18, arrived Qantara on 3/5/18, and entrained on 5/5/18. The Fd. Amb. detrained at Lydda on 6/5/18, and on 14/5/18 it joined 75th Div. at Wilhelma. (Also see note 42.)

54 Bn. left Ferozepore on 29/6/18, embkd. at Bombay on 2/7/18, disembkd. at Suez on 13/7/18, and went to Tell el Kebir until 23/7/18. Bn. reached Lydda on 24/7/18, and on 3/8/18 joined 232nd Bde. near Rantis.

55 Bn. was formed at Basra on 24/5/18 from 4 Cos. of 102/Grendrs., 108/Inf., 119/Inf., and 122/Rajputana Inf. Bn. embkd. on 3 and 19/6/18, disembkd. at Suez on 5/7/18, left Qantara on 16/7/18, reached Lydda on 17/7/18, and on 25/7/18 joined 233rd Bde. near Rantis.

56 Bn. was formed at Amara on 24/5/18 from 4 Cos. of 24, 25, 26, and 31/Punjabis. Bn. moved to Basra on 28-29/5/18, embkd. on 22/6/18, disembkd. at Suez on 11/7/18, and went to Qantara. Bn. entrained on 17/7/18, reached Lydda on 18/7/18, and on 26/7/18 joined 234th Bde. near Rantis.

57 Bn. began to mobilize at Sialkot on 21/12/17, entrained on 15/2/18, embkd. at Bombay on 18/2/18, disembkd. at Suez on 4/3/18, and went to Qantara until 21/3/18. Bn. reached Lydda on 22/3/18; and on 20/7/18 Bn. joined 75th Div. near el Lubban.

75TH DIVISION

FORMATION, BATTLES, AND ENGAGEMENTS

The division was formed in the field in 1917 ; it had no existence before the Great War.

On the 16th March, 1917, the War Office gave permission to G.O.C., E.E.F., to form an additional British division from the Territorial Force battalions which were arriving from India. On the 7th April, the War Office allotted the number 75 to this new division. Its three infantry brigades were to be numbered 232, 233, and 234.

The 232nd Brigade began to form at Moascar on the 14th April. On the 24th May, however, the War Office issued an order that Indian battalions were to be incorporated in the 232nd, 233rd, and 234th Brigades, so as to expedite the formation of the 75th Division ; and, in accordance with these later instructions, the 233rd Brigade began to form at Zeitun on the 25th May. Then, on the 11th June, the War Office cabled that the organization of the infantry of the 75th Division was to consist of mixed brigades of one British and three Indian battalions each ; but this indianization of the 75th Division could only be carried out gradually. On the 25th June the 234th Brigade began to assemble at el'Arish ; and on the same day the 75th Division came into existence at el'Arish.

The assembly of the division was a gradual process : one field company, the signal company, the mobile veterinary section, and the divisional train joined in July, 1917, and the field ambulances arrived in August. But, even after concentration, the arrangement of the battalions in the infantry brigades had to be changed on more than one occasion until, in July and August, 1918, the final organization of the brigades was completed. Then only did the 75th Division take on its final shape.

To complete the division rapidly with the necessary artillery was a real difficulty. On the 6th June the War Office cabled that a field artillery brigade (CLXXII) of four 6-gun 18-pdr. batteries would be sent to Egypt directly shipping became available. The brigade duly reached Alexandria on the 23rd July. This brigade formed the nucleus for two brigades of the 75th Division Artillery ; but, owing to the shortage of 4·5" howitzers, it was October, 1917, before each of the brigades was completed by the arrival of its howitzer battery. The third artillery brigade was provided by South Africa. After it reached Egypt the I South African Brigade was reorganized in two 6-gun batteries, and in September, 1917, the two batteries exchanged their 13-pdr. equipments for 18-pdrs. ; it was April, 1918, however, before a howitzer battery arrived and completed the I South African Brigade. (See Table.)

During the three years of its existence the 75th Division served in Palestine and Egypt, and was engaged in the following operations :—

1917

INVASION OF PALESTINE

27 Oct.–7 Nov. ... ... **THIRD BATTLE OF GAZA** [XXI Corps].
6 and 7 November ... **Capture of Gaza** [XXI Corps].

---

13 and 14 November ... **Capture of Junction Station** [XXI Corps].
20–24 November ... ... **Battle of Nabi Samweil** [XXI Corps].

1918

11 and 12 March ... ... **Tell 'Asur** [XXI Corps].
9–11 April ... ... **Berukin** [XXI Corps].

THE FINAL OFFENSIVE

THE BATTLES OF MEGIDDO

19 September ... ... **Battle of Sharon** [XXI Corps].

75TH DIVISION

At the end of the fighting on the 19th September, 1918, the division went into XXI Corps Reserve near et Tire, and until the 3rd October (when the division was transferred to G.H.Q.) it was employed on salvage work and road-making. On the 22nd October the division began to move to Haifa ; and at noon on the 31st October the Armistice with Turkey came into force.

By the 13th November the division concentrated in the Lydda area. The 232nd Bde., which was at Tul Karm (on the L. of C.), rejoined the division on the 14th. Between the 2nd–10th December the division moved back to Qantara and was transferred to XX Corps. On the 27th the light trench mortar batteries were disbanded. On the 6th January, 1919, the divisional education camp opened and a course of lectures was started. On the 18th January directions were issued that certain of the Indian battalions would return to India, as shipping became available ; and by the end of February two battalions had left and four more were awaiting passage. The 18-pdr. field batteries (except South African batteries) were reduced to 4 guns each on the 1st February, and general demobilization proceeded slowly. On the 20th February notification was received that the 75th Division had been selected for the Army of Occupation. XXXVII Brigade, R.F.A., was to be retained to form the divisional artillery, three companies of sappers and miners would form the divisional engineers, one British battalion and six Indian battalions would join to complete the infantry, and the machine-gun battalion and signal company would remain. By the middle of March divisional headquarters were at Alexandria with one infantry brigade, and the other infantry brigades were at Heliopolis and Ismailia. On the 23rd March XXXVII Brigade, R.F.A., became CXCI Brigade ; on the 25th a composite infantry brigade (Br.-Gen. Hon. E. M. Colston) was formed, and it moved to Cairo on the 26th and 27th.

Divisional headquarters moved to Ismailia on the 5th April, and on the next day CLXXII Brigade, R.F.A., was transferred to 7th (Meerut) Division. I South African Brigade left 75th Division on the 28th April, and on the 29th the Brigade embarked for South Africa. Headquarters, Egypt, handed over to XX Corps on the 25th April, and XX Corps then included 10th, 54th, and 75th Divisions. The 75th Division now became responsible for the Eastern Delta up to the Suez Canal. On the 1st June this command was renamed 75th Division Area : it included Zagazig, Belbeis, and Benha sectors, as well as Port Said, Ismailia, and Suez areas, with divisional headquarters at Ismailia. Many additional units were attached to the division for the necessary garrisons and protective work in this large district. Starting in July, however, the internal trouble in Egypt showed signs of dying down, and units began to return to their home-lands. The divisional ammunition column was disbanded on the 16th August, and on the 19th a similar fate overtook CXCI (formerly XXXVII) Brigade, R.F.A. The divisional artillery then consisted of X Indian Mountain Artillery Brigade. On the 27th August Major-General Palin went on leave to England and Br.-Gen. Keily assumed temporary command of 75th Division. The 232nd Brigade was disbanded on the 17th October. On the 26th November Major-General Sir Philip Palin returned from leave and resumed command of the division.

In January, 1920, 75th Division began to dwindle, and in February the G.O.C. was informed that the division would disappear and the two infantry brigades would be amalgamated. On the 16th March the 233rd Brigade (commanded since the 16th October, 1919, by Br.-Gen. E. H. Wildblood) was broken up, and its units were absorbed by the 234th Brigade (Br.-Gen. Keily).

Finally, at noon on the 1st April, 1920, 75th Division Area and troops were transferred to 10th Division, and the 75th Division ceased to exist.

APPENDICES

1, 1A, 2, 3, & 4;
5, 6, 7, 8, 9, & 10.

CENTRAL FORCE

In the narratives of the home-service 2nd-line Territorial Force divisions the Central Force is mentioned several times and therefore requires a short description.

On the outbreak of the Great War the forces intended for Home Defence (after the departure of the Expeditionary Force) were organized in a group of Armies which was designated General Force, with Headquarters at the Hotel Metropole, London. During August, however, the name was changed and it was known thereafter as Central Force, a more suitable designation. Central Force was made up of the Mounted Division (Headquarters, Bury St. Edmunds), First Army (Headquarters, Bedford), Second Army (Headquarters, Aldershot), and Third Army (Headquarters, Luton)[1]—a total of 10 mounted brigades, 9, 1st-line Territorial Force divisions, and 4 cyclist battalions. By November, 1914, Second Army Headquarters had moved from Aldershot to Tunbridge Wells. Central Force although formed in Eastern Command did not form part of it. Nevertheless from June, 1915, the same General Officer acted as Commander of both Central Force and Eastern Command, and Central Force Headquarters moved from Hotel Metropole to Eastern Command Headquarters at Horse Guards, Whitehall.

In February, 1915, Central Force was composed of the following formations : 1st Mounted Division (Bury St. Edmunds), 2nd Mounted Division (Hanworth), First Army (Cambridge), Second Army (Tunbridge Wells), and Third Army (Dunmow), a total of 13 mounted brigades, 11 Territorial Force divisions (7, 1st-line and 4, 2nd-line), and 3 cyclist battalions.

By November, 1915, however, Central Force was almost entirely composed of 2nd-line Territorial Force formations, and it then included : 1/1st Mounted Division (Norwich), 2/2nd Mounted Division (King's Lynn), First Army (Mundford), Second Army (Tunbridge Wells), and Third Army (Dunmow), a total of 13 mounted brigades (3, 1st-line) and 8, 2nd-line Territorial Force divisions[2] ; with 1 armoured train (North Walsham), 2 heavy batteries, 10 cyclist battalions, and 1 infantry battalion.

On Saturday, 11th December, 1915, G.O.C.-in-C. Central Force held a conference at the Horse Guards and described the forthcoming reorganization of Central Force: Third Army was to disappear forthwith, the commander would be transferred to First Army; the Horse Guards also had to be vacated to make room for the Commander-in-Chief and Headquarters Staff of the Forces at Home. Consequently, between Friday, 24th December, 1915, and Saturday, 15th January, 1916, Central Force Headquarters, and Eastern Command Headquarters, moved from Horse Guards, Whitehall, to 50, Pall Mall.

The end of Central Force was approaching, and on Sunday, 12th March, 1916, it ceased to exist. The troops were reorganized and placed under the direct orders of the Field-Marshal Commanding-in-Chief Home Forces (F.-M. Viscount French) for training and operations; for administration the troops remained under Eastern Command. At the same time Central Force and Eastern Command Headquarters amalgamated under the General Officer who since June, 1915, had acted as G.O.C.-in-C. Central Force and Eastern Command. The Armies were re-formed and became Northern Army (General Sir Bruce M. Hamilton, with Headquarters at Mundford) and Southern Army (General Sir A. H. Paget, with Headquarters at Brentwood).

---

[1] The Commanders of Central Force and of the three Armies are given in Appendix 1A.

[2] The narratives of the 2nd-line divisions included in this Part show the state of preparedness of these divisions for any active operations in November, 1915.

APPENDIX 1A

COMMANDERS of CENTRAL FORCE and of FIRST, SECOND, and THIRD ARMIES, HOME DEFENCE FORCES

CENTRAL FORCE

G.O.C.-in-C.

Formation ... ... General SIR IAN HAMILTON (until appointed to command M.E.F. on 12/3/15).

13 March, 1915 –12 March, 1916 ... ... General SIR H. M. L. RUNDLE.

FIRST ARMY

G.O.C.

Formation ...General SIR BRUCE M. HAMILTON.

22 June, 1915 –21 Nov., 1915 General SIR H. L. SMITH-DORRIEN [apptd. to command British Forces, East Africa, 22/11/15].

11 Dec., 1915 –12 Mar., 1916 Lt.-Gen. SIR A. E. CODRINGTON.

SECOND ARMY

G.O.C.

Formation ...Lt.-Gen. Hon. SIR F. W. STOPFORD.

7 June, 1915 –12 Mar., 1916 Lt.-Gen. C. L. WOOLLCOMBE.

THIRD ARMY

G.O.C.

Formation ... ... Lt.-Gen. SIR W. E. FRANKLYN.

6 September, 1914 –11 December, 1915 ... ... Lt.-Gen. SIR A. E. CODRINGTON [transferred to First Army; and Third Army disappeared].

GRADUATED BATTALIONS

Graduated battalions will be found in 8 of the divisions contained in this Part, and by the middle of March, 1918, the infantry of 4 home-service Territorial Force divisions was almost entirely made up of these battalions.

In 1916 regimental reserve units (including Territorial Force reserve units) were unable to cope with the numbers of recruits, and one expedient adopted for dealing with receipt, administration, training, and disposal of recruits was the formation of the corps of the Training Reserve. In this scheme the battalions comprising the various Reserve Infantry Brigades became Training Reserve Battalions, and the brigades became Reserve Brigades. Redundant battalions were broken up, some battalions were amalgamated, and the remainder (112) became 1st–112th Battalions, Training Reserve. To these 112 battalions were allotted all the recruits who were not required for regimental reserve (including T.F.) units. The units and men belonged to the corps of the Training Reserve; the officers, warrant officers, and non-commissioned officers were only attached to the units for administration and training, but continued to belong to their own corps.

The scheme was then developed to provide for the progressive training of recruits under 19 years of age. 42 (of the 112) battalions were selected for this purpose: 14 became Young Soldier Battalions and the other 28 became Graduated Battalions; both classes still belonged to the Training Reserve.

The Young Soldier Battalions received recruits, and gave them their initial training. Two of the Graduated Battalions were definitely linked to each Young Soldier Battalion, and the latter passed one company of recruits to one of its Graduated Battalions, and in due course sent another company of recruits to its other Graduated Battalion. At the outset recruits passed from Young Soldier to Graduated Battalions according to age. Later on a change was made and the stage reached in the recruit training was the criterion in the place of age. Normally recruits completed recruit training in the Graduated Battalions, and were then drafted abroad direct. In cases in which special clothing (kilts, etc.) was required the recruits were sent from Graduated Battalions to Regimental Reserve Battalions, en route for overseas.

In due course it was decided that the men in the Graduated Battalions could be used for Home Defence whilst finishing their recruit training. In accordance with this decision, from July, 1917, Graduated Battalions took the place of other units in the home-service divisions, but they were not employed in unallotted brigades. When this transfer of Graduated Battalions to the home-service divisions took place, the Graduated Battalions (still units of the Training Reserve) dropped the former numerical designations and were given high numbers (201st onward) as infantry battalions. Additional Young Soldier and Graduated Battalions were formed, and the latter were also employed in home-service divisions.

The Graduated Battalions were organized in 4 companies according to age, thus: 1 company for recruits varying between 18–18¼ years; 1 company from 18¼–18½; 1 company from 18½–18¾; and 1 company from 18¾–19 years of age. The whole of the last-named company would then be drafted to France and another 18–18¼ company joined. In this way, every three months there was a company of 19-year old men ready for drafting.

Later in 1917, it was decided that all Young Soldier and Graduated Battalions should be identified with and affiliated to Regiments of Infantry of the Line. In accordance with this decision, by the end of October, 1917, all Young Soldier Battalions became 53rd Battalions, and all Graduated Battalions became either 51st Battalions or 52nd Battalions of the regiments to which they were affiliated.

Although enlistments for the Training Reserve ceased at noon on the 11th November, 1918, yet many Graduated and Young Soldier Battalions continued to serve long after that date. Some battalions, indeed, went to France and to the Army of the Rhine.

APPENDIX 3

THE 90-mm. FIELD GUN

Even early in 1915 there were no reasonably modern field artillery equipments available in England for issue to the newly-formed, and now concentrated, 2nd-line Territorial Force divisions. Later on, when the 1st-line Territorial Force divisional artilleries had been re-equipped with 18-pdr. Q.F. guns and 4·5″ howitzers, their original equipments (15-pdr. B.L.C. guns and 5″ howitzers) were handed over to the 2nd-line divisional artilleries. At the beginning of 1916 the 2nd-line divisional artilleries were finally re-armed with 18-pdr. Q.F. and 4·5″ howitzer equipments, which by this time had become available. But early in 1915, when the 2nd-line divisional artilleries first concentrated at their war stations, the immediate necessity was to provide them with any armament.

In many 2nd-line divisional artilleries dummy wooden guns and dummy wooden sights were made, and the wooden guns were mounted on handcarts. In this way some preliminary instruction could be given in gun drill and driving drill. However, many of the 2nd-line divisions (four by the 4th March, 1915) were posted to Central Force and allotted a part in Home Defence ; and, in the emergency of an invasion, the employment of ' Quaker ' guns would have entitled even the Chinese to smile.

To ease what was rapidly becoming a serious situation, recourse was had to France. As far back as 1897 France had begun to re-arm with the celebrated 75-mm. Q.F. field gun, and the immediate predecessor of the 75-mm. Q.F. was the 90-mm. B.L. field gun. Naturally in 1915 no spare 75-mm. were available, but some of the now rather old-fashioned 90-mm. equipments were still in store, as well as a small proportion of 90-mm. ammunition. With great generosity, France placed these guns and the ammunition at the disposal of the British military authorities for training the 2nd-line divisional artilleries, as well as for use in an emergency.

This 90-mm. B.L. field gun was equipped with both common shell (with a black powder bursting charge) and shrapnel shell. The gun had a sight (graduated in metres) which was used in conjunction with a level, graduated in degrees. The time-fuze, for use with the shrapnel, was graduated in seconds. This fuze could be set either by boring, or by a fuze-setter similar to the setter used with the 75-mm.

Unhappily only a few of these equipments were still available in 1915 (18 years after their supersession), consequently only 4 equipments could be issued to each field-gun brigade, in the fortunate divisions selected to receive them. The earliest 2nd-line divisional artillery to obtain 90-mm. equipments did so in March, 1915 ; whereas another division had to wait for them until August, 1915. Only 20 rounds were still available to issue with each 90-mm. gun, and this ammunition had lain in store for nearly a quarter of a century. The gun was quite unknown to those who were now called on to use it ; no gun handbooks were available, the graduation of the sights proved to be a stumbling-block, and to many the setting of the fuzes provided an insuperable problem.

The 90-mm. guns, however, were real weapons and a distinct advance on the home-made ' Quaker ' guns. At any rate gun drill and driving drill could be more realistically carried out, without all ranks having to overwork their imaginations ; but the scarcity of ammunition still prohibited any gun practice. Valuable as they were for drill, it is fortunate that no 2nd-line divisional artillery had to employ the 90-mm. guns actively in Home Defence.

WORK OF THE ARMY ORDNANCE DEPARTMENT[1] AT HOME, 1914-1918

This Appendix summarises part of the work performed, in the Eastern Command during the War, by the Army Ordnance Department in equipping some of the sixteen divisions described in this Part (which were raised at home after the outbreak of War) and in supplying some of the nine divisions which served at home.

Between the 4th August, 1914, and the 4th August, 1919, the following numbers of officers and men served at the Eastern Command Depots at Colchester, Chatham, and Dover:

	Officers	Inspectors of Ordnance Machinery.	Other Ranks.
Colchester	122	6	2,356
Chatham	86	39	2,513
Dover	157	39	2,828

These officers and men equipped no fewer than 31 divisions, as well as hundreds of various units. Some idea of the work accomplished can be appreciated when it is realized that by the 4th August, 1919, the 3 Depots had issued:

628,000,000 rounds, S.A.A.,
8,000,000 blankets,
161,000 tents,
40,000 vehicles, and
68,700 bicycles.

Many of the blankets and tents were issued as often as three times, and on each issue all indents and vouchers were necessarily repeated. This work alone involved over 4,000,000 ledger entries.

Rapid changes of " Marks " of stores, as well as local purchases and new issues, all increased the ledger headings. Between 31st March, 1914, and 31st March, 1919, in one of the Eastern Command Depots the ledger headings increased from 3,178 to 5,567.

The weights of the stores handled at the three Eastern Command Depots were as follows:

Colchester	33,000 tons, in one year;
Chatham	207,000 tons, during the War;
Dover	35,279 railway truck-loads, during the War.

The three Eastern Command Depots dealt with 673,000 indents for general equipment and stores (exclusive of clothing). In the Eastern Command (during the War) clothing was only issued from Dover[2], and this Depot received 23,600 indents for clothing.

[1] Became Royal Army Ordnance Corps, 25/11/18 (Army Order, 363/1918).
[2] Clothing for all troops outside the Dover area was obtained either from Pimlico or from Weedon.

APPENDIX 4

In the early days of the War resort was made to local purchase to supplement issues which were not available from Army Ordnance Depots. In the Eastern Command £474,700 was expended in this manner. The system of local purchase helped to relieve a somewhat difficult situation ; though, in the case of purchases by officers commanding units, zeal occasionally outran discretion: one commanding officer purchased saddlery at a cost of £25,000.

Lord Kitchener's appeal for blankets had a splendid and instantaneous response. In the Eastern Command, 17,100 blankets were sent in as a result, and this prompt and liberal donation saved much discomfort to men who had just joined.

At the outbreak of War, and for many months thereafter, all unserviceable clothing was sold to contractors. The shortage of woollens and clothing, however, decided the authorities to open a Salvage Depot where all discarded clothing and necessaries could be received, sorted, and if possible repaired. In August, 1916, this Clothing Reception Depot was opened at Huntingdon. Everything received at this Depot was separated into 2 classes :

(i) Fit for repair. These garments were cleaned, repaired, and re-issued.

(ii) Unfit for further use. The garments were all carefully sorted, and all brass hooks and buttons were cut off. The unserviceable garments were then sent either to a rag market or to a manufacturer of cloth.

Between 1st October, 1918, and 31st March, 1919, this Salvage Depot handled :

(a) Unserviceable and surplus garments 3,669,161

(b) Of the foregoing, found fit for further service 936,355
Value at half-vocabulary rates of (b) £210,337
Value of produce £88,677

To effect this, the estimated cost of the Depot (including rent, rates, taxes, wages, and all incidental expenses) was £23,510. The staff was one Ordnance Officer (3rd Class) and one Temporary Officer. The great benefit to the Public requires no emphasis.

WAR ESTABLISHMENT OF 57th DIVISION (England, 1915),

Appendix 5.

57th (2nd/WEST LANCASHIRE) DIVISION (England, 1915).

Authority—W.E., Part IX (T.F.-2nd-Line), d/d. 6/Sept./1915.

Divnl. H.Q.

Infantry :
3 Brigades
(12 Inf. Battalions, with 2 machine guns each).

Mounted Troops :
1 Yeomanry Squadron ;
1 Cyclist Company.

Artillery :
H.Q., Divnl. Artillery ;
3 Field Artillery Brigades (9 batteries—15-pdr. B.L.C.) and 3 B.A.C.s ;
1 Field Artillery (How.) Brigade (2 batteries—5" How.) and 1 (How.) B.A.C. ;
1 Divnl. Ammn. Coln.

Engineers :
H.Q., Divnl. Engineers ;
2 Field Companies.

Signal Service :
1 Signal Company.

3 Field Ambulances.
1 Sanitary Section.
1 Mobile Veterinary Section.
1 Motor Ambulance Workshop.
1 Divnl. Train.

WAR ESTABLISHMENT, SEPTEMBER, 1915 (ENGLAND).

All Ranks	17,212	
Horses and Mules	4,156	
Guns	44	
15-pdr. B.L.C.		36
5" Hows.		8
Trench Mortars		
Stokes		
Medium		
Machine Guns	24	
Vickers		24
Lewis		
Carts and Vehicles	768	
Cycles	491	
Motor Cycles	16	
Motor Cars	13	
Motor Lorries	5	
Motor Ambulances	21	

58th (2nd/1st LONDON) DI

Author

Divnl. H.Q.

Infantry :
3 Brigades
(9 Inf. Battalions, w

3 Light Trench Mortar
(8, 3" Stokes Mortar

Artillery :
H.Q., Divnl. Artillery ;
2 Field Artillery Bri
(8 batteries—6, 18
2 Medium Trench M
(6, 2" Mortars eac
1 Divnl. Ammn. Col

Engineers :
H.Q., Divnl. Engineers
3 Field Companies.

Signal Service :
1 Signal Company.

Pioneers :
1 Pioneer Battalion
(12 Lewis Guns).

Machine-Gun Unit :
1 Machine-Gun Battali
(4 Companies, with

3 Field Ambulances.
1 Mobile Veterinary Se
1 Divnl. Employment
1 Divnl. Train.

WAR ESTABLISHMENT,

Appendix 6.
ce, 1918).
t VII, d/d. 31/Oct./1918.

uns each) ;

2, 4·5" How.) ;

s each).

Appendix 7.

60th (2nd/2nd LONDON) DIVISION (Palestine, 1918).
Authority—W.E., Part XI (Egypt), d/d. 11/Nov./1918.

Divnl. H.Q.

Infantry :
3 Brigades
(12 Inf. Battalions—3 British and 9 Indian—with 16 Lewis guns each) ;
3 Light Trench Mortar Batteries
(8, 3" Stokes Mortars each).

Artillery :
H.Q., Divnl. Artillery ;
3 Field Artillery Brigades
(9 batteries—6, 18-pdr. Q.F. and 3, 4·5" How.) ;

1 Divnl. Ammn. Coln.

Engineers :
H.Q., Divnl. Engineers ;
2 Field Companies ;
1 Field Company, Sappers and Miners.

Signal Service :
1 Signal Company.

Pioneers :
1 Indian Pioneer Battalion.

Machine-Gun Unit :
1 Machine-Gun Battalion
(3 Companies, with 16 Vickers M.G.s each).

3 Combined Field Ambulances.
1 Sanitary Section.
1 Mobile Veterinary Section.
1 Divnl. Train.

(FRANCE). | **WAR ESTABLISHMENT, NOVEMBER, 1918 (PALESTINE).**

(France)	(Palestine)		
	19,929		**All Ranks.**
	6,052*		**Horses and Mules.**
	48		**Guns.**
36		36	18-pdr. Q.F.
12		12	4·5" Hows.
	24		**Trench Mortars.**
24		24	Stokes.
12			Medium.
	240		**Machine Guns.**
64		48	Vickers.
336		192	Lewis.
	720		**Carts and Vehicles.**
	270		**Cycles.**
	29		**Motor Cycles.**
	9		**Motor Cars.**
	4		**Motor Lorries.**
	21		**Motor Ambces.**

* Includes 117 camels and 52 donkeys.

Appendix 8.

73rd DIVISION (England, 1917).

Compiled from Weekly Return of the British Army at Home and War Establishments, Part XIV (Home Service), August, 1917.

Divnl. H.Q.

Infantry:
3 Brigades
(9 Inf. Battalions, with 12 machine guns each).

Mounted Troops:
1 Cyclist Company.

Artillery:
H.Q., Divnl. Artillery;
2 Field Artillery Brigades
(6 batteries—4, 18-pdr. Q.F. and 2, 4·5″ How.);
1 Divnl. Ammn. Coln.

Engineers:
H.Q., Divnl. Engineers;
3 Field Companies.

Signal Service:
1 Signal Company.

3 Field Ambulances.
1 Sanitary Section.
1 Mobile Veterinary Section.
1 Divnl. Train.

WAR ESTABLISHMENT, NOVEMBER, 1917 (ENGLAND).

All Ranks	13,306	
Horses and Mules	2,034	
Guns	32	
18-pdr. Q.F.		24
4·5″ Hows.		8
Machine Guns	108	
Lewis		108
Hotchkiss		
Carts and Vehicles	321	
Cycles	603	
Motor Cycles	20	
Motor Cars	16	
Motor Lorries and Vans	131	
Motor Ambulances	24	

69th (2nd/East Anglian)

Authority—W.E., Pa

Divnl. H.Q.

Infantry:
3 Brigades
(12 Inf. Battalion

Mounted Troops:
1 Cyclist Company.

Artillery:
H.Q., Divnl. Artille
2 Field Artillery
(8 batteries—6,
1 Divnl. Ammn.

Engineers:
H.Q., Divnl. Engin
3 Field Companie

Signal Service:
1 Signal Company.

3 Field Ambulances
1 Sanitary Section.
1 Mobile Veterinary
1 Divnl. Train.

WAR ESTABLISHMEN

Appendix 9.

gland, 1918).

Service), d/d. 19/March/1918.

ine guns each).

d 2, 4·5" How.) ;

Appendix 10.

THE CYCLIST DIVISION* (England, 1918).

Authority—W.E., Part XIV (Home Service), d/d. 19/March/1918.

Cyclist Division H.Q.

3 Cyclist Brigades
(9 Cyclist Regts. or Bns.—16 machine guns each—and 3 signal sections, 3 S.A.A. columns, 3 brigade field ambulances, and 3 brigade trains).

Artillery :
H.Q., Cyclist Division Artillery ;
2 R.F.A. Batteries (6, 18-pdr. Q.F. each) and
2 Ammunition Columns.

Signal Service :
1 Cyclist Division Signal Company.

A.S.C. :
H.Q., Cyclist Division A.S.C.

18 (ENGLAND).

WAR ESTABLISHMENT, MARCH, 1918 (ENGLAND).

(Appendix 9)			
	5,580		All Ranks.
	271		Horses and Mules.
	8		Guns.
36		8	18-pdr. Q.F.
8			4·5" Hows.
	144		Machine Guns.
192			Lewis.
		144	Hotchkiss.
	31		Carts and Vehicles.
	4,607		Cycles.
	120		Motor Cycles.
	38		Motor Cars.
	143		Motor Lorries.
	12		Motor Ambulances.

* The Cyclist Division was included in Part 2A, pp. 19–26.

INDEX OF FORMATIONS

BRIGADES AND DIVISIONS

BRIGADES

Artillery—

R.F.A. ; R.F.A., T.F. ; etc.—

XII, 79 ; 80 (note 28) ; 82.
XXXVII, 126 ; 128 (note 34) ; 129 ; 130.
XLIII, 79 ; 80 (note 28) ; 82.
XLIV, 118 ; 119 (notes 24 and 39) ; 121.
XLIX, 77 ; 82 fn. ; 102 ; 103 (notes 37 and 51) ; 105.
CXVII, 118 ; 119 (notes 25 and 40) ; 121.
CLXXII, 126 ; 128 (note 35) ; 129 ; 130.
CXCI, 130.
CCLXVIII, 118 ; 119 (notes 26 and 41) ; 121.
CCLXXXV (2nd/I West Lancashire), 3 ; 4.
CCLXXXVI (2nd/II West Lancashire), 3 ; 4.
CCLXXXVII (2nd/III West Lancashire), 4 ; 5 (note 22).
CCLXXXVIII (2nd/IV West Lancashire), 4 ; 5 (note 2).
CCXC (2nd/I City of London), 12, 13 ; 14.
CCXCI (2nd/II London), 12, 13 ; 14.
CCXCIII (2nd/III London), 11 ; 12 ; 13 (note 20) ; 14.
CCXCV (2nd/I North Midland), 19 ; 20 ; 23 ; 35 ; 43.
CCXCVI (2nd/II North Midland), 19 ; 20 ; 23 ; 35 ; 43.
CCXCVII (2nd/III North Midland), 20 ; 21 (note 18).
CCXCVIII (2nd/IV North Midland), 20 ; 21 (note 19).
CCC (2nd/V London), 28 ; 29 (note 12).
CCCI (2nd/VI London), 28, 29 ; 30.
CCCII (2nd/VII London), 28, 29 ; 30.
CCCIII (2nd/VIII London), 28, 29 ; 30 (note 39).
CCCV (2nd/I South Midland), 36 ; 37 (note 11).
CCCVI (2nd/II South Midland), 36, 37 ; 39.
CCCVII (2nd/III South Midland), 36, 37 ; 39.
CCCVIII (2nd/IV South Midland), 36 ; 37 (note 14).
CCCX (2nd/I West Riding), 44 ; 45.
CCCXI (2nd/II West Riding), 44 ; 45 (note 10).
CCCXII (2nd/III West Riding), 44 ; 45.
CCCXV (2nd/I Northumbrian), 52 ; 53 (notes 32, 33) ; 54.
CCCXVI (2nd/II Northumbrian), 52 ; 53 (notes 32, 34) ; 54.
CCCXVII (2nd/III Northumbrian), 52 ; 53 (notes 32, 35) ; 54.
CCCXVIII (2nd/IV Northumbrian), 52 ; 53 (notes 32, 36) ; 54.
CCCXX (2nd/I Highland), 56, 57 ; 58 ; 59.
CCCXXI (2nd/II Highland), 56, 57 ; 58 ; 59.
CCCXXIII (2nd/III Highland), 56 ; 58 (note 10) ; 59.
CCCXXV (2nd/I Lowland), 62, 63 ; 64 ; 65.
CCCXXVI (2nd/II Lowland), 62, 63 ; 64 ; 65.
CCCXXVII (2nd/III Lowland), 62 ; 65.
CCCXXVIII (2nd/IV Lowland), 62 ; 64 (note 8) ; 65.
CCCXXX (2nd/I East Lancashire), 69 ; 70 ; 71 ; 73 ; 74.
CCCXXXI (2nd/II East Lancashire), 69 ; 70 ; 71 ; 73 ; 74.
CCCXXXII (2nd/III East Lancashire), 70 ; 71 (note 10) ; 73.

R.F.A.—*Continued.*

CCCXXXV (2nd/I Home Counties), 78 ; 80 (note 16) ; 81 ; 82.
CCCXXXVI (2nd/II Home Counties), 78, 79 ; 80 (note 23) ; 81 ; 82.
CCCXXXVII (2nd/III Home Counties), 78, 79 ; 80 (note 23) ; 81 ; 82.
CCCXXXVIII (2nd/IV Home Counties), 78 ; 80 (note 11).
CCCXL (2nd/I Welsh), 86 ; 88 (note 18) ; 89.
CCCXLI (2nd/II Welsh), 86 ; 89.
CCCXLII (2nd/I Cheshire), 86, 87 ; 89 ; 90.
CCCXLIII (2nd/IV Welsh), 86, 87 ; 89 ; 90.
CCCXLV (2nd/I East Anglian), 94 ; 96 (note 17) ; 97.
CCCXLVI (2nd/II East Anglian), 94, 95 ; 97 ; 98.
CCCXLVII (2nd/III East Anglian), 94 ; 96 (note 11) ; 97.
CCCXLVIII (2nd/IV East Anglian), 94, 95 ; 97 ; 98.
CCCL, 102 ; 103 (note 52) ; 105.
CCCLI, 102 ; 103 (note 53) ; 105.
CCCLII, 108 ; 109 (note 36) ; 110.
CCCLIII, 108 ; 109 (note 36) ; 110.
CCCLIV, 114, 115 ; 115 (notes 10 and 36) ; 116.
CCCLV, 114, 115 ; 115 (notes 10 and 36) ; 116.
I Cheshire, 85.
1st/I City of London, 11 ; 14.
I East Anglian, 93.
II East Anglian, 93.
III East Anglian, 93.
IV East Anglian, 93.
2nd/IV East Lancashire, 70 ; 71 (note 4) ; 73.
1st/IV Home Counties, 19 ; 78 ; 80 (note 4).
1st/II London, 11 ; 14.
1st/III London, 11 ; 14.
1st/IV London, 11 ; 14.
2nd/IV London (H.), 12.
III Portuguese, 19.
IV Portuguese, 3.
I South African, 126 ; 128 (note 36) ; 129 ; 130.
I Welsh, 85.
II Welsh, 85.
IV Welsh, 85.
2nd/IV West Riding (H.), 44 ; 45 (note 3).

R.G.A. ; R.G.A., T.F.—

Mountain—

VIII, 125.
IX, 125.
X (Indian), 130.
IV (Highland), 58.

Detachments and Forces—

Bethell's Force, 69 ; 74.
James's Force, 23 (fn.).
XI Corps Mounted Troops, 3 ; 19.

Dismounted Brigades—

2nd, 119 (note 2).
3rd, 119 (note 9).
4th, 119 (note 16).

Infantry Brigades and Infantry Brigades, T.F.—
3rd (Provisional), 93.
5th (Provisional), 93.
6th (Provisional), 105.
8th (Provisional), 110.
9th (Provisional), 116.
162nd (1st East Midland), 11.
170th (2nd/1st North Lancashire), 2 ; 3 ; 4 ; 5 ; 6.
171st (2nd/1st Liverpool), 2 ; 4 ; 5 ; 6.
172nd (2nd/1st South Lancashire), 2 ; 4 ; 5 ; 6.
173rd (3rd/1st London), 10 ; 11 ; 12, 13 ; 13 (note 8) ; 14.
174th (2nd/2nd London), 10 ; 12, 13 ; 14.
175th (2nd/3rd London), 10 ; 11 ; 12, 13 ; 14.
176th (2nd/1st Staffordshire), 18 ; 20 ; 21 ; 23.
177th (2nd/1st Lincoln and Leicester), 18 ; 20 ; 21 ; 23.
178th (2nd/1st Notts. and Derby), 18 ; 20 ; 21 ; 23.
179th (2nd/4th London), 26 ; 28, 29.
180th (2nd/5th London), 26 ; 28, 29 ; 32.
181st (2nd/6th London), 26 ; 28, 29 ; 32.
182nd (2nd/1st Warwickshire), 34 ; 36, 37 ; 39.
183rd (2nd/1st Gloucester and Worcester), 34 ; 36, 37 ; 39.
184th (2nd/1st South Midland), 34 ; 36, 37 ; 39.
185th (2nd/1st West Riding), 42 ; 44.
186th (2nd/2nd West Riding), 42 ; 44.
187th (2nd/3rd West Riding), 42 ; 44.
188th (2nd/1st Northumberland), 50 ; 52 ; 53 (note 20) ; 54 ; 110.
189th (2nd/1st York and Durham), 50 ; 52 ; 53 (note 24) ; 54 ; 116.
190th (2nd/1st Durham Light Infantry), 50 ; 52 ; 53 (note 28) ; 54 ; 105.
191st (2nd/1st Seaforth and Cameron), 55 ; 56, 57 ; 58 ; 59.
192nd (2nd/1st Gordon), 55 ; 56, 57 ; 58 ; 59.
193rd (2nd/1st Argyll and Sutherland), 55 ; 56, 57 ; 58 ; 59.
194th (2nd/1st South Scottish), 61 ; 62, 63 ; 64 ; 65.
195th (2nd/1st Scottish Rifle), 61 ; 62, 63 ; 64 ; 65.
196th (2nd/1st Highland Light Infantry), 61 ; 62, 63 ; 64 ; 65.
197th (2nd/1st Lancashire Fusilier), 68 ; 70 ; 71 (note 24) ; 72 ; 73.
198th (2nd/1st East Lancashire), 68 ; 70 ; 72 ; 73.
199th (2nd/1st Manchester), 68 ; 70 ; 72 ; 73 ; 74.
200th (2nd/1st Surrey), 76 ; 78, 79 ; 80 (note 31) ; 81 ; 82.
201st (2nd/1st Middlesex), 76 ; 78, 79 ; 81 ; 82.
202nd (2nd/1st Kent), 76 ; 78, 79 ; 81 ; 82.
203rd (2nd/1st North Wales), 84 ; 86, 87 ; 89 ; 90.
204th (2nd/1st Cheshire), 84 ; 86, 87 ; 89 ; 90.
205th (2nd/1st Welsh Border), 84 ; 86, 87 ; 89 ; 90.
206th (2nd/1st Essex), 92 ; 94, 95 ; 97 ; 98.
207th (2nd/1st East Midland), 92 ; 94, 95 ; 97 ; 98.
208th (2nd/1st Norfolk and Suffolk), 92 ; 94, 95 ; 97 ; 98.
209th, 99.
210th, 99.
211th, 99.
212th, 101 ; 102 ; 103 (note 39) ; 105.

Infantry Brigades—*Continued.*
213th, 101 ; 102 ; 103 (note 44) ; 105.
214th, 76 ; 79 ; 80 (note 31) ; 82 ; 101 ; 102 ; 103 (note 48) ; 105.
215th, 107 ; 108 ; 110.
216th, 107 ; 108 ; 110.
217th, 107 ; 108 ; 110.
218th, 112 ; 114, 115 ; 116.
219th, 112 ; 114, 115 ; 116.
220th, 112 ; 114, 115 ; 116.
229th, 117 ; 118 ; 119 (note 2) ; 121.
230th, 117 ; 118 ; 119 (note 9) ; 121.
231st, 117 ; 118 ; 119 (note 16) ; 121.
232nd, 124 ; 126 ; 127 (note 2) ; 129 ; 130.
233rd, 124 ; 126 ; 127 (note 8) ; 129 ; 130.
234th, 124 ; 126 ; 127 (note 14) ; 129 ; 130.
2nd/1st London, 10 ; 12 ; 13 (note 2) ; 14.
South African, 68 ; 69 ; 70 ; 71 (note 45) ; 74.

Mixed Brigades—
223rd, 93.
225th, 93.
226th, 27 ; 77 ; 104.
227th, 85.

Mounted Brigades—
1st Scottish Horse, 51.
2/1/Welsh Border, 51.

DIVISIONS

Cyclist—
The Cyclist, 143.

Infantry and Infantry, T.F.—
57th (2nd/West Lancashire), 1—7 ; 140.
58th (2nd/1st London), 9—15 ; 140, 141.
59th (2nd/North Midland), 17—23.
60th (2nd/2nd London), 25—32 ; 141.
61st (2nd/South Midland), 33—39.
62nd (2nd/West Riding), 41—47.
63rd (2nd/Northumbrian), 49—54.
64th (2nd/Highland), 55—59.
65th (2nd/Lowland), 61—65.
66th (2nd/East Lancashire), 67—74.
67th (2nd/Home Counties), 75—82.
68th (2nd/Welsh), 83—90.
69th (2nd/East Anglian), 91—98 ; 142, 143.
70th, 99.
71st, 101—105.
72nd, 107—110.
73rd, 111—116 ; 142.
74th (Yeomanry), 117—122.
75th, 123—130.

ADDITIONAL UNITS

Artillery—

R.G.A., T.F.—

Heavy Batteries—
1st/1st Devon, 93.
1st/1st East Anglian (Essex), 93 ; 97.
2nd/1st East Anglian (Essex), 93 ; 97.
2nd/1st Highland (Fifeshire), 58 ; 59.
1st/1st Home Counties (Kent), 77.
2nd/1st Home Counties (Kent), 77 ; 81, 82.
1st/1st Lancashire, 3.
2nd/1st Lancashire, 3 ; 69.
1st/2nd Lancashire, 69.
2nd/2nd Lancashire, 69 ; 73 ; 77 ; 82.
1st/1st London, 11 ; 14.
2nd/1st London, 11 ; 73 ; 77 ; 104.
2nd/2nd London, 27 ; 35 ; 73 ; 77 ; 104.
2nd/1st Lowland (City of Edinburgh), 64; 65.

Artillery—*Continued.*

R.G.A., T.F.—*Continued.*

Heavy Batteries—*Continued.*

2nd/1st North Midland, 19.
2nd/1st North Riding (Northumbrian), 51; 54.
2nd/1st South Midland (Warwickshire), 35; 77; 82.
1st/1st Welsh (Caernarvonshire), 85.
2nd/1st Welsh (Caernarvonshire), 85; 90.
1st/1st Wessex (Hampshire), 19; 27; 35.
2nd/1st Wessex (Hampshire), 19; 27; 35.
2nd/1st West Riding, 43.

Cyclists—

Cyclist Battalions—

2/7/Devon, 113.
1/8/Essex, 113.
2/1/Hertfordshire Yeomanry, 79; 104.
1/1/Kent, 3.
2/1/Kent, 77.
2/25/London, 85.
1/6/Suffolk, 85.
2/6/Royal Sussex, 85.
2/1/Warwickshire Yeomanry, 79; 104.

Printed under the Authority of His Majesty's Stationery Office
By C. Tinling & Co. Ltd., Liverpool, London and Prescot

S.O. Code No. 70-307-2-2.

Wt3590/1029 8.37 520 CT&CoLtd Gp51-8755.

Printed in the United Kingdom by
Lightning Source UK Ltd., Milton Keynes
141598UK00001B/11/A

9 781847 347398